POLITICS OF THE ADMINISTRATIVE PROCESS

SEVENTH EDITION

CQ Press, an imprint of SAGE, is the leading publisher of books, periodicals, and electronic products on American government and international affairs. CQ Press consistently ranks among the top commercial publishers in terms of quality, as evidenced by the numerous awards its products have won over the years. CQ Press owes its existence to Nelson Poynter, former publisher of the *St. Petersburg Times*, and his wife Henrietta, with whom he founded Congressional Quarterly in 1945. Poynter established CQ with the mission of promoting democracy through education and in 1975 founded the Modern Media Institute, renamed The Poynter Institute for Media Studies after his death. The Poynter Institute (*www.poynter.org*) is a nonprofit organization dedicated to training journalists and media leaders.

In 2008, CQ Press was acquired by SAGE, a leading international publisher of journals, books, and electronic media for academic, educational, and professional markets. Since 1965, SAGE has helped inform and educate a global community of scholars, practitioners, researchers, and students spanning a wide range of subject areas, including business, humanities, social sciences, and science, technology, and medicine. A privately owned corporation, SAGE has offices in Los Angeles, London, New Delhi, and Singapore, in addition to the Washington DC office of CQ Press.

POLITICS OF THE ADMINISTRATIVE PROCESS

SEVENTH EDITION

Donald F. Kettl

University of Maryland

FOR INFORMATION:

CQ Press
An Imprint of SAGE Publications, Inc.
2455 Teller Road
Thousand Oaks, California 91320
E-mail: order@sagepub.com

SAGE Publications Ltd.
1 Oliver's Yard
55 City Road
London EC1Y 1SP
United Kingdom

SAGE Publications India Pvt. Ltd.
B 1/I 1 Mohan Cooperative Industrial Area
Mathura Road, New Delhi 110 044
India

SAGE Publications Asia-Pacific Pte. Ltd.
3 Church Street
#10-04 Samsung Hub
Singapore 049483

Acquisitions Editor: Carrie Brandon
Development Editor: Anna Villarruel
eLearning Editor: John Scappini
Editorial Assistant: Duncan Marchbank
Production Editor: Bennie Clark Allen
Copy Editor: Christina West
Typesetter: C&M Digitals (P) Ltd.
Proofreader: Talia Greenberg
Indexer: Jean Casalegno
Cover and Interior Designer: Scott Van Atta
Marketing Manager: Amy Whitaker

Printed in Canada

Library of Congress Cataloging-in-Publication Data

Names: Kettl, Donald F., author.

Title: Politics of the administrative process / Donald F. Kettl, University of Maryland.

Description: Seventh edition. | Los Angeles : CQ Press, [2018] | Includes bibliographical references and index.

Identifiers: LCCN 2016046836 | ISBN 9781506357096 (pbk. : alk. paper)

Subjects: LCSH: Public administration—United States—Textbooks.

Classification: LCC JK421 .K4817 2017 | DDC 351.73—dc23
LC record available at https://lccn.loc.gov/2016046836

16 17 18 19 20 10 9 8 7 6 5 4 3 2 1

BRIEF CONTENTS

CONTENTS

FIGURES, TABLES, AND BOXES

FIGURES

TABLES

BOXES

PREFACE

With this seventh edition of *The Politics of the Administrative Process*, I'm celebrating eighty years of intellectual history. The book stands on the shoulders of James W. Fesler, one of the greatest scholars that the field of public administration ever produced. He established himself as an assistant professor during Franklin D. Roosevelt's New Deal. He contributed to winning World War II by serving as historian of the War Production Board, a position that might sound dull but which, in fact, helped keep track of the critical decisions the country made in allocating rubber and steel to the war effort. After the war, he went to Yale University, where he served as chair of the political science department and built it into the number-one-ranked program in the country. He helped develop a generation of scholars. His last doctoral student is the author of this seventh edition.

The culmination of his career was his public administration textbook, *Public Administration: Theory and Practice*, which appeared in 1980.[1] That book morphed into *The Politics of the Administrative Process*, whose first edition appeared in 1991, and we coauthored the book through its fourth edition in 2009. Jim brought to the book insights into history and current affairs. Many of the historical references in the book come from Jim's deep appreciation for the lasting issues. He loved the story of the struggles to keep the windows clean in a king's palace. Cleaning the outside was the job of one department, the inside of another, and the two departments were never in sync. Coordination of such a basic issue was something the king never mustered.

And Jim loved puns, especially bad ones—the more tortured the pun, the better. In fact, one of his proudest moments came in a column by William Safire, the distinguished *New York Times* columnist, who wrote a regular column called "On Language." In a 1996 column, Safire cited a pun Jim had concocted. It's worth quoting Safire directly:

> The Roman orator Cicero, launching his attack on the politician he suspected of plotting an assassination, expressed his revulsion at the degeneration of high principle in his era with O tempora! O mores! ("'O, the times! O, the bad new principles!'") With this as background comes the cry of the Latin-trained Japanese chef deep-frying an eel: "O tempura! O morays!"[2]

Jim celebrated the pun's publication in the *Times*. He loved the way it told a bigger story: Jim's affinity for history, connections across cultures, and the knack for bringing lasting issues into today's focus (even if, in this case, the connections are especially painful).

With the book's seventh edition, it's not only worth celebrating the eighty years of intellectual life captured in this book (Jim's first edition long predated the dawn of personal computers), not only from his own typewriter but in the work carried forward since his death in 2005. It's also worth going back to the foundation that Jim so carefully built: a search for fundamental questions that endure, the deeper their roots the better; the quest for a connection between theory building and practical applications; and the commitment to making government work well for its citizens. That last point was especially important for Jim. After all, he cut his professional teeth during the New Deal, when the country faced enormous challenges, it wasn't clear whether the government was up to solving them, and a new generation of scholars worked hard to figure out how government could best help millions of Americans deal with enormous hardship.

I point to Jim's great contributions to the field—and to this book—in launching this new edition, because today's historic distrust of government would greatly worry him. He would understand from history that there are deep roots to many of these issues. He would point to the fact that other nations have struggled with similar issues. And, more than anything else, he'd want to find ways of making government work better so it could serve citizens—and rebuild their trust in the organizations to which he devoted his life.

That's the focus of this edition. "Public administration" sometimes takes on an aura of something just the insiders need to worry about. It's sometimes something that seems almost no one can do anything about. Students sometimes think it's boring, or a career to which they can't imagine devoting themselves.

But here's my request: just read the first few pages of Chapter 1, which tells the story of lead poisoning in the water of Flint, Michigan. It's hardly just an inside game. It's certainly not boring. It's worth figuring out how to do it right. It is central to the Trump administration's challenges. And it's one of the most important things to which it's possible to devote a career.

So this book is not only a celebration of Jim Fesler's life and career (and his occasional penchant for punning). It's a call to focus our energy on making government work and restoring our confidence in it.

ORGANIZATION OF THE BOOK

Following a careful look at politics and administration in **Chapter 1**, *The Politics of the Administrative Process* explores the important issues in five parts. Part I considers what government does and how it does it. **Chapter 2** lays out government's strategies and tactics, as well as the growth of government's reliance on nongovernmental partners to do its work. **Chapter 3** examines the basic issues of administrative responsibility and the meaning of the "administrative state."

Part II moves on to probe the theories underlying organizations and their structure. **Chapter 4** charts the basics of organizational theory. **Chapters 5** and **6** analyze the structure of the executive branch and the problems that periodically hamper good organizational performance. **Chapter 7** examines the enduring instinct of policymakers and administrators alike to reform organizational structure.

Part III addresses the role of people inside these organizational structures and looks at the challenge of recruiting younger employees to public service, as baby boomers move to retirement. Civil service systems have long defined the basic rules and procedures for hiring and firing government workers, and that constitutes the focus of **Chapter 8**. **Chapter 9** asks how government can make the most of the intellectual capital its employees bring to the job.

Part IV carefully examines how administrative agencies accomplish their missions. Administration is about making decisions, and **Chapter 10** analyzes the theories about this process. **Chapter 11** applies these theories to budgeting, which is the most important administrative decision and which drives much of administrative action. **Chapter 12** explores how implementers transform decisions into practice.

Part V takes on the theme of government accountability, with **Chapter 13** probing the strategies of regulation and the courts. **Chapter 14** concludes the book by returning to the central overarching themes of executive power, politics, and accountability and examines, in particular, the control of administration by legislatures.

KEY FEATURES

Building on the book's full-color design, this edition offers several new features. First, each chapter has a **Diving into Data** feature, which explores how numbers and evidence can help sort through the fundamental questions of public administration. Many of the "data dives" have especially lively graphics to help the issues come alive. These sections are important, not only to bring new insight into the basic issues but also to give students practice in some of the cutting-edge approaches in especially high demand by employers.

Second, all of the graphs and most of the photos are new for this edition. I've kept some of the old classics—ones that Jim Fesler would have especially appreciated—but the graphic arts in the book are fresh and lively.

The book explores three big themes and how they affect public administration—politics, performance, and accountability. There is a special **Ripped from the Headlines** box in each chapter to examine how one of the themes connects with the topic of the chapter. Each of the "Ripped from the Headlines" boxes is new for this edition. For example, a box on harsh news coverage of a NASA space mission cuts to the underlying issues of what *good* public administration looks like. One box examines the surprising coordination issues that came from a small community's decision to license a marijuana farm, while another box looks at challenges for rooting out sexual harassment in the National Park Service. In one chapter, a box asks: Can state governments play a role in stopping earthquakes? These boxes bring alive the theoretical issues in each of the book's chapters.

Learning objectives open each chapter. Readers will also find **key concepts** bolded within the text and listed at the end of each chapter for ease of review, and a comprehensive **glossary** at the back of the book defines all of the key concepts. Each chapter concludes with a list of resources **for further reading** and a discussion of **suggested websites** to aid further study.

Each chapter features a new **case study**, as well as favorites from previous editions. The cases play a crucial role in bringing home the key points in the chapter text. The issues and situations presented in each case bring the chapter material to life—they show how these concepts actually play out in the real world. For example, in Chapter 12, on implementation, I discuss the complications arising in the rollout of President Obama's health insurance program, a major reform initiative that proved to be a tremendously complicated undertaking. This was the signature program in the president's agenda, but the launch of its website undermined the president's promises, weakened his credibility, and set the stage for Donald Trump's election. For thousands and thousands of health insurance hopefuls, negotiating the website proved painful or impossible. The case provided one more example of why management matters—no policy idea can be good if it fails in execution, and failed execution itself can become a point of enormous political contention.

In addition, each case ends with a "Questions to Consider" section, which challenges students to think critically about the big issues at play, to connect the ideas in the chapter with real-world examples, and to foster discussion among students about how they would solve the problems.

New cases for this edition include the following:

- Permission Slips for Oreos
- Are Private Markets Better than Government?
- Humvees in Ferguson
- What Should Government Do about Sharks?
- How to Fix the VA?
- Who's in Charge When Fires Strike?
- The War on Zika
- What Do We Owe Vets?
- Big Reform Ideas from House Republicans
- What Are You Eating for Breakfast?
- Lessons on Budgeting from *House of Cards*
- Better Numbers, Lower Crime
- What a Box of Honey Nut Cheerios Says about Today's Politics
- Lobbying for EpiPens and Uber

DIGITAL RESOURCES

for CQ Press

SAGE edge offers a robust online environment featuring an impressive array of tools and resources for review, study, and further exploration, keeping both instructors and students on the cutting edge of teaching and learning. I am thankful for the work of Michael Keeney, who revised or authored many of the resources listed below.

SAGE EDGE™ FOR INSTRUCTORS

Instructors receive full access to the password-protected **SAGE edge Instructor Resources Site. SAGE edge for Instructors** supports your teaching by making it easy to integrate quality content and create a rich learning environment for students. Instructors can access these resources at **http://edge.sagepub.com/kettl7e.**

- A **Microsoft® Word test bank** of more than 700 multiple-choice, true-or-false, and essay questions has been crafted specifically for the book. The test bank provides you with a diverse range of pre-written options as well as the opportunity for editing any question and/or inserting your own personalized questions to effectively assess students' progress and understanding.
- An **electronic test bank** contains multiple-choice, true-or-false, and essay questions for each chapter. The test bank provides you with a diverse range of pre-written options as

well as the opportunity for editing any question and/or inserting your own personalized questions to effectively assess students' progress and understanding.

- Editable, chapter-specific **Microsoft® PowerPoint® slides** offer you complete flexibility in easily creating a multimedia presentation for your course.
- **Sample course syllabi** provide suggested models for structuring your course for six, fourteen, or sixteen weeks.
- An **instructor's manual** provides chapter overviews, lecture outlines, and chapter-by-chapter talking points for discussion.
- **Graphics from the book**, including all of the tables, figures, and infographics, are available in .ppt, .pdf, and .jpg formats for use in lectures, assignments, or tests.

SAGE EDGE™ FOR STUDENTS

SAGE Edge for Students helps improve performance, enhance learning, and offers a personalized approach to coursework in an easy-to-use environment. Students can access these resources at **http://edge.sagepub.com/kettle7e**.

- Mobile-friendly **eFlashcards** strengthen understanding of key terms and concepts.
- Mobile-friendly **practice quizzes** allow for independent assessment by students of their mastery of course material.
- Access to a **case study archive** with 39 additional cases written by me, along with questions to consider that encourage critical analysis and help students apply concepts.
- Access to a selection of annotated full-text **journal articles**, from such SAGE journals as *Public Personnel Management*, *Public Policy and Administration*, *The American Review of Public Administration*, and *Administration and Society*, among others. Each article comes with **Critical Analysis** questions to help students link this scholarship to discussion in the text.
- **Data-based exercises** offer students the opportunity to use publicly available federal data, from sources such as OMB and GAO, to apply concepts learned in the text.
- Annotated links to **video and multimedia content** support and add depth to the book's case studies.
- **Chapter summaries with learning objectives** reinforce the most relevant material.
- A customized online **action plan** includes tips and feedback on progress through the course and materials, which allows students to individualize their learning experience.

ACKNOWLEDGMENTS

As I've noted, this book builds heavily on the pathbreaking work that Jim Fesler did, in his career and especially in the early editions of the book. He would be the first to remind us that the problems we're struggling with—determining what government should do and how best to do it—stretch to the very meaning of government. Moreover, Jim found great reassurance in discovering those roots. That did not lessen the huge conflicts over big issues, but it did help explain why the battles were worth fighting—and which fundamental issues will continue to shape the enduring issues about government and its administration. Jim's great contribution lays in explaining which fights we can win, which will endure, and why the battles matter.

In preparing this new edition, I'm especially grateful to the entire SAGE/CQ Press team. In particular, let me thank Charisse Kiino, Executive Director; Carrie Brandon, Senior Acquisitions Editor; Anna Villarruel, Associate Development Editor; Bennie Clark Allen, Project Editor; John Scappini, Associate eLearning Editor; and Duncan Marchbank, Editorial Assistant. Christina West did an outstanding job of copyediting the manuscript. In addition, I want to thank the following individuals for their exceptionally useful and perceptive reviews: Terry Curl, Golden Gate University–San Francisco; Joan Gibran, Tennessee State University; Herbert Gooch, California Lutheran University; Dave Ivers, Eastern Michigan University; Charley Jacobs, St. Norbert College; Patricia Jaramillo, University of Texas at San Antonio; Miguel Gonzalez Marcos, George Washington University; Ramona Ortega-Liston, University of Akron; Michelle Pautz, University of Dayton; Luke Perry, Utica College; Carlene Thornton, University of West Florida; Joe Wert, Indiana University Southeast; and Su Xuhong, University of South Carolina.

I want to thank the instructors around the country who have used this book to help their students understand the genuine excitement of this field—and the students, who will be leading the next generation of efforts to deliver better services to citizens.

Finally, let me especially thank my wife, Sue. She's been an invaluable friend, partner, strategist, and touchstone. She's lived every chapter of this book, and her insights have made every edition better. She has my deep and lasting thanks.

NOTES

1. James W. Fesler, *Public Administration: Theory and Practice* (Englewood Cliffs, N.J.: Prentice-Hall, 1980).
2. William Safire, "Punmeister," *New York Times* (September 22, 1996), http://www.nytimes.com/1996/09/22/magazine/punmeister.html.

ABBREVIATIONS AND ACRONYMS

AARP	American Association for Retired Persons
ACLU	American Civil Liberties Union
AFL-CIO	American Federation of Labor and Congress of Industrial Organizations
AFSCME	American Federation of State, County, and Municipal Employees
AIDS	Acquired immunodeficiency syndrome
APA	Administrative Procedure Act of 1946
ATF	Bureau of Alcohol, Tobacco, Firearms and Explosives
BBA	British Bankers' Association
BIA	Bureau of Indian Affairs
BOB	Bureau of the Budget
CBO	Congressional Budget Office
CDC	Centers for Disease Control and Prevention
CFR	Code of Federal Regulations
CIA	Central Intelligence Agency
CMS	Centers for Medicare and Medicaid Services
CPSC	Consumer Product Safety Commission
DHS	Department of Homeland Security
DMV	Department of Motor Vehicles
DOD	Department of Defense
EPA	Environmental Protection Agency
FAA	Federal Aviation Administration
FBI	Federal Bureau of Investigation
FCC	Federal Communications Commission
FDA	Food and Drug Administration
FDIC	Federal Deposit Insurance Corporation
Fed	Federal Reserve Board
FEMA	Federal Emergency Management Agency
FHWA	Federal Highway Administration
FLRA	Federal Labor Relations Authority
FPS	Federal Protective Service
FTC	Federal Trade Commission
GAO	Government Accountability Office (formerly General Accounting Office)
GDP	Gross domestic product
GIS	Geographic information system

GPP	Government Performance Project
GPRA	Government Performance and Results Act
GS	General Schedule of Classification and Pay
GSA	General Services Administration
HHS	Department of Health and Human Services
HIV	Human immunodeficiency virus
HR	Human resources
HUD	Department of Housing and Urban Development
ICE	Immigration and Customs Enforcement
IRS	Internal Revenue Service
KSA	Knowledge, Skills, and Abilities
MBO	Management by objectives
MSPB	Merit Systems Protection Board
NAPA	National Academy of Public Administration
NASA	National Aeronautics and Space Administration
NATO	North Atlantic Treaty Organization
NHTSA	National Highway Traffic Safety Administration
NIH	National Institutes of Health
NIMBY	"Not in my backyard"
NMA	National Motorists Association
NPR	National Performance Review
NSC	National Security Council
NYPD	New York Police Department
OECD	Organization for Economic Co-operation and Development
OFPP	Office of Federal Procurement Policy
OGE	Office of Government Ethics
OMB	Office of Management and Budget
OPA	Office of Price Administration
OPM	Office of Personnel Management
OSHA	Occupational Safety and Health Administration
PART	Program Assessment Rating Tool
PhRMA	Pharmaceutical Research and Manufacturers of America
PPBS	Planning-Programming-Budgeting System
RIF	Reductions in force
SCOTUS	Supreme Court of the United States
SEC	Securities and Exchange Commission
SEPTA	Southeastern Pennsylvania Transportation Authority
SES	Senior Executive Service
SSA	Social Security Administration
SWAT	Special Weapons and Tactics
TABOR	Taxpayer Bill of Rights
TQM	Total quality management
TSA	Transportation Security Administration
TVA	Tennessee Valley Authority
USDA	U.S. Department of Agriculture
VA	Department of Veterans Affairs
WSSC	Washington Suburban Sanitary Commission
ZBB	Zero-base budgeting

ABOUT THE AUTHOR

Donald F. Kettl is professor and former dean in the School of Public Policy at the University of Maryland. He is also a nonresident senior fellow at the Volcker Alliance, the Partnership for Public Service, and the Brookings Institution.

Kettl is the author or editor of many books and monographs, including *Escaping Jurassic Government: How to Recover America's Lost Commitment to Competence* (2016), *The Politics of the Administrative Process* (2015), *System under Stress: The Challenge to 21st Century Governance* (2014), *The Next Government of the United States: Why Our Institutions Fail Us and How to Fix Them* (2008), and *The Global Public Management Revolution* (2005). He has twice won the Louis Brownlow Book Award of the National Academy of Public Administration for the best book published in public administration. In 2008, Kettl won the American Political Science's John Gaus Award for a lifetime of exemplary scholarship in political science and public administration. He was awarded the Warner W. Stockberger Achievement Award of the International Public Management Association for Human Resources in 2007 for outstanding contributions in the field of public-sector personnel management.

He holds a PhD in political science from Yale University. Prior to his appointment at the University of Maryland, he taught at the University of Pennsylvania, Columbia University, the University of Virginia, Vanderbilt University, and the University of Wisconsin–Madison. He is a fellow of Phi Beta Kappa and the National Academy of Public Administration.

Kettl has consulted broadly for government organizations at all levels in the United States and abroad. He has appeared frequently in national and international media, including National Public Radio, *Good Morning America, ABC World News Tonight, NBC Nightly News, CBS Evening News,* CNN's, *Anderson Cooper 360,* and *The Situation Room,* the Fox News Channel, the *Huffington Post, Al Jazeera,* as well as public television's *News Hour* and the BBC. He is a regular columnist for *Governing* magazine, which is read by state and local government officials around the country. He chaired two gubernatorial blue-ribbon commissions for the Wisconsin state government, one on campaign finance reform and the other on government structure and finance. Kettl is a coshareholder of the Green Bay Packers, along with his wife, Sue.

1

ACCOUNTABILITY

Brett Carlsen/Stringer

In March 2016, Flint Mayor Karen Weaver talked with residents about the continuing problems with the city's water system. The National Guard helped city officials distribute bottled water to residents struggling with lead-contaminated water.

No complaint about public administration gets repeated more often than that it's inefficient—and that we'd be better off running government more like a business. In 2013, Microsoft cofounder Bill Gates complained about government's dysfunction and argued, "You don't run a business like this." Government, he said, was on "a non-optimal path." Gates concluded, "a business that is maximizing its output would proceed along a different path."[1]

This is precisely what Michigan Governor Rich Snyder promised when he took office in 2010. He campaigned using #onetouchnerd as his Twitter hashtag. Snyder was such a rising star that insiders openly discussed him as a possible vice presidential running mate in 2012 for Republican nominee Mitt Romney. By 2016, however, critics suggested his hashtag ought instead to be #onedonedude. Under Snyder's administration, the city of Flint switched its water supply from the city of Detroit to the Flint River. The change, his analysts concluded, would save taxpayers millions of dollars—and that was what "running government like a business would mean." Almost immediately, however, Flint residents began complaining that their water smelled, tasted, and looked funny. Even worse, nine people died from Legionnaires' disease, which investigators suspected was connected to the water switch. The lead poisoned thousands of children—for life. Tens of thousands of citizens resorted to bottled water for drinking, cooking, and even bathing. "We were an experiment in their philosophy of government," explained State Senate Minority Leader Jim Ananich, a Democrat and tough critic of Governor Snyder. "But unfortunately, it failed."[2]

The water from the Flint River, as it turned out, was far more corrosive than the water the city had been getting from Detroit. The Flint water ate away at the pipes carrying it, which in turn caused higher levels of lead and coliform bacteria. The state could have added anticorrosion chemicals to the water, but officials initially concluded it wasn't necessary. In the end, the plan to save taxpayers money ended up costing far more tax dollars and led to far greater misery than officials had ever imagined. In an early 2016 interview, a reporter speaking to Snyder noted that critics had "called this [his] Katrina," referring to the failed governmental response to the 2005 monster hurricane that devastated New Orleans and much of the Gulf Coast. He told a reporter, "It's a disaster."[3]

But Snyder then went on to criticize just about everyone. "This was a failure of government at all levels. Local, state and federal officials—we all failed the families of Flint," he told a congressional hearing in Washington, D.C., on March 17, 2016. He blamed the state's Department of Environmental Quality and argued that "bureaucrats created a culture that valued technical competence over common sense—and the result was that lead was leaching into residents' water." Snyder then singled out the U.S. Environmental Protection Agency (EPA), stating that "Inefficient, ineffective and unaccountable bureaucrats at the EPA allowed this disaster to continue

CHAPTER OBJECTIVES

- Understand the three intertwined themes of the book: politics, performance, and accountability

- Explore the history of the administrative process

- Explore the dimensions of accountability of administration

The Water Crisis and the Children of Flint, Michigan

Following the switch in Flint's water system, there was a debate about how much the change might have affected children's health. The issues centered on two parts of the debate: whether the change, in general, increased the lead in Flint's water; and whether some neighborhoods were more affected by the change than others. Here is a table showing the research.

Percentage of Elevated Blood Lead Levels in All Children Aged Younger Than Five Years

	All Flint (N=1,746)	High Water Lead Flint (N=742)	Rest of Flint (N=1,004)	Non-Flint (N=1,670)
PRE-SWITCH	2.1%	2.5%	1.8%	0.6%
POST-SWITCH	4.0%	6.3%	2.4%	1.0%

Source: Siddhartha Roy, "Pediatric Lead Exposure Presentation from Hurley Medical Center Doctors Concerning Flint MI," *Flint Water Study Updates* (September 24, 2015), http://flintwaterstudy.org/2015/09/pediatric-lead-exposure-presentation-from-hurley-medical-center-doctors-concerning-flint-mi/.

QUESTIONS

1. Do the data show that lead levels in children's blood changed after the switch to the new water system?
2. Some of the data are from "high-water lead Flint"—homes with the highest concentration of lead. Does this suggest that the lead problem had more impact in some neighborhoods than others?
3. How does the level of lead in children's blood in Flint compare with other communities surveyed?

unnecessarily." Flint resident Nakiya Wakes went to that hearing to try to get answers but left without the accountability she sought. But, at the least, she did get to take a shower in uncontaminated water—and she could drink water right out of the tap during her visit to Washington.[4]

Not only did "running government like a business" fail in this case, but it also created a vast public health disaster for the city's residents. It also set off a wave of finger-pointing, with Democrats blaming a Republican governor and Republicans blaming the EPA and the Democrats in the Obama administration. The state government blamed local authorities and all of them complained about the feds. Left with undrinkable water and poisoned children, the residents of Flint, 57 percent of whom were black, wondered why their government had failed them.

Sadly, this case reinforces the biggest challenge facing American government as it heads into the second quarter of the 21st century: the profound distrust Americans have for their political institutions. Two distinguished scholars of the political system, Thomas E. Mann and Norman J. Ornstein, contended not only that the system was broken but also that *It's Even Worse Than It Looks*, as the title of their 2012 book put it.[5] Presidential candidates have squabbled over who's to blame, and Congress has found itself tied in knots, unable to get much of anything done. But nothing is more fundamental to the distrust of government than the concern that too much of government just doesn't work well: that Americans find themselves paying high taxes for programs that underdeliver. Bureaucracy is the centerpiece of distrust. Nothing is more important to understanding the relationship between citizens and their government than understanding how government delivers what it promises. Nothing is more important to the future of American democracy than ensuring that programs work for citizens. At its very core, that is the story of the politics of the administrative process.

Although distrust has hit a boiling point in the United States in recent decades, there is nothing really new about the problem. Our founders, after all, used distrust of King George III as the foundation for a revolution. Their view of the king could not have been lower. Their aspirations for the new country could not have been higher. The Declaration of Independence has soaring, inspirational words: "We hold these truths to be self-evident, that all men are created equal, that they are endowed by their Creator with certain unalienable Rights, that among these are Life, Liberty, and the pursuit of Happiness." Stop and think: the revolutionaries who founded our government wanted to protect their liberty—and they wanted a government that would allow them to be happy. When was the last time you thought about "happiness" and "government" in the same sentence? (Actress Goldie Hawn, in fact, makes just this point in the 1984 movie, *Protocol.*) Then there's our basic framework, captured in the Constitution. It starts with a foundation in "We the People" and pledges justice, domestic tranquility, defense, the general welfare—and "the Blessings of Liberty to ourselves and our Posterity." Yet the 2016 presidential campaign swirled around charges that the rich and powerful had captured the system, steering the government to enrich itself at the expense of we the people.

We're the "posterity," living and walking today, but we're often not feeling especially happy about our government. The revolutionary DNA is still in our body politic. We battle over whether to shrink government to cut taxes or expand it to provide more protections. We quite deliberately vote opposing forces into office and then complain about congressional gridlock. But that doesn't stop much of the rest of the world from admiring our commitment to freedom and the society our government has built. In fact, we are often a puzzle to people in other parts of the world, who admire our government and are amazed at the way we govern ourselves. Those who look at us carefully from a distance understand what we often overlook: both our progress and our battles flow from our uneasy relationship with government, from our simultaneous efforts to empower and control it, and from our ceaseless struggles to figure out how to secure justice, defense, and the general welfare while seeking tranquility and happiness. The politics of the administrative process is the struggle to balance our lofty expectations for government with our deep distrust of it.

It's one thing to argue the case for justice, but it's another to make our state prisons secure without abusing inmates. It's one thing to argue for domestic tranquility, but it's another to determine how much force local police should use in fighting neighborhood crime. It's one thing to promise to defend the country from terrorists, but it's another to find just the right balance of weapons to protect the country without bankrupting it and undermining our freedoms. It's one thing to advance the general welfare, but it's quite another to decide which citizens whose homes are destroyed by a superstorm should get federal aid. (And how many times should we pay to rebuild the same property? One study found that we've paid to rebuild 2,109 properties at least ten times. One Louisiana home has gotten flood insurance payments forty times.[6]) It's our answer to the basic administrative questions, on the front lines of government, that define what our government really is and what values we protect.

No matter how bold or simple our policies, no matter how powerful our rhetoric, nothing in government has any meaning until we administer it.

For example, we have a clear national policy about the many oil-drilling platforms in the Gulf of Mexico. When companies extract the oil, our laws and regulations say they should keep their workers safe and ensure that their practices don't pollute. But on the evening of April 20, 2010, everything went tragically wrong. Workers on the *Deepwater Horizon*, a highly specialized drilling platform—part boat, part oil rig—noticed a highly explosive burst of methane gas moving up the pipes. One crew member raced to trigger the blowout preventer, a massive device on the ocean floor a mile below that was designed to seal the drilling pipe in case of trouble, but it failed. Explosions rocked the rig and the decks became sheets of flame. Some workers scrambled for the lifeboats. Other workers, facing a choice between the flaming cauldron and the dark sea 75 feet below, took the seven-story dive into the inky water. Rescuers fished some of the crew out of the water, but the *Deepwater Horizon*'s accident cost the lives of eleven crew members. The massive fire burned for a day and a half until the rig sank to the bottom, leaving oil gushing from the broken pipes. More than 4 million barrels of oil flowed into the Gulf, contaminating beaches, marshes, and wetlands in the largest oil spill in history.

One worker later reported, "There was no chain of command. Nobody in charge."[7] It quickly became clear that the spill was an epic disaster, whose full dimensions were truly unknown. No one really knew what was happening on the floor of the Gulf of Mexico, so deep that only unmanned submarines could reach the source of the spewing oil, so dark that submarines had to bring their own lights to see anything, and pressure so great that awkward remote-control arms proved to be the only way workers could work to contain the spewing oil.

At first, BP assured everyone that it would get the spill under control and that the company would deal with the environmental damage. At every step, though, television coverage undermined the corporation's pledge of quick, effective relief. Video of the out-of-control fire gave way to new shots of oil slicks on the water's surface and sludge-coated birds on the shoreline. Exasperated by the intense news coverage, BP's chief executive, Tony Hayward, told reporters, "I would like my life back." That infuriated Gulf residents who worried, "Our way of life is over," as Tom Young, a Louisiana fisherman, told a reporter. "It's the end, the apocalypse and no one outside of these few parishes really cares. They say they do, but they don't do nothing but talk. . . . Where's the person who says these are real people, real people with families, and they are hurting?" Hayward asked.[8] BP didn't know how much oil was flowing out of its well and couldn't seem to stop it. State and local governments pleaded for help.

BP called the spill "a well control event" that "allowed hydrocarbons to escape." In plain English, the spill was the result of a blowout caused by the failure of private companies to manage their operations safely, including BP and its two major contractors: Transocean, the world's largest ocean drilling company and the operator of the *Deepwater Horizon*, and Halliburton, a company that supplies a wide range of support services including, in this case, cementing the well on the floor of the Gulf. The spill was a private-sector failure—but congressional investigators began asking whether the federal government was doing enough. President Barack Obama decided that the federal government needed to act, and he appointed Coast Guard Commandant Admiral Thad Allen as the "national incident commander" to coordinate the response. As a tough and burly commander who had distinguished himself in leading the government's response to Hurricane Katrina five years earlier, Allen had become the federal government's go-to leader for impossible jobs. In the months that followed, Admiral Allen struggled to pull together the many players—and the thousands of workers—who were involved in the response effort.

In short order, a failure by a private company to manage its drilling operations became a demand for government to respond: private problems became public problems. The government response, in turn, was not just a program to be managed but a vast, complex, interconnected network to be built, across many government agencies, levels of government, and public-private connections. Overcoming the ooze depended on how well that network worked. There was enormous political pressure. Fishermen fearful of going out of business and a Republican governor with presidential ambitions, Louisiana's Bobby Jindal, had to join with the Democrats in the Obama administration. BP had to contain the oil, repair its image, and fend off the inevitable lawsuits. Residents along the Gulf just wanted the assault on their lives and their beaches to stop.

The Flint water crisis and the BP spill both capture the essence of modern government: We the people identify problems that we expect the government will solve, to promote the general welfare. How does it do so? Government, on behalf of us all, sets goals and then creates complex organizations to meet those goals. The Flint and BP crises also capture a fundamental challenge: Does government have what it takes to do what its citizens expect?

These challenges are huge, so the story can sometimes be depressing. But this book is built on optimism, out of an enduring belief that government can get smarter, serve citizens better, and support the fundamentals of American democracy on which the country depends. To a degree often not appreciated, government depends on *public administration* as the connection between those who make policy and the citizens who expect results. Running through public administration, moreover, are three enduring themes.

The first theme is *politics*. Many people often see administration as the business of the detail, which can't possibly be interesting. In reality, because no decision—especially no political decision—has any value except in the way it's implemented, public administration inevitably shapes and is shaped by politics. *Politics (and, therefore, public administration) is about the choices among values*, including which values get emphasis and which don't. That is the very fabric of public administration. Which neighborhoods get extra police protection? Who gets the speedy line through airport screening? When it snows, which highways are plowed first—and which see plows last? Each of these is a matter of detail richly wrapped in politics, and all administrative acts have political meaning. Indeed, the story of Flint's water crisis, at its core, is a political tale.

The second theme is *performance*. Public administration exists to get things done. How well does it work? How long does it take to respond to a house fire or report of a mugging? Do Social Security recipients get their checks on time and in the right amounts? Do state prisons keep prisoners inside, protecting citizens outside without abusing inmates inside? We expect public administration to work well, delivering effectiveness (high-quality goods and services) and efficiency (goods and services at the lowest cost to taxpayers).

The third theme is *accountability*. The prospect of a powerful bureaucracy out of control rightly terrifies citizens. The fear of a despotic government, after all, drove colonial Americans to revolt against the king. It brought down the Nixon administration in 1974. Worries that Obamacare will unleash a powerful, out-of-control bureaucracy helped propel Donald Trump into the White House in 2016. Accountability is a *relationship*. It is about *answerability to whom, for what*. When we debate whether public administration is accountable, we are asking to whom individual administrators must answer (legislative bodies like the city council, state legislature, and congressional committees, as well as administrative superiors up the chain of command) and for what activities they must answer (including the value judgments they make and the performance they demonstrate).

These three themes shape the big debates about public administration, because they frame the fundamental debate about the *power* of government. In 2013, for example, Louisiana Governor Bobby Jindal staged an attack on what he labeled the "two central philosophies of the Obama administration—the massive expansion of the size and power of the federal government and a lack of trust in the American people." What evidence did he present? He pointed to conflicting stories that the administration had presented about the attack on the American mission in Benghazi, Libya; mismanagement within the Internal Revenue Service; and "disastrous attempts to enforce Obamacare," the administration's health care reform.[9] And what does this evidence have in common? All focus on how administrative agencies to exercise power on behalf of government. Jindal suggested that the agencies were unaccountable to the people, that they were not performing on behalf on the public interest, and that they were the focus of administration decisions that, in Jindal's view, represented the wrong political decisions. Of course, Jindal's attack was itself political. How could it be otherwise? What government does is about politics—and political decisions take their meaning in the ways public administrators carry them out. Government's power centers on public administration.

These themes also capture the inevitable tradeoffs at the core of government power. Steps to increase accountability, including more rules to restrict administrators' power, can reduce efficiency by multiplying red tape. Streamlining government to make it more efficient can risk making administrators less accountable. At every stage, these basic questions frame the size and role of government, and there's nothing more fundamental to politics than that.

Public administration is about everything that's important about government, and everything that's important about government touches on or flows through public administration. Those twists and turns are often hidden, and the issues can be subtle. But if we care about government—especially if we care about making government work better—we need to pay very careful attention to the politics of the administrative process. And that's the mission of this book.

For example, consider the mundane problem of plowing snow from city streets. Could it possibly be about politics? Just ask former New York mayor John Lindsay. Following a blizzard in February 1969, much of the city was impassable for days. Almost 40 percent of the city's snow removal equipment was sidelined because of poor maintenance, and the borough of Queens was especially isolated. When Lindsay used a four-wheel-drive vehicle to make his way to the snow-bound residents, they booed him and called him a bum. He managed to win reelection, but the story haunted him for the rest of his career and undermined his 1972 presidential campaign. A 1979 storm in Chicago torpedoed the campaign of Chicago Mayor Michael A. Bilandic. Washington Mayor Marion S. Barry Jr. suffered for years after a blizzard hit his city while he was enjoying sunny weather in Southern California, where he was attending the Super Bowl.[10] A senior official in a Midwest city once confided in me that there was a

After a string of fierce Boston snowstorms, firefighters from Engine Company 3, Dana Nunan and Matthew Brady, dig out a hydrant on Albany Street.

special snow removal plan for election day, to ensure that the precincts most likely to vote for the mayor got plowed out first.

It's not especially surprising to discover that officials use government power to advance political purposes—or that administrative actions like snow plowing have political consequences. This is an echo of a great scene in the movie *Casablanca*, which might well be the best film of all time. Police Captain Louis Renault loves Casablanca's nightlife but the Nazis who occupy the city expect him to enforce public order, in the way they want it done. When the Nazis insist he crack down on his friend Rick's casino, Renault picks an ironic pretense. "I'm shocked, shocked to find that gambling is going on in here!" he tells everyone—just before his favorite dealer hands him his own winnings. We should be no more shocked to discover that politics surrounds the exercise of public power through public administration.

HISTORICAL ROOTS

These tensions and tradeoffs have deep roots in American history. We might not like politics or government much, but we like bureaucracy even less. Our founders rebelled against King George III, but the prime complaints were against his administrators. The Boston Tea Party was a public act of rebellion against the king's tax collectors. (For a small historical tidbit, check the modern heritage of colonial brewer Sam Adams, who was a ringleader of the Tea Party and whose name lives on today.) The Declaration of Independence specifically condemns King George III, saying, "He has erected a multitude of New Offices, and sent hither swarms of Officers to harass our people and eat out their substance." Signing the document required tremendous bravery on the part of the signatories, but declaring independence was the easy part. First they had to win the war against the world's most powerful army, and then they had to make independence stick by learning how to govern. The new government, in fact, failed an early test of governing, when it stumbled in putting down a rebellion in 1786, led by Daniel Shays in western Massachusetts. The founders concluded that protecting their hard-won democracy required a stronger government. That led in 1787 to another major Philadelphia convention, this time to write a constitution.

Determining the role of administrators in the new constitutional system, however, proved difficult. No one wanted to recreate the tyranny against which the founders had rebelled, but a weak government risked inviting invasion and conquest. The founders famously and delicately balanced government's power through the legislative, judicial, and executive powers. They finessed the tough question about how to exercise those powers, especially the administrative powers. Article II of the Constitution vests "the executive power" in the president, but the definition of executive power is fuzzy and the founders carefully balanced the exercise of this power through the powers given to the other two branches. Trying to define executive power further risked fracturing the fragile coalition that brought the new country together. What they left out couldn't draw political fire, and they left to future leaders how to administer the nation they worked so hard to create.

There is profound irony here. The founders were determined to prevent a recurrence of the abuse of power that prompted the revolution, but when they had the chance to define the power of the new government, they sidestepped the question. From its first moments, American public administration was grounded in politics—the political battle against the king, followed by the delicate political balance to get the Constitution ratified. The political issues about public administration colored Washington's two presidential terms, as

John Adams and other Federalists battled with Thomas Jefferson and his Democratic-Republican colleagues about how far the government's power should go. Defining the nature of executive power produced the first big divisions in the new nation, fueled a feud that cost the life of the former Secretary of the Treasury in a duel, and fed the creation of political parties with very different views on how that power ought to be exercised. (The story is so gripping, in fact, that it led to a hit Broadway musical, *Hamilton*.) The discovery that government power was about public administration and that public administration was about politics was about as surprising as Captain Renault's discovery that there was gambling—gambling!—going on in the casino where he did his betting.

The struggles change with the times, but the basic issues are as old as the United States: creating an administration strong enough to do the public's work but accountable enough to prevent the tyranny that the nation's founders sought to guard against. That leads us to a more detailed examination of the puzzle of *accountability*.

THE MEANING OF ACCOUNTABILITY

We use the word **accountability** a great deal, but we rarely stop to ask ourselves what it means, how it works, what we seek to control, or who controls whom. The word has its origins, as far back as the 1200s, in the notion that something ought to be capable of being counted. Medieval kings wanted to know what happened to their money. The issue is even more important in a modern democracy. So let us examine these issues in turn.

What Is Accountability?

Accountability is a relationship between people (who is accountable to whom?) about actions (what are they accountable for?). It is the foundation of bureaucracy in a democracy, because accountability depends on the ability of policymakers to *control* administrators' actions. Control, in turn, can be either *positive* (requiring an agency to do something it ought to do) or *negative* (seeking to prevent an agency from doing something it should not do). Sins of omission as well as acts of commission are subject to investigation, criticism, instructions, and sanctions.

The principal focus of control is on discovering bureaucratic errors and requiring their correction—a largely negative approach that tends to become dominant for several reasons. First, it is easier to see—and to criticize—sins of commission, for they tend to be the stories that attract media attention; the more intense the news coverage, the stronger the policymakers' reaction is likely to be. In 2004, the abuse of Iraqi prisoners by a small group of American soldiers generated news stories for months, while the effective military service—and considerable suffering—of other American troops in Iraq received little attention in comparison. Second, an external control body (such as Congress, a state legislature, or a city council) can more easily identify specific problems to be solved than it can devise a broader strategy to be followed. Oversight hearings promptly focused on the behavior of that handful of troops, but Congress struggled to sort out the far more complex issues underlying American policy in the region. When lead poisoning crippled the water system in Flint, Michigan, in 2015 and 2016, local and state investigators, along with federal regulators, worked to figure out the source of the problem and how to fix it. Our discussion focuses on efforts of policymakers to shape administrative behavior. It therefore focuses primarily on the negative aspects of external control: correcting bureaucratic behavior that policymakers believe is not in the public interest. However, we must explore that issue also in the context of the often confusing dynamics of the underlying policy.

But do policymakers actually *want* to control administrators? Often they do not. If policymakers precisely specify policy goals, that would make them more directly responsible for the results. Policymakers often like to keep some distance between the decisions they make and the consequences that flow from them. When problems occur—from accidents in the space program to the slow response time of fire trucks—reporters and top officials like to prowl for someone to blame. An unbroken chain from top policymakers to the front line would put the blame for problems directly into the laps of elected officials. Top officials certainly do not want to encourage problems, but they also do not want the finger of blame pointing directly at them when problems inevitably occur. When the independent commission investigated the September 11, 2001, terrorist attacks, commission members discovered that the web of responsibility was so unclear that it was impossible to fix the blame. Despite heavy pressure to hold someone accountable for failures in intelligence and security, no one was fired. When Hurricane Katrina in 2005 produced the worst administrative failure in American history, only the administrator of the Federal Emergency Management Agency, Michael Brown, lost his job, despite manifest problems throughout the federal, state, and local policy systems. Despite his city's huge problems in responding to the storm, New Orleans Mayor Ray Nagin was reelected.

Even if elected officials actually wanted a clear chain of accountability, it would create a "gotcha" effect: if administrators knew they would have to answer for every problem, they would make sure no one could see any problems they would have to answer for. Administrative problems rarely have simple solutions or leave a clear trail. How likely is it that some drugs will cause deformities in humans, or that landing an airplane in a thunderstorm is likely to be unsafe? How can a dangerous chemical dump best be cleaned? When a storm wobbles between snow, ice, and rain, when is it best to plow the roads, and how many chemicals should be applied to keep them clear (and what damage to the environment and to the roadway might the chemicals cause)? If we create a climate that punishes risk-taking, we are likely to get too-safe decisions that prevent government from doing its job. Excessive controls increase red tape and delay action. Finger-pointing leads to administrators digging deep foxholes instead of taking risks to achieve high performance. So much energy can be spent attempting to control administrative activities—and filing the paperwork to document that the control standards have been met—that there may be little money or time left to do the job. Controls that are too tight, therefore, may actually *reduce* administration's responsiveness to its public. Indeed, as British scholar Peter Self put it, "The tensions between the requirements of responsibility or 'accountability' and those of effective executive action can reasonably be described as *the* classic dilemma of public administration."[11]

Discretion is inevitable—and desirable—in administrative action. Policymakers can never specify all of the steps a complex program requires, and frontline administrators inevitably have to use their judgment in making programs work. Even if legislators could specify all of the steps, the legislative process—from city councils to the halls of Congress—makes that impossible, because reaching compromise on hard problems usually means blurring the lines. Moreover, not all circumstances are the same, and good administration requires adapting general policies to special needs. When first responders arrive on the scene of a serious traffic accident or a building collapse, what should they do first? How should firefighters approach a burning building, since everyone is different? Good responses depend on good training and professional judgment. That always requires discretion. We want to give administrators enough room to make the right decisions, yet we want to hold them accountable.

Barton Gellman/Getty Images

Edward Snowden, who formerly worked as a contractor for the National Security Agency, posed in December 2013 for a photo during an interview with government officials in Moscow. He had travelled the world looking for temporary asylum to escape prosecution in the United States.

Administrators must follow the law and meet the goals of public policy—at the same time.

Finding the right balance is an eternal challenge—and who makes the call? Who ultimately is accountable for what? The ancient Romans, in fact, worried about the problem—including the question, "*Quis custodiet ipsos custodes?*"—"Who is to watch the watchers?" as Juvenal put it[12] We all want accountability, but there is no absolute standard for accountability and who holds accountable those in charge of accountability. Accountability is a relationship and, like all relationships, it constantly changes—and is often full of tension.[13]

The responsibility of individual administrators underlies the accountability debate. Can—should—must administrators follow the orders of top officials? Or: can—should—must they become "whistleblowers," divulging to the public activities that they believe are wrong? On one hand, the answer seems clear. The post–World War II war crimes trials established that following orders was no defense against administrators who committed heinous acts. It's clear that administrators must exercise their own judgment. On the other hand, if administrators each exercised their own individual judgment as they went about their daily work, coordination would evaporate, the work wouldn't get done, and there would be little meaning to accountability.

Over the years, we've had a very mixed view of **whistleblowers**—individuals who take it upon themselves to disclose activities they believe are wrong. In a fascinating background story, *Wall Street Journal* reporter Ben Zimmer explains that the phrase "blowing the whistle" seems to have entered American language in the early part of the twentieth century, when fans expected sports officials to blow their whistles to stop play. If a football player committed a penalty or a boxer had beaten his opponent, fans called on referees to blow the whistle. A few decades later, during the 1930s, a new meaning crept in. "Blowing the whistle" took on the meaning of someone revealing a dramatic secret, often breaking a code of silence to authorities as a "snitch" or a "rat." In the 1970s, consumer advocate Ralph Nader deliberately changed the meaning. He challenged those with important information on misconduct, in either private companies or the government, to come forward, even if that meant "blowing the whistle against the system."[14]

This raises a fundamental question about accountability. How much obedience do government officials owe to organizational superiors and elected officials—and how much discretion should officials exercise on their own? Because there is no firm answer to that question, there is no single, clear approach to accountability. Accountability is, at once, the bedrock on which administrative power in a democracy builds and a puzzle that requires endless work in search of solutions.

Approaches to Accountability

In the United States, the effort to resolve this dilemma has focused on three big issues: the search for *legal boundaries* to constrain and channel administrative action, what we call the **rule of law**; the *political challenges* that have surfaced when administrative realities stretch those legal boundaries; and *evolving policy problems* that increasingly confound the strategies and tactics to hold governmental power accountable and to ensure that administration serves the public interest.

LEGAL BOUNDARIES. The problem of balancing governmental power with individual freedom, of course, is nothing new. When King John met England's nobles in Runnymede in 1215, they pledged him fealty—but only after the king agreed to limits on his power, which were captured in the Magna Carta, an important document that has since shaped the way we think about constraints on governmental power.[15] The debate has been endless, but two things are clear. One is that the uneasy pact forged at Runnymede helped establish the basis for the modern state. The other is that the rule of law emerged as the guide for setting the balance between governmental power and individual liberty. Kings (and later queens) found power useful to work their will. Citizens sometimes found the exercise of that power overbearing and expensive. Across a wide range of issues, King John and his successors agreed to accept limits on their power in law, even though the British monarchs claimed that their power flowed from divine right.

The *rule of law* thus became enshrined in English common law. In practice, the rule of the sword often pushed aside written agreements, and it took centuries for kings to realize that modern government required real accountability to the people. It's not surprising, therefore, that the story of the rule of law is the story of struggle and conflict.[16] The rule of law seeks to define and protect the basic rights of citizens against a too-powerful government, although claims of the Magna Carta's historical impact have been much exaggerated.[17] Its most important contribution, however, is this: it establishes the importance of having a system where everyone knows the rules and where the rules apply to everyone. Finally, the rule of law creates the foundation for administrative accountability. Since government in action is often the action of administrators, the rule of law provides the mechanism for constraining how administrators exercise their power. It tells them what they can do and what will happen to them if they step beyond their boundaries.[18]

This basic outline, of course, is far clearer in theory than it ever was in practice, but the rule of law provided at least a basic blueprint for the founders of the United States. In *Common Sense,* Thomas Paine wrote that "a government of our own is a natural right," with that right protected by the law, because

> in America the law is king. For as in absolute governments the king is law, so in free countries the law ought to be king; and there ought to be no other. But lest any ill use should afterwards arise, let the crown at the conclusion of the ceremony be demolished, and scattered among the people whose right it is. (1791)

The rule of law was central to the colonial founders as they tried to create their new government. Paine, and others, argued that citizens could establish that government because they would also bind its power.

The Articles of Confederation, the principles that guided the nation in the uneasy days between independence from the British crown and the adoption of the 1787 Constitution, was a clumsy first effort. But the Constitution that followed is a web of crosscutting restraints on government and the basic strategy for administrative accountability in American government: give the government power but set legal bounds to limit the dangers of its use. In the United States, the founders did not trust a single check. Multiple backstops, through separated institutions sharing authority, provided the extra insurance that the wary founders wanted. But this balance of powers was an unsteady deal. In the nation's first decades, officials created a national bank only to close it; they tried a second time and closed it again. Alexander Hamilton's powerful argument for government's help in promoting the economy repeatedly encountered a hurricane of citizen opposition.

The conflict became razor-sharp during the Progressive Era, toward the end of the nineteenth century. In tackling the problems of rising corporate power and the enormous potential of the industrial age, the **Progressives** faced a dilemma. They were convinced that stronger government, with new programs and stronger agencies, was necessary to drive the country forward and to constrain the giant private companies. But they also knew that citizens would be nervous about a more powerful government, for the American Revolution against King George III's tyranny remained in the country's collective consciousness. How could the government grow without creating bureaucratic tyrants? For the Progressives, the answer lay in the rule of law. (It's important to note that, for the early Progressives, they focused on creating strategies to make government work better. Only in subsequent decades did "Progressive" come to be associated with "big government.") Before being elected president, Woodrow Wilson, then a political scientist at Princeton University, famously sketched a solution:

> If I see a murderous fellow sharpening a knife cleverly, I can borrow his way of sharpening the knife without borrowing his probable intention to commit murder with it; and so, if I see a monarchist dyed in the wool managing a public bureau well, I can learn his business methods without changing one of my republican spots.[19]

Wilson, along with his fellow Progressives, contended that government administrators could be empowered to do government's work without threatening individual rights because the rule of law would hold them accountable. Delegation of power to administrators from elected officials and hierarchical control through authority controlled the use of power within administrative agencies. Separating politics from administration, in what became known as the **politics-administration dichotomy**, was their strategy for an effective administrative state in a modern democracy: politicians would determine policy, and administrators would carry out that policy within the bounds set by elected officials.[20]

The Progressives' reliance on the rule of law was an elegant solution to a very tough problem. As they contemplated the twentieth century, they concluded that government would have to become far stronger. Caught between the growing corporate power of the railroad barons and captains of industry and the limitless opportunities of industrial and territorial expansion, the reformers found in the rule of law a way to fit old theories to the new prospects. The rule-of-law formulation was not the last word for the Progressive movement, any more than it was for King John, but it provided a way to expand government in the twentieth century while holding it accountable.

POLITICAL CHALLENGES. Of course, big problems soon strained this neat formula. Herbert Hoover and his advisers fumbled in their response to the 1929 stock market crash. When Franklin D. Roosevelt launched the New Deal to attack these problems, critics complained it was a vast and unconstitutional overreach of power. The rule of law had real appeal, both because of its common law and historical roots and because it provided a logical answer to the nation's pragmatic problems. But the theory inevitably collided with politics, as John M. Gaus reminded everyone: "A theory of public administration means in our time a theory of politics also."[21] Not only did the rule of law fit uneasily between governmental power and individual liberty, it rested on the inescapable reality, captured so well by Gaus, that administration has always been about politics. Political pressures maneuvered King John into putting his seal on the Magna Carta, and they have swirled around the rule of law since then.

In his 1936 essay "The Responsibility of Public Administration," Gaus noted that cracks had appeared in the rule of law from the earliest times. He described a replica of a Babylonian monolith, which displayed a carving of the Code of Hammurabi from 2000 B.C. Above the code is a relief of Hammurabi receiving the command to establish a just law from the sun-god, Shamash. That, Gaus pointed out, established the "earliest conception of political responsibility": "Somewhere in the wisdom of God was to be found the absolute code, the fixed standard, which the ruler was to follow." However, he continued,

> the inadequacy of such a conception of responsibility is obvious. Responsibility is accountability, but who, under such conditions, could call power to account? Is God's will always so clear? Should not, then, His vicar interpret him? But can one be sure that the vicar is correct in his interpretation?[22]

That's the core conflict for administrative accountability and the rule of law. It's hard to beat an accountability system coming directly from God. But it's also impossible to translate, with complete transparency and total predictability, the rule of law directly into administrative action. As administrators interpret the rule of law to bring the law to life, the law slips in its hold on their rule. Gaus concluded in his essay that "neither the electorate nor the legislature can express in concrete detail the specific policy which it desires the administrative organization to enforce,"[23] so administrative discretion is the inevitable result of any administrative act. Indeed, the dilemma of building sufficient capacity to allow Congress to oversee executive branch actions is a puzzle that has echoed through the American Political Science Association lectures given in Gaus's name.[24]

What solution does Gaus offer? If forces external to the administrator cannot adequately shape the exercise of discretion, then democracy must necessarily rely on the administrator's professional norms. Gaus's argument set the stage for one of the most trenchant battles of public administration theory, the 1940 debate between Herman Finer and Carl J. Friedrich on whether professional training or external controls could best hold administrators accountable.[25] The battleground was the rule of law, as Finer made the case for the long tradition of administration held accountable by legal standards. But Friedrich echoed Gaus in making an inescapable point: if the law cannot fully control administrative action, then how can administrators be held accountable? For Gaus and Friedrich, the case for relying on professional norms was the inescapable conclusion. They argued that government had to rely on what it had at its disposal. That, in turn, not only makes public administration about politics, since it brings the value judgments of administrators squarely into the process; it also brings in the question of *whose* political values shape administrative action.

EVOLVING POLICY PROBLEMS. Resorting to pragmatism beyond the law was perhaps inevitable, but it also set the stage for a fierce debate about administrative theory and practice. The Magna Carta was important because it established the premise that law could limit the king's power, but the Runnymede meeting did not erase the enormous pressures on the exercise of political power that came before or after. The United States relied on the rule of law to define and protect individual rights, but few rights have ever been absolute and the debate over how to shape them has always involved substantial cross-pressures. As governmental programs became more complex in the first half of the twentieth century, and especially as

Why We Can't Have Nice Things, Explained
Theme: Politics

On June 1, 2016, Fox News anchor Greta Van Susteren saw a story that appeared on *NBC Nightly News*. In 2015, a National Aeronautics and Space Administration (NASA) spacecraft had flown by Pluto and captured truly remarkable photos. On that June day, NASA released the pictures. Van Susteren wasn't impressed and tweeted, "Why did they wait until NOW to release these? [P]ics taken in 2015 and we pay their salaries in tax dollars."

Through some careful digging, *Washington Monthly* reporter Nancy LeTourneau discovered that there was a complicated but interesting story about why it took so long for NASA to release these photos.

First, Pluto is a very, very long way from Earth. The distance: 3 billion miles. Even at the speed of light, it takes radio signals 4.5 hours to travel back home from Pluto. Second, the photos are high resolution, so there are a lot of data in each photo. Third, the spacecraft took a lot of photos.

The June 1 photo showed remarkable detail from the best photos ever taken of Earth's distant neighbor. NASA released the June 1 photo when it arrived and, given the huge volume of data and the long distances, NASA expected it would continue receiving photos until the end of 2016.

But instead of doing a story on NASA's triumph, Van Susteren "used her platform to spin the age-old tale about the inefficiency of government in spending our tax dollars," wrote LeTourneau. "That is as good of an example as I've seen to explain why we can't have nice things," she concluded.

Source: Nancy LeTourneau, "Why We Can't Have Nice Things," *Washington Monthly* (June 1, 2016), http://washingtonmonthly.com/2016/06/01/why-we-cant-have-nice-things-4/.

more public programs involved partnerships with the multiple levels of government and with the private sector, strains on the rule of law hit the breaking point. Gaus argued:

> In a state in which the powers of government intermesh widely with those of industry, commerce, and finance the traditional restraints upon the discretion of the administrator through making him responsible to the electorate, the courts, and the legislators are inadequate.[26]

Although Gaus wrote this in 1936, he could easily have been describing BP and the *Deepwater Horizon* accident: big problems that blur the legal boundaries in ways that make it hard to define who is responsible for what action.

Those changes in the complexity of governmental programs accelerated during the 1930s. Franklin D. Roosevelt's New Deal programs, in particular, not only reinforced the challenge of politics in accountability and pushed more reliance onto the professional norms of administrators, they also brought more players from a wider variety of organizations into the pursuit of public policy. World War II, as it spawned a massive network of private contractors to help the war effort, accelerated the trend. These steps, in turn, had two effects.

First, it became far more difficult to rely on any single rule-of-law standard to guide administrative action. There was a theoretical simplicity in the basic model—policymakers could track the exercise of discretion by administrators through the hierarchy and through the rule of law. Complicating that chain through new partnerships, where each member operated inside its own traditions, made it much harder to define and enforce a single rule of law to guide that partnership.

Second, different governments—and different government agencies—have very different cultures, and that makes it hard to ensure that any single set of professional norms can shape administrative behavior. The federal government has a different culture than its state and local partners, and the cultures of each government agency often have surprising variations.

Professionals in the government's private and nonprofit partners often live by far different cultures that stretch far beyond the typical profit-making or public good motives presumed to be at the core of their missions. Community-based organizations are very different from international environmental protection organizations, and they differ tremendously from defense contractors and road builders. There have even been famous squabbles at the scene of local incidents, where police officers and firefighters have thrown punches over who was in control. In fact, when Tony Hayward complained in the BP case that he wanted to "get my life back," he demonstrated the frustration of a private-sector executive operating within the realm of public policy, in harsh public light. Combining private actors and public expectations created a very nasty mix.

In 1933, President Franklin D. Roosevelt signed a law creating the Tennessee Valley Authority, which for the first time brought inexpensive electric power to many in the nation's South.

The rule of law, of course, was always more powerful in theory than in practice. But the rise of such mixed federal-state-local-public-private actions further undermines the theory's applicability. Since no single model of accountability is likely to work, how can government be effective, efficient, responsive, and accountable in the world of twenty-first-century politics?

Elements of Accountability

When we look at how we hold government in check, we focus on three elements of accountability: fiscal, process, and program.[27] In **fiscal accountability**, we seek to ensure that agency officials spend money on the programs they are charged with managing—and only on those programs. This issue cuts both ways. On the one hand, we want to make sure that, in fact, the money is spent. A recurring complaint in the early 2000s was that the U.S. Department of Homeland Security was too slow in distributing funds to state and local governments for strengthening their security efforts. On the other hand, we want to make sure that the money is spent according to the law and is not wasted. In 2011, for example, Fox News pundit Bill O'Reilly and *The Daily Show* host Jon Stewart tangled over charges that the U.S. Department of Justice paid $16 for each muffin served at a Washington conference. A vast number of very senior Obama administration officials spent a huge amount of time tracking down the story, which turned out to be "mostly untrue," according to a later analysis by fact checkers. In reality, the $16 muffin included beverages, some fruit, a fee for the meeting space—and the muffin. Although the muffin was not cheap, it certainly was not a vastly overpriced baked good.[28] But the tale underlines the fact that there's nothing like a headline on wasted government money to fuel political conflict.

Process accountability is concerned with *how* agencies perform their tasks. While we often argue about the meaning of procedural fairness, government agencies regularly find themselves charged with unfair treatment. Massive problems in the 2000 presidential election focused national attention on the voting machines that many state and local governments used and whether problems with those machines had prevented some votes from being counted. Those complaints about process led to a massive investment in new machinery for future elections. Despite the investment, however, many voters waited hours after closing time in the 2012 presidential election to cast their ballots.

Program accountability is the newest and most difficult objective of control systems. Is a public program achieving its purpose, as defined in law? The U.S. Government Accountability Office, the investigative arm of Congress, has increasingly conducted program analyses to measure how well federal agencies answer this question. At the local, state, and federal levels, governments have developed sophisticated performance measurement systems to gauge how well programs meet their goals. These new systems increasingly try to put hard numbers on the tough question of whether programs actually work.

Everyone agrees that citizens deserve accountability for their hard-earned tax dollars. But we tend to measure accountability in these three different ways—sometimes relying more on one standard than another and rarely trying to reconcile all three into an overall picture of an agency's performance.

Holding Administration Accountable

The related problems of making administration work efficiently and ensuring that it is democratically accountable are deep and lasting. Administrators can follow the basic doctrine of accountability, through the hierarchical system of delegated authority. When that leaves gaps, they can use their best judgment to discover the intent of the policy, rely on their professional judgment to determine how best to achieve that intent, and consult with the controllers to resolve uncertainties.[29]

But this is certainly not a magic solution. Administrators may face multiple controllers, and these controllers may not always agree on an agency's priorities. Congress might pass a law that conflicts with the president's priorities. That can leave agency heads, appointed by the president, to choose which to obey. Appointees who choose the legislature's course could find themselves replaced by appointees more willing to follow the president's wishes. Those who follow Congress might find their funds slashed or their time taken up by endless oversight hearings. Seeking clarity from Congress, furthermore, can be difficult, since there is no "Congress" to talk to—only a congressional committee or its chair (or sometimes its staff), whose interpretation may not conform to the view of Congress as a whole, whose muddy legislation is often the source of uncertainty to begin with. At the state and local levels of government, of course, the same problems occur. And because the implementation of public policies often depends on coordinating federal, state, and local actions, these uncertainties often make it even harder to know what accountability means.

Administrators must solve these problems in a world full of uncertainty and political conflict. In doing so, they inevitably must rely heavily on their own internal compasses—their personal character, professional training, devotion to the public service, and respect for faithful execution of the law. When controllers give conflicting directions or confusing signals, administrators face a conflict of loyalties. In the classic collection of options, they can choose **voice**: remaining in their positions and fighting for what they think is right, even if that risks dismissal. Or they can choose **exit**: resigning, possibly with a public attack on the controller whose mandate they condemn.[30] But administrators know that the exit option may put the policies they care about at even greater risk, for they can be replaced by people who will bend more easily to the very pressures they have battled against. In fact, the idea of a conscience-driven exit from government is more popular in the press than in reality, because civil servants often have families to support, college tuition to pay, and relatively few available job options. In contrast, most high-level political appointees, cushioned by established reputations and extensive contacts outside government, can often exit to private-sector jobs at higher salaries. Furthermore, an attack by a resigning official is usually only a one-day media event, so anyone deciding to resign in protest must weigh the short-term political effect against the long-term personal impact.

In the end, the solution to the problem of accountability hinges on the balance between forces that come from outside administrators, including efforts by outside controllers, and forces that emerge from administrators themselves, including their character, background, and training. Theorists for generations have debated which forces are—and should be—more important. Should we assume that external controllers can never know enough about an administrator's actions, and that setting the administrator's internal compass is most important? Or should we insist on extensive external controls to compensate for the tendency of administrators sometimes to stray off course? Friedrich and Finer were unable to resolve this debate in the 1940s. Subsequent scholars and practitioners have not done any better. Accountability, in the final analysis, is a fine balance between external and internal controls. This balance, in turn, depends ultimately on ethical behavior by administrators.

The detention of Iraqi prisoners at Abu Ghraib prison outside Baghdad created security worries, as well as international outrage at the treatment of the prisoners held there.

Wathiq Khuzaie/Getty Images

GOVERNMENTAL POWER AND ADMINISTRATIVE ETHICS

Citizens and elected officials alike demand a higher standard of ethics than typically prevails in the private sector. Indeed, that ethical upgrade often comes as a shock for political appointees who come to government from the private sector.[31] As Calvin Mackenzie writes,

> At one time or another in their work lives, most business leaders have found jobs in their own companies for family members or friends, have entered into contracts with firms in which they had a financial interest, or have accepted substantial gifts from people with whom they regularly do business. . . . When public officials engage in similar activities, however, they break the law.[32]

The pursuit of high **ethical behavior** in government raises a different tradeoff. On the one hand, we want skilled employees who can ensure that government's work is done well. In particular, we don't want to make the process of screening and hiring officials to be so burdensome, in the pursuit of high ethical standards, that we drive away good people. On the other hand, the public expects that those who exercise the public's trust will meet high standards and that, in particular, they will not use their power to line their own pockets, advantage their friends, or trade

As President Barack Obama gave a major speech in 2014 about reforming the National Security Agency, activists protested outside. The debate focused over what permission intelligence agencies needed in advance to examine the telephone records of U.S. citizens.

in the future on the relationships they developed in public service.

In his 2008 inaugural address, Philadelphia Mayor Michael A. Nutter emphatically made the point that this issue crosses all governmental boundaries. "There is nothing government does that cannot be done ethically and transparently," he said. His goal, he told Philadelphians, was "a government that serves all of us, not a few."[33] Nutter's speech underlined the recurring central themes of public administration: creating governmental power to serve citizens; holding that power accountable to elected officials and ultimately to voters; exercising power ethically, according to high standards of public service; and ensuring accountability through transparency.

THE PUBLIC SERVICE

In the end, the quality of government's work depends on the quality of the individuals recruited and retained in the public service, on their respect for bureaucratic accountability and ethical behavior, and especially on their commitment to the constitutional, democratic system. Instilling such values is a task for society. It depends on communication by family, schools, and peers. It also depends on creating a system that is accountable within our political system—especially since, in so many ways, the politics of the administrative process shapes the performance of American government.

Those capabilities encompass much more than they did in the past. Public administration is no longer primarily the direct execution of governmental programs. Much of it now is administration by proxy, with complex partnerships among government agencies, for-profit companies, and nonprofit organizations responsible for the implementation of government programs. That, in turn, multiplies the problem of public ethics, since many private and nonprofit employees find themselves doing the public's work, during at least part of their time, but often without a clear signal that they are entering the public realm.

An ethical government begins with ethical public servants—public servants devoted to the fundamental challenge of helping "to form a more perfect union, establish justice, insure domestic tranquility, provide for the common defense, and secure the blessings of liberty to ourselves and our posterity."[34] Encouraged by such possibilities, they will recognize that the public service, as President George H. W. Bush said, is "the highest and noblest calling."[35] In running for the presidency in 2008, Barack Obama was more direct. His goal, he said, was "to make government and public service cool again."[36] Few vocations offer greater promise for improving the lives of so many of the world's citizens. Charting the course is the fundamental challenge of this book.

CASE 1.1

Do NOT Read This Case! The NSA's Surveillance Program

In July 2013, U.S. Department of Homeland Security employees received a message warning them not to use their home computers or personal smartphones to look at an article on the *Washington Post* website. The website, it turns out, contained a "top-secret" slide leaked by former intelligence analyst Edward Snowden. If an agency employee viewed the top-secret material from an unclassified computer, it would constitute "classified data spillage," which had to be reported to supervisors, like a toxic chemical spill.

Here's the email, as the *Post* reported it:

From: [REDACTED]

Sent: Friday, July 12, 2013 9:50 AM

Subject: SECURITY ALERT ***Washington Post Article***

Importance: High

FYSA . . . From DHS HQ

Per the National Cybersecurity Communications Integration Center:

There is a recent article on the Washington Post's Website that has a clickable link titled "The NSA Slide you never seen" that must not be opened on an Unclassified government workstation. This link opens up a classified document which will raise the classification level of your Unclassified workstation to the classification of the slide which is reported to be TS/NF.

If opened on an Unclassified system, you are obligated to report this to the SSO as a Classified Data Spillage (Opssecurity@hq.dhs.gov <mailto:Opssecurity@ hq.dhs.gov><mailto:Opssecurity@hq.dhs.gov<mailto: Opssecurity@hq.dhs.gov> >).

Again, please exercise good judgment when visiting these webpages and clicking on such links. You may be violating your Non-Disclosure Agreement in which you sign that you will protect Classified National Security Information. You may be subject to any administrative or legal action from the Government.[1]

What caused all the fuss was a PowerPoint slide revealing the basic structure of the federal government's PRISM program.[2] No one but highly placed insiders had previously even known about the program. Through PRISM, the National Security Agency (NSA) worked with a wide variety of information technology companies, including Apple, Google, Skype, Yahoo, and Facebook, to collect information on the communications of individuals that the NSA wanted to investigate. The companies shared the information with NSA, which then put its analysts to work to determine whether any of the communications constituted a threat to national security. How many "targets" was NSA investigating? At the time of Snowden's leak, there were 117,675 targets. Other Americans, however, might have had their communications shared with NSA "incidentally," as a result of the agency's work.[3]

So if you have a top-secret security clearance and if you read this case, you must immediately go to your supervisor to report a "classified data spillage." If you don't have a top-secret clearance, you've just read something you weren't supposed to see to begin with. Either way: Do NOT read this case!

QUESTIONS TO CONSIDER

1. What do you think about this government surveillance program, which allows the NSA to work with popular service providers like Facebook, Google, and Skype to collect personal information without the user's knowledge? On the one hand, terrorists frequently use the Internet to plan attacks. On the other hand, such surveillance is clearly an invasion of individual privacy.

2. The memo to employees might seem silly to some. But the government has a broad policy on not allowing users to look at classified information on unclassified computers. Why? Unclassified computers can be infiltrated by viruses and spyware, which allow others to capture anything that goes across the screen. (The Central Intelligence Agency and the NSA do not allow cell phones inside their buildings' secure zones.) If you were a manager, how would you handle this situation?

3. Perhaps nothing more sharply frames the problem of accountability in modern government than determining how to safeguard the personal communications of individual Americans while preserving national security. What kind of accountability system would you design to find the balance?

NOTES

1. Josh Hicks, "DHS Warns Employees Not to Read Leaked NSA Information," *Washington Post* (July 15, 2013), http://www.washingtonpost.com/blogs/ federal-eye/wp/2013/07/15/dhs-warns-employees-not-to-read-leaked-nsa-information.

2. To view the slide, go to http://www.washingtonpost .com/business/economy/the-nsa-slide-you-havent-seen/2013/07/10/32801426-e8e6-11e2-aa9f-c03a72e2d342_story.html.

Snow Removal in the Blizzard of 2010: Who Gets Plowed First?

Throughout much of the East Coast, the winter of 2010 was painfully burned into everyone's memory. Children looking forward to snow days had their dreams fulfilled—and then some. By mid-February, the Washington, D.C., area had already shattered the all-time record for snow, with 55 inches of accumulation. For a time, Baltimore, Maryland, had more snow than Buffalo, New York. Many football fans found themselves stuck at home instead of partying with friends for the Super Bowl. Some local universities were shut down for a week as the snow removal crews struggled to dig out the sidewalks and parking lots.

Most people in the area tried to bring good humor to the onslaught, but in some neighborhoods snow plow drivers were threatened by angry residents. Stuck for days and watching the plows drive by without dropping their blades, some residents of a neighborhood in Prince George's County, a Washington, D.C., suburb, told several snow plow drivers that they were going to "throw them out of their trucks and beat them up" if they didn't stop to plow their streets. Other drivers called 911 for reinforcements when angry taxpayers made threats. A county spokesperson said that the drivers "are working as hard as they possibly can." She explained, "I understand people are frustrated. . . . Obviously we know we have work to do and we're trying . . . just as hard as we can. We want to go home."[1]

In nearby Arlington County, across the Potomac River, county officials pointed to their snow removal priority plan with a sophisticated map that charted which streets the plows worked on first. Plowing starts when the snow becomes two to four inches deep. The snow crews focus on priority areas: snow emergency routes marked with bright signs, main arteries, roads leading to hospitals and fire stations, and the areas around subway stations and police stations. Crews work twelve-hour shifts, get twelve hours off for food and sleep, and then come back to work again.[2] Even that effort struggled to keep up with 2010's blizzard of the century, and for months afterward residents complained about being marooned. Why, they asked, couldn't the government plow them out faster?

QUESTIONS TO CONSIDER

1. Assume you are the head of the department of public works of your county. You're in charge of snow removal. What streets would you plow first?

2. What would you say to residents whose streets end up at the bottom of the plowing priority list? After all, they will tell you: they pay taxes, too!

3. Following the blizzard, Arlington County considered an ordinance that would require local residents to join with the county in the snow removal effort. In particular, "the ordinance first would require all property owners to remove snow and ice adjacent to their property, creating a path that is a minimum of thirty-six inches wide (to accommodate wheelchairs, strollers, and adults with children in hand) within twenty-four hours after the snow stops falling, when accumulations are less than six inches, and within thirty-six hours when six or more inches of snow accumulate. Failure to comply with the ordinance could result in a civil penalty." Would you favor the passage of such an ordinance, which brings individual citizens into a partnership with government in providing public services? What would you do for older and disabled residents, who might not have the physical strength to shovel their sidewalks? Just how far should a government's reach into an individual's property go?

4. One official of a Midwest town once admitted that the town had a special snow removal plan for election day. If it snowed, he said, there was a plan to make sure that the "right" neighborhoods—those most likely to vote for the mayor—were plowed first. The other neighborhoods—those most likely to vote for the mayor's opponent—would have to wait much longer. Do you think that this is a proper use of government's power, or of the way that administrative decisions shape values in society?

NOTES

1. Jonathan Mummolo, "Snow Removal Workers Threatened in Prince George's, Official Says," *Washington Post* (February 11, 2010), http://voices.washingtonpost.com/annapolis/2010/02/snow_removal_workers_threatene.html.

2. Arlington County Government, "Snow Removal Process & Phases," https://emergency.arlingtonva.us/weather/snow-ice/snow-removal-phases/.

CASE 1.3

In Riverhead, New York, town officials launched an aggressive campaign to find backyard swimming pools whose owners hadn't obtained the required permits to build them. As the town's chief building inspector, Leroy Barnes Jr., explained, "It's a safety issue more than anything else." Faulty plumbing could cause water damage to neighboring properties. If electrical wiring for lights or filters were installed improperly, someone could be electrocuted. In addition, the town's ordinance required pool owners to install a fence around the pool to prevent small children from wandering in and accidentally drowning. The campaign, in this small town near the tip of Long Island, found 250 pools that had been constructed but whose owners had not received the requisite permits. In addition, the aggressive inspection program produced $75,000 in fees from violators.[1]

Barnes, however, quickly found himself under fierce attack from the American Civil Liberties Union (ACLU) and scores of angry townspeople. It wasn't because of the campaign to find violators, at least on the surface. Rather, it was because Barnes had cleverly used the Google Earth search program to find the pools. He used the program's online satellite feature to find pools, identify the address, check the address against the town's database of permits, and find pools that did not have the permits required by law. Town officials wondered what all the fuss was about. After all, Google Earth is available to any user, on any computer. It doesn't show anything that anyone anywhere can't see. Why can't the town use publicly available information to enforce its laws?

"Technically it may be lawful," replied Donna Lieberman of New York's ACLU, "but in the gut it does not feel like a free society kind of operation."[2] Some local residents complained that it felt creepy to know that the town was peeking into their lives via satellite. Critics pointed out that the Fourth Amendment to the Constitution prevents government officials from conducting unlawful searches. Using remote satellites without a search warrant crossed the line, they argued.

Just how far should government go in combining emerging technology with its vast power? In Greece, as well as New York, government officials are using Google Earth to track down pools without permits in order to collect fines. Enterprising private citizens are also making innovative use of satellite surveillance. Thieves in the United Kingdom are using the technology to identify backyard ponds stocked with exotic fish, which they steal and sell for large sums. A private company is already using private satellites to photograph the parking lots of Walmart stores. Counting the cars tells analysts which communities have the fastest-growing economies. If private companies are doing it, should government be restrained from using the same readily available technology to enforce its laws?

It's easy to see even bigger issues in the future. If governments pass aggressive energy-saving laws to restrict backyard barbeques (too many hydrocarbons being released) and to require better insulation of homes (to prevent energy from being wasted), should the government be able to use remote-sensing devices to detect heat emissions? Private companies are now trying to sell special vans to local police that provide a comprehensive scan of every passing car. The scan can detect illegal items onboard without a search warrant. Should local police buy these disguised vans to locate contraband and possible terrorist threats—and deploy them without search warrants? What about antiterrorism forces in the Federal Bureau of Investigation? The federal government's Transportation Security Administration is deploying new scanners that can look through an airplane passenger's clothing to see, well, just about everything. Passengers boarding planes know that they are subject to searches, although there's always a debate about just how intrusive those searches ought to be. But should drivers steering their cars past a van parked on the side of the road have any expectation of privacy, even if they are carrying something illegal under the seat or in the trunk?

Public complaints in Riverhead forced town officials to end the Google Earth project, even though the information was available to everyone on the web and it was used to find people who had broken local ordinances. But it raised very tough questions about how government officials should exercise discretion in doing their jobs—and how they should wield their power.

QUESTIONS TO CONSIDER

1. Do you think there was anything wrong with the town's decision to use Google Earth to detect individuals who had broken local laws by installing pools without obtaining the required permits?

2. How should local officials, like Leroy Barnes, be held accountable for their actions?

3. Sam Adams, in addition to brewing beer, also helped lead the revolt that culminated in the Boston Tea Party, during which colonists tossed tea into Boston Harbor to protest the power of the English king. What do you think he and his fellow revolutionaries would think about the use of Google Earth to detect lawbreakers?

NOTES

1. Russell Nichols, "Is Google Earth Eyeing Your Pool?" *Government Technology* (August 17, 2010), http://www.govtech.com/policy-management/Is-Google-Earth-Eyeing-Your-Pool.html?topic=117688#.

2. Ibid.

 CASE 1.4

Permission Slips for Oreos

Just by sending a frustrated tweet, a suburban Philadelphia mother set off a tsunami. "Insanity!" the woman fumed. "I have to sign a permission slip so my middle-schooler can eat an Oreo." She was telling the truth, and her tweet inadvertently launched a national debate over whether a lawsuit-crazed society had finally gone too far.

The cookie in question was actually a Double Stuf Oreo. The permission slip came one day in March from Darlene Porter, a teacher at Welsh Valley Middle School in the suburbs of Philadelphia. The purpose: an experiment on the Earth's tectonic plates.

According to the permission slip, students would "model plate movement and observe earth's features," using the cookie to "simulate the [three] types of plate boundaries." But then came the crucial part. "The students may eat the Oreo after the investigation if this is okay with you. The students do NOT have to eat the Oreo if they do not wish to do so." A warning at the end: "Without a signed permission slip, my child understands that he/she will not be able to sample the Oreo."

The story exploded on social media. Dutchman61 complained about "the shear [*sic*] idiocy of what our schools and institutions have become. And the really ugly truth is that there are idiots who would sue if their kid was allowed to have an Oreo." From Scotland, AMCK1997 was sympathetic to the reasons for the permission slip, arguing a lawsuit could cost the teacher her job. Still, he concluded, "it does seem a bit ridiculous."

Doug Young, the school district's spokesman, told the press, "It's one teacher who was really trying to do her due diligence, quite honestly." A parent with an allergy tried to help by sending in gluten-free Oreos. And the mother who kicked off the battle made it clear that she didn't blame the teacher. "I fault our crazy culture," she said.

Was the Oreo fracas just one more indignity imposed by a super-suing, overregulated society? Or, given what we know about the way food affects kids' health, was it an enlightened step forward? One school employee defended the cookie warning. "There are many children in the school I work at that have severe food allergies," she wrote. "This mother needs to chill out and be happy that the teacher is concerned that one of her students has food allergies."

The incident underscores a bigger divide among parents over how much supervision of children is too much supervision. One blogger wondered whether so-called helicopter parents in 2024 would give their kids swallowable sensors that would tell a smartphone if the kids were eating too much sugar, fat, or gluten. By then, this writer imagined, "letting kids do anything on their own will be considered completely irresponsible, or even insane."

Humor columnist Dave Barry looked back to the 1960s. His parents, Barry reminisced in the *Wall Street Journal*, "didn't worry about consuming trans fats, gluten, fructose, and all the other food components now considered so dangerous they could be used to rob a bank ('Give him the money! He's got gluten!')." A school nurse voiced the same sentiments. "You would not believe the insanity of the parents nowadays," she wrote. "Gluten! Sugar! Allergies! There are parents who live in perpetual fear and want everyone else to be afraid with them. Sadly, most school districts give in to these demands."

For some kids, however, gluten is truly no joke. The U.S. Food and Drug Administration has found that in some cases, gluten can cause serious gastrointestinal problems and life-threatening metabolic problems. Later in life, some of those with celiac disease, which is worsened by gluten, develop problems ranging from epilepsy and infertility to neuropathy and high-mortality cancer. Science has come a long way since the 1960s, when many children suffered from problems that researchers have since learned can be prevented. And some of that prevention comes from being careful with what the kids eat.

In fact, concerns about kids' reactions to allergens aren't just a matter of regulatory excess. Chicago Public Schools stock epinephrine autoinjectors, which allow the staff to treat potentially fatal anaphylaxis—difficulty in breathing and a possible heart attack—that can result when sensitive kids are exposed to certain foods. In the 2013–2014 school year, there were thirty-eight emergency injections. Half of the shots were for kids with a first-time reaction who had never had problems before. All survived. In the end, being extra careful about exposing kids to things that can hurt them is much more than an opportunity for blogger flippancy. Precautions have to be balanced with common sense, but it's a mistake to sacrifice science to sarcasm.

Still, there's one other comment that deserves careful attention. One blogger wasn't worried about intrusive school nannying, but had an entirely different problem to complain about. How could the teacher use Double Stuf Oreos, he wanted to know, when Hydrox cookies were an obviously better choice for the experiment?

QUESTIONS TO CONSIDER

1. Is this a case simply over the top? Here's a clever and creative teacher trying to do a demonstration for students—but asking parents to sign a permission slip before a child could eat an Oreo?

2. Consider how you'd feel if your child had a gluten allergy and might be affected by eating an Oreo in the

classroom. Would you want to subject the entire class to the burden of collecting permission slips for your child?

3. Just how should government set a balance in the behavior and accountability of its officials, between providing flexibility in the way they do their jobs and ensuring that nothing in the way they do their jobs could harm anyone?

4. How does this affect the meaning of *accountability* in the day-to-day operation of government agencies, like public schools?

———————————————

Note: This case comes from my column in *Governing* (June 2015), http://www.governing.com/columns/potomac-chronicle/gov-school-lunch-regulations.html.

KEY CONCEPTS

accountability   8

ethical behavior   17

exit   16

fiscal accountability   15

politics-administration dichotomy   12

process accountability   15

program accountability   16

Progressives   12

rule of law   10

voice   16

whistleblowers   10

FOR FURTHER READING

Burke, John P. *Bureaucratic Responsibility.* Baltimore: Johns Hopkins University Press, 1986.

Finer, Herman. "Administrative Responsibility in Democratic Government." *Public Administration Review* 1 (Summer 1941): 335–350.

Friedrich, Carl J. "Public Policy and the Nature of Administrative Responsibility." In *Public Policy*, edited by Carl J. Friedrich and Edward S. Mason, 3–24. Cambridge, Mass.: Harvard University Press, 1940.

Gruber, Judith E. *Controlling Bureaucracies: Dilemmas in Democratic Governance.* Berkeley: University of California Press, 1987.

Hirschman, Albert O. *Exit, Voice, and Loyalty: Responses to Decline in Firms, Organizations, and States.* Cambridge, Mass.: Harvard University Press, 1970.

Landau, Martin. "Redundancy, Rationality, and the Problem of Duplication and Overlap." *Public Administration Review* 29 (July–August 1969): 346–358.

Rohr, John A. *Ethics for Bureaucrats: An Essay on Law and Values.* 2nd ed. New York: Marcel Dekker, 1989.

SUGGESTED WEBSITES

Extensive discussion on federal ethics laws and policies can be found on the website of the U.S. Office of Government Ethics, **www.oge.gov**.

More broadly, the Council on Governmental Ethics Laws, **www.cogel.org**, tracks policies on ethics. In addition, many state and local governments have their own sites—which search engines can readily locate—detailing laws and regulations on ethics.

SAGE edge™
for CQ Press

WANT A BETTER GRADE?

Get the tools you need to sharpen your study skills. Access practice quizzes, eFlashcards, video, and multimedia at **edge.sagepub.com/kettl7e.**

PART I

The Job of Government

Public administration does not exist as an abstract concept. It gets its meaning from how public administrators do their jobs, as they translate policy decisions into practical results. But not all practices or administrators are the same. At different levels of government, the process can look very different, ranging from the distant and hush-hush world of the Central Intelligence Agency to the frontline work of police officers and firefighters we see every day.

So if we want to understand what public administration really is, we must begin by looking at what public administrators actually do. Even more fundamentally, we must understand the connections between citizens, the officials they elect, and the administrators they empower—and how all of this combines to shape what government actually does. That, in turn, is the key for holding public administrators accountable for *what* they do and *how* they do it.

2

WHAT GOVERNMENT DOES—AND HOW IT DOES IT

Michael Robinson Chavez/The Washington Post via Getty Images

After years of neglecting maintenance issues, officials in Washington's Metro system announced in 2016 that they would shut down portions of the system throughout the coming year to make repairs. Commuters and employers scrambled to find other ways of getting to work.

One very early morning not long ago, I struggled out of bed for an early-morning trip to Washington, D.C., from the Philadelphia apartment where we were then living. I rode an elevator down to the lobby and caught a trolley to the 30th Street train station. I emerged from the underground tunnel at the station just as the sun was coming up and just in time to scoot across the street as the "Don't Walk" signal began flashing. As I waited for the Amtrak train, the barking of a bomb-sniffing dog echoed throughout the concourse. The dog had not spotted a suspicious package—he was a pup in training and was struggling to focus on the job instead of all the fascinating people milling around the platforms and the breakfast snacks just out of his paw's reach. The train, fortunately, was on time, and it was a pretty ride, with the rising sun shining on the Chesapeake Bay, before rolling into Union Station at the foot of Capitol Hill. A quick trip on Washington's Metro subway got me to a meeting in a nearby federal office building.

This tale, of course, is about more than the trip of a sometime road warrior and textbook author. It is also a map of government—and government administration—in action. The Philadelphia elevator had an inspection sticker certifying that the Pennsylvania Department of Labor and Industry had found the elevator safe, for which I was grateful (since it would have been a fourteen-flight fall down the shaft to the basement). The inspection might have been performed by a private company licensed by the state, but the state government stood behind the certificate pasted on the elevator's wall. The Southeastern Pennsylvania Transportation Authority (SEPTA), a regional organization stretching across a collection of local governments and three states, ran the trolley. The city of Philadelphia's Traffic Engineering Division managed the "Walk/Don't Walk" signal. The excited puppy was an employee of Amtrak's own police department, and he had the vest to prove it. Amtrak is really the National Railroad Passenger Corporation, a quasi-governmental corporation that operates like a private company but is controlled by government officials and subsidized by public money. Maryland's Chesapeake Bay is more scenic because of the efforts of Pennsylvania, Virginia, and Maryland, in concert with the U.S. Environmental Protection Agency, to ensure the waterway is clean. Like SEPTA, Washington's Metro system is a regional transportation authority, involving two states and the District of Columbia. Its stations contain hidden security devices to detect terrorist threats, with security provided by a complicated network of federal, state, regional, and local law enforcement agencies. Before I had fully awakened, I had encountered the vast reach of public administration.

None of us can even start our days without bumping into government. The water we drink, the cars we drive, the bicycles we pedal, the streets we walk—all are the products of government bureaucracy in action. We take it all for granted, but we expect the highest levels of service. Indeed, over the years, public administration's role in society has become so pervasive that we often speak of the rise of the **administrative state**.[1] In fact, political scientist Dwight Waldo wrote a

Trust in the Federal Government

Just about everyone complains about how much government has become disconnected from citizens. Trust in government is low. But how has it changed over the years? Consider this chart.

Percentage Who Trust the Government in Washington "Always" or "Most of the Time"

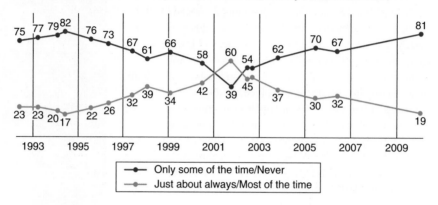

How much of the time do you think you can trust government in Washington to do what is right—just about always, most of the time, or only some of the time?

- Only some of the time/Never
- Just about always/Most of the time

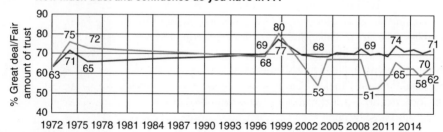

How much trust and confidence do you have in . . .

% Great deal/Fair amount of trust

- The local governments in the area where you live when it comes to handling local problems?
- The government of the state where you live when it comes to handling state problems?

Source: Gallup, "Americans Still More Trusting in Local Over State Government" (September 19, 2016), http://www.gallup.com/poll/195656/americans-trusting-local-state-government.aspx; and "Trust in Government" (2016), http://www.gallup.com/poll/5392/trust-government.aspx.

QUESTIONS

1. What is the overall trend of the public's trust in government?

2. Can you identify reasons for some of the up-and-down changes in the overall trend?

3. Suppose you were president of the United States. Do you believe that there is anything you could do to affect the public's trust in government?

doctoral dissertation by this title and published it in 1948. Since then, bureaucratic power has been the focus of huge debate. Some critics have condemned the growth of government and its power. More sympathetic observers have seen it as part of an inevitable—even desirable—reaction to the growing complexity of social problems and Americans' demands to solve them. Some fear that the growth of government has empowered nameless, faceless bureaucrats with greater control over our lives. Others point to government's help in solving big problems. Some plead for making government work more like a business. Others argue that government and business are so fundamentally different that corporations can't teach public organizations very much. But one thing seems certain: when trouble strikes, whether it's a giant superstorm that savages the East Coast or a tornado that pulverizes an Oklahoma city, or a terrorist attack in San Bernardino or a water crisis in Flint, Americans look to their government for help.

These debates have produced a wide array of approaches to the study of public administration, but one issue dominates: **administrative responsibility**. Americans expect—they insist—that the bureaucracy be held accountable to elected officials and, through these officials, to the people. Critics sometimes complain that government bureaucracy has no bottom line. In fact, government does have a bottom line: administrative responsibility, not only for administering programs efficiently but also for ensuring that both the process and its results are accountable to elected officials and, ultimately, to the people. Americans care deeply about what government does—whether its agencies pick up the trash promptly and regularly or prevent dangerous food products from being sold in stores—and about how it does it, including making sure that people are treated fairly and that government officials do not abuse their power. How government works is key to the politics of the administrative process. And nothing is more central to these politics than the ongoing, often fierce debate about the size of government.

THE SIZE OF GOVERNMENT

Especially since the end of World War II, citizens have demanded far more services from government—better roads, a stronger safety net, safer food, better mass transit, more effective schools, and even better public colleges and universities. New programs and more ambition led to the creation of more government agencies, more government workers, and more government spending. As Dwight Waldo pointed out, this not only led to a bigger bureaucracy; it also created demand for ensuring that a bigger bureaucracy did not threaten our strong and vibrant democracy.[2]

Five Myths about "Big Government"

Americans often complain about "big government" and legions of politicians have campaigned for office by running against it. Most of what we think we know about big government, however, is wrong. Consider these five myths.

1. WASHINGTON IS THE CENTER OF THE "BIG GOVERNMENT" PROBLEM.
In his first inaugural address, Ronald Reagan boldly argued, "Government is not the solution to our problem; government is the problem."[3] Nothing looms bigger in Reagan's diagnosis than that the best way to drive the country forward is to take power out of Washington and send it back to the states and to the people.

The only problem with that argument is that we did it—long ago. Most American government isn't federal, and most federal government isn't in Washington. Just one-sixth of all government employees in the United States work for the federal government. Nearly two-thirds work for local governments as teachers, firefighters, police officers, emergency responders, and sanitation workers. Most government in the United States is local government.

How about federal workers? About five in six federal employees work outside the Washington metropolitan area. Most federal government in the United States is local government, too: the workers who process Social Security applications, manage air traffic control, provide security at airports, and take care of the national parks. So, one of six government employees works for the federal government, and one of six federal employees works in Washington, D.C. Federal employees in the D.C. area make up fewer than 2 percent of all government workers in the country. Washington isn't the center of real government action in this country. We'll circle back to this issue shortly.

2. LET'S TAKE GOVERNMENT BACK TO THE REAGAN "SMALL GOVERN-MENT" DAYS. Suppose we wanted to take government back to the same size it was in Reagan's last days in office. That would take some doing: we'd have to go on a hiring binge and bring in 400,000 *more* federal employees. At the end of Reagan's term, the federal government had just over 3 million civilian employees, compared with just over 2.6 million in 2016. In the meantime, of course, we created the Transportation Security Administration (TSA) after September 11, 2001, and we made all the airport screeners into federal workers. So a real back-to-Reagan strategy would require hiring even more feds—51,000 additional employees, in fact, to account for the TSA. The federal workforce, after taking account of airport screeners, is now 15 percent smaller than in Reagan's day.

But what about federal spending? Isn't that also a gauge of "big government"? Yes, it is—but government spending as a share of the economy is just about the same now as it was at the end of the Reagan years: 20.5 percent of the gross domestic product in 1989 versus 20.7 percent in 2015. What's changed is what's inside. Spending on **entitlements**—government spending to which recipients are automatically entitled by law, usually through a formula enacted in law—grew from 47 percent to 69 percent of all federal spending from 1989 to 2016. Most of that, of course, is in Social Security and Medicare. Big government or not, no one really wants to cut these two programs.

If we really wanted to go back to the Reagan days, in terms of how much discretionary spending we budget, we'd have to *boost* defense spending from 3.3 to 5.5 percent of the economy. That would be a budget-buster. Or, if we decided to do that, we'd have to *cut entitlements* by nearly a third to get back to the Reagan days. That would take away billions from the Social Security checks of retirees and billions more from the health care on which they rely.

3. LET'S CUT GOVERNMENT BY CUTTING BACK ON THE NUMBER OF FEDERAL EMPLOYEES. A host of plans have surfaced during presidential campaigns. In the 2016 election, for example, Ted Cruz proposed eliminating 150,000 federal jobs. In his transition, President Donald Trump said he'd impose a hiring freeze upon taking office. There's an underlying assumption that every government agency has enough fat in it that it would be easy to make big cuts and no one would really notice the difference.

However, we've already pushed much of the federal government's work out the door. Nine of every ten dollars in the Department of Energy, one of the departments often proposed to be abolished, are already being spent on contractors, mostly on maintaining the nation's nuclear weapons arsenal, cleaning up the waste from two generations of weapons production, and researching the next generation of nuclear weapons defense. We wouldn't do away with these functions if we closed down the department—and we'd continue to rely on contractors to do the job. We spend about $450 billion per year on contracts throughout the federal government, on everything from drones and advanced fighters to planning and support in civilian agencies.

Consider how we manage Medicare and Medicaid, the federal government's health care programs for the elderly and the poor, and the Children's Health Insurance Program. Together, these programs account for 25 percent of all federal spending—but they are managed by just 0.2 percent of all federal employees, who work in the Centers for Medicare and Medicaid Services (CMS). It would be hard to imagine cutting back even more. As it is, every CMS employee is responsible, on average, for $144 million in spending. That's simply stunning. Cutting back on government employees here—and throughout the government—puts enormous amounts of money and services for citizens at risk, because many federal employees don't deliver services. They leverage the nongovernmental partners who do, and weakening their leverage puts money at risk.

4. LET'S CUT WASTE, FRAUD, AND ABUSE. One of the things that everyone seems to know about the federal budget is that it's full of waste, fraud, and abuse. The media are full of programs that don't seem to work, like the Department of Veterans Affairs' long waiting list for vets, and anecdotes about waste, like featherbedding employees. In fact, a Google search on "lazy government workers" produces approximately 14.8 million hits.

A look at the government's biggest problems, however, shows both that there's a lot of waste in government *and* that it's possible to cut it—but that this takes hard day-to-day work, not an axe. There's no line item for waste in the budget to slash. Rather, the problems are marbled into the government's operations and excising them takes extraordinary skill. Moreover, consider the Government Accountability Office's (GAO) list of the worst-of-the-worst, its "high-risk list" of thirty-two programs most prone to problems.[4] At least twenty-five of the thirty-two programs are there because managers are struggling to deal with huge problems in navigating complex programs across boundaries—contracts with private companies, arrangements with state and local governments, or coordination with other agencies that share a piece of the problem. Since 1990, the GAO has put fifty-seven programs into this hall of shame, but twenty-three of them (40 percent) have escaped. How? Good managers are doing good management.

The GAO found that about one in every ten Medicare dollars is part of government's improper payments problem. But that can't be reduced by decree or willpower. It would take careful sleuthing to track down unscrupulous health care providers charging twice for the same wheelchair or padding the bills for drugs. And that requires government managers who know what they're doing.

Cutting waste, fraud, and abuse is certainly possible. But doing so usually requires more good managers who know how to cut out the marbled waste without destroying the steak. An axe, swung haphazardly, would only make waste worse and turn government's steak into an indigestible pulp.

5. ABOLISHING AGENCIES WILL SHRINK THE GOVERNMENT. There is a long list of federal agencies that candidates have proposed for the chopping block, including the Environmental Protection Agency (EPA) and the Departments of Education, Energy, Commerce, and Housing and Urban Development (HUD). However, it's a lot easier to erase the names of agencies than to wipe out the functions they perform—and on which citizens depend. Who would operate the satellites, collect the data, and run the supercomputer models that predict the paths of storms like Superstorm Sandy (as the National Weather Service does in Commerce)? Who would take care of the nation's nukes (as the National Nuclear Security Administration does in Energy)? Who would run the nation's student loan programs, now larger than credit card debt, auto loans, and homeowner lines of credit (as Education does)? Who would help communities reduce lead paint exposure in homes (as HUD's Office of Lead Hazard Control and Healthy Homes does)? No one likes the IRS. In fact, no one has ever really liked revenue agents. In the Gospels, Jesus is criticized for daring to talk and eat with a tax collector. However, to pay for what we expect government to do, someone must pay the taxes and someone must collect them.

None of this is an excuse for government doing stupid things, or for doing well-intentioned things in inefficient ways. But if we're really serious about cutting down government's reach into our lives, we need to get past the myths of big government—and figure out how to make the government we insist on work well. That doesn't require more government, but it surely requires a smarter one. And, at the core, it requires an effective public administration. So let's explore the question of government, its size, and its functions, in more detail.

Number of Governments

The first step is counting the number of governments we have in the United States. That step turns out to be much more complicated than it might first appear. We have, of course, one federal government and fifty state governments. But, as Table 2.1 shows, the United States has a very large number of local governments—more than 90,000 in fact. Local governments are the foundation of public administration in the United States, from police and fire to sanitation and education. In fact, the public administrators citizens are most likely to see and connect with are local government officials.

More than half of local governments are **special-purpose governments**, such as school districts and special districts, with functions including water and sewer systems, airport operation, cemeteries, dikes and drainage, regional fire protection, flood control, libraries, mosquito control, parks, regional bus service, weed removal, and garbage collection. These districts have three things in common: a narrow focus on which they concentrate their work; some kind of governance structure, often through appointed or elected boards; and taxing authority, either through general taxes or special **user fees** (where citizens pay for the services they get, like bus fares or water bills).

HBO's *Last Week Tonight*, hosted by comedian John Oliver, actually spent most of one episode exploring these special districts.[5] He found that these special districts spend more money than all of the Russian military and that many of them have board meetings so sparsely attended that, in some cases, only a couple of board members are present. In a 2012 study, Kentucky's state auditor, Adam H. Edelen, found that these special districts were "the most prevalent and least understood level of government" in the state. Edelen was surprised by what he found. "It is a scandal that for generations no Kentuckian could answer basic questions as to the number of special districts, nor how much they tax, fee, spend, or hold in reserves," he stated. These special districts cost Kentucky taxpayers more than the cost of running their counties. Their work, Edelen concluded, was critical to the services that citizens expect, but the lack of transparency and accountability was "scandalous." The districts, he said, constituted a collection of "ghost governments" that required upgrades in technology, training, and rules to improve the way they answered to citizens.[6]

Not all special district governments share these problems. Many special-purpose governments are large, robust, and professional, like the school districts that provide education in many of the nation's cities. But these governments raise particular challenges for public administration, especially since, as Table 2.1 shows, they have been on the rise, more than quadrupling in number since 1942.

Some parts of the country, moreover, tend to have more local governments than others, special-purpose and otherwise (see Figure 2.1). The Midwest tends to have far more

Table 2.1	Number of Government Units		
	1942	**2012**	**Change: 1942–2012**
Federal	1	1	0 %
State	48	50	4 %
Local	155,067	90,056	−42 %
County	3,050	3,031	−1 %
Municipal	16,220	19,519	20 %
Towns	18,919	16,360	−14 %
School district	108,579	12,880	−88 %
Special district	8,299	38,266	361 %
Total	155,116	90,107	−42 %

Source: U.S. Bureau of the Census, *Statistical Abstract of the United States; Census of Governments.*

Figure 2.1	Regional Characteristics of Local Governments

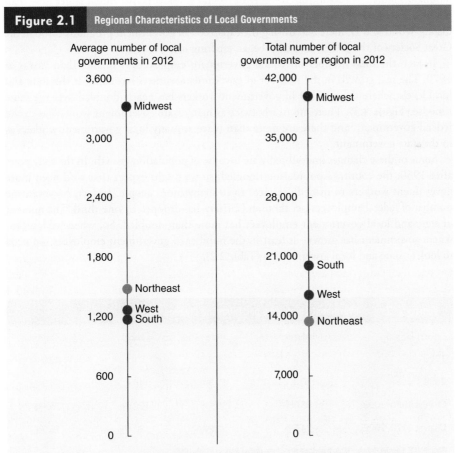

Source: U.S. Bureau of the Census, *2012 Census of Governments: Organization Component and 2010 Census,* http://www2.census.gov/govs/cog/g12_org.pdf.

local governments, both in total and by state, than any other part of the country. There's a large variety of cultural reasons that explain this, from the instinct of the region's settlers to create large numbers of small towns to a high reliance on special districts. This is all part of the rich fabric of government in the United States—and of local government in particular.

Government Employment and Spending

Measuring the size of government, beyond counting the number of governmental units, turns out to be very difficult.[7] But let's start looking at the size of government by looking at the number of government employees.

As we saw in the last section, one of six government employees works for the federal government, and one of six federal employees works in Washington, D.C. At the federal level, the total number of federal employees grew rapidly in the last century, from just 231,000 in 1901 to 2.1 million in 2014.[8] That's more than a ninefold increase. However, over the same time period, the U.S. population has grown as well. As a share of the population, as Figure 2.2 reveals, the number of federal employees isn't much larger now than it was in 1920, after factoring in population growth. Federal employment grew rapidly during World War II, increased during the expansion of government programs through the Great Society of the 1960s, and then began tapering off.

In fact, the total number of federal government employees is smaller than it was in 1970. The real growth in the number of government workers has come at the state and local levels, where the number of government workers has nearly doubled over the same time (see Figure 2.3). There are nearly twice as many state government workers as in the federal government, and there are more than twice as many local government workers as in the state government.

Some of these changes undoubtedly are because of population growth. In the sixty years after 1950, the country's population doubled, so we might expect that we'd need more government workers to provide services to so many more people. In fact, however, the number of federal employees per thousand citizens has dropped by one-third. The number of state and local government employees has more than doubled. So, when we look for where government has grown, at least in the number of government employees, we need to look at state and local governments (Table 2.2).

Table 2.2	Government Employees per Thousand Citizens			
	Federal	State	Local	Total
1950	13.9	6.9	21.2	42.0
2009	10.3	17.3	46.4	74.0
Change 1950–2009	−33.8%	150.1%	122.5%	75.4%
Change 1970–2009	−34.5%	29.2%	30.8%	16.0%

Source: U.S. Census Bureau, *Historical Statistics of the United States: 1789–1957*.

| Figure 2.2 | Federal Civilian Employees per Million Americans, 1990–2010 |

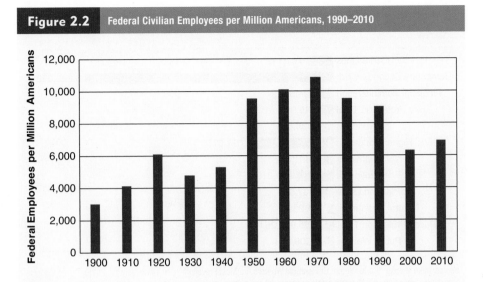

Source: U.S. Bureau of the Census; U.S. Office of Management and Budget, *Budget of the United States Government: Historical Tables.*

Note: Federal employees includes all executive branch civilian employees but excludes the Postal Service.

| Figure 2.3 | Government Workers in the United States |

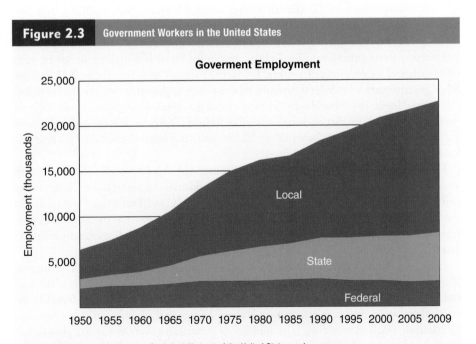

Source: U.S. Bureau of the Census, *Statistical Abstract of the United States*, various years.

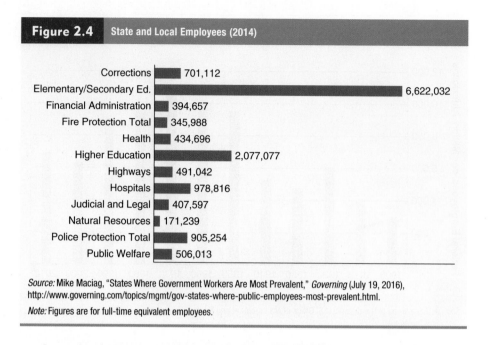

Figure 2.4 State and Local Employees (2014)

Corrections	701,112
Elementary/Secondary Ed.	6,622,032
Financial Administration	394,657
Fire Protection Total	345,988
Health	434,696
Higher Education	2,077,077
Highways	491,042
Hospitals	978,816
Judicial and Legal	407,597
Natural Resources	171,239
Police Protection Total	905,254
Public Welfare	506,013

Source: Mike Maciag, "States Where Government Workers Are Most Prevalent," *Governing* (July 19, 2016), http://www.governing.com/topics/mgmt/gov-states-where-public-employees-most-prevalent.html.

Note: Figures are for full-time equivalent employees.

And what do state and local employees do? The largest categories are for teachers, in elementary and secondary schools (at the local level) and in colleges and universities (at—mostly—the state level). After that come hospital workers, police officers, and corrections officers. In fact, there are three times as many elementary and secondary teachers as there are civilian employees in the *entire* federal government (see Figure 2.4).

Compared with other countries, in fact, the United States is distinctive in having such a large share of its government workers below the national level (see Figure 2.5). It joins other governments with federal systems, where power is shared across the national and subnational levels, in having about 15 percent of all government employees in the national government. Compare that with countries like Ireland, Turkey, and New Zealand, where the national government performs almost all functions and where the national government has almost all government employees.

How does American government *spending* compare with other countries? Compared with spending at all levels of government among major industrialized nations, the United States ranks near the bottom, about the same as Estonia, Russia, and Brazil (see Figure 2.6). In contrast, Denmark, Sweden, Finland, and France spend almost twice as much on their governments, as a share of their nation's wealth. At least in terms of spending, Americans think that their government is big—but in many countries, it's much bigger.

How does this add up? It's scarcely a portrait of explosive, big government. The number of employees has grown, but only in proportion to population growth, and mostly at the state and local government levels. There hasn't been a large increase in the number of feds. On the international stage, American government is about average in the number of employees, and it's relatively small in spending. The number of American governments has grown, but mainly to serve special purposes that have accompanied the growth of the nation's populations. These conclusions certainly don't match popular perception, but they're the underlying bedrock of public administration.

| Figure 2.5 | Government Employment around the World |

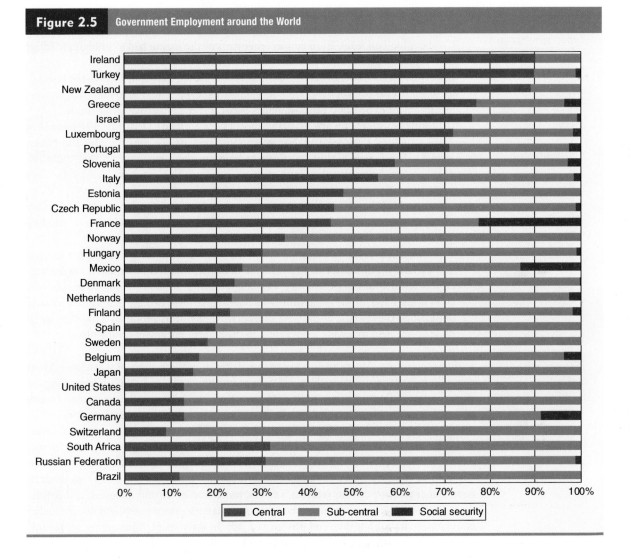

Central   Sub-central   Social security

WHAT GOVERNMENT DOES

Government is a complex collection of services, much of which are hard for us to see and, sometimes, to avoid taking for granted. Consider these snapshots of government in action:

- The Social Security Administration distributed 59 million monthly payments, totaling $870 billion in benefits, in 2015. The benefits amount to nearly 40 percent of the income of the elderly. Among the elderly, more than one in five married couples and almost half of unmarried persons rely on Social Security for 90 percent or more of their income. The program has been a major force in dramatically reducing the poverty of older Americans.[9]
- In 1989, the Federal Deposit Insurance Corporation (FDIC), best known for its bank-window stickers promising $100,000 insurance for each account, took over the

management of two hundred financially troubled savings-and-loan institutions. As part of this process, the FDIC found itself the temporary owner of 12 percent of the Dallas Cowboys football team. Even fans in other parts of the nation had to grudgingly admit that, for a time, the Cowboys were America's team.[10]

- Inspectors for the Food and Drug Administration, alerted in March 1989 to the possibility that terrorists might attempt to poison imported fruit, managed to find two grapes—in a shipment of 364,000 crates of grapes—that had been injected with cyanide.[11]

- In just the month of January 2016, the City of New York Fire Department responded to 2,421 structural fires, with an average response time of just four minutes and fifteen seconds. There were almost ten times as many medical emergencies that month—21,527—and help arrived in four minutes and forty-five seconds, even in the city's famously snarled traffic.[12]

- The Port of Los Angeles is the nation's busiest port. Managed as a department of the City of Los Angeles, its facilities handle more than $270 billion in cargo per year, including 164,231 imported cars.[13]

- Ohio State University enrolls more than 64,000 students, making it the largest campus in the country. The University of Michigan, of course, would counter that it has the largest football stadium in the country. The "Big House" seats almost 110,000 people, and every seat is filled for the game with Ohio State. Since these two Big Ten schools are state universities, they're part of the state bureaucracy. Engineers promised a big increase in noise on the field following renovations, in the hope of rattling opposing players.

The scope of the American government's activities is nothing short of remarkable. From controlling drug safety to researching AIDS, from protecting the food supply to protecting the nation's finances, from arresting criminals to protecting waterfalls, government agencies oversee an amazing variety of services. Public administration is central to all of these functions.

Not surprisingly, the functions of government are different at each level of government. As Table 2.3 shows, the federal government has primary responsibility for national defense, although the states run the National Guard. The federal government also runs the Postal Service and conducts space exploration, and it spends more than the other two levels of government put together on veterans' services, protection of natural resources, and entitlement programs like Social Security. State governments have primary responsibility for higher education, welfare, highways, and prisons and jails. In some states, liquor stores are government-owned monopolies. In Pennsylvania, for example, a former liquor control board commissioner was also a wine aficionado, and state liquor stores featured his "chairman's selections"—a government official was also serving as the state's quasi-official wine steward. Finally, local governments carry primary responsibility for basic services such as fire protection, police, and elementary and secondary education. For a few services, including health and hospitals, governmental responsibilities are balanced among the levels of government.

Although most government functions are concentrated in one level of government, there's almost no area in which a level of government has exclusive responsibility for any major function. Federal and state governments provide aid to local schools and set broad policies. Local governments pass resolutions on foreign policy questions. In short, America's public administration system is part of the nation's system of federalism, and that system is a world of blended functions. On any issue that matters, many Americans want a voice, and there are few barriers to governments getting involved in important questions. This blended system is a logical product of America's politics and rich history, but it also creates many of its

Table 2.3	Concentration of Government Spending		
Level of Government with Primary Responsibility			
Federal	**State**	**Local**	**Mixed**
Defense	Higher education	Elementary education	Health
Postal Service	Welfare	Libraries	Hospitals
Space	Highways	Police	
Veterans' services	Corrections	Fire	
Natural resources and environment	Inspections	Parks	
	Liquor stores	Housing and community development	
Social Security		Sanitation	
Homeland security		Utilities	

Note: "Primary responsibility" means accounting for more than 50 percent of direct government spending for the function.

administrative cross-pressures. Political imperatives lead to shared policymaking; shared policymaking means that no single level of government has full responsibility for anything. This fundamental political reality muddies accountability and vastly complicates performance.

HOW GOVERNMENT DOES IT

This story of mixed policymaking and policy administration is the cornerstone of American public administration. It explains how government could extend its reach without expanding its workforce. And it explains why accountability and performance so often seem difficult, since rarely is anyone fully in charge of anything and many hands share responsibility for results.

One helpful way of understanding the work of government is to see public administration not just as a collection of departments, bureaus, and agencies but as a collection of basic tools, which organizations and their leaders operate. As Christopher C. Hood puts it:

We can imagine government as a set of administrative tools—such as tools for carpentry or gardening, or anything else you like. Government administration is about social control, not carpentry or gardening. But there is a toolkit for that, just like anything else. What government does to us—its subjects or citizens—is to try to shape our lives by applying a set of administrative tools, in many different combinations and contexts, to suit a variety of purposes.[14]

Some of these tools are **direct tools**—including the provision of goods and services, such as police and fire protection; income support, such as Social Security; and the cost of doing business, such as basic organizational management and the payment of interest on the national debt. As we move from the federal to the state and then to local governments, the administrative tools are more likely to be direct: from local ambulances to libraries, or from schools to criminal justice, local administration is most likely to be **direct administration**. This is the approach that

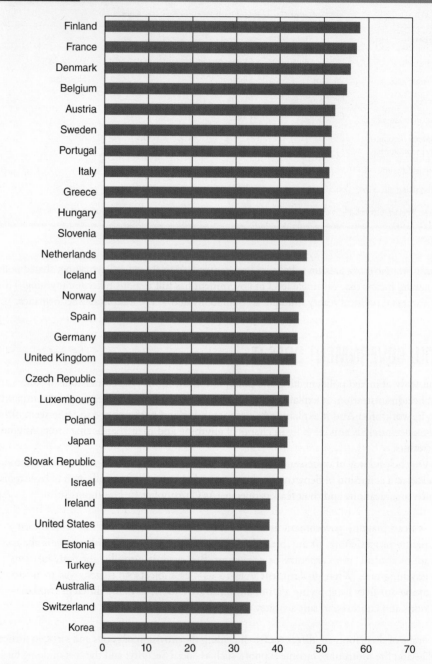

Figure 2.6 Government Spending (as a Percentage of Gross Domestic Product, 2013)

Source: Organization for Economic Co-operation and Development, OECD National Accounts Statistics (database).

comes to mind most often when we think of government, and it matches the model that citizens and policymakers alike carry around in their heads. Government is a vending machine into which policymakers load programs, insert money, and wait for goods and services to pop out. When the wrong things come out of the machine, the answer is to tinker with its mechanisms. If the price goes up, then the machine can be reset to take more money. As long as government was direct, the vending machine fit the popular model, and improving public administration remained a matter of adjusting its parts.[15]

But government has also undergone a quiet revolution—the development of a government by proxy through **indirect tools** of action.[16] Such indirect tools include contracting out governmental programs to nongovernmental partners; disbursing grants to encourage other levels of government to do things they might not otherwise have done; regulating behavior to change private-sector actions; handing out vouchers to allow citizens to purchase services from private organizations; and administering loan programs to enhance the ability of individuals and private organizations to borrow private money to pursue public goals. We will return to a detailed examination of these issues when we examine policy implementation in Chapter 12, but a brief excursion through these tools now will help set the stage for the discussions to follow.

Contracts

While governments have always relied on **contracts**—to feed and supply armies, for example—their use has increased markedly since World War II. The growing complexity of government has led to greater reliance on private-sector experts and outside organizations. In a contract, government administrators sign a formal agreement with private parties: the government agrees to pay a certain amount of money in exchange for a good or a service.

The reach of contracts is long and sweeping. Consider America's long and painful war in Afghanistan. Just a month after the terrorist attacks of September 11, 2001, the United States and a collection of allies launched a major counterattack to root out the al Qaeda organization that had planned the September 11 attack, to disrupt any future attacks, and to get al Qaeda's leader, Osama bin Laden. The Obama administration finally did get bin Laden, in a daring 2011 raid by Navy Seals in neighboring Pakistan, but the war dragged on for years afterward. From the beginning, the Pentagon's strategy was to keep the size of deployed forces as small as possible. Following a surge of troops in 2011, for example, there were nearly 100,000 soldiers in the country. But supporting the troops was a vast army of civilian contractors. At the end of 2008, for example, there were 2.2 contractors for every U.S. soldier, including American and international workers, as well as tens of thousands of local contractors hired to support the war effort. For most of the war, American troops accounted for less than half—and sometimes only a third—of the force sent to root out al Qaeda.[17] Recruiting enough soldiers to fight the war would have been very difficult, and the contracting strategy allowed the military extra flexibility. But relying on so many contractors vastly complicated the war-fighting effort and the problem of ensuring accountability for the use and support of force.

Contract administration thus requires the government to employ officials to set the standards for contracts, to negotiate effective programs at low prices, and to oversee the results that contractors produce. While newspaper stories about Pentagon contracting scandals remind us about both the scope of federal contracting and how difficult it can be

Profiting from Red Tape
Theme: Performance

We tend to think about "red tape" as a bad thing that helps no one. But two employees at the Consolidated Mail Outpatient Pharmacy, operated by the U.S. Department of Veterans Affairs, thought they found a way to help themselves.

The pharmacy is part of the department's system for helping vets—and for making the system more efficient. Doctors send prescriptions to the central pharmacy, which then fills the prescriptions and mails the drugs to vets around the country. The employees thought they figured out a way to make some quick money. They worked out a deal with a supplier to buy a product from a supplier at twice the usual price. What were they buying? Red tape. (Really!) They put in an order for 100,000 rolls of tape, designed to prevent tampering with the drugs, with markings that said "security" on it. The retail value was $2.50 a roll. They made the purchase at $6.95 and pocketed $1 per roll for themselves.

This is a case of government employees who actually tried to find a way to profit from red tape. Until, that is, they were caught, tried, and convicted—and sentenced to fifteen years in jail.

Source: Freakonomics Radio, "Government Employees Gone Wild: Full Transcript" (July 17, 2013), http://freakonomics.com/2013/07/17/government-employees-gone-wild-full-transcript/.

---

to administer contracts well, they disguise the degree to which government at all levels relies on contracting. From the management of cafeterias in federal office buildings to the construction of roads by local governments, contractors play an important role in many governmental activities. The effective management of contracts poses a growing challenge for public administrators.

Grants

Much governmental activity occurs *between* levels of government. Sometimes one level of government wishes to provide financial assistance to another level—often to encourage other governments to do what they could not otherwise afford or might not otherwise choose to do. Sometimes one level of government wants to induce another level to perform a certain service in a particular way. For example, the federal government created the interstate highway system to encourage state governments to build modern high-speed roads; it provided 90 cents of every construction dollar, and the states naturally found the funds irresistible. In fact, the use of this tool dates from the Ordinance of 1787—before the drafting of the Constitution—which provided land grants to the states for education. Since then, **federal grants** have been used for everything from supporting land-grant colleges to helping states provide medical care for the poor. Many state governments provide a large share of the support for local schools, to help improve the quality of education and to level out the financial disparities among local governments. As Donald Haider argues, "federal grants are the oldest, most widely used, and probably the best-understood tool that the federal government has available to carry out public policy."[18]

The administration of grants differs significantly from direct administration and from administration through contracts. Administrators at one level must supervise administrators at another, but they cannot command actions or write contracts. Most often, grants work by providing incentives for state and local governments to act, but also to use their own judgment on how to administer programs. This creates another complex front on which to weigh the issues of politics, performance, and accountability, and it incorporates new challenges for administration.

Regulations

As the beginning of this chapter makes clear, we can't even get out of bed in the morning without encountering government regulation, for it dictates the disclosures about the content of the bed on which we sleep, the strength of the floors on which we walk, the safety of the electricity that powers our alarm clocks, the labels on our orange juice, and almost everything else we touch before we even leave our homes. We often refer to this as the world of **red tape**. The term has long historical roots; it comes from the brightly colored ribbon used to tie up documents presented to the English king in centuries past. After the American Civil War, veterans had to show proof of their service to receive their pensions. The war records were bound in red ribbon, so government officials had to "cut the red tape" to get to the papers. Since then, "red tape" has captured the image of a government tied up in its own rules. We often complain bitterly about red tape and look for

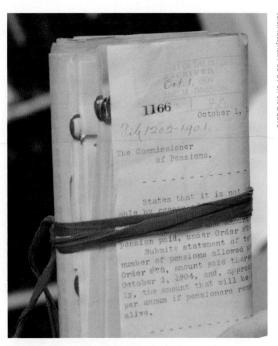

After the Civil War, the government collected the service records of soldiers and organized them by tying them with red ribbons. When soldiers applied for pensions, the records needed to verify their claims were literally "tied up in red tape." To approve their applications, officials had to "cut the red tape." Those phrases have lived on to this day.

someone with a sharp knife to cut through complications. This is one more way that government can increase its reach into our lives without increasing its size. A relatively small number of government administrators can write rules that affect us all. But we often want this to happen—we expect government to ensure that our elevators and cars are safe, that companies don't pollute our drinking water, and that we get a fair shake at tax time. We might hate the process, but we also insist that it work well. Regulation is one more way that the government increases its reach into our lives without increasing its size.

Regulatory programs can significantly expand government's power while spending relatively little money. A mere handful of government regulators can promulgate extensive and costly rules that apply to entire industries or large segments of the population. Even the volume of **regulations**—there are more than two hundred volumes in the *Code of Federal Regulations*, the federal government's compendium of rules—does not provide a really good gauge of the size or scope of federal regulations. The rules are wide ranging: there are twenty volumes of rules on agriculture, eighteen covering the IRS's tax regulations, and one on the Panama Canal. A casual look around us shows the breadth and importance of regulation by all levels of government. Federal food experts found the tainted grapes. State regulators check the management of many banks and insurance companies. Local inspectors ensure the accuracy of the scales grocery stores use to measure and charge for our food. Everything from the cars we drive, the gas we put in them, the bicycles we peddle, the clothes we wear, the banks we use, the air we

Joe Raedle/Getty Images

Vice President Joe Biden visited Miami in 2009 to point to the administration's investment in local infrastructure, as part of the American Recovery and Reinvestment Act. The programs were part of a national effort by the federal government to jump-start the economy following the 2008 economic collapse.

breathe, the food we eat, and the airplanes in which we fly is covered by regulations—and by public administrators who write and enforce these rules.

Tax Expenditures

Governments at all levels include a wide variety of features in their tax codes to give individuals and taxpayers special advantages in paying their taxes. These features do more than ease taxpayers' burdens. They serve as incentives to promote many different social and economic policies to encourage taxpayers to do some things and avoid doing others. Such tax advantages are called by a variety of names—tax breaks, tax loopholes, and **tax expenditures** (which is the term we use, to emphasize their relationship to regular spending). Tax expenditures reduce the cost of homeownership and thus encourage taxpayers to buy rather than rent their homes, for example. The federal tax deduction for mortgage interest and local property taxes, which makes family homes much cheaper to own, will cost the federal government \$104 billion in 2017.[19] The interest taxpayers earn on state and local government bonds is another example of a tax expenditure that is exempt from income taxes, which thereby reduces the cost of state and local government borrowing. The special tax breaks for oil and gas exploration encourage more exploration for these resources.

Most state income taxes use federal tax law to structure their systems, so federal tax expenditures spill over into the state level as well. Moreover, many local governments have devised their own special tax preferences, especially those designed to promote economic development. Many local economic growth programs, including enterprise zones and tax increment financing zones, create special tax abatements to encourage investment in economically depressed areas. For many economic development projects, the tax breaks can provide incentives. State and local governments view them as investments in the future.

Proponents of tax expenditures often promote them as "free" programs. The government does not have to budget or spend any money on these programs, and that hides their cost—which, of course, is real. They are scarcely free: tax expenditures cost the government money, by taking away from current and future revenues instead of adding to the pool of money for spending. Moreover, because their cost is relatively hidden—estimates for federal tax expenditures are buried deep inside the budget in a place only real tax policy wonks can find them—once tax expenditures are created, there usually is no process for renewing them or for assessing their effectiveness. But they can be very complex to administer. Tax expenditures require tax administrators to write and enforce rules, which can be, as anyone who has encountered the IRS can testify, a very difficult process. Those problems constantly embroil the IRS in controversy and political conflict.[20]

Loan Programs

The federal government has become the largest lender in the country. From guaranteeing student loans to extending credit to farmers, the federal government provides financial assistance through a broad range of **loan programs**. (Other levels of government have their own programs as well, but the federal government plays the most important role in this area.) Federal lending began during the Great Depression, but it grew dramatically during the late 1970s and early 1980s. As budget deficits swelled, members of Congress seeking new ways of funding federal programs found that loans provided an easy answer. As Rep. Willis D. Gradison Jr. (R-Ohio) put it, federal loans are "a technique used during a period of budget stringency to do good things where the cost doesn't show up until later." The result is a huge but hidden support of the lending markets. Federal lending has increased dramatically, with more that $2.6 *trillion* in loan guarantees and more than $1.2 *trillion* in direct loans (see Figure 2.7). Lending programs, already rising in the 2000s, got a big boost during the economic crisis late in that decade. Student loan programs, in particular, increased dramatically, to a level higher than credit card loans, mortgage equity lines of credit, and car loans.

Although the federal government dominates government credit policy, lending programs are administered in a highly decentralized fashion. Loans for college students and home mortgages, for example, are administered by local banks under the supervision of state and federal agencies. Government loan programs, thus, are part of the subtle and complex public-private mixture of administrative strategies that have grown in the American system, especially since 1945.

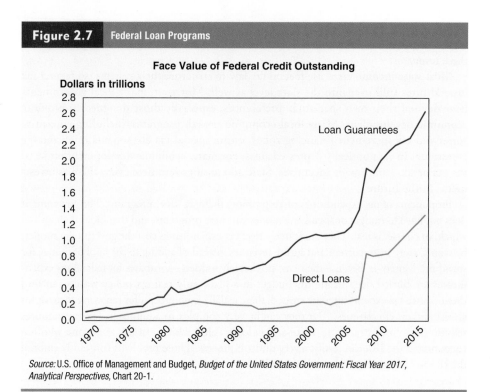

Figure 2.7	Federal Loan Programs

Face Value of Federal Credit Outstanding

Source: U.S. Office of Management and Budget, *Budget of the United States Government: Fiscal Year 2017, Analytical Perspectives,* Chart 20-1.

IMPLICATIONS FOR PUBLIC ADMINISTRATION

Our broad discussion of what the government does and how it does it leads to three broad implications.

1. THE JOB OF GOVERNMENT VARIES BY LEVEL. Local governments tend to concentrate on direct provision of goods and services. State governments provide many goods and services directly as well, but they also play a crucial intermediary role in the American federal system by transferring money to local governments (especially for public schools) and administering grants from the federal government (especially for welfare and Medicaid). The federal government, by contrast, devotes most of its administrative energy to national defense and the transfer function. Different levels of American government tend to do different things. That means public administration in America also varies by the level of government.

2. THE JOB OF GOVERNMENT VARIES BY FUNCTION. The growth of transfer functions emphasizes that different kinds of governmental programs require different administrative approaches. Providing goods and services, from education to national defense, requires sharp technical skills. For example, education administrators work to develop the best techniques: the best way to train teachers, the right kind of audiovisual aids, textbooks that do not promote stereotypes or advance the "wrong" values, and tests that most appropriately measure students' achievements. In direct provision of goods and services, most administrative action is internal to the government's bureaucracy. By contrast, administering transfer programs involves extensive action external to the government bureaucracy. Instead of mailing checks for welfare and Social Security, government could directly provide such services as government-run shelters for those who could not afford their own homes, government-run kitchens for those who could not afford food, and so on. Transfer payments serve both to make the government's administrative task easier and to preserve dignity and free choice for the recipients. They also fundamentally change the administrative task: instead of providing the necessary services, the government seeks to determine the size of the check to which the law entitles a recipient. That is a very different kind of government-citizen interaction than would be involved in direct services, and it requires a different collection of administrative skills. Thus, the job of government varies with the job it does.

3. THE JOB OF GOVERNMENT VARIES BY WHO FINALLY PROVIDES THE GOODS AND SERVICES. Even services that formerly were offered directly by government are now being provided instead through contracts, intergovernmental grants, tax expenditures, and loan programs. Just as in transfer programs, much of the administrative work is external to the government bureaucracy. When contractors manufacture weapons for defense or collect local garbage, government officials are "in the uncomfortable position of being held responsible for programs they do not really control."[21] There is, in short, a difference between who *provides* a service, by creating a program and paying for it, and who *produces* it by actually administering the service.[22] As government has grown bigger, more and more of its growth has come about through providing more services but relying on nongovernmental agents and organizations—or sometimes governments at other levels—to produce them.

Such **government by proxy**—the use of third-party agents to deliver programs that the government funds—is different from transfer programs because the responsibility of government officials extends far beyond simply ensuring that checks are mailed out correctly, and it is different from directly administered programs because government officials do not control those who finally provide the service. Each government tool requires a different approach to administration, tailored to its special problems and needs. We explore this problem in more depth in Chapter 12. For now, it's important to note that the job of government varies with who ultimately delivers the service.

This complexity, in turn, is part of the problem of trust in government, because it's hard to trust a government in which no one seems clearly in charge. The growing problem of trust in government is inescapable. In 1958, 73 percent of Americans said they trusted government "just about always" or "most of the time." By 2015, it was 24 percent and had been bouncing along the bottom for a decade (see Figure 2.8).[23] Even worse, by 2015, the share of Americans who said they were "frustrated" about the federal government rose to 57 percent and the number who were "angry" about Washington hit 22 percent.[24] Of course, Americans have always been ambivalent about their government. After all, one of the things that distinguishes the United States of America from many of the world's other nations is that it was founded through a revolution. Its citizens rejected their king, fought off the world's most powerful army, and dedicated themselves to the idea that they would never again permit such concentrated governmental power to rob them of their liberty.

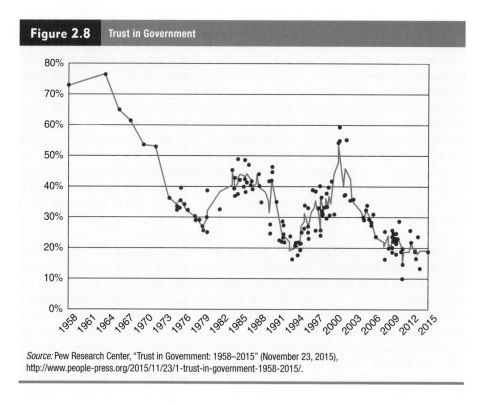

Figure 2.8 Trust in Government

Source: Pew Research Center, "Trust in Government: 1958–2015" (November 23, 2015), http://www.people-press.org/2015/11/23/1-trust-in-government-1958-2015/.

On the other hand, Americans have always expected government to protect them. The Marine Corps hymn celebrates the Marines' role in protecting the nation "from the halls of Montezuma" (the site of a famous battle in the Mexican-American War in 1847) "to the shores of Tripoli" (a battle against North African pirates in 1805). From these early battles to the effort to stop and clean up the tainted drinking water in Flint, Americans expect their government to work for them—but they never like the governmental power that goes along with its job. As one Republican strategist told the *Washington Post*, "Americans don't want government to work." Why is that so? "They want it to stop working because they suspect every time it does work, they pay a price."[25] There's a deep paradox here—a fear of a government so powerful it could erode their liberty and the insistence on a government powerful enough to solve almost any problem. That's a tall order, if not an impossible job, and public administrators find themselves always squeezed in this paradox.

CONCLUSION

If there truly is a crisis of confidence in American government, its roots are not necessarily in "big government." While government unquestionably has gotten bigger, it has not become more concentrated. Its growth has come through entitlements and loan guarantees and contracts, as well as through an expansion of services that citizens expect—and demand. In fact, the "size of government" issue is really a reflection of government's growing complexity. More and more, governmental programs rely on intricate relationships among levels of government or between government and private contractors or other agents. That web, in turn,

New York Mayor Michael Bloomberg championed a campaign to ban the sale of large sodas and other sugary drinks in the city's movie theaters, restaurants, and street carts. He argued that it would reduce obesity. Opponents contended that the city's actions were an erosion of individual choice.

has disconnected decisions about raising money from the ways we spend it. Those responsible for the performance of governmental programs are not always within the same level of government, and often they are not within government itself.

That complicates the task of accountability. Traditional approaches to accountability, as we see in the next chapter, depend on a direct link between government policymakers and the administrators executing governmental decisions. When the chain of implementation stretches beyond a government agency to another level of government—or even to nongovernmental partners—traditional approaches to government are strained. This certainly does not mean that the growth of government's reliance on indirect tools makes accountability impossible. Nor does it necessarily make it more difficult, although holding government's partners accountable often requires different and more complex approaches. But it does mean that today's accountability is often different from the accountability system that government has been used to in the past, and that raises new challenges for government accountability.

Indeed, from filling out income tax forms to borrowing money through student loans to working as government contractors, all citizens have become more involved in the performance of governmental programs. Public functions are more intricately interwoven with the private sector, and this interweaving brings new complexities into the administration of government. If government depends both on public and private values, whose values are to prevail in the inevitable conflicts, and who will work out solutions to these conflicts?

These fundamental issues, which underline the crucial problems of accountability and performance in public administration, will follow us through this book as we explore the value of traditional theories of management, both public and private, and as we examine the challenges of the new approaches, both to existing notions of public administration and to lasting values of American democracy.

CASE 2.1

Pennsylvania: Who Is in Charge of Homeland Security?

In late 2010, investigative journalists at the ProPublica non-profit website got their hands on a copy of "Pennsylvania Intelligence Bulletin No. 131," a twelve-page newsletter distributed to law enforcement officials and managers of some private-sector operations by the state's Office of Homeland Security. In the coming weeks, the newsletter warned, officials in Cranberry Township would be holding a hearing on drilling for natural gas in a shale formation. Near the Delaware River in Philadelphia, a group had scheduled a screening of the movie *Gasland*, a documentary that explored whether new natural gas wells risked contaminating the nation's water supply. The movie, the bulletin warned, was controversial and might pose a threat to homeland security.[1] How controversial was the film? The movie won a documentary award at the Sundance Film Festival and was later broadcast on PBS.

But the bulletin didn't stop there. Antiwar activists planned a short car caravan through a small town to stop at a defense contractor's facility. The newsletter listed other looming dates: Eid, the end of the Ramadan month of fasting for Muslims, and the Jewish high holidays, which "may present additional risk factors" because there would be "very high attendance at Jewish houses of worship and public gatherings." A few days later, an animal rights group planned to protest against a rodeo. Gay and lesbian activists planned a PrideFest event.

All of this information came from the state's Office of Homeland Security, through the Institute of Terrorism Research and Response, a private contractor hired with $125,000 of grant money. The source of the grant money? A federal program designed to help state and local governments identify threats to "critical infrastructure"—power plants, bridges, water systems, and other facilities that, if attacked by terrorists, might cause big disruptions.

Governor Ed Rendell, a Democrat winding down his term, was furious. "Tell me," he wondered out loud, "what critical infrastructure does the gay and lesbian PrideFest threaten?" He went on, "How in the Lord's name can we consider them to be terrorists?" An antidrilling activist asked, "I remember when Iran, Iraq, and North Korea were enemies of the state." He went on, "When did Lassie, Mother Nature, and vegetarians become the Axis of Evil?"

Embarrassed supporters of the newsletter quietly told reporters that the natural gas industry had suffered some acts of vandalism, and that environmental activists were "beginning to morph—transitioning to more criminal, extremist measures." The newsletter, a spokesperson for the state office overseeing the Office of Homeland Security said, helps "increase situational awareness for public safety officials."[2]

Reporters discovered that an organization, Good Schools Pennsylvania, which was founded by the governor's own policy adviser, previously appeared in a warning. Rendell said he was "deeply embarrassed" and promised to terminate the contract. He said he wouldn't fire the head of the Office of Homeland Security, however, because "there's shared responsibility here." It turns out that some members of Rendell's staff knew that the contractor had been tracking innocent activities around the state for several months.[3]

Just what was the Institute of Terrorism Research and Response? Its website says that it is an "American and Israeli nonprofit corporation created to help organizations succeed and prosper in a world threatened by terrorism," with offices in Philadelphia, Washington, London, and Jerusalem. Its head was a former police officer from York, a small town in south-central Pennsylvania, who had worked in military and counterterrorism operations in Israel.

Tom Ridge, the Republican former Pennsylvania governor, founding director of the Office of Homeland Security, and adviser to the shale oil company that was the object of some of the demonstrators, said he found the program "rather bizarre." Had he had any role in the contract, Ridge was asked? "Hell, no," he replied.[4]

QUESTIONS TO CONSIDER

1. After the September 11, 2001, terrorist attacks, experts worried that a new round of small but carefully targeted terror attacks against "critical infrastructure" could cripple American cities by shutting off power, poisoning water, or blocking traffic. Does the broader strategy to identify possible threats to this critical infrastructure strike you as a wise idea?

2. Who is accountable for this action? The money flowed from the U.S. Department of Homeland Security to the Pennsylvania Office of Homeland Security to a private contractor. If you wanted to fire someone, who would you fire? The federal official who awarded the grant? The state official who managed the contract? The contractor? Would you fire the official in charge at each step—or the higher-level officials who were in charge of the agencies? Or would you just terminate the contract?

3. What steps do you think government ought to take to control the actions of contractors who spend taxpayers' dollars in the government's name?

4. More generally, is the analysis of possible threats to homeland security something that can—and should—be contracted in part to private organizations, which might have more expertise than government agencies? Or is it an activity, full of implications for individual freedom, that the government ought to keep within its own organizations?

NOTES

1. See Pennsylvania Intelligence Bulletin, no. 131 (2010), https://www.propublica.org/documents/item/pennsylvania-intelligence-bulletin-no.-131-aug.-30-2010.

2. Angela Couloumbis, "Rendell 'Appalled' by State's Tracking of Activists," *Philly.com* (September 15, 2010), http://articles.philly.com/2010-09-15/news/24975314_1_rendell-peace-activists-bulletin.

3. Donald Gilliland, "Gov. Ed Rendell's Top Staffers Knew of Homeland Security Tracking Protesters in July," *Patriot-News* (September 15, 2010), http://www.pennlive.com/midstate/index.ssf/2010/09/rendells_top_staffers_knew_of.html.

4. Joe Smydo, "Shale Adviser Ridge Calls Anti-Terror Pact 'Bizarre,'" *Pittsburgh Post-Gazette* (September 16, 2010), http://www.post-gazette.com/stories/local/state/shale-adviser-ridge-calls-anti-terror-pact-bizarre-264195.

 # CASE 2.2

Reading License Plates: Collecting Data on American Citizens

If there's any part of government that citizens seem to take for granted, it's the license plate. They're everywhere. Some states just have one, at the rear of the car. Some have both. Some states take fierce pride in the slogans on the plates. "Live free or die" has been on New Hampshire license plates for years. Since 2000, Washington, D.C., has put "Taxation without representation" on its plates to protest the lack of full congressional representation for its citizens. D.C. plates with the phrase have gone on the presidential limousine during the Clinton administration, off during the Bush administration, and back on for the Obama administration. Wisconsin is proud of its "America's Dairyland" plates, and Maryland residents have a choice of plates that proclaim "Treasure the Chesapeake."

Whatever plate might be on your car, though, you might not know that police around the country are keeping a close eye on it—and you. Technological advances have made it possible for police to mount relatively inexpensive cameras on road signs, overpasses, police cars, and buildings around the country. The cameras have amazing resolution. They can capture the license plate number as well as the location, date, and time of the scan; pour it into an enormous database; and compare the information with "most wanted" information in national databases. These systems around the nation collect thousands of license plate numbers every minute.

The data systems are tremendously valuable for tracking the movement of suspects, but in the process they also collect enormous amounts of information on everyone else. As a report by the American Civil Liberties Union (ACLU) showed, "enormous databases of innocent motorists' location information are growing rapidly. This information is often retained for years or even indefinitely, with few or no restrictions to protect privacy rights."[1]

Police officials like not only the ability to scan enormous numbers of license plates in the hunt for suspects, ranging from individuals who have abducted children to possible terrorists. They also like the ability to keep a long-running database. As David J. Roberts, a senior program manager for the International Association of Chiefs of Police, put it, "We'd like to be able to keep the data as long as possible, but it does provide a rich and enduring data set for investigations down the line."[2] An individual whom police identify as part of one crime might be connected with others by tracking license plate numbers back through the system. Camera systems are even used on many campuses, with college police departments quietly tracking every car that enters the campus.

©iStock.com/makok

The ACLU worried that the systems collected vast amounts of information about completely innocent citizens. In Maryland, for example, it discovered that the license plate readers scanned 29 million plates, but only 0.2 percent (1 in 500) were "hits," that is, associated with any wrongdoing.[3] In many jurisdictions, the information remains in storage for a long time, as Figure 2.8 shows.

Three communities in the ACLU survey—Grapevine, Texas; Mesquite, Texas; and Yonkers, New York—kept the information indefinitely. To safeguard citizens' privacy, the ACLU recommended a five-step policy (see Table 2.4).

Figure 2.9	License Plate Data Retention Policies for Selected States

MILPITAS, CA
Population: 67,000
Data policy: None
Stored plate reads: 4.7 million
(as of 8/2/12)

MINNESOTA STATE PATROL
Population: 5.3 million
Data policy: Delete after 48 hours
Stored plate reads: Less than 20,000

GRAPEVINE, TX
Population: 47,000
Data policy: None
Stored plate reads: 2 million
(as of 8/29/12)

JERSEY CITY, NJ
Population: 250,000
Data policy: Delete after 5 years
Stored plate reads: 10 million (estimated)
(as of 8/2/12)

Source: American Civil Liberties Union, *You Are Being Tracked: How License Plate Readers Are Being Used to Record Americans' Movements* (New York: July 2013), p. 17, https://www.aclu.org/files/assets/071613-aclu-alprreport-opt-v05.pdf.

Table 2.4	**ACLU Recommendations on License Plate Cameras**

License plate readers may be used by law enforcement agencies only to investigate hits and in other circumstances in which law enforcement agents reasonably believe that the plate data are relevant to an ongoing criminal investigation.

The government must not store data about innocent people for any lengthy period. Unless plate data have been flagged, retention periods should be measured in days or weeks, not months and certainly not years.

People should be able to find out if plate data of vehicles registered to them are contained in a law enforcement agency's database.

Law enforcement agencies should not share license plate reader data with third parties that do not follow proper retention and access principles. They should also be transparent regarding with whom they share license plate reader data.

Any entity that uses license plate readers should be required to report its usage publicly on at least an annual basis.

Source: American Civil Liberties Union, "You Are Being Tracked: How License Plate Readers Are Being Used to Record Americans' Movements" (2013), http://www.aclu.org/alpr.

QUESTIONS TO CONSIDER

1. Are you surprised by the findings of the ACLU report? Does the license plate camera system worry you?

2. Would you recommend adopting the ACLU's proposals on license plate cameras?

3. If you were the chief of police of your community, and if you were using such a system, how would you respond to a reporter's questions about the system?

NOTES

1. American Civil Liberties Union, "You Are Being Tracked" (2013), http://www.aclu.org/alpr.

2. Craig Timberg, "License-Plate Cameras Track Millions of Americans," *Washington Post* (July 17, 2013), https://www.washingtonpost.com/business/technology/license-plate-cameras-track-millions-of-americans/2013/07/17/40410cd0-ee47-11e2-bed3-b9b6fe264871_story.html.

3. American Civil Liberties Union, *You Are Being Tracked: How License Plate Readers Are Being Used to Record Americans' Movements* (New York: July 2013), p. 17, https://www.aclu.org/files/assets/071613-aclu-alprreport-opt-v05.pdf.

CASE 2.3

Wasting Away? Fifty Examples of Government Waste[1]

In late 2009, the conservative Heritage Foundation released a list of fifty examples of government waste. The examples fell into six categories, according to the foundation's analysts:

1. Programs that should be devolved to state and local governments
2. Programs that could be better performed by the private sector
3. Mistargeted programs whose recipients should not be entitled to government benefits
4. Outdated and unnecessary programs
5. Duplicative programs
6. Inefficiency, mismanagement, and fraud

And here's their list:

1. The federal government made at least **$72 billion** in improper payments in 2008.

2. Washington spends **$92 billion** on corporate welfare (excluding expenditures under the

Troubled Assets Relief Program [TARP]) versus $71 billion on homeland security.

3. Washington spends **$25 billion** annually maintaining unused or vacant federal properties.

4. Government auditors spent the past five years examining all federal programs and found that 22 percent of them—costing taxpayers a total of **$123 billion** annually—fail to show any positive impact on the populations they serve.

5. The Congressional Budget Office published a "Budget Options" series identifying more than **$100 billion** in potential spending cuts.

6. Examples from multiple Government Accountability Office (GAO) reports of wasteful duplication include **342** economic development programs; **130** programs serving the disabled; **130** programs serving at-risk youth; ninety early childhood development programs; **75** programs funding international education, cultural, and training exchange activities; and **72** safe water programs.

7. Washington will spend **$2.6 million** training Chinese prostitutes to drink more responsibly on the job.

8. A GAO audit classified **nearly half of all purchases** on government credit cards as improper, fraudulent, or embezzled. Examples of taxpayer-funded purchases include gambling, mortgage payments, liquor, lingerie, iPods, Xboxes, jewelry, Internet dating services, and Hawaiian vacations. In one extraordinary example, the Postal Service spent **$13,500** on one dinner at a Ruth's Chris Steakhouse, including "over 200 appetizers and over $3,000 of alcohol, including more than forty bottles of wine costing more than $50 each and brand-name liquor such as Courvoisier, Belvedere, and Johnny Walker Gold." The eighty-one guests consumed an average of $167 worth of food and drink apiece.

9. Federal agencies are delinquent on nearly 20 percent of employee travel charge cards, costing taxpayers **hundreds of millions of dollars** annually.

10. The Securities and Exchange Commission spent **$3.9 million** rearranging desks and offices at its Washington, D.C., headquarters.

11. The Pentagon recently spent **$998,798** shipping two 19-cent washers from South Carolina to Texas and **$293,451** sending an 89-cent washer from South Carolina to Florida.

12. **Over half of all farm subsidies** go to commercial farms, which report average household incomes of $200,000.

13. Health care fraud is estimated to cost taxpayers more than **$60 billion** annually.

14. A GAO audit found that ninety-five Pentagon weapons systems suffered from a combined **$295 billion** in cost overruns.

15. The refusal of many federal employees to fly coach costs taxpayers **$146 million** annually in flight upgrades.

16. Washington spent **$126 million** in 2009 to enhance the Kennedy family legacy in Massachusetts. Additionally, Senator John Kerry (D-Mass.) diverted $20 million from the 2010 defense budget to subsidize a new Edward M. Kennedy Institute.

17. Federal investigators have launched more than **twenty criminal fraud investigations** related to the TARP financial bailout.

18. Despite trillion-dollar deficits, there were 10,160 earmarks in 2008, which included **$200,000** for a tattoo removal program in Mission Hills, California; **$190,000** for the Buffalo Bill Historical Center in Cody, Wyoming; and **$75,000** for the Totally Teen Zone in Albany, Georgia.

19. The federal government owns more than **50,000 vacant homes**.

20. The Federal Communications Commission spent **$350,000** to sponsor NASCAR driver David Gilliland.

21. Members of Congress have spent **hundreds of thousands** of taxpayer dollars supplying their offices with popcorn machines, plasma televisions, DVD equipment, ionic air fresheners, camcorders, and signature machines—plus **$24,730** leasing a Lexus, **$1,434** on a digital camera, and **$84,000** on personalized calendars.

22. More than **$13 billion** in Iraq aid has been classified as wasted or stolen. Another **$7.8 billion** cannot be accounted for.

23. Fraud related to Hurricane Katrina spending is estimated to top **$2 billion**. In addition, debit cards provided to hurricane victims were used to pay for Caribbean vacations, NFL tickets, Dom Perignon champagne, "Girls Gone Wild" videos, and at least one sex change operation.

24. Auditors discovered that **900,000** of the 2.5 million recipients of emergency Katrina assistance provided false names, addresses, or Social Security numbers or submitted multiple applications.

25. Congress recently gave Alaska Airlines **$500,000** to paint a Chinook salmon on a Boeing 737.

26. The Transportation Department will subsidize up to **$2,000 per flight** for direct flights between Washington, D.C., and the small hometown of Congressman Hal Rogers (R-Ky.)—but only on Monday mornings and Friday evenings, when lawmakers, staff, and lobbyists usually fly. Rogers is a member of the Appropriations Committee, which writes the Transportation Department's budget.

27. Washington has spent **$3 billion** re-sanding beaches—even as this new sand washes back into the ocean.

28. A Department of Agriculture report concedes that much of the **$2.5 billion** in "stimulus" funding for broadband Internet will be wasted.

29. The Defense Department wasted **$100 million** on unused flight tickets and never bothered to collect refunds even though the tickets were refundable.

30. Washington spends **$60,000 per hour** shooting *Air Force One* photo-ops in front of national landmarks.

31. Over one recent 18-month period, Air Force and Navy personnel used government-funded credit cards to charge at least **$102,400** on admission to entertainment events, **$48,250** on gambling, **$69,300** on cruises, and **$73,950** on exotic dance clubs and prostitutes.

32. Members of Congress are set to pay themselves **$90 million** to increase their franked mailings for the 2010 election year.

33. Congress has ignored efficiency recommendations from the Department of Health and Human Services that would save **$9 billion** annually.

34. Taxpayers are funding paintings of high-ranking government officials at a cost of up to **$50,000 apiece**.

35. The state of Washington sent $1 food stamp checks to 250,000 households in order to raise state caseload figures and trigger **$43 million** in additional federal funds.

36. Suburban families are receiving large **farm subsidies for the grass in their backyards**—subsidies that many of these families never requested and do not want.

37. Congress appropriated **$20 million** for "commemoration of success" celebrations related to Iraq and Afghanistan.

38. Homeland Security employee purchases include 63-inch plasma TVs, iPods, and **$230** for a beer brewing kit.

39. Two drafting errors in the 2005 Deficit Reduction Act resulted in a **$2 billion** taxpayer cost.

40. North Ridgeville, Ohio, received **$800,000** in "stimulus" funds for a project that its mayor described as "a long way from the top priority."

41. The National Institutes of Health spends **$1.3 million** per month to rent a lab that it cannot use.

42. Congress recently spent **$2.4 billion** on ten new jets that the Pentagon insists it does not need and will not use.

43. Lawmakers diverted **$13 million** from Hurricane Katrina relief spending to build a museum celebrating the Army Corps of Engineers—the agency partially responsible for the failed levees that flooded New Orleans.

44. Medicare officials recently mailed **$50 million** in erroneous refunds to 230,000 Medicare recipients.

45. Audits showed **$34 billion** worth of Department of Homeland Security contracts contained significant waste, fraud, and abuse.

46. Washington recently spent **$1.8 million** to help build a private golf course in Atlanta, Georgia.

47. The Advanced Technology Program spends **$150 million** annually subsidizing private businesses; 40 percent of this funding goes to Fortune 500 companies.

48. Congressional investigators were able to receive **$55,000** in federal student loan funding for a fictional college they created to test the Department of Education.

49. The Conservation Reserve program pays farmers **$2 billion** annually not to farm their land.

50. The Commerce Department has lost **1,137 computers** since 2001, many containing Americans' personal data.

QUESTIONS TO CONSIDER

1. Look over the list. Which examples do you think are the most serious? Are there programs on the list that you think are, in fact, not wasteful?

2. Assume that in at least some of these cases, someone thought there was a good reason to fund the programs. Can you identify five such programs and craft an argument that could be used to support the programs?

3. Pick five programs you think are simply bad ideas. They are likely to be decisions made by elected officials. What steps would you take to end them?

4. Responding to some of these problems might require administrative changes. Can you pick one program on this list that you think you could improve through better public administration? What steps would you take to strengthen its administration to reduce waste?

NOTE

1. Excerpt from Brian Reidl, *50 Examples of Government Waste*, Heritage Foundation (October 6, 2009), http://www.heritage.org/research/reports/2009/10/50-examples-of-government-waste. The citations to the original sources can be found at the Heritage Foundation website. Emphasis is in the original.

Are Private Markets Better Than Government?

It's no secret that Americans like private markets better than they like government. In a 2014 Pew Research Center poll, 70 percent of Americans said they believed they were better off in a free-market system. Only in South Korea and Germany do citizens like markets more.

From environmental policy to health care, this basic finding has framed the critical decisions of government in recent years. If we want to take on a new policy challenge, citizens and policy experts seem to agree, it's better to trust the states than Washington. And the states should do as much as possible through private markets.

The strategy has launched some remarkable policy innovations. But most of the time, it hasn't worked out so well in practice.

Take the movement to reduce carbon emissions. In the 2000s, many states embarked on a revolutionary cap-and-trade strategy. They would set a cap on acceptable greenhouse gas levels, businesses would pay for the right to emit the gases, and the hidden hand of the market would reduce pollution by the largest amount at the lowest cost. By 2008, according to a count by the University of Michigan's Barry Rabe in the journal *Governance*, twenty-three states had joined the effort. It seemed a perfect solution. New markets developed, and regional consortia planned to reduce greenhouse gases by 10 percent or more within a few years.

But that perfect solution didn't last long. Rabe found that, within five years, more than half the states had walked away from their cap-and-trade commitment. The market-based alternative to command-and-control regulations evaporated as a state-based policy tool.

Then there's the marketplace system at the core of the Affordable Care Act. It's easy to forget that the Obama administration originally was trying to avoid using a Washington-driven hammer. Instead, the plan aimed to provide health insurance to everyone by encouraging the states to do the job—and having the states work through market-based insurance exchanges to make the policies available.

Relying on state-based markets seemed a logical step, both ideologically and pragmatically. It stood to minimize complaints about big government by pushing policy implementation into the private sector, and it echoed the Pew poll results. After all, there's scarcely a more popular refrain than the one that proclaims government should be run more like a private business. But as in the cap-and-trade example, this market-based strategy just didn't work well. State implementation proved wildly uneven. Federal policymakers found themselves without the results they sought. And everyone came away more convinced than ever that government couldn't solve problems like this, even though many of the problems were rooted in private-market failures.

By the end of 2015, thirty-eight states had declined to set up health care exchanges, leaving the federal government to step in and create them. Three states—Hawaii, Nevada, and Oregon—tried the exchange approach and backed out when enrollment was lower and costs were higher than expected. Some states, like Maryland and Washington, enthusiastically embraced the exchanges but fumbled the launch. Pressed by angry Republicans, who criticized the states' lack of accountability for federal funds, the Obama administration took back $200 million in grants it had made to states that had struggled to launch their exchanges.

Why did these efforts fail?

Part of the answer has to do with the partisan makeup of the statehouses. Republicans hold thirty-one of the fifty governorships, and many of the Republican governors came to office touting free markets and smaller government. In most states, the champions of aggressive policy innovation are on the run. Fewer citizens in these conservative states believe that climate change is manmade, and that reduces the incentives for state-level action. The fumbled launch of the Affordable Care Act website eroded public support for health care reform. The appetite for strong state policy initiatives has gradually evaporated.

Moreover, as Rabe points out, managing the pollution market mechanisms turned out to be hard, and financially strapped states had a shrinking capacity to do the job well. That was even truer for the health exchanges, where some of the most ambitious states stumbled despite their aggressive efforts.

The fundamental flaw lies in two assumptions: that markets always work better than governments and that markets will run themselves if government gets out of the way. The first assumption is the stuff of fierce ideological debate, but the second is really a settled question. Markets just don't run themselves in delivering public goods, because most of the time they are being asked to do things they aren't used to doing. And because policymakers tend to assume that the markets will take care of themselves, they often don't build governmental capacity to steer the process. The reformers then end up running after problems as they develop down the line.

It's tempting to dance around the big battles over the size of government by assuming private markets can step in and fix everything. Too often, we end up abandoning the markets, disappointing the customers and undermining everyone's confidence in leadership. There's no sidestepping the fact that government requires governing.

QUESTIONS TO CONSIDER

1. Consider the case for action through markets and through government. What are the pros and cons of each?

2. Government's critics often argue that government ought to be run more like the private sector. What lessons does this case teach about that argument?

3. Does reliance on private markets to achieve public purposes eliminate the need for a government role? What are the implications for government of relying more on the private sector for such missions?

Note: This case comes from my column in *Governing* (February 2016), http://www.governing.com/columns/potomac-chronicle/gov-free-market-failures-government.html.

KEY CONCEPTS

FOR FURTHER READING

Hood, Christopher C. *The Tools of Government.* Chatham, N.J.: Chatham House, 1983.

Kerwin, Cornelius. *Rulemaking: How Government Agencies Make Law and Write Policy.* Washington, D.C.: CQ Press, 2003.

Kettl, Donald F. *Government by Proxy: (Mis?) Managing Federal Programs.* Washington, D.C.: CQ Press, 1988.

Kettl, Donald F. *The Next Government of the United States: Why Our Institutions Fail Us and How to Fix Them.* New York: Norton, 2009.

Salamon, Lester M., ed. *The Tools of Government: A Guide to the New Governance.* New York: Oxford University Press, 2002.

SUGGESTED WEBSITES

For research on how the federal government spends its money, the basic source is the federal budget, published by the Office of Management and Budget, **www.white house.gov/omb**. OMB annually publishes two useful reports: *Analytical Perspectives,* which provides background information on issues such as federal taxing, spending, and lending programs, and *Historical Tables,* which provides long-term data on federal budget trends. Many of the key budget tables are available for download in Excel format.

In addition, the Congressional Budget Office, **www.cbo.gov**, assembles federal budget data and is especially useful for tracking trends in entitlement and discretionary spending and in federal government revenue.

The best source of information about trends in state and local government finances is the U.S. Census Bureau, **www.census.gov**. For international comparisons, the "statistics" portal at the Organization for Economic Co-operation and Development website, **www.oecd.org**, is valuable. OECD is an international organization that tracks the policy and financial issues facing nations around the world.

for CQ Press

WANT A BETTER GRADE?

Get the tools you need to sharpen your study skills. Access practice quizzes, eFlashcards, video, and multimedia at **edge.sagepub.com/kettl7e.**

3

WHAT IS PUBLIC ADMINISTRATION?

The government's response to the enormous devastation of Superstorm Sandy in November 2012 was a huge change from the problems that surrounded Hurricane Katrina's assault on the Gulf Coast in 2005. As with the case of Loretta Abruscato, here, aided by New York National Guard troops, government at all levels responded far more effectively to citizens' needs, thanks to the careful analysis that happened in response to the failures seven years earlier.

The ageless debates about *bureaucracy* has always formed the core of public administration. The term *bureaucracy* itself has deep roots, in fourteenth-century France. At the Chamber of Accounts, field administrators placed their financial records on a brown woolen cloth, *la bure*, which covered the table facing the king's auditors. The room came to be called "the bureau," and the way these officials did their work became known as "bureaucracy." From the king's point of view, the most important thing, of course, was making sure that the financial records were correct and that no one was cheating the crown, so "bureaucracy" quickly became connected with "accountability." It didn't take long for the term to take on the negative meaning we sometimes associate with it. In an 1836 novel, French author Honoré de Balzac characterized the bureaucracy as "a gigantic power manipulated by dwarfs" and as "that heavy curtain hung between the good to be done and him who commands it."[1] Bureaucracy is something we all love to hate—and it's something we can't live without. The tensions go back many centuries.

There is a deep contradiction buried in this ageless debate.[2] On one hand, bureaucracy is viewed as a device that cripples government: red-tape-bound civil servants are seen as inefficient, unresponsive, negative, bored, impolite, and unhelpful to citizens seeking services. On the other hand, bureaucracy is feared for the power it concentrates: officials sometimes are seen as all-too-efficient in gathering power and arbitrarily deciding matters without providing citizens due process. How can both be true: a bureaucracy so inefficient it can't accomplish much of anything but also so powerful that it threatens our liberty? This is not only the central problem of bureaucracy in modern life. It's the ageless dilemma of bureaucracy itself.

At its core, the term *bureaucracy* has a neutral meaning. Indeed, bureaucracy is not even a public-sector term—it's a basic description for the organization and structure of complex organizations, and private companies have bureaucracies, too. Apple and Microsoft, the American Red Cross and the American Cancer Society, the power company and Facebook all are bureaucracies. The oldest continuously functioning bureaucracy in the world is the Roman Catholic Church. (The New Testament records that after the ascension of Jesus, the new church immediately created a formal organization to carry on the work of its charismatic founder.) In this book, we will use *bureaucracy* to refer to complex public organizations: the formal, rational system of relations among persons vested with administrative authority to carry out public programs. In Chapter 4 we examine this interpretation of bureaucracy—and some of its alternatives—more fully.

Even though the term *bureaucracy* itself is neutral, the negative meanings are never far away. The often contradictory images of bureaucracy point to very real problems of large-scale administration. They also shape the politics

CHAPTER OBJECTIVES

- Understand what makes public administration "public"
- Discuss what public administration is
- Look at the deep historical debates that have shaped the study of public administration

of public administration. As presidential candidates, both Jimmy Carter and Ronald Reagan campaigned on bureaucracy-bashing themes; Bill Clinton dealt with calls to shrink the bureaucracy; both Presidents Bush campaigned on a conservative agenda to reduce government (even though they both actually increased it); and John McCain and Barack Obama sparred over who could best promote change in the way Washington does business. Obama and Mitt Romney replayed many of the same themes in 2012. In the 2016 presidential campaign, an army of candidates competed to convey the strongest antibureaucracy theme. And this isn't just a federal phenomenon, of course. Candidates at all levels of government often work hard to make the case that they can come in and fix what ails government.

The negative image of bureaucracy is universal. A foreign prime minister once complained, "Creating the appearance of work, taking cover behind hollow rhetoric, bureaucracy may hold back the improvement of the economic mechanism, dampen independence and initiative, and erect barriers to innovation." A second said, "Bureaucratism remains a serious problem in the political life of our party and state. The overstaffing, overlapping and unwieldiness of Government organs, confusion of their responsibilities and buck-passing are . . . major causes of bureaucratism. We must therefore reform these organs from top to bottom." The first speaker was prime minister of the former Soviet Union; the second, an acting prime minister of the People's Republic of China.[3] Government officials around the world share the basic instinct to reform "bureaucracy."[4]

If almost everyone hates bureaucracy and red tape, why don't we abolish them? The answer is that government can't deliver complex goods and services any other way—and, no matter how much they complain, citizens expect that the work *will* get done. Complexity and red tape are part of all large organizations. That's even more the case for government, where public policy embraces many complex and competing goals.[5] We might not much like paying taxes or dealing with rules, but we usually like much of the government we get and resist efforts to cut back on the services we receive. Americans want bureaucracy cut—except for *their* bureaucracy and the programs that serve *them*. The challenge of public administration revolves around these dilemmas.

THE MEANING OF PUBLIC ADMINISTRATION

Despite the long-standing importance of **public administration**, analysts and scholars have never agreed on a common definition.[6] In a system that ranges from delivering mail, collecting trash, and licensing motor vehicles to launching cameras and spacecraft on Mars, dispatching Peace Corps volunteers all over the world, helping citizens recover from hurricanes, and tracking dangerous storms with satellites, a concise definition is impossible.

One approach might be breaking public administration in half, defining *administration* and then *public,* but that doesn't work. Scholars have sometimes used phrases like *administration is executing,* but that phrase needs further definition. Other writers characterize administration as cooperative human action that has a high degree of rationality, which maximizes the realization of certain goals.[7] But this formulation could include people who use text messages to create a flash mob. Still other writers, operating at a less abstract level, say that administration is concerned with "how, not what," with "means, not ends," with "process, not substance," with "efficiency, not other values." But this approach only provokes more debates, rather than providing a clear definition.

A better starting point for understanding the meaning of *public* administration is to distinguish it from *private* administration. We begin by evaluating the argument that administration is administration wherever it exists, whether in the public or the private sector. Next we examine policy execution versus **policymaking** (or policy formulation). This separates the administrative processes, in which government administration shares similarities with private administration, from the distinctly public nature of governmental decisions. Finally, we emphasize the ways that administrative responsibility in public administration differs in both form and content from its analog in private enterprises. Of central importance to public bureaucracies, administrative responsibility defines the very essence of our puzzle—and of this book.

Public versus Private Administration

Public administration is *public:* it is the administration of governmental affairs. Yet it is also *administration*, an activity essential to all large organizations. For years, experts have debated the questions: Are its basic features the same as other types of administration? Is it simply a subset of more generic management issues? Or does it have special, distinctly public elements that require separate attention? This, after all, is a central puzzle in the Flint water case, with which we began this book. Several schools of thought seek to answer these questions.

A generic approach to administration begins with sociologists who specialize in **organizational theory**, along with many scholars of management from business schools. At the most fundamental level, some organizational theorists contend that administration is administration, whatever its setting, and that the problems of organizing people, leading them, and supplying them with resources to do their jobs are always the same.[8] More practically oriented thinkers have argued that that "political conflict is at the center of management life"; that management is always fundamentally about managing that conflict, regardless of its organizational setting; and that such conflict management is the core of administration, public and private.[9] Most broadly, Barry Bozeman has argued that "all organizations are public because public authority affects some of the behavior or processes of all organizations." Thus, organizations are neither purely public nor purely private; but all organizations, Bozeman contends, share public and private features independent of their legal or formal status.[10] In fact, a leading British political scientist, William A. Robson, has noted that "modern American theory is heavily committed to the view that one can discuss every kind of administration in a generalized manner," by seeking to understand the fundamental features of administration.[11]

Over time, in fact, the distinction between the public and private sectors has gradually become more blurred. As Dwight Waldo pointed out in 1980, "In the United States—and I believe much more widely—there is a movement away from a sharp distinction between *public* and *private*, and *toward* a blurring and mingling of the two."[12] As government becomes more involved in business, and as more business organizations are incorporated into the provision of public services, such blurring is inevitable. But that, of course, only complicates our central question: Is there something distinctly *public* about public administration?

Private-sector managers who move into top public-sector positions have universally found large, crucial differences between the two sectors.[13] Scholars have emphasized two important distinctions. First, and most crucially, is the *what*: public organizations do the public's business—they administer law. Second, there is the *how*: compared with private companies, public organizations use fundamentally different processes and work in very different environments.[14]

DIVING INTO DATA

Created as part of Lyndon B. Johnson's "Great Society" programs in 1965, Medicare and Medicaid have become two of the most important elements of government. Consider these basic facts about the programs.

The Centers for Medicare and Medicaid Services (CMS) is in the U.S. Department of Health and Human Services. Medicare provides health care to older Americans while Medicaid provides for poorer Americans and children's health care.

Share of total federal budget:

25%

CMS workers as a portion of all federal employees:

.02%

Average federal spending for which each CMS employee is responsible:

$144 Million

Improper Payments Made for Fiscal Year 2014

Medicare

$58 Billion

Medicaid

$17 Billion

Error Rate in Program Payments for Fiscal Year 2014

Medicare

12%

Medicaid

7%

Source: Donald F. Kettl, *Escaping Jurassic Government* (Washington, D.C.: Brookings, Institution Press, 2016); and U.S. Government Accountability Office, *Improper Payments: Government-Wide Estimates and Use of Death Data to Help Prevent Payments to Deceased Individuals*, Report GAO-15-482T (March 2015), at http://www.gao.gov/assets/670/669026.pdf.

QUESTIONS

1. Are you surprised at the relatively small number of federal government employees responsible for managing such large programs?
2. Who do you think is responsible for managing the program's operations, since federal employees are not (hint: for-profit and nonprofit hospitals, clinics, and health care providers)?
3. Do you think that the improper payments and error rates represent a serious problem? What information do you need to answer this question?
4. What steps would be required to attack this problem?

THE CRITICAL ROLE OF PUBLIC AUTHORITY. The most fundamental distinction between public and private organizations is the rule of law. In general, public officials must do what the law requires, and they cannot do anything that the law does not. Private officials can choose to do what they like, as long as the law does not forbid it. Every action taken by a public administrator ultimately "must be traceable to a legal grant of authority; those of private firms need not be," as Harold F. Gortner, Julianne Mahler, and Jeanne Bell Nicholson argue.

> Managers of private firms can generally take any action, establish any policy, or use any means of operation not specifically prohibited. Public managers, in contrast, may not do so in the absence of specific grants of authority. Private organizations can act unless proscribed or forbidden; public ones may act *only* if the authority is granted. As a veteran public manager remarked . . . "For the private organization, it is a matter of 'go until I say stop'; but to the public manager the message is 'don't go unless I tell you to.'"[15]

Public administration exists to implement the law, and the constitutional system creates the authority for doing so. In the American system, authority flows from the people to those they elect to govern them. Of course, when a legislature passes a law and an executive signs it, the law does not implement itself. That is the task the legislature delegates to an administrator, and it is this chain of authority, flowing from the people through elected institutions to the public administrator, that makes public administration distinctively public. Faithful execution of these laws is the highest calling of public administrators. It is the core of administrative responsibility.

Public management scholar Steven Kelman points to a fundamental difference between public and private management. All organizations, he says, must balance goals and constraints. Goals are the good things organizations try to do—the value they produce, the objectives they seek to accomplish. Constraints are the negative forces they must work around and the rules they must obey in pursuing their goals. Ideally, organizations would find the right balance that ensures good results and strong accountability. For private organizations, the balance leans toward the goals and, with fewer constraints, free-wheeling tactics can sometimes lead to financial disaster, as the 2008 financial crisis showed. With additional constraints, government sometimes struggles to accomplish the objectives that policymakers set for it. This, Kelman says, is "the Katrina problem"—red tape that restrains

AP Photo/The Star-News, Matt Born

Public libraries are an important government-funded service. In many communities, like this one in Wilmington, North Carolina, public libraries are not only repositories of books—they are increasingly gateways to the information age.

the ability of government to do its job. Public and private organizations both share the need to balance goals and constraints, but the forces underlying their operations tend to push them in different directions. That dynamic, in turn, frames very different problems for their leaders and for the people they serve.[16]

PROCESSES THAT MAKE PUBLIC ADMINISTRATION PUBLIC. Although these differences are not fixed in law, there typically are important distinctions between public and private organizational processes.[17] Here are the most fundamental differences:

- *Career service.* Whereas private-sector organizations tend to be led by individuals who devote their careers to the organization, American public bureaucracies tend to be headed by relative amateurs whose tenure is of short duration. Assistant secretaries in federal departments, for example, typically serve only eighteen months and spend much of their time in office simply learning their jobs.
- *Performance measures.* The private sector has the market in which to test its performance. Few public-sector organizations, by contrast, have any "direct way of evaluating their outputs in relation to the cost of the inputs used to make them," as Anthony Downs puts it.[18] For public administrators, compliance with the law is the ultimate **performance measure**, but laws often are vague and give little guidance.
- *Competing standards.* Whereas efficiency is the ultimate private standard, public administrators are expected to manage both efficiently and equitably. These two standards often compete: what is fair often is not the most efficient, and vice versa. As economist Arthur Okun notes, the balance between equality and efficiency is "the big tradeoff."[19]

- *Public scrutiny.* Far more than in the private sector, public administrators work under public scrutiny. Public administrators labor under laws whose very titles, such as "Government in the Sunshine," underline the role of public **oversight**, covering both internal and external operations. This "goldfish-bowl effect" is in stark contrast with the much more limited public scrutiny that private organizations receive. Dealing with the media has long been a feature of public administrative activity.[20]
- *Persuasion.* In the private sector, managers tend to manage by authority. They give orders and expect them to be obeyed. In the public sector, by contrast, administration depends far more on persuasion and the balancing of conflicting political demands.
- *Scope of authority.* Government officials are legally required to administer the law—and the federal **Antideficiency Act** explicitly forbids officials from spending money on any purpose not explicitly *authorized* by law.[21] (This is what forces the government to shut down if Congress fails to pass a budget on time. Government officials may not spend any money, even to turn on the lights or use their computers, if Congress has not approved it.) In the private sector, by contrast, officials are allowed to do anything not explicitly *forbidden* by law.[22]
- *Oversight.* Public administrators must answer not only to their superiors but also to legislators and the courts. Administrators must appear before legislative committees to explain their activities and must answer complaints raised in court. If the private sector has one bottom line—the annual or quarterly financial statement—the public sector has several: accountability to higher-level administrative officials, to the chief executive, to legislators, to the courts, and ultimately to the public.

We tend sometimes to separate public and private activities by the profit motive. To be sure, this is an important difference, but it does not clearly distinguish the two sectors. Private organizations sometimes put other goals before profitmaking. Some nongovernmental organizations are **nonprofit** and exist to advance social agendas. On the other hand, some public organizations, such as the U.S. Postal Service, simulate the market by imposing fees and charges and (try to) break even. In fact, reformers have tried to make public organizations more efficient by pushing more market-based strategies on public organizations.

Most fundamentally, however, public organizations are public because they administer the law and because their existence springs from the law. Moreover, public organizations typically operate in a different environment from that of private organizations. Wallace Sayre once wryly suggested that "business and public administration are alike only in all unimportant respects."[23] Public administration is *public* because it does the public's business, as defined in laws passed on behalf of the people.

Policy Execution versus Policy Formation

Public administration shares with private administration many basic features of policy execution. From managing computer systems to processing forms, the basic work often is similar. But public-sector execution differs fundamentally in the goals to be served and the standards by which its achievements are judged. Indeed, part of what makes public administration public is its execution of the will of the people as defined by governmental institutions. Because public administration contributes to the shaping and execution of policies, it is often very different indeed from private administration. We look first at the more familiar function—policy execution.

POLICY EXECUTION. Consider what it means when we say that the government has "adopted" a policy. In our system, this normally means that the elected policymakers have enacted a law forbidding, directing, or permitting members of the society to behave in specified ways. Then what happens? The law is merely a text printed on paper. The task of public administration is to translate the print from statute books into changed behavior by members of society—individuals, groups, organizations, and businesses—in other words, to convert words into action, form into substance.

Execution of policy is a complex task. It means expanding some individuals' opportunities by extending governmental services and protections to them. It means regulating some individuals' freedom by drawing taxes from them, discovering and prosecuting those who engage in forbidden behaviors, granting or denying permission to engage in certain activities (for example, licensing radio and television stations and selling prescription drugs), and manipulating the environment of subsidies and interest rates. The government administers some enterprises itself, either as monopolies or as competitors of private enterprises: local libraries and the Social Security Administration function largely as monopolies; the U.S. Postal Service and the Tennessee Valley Authority compete with private companies. Reformers have increasingly sought to bring private competition into local schools, and public schools increasingly have to compete with private schools and parents schooling their children at home. The government also administers the defense establishment and foreign affairs, including hundreds of outposts over the world. The range is immense, and the pattern mixes old and new concerns.

Authorizing these governmental activities, giving policy direction, and providing the necessary resources are among the central tasks of the elective legislature and chief executive. But this merely permits something to happen; it does not *make* something happen. Administration translates paper declarations of intent into reality. It shapes the behavior of citizens to match policy goals and delivers the benefits promised in legislation.

Administration as execution cannot be taken for granted. Weak or unresponsive administration will enfeeble the political system. For example, in many developing countries the critical problem is not so much the government's political instability as it is the government's incapacity to carry out its decisions. Public policies, no matter how bold or innovative, are worthless if government cannot carry them out. When Hurricane Katrina submerged New Orleans in 2005, official governmental policy was to provide help quickly, but the government failed, not because its officials did not want to help but because executing the policy proved tremendously complex. Five years later, much of the Gulf Coast was under assault from BP's oil spill. Everyone wanted it to stop—that was the clear governmental policy—but it took months to figure out how. The Obama administration desperately wanted its health care reform to work, but when its website went live on October 1, 2013, the site was so flawed that almost no one could sign up for insurance. *Making* policy does not ensure that policies produce results.

POLICY FORMATION. Administration's second role is to help decision makers form policy. Its role plays out at two stages: (1) before the legislature and chief executive have made the policy decisions for which they're responsible and (2) after elected officials have enacted statutes or issued executive orders, and then delegated to administrators the job of interpreting these actions. In the first stage, proposals for new laws flow from many sources, and the special expertise of administrative agencies makes them prime players. Government agencies possess much factual information about their specific field, retain an expert staff to analyze data, discover the defects in existing statutes after applying them, and exhibit devotion to the program's objectives. Often, though not always, the agency is trusted as a less biased source of information than other available sources, such as organized interest groups.

In recent years, two developments have enhanced administrators' role in this early stage of policymaking. First, as policy has become ever more technical, so has the specialized competence of administrative staffs. Regulating oil wells and building bridges, for example, must be guided by sophisticated information, analysis, and advice from engineers. Expert knowledge and advice are essential to policy development for national defense weaponry, space exploration, public health, research and development, education, poverty, urban renewal, energy, air and water pollution, police, fire, sanitation, water, and a host of other program areas. Within government, most experts are in the administrative agencies. Second, the chief executive's role as an agenda setter has grown. The chief executive—president, governor, mayor, county executive—initiates most of the proposals that legislatures review. Typically the executive shapes this program through consultation with the agency-based experts of the executive branch. Although they are not the only sources of the executive's ideas, agency experts are strategically situated to initiate and counsel on policy proposals in the search for the executive's support. And to complete the circle, the executive's need for expert help has grown as public policy problems have become increasingly technical.

The second stage of the policy formation process occurs after the laws are on the books. In most cases, the statutes are not clear enough so that what happens afterward can be regarded as execution in the narrow sense. Legislative behavior sometimes produces highly detailed statutes and other times results in only a fuzzy identification of a problem that administrators must wrestle with. In effect, administrators make policy by trying to decide what the legislators meant and acting on it.

There are several reasons for delegating such extensive policymaking power. In a new policy field in which there is little experience to build on, the legislature may only wave vaguely in the direction that action should take. In a field in which technology or other features change rapidly, the statute must permit flexible action by the agency, rather than requiring frequent returns to the legislature for enactment of new language. Congress, for example, could never possibly anticipate all the steps of putting satellites into space. (There was a time when the computer code for a rocket launch was the most complicated on Earth. The smartphone in your pocket is more powerful than the computer that put a man on the moon.) Some subjects, such as licensing liquor stores and operating taxis, simply do not lend themselves to the specification of criteria that would confine administrative discretion. Statutes often do specify some conditions (for example, requirements that liquor store owners must not have criminal records and that liquor stores not be located near schools), but they offer few guidelines about how to choose among the numerous applicants who meet these simple criteria. In addition, ingenious entrepreneurs can often generate clever ways of evading any highly specific prohibitions in a statute. Congress broadly forbids "unfair methods of competition . . . and unfair or deceptive acts in commerce," leaving the administrative agency and the courts to refine those vague terms "unfair" and "deceptive."

At times, the legislative process is so stormy and full of crosscurrents that the resulting statutes incorporate contradictory policy guidelines, leaving agency managers to use their own judgment in reconciling the contradictions. Sometimes, too, a compromise leads to legislative language that papers over disagreement, but that gives administrators a wide range for interpretation. Most agencies, furthermore, administer many statutes passed at different times and

The Prison Becomes a Marijuana Farm
Theme: Accountability

The city council of Coalinga took a pair of votes in July 2016 that promised big changes for the city—and big challenges for local public administrators. The town of 16,000 in California's San Joaquin Valley voted to allow the commercial cultivation of marijuana within the city limits—and to sell a closed prison to a private company, Ocean Grown Extracts, to create a "medical cannabis oil extraction plant." The $4.1 million sale immediately helped the town balance its budget.

The town's mayor pro tem, Patrick Keough, explained, "It's like the Grateful Dead said: 'What a long, strange trip it's been.'" It was democracy in action, he contended. "We listened to the citizens and created a package that was reflective of our population." City officials also believed that the vote would help prevent Coalinga from lagging behind other towns trying to get into the cannabis cultivation business.

But the vote didn't come without strings, and the requirements promised to keep local police and public administrators busy. The owner would be responsible for any liability issues, which could prove an issue as long as federal law prohibits the use of marijuana. All employees would be subject to a background check and receive a local government permit to work on the site, which the Coalinga Police Department would keep on file.

The facility would be required to have locked gates and would not be open to the public. The operators would need to have video surveillance twenty-four hours per day, with the feed provided to the police department. It could not have any signs and the facility's operators would need to have odor control, so passersby couldn't smell cannabis. And each of the plants would be required to have an electronic tracking device. The police chief, fire chief, and city planner would be required, sixty days in advance, to certify that the facility met all fire safety and building codes. The policy change required even bigger changes for the local public administrators.

Source: Rory Appleton, "Coalinga Legalizes Medical Marijuana Operation," *Fresno Bee* (July 7, 2016), http://www.fresnobee.com/news/local/article88377122.html.

---

mirroring different legislative preferences, leaving administrators to reconcile the accumulated instructions. Finally, the legislature may not appropriate sufficient funds to enable an agency to carry out a program as enacted. Unless the legislature itself gives specific direction, the agency must then decide whether to spread the money thinly or choose which of its objectives it will pursue with vigor and which it will slight.

In short, public administration shapes policy on the way up, executes policy after it has been made, and exercises discretion about policy questions on the way down.

THE POLITICS-ADMINISTRATION DICHOTOMY. As scholars studied public administration early in the twentieth century, they separated policy—the political work of shaping public decisions—from administration—the detailed work of carrying them out. As we saw in Chapter 1, this dichotomy came from the goal of defining a distinctive field of study and, even more so, from the efforts to reform city, state, and national governments in the late nineteenth and early twentieth centuries by rooting out pernicious political corruption. Establishing a neutral realm for administration, protected by civil service laws and governed by a drive for efficiency, would dry up the patronage resources of political machines and leave policymaking organs of government more directly accountable to the people.

Today, the dual goals of assuring a nonpartisan body of civil servants remain unchanged: loyal service to officials from different political parties and the achievement of efficient administration. The obvious fact that administrative staffs share in policy formation—as well as the fuzzy line between policy and administration—has led many students to reject the policy-administration dichotomy. Analysts have tried to reestablish the distinction by forbidding administrators from participating in political activities, but that line may waver. Civil servants need to be respectful of the policy goals of elected officials and sensitive to the political implications of their policy suggestions. But civil servants have other obligations as well—to long-range policy goals, continuity and consistency, effective administration, and resistance to corruption. Furthermore, they must balance an administration's preferences against legislative and judicial mandates.

Civil servants have responsibilities different from those of politically elected officials. Policy and administration are certainly intertwined, but the motivations and behaviors of policy-makers and public administrators are very different. Separating them is a core issue of public administration.

Administrative Responsibility

Every well-developed organization has some system for holding subordinates accountable to their superiors. Nowhere is the system so complex and confining as in government.[24] Statutes and regulations specify elaborate procedures that seriously limit administrators' discretionary authority. Legislative committees call administrators to testify about complaints that have arisen on the programs they manage. Members of legislative staffs closely monitor administrative actions in agencies of interest to their superiors. Budget offices typically review proposed regulations and information-gathering proposals in addition to reviewing financial requests and setting personnel ceilings.

From the career administrators' perspective, this is a formidable control system. Yet as we suggested earlier, administrative responsibility goes beyond these external controls on behavior. There are also norms for behavior that are internalized by administrators themselves. First, knowing that they serve in government, they must be sensitive to the legitimate roles of other parts of the government, including institutions charged with legal control of their behavior. Second, they have a loyalty to their agencies and the programs entrusted to them. Third, in a civil service now populated by professional experts, they have absorbed their professional standards and are motivated to be recognized by their fellow professionals outside the government. All these commitments shape administrative responsibility, even though at times they may not all point in the same direction.[25]

That leads to a fundamental problem of accountability. External controls on bureaucracy often lead to red tape. External controls can replace external oversight, but that requires enhanced trust between the political and the civil service strata of government. And that, in turn, sets up some of the most fundamental debates about the study of public administration.

Now, to be sure, the debate about the differences between public and private administration sometimes get overblown. As we shall see in this book, public administration is relying far more on private partners for the administration of governmental programs. In the private sector, public policies create limits on hiring and firing, and companies sometimes push short-term profits to the side in pursuit of longer-term relationships with suppliers and customers. Moreover, the debate sometimes gets caught in fierce ideological battles that have more to do with trust in government than fundamental analytical differences. There is often more heat than light in these debates. But at the core, the light is useful: it helps illuminate those features that lie at the core of public administration—and of the important issues we examine in this book.

A congressional investigation into a conference sponsored by the federal General Services Administration brought tough congressional questions about events featuring a professional mind reader, a clown, and a team-building exercise for building bicycles. Inspector General Brian Miller (left) produced a report on the conference, which led agency administrator Martha Johnson (center) to resign. Jeff Neely, regional commissioner (right), organized the conference.

THE STUDY OF PUBLIC ADMINISTRATION

How, then, should we think about "public administration"?[26] Dwight Waldo suggests that we face a difficult task. He points out that public administration has roots deep in historic crosscurrents, including the political ideas of the small Greek city-state (the *polis*) and the large-scale administration of the Roman Empire, both of which helped shape the American system.[27] One way of addressing this task is claiming that administration and policy (or politics) are separate spheres. Woodrow Wilson and Frank J. Goodnow, writing in the late nineteenth and early twentieth centuries, took this view.[28] Nicholas Henry identifies 1900–1926 as the period when the politics-administration dichotomy reigned. He then traces later periods: 1927–1937, when students affirmed the existence of clear principles of public administration; 1938–1950, marked by rejection of the politics-administration dichotomy and loss of confidence in principles; the reaction of 1950–1970, years of reorientation to public administration as political science; overlapping and contradicting that reorientation, a 1956–1970 emphasis on management, often borrowing from business management, together with the rise of public policy studies (focused on effective achievement of policy objectives); and, finally, the post-1970 reversion to a specific focus on public administration. That work is often lodged in distinct schools of public administration that are hospitable to management methods but are sensitive to the public-interest commitment of administrators of governmental affairs.[29]

In our study, we need to confront three questions in trying to frame a general approach to the field. First, does public administration have meaning apart from its historical context?

Second, does it have meaning regardless of place, circumstance, and level of government? Third, if we make even limited generalizations, how shall we proceed? To such fundamental questions, we must offer perplexing answers:

1. Public administration is timeless but is time-bound.[30]

2. Public administration is universal but is also culture-bound and varies with situations.

3. Public administration is complex but is intelligible only by a simplified model or a step-by-step combination of such models.

We consider the first two puzzles together, because time and space are related variables.

Public Administration in Time

Public administration has a longer history and a wider geographic range than almost any other aspect of government. It is far older than American government—it has been the instrument of ancient empires, monarchies, democracies, and dictatorships, in both developed and developing countries. Carl J. Friedrich has cogently argued that the achievement of representative government in Western Europe depended on the prior development of effective bureaucracies by undemocratic regimes.[31] Indeed, revolutions that seek to transform the structure of political authority also struggle to control the bureaucracy.

In the United States, public administration received scant discussion from the nation's founders for decades after the writing of the Constitution. As he traveled the United States in 1835, Alexis de Tocqueville was amazed at the neglect of the subject in the young nation, compared with experience in his native France:

> The public administration is, so to speak, oral and traditional. But little is committed to writing and that little is soon wafted away forever, like the leaves of the Sibyl, by the smallest breeze. . . . The instability of administration has penetrated into the habits of the people . . . and no one cares for what occurred before his time: no methodical system is pursued, no archives are formed, and no documents are brought together when it would be very easy to do so. . . . Nevertheless, the art of administration is undoubtedly a science, and no science can be improved if the discoveries and observations of successive generations are not connected together in the order in which they occur. . . . But the persons who conduct the administration in America can seldom afford any instruction to one another. . . . Democracy, pushed to its furthest limits, is therefore prejudicial to the art of government; and for this reason it is better adapted to a people already versed in the conduct of administration than to a nation that is uninitiated in public affairs.[32]

To deal with these issues, Woodrow Wilson wrote that "the poisonous atmosphere of city government, the crooked secrets of state administration, the confusion, sinecurism, and corruption ever and again discovered in the bureau at Washington forbid us to believe that any clear conceptions of what constitutes good administration are as yet very widely current in the United States."[33] Noting that "the functions of government are every day becoming more complex and difficult" and "are also vastly multiplying in number," Wilson pleaded in his 1887 essay for "a science of administration which shall seek to straighten the paths of government, to make its business less unbusinesslike, to strengthen and purify its organization, and to crown its duties with dutifulness." Such a science, he noted, existed on the European continent, especially in Prussian and French practice. He anticipated that comparative study would yield "one rule of good administration for all governments alike. So far as administrative functions are concerned, all governments have a strong structural likeness; more than that, if they are to be uniformly useful and efficient, they must have a strong structural likeness."

From one point of view, then, public administration has universal elements, independent of time, place, and political system. Those who serve in any public bureaucracy must be selected, paid, given specific assignments, controlled, disciplined when necessary, and so on. To pay them and to support other governmental activities (minimally, provision for military forces and construction of roads), a revenue system must be devised, the receipts allocated by some kind of budgetary system, and accounting and other recordkeeping methods worked out.

To say that there are such universal elements implies that governments everywhere can accumulate experience, and that this constitutes a reservoir on which governments can draw to avoid repeating mistakes. As Wilson stated, "the object of administrative study is to rescue executive methods from the confusion and costliness of empirical experiment and set them upon foundations laid deep in stable principle." However, despite expectations that more than 100 years of public administration study should by now have yielded stable principles, that has not yet happened. Wilson based his analysis on a perception of administration as a neutral instrument, distinct from policy, politics, and particular regimes. Such a perception seemed essential to define a distinct field of study, separate from the study of policy and politics. It may also have sprung from the **neutrality doctrine** of civil service reformers, who had succeeded in getting the Pendleton Civil Service Act passed just four years before Wilson's essay appeared in the 1887 volume of *Political Science Quarterly.* But it was an especially critical assumption for Wilson's thesis that "nowhere else in the whole field of politics, it would seem, can we make use of the historical, comparative method more safely than in this province of administration." That is, we can learn administration from the Prussian and French (Napoleonic) autocracies without being infected by their antidemocratic political principles.

Wilson's line of argument framed two contradictory themes. One was that administration must be fitted to the particular nation's political ideas and constitutional system. The science of administration, Wilson wrote,

> is not of our making; it is a foreign science, speaking very little of the language of English or American principles. . . . It has been developed by French and German professors, and is consequently in all parts adapted to the needs of a compact state, and made to fit highly centralized forms of government. . . . If we would employ it, we must Americanize it, and that not formally, in language merely, but radically, in thought, principle, and aim as well. It must learn our constitutions by heart; must get the bureaucratic fever out of its veins; must inhale much free American air.

Wilson advanced a second theme that blurs the distinction he made elsewhere between policy and administration. He contended that the

> lines of demarcation, setting apart administrative from nonadministrative functions . . . run up hill and down dale, over dizzy heights of distinction and through dense jungles of statutory enactment, hither and thither around "ifs" and "buts," "whens," and "however," until they become altogether lost to the common eye.

Wilson suggested "some roughly definite criteria": "public administration is detailed and systematic execution of public law," "every particular application of general law," "the detailed execution" of "the broad plans of governmental action," the "special means" as distinguished from the "general plans." Yet he went on to plead for the vesting of "large powers and unhampered discretion" as the indispensable conditions of administrative responsibility.

Here, then, are Wilson's basic contradictions: he contends that public administration needs to be interpreted in the light of a particular country's political ideas and form of government, but at the same time he sees it as a neutral instrument. He seeks a goal of "one rule of good administration for all governments alike," but he notes that different settings can produce different problems. He explains that administrators have large powers and great discretion, but he says that the administrative cannot readily be distinguished from the nonadministrative aspects of government.

Much of the literature on administration since Wilson's time has struggled with the same contradictions with which he struggled. Each of the positions he embraced has just a piece of the whole truth. A number of problems are common to all or most public bureaucracies. Most of these issues flow from a simple question, which Wilson laid out: How can government do things "with the utmost possible efficiency and at the least possible cost either of money or of energy"? Yet there are also problems, some of them among the most critical for administration, that require different criteria and different answers in dissimilar social and political systems, at the several stages of national development, and even in the individual agencies of a single government.

Western models have not proved good matches for understanding bureaucracy in non-Western political systems. And when developing countries have looked to the West for models, they have struggled to choose which ones to follow. A substantial comparative administration movement appeared in the 1960s, but the movement virtually evaporated until the global public management revolution that began in the late 1980s helped to rejuvenate it. Time and space are interlinked in the recent and growing literature on the history of governmental administration.[34] Moreover, as Christopher Pollitt argues, the deep traditions of behavior and culture have a powerful influence over administrative action. The pace of social change has accelerated around the world, and "this makes considerations of time and of the past even *more* important, not less so."[35] We need to understand where administration comes from to understand how the past shapes the way we think about the present and future.

Complexity and Simplicity

Any real organizational system is extremely complex, and it is therefore impossible to describe any such system fully. It might appear to be a reasonable assumption that the main features of the system can be described—for example, by a single model that simplifies *total* reality in order to clarify *essential* reality. Even this assumption is wrong, however, for three reasons.

First, the complexity of any large-scale organization is not a puzzle that a single key will unlock. Instead, there are so many ways of looking at an organization that no single model can suffice as a model, as can be seen from the following list of complicating factors[36]:

- *Interconnections of policymaking and execution.* An organization (as we have seen) both shapes policy and executes it, and they intertwine in ways that are sometimes both supportive and awkward.

- *Coordination.* An organization is a way of both dividing up and coordinating work.
- *Relationships of power.* An organization is both a formal, prescribed structure of relationships among offices and organization units and an arena in which ambitious persons and units work to expand or at least maintain their status and power.
- *Floating in the seas of time.* An organization both persists over time despite changes in its personnel (complete change in the case of long-lived organizations) and at any single point in time contains a particular group of individuals, each with a special set of psychological needs and frustrations.
- *Top-down and bottom-up.* An organization is both a top-down system of authority, conformity, and compliance and a bottom-up system for the flow to the top of innovative ideas, proposed solutions to problems, claims on resources, and reports of trouble signs in program execution and content.
- *Information.* An organization is an information generation system, a storage and retrieval file, and a communication network, subject to overloads of information, misreading of signals, and supplementations and wire crossing by informal grapevines.
- *Headquarters and field.* An organization usually includes both a headquarters staff and a far-flung field service, the former organized by functions and the latter by geographical areas—a feature that hinders their effective linkage.
- *Values.* An organization's decision-making process must embrace the broad choices in which the personal value preferences and educated guesses of officials play a large part. It must provide for other major choices for which quantified data and other scientific evidence can clarify the options and reduce the role of mere hunches, and it must program the narrow choices capable of routine handling by clerks and automatic data-processing machines.
- *Inside and outside.* An organization looks both inward and outward, having to maintain internal effectiveness and adapt to the external environment in which it encounters the pressures of other organizations, temporary crises of the society and the economy, occasional wrenching change, and the often poorly articulated needs of the customers of its service.
- *Physical and organic models.* An organization is sometimes compared to a physical system such as a machine, and sometimes to an organic biological system such as that of an animal or a living plant.
- *Success.* It can be judged successful if it simply survives, or it can be so judged only if it achieves the purpose that justifies its existence.

Second, it is hard to produce a single model because most writers on organizations have sought to describe organization in the abstract. Realities are often far more complex, and theorizing has often become disconnected from concrete experience.[37]

Third, organizational theorists do not agree on a single theory or model. Theories and models of organization abound. Each one usually seeks to define, in its own way, the essence of organizations but, in fact, each theory tends to focus on a limited number of organizational characteristics. The complexity of an organization can be accurately portrayed only by a combination of the partial truths that most models have expressed. We can imagine each model's bit of truth being mapped on a transparent sheet of paper; when one is placed on top of another, the series of overlays comes closer to the real organization than any single sheet does.[38]

In Chapter 4, we move from this foundation—the nature of public administration—to explore the basic building blocks of organization theory.

CASE 3.1

The Administrative State: Enforcement of Speeding Laws and Police Discretion

Attention, motorists! Driving through the East Coast? You might want to check out a website sponsored by the National Motorists Association (NMA), called the National Speed Trap Exchange, at www.speedtrap.org. Here's what its writers have to say about a particularly notorious stretch of the Interstate 83 highway near York, Pennsylvania:

> The Interstate goes from 65 to 55 mph but with absolutely no change in the highway construction, condition, or population densities as it's out in the country. It just so happens that just off the Loganville exit is a state police barracks which makes it awful convenient for them to work this stretch of road.[1]

A reader chimes in with her two cents below that entry:

> My mother lives in PA, and I have seen troopers measuring speed in that area—especially where that little cut-out is on the southbound hill of I-83. Troopers in PA have to use stationary radar, so they have learned to be quite creative with their hiding places.

Even if we'd like to spare this person a ticket on her way to her mother's house, doesn't it seem a little, well, *dishonest* to share this kind of information? Isn't the speed limit the speed limit—in other words, the law—after all?

Ethically challenged? Maybe. But, in fact, the idea that the speed limit is whatever the officially posted limit sign says it is misses the point. The posted limit may be the official maximum, but everyone knows that these posted limits often have little meaning in reality, a fact that the NMA apparently both recognizes and embraces.

Sometimes, traffic moves along at barely a crawl. Congestion, poor road engineering, and the unpredictable behavior of drivers can limit speeds. On clogged roads, the posted limit can seem a distant dream instead of a realistic limit. On wide-open roads, in contrast, many drivers have discovered that if they drive at the posted limit, most other traffic goes flying past them.

©iStock.com/chapin31

So what is the real speed limit? It's the speed at which one can safely drive without being pulled over by the police or a state trooper and issued a citation. On an interstate highway, the conventional wisdom is that a driver can drive at 5, or perhaps 7, miles per hour over the posted limit with little fear of being stopped and ticketed.

Does that mean that if the posted speed is 65 mph, the speed limit is *really* about 72 mph? Not quite. If a driver is clocked by radar at going 71 in a 65-mph zone, the fact that the driver's speed is under the conventional-wisdom limit would be no defense in traffic court. Police officers can—and do—issue citations for driving at that speed. But if the police stopped everyone going just a bit over the posted limit, they would spend all their days and nights stopping just about everyone. Aggressive speeders might then get a free pass, because the police would be so busy stopping people driving just a few miles over the limit that they might not catch the super-speeders, drunk drivers, and others who are reckless on the road. As a result, the highway death toll might shoot up. In short, the real speed limit is determined less by what the posted limit is than by how the police choose to enforce it.

It is one thing for elected officials to pass a law, create a policy (such as a speed limit), and post it for all to see. It is quite another to translate that policy into action. When it comes to the speed limit, how that process works depends on the discretion that police officers and state troopers exercise as they patrol the nation's highways. The police invest a great deal of time in deciding how best to exercise that discretion: where most effectively to concentrate their energy, according to their best judgment about how to save the most lives, improve traffic flow, and (sometimes) increase the flow of cash to the local government.

Governmental policy on the control of speeding depends not only on how the police translate the official limits into their operating plans but also on how individual police officers, often operating alone in cars with no supervision, decide to exercise their own discretion. Should a police officer ticket a husband who is driving fast to get his wife to the hospital because she is in labor? Should the officer just issue a warning to someone who says, "Gee, officer, this is my first ticket"? Should the officer concentrate on easy pickings—drivers with out-of-state licenses who will most likely want to settle quickly so they can get on their way? And should the officers' commanders—and the elected officials who set policy—worry if different officers make these decisions in different ways, so that the real speed limit depends ultimately on the subjective discretion of the individual officer operating the radar in the police car?

The work of government bureaucrats (for that is what police officers are) extends far beyond enforcement, reaching into policy planning, development, and research. Some of the world's leading experts on traffic safety work for the U.S. Department of Transportation's Federal Highway Administration (FHWA). A fascinating study conducted by the FHWA in 1992 found that changes in the speed limit—lowering it by as much as 20 mph or raising it by as much as 15 mph—had little actual effect on drivers' speed. Moreover, the FHWA found, *most* drivers regularly exceed the speed limit. Lowering the speed limit below the 50th percentile (that is, to a speed lower than that at which half the drivers drive) did not reduce accidents—but it did increase the number of violations.

Where should state and local governments set the speed limit? The FHWA determined that it should be set at the 85th percentile (the speed on any given road at which 85 percent of the drivers drive slower and 15 percent drive faster). Because most accidents are caused by people who drive *very* fast, setting the limit at the 85th percentile would allow most drivers to drive as fast as is reasonable and safe, and it would allow the police to focus their attention on those drivers who are most likely to cause accidents.[2]

Having that FHWA data in hand isn't the end of the story, however. Policymakers often resist such seemingly sound advice on setting the speed limit as different constituents weigh in on the ramifications of raising or lowering the limit. Higher speeds burn more gasoline, so environmentalists often favor lower limits. In many western states, drivers chafe at even high limits and press for even higher limits—as high as possible—and enforcement as loose as possible. A string of accidents on a stretch of road can create enormous pressure on policymakers and police officers for a crackdown. Citizens demand that governments respond to their preferences. When it comes to speed limits, policymakers need—and want—administrators to be accountable, because if lax enforcement of speeding laws causes accidents, the political costs for politicians can be very high. But when it comes to setting and enforcing speed limits, that's a tough tradeoff. In the end, one thing is clear: the posted speed limit is one thing, but the government's actual policy against speeding may be quite another.

QUESTIONS TO CONSIDER

1. The announced policy on speeding usually does not match the policy as the police actually enforce it. Why? What forces are at work?

2. Should citizens worry that there seems to be such a gap between policy and administration?

3. Where the speed limit policy posted on traffic signs and the actual enforcement behavior of the police differ, what issues are potentially the most difficult to resolve?

4. Police are bureaucrats—but so are the technical experts who have conducted published studies on the speed limits. What impact can—and should—government's bureaucratic experts have on its policy?

5. Who is responsible for what in this surprisingly complex system: framing policy options, setting overall policy, setting patrol strategies, and enforcing the policy on the roads? What does this tell us about the politics of the administrative process?

NOTES

1. See National Speed Trap Exchange, http://www.speed trap.org/city/10210/York.

2. Federal Highway Administration, U.S. Department of Transportation, *Effects of Raising and Lowering Speed Limits*, Report FHWA-RD-92-084 (October 1992). See also Elizabeth Alicandri and Davey L. Warren, "Managing Speed," *Public Roads* (January–February 2003), https://www.fhwa.dot.gov/publications/publicroads/03jan/10.cfm.

Should Private Contractors Be Guarding Government Buildings?

Vernon Hunter and his wife, Valerie, both worked for the Internal Revenue Service (IRS) in Austin, Texas. They both loved their jobs, but Vernon, age 67, was thinking about leaving the government and spending some quiet years in retirement. For Vernon, a Vietnam War vet, those thoughts ended abruptly in February 2010. Joseph Stack, a man with a long grudge against the IRS, posted a hate-filled diatribe on the web, set fire to his own home, drove to an airport, and took off in his plane. He seemed to have aimed it directly at the portion of the building occupied by the IRS. Valerie heard the explosion, and when she couldn't find Vernon right away, she assumed he was helping others out of the fire. Only later did she discover that Vernon died in the explosion caused by the plane's fuel tank.

Attacks on government buildings have worried security officials even more since the September 11, 2001, terrorist attacks. Timothy McVeigh's 1995 assault on the Alfred P. Murrah Federal Building, an Oklahoma City federal government building, with a truck bomb that killed 168 people showed how vulnerable government facilities could be. Other attacks, including Russell Eugene Weston Jr.'s 1998 attempt to shoot his way into the U.S. Capitol and James W. von Brunn's 2009 attack on Washington, D.C.'s Holocaust Museum, showed the risk. But just how vulnerable are government buildings to such attacks?

Government investigators decided to find out. The Government Accountability Office, Congress's investigatory agency, sent undercover operatives into federal buildings with guns, knives, and fake bombs. In eighteen tests, the guards detected the weapons—but they missed them thirty-five times, for a two-thirds failure rate. At one facility, an investigator put a bag containing a fake bomb onto a belt for an X-ray check. The guard missed it and the investigator was able to pick up the bag and carry it into the building. In another test, an inspector put a bag holding a fake gun on the belt. The guard caught this one and held the inspector off in a corner—but without a further search or handcuffs, as the rules required. As the guards concentrated on the first decoy, a second inspector walked right through the checkpoint with two knives—and without being stopped. In a broader check, investigators were able to get into ten different facilities with the materials they needed to build a bomb.[1]

Is this a failure of government security? The answer to that is clear. But is it a failure of government security guards? That, as it turns out, is a far tougher question. The agency responsible for security in federal buildings, the Federal Protective Service (FPS), employs 1,225 persons—but is responsible for 2,360 federal facilities. How does it plug this gap? With 15,000 private security guards, working under contract to FPS. In fact, though most visitors never notice it, the shoulder patches on the arms of most guards protecting the majority of most federal buildings show they work for private companies.

The Secret Service guards the White House. But for many years, the guards charged with preventing terrorists from storming the facilities manufacturing parts for nuclear weapons—including sites stocked with plutonium, perhaps the most dangerous substance on the planet—were from private companies. On a visit to one such plant, I talked with a guard who proudly told me he was trained on twenty-one different weapons. He worked for Wackenhut, one of the world's largest private security companies.

But the combination of rising threats and the government's high reliance on private guards has made many members of Congress uneasy. Rep. Sheila Jackson Lee (D-Tex.) has argued that FPS ought to be required to shift more of its guards from private contractors to federal employees. She pointed to the decision to federalize airport inspectors after the September 11, 2001, terrorist attacks. "Many of us believe that it may be time to un-privatize the contractors of the Federal Protective Service or at least put in higher requirements," she said.[2]

QUESTIONS TO CONSIDER

1. Do you think that it matters *who* provides security at government facilities? Why? Fans of contracting say that whoever can do the job for the lowest cost ought to get the work. Opponents counter that protection is an inherently governmental activity that ought to be performed by government employees.

2. Do you like the idea of arming private employees and allowing them to shoot to kill, in the interest of protecting government buildings and their employees? Or should lethal force be a power given only to government guards doing the government's work?

3. More generally, how would you sort out the work that you think government ought to perform? And who ought to perform that work on behalf of government?

NOTES

1. U.S. Government Accountability Office, *Homeland Security: Federal Protective Service's Contract Guard Program Requires More Oversight and Reassessment of Use of Contract Guards*, GAO-10-341 (April 2010), http://www.gao.gov/new.items/d10341.pdf.

2. Ed O'Keefe, "Legislation Would Federalize Private Guards Who Protect U.S. Government Buildings," *Washington Post* (September 14, 2010), http://www.washingtonpost.com/wp-dyn/content/article/2010/09/13/AR2010091306355.html.

CASE 3.3

Crisis of Water in Maryland

What could be worse than days of temperatures in the mid-90s with steamy humidity, thought residents of Prince George's County, Maryland, than the announcement by their local water district that all water would be turned off for days? Residents scrambled to buy cases of bottled water in neighborhood stores. Many filled their bathtubs to the brim. Others scrambled for anything they could find that could hold water, from recycling bins to trash cans. With oppressive temperatures in the forecast for days, residents feared they were in for a very tough time.

The source of the problem was a 48-year-old valve, 4.5 feet in diameter, that threatened to burst not far from the Washington Beltway. Just a few weeks before, the Washington Suburban Sanitary Commission (WSSC), a special-district government that supplies water and waste treatment to the region, had installed a new acoustic cable through the water pipe to detect problems before they exploded suddenly in a massive water-line break. Just a few months before, a water main burst on the other side of the city, creating a 20-foot deep crater and sending a geyser 40 feet into the air. Problems with a main water-supply line are never good, but they're worst when they happen by surprise and cause blast-like damage in the process.

Officials from WSSC were proud that their new equipment had caught the problem before it ruptured. Their plan was to shut off the water, repair the valve before it blew, and then get the system back on line as soon as they could. The valve was at an especially hard-to-reach spot, and they had to begin by building a road to the site to bring in equipment before they could start repairs, all the while hoping that the pipe wouldn't burst before they could fix it.

WSSC recommended that residents stockpile at least 2 gallons of water per person per day, and that set off the scramble. Supermarkets called their suppliers for extra truckloads of bottled water. Restaurants inside the affected area shut down, since there would be no water for cooking or dishwashing. A major resort hotel sent all of its guests home, since there would be no water for laundries, restaurants, sinks, or toilets. Firefighters made plans to respond to alarms with big tanker trucks, since fire hydrants wouldn't work. Scott Peterson, the county executive's spokesman, told reporters that the "economic impact of this event will be the equivalent of a natural disaster hitting the county."[1] The shutdown story made news around the country and worried residents prepared for a long siege.

But hours into the repairs, workers managed a minor miracle. Two workers, exposed to miserable heat and working 4 feet below ground level, found a way to repair the valve without having to shut down the pipe, and the water never stopped flowing. They managed to get the valve unstuck and to make the 400 turns required to put it back

in operation. "No one thought these guys were going to pull this off," the WSSC spokesperson happily explained.

County Executive Rushern Baker III, however, was in no mood to celebrate. He was stunned to discover that his county had gone through such wrenching preparations, only to have no interruption in service. "When did they first know about this other option, and how soon were they able to tell us other than this morning?" Baker wondered. "We are going to ask some very tough questions. We are going to have a very long and lengthy discussion about how we can make sure this doesn't happen again." Jim Neustadt, speaking on behalf of WSSC, explained, "The bottom line is our experts make the best decisions they can with all the information we have available. We have to protect the public, and that's what we felt we were doing."[2]

There wasn't a soul in the county who wasn't immensely relieved that their water continued to flow. But after the catastrophic explosion several months before, followed by what local officials viewed as warnings of risk without transparency, tough questions lay ahead for WSSC's leaders.

QUESTIONS TO CONSIDER

1. Suppose you were an administrator charged with the public health and safety of your community, and you learned that your water, within hours, would be shut off for days. What would you do? How would you communicate with citizens? How would you protect essential services?

2. Consider the situation that WSSC faced. Its top officials did not believe that its team was likely to be able to repair the water line without shutting it off—and if it had to shut it off, service would be out for days. Officials did not tell the public or Prince George's County government officials that there was a chance that its workers could make the repairs without shutting off the water. Do you believe that WSSC handled the situation properly? If they told everyone that there was a chance that a shutoff might not be necessary, they risked having thousands of citizens who failed to make preparations if the shutoff happened, at a time of extreme heat. They did not share the word, but then received harsh criticism from the county executive.

3. County Executive Baker was in a difficult situation. WSSC is a special-district government, providing water and sewage service to his county and to a neighboring county. It was not under the political or operational

control of either. WSSC was making decisions that affected his constituents, but he had no control over WSSC's actions. What strategies could—and should— Baker use in this case?

NOTES

1. Katherine Shaver and Ashley Halsey III, "Prince George's Residents Brace for Water Shut-off,"

Washington Post (July 16, 2013), http://www .washingtonpost.com/local/prince-georges-residents- brace-for-water-shut-off/2013/07/16/abdaa72c- ee05-11e2-9008-61e94a7ea20d_story.html.

2. Ashley Halsey III and Katherine Shaver, "Prince George's Water Shut-off Averted," *Washington Post* (July 17, 2013), https://www.washingtonpost .com/local/prince-georges-copes-with-water- restrictions/2013/07/17/12c44bcc-eed4-11e2- 9008-61e94a7ea20d_story.html.

CASE 3.4

Humvees in Ferguson

In the days after the tragic shooting of Michael Brown in Ferguson, Missouri, in August 2014, news programs ran video after video showing local police around the country armed with machine guns and driving heavily armored vehicles. The *New York Times* described a desert-khaki- painted MRAP—for mine-resistant ambush protected vehicle—sitting next to a snowplow in the municipal garage of Neenah, Wisconsin. And a report from *The Chronicle of Higher Education* revealed that the University of Central Florida in Orlando owns a grenade launcher, retooled to fire tear-gas canisters.

Hundreds of communities and campuses across the country have been the recipient of hand-me-down military equipment, from machine guns and armored vehicles to helicopters and night-vision goggles. All the equipment comes from the Department of Defense's 1033 program, which gives police departments wartime gear that the military no longer needs.

Better that it's shipped to local cops, the reasoning goes, than get tossed away. After all, local police surely can never be too prepared for the vast array of threats they face.

But the idea of an MRAP tooling around Wisconsin or a Humvee making the rounds on a college campus raises concerns among critics who question whether the feds are kindling racial tensions through a policy of super-arming cops. As Eastern Kentucky University criminal justice professor Peter Kraska told a reporter, a "small agency can go rapidly from one of protecting and serving to one of viewing the community as the enemy and a potential threat."

That worry, in fact, led President Obama to call for a full review of the program. With Ferguson's heavily armed cops tossing tear gas from behind armored vehicles, pundits suggested that the feds and their 1033 program had fueled the tensions on the city's streets.

They were wrong. Almost none of Ferguson's weaponry, as it turns out, came from the 1033 program. The town's police department did pick up a couple of Humvees, a cargo trailer, and a generator through the program, but nothing in the center of the controversy came from the Pentagon.

Ferguson and St. Louis police departments bought almost everything seen on television with their own money.

Most of the equipment in the program isn't even weaponry—Yale University received men's trousers and Nashville's police department got Zodiac boats, which its officers used in the 2010 floods to rescue stranded residents. With cops sometimes finding themselves not only in difficult tactical situations but also under assault, giving them the best protection makes sense. The real issue isn't so much the feds fueling racial tension with the equipment, as it is that the equipment has come to symbolize ongoing frictions in many communities between local police and their citizens.

Many police departments have long-standing racial tensions with citizens, especially in those places where the composition of the police force doesn't match that of the locality. In Ferguson, where two-thirds of the population is black, fifty of the fifty-three police officers are white. Ferguson isn't alone. In nearby Grandview, the police force is 92 percent white while the population is 55 percent nonwhite. Kansas City, Kansas, is doing a bit better. Its police department is 72 percent white while its population is 60 percent nonwhite.

Virtually all of these officers, it should be said, are incredibly dedicated and go to work every day facing a very tough mission. Diversity is much more complex than a numbers game, and some diverse departments have their own struggles with community relations. But with so many cities demonstrating the effectiveness of community policing, a racial gap between officers on the force and citizens on the streets can vastly complicate the community connection. As one black Ohio resident told a reporter about the nonblack cops he encountered, "The police come here, they do their jobs, they don't try to get to know anybody." And, he continued, "The police don't wave."

Cops who connect with the communities they serve, criminal justice experts believe, prove more effective in building relationships, generating trust, and de-escalating conflicts.

There isn't good evidence on whether racial diversity makes police forces more effective, or whether police officers of different races treat the people they encounter any differently. Moreover, hiring more black officers doesn't wipe away police-community tensions, and increasing diversity is a hard road, experts say. It seems to matter much more whether top officials support efforts by their officers to build neighborhood ties.

It's easy to point to video of heavily armed cops as the cause of the racial problem, with the Pentagon driving a top-down racial wedge into local communities. That's wrong.

Far more important is the bottom-up effort to strengthen the relationship between police officers and the citizens they serve. The way in which cops and communities connect has become one of the most important front lines in the continuing struggle over civil rights. Federally delivered MRAPs aren't so much the cause of the problem as they are a powerful symbol that a great deal of work still needs to be done to make that connection.

QUESTIONS TO CONSIDER

1. What do you think of the federal government's program to supply state and local governments to purchase military equipment for their police forces? Is it a good way of providing them with additional resources—or does it risk worsening citizens' relationships with the police?

2. Consider the racial makeup of the Ferguson police department, at the time of Michael Brown's shooting. Does the mismatch between the racial composition of the police department and of the community cause you concern?

3. What strategies do you think would be most effective in improving relationships between the community and local police?

Note: This case comes from my column in *Governing* (December 2014), http://www.governing.com/columns/potomac-chronicle/gov-police-ferguson-militarization.html.

KEY CONCEPTS

Antideficiency Act 65
neutrality doctrine 72
nonprofit 65
organizational theory 61

oversight 65
performance measures 64
policymaking 61
public administration 60

FOR FURTHER READING

Fry, Brian R. *Mastering Public Administration: From Max Weber to Dwight Waldo.* 3rd ed. Washington, D.C.: CQ Press, 2013.

Goodsell, Charles T. *The Case for Bureaucracy: A Public Administration Polemic.* 4th ed. Washington, D.C.: CQ Press, 2004.

Okun, Arthur. *Equality and Efficiency: The Big Tradeoff.* Washington, D.C.: Brookings Institution, 1975.

Pollitt, Christopher. *Time, Policy, Management: Governing with the Past.* Oxford: Oxford University Press, 2008.

Waldo, Dwight. *The Administrative State: A Study of the Political Theory of American Public Administration.* New York: Ronald Press, 1948.

Wilson, Woodrow. "The Study of Administration." *Political Science Quarterly* 2 (June 1887). Reprinted in *Political Science Quarterly* 56 (December 1941): 481–506.

SUGGESTED WEBSITES

The Internet contains a vast reservoir of information about public administration and public organizations. A good place to explore the subject is with the associations that focus most on the field: the American Society for Public Administration, **www.aspanet.org**, and the National Academy of Public Administration, **www.napawash.org**.

Moreover, the federal government has an excellent search engine that provides easy access to the huge amount of data, reports, and programs produced by the government: **www.usa.gov**. Most state and local governments have their own websites as well, and **www.statelocalgov.net** provides an easy index of them.

for CQ Press

WANT A BETTER GRADE?

Get the tools you need to sharpen your study skills. Access practice quizzes, eFlashcards, video, and multimedia at **edge.sagepub.com/kettl7e.**

PART II

Organizational Theory and the Role of Government's Structure

The organization is the basic building block of public administration. Done badly, its work can create all of the pathologies that make bureaucracies appear "bureaucratic." Done well, bureaucracies make it possible to accomplish the complex tasks that society wishes to pursue—and often, it's the only way to make these programs work. There is a long intellectual history of thinking about how best to structure bureaucratic organizations. Given the problems of organizations, there is also an equally long history of reform.

Every option about changing bureaucracy is inevitably a *political* choice, one that emphasizes some values over others. Because these are political decisions, there are tradeoffs among competing values. Because there are tradeoffs, no choice is very stable for very long. The values of individuals shift and change, and so do the ways they arrange organizational structure. In the chapters that follow, we examine the basic foundations of organizational theory, the strategies to reform it, how organizational structure affects the behavior of political executives, and how efforts to reorganize bureaucracy can improve the way it functions.

4

ORGANIZATIONAL THEORY

Some management experts use team-building exercises, like this rope exercise that demands cooperative problem solving, to promote collaboration in the workplace.

In any large-scale organization, the basic building block is structure—a formal arrangement among the people engaged in the organization's mission. Within that structure, the fundamental concept is **hierarchy**, the top-down delegation of authority from higher officials to lower ones. The top official sets policy for the organization and then delegates responsibility to subordinates, so all employees know who is supposed to do what and who they are responsible to. The chain of authority ensures accountability from top officials all the way through the organization to its front lines. The result is the familiar organizational chart that dominates both the abstract model and the operating reality of complex organizations (see Figure 4.1). In the traditional approach, hierarchy defines the basic shape of organizations, and authority shapes the fundamental relationships.

This hierarchical model is the dominant model for organizing complex work. Over time, however, four major challenges to hierarchy have arisen. The **humanist approach**, rooted in the dynamics of human relations, condemns the impersonality of bureaucratic hierarchies and pleads for the humanizing of organizations. The **pluralist approach**, emphasizing the realities of political life, focuses on a fundamentally political model of organizational interactions. The **government-by-proxy approach**, introduced in Chapter 2, notes that government shares power with other governments, private organizations, and mixed public-private enterprises, as well as within its own **organizational structure**, and so develops a mixed model. The **formal approach** returns to a structural perspective but adds a very different theoretical twist.

There is little agreement on which theoretical approach works best. Furthermore, there is currently no consensus on which approach best fits the public sector. Together, though, these competing models frame the big debates about organization theory. In this chapter, we examine competing theories and explore their implications.[1]

THE STRUCTURAL APPROACH TO LARGE ORGANIZATIONS

Because **structure** is so fundamental to complex organizations, reformers usually focus on changing it when problems develop. People matter, of course, but in organizations what matters is how structure shapes the ways they interact. Students of administration tend to focus on bureaucratic positions—and the patterns of behavior in them—more than on the people who hold the jobs.

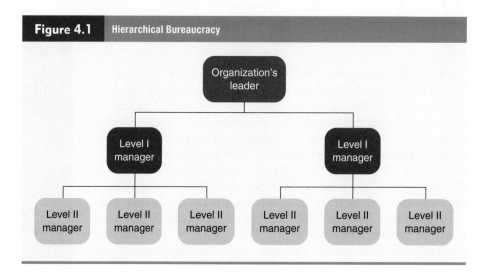

Figure 4.1 Hierarchical Bureaucracy

This concept builds on the concept of *role* in sociology and psychology: a person's formal position in the organization defines the person's tasks and relationships. As Daniel Katz and Robert L. Kahn wrote:

> In any organization we can locate each individual in the total set of ongoing relationships and behaviors that make up the organization. The key concept for this is *office* [i.e., position], by which is meant a particular point in organizational space; space in turn is defined in terms of a structure of interrelated offices and the patterns of activities associated with them. . . . Associated with each office is a set of *activities* or expected behaviors. These activities constitute the *role* to be performed, at least approximately, by any person who occupies that office. . . .
>
> To a considerable extent the role expectations . . . are determined by the broader organizational context. The technology of the organization, the structure of its subsystems, its formal policies, and its rewards and penalties dictate in large degree the content of a given office. . . . The structural properties of organization are sufficiently stable so that they can be treated as independent of the particular persons in the role-set.[2]

The structure of an organization, therefore, shapes the fundamental tasks, relationships, and expectations for people in administration. There are, of course, many big ideas behind the structure, from representative government, through the officials they elect, to the complex job of carrying out governmental policy, through a large, powerful, unelected bureaucracy. This chapter and the one that follows explore these issues.

Authority and Hierarchy

If structure is the building block of organization, authority and hierarchy are basic building blocks of structure. Authority and hierarchy deal with the central issue of the politics of the administrative process: power—who has it and how they use it. In democratic systems, the people consent to be governed by constitutional systems, which convey power to the government. (Of course, that certainly doesn't mean that citizens always agree with how government officials exercise that power.) And that, in turn, creates a two-way relationship: the people convey power to government, and the government expects the people to comply with its decisions. Most citizens do so voluntarily. Sometimes the government must exercise a heavier hand, whether to collect taxes or enforce speed limits. But, at the core, government's basic work builds on **authority**—the rightful power to make decisions within constitutionally defined limits, with the expectation of widespread compliance.[3]

Constitutions vest authority in designated major institutions (e.g., legislature, courts, executives) and the people in those bodies. In addition to granting authority, constitutions also limit how government officials use it. Government's authority ultimately flows from the people's grant of power.

The authority of public administrators builds on this foundation. In exercising their power, the major institutions *delegate* the power to carry out their decisions to administrators. Note, though, that the idea of delegated authority has two applications. First, an administrative agency can expect most citizens to comply with its decisions because the government agency carries the legitimacy of government. Second, the legislature, the courts, and the chief executive expect administrators to comply with *their* decisions because they exercise the power that flows from the people. Now, put these two applications together: citizens must follow the decisions of administrative agencies, as long as agencies' demands fit with the relevant constitutional, legislative, judicial, and executive limitations and instructions.

Thus, the roles of administrative structure and authority tap into the most fundamental questions of government and its power. These questions have roots in such great political questions as the nature of "the State," the legitimacy of governments themselves, the limits to their powers, and the rights of revolution and civil disobedience. The answers have implications just as big, including how policymakers delegate power, the legal liability of government executives and their agencies for wrongs done private citizens, and the right of public servants individually to expose wrongdoing and even to strike. Public administration is government in action. Its role cannot be understood without understanding its relationships to these great political, doctrinal, and moral issues.

PROPOSITIONS ABOUT THE ROLE OF AUTHORITY IN PUBLIC ADMINISTRA-TION. Six basic propositions flow from the view of public administration as a structuring of authority:

1. *Principals and agents.* In a democracy, the **principals** are the elected officials who make policy on behalf of the people and delegate responsibility to **agents**, who are the administrators charged with carrying out the law. This, in fact, is where the concept of **agencies** comes from—agencies are the agents established to do the principals' work.

2. *Narrow, defined specialization.* The law assigns each agency to a particular field of activity and a set of responsibilities. It cannot legitimately exercise power outside this field.

3. *Internal specialized structure.* The agency has an internal structure that divides responsibilities among bureaus (or whatever its principal units are called) and among individual positions.

4. *Rules of the game.* The agency has a set of procedures that identify which units and position holders do what, how, and when, as work flows through the agency.

5. *Staff of experts.* The agency has a staff of officials and employees who perform the agency's responsibilities. Principals hire agents because they expect the agents to be experts in the work to be done.

6. *Outside definition of roles and responsibilities.* Other parts of the government—such as the legislature, chief executive, and judiciary—have authority to abolish the agency; to increase or decrease its activities and responsibilities; to fix the amount of funds it can use; to appoint some staff members and specify how others shall be chosen; and to impose structural and procedural requirements on its organization and operation.

Thus, a government agency does not spontaneously spring into being. Rather, bodies with constitutional responsibility create it. The agency cannot choose its own objectives. Rather, its mission is the product of law. These formal rules and procedures create the foundation for the agency's power and ground it in the constitutional system—and seek to ensure that agencies promote the interests of citizens as a whole instead of the interests of special groups.

Authority guides these propositions, but it does not guarantee that public administrators will work without problems. The lawmaking body may create an agency that is not needed. The law might be vague about the agency's responsibilities, and they might overlap those of other agencies. In fact, the very nature of politics often *creates* agencies with vague and overlapping responsibilities—since the fuzzier the goals, the easier it often is for legislators to get a majority. An agency's internal structure may be poorly designed to accomplish its mission because special interests might try to steer its work to benefit them. Agencies sometimes generate such powerful allies that elected officials might hesitate to challenge their power. But, despite these challenges, structure and authority define the basic issues in the exercise of bureaucratic power, and they set up the big problems for which leaders and theorists have, for a very long time, searched for solutions.

Two Models: Classical and Bureaucratic

Two schools of administrative theory flow from this foundation: the classical and the bureaucratic. Both see the fundamental organizational problem as defining the agency's mission and then setting up internal units and subunits, each charged with a specified portion of the agency's activities. They both develop a theory for the relationship of higher-level units to lower-level units, along what is usually called the **chain of command**.

Both the classical and the bureaucratic schools rely on the values of legitimacy, power, and rationality. Both schools view organizations simply as neutral, rational instruments for achieving whatever policy objectives (that is, political values) the state's rulers may choose. They differ in *how* they do so.

THE CLASSICAL MODEL. The **classical theory** of organization begins by defining clear jurisdictions of authority and responsibility. The theory then subdivides these jurisdictions down the chain of command, to the front lines. Its prime goal is **efficiency**, which focuses on creating *specialized* functions and *coordinated* responsibilities. The theory reached its sharpest focus in the 1930s, when organizational theorist Luther Gulick published its most persuasive description.[4] The classical theory still has great

Cyber Leadership
Theme: Politics

In December 2015, Virginia Governor Terry McAuliffe took aim at one of the biggest problems his state faced. "I am dead set in making Virginia the leader of cybersecurity," he said. In fact, during his year as chair of the National Governors Association, he campaigned to make cybersecurity an issue on which every governor must focus.

As McAuliffe told a reporter in July 2016, "since January 1, we have had 53 million cyber attacks which is about 1 every 4 seconds. About 300,000 per day. We've blocked 42,000 of malware [attacks], we've stopped about 131 'very serious' cyber attempts into our system." He pointed to the health care information that states collect, especially as part of the Medicaid program, and the vast quantity of data in the states' tax records.

McAuliffe deliberately didn't call out any state by name, but he contended that "five states are doing a very good job, 20–25 are making significant progress and about 20 are in very bad shape." As he pointed out, "until all 50 states have done what they need to do to protect themselves, you're only as good as the weakest link on the chain."

Why does this matter? It's not only the state government's records, McAuliffe explained. It's also the businesses in the state, the financial systems that surround them, and the ability of states to attract jobs: "your ability to do commerce," as he put it.

For state governments, the rise of cyber threats not only marked a big policy challenge. It also posed a stark management challenge. Cyber problems don't follow hierarchical lines—and responding to the threats required a response that crossed hierarchical boundaries.

Source: Michael Grass, Quinn Libson, and Dave Nyczepir, "McAuliffe on Cybersecurity: 'It's Something That Every Governor Needs to Focus On,'" *Route Fifty* (July 18, 2016), http://www.routefifty.com/2016/07/terry-mcauliffe-national-governors-association-cybersecurity/130007/?oref=rf-today-nl.

value—it is both a theory in itself and the foundation for other approaches. Critics often argue that it pays too much attention to authority and relies too much on defining boundaries, but it is nevertheless the touchstone for modern administration.

Gulick contended that public administration builds on six principles:

1. *Bases of organization.* Organizations can be structured according to four different strategies:
   a. Purpose (e.g., defense, education, police, fire)
   b. Process (e.g., accounting, engineering, purchasing)
   c. Clientele (e.g., Indians, children, veterans, the elderly)
   d. Place (e.g., neighborhoods, New England, Mississippi, Latin America)

2. *Mutually exclusive alternatives.* When policymakers design an organization, they must recognize that the four bases of organization are mutually exclusive. They must choose one, build on its advantages, and develop strategies to deal with the lost contributions of the other approaches. For example, it is virtually impossible to create an organization based on both purpose and place, or on both clientele and process. There can be a neighborhood-based agency that manages all programs affecting a particular area, but that comes at the cost of functional specialization (like the expertise that firefighters and police officers perform citywide). There can be an agency—say, a police department—that develops a specialized capacity in crime control, but it is hard to build deep expertise in complicated issues like crime

scene investigation and drug control on a neighborhood-by-neighborhood basis. There can sometimes be specialized offices within the broad strategy. For example, the New York City Police Department (a purpose-based agency) has a special unit dedicated to Times Square (a place-based operation). But, in general, governments face a basic strategic choice: what building block they will use for their fundamental structure.

3. *Focus on purpose at the top.* Governments most often solve this problem by organizing their executive branch by purpose and by bringing together all activities that contribute to this purpose.

4. *Span of control.* There's a limit to how many subordinates any executive can oversee, what theorists have long called the **span of control.** The best span of control, however, is subject to fierce debate. A smaller span of control allows executives to pay more attention to each subordinate, but this increases the number of layers from the top to the bottom of the organization. If an executive has a larger span of control, the number of layers decreases, but the executive must supervise more subordinates. There's no easy answer to this dilemma.

5. *Single head for agencies.* Administrative authority and responsibility should be vested in single administrators. Boards and commissions can be useful for policymaking, because they make it easier to represent many different points of view. But this can frustrate the need to provide clear-cut decisions for agencies to administer. This leads to the principle of **unity of command**, with one person responsible for those in subordinate positions.

6. *Separate line and staff.* Line activities and staff activities should be sharply distinguished. **Line activities** are those operations *directly* related to the major purpose of the agency. In a fire department, for example, firefighters on trucks do most of the department's frontline work. **Staff activities**, in contrast, *assist* the work of the line officials. In the fire department example, fire marshals do staff work, reducing the risk of fires. Staff functions include research, policy, and program analysis as well as planning, budgeting, personnel administration, and procurement of supplies. Line executives exercise powers of decision and command. Staff officials are—or should be—restricted to advising and providing raw materials. In practice, we often use *staff* as a generic term for all agency employees. In the formal sense, however, "staff" refers to individuals in support positions. In practice, the distinctions between line and staff often blur in practice, especially with budget officials—in their staff role—exercising substantial power over what line officials actually do.

At the core of the classical model is designing organizations to maximize efficiency. Closely related are ideas we will explore later in the book, including a civil service of qualified persons selected by merit and a single-budget system for the whole executive branch. The classical model also anticipates a rational decision-making process, through which higher officials draw on the specialized knowledge at lower levels to make their decisions and use the hierarchy to transmit those decisions throughout the organization. Much of the rest of this book is about the challenges to this theory that have been raised over time, but it remains the foundation on which much of the field has been built.

THE BUREAUCRATIC MODEL. Closely related to the classical model is the **bureaucratic model**, which is most commonly associated with Max Weber, a German sociologist. The bureaucratic model is less based on formal structure than the classical model and focuses more on the roots of authority within organizations. Weber is one of the organization theory's best-known theorists, but that's ironic. He died in 1920, but his work was not translated into English until 1946, when his impact grew enormously.[5]

Weber was interested in how organizations can be stable and, in particular, why people feel obligated to obey commands. He suggested that a stable system of authority cannot depend purely on subordinates' sense of self-interest, nor on their liking or admiration of their superior, nor on their sense of an ideal world. Instead, a stable pattern of obedience rests on the subordinates' belief in the legitimacy of the system of authority. That leads them to defer to superiors and, ultimately, to the source of command in that system.

Weber found it useful to think in terms of three "pure" models of legitimate authority: traditional, charismatic, and rational-legal. **Traditional authority** rests on the belief in the sacredness of traditions ("what actually, allegedly, or presumably has always existed"); it thus depends on the loyalty of individuals to someone who has become "chief" in a traditional way. **Charismatic authority** rests on personal devotion to an individual because of the exceptional sanctity, heroism, or exemplary character of this person. Because of the roots of these approaches, the bureaucratic model holds that they lack rationality.

By contrast, **rational-legal authority** (Weber used both terms interchangeably) rests in "the legally established impersonal order." He found it useful to describe this as an "ideal type" of bureaucracy. For Weber, that didn't mean his idea of the perfect plan, but rather the basic characteristics of a bureaucratic system. Obedience is due to "the persons exercising the authority of office under it only by virtue of the formal legality of their commands and only within the scope of authority of the office."[6] Weber describes how the "official duty . . . is fixed by *rationally established* norms, by enactments, decrees, and regulations, in such a manner that the legitimacy of the authority becomes the legality of the general rule, which is purposely thought out, enacted, and announced with formal correctness."[7] Weber also describes the basis of why obedience is owed to the person in authority: persons in a corporate body, "in so far as they obey a person in authority, do not owe this obedience to him as an individual, but to the impersonal order."[8] Weber's rational-legal approach establishes the basic structure for accountability, because it describes the flow of power and responsibility from top officials to those at the bottom of the organization.

To Weber, such a bureaucratic structure leads to efficiency. He wrote:

> Experience tends universally to show that the purely bureaucratic type of administrative organization . . . is . . . from a purely technical point of view, capable of attaining the highest degree of efficiency and is in this sense formally the most rational known means of carrying out imperative control over human beings. It is superior to any other form in precision, in stability, in the stringency of its discipline, and in its reliability. It thus makes possible a particularly high degree of calculability of results for the heads of the organization and for those acting in relation to it.[9]

To achieve such efficiency, Weber explains, an organization requires two conditions, similar to those in the classical approach. First, laws and administrative regulations establish "fixed and

German social scientist Max Weber not only championed economic reform but also produced an analysis of "ideal types" of bureaucracy, which continues to influence the way scholars and practitioners think about theories of organizing complex work.

official jurisdictional areas" as part of a systematic division of labor, with each area being assigned "regular activities . . . as official duties" and given "the authority to give the commands required for the discharge of these duties" (subject to rules delimiting the use of coercive means for obtaining compliance). Members of the bureaucracy can be efficient only if their responsibilities are sharply defined. Second, "the principles of office hierarchy and of levels of graded authority mean a firmly ordered system of super- and subordination in which there is supervision of the lower offices by the higher ones." Efficiency also depends on clear patterns of hierarchy and authority, from the top to the bottom of the organization.[10]

Weber, like the classical theorists, fills out the model by defining the characteristics of a full-fledged rational bureaucracy. He argues that officials should be full-time, salaried, and selected on the basis of technical qualifications. But, again as with the classical theory, the human beings who constitute "the bureaucratic machine" seem stripped of their human differences:

> The individual cannot squirm out of the apparatus in which he is harnessed . . . the professional bureaucrat is chained to his activity by his entire material and ideal existence. In the great majority of cases he is only a single cog in an ever-moving mechanism which prescribes to him an essentially fixed route of march.[11]

This "cog in a machine" image has long attracted fierce criticism of Weber's work, as well as endless parodies: from Charlie Chaplin's famous silent movie *Modern Times* to the satire on the Korean War, *M.A.S.H.*, which led to a long-running television comedy, and on to long-running comedies like *Parks and Recreation* and *The Office,* which had both British and American versions.

Classical theory and bureaucratic theory have many similarities, but there is one important difference. Many modern students of administration have scathingly attacked classical theory, but bureaucratic theory tends to be respected. To some theorists, classical theory seems impersonal and autocratic. Weber's bureaucratic theory, on the other hand, paints a richer canvas. To be sure, Weber has attracted much criticism. For example, critics have pointed out that he both emphasizes the importance of hierarchical authority and recognizes that bureaucracy builds on specialized, professional knowledge and technical competence among subordinates, expertise that gives subordinates a kind of authority that can conflict with the top-down patterns of organizational authority.[12] Despite these criticisms, however, Weber's concepts remain central to modern sociological analyses of bureaucratic organization.

DIVING INTO DATA

Government Employment as a Percentage of the Labor Force

Americans spend a lot of time debating the size of their government—especially the federal government. A look at government employment across many of the globe's most-developed countries leads to some interesting comparisons—and some surprises.

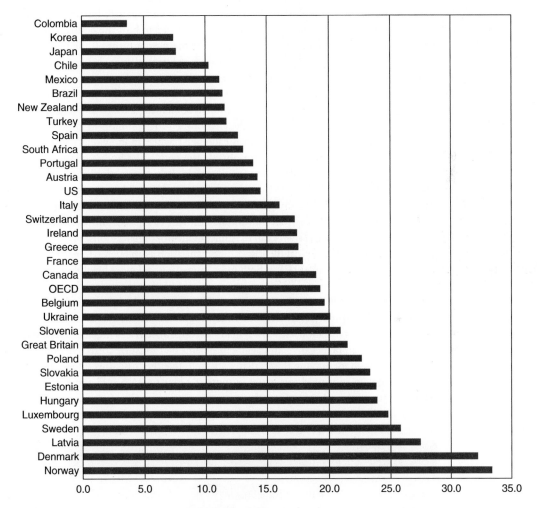

Source: OECD, *Government at a Glance, 2015* (Paris: OECD, 2015), Figure 3.2; and U.S. Bureau of Labor Statistics, "Employment by Major Industry Sector," http://www.bls.gov/emp/ep_table_201.htm. OECD data are for 2013; U.S. data are for 2014.

QUESTIONS

1. How does general government employment in the United States compare with government employment in other countries?
2. What would explain the way that America differs?
3. To what countries is the United States similar? Why?

SYSTEMS THEORY

Systems theory has arisen as a major alternative to the hierarchical approach.[13] It sees organizational work as a set of related parts, and it seeks to generalize about all organizations, public and private, large and small.

A system can be either closed or open. **Closed-system theorists** view an organization as a machine, which translates inputs into outputs but whose operation is substantially unaffected by its environment. A common example is the heating system of a house. We might set the thermostat for a given room temperature. When the temperature falls below the set point, the thermostat triggers the furnace, and the furnace burns fuel to heat the house. When the temperature rises to the level set on the thermostat, the thermostat turns off the furnace. The system's operation is self-contained—once set, it reads the temperature changes and performs its function, without anyone needing to intervene. We can set the thermostat and leave the house—for an hour or a month—and come back to a home heated to just the point we set.

Open-system theorists see an organization as something akin to a biological organism, such as an animal or a plant living in the environment. A common example is the human body's normal temperature of 98.6 degrees Fahrenheit: when an individual contracts a disease from outside the system (that is, from outside the body), the body's temperature rises in response and the body's own system—sometimes with help from a physician—tries to kill the disease and restore the temperature to normal. Systems theorists have tended to be fascinated with nature's processes for restoring normalcy. Their tendency to look at both the nature of the system and that of the forces that pull the system back to equilibrium has often led system theorists to produce static, rather than dynamic, models of organizations.

In organization theory, most theorists treat organization as an open system (that is, one that interacts with its environment). It is both more interesting and more helpful in understanding how it works. The essential elements are these: an organization is a system that receives **inputs** of resources (equipment, supplies, the energies of employees), which it **throughputs** and transforms to yield **outputs** (products or services). (Some of the inputs, of course, must go to maintaining the organization itself as a system.) An open system also includes a **feedback loop**. Some feedback can be negative, in flagging problems that must be corrected. Some feedback can be positive, in identifying things that work well. In either case, this information can help adjust the system so it produces better outputs at a lower cost. See Figure 4.2 for a graphic representation of the systems approach.

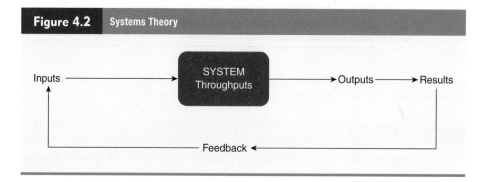

Figure 4.2   Systems Theory

Inputs → SYSTEM Throughputs → Outputs → Results

Feedback

The open-systems model has particular power in organization theory, in part because of its focus on how an organization does things and in part because it points to the organization's relationship with its environment. In an era of networked government and rising globalization, this systems approach has become even more powerful.

Systems theory helps focus two important elements of classical and bureaucratic theories: agency jurisdictions, which define **system boundaries**, and agency missions, which define **system purpose**.

System Boundaries

Boundaries are essential for both classical and bureaucratic theories. They define the authority and responsibility of each department and each bureau: what they should do, and what they should not. A system, too, must have boundaries, so that one can tell what is within the system and what is outside it. This inside-outside distinction is vital for two reasons. First, systems theorists need to identify what the system gets from and gives to the environment. These transactions occur at the system's boundaries. Second, the theory distinguishes two requisites for the survival of a system: its capacity to manipulate or adapt to its external environment and its capacity to suppress or moderate internal threats.

It is often difficult to see private corporations as neatly bounded systems. That's even harder in the public sector. One can assert, of course, that the U.S. Department of Agriculture or the California Environmental Protection Agency (EPA) is a distinct system with precise boundaries. More broadly, one can treat a department, its interest groups, and its relevant legislative committees as a system. Nevertheless, legal, political, and organizational realities allow the department much less clarity of boundaries than the basic systems approach requires. California's EPA is part of the state's executive branch, so many of its important decisions require the concurrence of other departments, the governor, and central agencies such as the budget office. Decisions directly affecting the environment may actually lie with other agencies or with the governor. The California EPA does have a distinctive identity within the executive branch, but its identity rests in its mission, not in how sharply its boundaries are drawn. The same holds true across government, from state highway departments to local fire departments.

System Purpose

Classical theory proposes that the executive branch should be organized at the top by major purpose. Systems theory goes much further. It asserts that every organizational system has a purpose, goal, or objective—translating inputs into outputs.

Systems theory borrows heavily from the idea of biological systems, which take in inputs (nutrients) from the environment, process the inputs, and turn them into outputs (activities or behaviors that characterize the organism's way of living). Of course, the first imperative of all organisms is simply to survive.[14] Systems theorists conclude that the same is true for organizations as well. Business corporations must take in more money than they spend or they cannot stay in business. According to systems theory, a corporation's long life is, therefore, a sign of the success of its system.

Systems theorists then argue that, unlike most organisms, humans are moral beings, and they seek a purpose beyond themselves. As Lord Ashby explained in the middle of the twentieth century, when writing about universities as organizations:

> Among living organisms it is assumed that the prime function is to survive. . . . Among social institutions one cannot make so simple an assumption. The biological analogy breaks down. It is not enough to say that the function of a university is to survive. It has functions over and above survival: in other words, it has purpose. . . . Unlike the biologist, the university administrator cannot eschew teleology; he must squarely face the fact that universities do not exist simply for their own sakes, as daffodils and sparrows and mice do; they have a purpose.[15]

Thus, systems theory focuses on an organization's purpose and how best to achieve it—how best to translate inputs into outputs. Systems theorists conclude that organizations need to be understood in terms of their purposes and that those purposes define the nature of organizations.

However, seeking identity by defining purpose is often difficult in practice. Especially in government agencies, organizational purposes often multiply and sometimes conflict. Let's return to the California EPA. Is it the department's purpose to encourage conservation? Or is it to promote the best use of resources to advance industries, like agriculture and tourism? Is its mission to seek the best interest of individual citizens or to protect large businesses? And if the answer is "both," how should it best balance the competing demands? The state legislature does not provide a simple answer, for the laws shaping the state's EPA embrace competing demands. The U.S. Forest Service often finds itself caught between competing priorities: encouraging the growth of wild forests—but stopping the fires that help forests regenerate themselves.

The multiple, fuzzy, and competing goals in many government agencies can actually help them cope with their political environment. The multiple goals give their leaders extra flexibility in navigating turbulent political waters—and the ability to enlist a wide variety of political allies in support. But this, in turn, raises challenges to systems theory and its focus on clear boundaries and purposes.

CHALLENGES TO THE TRADITIONAL THEORIES

The models and theories we've explored so far have much in common. Each offers a rather formal, abstract view of organizations, with a focus on clear goals and sharply defined boundaries. Systems theory views an organization as a "black box" that translates inputs into outputs. The classical model looks inside the black box and sees organizational units and subunits as clearly bounded and arranged to provide a pyramid-based, hierarchical structure of authority.[16]

Over time, these traditional theories have drawn fire from three directions. Humanists charge that the structural approaches are authoritarian—that they stifle the creativity of the human beings who work inside. Pluralists charge that the classical and bureaucratic models ignore the political system, give an unreal portrayal of the executive branch, and conflict with democratic values. Other critics from the government-by-proxy perspective contend that government agencies rely increasingly on other levels of government and on private and nonprofit organizations to administer public functions.

All three approaches, therefore, raise fundamental challenges to the structuralist perspectives embodied by Weber, Gulick, and systems theory. All of the challenges focus on the role that boundaries play in organization theory: how much sharp lines can define what organizations do and how they can do it better. We discuss each of these approaches in detail below.

THE HUMANIST CHALLENGE

The humanist challenge to the structural models looks inside the bureaucracy, focusing on the life of individual workers within the organization. Most of this challenge flows from work researchers have done inside large corporations.

Jobs, Productivity, and Happiness

Industrial managers have long recognized that a business organization's performance depends on the productivity of individual workers. Productivity, they believe, builds on the design of the job and the organization's ability to motivate workers to do the job well. The foundation of this approach is the **scientific management movement**, which developed the profession of industrial engineering in the early 1900s. One of the movement's foremost leaders, Frederick W. Taylor, conducted time-and-motion studies, where his efficiency experts, armed with stopwatches, studied which production techniques produced the best outputs in the shortest times. These studies helped improve the efficiency of assembly lines, which were beginning to revolutionize manufacturing.[17] Even then, critics argued that this single-minded pursuit of efficiency was dehumanizing. Taylor himself helped feed that criticism, writing that because of "the grinding monotony" of the work, "one of the first requirements for a man who is fit to handle pig iron as a regular occupation is that he shall be so stupid and so phlegmatic that he more nearly resembles in his mental make-up the ox than any other type."[18]

Such views reinforced the worry that bureaucracy squeezed the humanity out of individuals in the pursuit of efficiency. Critics argued instead that organizations ought to make the work more rewarding—and that happier workers would be more productive workers. That led to the humanist movement, which focused on the basic question of motivation: Why do individuals join an organization, stay with it, perform well, and leave?[19] Money helps, but it does not adequately explain variations among companies or among a single company's work groups. Important research in the late 1920s and 1930s at the Hawthorne Works of the Western Electric Company showed how variations in working conditions could affect the motivation and productivity of workers.[20] Researchers adjusted the level of light in the factory and found in one experiment that changes in the lighting increased workers' productivity, even when the lightning was reduced to the point they could barely see. The researchers called this the "Hawthorne effect"—workers respond to supervisors who pay attention to them. They established the point that motivating employees is important to organizations, and that planning for efficiency alone would never be enough.

This research gave birth to the **human relations movement**, which had great impact in the 1950s and 1960s. The humanists argued that happy workers were more productive, and their early research studies confirmed this. Happiness—or satisfaction, as it was usually called—was not a matter of monetary and promotional rewards but of the interpersonal relations in the small face-to-face group of fellow workers and their immediate supervisor. According to the humanists, an atmosphere that generates satisfaction does not flow from bureaucratic structure.

Instead, managers can increase satisfaction and productivity by involving workers in reaching decisions for the group. In such a system, the supervisor is not autocratic and directive; rather, the supervisor is informal, consultative, trusting, and concerned for the team members' welfare.

Although such arguments seemed promising, researchers found that (1) this strategy makes some workers happy but others unhappy—some workers like to participate in decision making but others resist having to share the risk and responsibility for big decisions; and (2) happy workers are not necessarily more productive workers.[21] Many research studies have consistently shown that "job satisfaction is related to absences and turnover; they have been equally consistent in showing negligible relationships between satisfaction and level of performance or productivity."[22]

Moreover, researchers have found that smarter and richer people with more accomplishments aren't necessarily happier. The combination could even make individuals less happy. The more individuals seek to conquer a field, the more they make comparisons with others, and the constant search for "how am I doing compared with everyone else" can lead to unhappiness. The goal of winning more awards and gaining more recognition can undermine the quest for satisfaction. Instead, some experts suggest that being happier lies in the quest for finding what a worker is good at and most enjoys doing—and doing more of it. This creates a world in which everyone has an opportunity to grow in the way that makes everyone happier, the argument goes.[23]

At the core, though, there's the important basic conclusion: happier workers are better workers; and the more organizations help workers be happy, the more productive they will be. In fact, California's dairy industry waged a campaign arguing that "happy cows make better milk." The ads were broadcast across the country—except in Wisconsin. The implication was that cows there, in the "dairy state," were less happy and that Wisconsin dairy products weren't as good. The campaign was powerful because it resonated with the way many people *think* motivation works.

Ideology

These findings created a strong argument for what theorists call "self-actualization" (creativity, self-direction, and the realization of one's full potential as a human being) and for the equality of workers (and thus minimal subordination to a leader's direction and maximal participation in decision making). Members of the human relations movement insisted that large, formal organizations, with their hierarchical authority structure, are repressive. These organizations would work better, the theorists argued, if they helped their workers "self-actualize." Chris Argyris wrote that organizational planners

> assume that efficiency is increased by a fixed hierarchy of authority. The man at the top is given formal power to hire and fire, reward and penalize, so that employees will work for the organization's objectives.
>
> The impact of this design-feature on human personality is clearly to make the individuals dependent on, passive and subordinate to the leader. The results are obviously to lessen their self-control and shorten their time-perspective . . . pushing individuals back from active toward passive, from being aware of long time-perspectives toward having only a short time-perspective. In all these four ways, the result is to move employees back from adulthood toward immaturity.[24]

| **Box 4.1** | **McGregor's Theory X and Theory Y** |

Theory X

1. The average human being has an inherent dislike for work and will avoid it if he or she can.

2. Because of this human characteristic of dislike of work, most people must be coerced, controlled, directed, or threatened with punishment to get them to put forth adequate effort toward the achievement of organizational objectives.

3. The average human being prefers to be directed, wishes to avoid responsibility, has relatively little ambition, and wants security above all.

Theory Y

1. The expenditure of physical and mental effort in work is as natural as play or rest.

2. External control and the threat of punishment are not the only means for bringing about effort toward organizational objectives.

3. Commitment to objectives is a function of the rewards associated with their achievement.

4. The average human being learns, under proper conditions, not only to seek but to accept responsibility.

5. The capacity to exercise a relatively high degree of imagination, ingenuity, and creativity in the solution of organizational problems is widely, not narrowly, distributed in the population.

6. Under the conditions of modern industrial life, the intellectual potentialities of the average human being are only partially utilized.

Source: Douglas McGregor, *The Human Side of Enterprise* (New York: McGraw-Hill, 1960), 33–49.

Not all theorists have agreed, however. Four attacks have been made against the human relations school.[25] First, critics believed that the research was flawed. Most of the early work was conducted by "true believers," and other scholars argued that researchers found what they went looking for: a connection between motivation and productivity.

Second, critics argued that the sweeping contrast of the bad hierarchies with ideal human-based organizations was overdone and based on simple assumptions. Many humanist researchers adopted Douglas McGregor's distinction between two different approaches to organization and management: Theory X, which relied on hierarchical authority, and Theory Y, which relied on motivation. McGregor advocated Theory Y.[26] (See Box 4.1 for a summary of McGregor's theory.) The simplicity of his argument built a powerful foundation for the human relations approach, but recent studies have rejected this simple contrast. Newer research leads to prescriptions for tailoring leadership and participatory styles to the particular circumstances.[27] However, this call to adapt strategies to specific situations frustrates the search for general propositions. That, of course, is the essence of theory building.

Third, critics argued that the human relations movement tended to treat jobs as if they were the worker's whole life. Critics made the obvious point that most people obtain important satisfaction off the job, and that some people go to work to earn enough money to be happy off the job. They don't always seek—or get—self-actualization on the job. Individuals can be relatively happy without their work making them so.

Fourth, critics said that the human relations movement tended to ignore the need of leaders to lead. Abraham Maslow, a psychologist much admired by humanists, made the point most sharply:

> The writers on the new style of management have a tendency to indulge in certain pieties and dogmas of democratic management that are sometimes in striking contrast to the realities of the situation.

With dogma occupying this front-rank position, it is not surprising that human relations theory has evaded the problem of the very superior boss. The participative kind of management, where subordinates work toward a good solution to a problem, is often an inappropriate setting for the superior boss. He is apt to get restless and irritated. . . . The less intelligent subordinates are also affected adversely. Why should they sweat for three days to work toward the solution of a particular problem when they know all the time that the superior can see the solution in three minutes. . . .

The relationship of the boss to the people whom he might have to order around or fire or punish is, if we are realistic about it, not a friendly relation among equals. . . . This hard reality ought to have some impact on the theories of participative, democratic management.[28]

Despite its uneven impact on organizational performance, the antibureaucratic school has had a profound effect on the study of organizations. It has become a rallying point for those seeking to move the study and practice of organizations past the structural approaches to new ones founded on interpersonal relationships. Improving those relationships, human relations theorists have long argued, has been the foundation for improving organizational performance. The reaction against treating individuals as mere cogs in the organizational machine remains a very powerful force.

THE PLURALIST CHALLENGE

The pluralist challenge to the formal, structural model emphasizes the central role of interest groups and how they shape a bureaucracy's behavior. It is a powerful argument that captures the rising role of interests and their increasing ability to bend the bureaucracy's will—and about how environmental forces can shape organizational behavior. In fact, Francis Fukuyama argues in a modern classic that the rise of interest groups has set the stage for a decline of political order and the rise of political decay.[29]

The pluralist model assumes that the interplay of groups shapes society and its government. Groups seek their own interest, with administration as an important battleground for winning their way—and for continuing the struggles they fought in the legislative and judicial arenas.[30] The model sees administration as fragmented, reflecting the fragmented nature of the legislature. Bureaucracies are a jumble of structures, pushed by political crosscurrents, instead of a neat, symmetrical pyramid. The task of administration, at least at its highest levels, is the same as the task of politics—to facilitate the peaceful resolution of conflicts, work out the differences in power among groups in our society, and use the interplay of these groups to seek the public interest.

Administrative organizations, according to the pluralistic model, are both the products of this constant battle and the arena in which the battles are often fought.[31] Their survival as individual agencies depends on their command of sufficient outside support to withstand assault by disadvantaged interests. Their top officials can retain their power only as they adjust their use of power to the preferences of the supporting groups—or if they succeed in winning sufficient support from other groups to break free from the original supporters. The chief executive appears in this model as the spokesperson not for the nation in the sense of "all the people," but for the specific combination of forces that makes it possible to attain, retain, and exercise power and that makes it possible to retain and exercise power. This is true for mayors, governors, and presidents.

To survive, administrative agencies must be responsive to legislatures, and especially to their committees and subcommittees, since they shape the laws to be administered and the money that pays for them. In this model, bureaucracy is one more arena among many in which the battle of political interests plays itself out.

Organizational Culture

One variation of the pluralistic approach emphasizes the importance of **organizational cultures**.[32] Agencies have many differences, and these differences generate different ways of doing business. Some have such strong interest group support that they have substantial autonomy within the executive branch. The interest groups' influence dominates the organization's life. Some have such records of devotion to the public interest (like Teach for America) or to professional standards (like the Justice Department) that they can resist interest group pressure. Others are orphans in the storm, the easy victims of external pressures. An agency physically consolidated in one building differs from one whose headquarters, units, and staff members are scattered among many buildings or among capitols, suburbs, and distant cities.[33] Following the September 11, 2011, terrorist attacks, Congress created the Department of Homeland Security to "connect the dots" among related security issues. However, because most of the twenty-two existing agencies that comprised the new department remained in their existing buildings, blending the culture into a single, new approach proved impossible.

The organizational culture approach stresses the differences among agencies, which flow from their mission and staffing. One can enter a state liquor-control agency or a prison and sense a different atmosphere from that in, say, a banking or insurance department or a labor department. Sanitation departments are very different from police departments, and police departments have a very different culture than fire departments. In Washington, D.C., "one has only to walk into the ancient Treasury Department building . . . to sense the atmosphere of a conservative financial institution."[34] That is even the case with the Federal Reserve, which has the feel of a Greek temple that oozes power and independence, and which is reflected in the Fed's organizational culture.[35] The Secret Service has resisted efforts to integrate it strongly into the Department of Homeland Security because its employees have resisted surrendering the Secret Service's symbols, like the Secret Service star, and its autonomy to the broader department. Moreover, critics have pointed to the forced merger of the Secret Service into the Department of Homeland Security as the source of many of the problems with which the Service struggled in the 2010s, including staffing and the struggle to maintain security over the White House grounds. In many jurisdictions, collaboration between police and fire departments has proven difficult because they have such different cultures. Sometimes the cultural differences have, quite literally, led to fist fights about who was in charge at the scene of major incidents.[36]

Critics have sometimes dismissed organizational culture as too fuzzy an idea to guide either theory or practice. However, after the space shuttle *Columbia* disintegrated on reentry from orbit on February 1, 2003, killing all seven astronauts on board, the National Aeronautics and Space Administration (NASA) went through a deep soul-searching investigation about how the accident had happened. Subsequent investigation revealed that the accident had been caused by hot gases pouring through a hole in the leading edge of

Hal Gehman, who headed the NASA-convened board that investigated the February 1, 2003, *Columbia* space shuttle accident, asked a question during a public hearing six weeks after the disaster. The board found that NASA had slipped back into many of the same problems that had contributed to the *Challenger* disaster years before.

the right wing and eating away at the internal support, until the wing gave way and the *Columbia* broke up; the hole, in turn, had been caused by the impact of a piece of insulation at launch. NASA's cameras had caught the impact, but attendees of meetings held while the shuttle was in orbit had concluded that it posed little risk. Investigators later determined that NASA had developed a culture that was unreceptive to airing and resolving problems. In fact, an extensive survey of NASA employees a year after the disaster showed that "there appear to be pockets [within NASA] where the management chain has (possibly unintentionally) sent signals that the raising of issues is not welcome. This is inconsistent with an organization that truly values integrity." How should NASA solve the problem? NASA's report concluded, "There is an opportunity and need to become an organization whose espoused values are fully integrated into its culture—an organization that 'lives the values' by fostering cultural integrity."[37]

Critics sometimes wonder whether there's anything real at the bottom of what can seem like a soft analysis of cultural differences. NASA's top officials, however, concluded that its organizational culture contributed to the *Columbia* disaster. A piece of foam broke off the shuttle on launch, struck the wing, created a hole, and that led to hot gases tearing the shuttle apart as it prepared to land. Culture problems within NASA had hindered communication about the recurring problem that foam had caused on launch. NASA administrator Sean O'Keefe said bluntly, "We need to create a climate where open communications is not only permissible, but is encouraged."[38] Together with outside experts brought in to help prevent future disasters, NASA's leader concluded that its culture had contributed to the accident, and that the agency needed to invest hard work to change it.

Assessment

The hierarchical and pluralistic models provide different insights. The pluralistic model yields a pragmatic description of the role of politics in administration. But because this model builds so much on the fragmentation of the political system, it's often better at *describing* the internal tensions than *providing* a guide on how to improve administration. It is much better at describing what *is*, compared with what *ought to be*. The organizational culture approach, moreover, provides a stark warning that change is hard and might prove fleeting, because cultures are deep-seated, rooted in particular functions and histories, and change slowly and incrementally.

The hierarchical model, in contrast, draws strength because of its deep roots. It's the pattern that everyone knows, and it's the one that reformers turn to when problems arise. For example, the hierarchical model drove the reformers who sought to improve homeland security after the September 11 terrorist attacks by creating the new Department of Homeland Security, designed to bring related agencies together under the same bureaucratic umbrella. It was a classic case of pursuing the hierarchic model and its prescriptions for clarifying missions and responsibilities, but subsequent cases have shown that many dots remained unconnected.

In October 2013, the U.S. Department of Justice shut down an underground web business that specialized in peddling illegal drugs, including heroin and cocaine, called "Silk Road." The site was doing millions of dollars of business before a multi-agency investigation arrested the dealer, who went by the alias "Dread Pirate Roberts," a fictional character in the movie *The Princess Bride*.

In the United States, our most fundamental organizational challenge is trying to create hierarchical arrangements in a pluralistic government. That, in turn, helps reinforce the ongoing dilemma of policy and administration. Administration is inevitably part of the effort to resolve political differences. Hierarchy is a search for control and efficiency. There simply isn't an easy way of balancing these conflicting instincts. The role of government in a democracy has always been to build energy to accomplish important objectives, whether for national security against foreign enemies, for provision of basic services like water and roads, for maintenance of the legal system, or for the affirmative promotion of economic and social welfare at all levels of government. That inevitably highlights the efforts to improve coordination, rationality, and legitimacy, which in turn emphasizes the hierarchical model. But those efforts, in turn, need to negotiate a world full of interest groups, fragmented congressional committees, other levels of government, nonprofit organizations, and other agencies with sometimes-competing missions and cultures. Administration is embedded in politics, and it always has a heavy political flavor.

FORMAL MODELS OF BUREAUCRACY

By the 1980s, many theorists were unhappy with the development of the various theories of public bureaucracy. They liked the fundamental simplicity of the hierarchical model, but they found that it did not produce clear propositions about how best to organize bureaucracy. They did not believe that the systems model produced enough insight, and they found the human relations approach too imprecise. Theorists instead adapted economic theory to produce formal models of bureaucracy.[39]

The formal approach fundamentally transformed the theory of public administration. Theorists began with elemental questions. They identified individuals as the basic building blocks of economic systems. What motivates them? How do these motivations shape their behavior? How does their behavior shift as they come together in formal organizations? Traditional public administration assumed that authority relationships between superiors and subordinates shaped the basic relationships within an organization: individuals did what they did because superiors asked them to do it. The formal approach, by contrast, began with the proposition, borrowed from microeconomics, that individuals seek to maximize their self-interest: workers agree to work because the work provides them with valued rewards, such as pay and fulfillment; employers agree to pay workers to get the job done, and the market determines how much employers must pay and what employees will agree to accept.

These basic assumptions have led to approaches that view bureaucracies as networks of contracts, built around systems of hierarchies and authority.[40] Each of these networks consists of relationships between superiors and subordinates, and each relationship has a variety of **transaction costs**—especially the cost to the supervisor of supervising the subordinate. As originally developed by Nobel laureate Ronald Coase in 1937, this theory has made several advances.[41] Beginning with the motivations of individuals, it explains how they fit into organizations. It explores the problems that such motivations can cause within organizations and identifies the problems that supervisors have in overseeing subordinates. By building on the concept of a contract between individuals and the organization, the theory links organizational theory to economics and its related ideas.

Principals and Agents

From this foundation, theorists developed the **principal-agent theory**, an approach that details the contracts between superiors and subordinates. This approach, a top-down alternative to hierarchical authority, stipulates that higher-level officials (principals) initiate the contracts and then hire subordinates (agents) to implement them. It also provides an alternative theory of accountability: workers (agents) are responsible to top-level officials (principals) not because they have been ordered to do so but because they have negotiated contracts in which they agreed to pursue specific actions in exchange for specific rewards. Principal-agent theory thus offers an elegant and theoretically powerful solution to basic problems—especially devising the best organizational structure and motivating the employees within it—with which traditional public administration struggled for nearly a century. In both cases, the measure of "best" is the same: the ability of the organization to produce the most efficient and responsive goods and services possible.

Because principals and agents operate through contracts, results will be only as good as the contracts. Theorists contend that predictable problems grow out of any contractual relationship. To write a good contract requires good information. But principals can never know enough about their agents to make sure they have selected the best ones, and that lack of insight can produce adverse selection problems, in which ill-chosen agents cannot or choose not to do what their principals want. Moreover, principals can never observe their agents' behavior closely enough to be sure that their performance matches the terms of the contract—this lack of knowledge can produce moral hazard problems, in which agents perform differently than the principals had in mind.

Principal-agent theory thus focuses on information and the incentives for using that information as the critical problems of public administration. Principals need to learn the right things about their agents before hiring them, and they need to improve their monitoring of agents' behavior to learn what results they produce. They can use this improved knowledge to adjust agents' incentives and to redesign organizations to reduce the risks from adverse selection and moral hazard. And because conventional wisdom and formal theory alike predict that bureaucrats resist change, principals can use this analysis to improve performance and oversight.

For public administration, this approach produces a straightforward theory: institutions headed by elected officials, such as the executives and legislators, create bureaucracies (that is, bureaucracies can be viewed as agents for the principals'—elected officials'—wishes). The principals design bureaucracies' incentives and sanctions to enhance their control, and when the principals detect bureaucratic behavior that does not match their policy preferences, they use these incentives and sanctions to change that behavior. Among the important sanctions are the president's appointment power and the budgetary leverage that the branches share.[42]

Principal-agent theory thus has introduced a simple, precise solution to the enduring puzzle of how principals should manage their relationships with their agents. Since these are market-based relationships, with costs and benefits on both sides, it makes sense to structure the relationship through a basic tool of the market, a contract, which specifies what the principal wants and what the principal will pay. When both the principal and the agent sign it, they resolve the uncertainties that otherwise would surround their relationship—and potentially undermine their work.

Moreover, principal-agent analysis has provided an inductive approach to theory building. Starting with a simple assumption—that individuals seek their self-interest—the theorists have built propositions about why individuals join organizations, how organizations structure their work, and what problems can emerge from such relationships. Those propositions, in turn, have produced hypotheses (for example, that rational bureaucrats seek to maximize their budgets) that seem to explain much commonly observed administrative behavior. Principal-agent theory not only has helped to develop an alternative explanation of bureaucratic behavior but has also identified the pathologies that, especially by the late 1970s, seemed so often to afflict bureaucratic behavior.

Criticism

The very popularity of principle-agent analysis, however, has stirred heavy criticism, especially from theorists who contend that a single-minded search for rationality robs the study of organizations of its very life. Economic theories of organization, Charles Perrow argues, represent "a challenge that resembles the theme of the novel and movie *The Invasion of the Body Snatchers*, in which human forms are retained but all that we value about human influence, and resentment of domination—has disappeared."[43] Even one of formal theory's strongest voices, Terry M. Moe, agrees, commenting that the inner workings of bureaucracies tend to evaporate from most of these models. Instead, they appear "as black boxes that mysteriously mediate between interests and outcomes. The implicit claim is that institutions do not matter much."[44] Theorists from the structural approach schools often add that the same goes for the people inside these institutions.

This debate leads to several important conclusions about the formal approaches to bureaucracy. First, although these approaches are intriguing, they are not theoretically mature. Their proponents frankly acknowledge that large holes remain in their arguments and that far more work needs to be done. In particular, even though the approaches build from models of individual behavior, many of the models are peculiarly people-free. Public administration, at the least, has demonstrated that bureaucratic behavior matters, and if they are to be successful, the formal approaches will need to become more sophisticated about modeling that behavior. Second, the approaches lead in different, even contradictory, directions. The theorists have engaged in lively, even heated, arguments among themselves about which formal approach is most useful, and the battles are nowhere close to resolution. Third, the theoretical propositions are far more elegant than their empirical tests. The behaviors they seek to model are extremely complex and not easily reducible to equations and statistics. To conduct empirical tests, the formalists must impose large constraints and look only at pieces of the puzzle. That, they contend, is a natural part of theory building.

Traditional public administration scholars have found the assumptions and models of the formal approach arbitrary and unrealistic; practically inclined researchers and practitioners have found them unpersuasive. Nevertheless, the formal models do provide theoretical elegance and a clear, logical set of propositions that many scholars find extremely powerful in a discipline that has long been searching for an intellectual anchor.

THE CHALLENGE OF INTERWOVEN GOVERNMENT

All of these theories share an assumption: that public administration works by having government employees carry out government programs through the government's own bureaucracies, and that government's bureaucracies have a line of sight to the front lines where services are actually delivered. However, to a steadily diminishing degree, that doesn't describe the way American government operates. As we saw in Chapter 2, much of the government's work happens outside the straightforward government hierarchy, through grants to other governments, contracts with private and nonprofit organizations, indirect tools like loans and regulations, and a host of similar strategies.

Moreover, government programs have become so complex that no problem that matters is managed by any single government organization.[45] The more government's service delivery system has become characterized by **interweaving**, as I describe it—interwoven with the work of other agencies, other levels of government, other sectors (including the for-profit and nonprofit worlds), and even other countries—the less classical theories fit practice. Our bureaucracies operate under the assumption of hierarchical control of vertically organized organizations. In fact, doing the government's work increasingly requires horizontally connected programs across the boundaries separating different organizations, levels of government, and sectors.[46]

The growth of interwoven government challenges the classic and bureaucratic models, because hierarchy and authority do not work well if the work doesn't occur mostly through the chain of command. Hiring, firing, and direct supervision of work are hierarchical powers that work poorly, if at all, when dealing with grants and contracts. To manage indirectly administered programs well, government must seek other forms of leverage, especially through negotiation, contract law, and performance measurement. That, in turn, requires the creative use of new tools.

The vast spread of these indirect tools makes it difficult for government to monitor all these outside agents. It cannot easily cancel large grants and contracts for violation of the prescribed conditions without damaging its programs and the public they serve. Consider just two examples. First, America fought the wars in Iraq and Afghanistan by hiring at least one contractor for every soldier, an enormous increase in the reliance on contractors compared with previous wars. Second, the federal government manages Medicare, Medicaid, and the Children's Health Insurance Program—which account for 25 percent of all federal spending—with just 0.2 percent of the entire federal workforce. That's a simple indicator for a very complex set of programs, in which the federal government leverages the work of state agencies (in the case of Medicaid, where the states have primary operating responsibility and make large financial contributions of their own to the program) and in which private and nonprofit health care providers actually provide the health care. It's a government-funded, privately delivered system, in which hierarchy doesn't begin to capture the way the programs actually work.

Some scholars have suggested that an approach built on interorganizational **networks** might help to explain these problems better.[47] Such networks, Eugene Bardach explains, consist of "a set of working relationships among actors such that any relationship has the potential both to elicit action and to communicate information in an efficient manner."[48] Pragmatic in its exploration of how organizations share common ground—missions, clients, and goals—and coordinate their work, this approach has been developed by administrative scholars who sought to explain the management of public programs but found existing theories lacking. For example, they have discovered that most social service programs work through complex networks: a chain of federal grant money, frequently supplemented by state grant funds, that is passed on to local governments and administered through governmental organizations, as well as for-profit and nonprofit contractors. These programs, in turn, connect with local schools, police departments, antidrug programs, programs managed through churches, and volunteer organizations, among others. The growth of this movement has given rise to extensive research into "collaborative governance."[49]

Network analysis is distinguished from other approaches by two characteristics. Scholars debate whether networks constitute an approach, a theory, a method, or a prescription, but there is rising recognition of the power of collaborative approaches to public administration. On one level, the network approach is important for what it is not: the approach is based neither on traditional hierarchical control of organizations nor on market-based transactions among them. Organizations help one another because they discover that collaboration advances their own goals as well. On another level, such interdependence has come to define more governmental programs. Traditional administration begins by assuming that the legislature delegates to government agencies the job of managing programs. In contrast, network analysis begins with the discovery that the management of programs depends on the interconnections among those who actually implement programs and that links of the implementation process often lie outside the bureaucratic chain of command. Some networks connect different agencies within a single department. For example, the performance of a state's human services department typically depends on the network connecting its child welfare, health, and social service agencies. Some networks, especially those for federal grant programs, connect different departments at different levels of government. The performance of governmental programs depends on how well these networks function.

Compared with traditional hierarchical authority, network analysis is in its relative infancy. Its proponents disagree about whether it is a broad-based theory or simply a useful approach. But in moving past the traditional theories of hierarchy and in exploring the pragmatic tactics that managers develop to tackle the problems of interwoven government, network analysis offers fresh insights for government's emerging issues.

At the core, however, the rise of interwoven policy is one of the great and inescapable challenges of public administration. It is a challenge to governmental effectiveness, since these programs are complex. But it is also a challenge to organization theory, since most of the existing theories do not fit interweaving well. From a practical sense, how should we manage programs where responsibilities are so broadly shared? From a theoretical sense, how should we capture the deep truths of a system that builds on hierarchy but doesn't operate hierarchically? These are cutting-edge puzzles for organization theory.

CONCLUSION

One of the remarkable things about public administration is that different theorists can look at the same basic question—how do government organizations work?—and reach fundamentally different interpretations.[50] They've produced a daunting array of theories. In all of these multiple and contradictory approaches, however, three broader propositions surface.

First, each approach focuses on an important truth about governmental organizations. Each has endured because it has captured at least an important nugget of reality for a large number of analysts, and because it produces an explanation for problems that other theories leave unanswered.

Second, none of these theories captures everything. Not all organizations are the same; not all small groups are the same; not all jobs are the same. We seek broad theories to explain the world of public administration; many of the theories do best in explaining the variations.

Third, some theories provide a broad framework for understanding administration without necessarily dealing with all the operating realities. How important is it that the theories capture these realities? A search for basic ideas inevitably leaves some things out. Because public administration is both a part of politics and because it seeks to provide guidance to administrators in solving real-world problems, leaving things out can leave frontline administrators without guidance for problems they have to solve.

Each of the approaches reviewed in this chapter contributes something that is true. Together they paint a rich portrait of a complex reality:

- The *formal model* of bureaucracy provides great intellectual power in laying out the foundations of bureaucracies and some of their most fundamental elements. However, critics have pointed out that the formal models provide little practical guidance to public administrators. In the minds of many theorists, they have not been supported by enough research. The challenge has become even greater as formal theory seeks to accommodate complexity by becoming more complex itself. That, in turn, has tended to lose some of the power of its approach, which came from its laser-like focus on a small number of important propositions.

- The *pluralist* approach emphasizes the societal and political environment in which powerful interest groups intervene in administration to achieve their objectives. It is especially powerful in explaining how the values of different interest groups shape administrative action. It has also proven useful in explaining the political setting of public administration. However, it has proven less useful in explaining how administrators can balance the need for hierarchical responsibility with the imperative for political responsiveness.

- The *humanist* approach, although flawed in several ways, usefully reminds us that individual workers' incentives and teamwork matter in gauging the effectiveness of administration. At the core, the answers to two questions remain unclear: (1) what responsibility do organizations have for motivating employees? and (2) how can organizations make individuals happier on the road to higher performance?

- A *systems* approach is simple to describe but very hard to apply. As with pluralism, its contribution lies in identifying the interplay between an administrative system and its environment. In addition, its attention to feedback reminds us that organizations learn from experience over time.

- The *structural* approach, with which we started, goes back to first principles about government, viewing authority—legitimate power—as the heart of the matter. Executive branch departments are agents that hold authority that is delegated and restricted by other elements of the constitutional system—legislatures, executives, and the courts. In turn, each such agency organizes a hierarchy for further delegating and restricting authority and for holding subordinates accountable for their use of such authority. Despite more than a century of criticisms of and complaints about this approach, it remains the foundation for both the theories and practice of public administration.

- The theory of *interweaving* brings new challenges to all of these approaches. As the administration of government's work becomes more of a complex partnership with a wide variety of actors, including many outside of government, making administration both effective and accountable becomes far more difficult. Indeed, it becomes even more difficult to understand what *public* administration is, since it relies so heavily on private administrators. The growing gap between these operating realities, on the one hand, and the theories of administration, on the other, frames some of the most fundamental challenges to the organizational theory of public administration.

This brings us to the first principles, linked to the concept of *authority*. It focuses on basic issues: Who is in charge of what, and how can each individual be held accountable for their actions? Classic theory surely has its challenges, but its great strength is in defining the most fundamental questions. It also provides the foundation for hierarchy, the basic building block of organizations and their operations. It's little wonder, therefore, that it remains the core of organizations, in both theory and practice.

Differences in Organizational Culture:
Is the FBI from Mars and the CIA from Venus?

Author John Gray has made a global reputation with his best-seller *Men Are from Mars, Women Are from Venus*. His argument: that men expect women to think and talk like men, that women expect men to think and talk like women, and that "our relationships are filled with unnecessary friction and conflict."[1]

Gray must be on to something. His Mars/Venus books have sold more than 30 million copies in forty languages. In fact, thanks to appearances on *Oprah* and *Live with Regis*, his first book was the best-selling book of the 1990s.

Some people think Gray's guide to male-female relationships helps explain the tensions between governments as well. Journalist Siobhan Gorman thinks so. She writes that the key agencies responsible for protecting the United States from terrorist attacks, the Central Intelligence Agency (CIA) and the Federal Bureau of Investigation (FBI), "have such different approaches to life that they remain worlds apart," and even White House—ordered relationship counseling might not be enough to bring them together.[2]

Prior to the September 11, 2001, attacks, U.S. government intelligence agencies spread across the nation and around the world had collected fragments of information, hints, and warnings about the potential attacks from numerous disparate sources. But the information never came together as a picture of the impending disaster. Even in retrospect, it isn't certain that the picture would ever have been clear enough for the government to stop the attacks. However, the country never found that out because high bureaucratic barriers prevented the flow of information.

In the months after the attacks, critics and reformers universally called on government to "connect the dots"—to do a much better job of interpreting the information collected by the various intelligence agencies. That process, they all concluded, would make America safer by helping top officials identify the greatest threats. Everyone agreed that the intelligence system needed better coordination and reached consensus that bureaucratic battles between the intelligence agencies were undermining the nation's security.

The national commission investigating the September 11, 2001, attacks confirmed that deep divisions between the nation's intelligence agencies had frustrated the government's ability to uncover valuable clues and, perhaps, take steps to prevent the attacks. Commission chairman Thomas Kean declared that the government had not been able to protect its citizens from attack because of "a failure of policy, management, capability and, above all, a failure of imagination." Who or what was to blame? Kean's commission answered, "There's no single individual who is responsible for our failures." The commission's recommendation? Create

a new cabinet-level national intelligence director to oversee the nation's network of fifteen different intelligence agencies.[3] A single head of intelligence, the commission argued, would improve coordination and break down the barriers that had prevented the sharing of intelligence before the attacks. This national intelligence director needed to be able to steer the agencies' investigations, coordinate the information they collected, and provide clear advice to the president. That complex assignment, the commission concluded, required a new position at the highest level of the federal government—with the power to hire and fire employees and to control the intelligence budget.

At the center of the organizational battle was a decades-old struggle between the CIA and the FBI. "It's not that [FBI agents and CIA officers] don't like each other, but they're really different people," explained Jim Simon, who had worked as an analyst in the CIA. "They have a hard time communicating."[4]

For years, the two agencies had coexisted uneasily: the CIA focused on digging out information abroad on threats to the United States, while the FBI concentrated on dangers inside the country. A tidy boundary, perhaps, but not one that the nation's enemies respected. In fact, it was one they were able to exploit in carrying out the September 11, 2001, attacks, in which foreign operatives burrowed into American society, only to pop up to stage the biggest assault on American soil since the Japanese attack on Pearl Harbor in December 1941. President Bush, congressional leaders, and the 9/11 Commission issued an inescapable challenge to the agencies: cooperate! "But the organizations' institutional cultures are so different," concluded Gorman, "that real coordination will be very difficult to achieve."[5]

Since its creation in 1947, in the early days of the Cold War, the CIA has focused on building long-term relationships with potential intelligence sources. A field agent may spend long hours engaging in conversation with a subject who is plied with good liquor, swapping tales, and building trust, in the hope that, when things begin to happen, the source may share some important information. Within this clandestine world, where it is always hard to predict what is going to happen where, the CIA—known as "The Company" to insiders—has encouraged a loose, nonhierarchical style of operating. Success here consists of digging out a critical piece of information and passing it along to top policymakers. Field agents often cut corners to make this possible, and then they melt back into the background.

By contrast, the FBI, founded in 1908, has long had an informal motto: "We always get our man." Dogged police work combined with careful training of its agents has always been the hallmark of the FBI. Knowing that their job is to catch and incarcerate criminals, this agency's operatives scrupulously avoid crossing legal lines so they won't jeopardize prosecutions. Success means putting bad guys behind bars, one case at a time.

FBI agents take up a case, track it to its completion, file it away, and move on; their work is linear. In contrast, CIA agents circle constantly around problems, pick up on leads until they either solidify or evaporate, and work them like a prospector panning for gold.

These different styles of work lead each agency to recruit a different kind of person. John Vincent, a twenty-seven-year FBI veteran, explains, "The type of people that go into the CIA is completely different from the type of people who go into the FBI." In the FBI, most employees "are pretty normal Joes off the street. The CIA guys—they're a different group of people. Most of the CIA guys I've met are very intelligent but wouldn't know how to put a nut on a bolt."[6] FBI agents, in Gorman's analysis, are from Mars.

Sixteen-year CIA veteran Ronald Marks says that's because, in the CIA, judgment is much more important than rules. "You have a source who will tell you X. Your judgment of that source is based on the time you've spent with them. You're dealing pretty much in a murky world." That, Marks concludes, is "the world of judgment."[7] As Gorman puts it, CIA agents are from Venus.

These different operating styles have led to very different antiterrorism strategies. The information-based, judgment-driven world of the CIA has focused on rooting out information about possible attacks in advance, even if the information does not come together in sharp focus. The conviction-based, rule-driven world of the FBI has focused on trying to arrest and convict terrorists, often after the fact.

Nevertheless, the stark realities of the post-9/11 world make it essential for the two agencies to cooperate. As the 9/11 Commission warned, "Countering transnational Islamist terrorism will test whether the U.S. government can fashion more flexible models of management needed to deal with the twenty-first-century world."[8] In fact, toward the end of its report the commission quoted the following stark conclusion, drawn from a study of the Pearl Harbor attack: "Surprise, when it happens to a government, is likely to be a complicated, diffuse, bureaucratic thing. It includes neglect of responsibility, but also responsibility so poorly defined or so ambiguously delegated that action gets lost."[9]

To prevent poorly defined, ambiguously delegated policy in the future—to prevent the government's bureaucratic problems from getting in the way of its war on terror—the commission argued that the nation needed a single, powerful director of national intelligence with the authority to force coordination between the FBI and the CIA, as well as the thirteen other intelligence agencies. That change, the commissioners concluded, was the only way to create a unified homeland security culture from the very different independent organizational cultures that had grown in the vast intelligence community.

But even a new organization, Gorman argued, might not solve the problem. Looking back at Gray's best-seller, Gorman wrote, "Mars and Venus can expect to need couples' counseling for a very long time."

QUESTIONS TO CONSIDER

1. What are the roots of the different organizational cultures in the FBI and the CIA? How do these cultures affect their work? In both good and bad ways?

2. How likely is it that the two agencies will be able to change their cultures?

3. Do you think that changes in the organizational structure can produce changes in the organizational culture? Is the 9/11 Commission's proposal a good idea? Why or why not? How else might an organization's culture change, if not by changes to its structure?

NOTES

1. John Gray, *Men Are from Mars, Women Are from Venus* (New York: HarperCollins, 1992), 10.

2. Siobhan Gorman, "FBI, CIA Remain Worlds Apart," *GovExec.com* (August 1, 2003), http://www.govexec.com/defense/2003/08/fbi-cia-remain-worlds-apart/14671.

3. Chris Strohm, "9/11 Commission Scolds Government over Attacks, Calls for Major Reforms," *GovExec.com* (July 22, 2004), http://www.govexec.com/defense/2004/07/911-commission-scolds-government-over-attacks-calls-for-major-reforms/17234. See the Commission's report, *The 9/11 Commission Report* (2004), http://www.9-11commission.gov/report/911Report.pdf.

4. Gorman, "FBI, CIA Remain Worlds Apart."

5. Ibid.

6. Ibid.

7. Ibid.

8. *The 9/11 Commission Report*, 406.

9. Thomas Schelling, foreword to Roberta Wohlstetter, *Pearl Harbor: Warning and Decision* (Stanford University Press, 1962), viii.

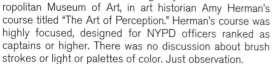
Learning to See in the New York Police Department: How Studying Art Makes You a Better Cop

It was a tough case, and the officers split up into two- or three-person surveillance teams. Their assignment: to study the scene carefully and try to figure out what was going on. The scene was puzzling—a man, with short hair and lots of muscles, was getting rough treatment. A buxom woman ripped the shirt he was wearing. One 52-year-old inspector, a longtime veteran of the New York Police Department (NYPD), quickly concluded it was the end of a trial and the victim was "possibly being led off to be tortured." The woman? Part of a lynch mob, he said.[1]

The case? A close-up examination of a seventeenth-century painting by Italian baroque artist Guercino depicting the biblical hero Samson, after Delilah betrayed Samson to the Philistines. The scene? A gallery in New York's Metropolitan Museum of Art, in art historian Amy Herman's course titled "The Art of Perception." Herman's course was highly focused, designed for NYPD officers ranked as captains or higher. There was no discussion about brush strokes or light or palettes of color. Just observation.

Herman's course began with instruction for medical students in 2004. One night as they were eating pizza, a friend asked Herman if she had thought about expanding her audience. Herman visited the New York City Police Academy to explain what she thought her course could accomplish. She remembered one of her early courses. One officer said, on looking at a painting with everyone looking up, that if he drove up on the scene, "I'd figure I had a jumper," someone poised to leap off a ledge. The picture was baroque artist Claude Lorrain's *Sermon on the Mount*.

Officers found great value in not only honing their powers of observation but also talking to their detectives about what to look for. Herman noted in class that one murder victim's body had not been found for more than a year because the commander had issued only fuzzy instructions about how and where to look for it. One of her students said that instead of telling his detectives to "search the block" for evidence like shell casings, he would order them to make their search more systematic, by telling them where to start, where to stop, where to look, and what to search for. A graduate, Lt. Dan Hollywood, said Herman's teaching on perception had helped him snag criminals lurking around Times Square. As coordinator of a twenty-four-person team of plainclothes officers, Hollywood said, "Instead of telling my people that the guy who keeps looking in one parked car

after another is dressed in black, I might say he's wearing a black wool hat, a black leather coat with black fur trim, a black hoodie sweatshirt, and Timberlands."

One FBI agent who took Herman's course went undercover for eighteen months as part of a task force trying to break up mob control over the sanitation business in nearby Connecticut. With his powers of observation sharpened, he helped provide the basis for search warrants that produced thirty-four convictions and that busted up $60–$100 million in garbage companies. "Amy taught us that to be successful, you have to think outside the box," said the task force's commander, Bill Reiner. "Don't just look at a picture and see a picture. See what's happening."

Herman follows her own advice, of course. On a subway, she nervously eyed two large men who, in turn, were eyeing her. They hadn't shaved and their clothes were shabby, and she prepared to hop off the train as soon as it stopped.

"Hey," one of the men said, noticing that she was noticing, "we took your course. We're cops."

QUESTIONS TO CONSIDER

1. In police department culture, could there be many things further removed than the study of art history? Consider how an organization's culture helps the organization accomplish its mission—and how bringing other cultural insights can help hone the ability to achieve results.

2. Choose one or two other local governmental organizations. Assess the culture that operates inside those organizations. How might that culture support the mission—and where do you think that culture might blind the organization to things it ought to know to get its job done? Can you suggest ways of providing the organizations with new insights?

3. Organizational culture is the product of the hierarchy, the informal norms that shape the organization, and the way that individuals approach their jobs. What lessons do the lessons from Herman's course suggest for organization theory?

NOTE

1. The case comes from Neal Hirschfeld, "Teaching Cops to See," *Smithsonian.com* (October 2009), http://www.smithsonianmag.com/arts-culture/teaching-cops-to-see-138500635/.

CASE 4.3

Ben Vienneau noticed a special offer from Canada's CHSJ Radio 94.1. The station was running a competition for an ultimate "wedding by the sea," featuring a ceremony, limo, reception, flowers, and a honeymoon—all worth $20,000. What did he have to do to win? Create a video, post it on YouTube, and get more people to click and vote than anyone else.

So he came up with a very unusual proposal to his girlfriend, Marcia Belyea. Ben talked his brother-in-law, who was a police officer, into driving up behind Marcia, hitting the siren and lights, and pulling her over. The officer, in full uniform, told her she had over $2,000 in parking tickets, put her in the back of the police car, and threatened to put her in jail for thirty days. She broke down in tears—until the officer told her, "We've agreed to waive the fine, OK, and let you go, if you take his hand in marriage."[1] Ben got down on his knee, told her "I love you so much. I want to spend the rest of my life with you." Marcia's worries turned into smiles as Ben slipped the ring on her finger—and the police officer asked to see the ring, "just for evidence," he said.

Ben put the video on YouTube, and it went viral. In the United States, television shows like *The View* and *Whoopi* picked it up. The video ran on ABC's *Good Morning America* and Perez Hilton's gossip website. All the publicity pushed them into the finals of the radio station's competition, and Marcia made a Facebook post asking people to vote for them and put them over the top.

The stunt started a wild online chat about whether what Ben—and his brother-in-law—did was okay. Some applauded the couple for being so much in love. Others said it was "a huge waste of taxpayers' money."

But almost no one wondered whether it was right for a police officer to use his government authority to set up the prank. The story echoed against another one from Charlottesville, Virginia, where a twenty-year-old University of Virginia student found herself surrounded by plainclothes police. She had just come out of a store, having purchased some sparkling water. Agents from the state's Alcohol Beverage Control agency mistook the water for a twelve-pack of beer. One agent jumped on the hood of her car. Another drew a gun. They pulled out identification but the woman, Elizabeth Daly, couldn't read it in the dark parking lot, at 10:15 p.m. Terrified by the officers—and not knowing that they were officers, because they were not in uniform—she tried to escape by driving out of the parking lot. In the process, she grazed a couple of the officers. A police car with a siren and flashing lights pulled her over a few blocks away.

There was no engagement ring waiting for Elizabeth. The agents charged her with three felonies and put her in jail overnight. They had mistaken her sparkling water for beer; they charged her with assaulting an officer.[2] They later dropped the charges and apologized.

Two women were driving cars. Both were pulled over by officers with sirens and flashing lights. Neither woman had done anything wrong. One was punked as part of an engagement for a radio station competition, by an officer in uniform. The other was a victim of mistaken beverages, by officers not in uniform.

And, by the way: Ben and Marcia won their dream $20,000 wedding by the sea in the radio station's Facebook competition.

QUESTIONS TO CONSIDER

1. Police officers, every day, take enormous personal risks to do their jobs. They often ride alone and have to make snap life-or-death decisions. Citizens count on their hard work to keep them safe. What kind of supervisory issues does that pose for police departments and their leaders?

2. Do you think that Ben's brother-in-law committed a harmless prank in helping Ben surprise Marcia? Or did he abuse his police power?

3. What, if anything, did Virginia's Alcohol Beverage Control agents do wrong? They suspected Elizabeth, who was underage, of buying beer, and they had staked out a store where they believed such purchases were frequent. They were not wearing uniforms, to make it easier to catch suspected lawbreakers. If you were their supervisor, would you make any changes to the procedures to prevent such an occurrence from happening again?

4. Are there any links between these two cases, especially in the trust that citizens must have for the police and the flexibility that police must have to do their jobs?

NOTES

1. "Fake Arrest Proposal" (July 1, 2013), http://www.youtube.com/watch?v=RAzXRezukdo.

2. K. Burnell Evans, "Bottled-Water Purchase Leads to Night in Jail for UVa Student," *Charlottesville Daily Progress* (June 27, 2013), http://www.dailyprogress .com/news/bottled-water-purchase-leads-to-night-in-jail-for-uva/article_b5ab5f62-df9b-11e2-81c4-0019bb30f31a.html.

CASE 4.4

What Should Government Do about Sharks?

In 1975, director Steven Spielberg discovered a powerful truth about the moviegoing public: we love to go to theaters and be terrified by the prospect of sharks on the loose. In *Jaws*, Spielberg told a powerful tale of a trio on the trail of a man-eater—the local sheriff, an oceanographer, and an experienced shark hunter. The movie spun off three sequels, a ride at Universal's Orlando theme park, and a series of cheeky *Sharknado* television movies. Some beachgoers couldn't put their toes into the ocean without hearing John Williams's haunting theme in their heads. And little wonder: the movie's tag line was "don't go in the water."

Forty years later, stories of shark attacks dominated the news, terrified swimmers, and preoccupied state and local officials trying to convince vacationers that it was safe to come to their beaches.

Colin Cook, for example, was sitting on his surfboard off a beach in Oahu when a shark attacked him from below. A surfer and a kayaker helped him to shore, where he received medical attention and survived. But the attack was the fifth recorded in Hawaii by October 2015.[1] By the Fourth of July weekend that year, North Carolina beaches recorded eight shark attacks, and swimmers were wary. The year, in fact, proved an especially bad one for shark attacks. Around the globe, there were ninety-eight attacks and six fatalities, according to the International Shark Attack File.[2]

But that, of course, raises an important series of questions: Is this a governmental problem? Can government do anything about it? Should government do anything about it—and, if so, how?

There are plenty of sharks in coastal waters. In the town of Surfside Beach, California—not far from Long Beach and Los Angeles—the Marine Safety and Lifeguards Department takes sharks seriously. It bought a Phantom 3 Professional, a quadcopter—that is, a drone. Its team sends the drone out regularly to monitor young great white sharks offshore and, in the busy summer of 2015, "Every time we've flown it we've seen sharks," said Joe Bailey, the department's chief. In the past, the town had sent out lifeguards on personal watercraft to patrol for sharks. The drones worked much better: they could cover more area, in less time, from an altitude that made it easier to spot the sharks.

But, in general, the risks from sharks are very low. In the previous decade, the average death toll from sharks around the world was six. One study estimated that the risk of dying from a shark bite was one in 8 million, compared with one in ninety for dying in a car accident. Sharks have far more to fear from humans than humans do from sharks, since we kill 100 million sharks a year.[3]

Experts attribute some of the fear about sharks to much better reporting. The combination of improved information

sharing and a news media always ready to pounce on shark stories, especially on slow-news days around the holidays, can make the risk seem larger than it is.

However, when attacks surged in mid-2015, local governments worked to put new restrictions in place. Near North Carolina's beaches, local officials created "swim only" beaches, where fishermen would be banned. Officials suspected that sharks might have been attracted to areas where fishermen and their bait were mixing with swimmers. Fishermen were furious, but officials countered that the restrictions were limited: to small areas, at limited times of the day and limited months of the year. The board of commissioners in Emerald Isle, North Carolina, enacted a ban on "chumming" (tossing ground-up fish into the water to attract big-game fish). And lifeguards along the beaches were extra-vigilant.

Still, as Patricia Smith, the North Carolina Division of Marine Fisheries public information officer, said, "Sharks are in the water, and swimmers are in the water, and sometimes this happens."

What about a campaign to kill the sharks? A Stanford University expert said that a shark-killing program in Western Australia cost $22 million. It was a "waste of money," he said. Moreover, "Most of the time when you go out and kill sharks, you kill the wrong shark."[4]

And, as George H. Burgess, director of the Florida Museum of Natural History's Program for Shark Research and curator of its International Shark Attack File, pointed out, thousands more people are killed driving to the beach than by sharks when they get there.

QUESTIONS TO CONSIDER

1. Consider the implications of these arguments for organization theory. What strategies would you use to deal with the shark problem? How would you organize an effort to deal with shark issues? What entities would you involve? How would you connect them? Note that the one thing that would not be a good answer would be a governmental unit, organized hierarchically, focused squarely on shark-fighting.

2. Is there in fact a "shark problem"? If so, is it a governmental problem? Why or why not? Who should decide the answer to this question?

3. To the degree that you think government should play some role in keeping the beaches safe, how much governmental control should there be? How much should government regulate behavior, compared with educating everyone involved?

4. What different political interests are involved in this issue? Consider fishermen, vacationers, hotel operators, restaurants, and environmental policy experts, among others. How does this constellation of political interests affect the way government approaches the issue?

NOTES

1. Andreas Preuss, "Fellow Surfer, Witnesses Assist Shark Attack Victim in Hawaii," *CNN.com* (October 10, 2015), http://www.cnn.com/2015/10/10/us/hawaii-shark-attack-injures-surfer/index.html.

2. Brian Clark Howard, "2015 Had a Record Number of Shark Attacks. Here's Why," *NationalGeographic.com* (February 9, 2016), http://news.nationalgeographic.com/2016/02/160209-2015-shark-attacks-el-nino-economy/.

3. Ibid.

4. Ibid.

KEY CONCEPTS

FOR FURTHER READING

Goldsmith, Stephen, and William D. Eggers. *Governing by Network: The New Shape of Government.* Washington, D.C.: Brookings Institution, 2004.

Goldsmith, Stephen, and Donald F. Kettl, eds. *Unlocking the Power of Networks: Keys to High-Performance Government.* Washington, D.C.: Brookings Institution, 2009.

Gulick, Luther. "Notes on the Theory of Organization." In *Papers on the Science of Administration*, edited by Luther Gulick and L. Urwick, 1–45. New York: Institute of Public Administration, 1937.

Katz, Daniel, and Robert L. Kahn. *The Social Psychology of Organizations.* 2nd ed. New York: Wiley, 1978.

Kettl, Donald F. *Escaping Jurassic Government: How to Recover America's Lost Commitment to Competence.* Washington, D.C.: Brookings Institution, 2016.

Khademian, Anne M. *Working with Culture: The Way the Job Gets Done in Public Programs.* Washington, D.C.: CQ Press, 2002.

McGregor, Douglas. *The Human Side of Enterprise.* New York: McGraw-Hill, 1960.

Moe, Terry M. "The New Economics of Organization." *American Journal of Political Science* 28 (1984): 739–777.

Perrow, Charles. *Complex Organizations.* 3rd ed. New York: Random House, 1986.

Simon, Herbert. *Administrative Behavior.* New York: Macmillan, 1947.

Weber, Max. *From Max Weber: Essays in Sociology.* Translated and edited by H. H. Gerth and C. Wright Mills. New York: Oxford University Press, 1958.

SUGGESTED WEBSITES

For an exploration of academic research about organizational theory, see the websites of the Public Management Research Association, **www.pmranet.org**, and the Academy of Management, **www.aom.org**. Both provide links to cutting-edge research in the field. In addition, the website prepared by Babson College Assistant Professor Keith Rollag, **http://faculty.babson.edu/krollag/org_site/encyclop/encyclo.html**, is a useful encyclopedia of the major terms in the organizational theory literature.

$SAGE edge™
for CQ Press

WANT A BETTER GRADE?

Get the tools you need to sharpen your study skills. Access practice quizzes, eFlashcards, video, and multimedia at **edge.sagepub.com/kettl7e.**

5

THE EXECUTIVE BRANCH

In May 2011, President Obama and his senior staff, including then-Secretary of State Hillary Clinton, intently tracked the final steps in the hunt for Osama bin Laden, from the White House Situation Room.

Structure is the basic building block of the executive branch. There are organization charts that diagram who reports to whom. There are agencies created by legislatures to do government's work. Relationships among the pieces are crucial. And everything—especially power—depends on where in the hierarchy an official works. According to Miles's Law, a famous saying named after noted Princeton professor Rufus E. Miles, "where you stand depends on where you sit."[1] The setting both defines the way that government officials see their jobs and describes how they connect with others in doing those jobs.

If structure is the building block, **coordination** is the goal. Organizations are repositories of the expertise that government needs to get its complex work done. Because no single organization can fully manage any problem that really matters, ensuring that organizations work together is essential.[2] That makes coordination the central challenge of the executive branch. "If only we can find the right formula for coordination," Harold Seidman wrote, "we can reconcile the irreconcilable, harmonize competing and wholly divergent interests, overcome irrationalities in our government structures, and make hard policy choices to which no one will disagree."[3]

Of course, we have never quite found the magic formula for coordination, but that hasn't stopped reformers from constantly searching for the best structure to make it happen. Reorganization is a constant impulse, and new plans for new structures follow every crisis. How can we best ensure security for passengers boarding airplanes? Before September 11, 2001, that was the job of the U.S. Department of Transportation, which often allowed local airports to hire private contractors to screen passengers and their luggage and which coordinated screening with air traffic control and other transportation functions. After the September 11, 2001, terrorist attack, Congress made airport screening a federal government function, with the Department of Homeland Security hiring public employees as screeners. In 2004, reformers in California boldly declared, "California's government must reorganize to meet the demands of modern California." Their report proposed a massive shift in the responsibilities of state agencies that seeks to align "programs by function, consolidates shared services and abolishes outdated entities." Pointing out that California is the fifth-largest economy in the world and that the state has a rich tradition of embracing new ideas, the review nevertheless charged that

> California's state government is antiquated and ineffective. It simply does not mirror the innovative and visionary character of our state. Instead of serving the people, it is focused on process and procedure. It is bureaucracy at its worst—costly, inefficient and in many cases unaccountable.

CHAPTER OBJECTIVES

- Understand the basic building blocks of executive branch structure

- Connect the role of individual leadership with the contributions of structure

- Examine the structure of the White House as an example of top-level executive management

- Consider the opportunities that electronic government creates for improving government's performance

The performance review recommended a fundamental restructuring of the state's eleven agencies, seventy-nine departments, and more than three hundred boards and commissions responsible for carrying out the state's functions.[4]

Government's complex mission and intricate structure are closely linked. In this chapter, we will begin by looking at the basic issues. Chapter 6 focuses on critical and persistent organizational problems. Structure matters—a lot. How structure affects organizations and the way they behave, however, is a deceptively complex puzzle.

EXECUTIVE BRANCH COMPONENTS

For centuries, organization by **function** has been government's foundation. Four functions have long been at the core, in the United States and around the globe: (1) managing money, including revenues, spending, and borrowing (as with a treasury or a finance ministry); (2) maintaining internal law and order (through the courts and a department for justice); (3) keeping the country safe (through departments for the military and navy); and (4) managing the country's foreign affairs (through a foreign ministry). Other functions soon began appearing, such as a postal service and an engineering construction service (for roads, bridges, waterways, and public buildings). Local governments created departments for police, fire, sanitation, and education. As governments took on new functions, new departments followed. There were departments for agriculture and trade, and later for social welfare, health, housing, and education. With the twentieth century came an emphasis on technology, science, energy, the environment, and economic planning.

The names of these units, however, can sometimes be confusing. The top level of organization is usually a "department," but there's no consistent logic about what makes a department a "department" (and outside the United States, "departments" are often called "ministries.") The federal Department of Veterans Affairs (VA) had been an independent agency. When the VA became a cabinet department in 1989, the change was primarily symbolic, to recognize the contributions of the nation's veterans. None of its operations changed. Sometimes the change works in reverse. In 1995, the Social Security Administration moved out of the Department of Health and Human Services and became an independent agency to insulate its huge spending from the annual budget battles. The National Aeronautics and Space Administration (NASA) and the Environmental Protection Agency (EPA) both have big missions and they are agencies independent of any cabinet department, but neither has "department" status. The head of the EPA has "cabinet rank," in Washington protocol; the head of NASA does not. The reasons are arbitrary; their bases are primarily political. Look around any state or local government, and the same holds true. There are so many terms to describe executive branch units (*bureaus, departments, commissions, offices,* and *agencies*) and the result can be confusing. We typically use *agencies* as the broadest, most generic designation—executive branch units, after all, operate as *agents* of the government.

At the core of the debates over government's structure, there is a paradox. We typically look to the top official—mayor, governor, or president—as the chief executive, but the structure this person manages is usually the product of legislative decisions. An executive can propose the creation of a new cabinet-level department, but its creation and budget are both legislative decisions. That's very different from the private sector, where executives have far greater power to create, abolish, staff, and fund the structures they manage. In government, executives are responsible for managing agencies whose missions, structures, and resources they do not fully control.

Environmental Protection in Wisconsin

I t's one thing to create an organization to do something important, like environmental protection. It's another to staff it adequately to do its job. In recent years, the number of attorneys in Wisconsin's Department of Justice, assigned to environmental protection, has shrunk under Wisconsin Attorney General Brad Schimel.

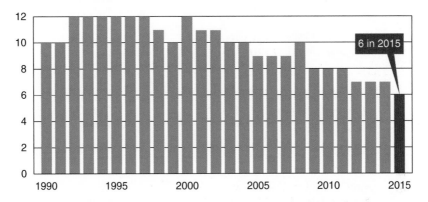

6 in 2015

Source: Steven Verburg, "Environmental Law Unit Shrinks Some More under Brad Schimel," *Wisconsin State Journal* (July 12, 2016), http://host.madison.com/wsj/news/local/environment/environmental-law-unit-shrinks-some-more-under-brad-schimel/article_044ad88c-bdb8-5ccc-a3ca-cc8132653b5b.html.

Between 1989 and 2009, the state's Department of Natural Resources sent between 105 and 179 cases to the unit. Between 2010 and 2016, the number of cases was higher than 100 only once. Fines against polluters in 2015 dropped to their lowest point since 1994.

QUESTIONS

1. What is the trend in the number of state government attorneys assigned to environmental protection? Is the trend significant?

2. What impact does that trend seem to have had?

3. What do you believe the connection is between the number of attorneys and the policy impact? Is this a good thing or a bad thing? How would you know? What additional data might you need to answer the question?

The Cabinet

Chief executives have traditionally gathered their agency heads together in a group that's come to be called the **cabinet**. That term has its roots in the Old French *cabine*, a gambling room, usually small and private to avoid prying eyes. That made the small, secluded chamber a natural place for the king's advisers to gather. In the sixteenth century, that confidential room evolved in England to the cabinet, a small room where the king met with his closest advisers. Over time, the meeting of the king's ministers grew into a more formal structure, and the American government incorporated the concept to describe the relationship between the president and department secretaries. A cabinet *"secretary"* comes from

Table 5.1	Federal Executive Branch Departments: Estimated Outlays and Employment, FY 2017	
Department	Outlays (millions of dollars)	Employees (thousands of full-time equivalent)
Department of Agriculture	151,485	90.5
Department of Commerce	10,546	45.6
Department of Defense	646,114	732.9
Department of Education	68,438	4.5
Department of Energy	30,373	16.1
Department of Health and Human Services	1,144,690	74.4
Department of Homeland Security	47,750	188.1
Department of Housing and Urban Development	40,738	8.4
Department of the Interior	15,040	66.7
Department of Justice	35,274	119.8
Department of Labor	50,962	17.7
Department of State	28,865	34.4
Department of Transportation	85,828	56.2
Department of the Treasury	618,290	103.0
Department of Veterans Affairs	180,220	366.5
Selected independent agencies		
Army Corps of Engineers	6,654	22.2
Environmental Protection Agency	8,693	15.6
General Services Administration	1,284	11.9
National Aeronautics and Space Administration	19,256	17.4
National Science Foundation	7,026	1.4

Source: U.S. Office of Management and Budget, *Budget of the United States Government, Fiscal Year 2017,* Historical Tables, Table 4.1, and *Analytical Perspectives,* Table 8-2.

Old English and refers to a high-level, confidential officer, who had the unusual ability to read and write. Its lower-level clerical meaning emerged much later.

Of the fifteen executive departments now operating at the federal level, three date from 1789 (State, Defense,[5] and Treasury). The newest is the Department of Homeland Security, established in 2002 (see Table 5.1). The departments range greatly in size, from the Department of Defense, which accounts for a third of all federal civilian employees, to the Department of Education, whose 4,500 employees would make it a small agency within many of the larger cabinet departments. In fact, it's smaller than the EPA, which does not have departmental status.

Moreover, as we saw in the earlier chapters, the nature of activities in these departments and agencies varies widely. Some departments and agencies perform relatively more of their missions themselves, like Interior, Commerce, and the General Services Administration, the federal government's landlord (see Figure 5.1). On the other hand, some departments and agencies rely very heavily on third parties, and their work is far more interwoven with the private and nonprofit sectors. That's the case especially for Education, with its vast portfolio

Figure 5.1   Spending per Employee

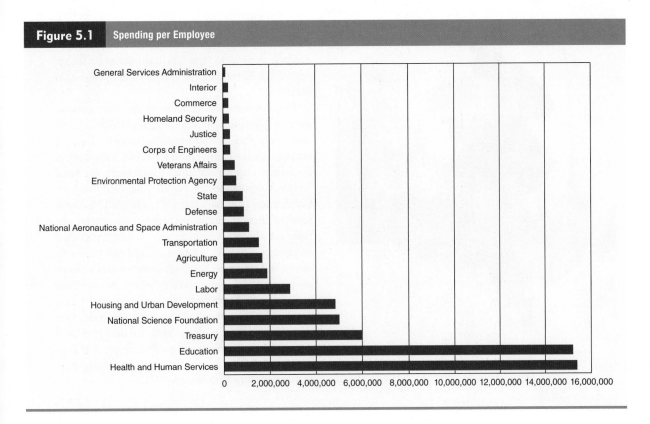

of grant and loan programs, and Health and Human Services, because of the enormous health care programs, Medicare and Medicaid.

Independent Agencies

Beyond the cabinet departments lie a large number of **independent agencies**, which account for about one-tenth of the federal government's employees and one-fifth of its spending. The Social Security Administration accounts for much of that spending and most of those employees. Other federal agencies range from the small, such as the American Battle Monuments Commission, to the hugely powerful, such as the Federal Reserve Board. Some agencies are regulatory, such as the Federal Communications Commission, which sets broadcast standards and manages licenses for the nation's broadcasters. Other agencies provide services, such as the Tennessee Valley Authority (TVA), which operates flood-control and power-generating dams in the southeastern part of the country. Then there are the super-secret spy agencies, including the Central Intelligence Agency and the National Security Agency.

Congress originally created independent agencies to insulate them from presidential control and legislative-executive politics.[6] Some agencies have enormous power over important parts of the economy. **Regulatory commissions** rely on complex tools—licensing, rate-fixing, and safety codes, for example. The federal government controls which drugs can be sold. Local

New York's old post office building bears the inscription, "Neither snow nor rain nor heat nor gloom of night stays these couriers from the swift completion of their appointed rounds." That surely was the case for Patrick Conley in Portland, Maine, even though the Postal Service's financial problems led to searching debates about how to reduce costs.

governments regulate taxis. State governments license barbers and tattoo parlors. The 2016 decision by Austin's voters to require Uber's drivers to be fingerprinted led the company to shut down its operations in the city.

Some of these independent agencies are **government corporations**, mostly engaged in lending, insurance, and other business-type operations.[7] Familiar examples are the Corporation for Public Broadcasting, the Federal Deposit Insurance Corporation, the Legal Services Corporation, the National Railroad Passenger Corporation (Amtrak), the TVA, and the U.S. Postal Service. These government corporations vary greatly. Some are wholly government owned, others are mixed enterprises with both government and private investments, and yet others have only private funding. Some are meant to be profit making; others are nonprofit organizations. Some support themselves from their revenues; others are wholly or partly dependent on government appropriations. Some are integrated into the regular departments; others float freely. And they vary in conformity to standard personnel, budgetary, and auditing practices and controls.

Over time, the independence of independent regulatory commissions has eroded. Chief executives, for example, can usually appoint a commission's majority and install members who share policy goals. Their budget offices review the commissions' budgets. However, years of political wrangling have made it nearly impossible for the Federal Elections Commission to work effectively.

At the state and local levels, the same issues hold true, in almost endless variety. The Railroad Commission of Texas, for example, is an independent regulatory commission whose mission grew from its early railroad days to one of the state's most powerful agencies. The commission develops and regulates Texas's vast oil, gas, and other energy resources. North Dakota has an Industrial Commission with great authority over the state's own vast energy resources. A three-member board, composed of the governor, attorney general, and agriculture commissioner, oversees the North Dakota commission. The pattern ripples throughout the country, but the same basic question occurs everywhere: Who holds the administrators accountable for what they do and how much they spend?

Bureaus

Within agencies, the principal operating organizations are **bureaus**. This general term covers many organizations within the larger departments. Bureaus have a wide variety of titles, such as Bureau of Motor Vehicles, Internal Revenue Service (IRS), Geological Survey, Antitrust Division, Federal Highway Administration, Homicide Division, Office of Energy

In 2011, the U.S. Transportation Security Administration created its "PreCheck" program, which allows frequent fliers who pay an extra fee to use a special airport security line and avoid taking off their shoes or removing liquids from their carry-on baggage.

Research, and the famous Federal Bureau of Investigation (FBI). *CSI*—the Crime Scene Investigation Bureau—became an immensely popular series of television shows. These operating units are so important in public administration that they give the field its name: *bureaucracy*—that is, a government by bureaus. (As usual, however, we often aren't consistent in calling bureaus "bureaus"—they can be services, divisions, or offices, among other things.)

Bureaus vary dramatically in size and significance. Some of them have long historical roots—longer, often, than those of the departments in which they are currently located. The Public Health Service system traces its origins to 1798, when Congress authorized marine hospitals to care for merchant seamen. Four years later, Congress established the Army Corps of Engineers and soon charged it with improving the navigability of rivers and harbors for civilian as well as military purposes. The Bureau of the Census in the Commerce Department finds its mission in the Constitution's 1789 provision requiring a decennial population census, although the bureau itself dates only from 1902. (Originally, the census was taken by U.S. marshals under supervision of the State Department; after 1850, the Interior Department did the job.) The Bureau of Land Management succeeded the General Land Office (established in 1812), some of whose records bear the signatures of George Washington and Thomas Jefferson.[8] Many other bureaus are old enough to have developed a distinctive culture—a sense of organic institutional life and a doctrine and tradition to which their staffs are dedicated.

As we have seen, bureaus do not easily abandon such culture simply at the command of the temporary officials who fill top executive branch positions.

One of the first things that state and local governments did as they became organized was to set up bureaus to deal with the safety, public health, and transportation of their citizens. At the local level, many such organizations date from before the birth of the nation. Even as he was tinkering with lightning rods and his famous stove, Benjamin Franklin created a lending library, a fire brigade, a night watchmen unit, a hospital, a militia, and a university. In his stimulating biography of Franklin, Walter Isaacson quotes the sage of Pennsylvania as writing, "The good men may do separately is small compared with what they may do collectively."[9] Franklin proved a remarkable architect of government bureaus.

Field Offices

Most of the time, we focus on the headquarters organization. That is the source of most big policy decisions and the most important political battles. The reality, of course, is that most government operations happen far from headquarters. At the federal level, for example, *just 12 percent* of the federal government's civilian employees are located in the Washington, D.C., metropolitan area. Seven of eight federal employees work in the field, from airport screeners and air traffic controllers to local Social Security Administration representatives and members of the foreign service in embassies around the world. In fact, in 2012, the federal government hired almost as many new employees in Texas as in Washington, D.C. At the state and local levels, most police officers patrol neighborhoods and rarely visit headquarters. Firefighters staff their equipment at stations around the city. Police sergeants conduct roll call in their precincts. State natural resource workers manage water and sewer permits and oversee hunters. Highway department employees work out of regional offices to build roads, patch potholes, and plow snow. The headlines focus on big battles in the state capitol or city hall, but most of government's work happens in the field.

There are two common strategies for organizing field work. Most bureaus work by function, with field offices organized by task, from police precincts and fire stations to motor vehicle offices and college campuses. But there is another strategy, based on area. This **areal system** dates from the Roman Empire, where the army commander controlled all of the government functions within a region. In such a system, each region has a single national official (which is called a *prefect* in some countries, with the structure called a **prefectoral system**) to oversee all national field agents in the area, regardless of their departmental and bureau affiliations.[10] The French prefectoral system, originated by Napoleon Bonaparte, is the model most widely copied.[11] The advantage of the area-based prefectoral system is coordination, because a single prefect is in charge of all government functions in the region. The disadvantage is specialization, since the coordinator is by necessity a broad generalist.

In the United States, the typical model is organization by function. This encourages specialization, but at what cost? This model has a major effect on coordination of activities in the field. For example, such efforts have proven especially difficult in homeland security, which involves coordination among not only multiple federal agencies but federal, state, and local governments as well.[12] Reformers often try to solve coordination problems by creating area-based offices; they sometimes replace area-based offices with functional experts. There is an inevitable tension between specialization and coordination choice, and no one has yet figured out an organizational strategy to get the right measure of both at the same time.[13]

LEADERSHIP OF THE EXECUTIVE BRANCH

The chief executive—mayor, county executive, governor, or president—might lead the executive branch, but the elements of the branch are the creatures of the legislature. We know organizations best by the private-sector model, which puts executives in charge. That often leads us to vastly underestimate the legislature's role in administration. Moreover, it's easy to overestimate the role of executives. The federal government is so vast that the president can never pay attention to more than a handful of public administration issues. The same is also true for cabinet secretaries, whose biggest nightmare is discovering a major issue about their department for the first time on the front page of the *Washington Post.* At the state and local levels, the executive branch is often little more than a heap of twigs. In most state governments, the governor is only one of five or six popularly elected executive officials, and executive heads of departments and agencies are often chosen by the legislature or by boards and commissions (whose members have overlapping terms) rather than by the governor. On the average, governors appoint less than half of their states' administrative officials (whether with or without legislative confirmation). Some mayors in so-called weak-mayor systems have similar handicaps. More strikingly, even those in strong-mayor systems (and city managers, too) find that many functions are vested in other local governments, including special districts for schools, transportation, and water that are a step removed from their control. In many states, the attorney general and the secretary of state (and sometimes other major positions as well, such as regents for the state university system) are elected independently of the governor. In fact, the state attorney general's election is often a stepping stone to the race for governor, and that often complicates the governor's job as executive. At the federal level, the president at least has appointment power over the key members of the cabinet; at the state level, that is often not the case. In her political biography of George W. Bush, Texas columnist Molly Ivins wrote, only partly in jest, that the Texas governor is the fifth most powerful person in the state, behind the lieutenant governor, attorney general, comptroller, and land commissioner, all of whom are independently elected.[14] In many local governments, positions such as clerk of courts, coroner, county clerk, district attorney, registrar of deeds, sheriff, and treasurer are often independently elected as well. The fragmentation of administrative organization means that, in many state and local governments, the chief executive may be responsible for the performance of state agencies, but many key officials with whom the executive must work have independent sources of political power.

Problems for Executive Management

The chief executive's primary job is to faithfully execute the laws. As we know, however, such execution is often difficult, for three reasons.

First, top elected executives rarely get their jobs because of their managerial ability and experience. Few have a lively interest in administrative matters, and they must tend to the politics to survive. Before Barack Obama became president, the largest organization he had run was his U.S. Senate office, which was microscopic in size compared with the executive branch. Presidents quite properly devote much of their energy to making foreign and domestic policy decisions and to resolving crises; they work to influence Congress and to build support with major interest groups and the public. Presidents know that they will not be judged by their administrative achievements, but they also know that their power depends on how well administration responds to their policies.[15] The same is true for governors, county executives, and

Can—and Should—Government Treat Citizens More Like "Customers"?
Theme: Accountability

The Obama administration made improving customer service one of the most important cross-agency goals in the president's management agenda. In a leading survey, "The US Customer Experience Index" conducted by Forrester Research, government showed improvement in 2016.

But it clearly has a long way to go. Among twenty-one industries that Forrester surveyed, the federal government ranked last.

The Forest Service was the federal government's top-rated agency, with a "good" index of interacting with the public. But, on average, federal agencies rated "poor," with some agencies scoring "very poor."

Not everyone agrees that citizens ought to be treated like "customers," since the customer relationship is based on market transactions and government is charged with administering programs passed by legislatures. But many reformers countered that government could—and should—improve citizens' interactions with government agencies. Moreover, they contend that citizens have come to expect better service from private companies and that, if government lags behind, it undermines public trust in government itself.

Source: Frank Konkel, "Despite Improvements, Government Still Bottom of the Barrel in Customer Experience," *Nextgov* (July 18, 2016), http://www.nextgov.com/technology-news/2016/07/despite-improvements-government-still-bottom-barrel-customer-experience/130003/.

mayors. One exception is when the government fails to solve major problems, which can prove fatal at the polls. For example, George W. Bush's "negative" ratings exceeded his "positives" following the debacle with Hurricane Katrina, and he never recovered politically.

Second, although top executives appoint cabinet and subcabinet officials, these officials often develop independent power bases among legislators and interest groups. Many of them don't stay on the job long. Presidential appointees, including department heads, their under-secretaries, and their assistant secretaries, often have brief tenures: two years is the median; a third remain in their positions for eighteen months or less, and only a third stay as long as three years.[16] Many of them are policy wonks who have never run a large organization. The door is always revolving at the top of the executive branch, at all levels of government. Moreover, most department heads rarely have a free hand in assembling their teams of subordinates, and that further weakens control over the executive branch operations.

Third, interdepartmental friction points have multiplied. As problems have become more complicated, most agencies find that they must work with others to get their job done, and that complicates the challenge of determining who is in charge of what. Because a department has relatively fewer things to itself, it is more difficult to hold the single department head responsible for its results. In New York City's Lower East Side, a September 2005 call for help led to a raging battle among emergency responders. A woman suffering from Alzheimer's disease was threatening to use a knife to cut herself. A fire department ambulance arrived to help. So did a volunteer Jewish ambulance crew. But an argument erupted between a member of the Jewish ambulance crew and a police officer. The police arrested the volunteer ambulance crew member and the battle spilled over into a noisy shouting match pitting the police against friends of the arrested crew member. New York State Assembly Speaker Sheldon Silver, who lived in the neighborhood, personally intervened to cool the tempers, but that

The annual Easter Egg Roll attracts an enormous crowd to the South Lawn of the White House. The tradition began in 1878 in the administration of President Rutherford B. Hayes and has continued since, except on a few days with bad weather and during World Wars I and II.

only enraged the police. Some officers contended that they had been forced to give the ambulance crew member preferential treatment because of political pressure. Supporters of the volunteer ambulance crew member contended that their volunteers could have given the woman better care, because they were from the neighborhood and spoke Yiddish. The dispute simmered for a long time. Should the city pay attention to the special neighborhood/area-based considerations in the case? Or should the functional specialization of the city's ambulance crew rule?[17]

Reinforcing these trends is the growing size, power, and reach of the executive office itself. Let's take a look at that at the federal level.

The Executive Office and the White House

As long ago as 1937, in transmitting to Congress the report of the President's Committee on Administrative Management (the Brownlow Committee), Franklin D. Roosevelt recognized the enormous burden of trying to manage the executive branch:

> The Committee has not spared me; they say what has been common knowledge for 20 years, that the President cannot adequately handle his responsibilities; that he is overworked; that it is humanly impossible, under the system which we have, for him fully to carry out his constitutional duty as Chief Executive. . . . With my predecessors who have said the same thing over and over again, I plead guilty.

> The plain fact is that the present Organization and equipment of the executive branch of the Government defeats the constitutional intent that there be a single responsible Chief Executive to coordinate and manage the departments and activities in accordance with the laws enacted by the Congress.[18]

As a first step, following the passage of the Reorganization Act of 1939, Roosevelt established the Executive Office of the President, transferred to it the Bureau of the Budget (from the Treasury Department), and set up its other units, among them the White House Office. The modern White House establishment was born.

From its relatively modest beginnings, with 570 employees in 1939, the Executive Office had expanded to include about 1,850 employees by 2013.[19] In addition, the White House has long had additional employees detailed to it from executive departments, many of them appointed to department rolls specifically for White House service.[20] "The swelling of the presidency," as Thomas Cronin has called it,[21] was not only quantitative.

Not only has the number of Executive Office employees increased, but their role has changed as well. In 1937, the Brownlow Committee proposed that six presidential assistants be added to the three White House secretaries (who dealt with Congress, the public, and the media). Contrast the powerful position of recent presidents' aides to the committee's stipulation of the role of the proposed assistants:

> These assistants, probably not exceeding six in number . . . would have no power to make decisions or issue instructions in their own right. They would not be interposed between the President and the heads of his departments. They would not be assistant presidents in any sense. . . . They would remain in the background, issue no orders, make no decisions, emit no public statements. . . . They should be men in whom the President has personal confidence and whose character and attitude is such that they would not attempt to exercise power on their own account. They should be possessed of high competence, great physical vigor, and a passion for anonymity.[22]

Surprisingly, eight former chiefs of staff to presidents from Eisenhower to Carter emphatically endorsed this description of the role of presidential assistants.[23] The "passion for anonymity" phrase has proven memorable, but it doesn't have much basis in reality.

The White House staff is now so large, multitiered, and specialized that it is increasingly hard to coordinate the coordinators.[24] In fact, says a Carter aide, "even those at the highest levels—assistants, deputy assistants, special assistants—don't see the President once a week or speak to him in any substantive way once a month," and that has since become even more pronounced.[25] Infighting among staff members to gain the president's ear has plagued every modern president. Even the tightly disciplined staff of George W. Bush found itself plagued by books and newspaper stories alleging deep rifts between key advisers. In the Obama administration, a large number of "czars" produced extra White House layers that distanced cabinet officials from the president and created new stovepipes inside the White House apparatus.

A frequent proposal to solve these problems is shrinking the size of the White House staff, but others have seen the staff's growth as the inevitable result of the president's increasing leadership responsibilities, which are attributed to a weakening of congressional leadership and of political parties, the rise of presidential use of public relations technologies, and other factors. "Instead of trying to wish it away," says political scientist Samuel Kernell, "the presence of a large, complex staff must be accepted as a given and its problems addressed forthrightly. . . . The President must give the staff clear direction and vigilantly oversee its performance."[26]

The White House office is full of policy advisers who cut large swaths across the government. In theory, their role is to provide a wide range of advice to the president in making policy. In practice, their growing power spills over into the operation of government programs, such that it's often difficult to separate advice from administration. In fact, presidents tend to like to hold close the control over administrative issues most important to them—although the Obama administration's neglect of details surrounding the launch of its landmark health reform program damaged the president greatly.

Of the major agencies of the Executive Office of the President, two warrant special attention: the **Office of Management and Budget** and the **National Security Council**.

The Office of Management and Budget

Chief executives have always needed help to manage the finances of their governments. At the federal level, that job began in the Bureau of the Budget, established in the Treasury Department in 1921 and moved to the new Executive Office of the President in 1939. In 1970, President Nixon renamed it the Office of Management and Budget (OMB). His intent was to elevate attention to management, but it's not surprising that the budget has always been the driving core of OMB's mission and culture. It has long been the largest unit of the Executive Office, accounting now for over a third of the executive employees.

At the center of OMB's power is its control of the budget process.[27] OMB analyzes the agencies' budget proposals, makes recommendations to the president for how much money should be provided, and compiles all of the requests into the budget that are formally transmitted to Congress. That gives OMB enormous power. However, because budgeting is virtually the only comprehensive decision-forcing process in the executive branch, the budget review gives OMB great insight into almost everything the federal government does, and that information is power over policy. In addition, OMB is the agency charged with implementing most government-wide policies, ranging from procurement standards to policies about websites, so its role takes OMB into every nook and cranny of the federal government's operations. Thus, in addition to budgetary review, OMB has important nonbudgetary functions:

- *Legislative clearance.* Agencies are required to submit to OMB their proposals for new legislation and amendments before transmitting them to Congress. OMB uses this legislative clearance function to ensure that agencies' proposals are "in accord with the president's program."
- *Review of legislation passed by Congress.* OMB is in charge of the time-pressured review of each bill passed by Congress and sent to the president for approval or veto. It rapidly canvasses the views of all concerned agencies about the appropriate action, ensures that the president is aware of those views when the president makes decisions, and often recommends what action the president should take.
- *Review of regulations proposed by agencies.* OMB reviews the principal regulations affecting the public that agencies propose to issue, which is a recent and powerful policy and management tool (as discussed in Chapter 13).

- *Management review.* OMB's efforts to improve administrative organization, management, and coordination in the executive branch are meant to help meet the president's responsibilities as the chief executive.
- *Intelligence about executive branch operations.* As they perform their jobs, OMB analysts are in constant contact with agency officials, about issues ranging from new rules to budget requests. OMB can therefore be a rich source of intelligence for the president, providing information on what is happening in all levels of policy generation and program management.

In the course of its life, the Bureau of the Budget and then OMB developed a tradition of serving both the long-term institution of the presidency and the short-term, incumbent president—a difficult balance to keep. Hugh Heclo has described the job as stressing "neutral competence."[28] OMB fills most positions in the agency with career civil servants, attracted by the opportunity for a powerful role and lasting impact. That, in turn, helps provide the White House with a longer-term institutional memory than would be possible in the normal four-year election cycle.[29]

This tradition of service to both the incumbent president and the institution of the presidency has been at the core of OMB's role. Its tradition of neutral competence came under enormous pressure during the Nixon administration, when the president's OMB directors and deputy directors were political activists, making political speeches, advocating the president's policies at congressional hearings, and defending massive impoundments of appropriated funds until a number of courts ruled the impoundments illegal. A new layer of political appointees was inserted between the director and the career civil servants: in 1974, nearly two-thirds of the heads of OMB's major offices and examining divisions had one year's experience or less in their posts (compared to one-tenth in 1960).[30]

In the 1980s, OMB enjoyed a resurgence of power. Reagan's first director of the budget, David Stockman, led the administration's top-priority policy of cutting spending on domestic programs; he centralized decision making in the bureau with little input from the agencies.[31] In other functions as well, some of them enhanced by legislation and executive orders, the bureau has become so fully in tune with the president's political objectives that it has recaptured roles earlier yielded to White House staff members. The dozen or so high-level political appointees in OMB, serving for one to three years, ensure that the political orientation will prevail and, as the budget has become even more central to federal policy in the 1990s and 2000s, the bureau's resurgence has continued. During the enormous budget battles of the 2010s, OMB was a central player in the ongoing negotiations.

The management side of OMB has struggled to play the role envisioned when the "M" was added to the Bureau of the Budget. In one view, "Management has become largely ad hoc, short-term responses to immediate political problems. The management 'initiatives' have been geared principally toward those activities which promise a quick political pay-off or have the potential for a salutary impact on budgetary 'spending.'"[32] Despairing of invigorating OMB's management work, a panel of the National Academy of Public Administration urged transfer of that work to a new Office of Federal Management, in the Executive Office.[33] Opponents argued that such an office would lack the power over agencies that inclusion in OMB confers: when budgeting and management improvement are in a single agency, budgeting is sure to predominate, but putting the management function into a new agency could well weaken the top-level focus on administration even further by separating it from the budgetary muscle that never fails to attract the attention of executive agencies and congressional committees. That logic underlay George W. Bush's management agenda to recouple administrative efforts with budgetary clout (see Chapter 7). This recurring debate demonstrates the sharp dilemmas in which central budget offices such as OMB always find themselves: the tension between long and short term, between management and budgeting, between inputs and performance. It also says a great deal about the role of public administration in a process that is inevitably political.

The National Security Council

The National Security Council (NSC) was established by statute in 1947, "to advise the President with respect to the integration of domestic, foreign, and military policies relating to the national security."[34] Its statutory members are the president, the vice president, the secretary of state, and the secretary of defense; also attending the meetings as statutory advisers are the chair of the Joint Chiefs of Staff and the director of the Central Intelligence Agency, and the president may ask others to attend as well.[35] An elaborate structure of interagency committees reviews foreign, defense, international economic, and intelligence policy issues and anticipates and manages crisis situations.[36] Recommendations on policy issues are submitted to the NSC but, its role being advisory, the president retains the decision-making responsibility.

Over time, the NSC has gradually become the focus of presidential foreign policymaking. Indeed, that growing power has regularly rankled secretaries of defense and, especially, secretaries of state. It is no wonder that some perceive that the United States has two State Departments.[37] Reinforcing the complaints is the growing size of the NSC's staff. In the George H. W. Bush administration, its size was about fifty. By the end of the Obama administration, it had grown to 350. Critics complain that the growing size and reach of the staff has led to increasing micromanagement of policy and operations from the White House. White House officials counter that, with foreign policy issues becoming more important and more complex, the president needs help.[38]

The NSC has become more important for several reasons. Its director has special access to the president and close proximity to the Oval Office. Disputes among executive branch agencies, like State, Defense, and the CIA, are frequent, and the president often looks to a close adviser to help arbitrate them. And, with a team of advisers close at hand, the NSC can often move quickly on fast-breaking policy issues. Add to that the fact that the NSC's head is appointed by the president without Senate confirmation. That gives the NSC an extra measure of operating flexibility.

Critics have argued that the NSC staff should be trimmed and that more power ought to be given back to the operating agencies. As one recently departed high-level official in the Obama administration explained, "If assistant secretaries, deputy assistants, don't have a sense of authorship and accountability, they tend to get beaten down." In addition, the official explained, "When large agencies—the Defense Department or State or others—don't feel as much a part of the takeoff, implementation tends to suffer. It's just human nature."[39] Presidents have fought efforts to shrink their NSC staff, because having trusted advisers close by gives them an extra measure of confidence in dealing with hard questions. But the NSC case frames the fundamental dilemma: How should administrative agencies balance the role of staff agencies like the NSC with the operational role of line agencies like State, Defense, and the CIA?

E-GOVERNMENT

The rise of desktop computers and the Internet in the 1990s led to a radically new approach to some of government's organizational problems. Government officials began recognizing that citizens did not necessarily need to come to government to transact public business. The spread of always-available electronic connections made it possible to build systems to allow citizens to file their taxes, renew their motor vehicle registrations, check on traffic congestion, obtain a police report, pay a traffic ticket, or apply for a job. In almost every government, citizens can connect electronically to access a vast array of services.

The IRS, for example, has increasingly encouraged taxpayers to file their taxes electronically. About 129 million taxpayers filed online for 2015—more than 90 percent of all returns, up from 31 percent in 2001.[40] The IRS saved money by avoiding the costs of printing, mailing, and then processing millions of paper returns. Electronically filed returns did not have to be hand-keyed into the IRS computer system, and they even proved more accurate than the paper filings, since private-market computer programs such as TurboTax and TaxCut had already double-checked the figures. Taxpayers received their refunds far more quickly, often in just two weeks, by electronic deposits made directly to their bank accounts. In Phoenix, Arizona, citizens can conduct a wide range of transactions with the government without having to leave their keyboards. They can get permits and pay taxes and fines. They can sign up for classes on irrigation and landscaping, get a parking permit or buy surplus city equipment, view city maps, or watch the city's online television channel, all at http://phoenix.gov/eservices. The array of e-government services has vastly expanded since the early 1990s, and it's now universal.

The growth of e-government, as the movement is known, has rapidly transformed the operations of many governmental services and has changed the way government connects with citizens.[41] President Obama developed more than 30 million Twitter followers. Newark Mayor Cory Booker had 1.3 million followers and became famous for tweeting from the cabs of snowplows as workers helped the city recover from storms.

E-government has raised several important implications. First, it has tremendous potential for improving government's performance. It allows government to deliver services on citizens' own schedules, allowing them to determine when they want to conduct transactions. Instead of visiting the motor vehicle administration or the tax office, citizens can often conduct transactions online. That can make their lives easier—and save the government money. The U.S. Customs and Border Protection agency developed a new series of "trusted traveler" programs, including the Global Entry program that allows air travelers to be screened in advance and then bypass long immigration lines when reentering the country, just by scanning their passport and fingerprints at a handy kiosk.

Second, e-government can enhance the ability of citizens to connect more easily with government. Web portals such as the federal government's USA.gov and the Commonwealth of Virginia's Virginia.gov allow citizens to think in terms of the services they want to access, without necessarily having to determine in advance which government agency provides them. For example, it often takes some time to figure out that in order to obtain a passport, one needs to obtain a photograph from a private photographer, visit a post office (run by the U.S. Postal Service), and submit a passport application to the U.S. State Department. On USA.gov, one can simply type in "passport" to find these instructions.

Third, the rise of e-government raises questions of access and equity. By 2013, nearly three-fourths of Americans had high-speed Internet access in their homes, and 84 percent had a computer. Senior citizens, less affluent Americans, and less educated citizens tended to use the Internet less.[42] Technological barriers are falling, but inequities remain. Moreover, the explosion

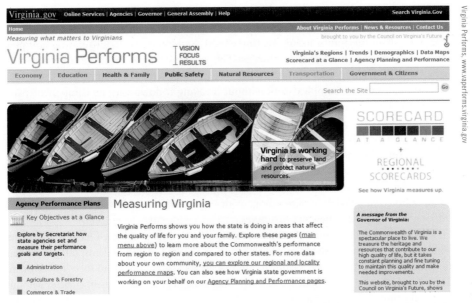

Virginia Performs, www.vaperforms.virginia.gov

Online services have transformed the way governments communicate with their citizens, and have led to fundamental efforts to measure and report government performance.

of technology has created new splits, between individuals who text or use social media (such as Twitter, Facebook, and emerging social networks or apps) and those who do not.

Fourth, the advent of e-government also raises significant organizational questions. Freed from dependence on traditional government bureaucracies, e-government can operate in a loose, even invisible network, which offers the chance for creating new virtual strategies for linking governmental organizations. Such technology is unlikely to solve government's eternal coordination problems, but it does offer new strategies and tactics for doing so. However, in attacking the problem through information systems instead of through bureaucratic hierarchies, e-government also has the potential for radically altering the existing patterns of bureaucratic behavior, authority, and power. It raises serious questions of security and privacy, to ensure that sensitive information is kept safe. Moreover, as Jane E. Fountain suggested, the e-government movement "may allow bureaucrats less opportunity to use their accumulated experience and judgment, or tacit knowledge, to consider exceptional cases that do not conform to standardized rule-based systems." Indeed, she concluded, "The state is being reconstructed as organizational actors enact new technologies to reshape relationships in the state and the economy."[43] Public officials have sometimes found themselves surprised by issues that bubble up in blogs, and they have sometimes scrambled to address virtual issues that they had not previously encountered through their traditional communication channels.

Given the tremendous changes in information technology over the past half-generation, it is hard to guess where the next generation will take us. Although, as one study concluded, "E-gov is not yet the 'killer app' among the available tools to contact government,"[44] it is clear that it will continue to develop, with government agencies creating strategies for new applications and other real-time links between citizens and their governments. These technological changes will present deep and fundamental questions for the operation of government—and for the future of democracy.

CONCLUSION

The executive function is about creating effective strategies for coordinating complex systems—and to deliver value to citizens. The goal has long been to ensure continuity between policymaking and administration, yet the best path is anything but clear. It is impossible to manage complex work without breaking it down into its component parts and then building strong competence in bureaus to carry it out. But dividing complex jobs into bureaus risks creating overlaps for some problems and gaps through which others may fall. Coordination is essential for administration, and organization is perhaps the most basic tool for achieving it. No matter how hard they try, however, government officials can never fully solve the coordination problem, and their efforts to solve some parts of the problem can sometimes create new and unexpected issues. The search for the solution to coordination problems is never-ending, with e-government and web-based technology offering hard-to-predict new opportunities.

This fundamental dilemma of administration points to three problems. One that afflicts the whole executive branch is the interconnectedness, in the end, of all problems; this means that top officials must break problems down into manageable parts in order to solve any of them. Top officials then face the challenge of developing enough expertise in their agencies without having the process break down into insulated units that don't talk to each other. The second is that executives must increasingly work through interwoven policy tools to get their work done. Third is the perennial distinction between those who carry out government's work—"line" officials—and those who provide advice—"staff" officials. Staff officials rarely want to stop at giving advice, but top officials don't want to simply follow the counsel of their line managers without careful checking by the staff. These are deep and enduring issues, and we turn to them in the next chapter.

CASE 5.1

The Boston Marathon Bombing: Effective Coordinated Response

In the week between the tragic bombing at the 2013 Boston Marathon and the surviving suspect's arraignment in his hospital room, we saw how far homeland security has come since the September 11 terrorist attacks. The message is overwhelmingly good.

We saw tremendous bravery in the moments after the bombs exploded, as citizens and first responders raced toward the victims without regard to whether more bombs were primed to explode. Civilians applied tourniquets to prevent some of the wounded from bleeding to death. The

field station, originally set up to treat chilled, dehydrated runners, quickly became a triage station. The city's network of ambulances, police, and hospitals responded magnificently, in large part because they had practiced over the years for just such a day.

In the immediate aftermath of the blasts, we learned again the fundamental lessons: all homeland security events are local, beginning with local consequences that require local officials to respond. We learned that effective response depends on robust relationships among people who have learned to work together before events happen. And we learned that skilled, problem-focused improvisation can fill in the gaps.

Moreover, we've also learned again that good homeland security is intergovernmental, interagency, intersectoral—and enlists ordinary Americans. While the FBI managed the scene, it was a regional Massachusetts Bay Transportation Authority SWAT team that took the suspect down. The first photos of the captured suspect showed federal tactical officers wearing FBI and ATF gear. And don't forget, during the manhunt for the suspect, it was a citizen who found him hiding in a boat. Citizens often worked the front lines, making "Boston Strong" more than a T-shirt message and demonstrating that "if you see something, say something" is far more than a cliché.

The very same week of the alleged bomber's arraignment, the opening of the George W. Bush Presidential Center recalled these same balance-of-responsibility questions. In the center's Decision Points Theater, visitors are asked to relive one of four big moments from the Bush presidency. Listening to briefings from former White House chiefs of staff, participants are immersed in the events as they unfold. In the case of Hurricane Katrina, for example, they're asked what should President Bush do—deploy federal troops or rely on local forces?

The contrast between Boston's lessons and the theater's questions could not be bigger. The Bush administration's initial response to Katrina was anything but successful, with citizens stuck at the Superdome and political support crumbling. During Katrina, the questions about who was in charge and whether to deploy federal troops or rely on local forces preoccupied the Bush White House. In Boston, we learned yet again that this is precisely the wrong question. We've been crippled most when we battle over who's in charge; we succeed best when we send out the best we have to those who need it most.

This is what retired Coast Guard Admiral Thad Allen calls "unity of effort" instead of "unity of command." After the battle between New Orleans, Baton Rouge, and Washington hamstrung the government's Katrina response and cost FEMA Director Michael Brown his job, President Bush sent in Allen. The no-nonsense admiral pushed the bureaucratic squabbling aside, figured out who had which assets to solve which problems, and promised everyone on the front lines that he had their backs. In remarkably short order, Katrina moved from a monument of government failure to a model of effective response.

In Boston, unity of effort drove success in the federal-state-local-private-public-nonprofit-civilian response, just as

it eventually did after Katrina when Allen took the helm. The badges on the uniforms didn't matter as much as the capacity to get the job done. And the job got done.

The prevention side remains a huge challenge, and stories continue to trickle out of dots unconnected among federal agencies. But on the response side, we've come light years since the painful days of the 2001 terrorist attacks and the 2005 hurricane. It's heartening to see that we know how to learn, and that we've been able to apply winning strategies to tragedies like Superstorm Sandy and the Boston Marathon bombing.

The Bush Presidential Center poses the big and irresistible "who's in charge" question. The remarkably brave response in Boston shows us why this is the wrong question. Effective response begins with a strong, integrated, practiced-in-advance local response coupled with a nimble problem-solving ability.

More fundamentally, we've learned again that our really important challenges are too big for any one agency, any one level of government, or even government itself to try to control. Someone has to be in charge to make sure that coordination happens. But the job of the field commander isn't barking orders; it's identifying the assets that are needed, who has them, and how to get them to where they're needed. In the end, what works is focusing more on solving that problem than solving who's in charge.

QUESTIONS TO CONSIDER

1. Consider the questions posed to visitors to the Bush presidential library. What would *you* do in the midst of a crisis like Katrina or the Boston Marathon bombing: Deploy federal troops or rely on local agencies?

2. Now step back. Are these cases so different that comparisons make little sense? If so, how would you sort out the question of who ought to respond to which problems? If you think they are alike enough to make comparisons, how would you draw lessons?

3. What lessons do these large-scale events have for organizational theory and effective government operations?

Note: This case comes from my column in *Governing* (June 2013), http://www.governing.com/columns/potomac-chronicle/col-boston-bombing-highlights-homeland-security-done-right.html.

CASE 5.2

Which Way for Cheese? Conflicting Policies at the U.S. Department of Agriculture

Not long ago, the Domino's pizza chain was in trouble. Sales were down and even the company's advertisements acknowledged it was not making a very good pizza. But Dairy Management, a nonprofit trade association, came riding to the rescue, with pizza design help and $12 million for a new marketing campaign. The result was a new pizza with 40 percent more cheese, and people loved it. Sales soared and the company began to climb out of the fast-food cellar.

Dairy Management also helped Taco Bell invent a new steak quesadilla, which mixed together pepper jack, mozzarella, and cheddar cheeses, along with a creamy sauce. People loved it, in part because it had eight times more cheese than most other items on the Taco Bell menu.

Dairy Management has become a huge player in the food business.[1] Americans eat an average of 33 pounds of cheese each year, and Dairy Management aims to increase that total. With its $140 million annual budget, it has worked with Pizza Hut to develop its Cheesy Bites pizza, with Wendy's on the Double Melt sandwich, and with Burger King on the Angus Bacon cheeseburger. The organization's goal is to convince Americans to eat more cheese—and to expand the market for cheese producers. In 2007, its efforts increased cheese sales of almost 30 million pounds, and cheese producers love it.[2] The association has been tremendously successful in bringing more cheese to restaurant menus and into supermarkets, and it was behind the wildly successful "Got Milk?" campaign.

Dairy farmers contribute to a fund to help promote the consumption of dairy products. The U.S. Department of Agriculture (USDA) collects the funds and disburses them under a program created by Congress.[3] The program is self-funded, but USDA oversees its operations to ensure the activities are consistent with the law that created the nonprofit corporation designed to encourage dairy production. In addition, USDA regularly reports on its operations to Congress.[4] Is it a governmental organization? No. Is it connected to the federal government? Yes, through the collection and distribution of money and through policy oversight.

In other parts of its operation, USDA is working hard to encourage Americans to make so-called healthier food choices. It's easy to blast past government-recommended levels of saturated fat consumption with a couple of slices of Domino's pizza. USDA's Nutrition.gov program is making an aggressive effort to encourage Americans to reduce their consumption of fatty foods, especially saturated fats. It points out that "a healthy eating plan is one that:

- Emphasizes fruits, vegetables, whole grains, and fat-free or low-fat milk and milk products.
- Includes lean meats, poultry, fish, beans, eggs, and nuts.
- Is low in saturated fats, trans fats, cholesterol, salt (sodium), and added sugars."[5]

First Lady Michelle Obama added her own voice to the healthy eating campaign. She told the American Restaurant Association that "One local survey found that 90 percent of those menus includes mac and cheese—our children's favorite; 80 percent includes chicken fingers; 60 includes burgers or cheeseburgers." It's important, she said, to "make a commitment to promote vegetables and fruits and whole grains on every part of every menu. We can make portion sizes smaller and emphasize quality over quantity. And we can help create a culture—imagine this—where our kids ask for healthy options instead of resisting them." She concluded by saying, "I hope that each of you will do your part to give our kids the future that we all know they deserve."[6]

QUESTIONS TO CONSIDER

1. What do you make of these contradictory policies within a single federal department: one that encourages the consumption of dairy products and another that urges their consumption in moderation?

2. Do you think it makes a difference that the USDA's role in the Dairy Management association is indirect?

3. If you were the leader of USDA, would you have an obligation to reconcile these competing programs? Or would you view it as an inevitable product of the political battles within American pluralism?

NOTES

1. See Dairy Management Inc.'s website, http://www.dairyinfo.com.

2. Michael Moss, "While Warning about Fat, U.S. Pushes Cheese Sales," New York Times (November 6, 2010), http://www.nytimes.com/2010/11/07/us/07fat.html.

3. See Dairy Today Editors, "Dairy Management, Inc. Answers New York Times Allegations"

(November 15, 2010), http://www.agweb.com/article/dairy_management_inc_answers_new_york_times_allegations/.

4. See U.S. Department of Agriculture, *Report to Congress on the National Dairy Promotion and Research Program and the National Fluid Milk Processor Promotion Program* (July 1, 2002), https://www.ams.usda.gov/sites/default/files/media/2012%20-%20Dairy%20Report%20to%20Congress.pdf.

5. See U.S. Department of Agriculture, "Finding Your Way to a Healthier You: Based on the *Dietary Guidelines for Americans*," http://health.gov/dietaryguidelines/dga2005/document/html/brochure.htm.

6. Michelle Obama, "Remarks by the First Lady in Address to the National Restaurant Association Meeting" (September 13, 2010), https://www.whitehouse.gov/the-press-office/2010/09/13/remarks-first-lady-address-national-restaurant-association-meeting.

CASE 5.3

Partly Cloudy? Wyoming Moves to Google Apps for Government

In October 2010, the state of Wyoming announced it was moving all 10,000 of its employees to Google Apps for Government (http://gov.googleapps.com). The result, Google proudly announced, would save the state $1 million per year and bring all state employees, for the first time, to a common electronic platform. "We welcome Wyoming to the cloud," Google said.[1]

It's always good, of course, to save a lot of money. But what is "the cloud"? In one respect, it's simply another name for the Internet. More broadly, it's a way of separating the details of computer systems from users—software providers create easy interactions with the key programs that users need, and then manage the back-end Internet systems in ways that are transparent (and therefore unimportant) to users. Web browsers provide the key point of connection to the world. Software and data are stored on servers. Computer analysts have long used cloud-like drawings to depict these connections, and "the cloud" has come to capture the broad approach of web-based computing.

For Google, it was one of a series of agreements it had negotiated with government agencies. Los Angeles and Orlando had both signed up with Google. So did government departments in Colorado, Kansas, and New Mexico. But its mega-competitor, Microsoft, was scarcely standing still. New York City signed a deal to bring 100,000 of its employees to Microsoft's cloud applications. The city built this arrangement into a much broader effort, nicknamed SimpliCity, to streamline the city's work and improve its service to citizens. In its previous system, the city managed forty different software licenses and even more maintenance and support packages. The cloud approach, city officials believed, would allow city officials to collaborate more easily across a single software platform.[2] In addition, New York Mayor Michael Bloomberg and Microsoft CEO Steve Ballmer also agreed that the city would host Microsoft's Imagine Cup 2011 worldwide finals, a global competition bringing high school and college students together to solve problems through technology. As Stephen Goldsmith, New York's deputy mayor for operations, explained, "We took advantage of the competitive moment," in an arrangement that would save $50 million in the next five years.[3]

©iStock.com/roccomontoya

QUESTIONS TO CONSIDER

1. As technology creates new opportunities, how do you think that government can—and should—use technology to increase its efficiency and provide better service to its citizens?

2. Do you think that competition between private companies, such as Google and Microsoft, enhances government's ability to get a good deal? How might this case have worked differently if either Google or Microsoft had been in the game as the sole provider?

3. Since the cloud relies on the Internet, the servers provide services that could be located anywhere. For example, some of the leading cloud computing companies are working to expand their operations to China. If you were a government information technology manager, would you be concerned about basing your mission on technologies that rely heavily on elements that aren't transparent to you? Would you use different strategies for different parts of your mission—perhaps maintaining the most confidential work on your own servers and relying on the cloud for the rest of your work—or would you worry that such a divided strategy might compromise the efficiencies you are seeking?

4. Many state and local governments have encountered serious difficulty in managing their information technology resources in recent years. The reason, most often, is that governments have not had sufficient expertise in-house to assess the claims and promises that private companies made. If you were a government official charged with making these decisions, what steps would you take to make sure that you were in the best position to make the best decisions for your government and for the citizens it serves?

NOTES

1. Dan Israel, "Wyoming Is Going Google" (October 27, 2010), http://googleenterprise.blogspot.com/2010/10/wyoming-is-going-google.html.

2. Marc LaVorgna and Jake Goldman, "Mayor Bloomberg Welcomes Students to the First Day of School at Gregorino Luperón High School for Science and Mathematics" (September 9, 2013), http://www1.nyc.gov/office-of-the-mayor/news/297-13/mayor-bloomberg-welcomes-students-parents-faculty-staff-the-first-day-school-at#/0.

3. Kevin McCaney, "NYC Gets Citywide Deal for Microsoft Cloud," *Microsoft Certified Professional Magazine* (October 21, 2010), http://mcpmag.com/articles/2010/10/21/nyc-gets-citywide-deal-for-microsoft-cloud-apps.aspx.

 # CASE 5.4

How to Fix the VA?

In December 2013, Dr. Sam Foote decided to retire from his post as an internist at the Phoenix VA hospital. He had spent a long career at the VA and had become increasingly concerned about issues at the Phoenix facility. Some veterans, he told *Arizona Republic* reporter Dennis Wagner, had died while awaiting care. Perhaps even worse, he said, VA staffers were falsifying records about how long vets were waiting for appointments.[1]

Foote's allegations triggered a national scandal. Investigators found similar problems at other VA medical centers, and the problem of falsifying wait times proved to be an epidemic throughout the VA. Auditors from the Government Accountability Office and the VA's own inspector general's office found a host of problems. News coverage was withering. Few interest groups are as well organized as those for veterans, and critics pounced on the department for failing those who had sacrificed so much to serve their country. Months of new revelations finally led to the resignation in May 2014 of VA Secretary Eric Shinseki, a former general, chief of staff of the U.S. Army, and decorated combat veteran who had won two Purple Hearts for being wounded in battle. The turmoil had undermined Shinseki's ability to lead the department, the White House concluded. In accepting the secretary's resignation, President Obama said, "We don't have time for distractions." Instead, "We need to fix the problem."[2]

Part of the effort to fix the VA led to the creation of a Commission on Government Care. The twelve-member commission met over two years to examine a host of options to fix the VA. One proposal that gained a great deal of early support was to privatize much of the VA's operations. The VA is the nation's largest health care system, managing more than 85 million outpatient visits a year by 8.3 million veterans. Critics argued that the VA had simply become too large, and its bureaucracy too wrapped in red tape, to serve veterans well. Moreover, despite the VA's vast network of hospitals and health care centers—152 major medical centers and 1,400 clinics—many vets faced long drives to get care.[3] Why not give vets vouchers, some reformers suggested, and allow them to seek care from local health care providers instead of forcing them to go to VA facilities?

The plan seemed to make great sense. And it also had the quiet backing of several important conservative groups, who favored private provision of services wherever possible and saw the choice program as an opportunity to shrink the number of government employees and to weaken a large government agency. The commission, however, was blunt in its assessment of the choice program: "Both the design and implementation of the law have proven to be flawed," it concluded.[4] The choice program in fact provided vets with little choice, and management of the program by the two contractors selected to administer it proved very troubled. Creating the administrative structure to connect vets with private providers, finding providers willing to accept the government's pay for the care they provided, and overseeing the quality of the care all proved to be far more difficult than reformers assumed at the beginning.

In addition, supporters of the VA argued that its health care system provided distinctive benefits to vets. For some conditions, like hearing loss or routine medical care, vets had similar issues as most patients. But for many conditions facing veterans, ranging from post-traumatic stress disorder to care for war wounds, community-based facilities often lacked the special skills needed to provide the best possible care.

Moreover, veterans really like the care they receive once they're inside the system. They like being recognized for their service, they like the chance to mingle with other vets, and they like the services they get.

The commission recognized the enormous challenges that the VA system faced, particularly in attracting enough health care providers to deal with the number of vets looking for care. Rather than funding vets to seek care outside the system, the commission argued that the VA itself should be transformed. Its key recommendations were as follows:

- The VHA [the Veterans Health Administration] Care System governing board . . . should develop a national delivery system strategy, including criteria and standards for creating the VHA Care System, comprising high-performing, integrated, community-based health care networks, including VHA providers and facilities, Department of Defense and other federally funded providers and facilities, and VHA-credentialed community providers and facilities.
- Integrated community-based health care networks should be developed with local VHA leadership input and knowledge to ensure that their composition is reflective of local needs and veterans' preferences.
- Integrated, community-based health care networks must include existing VHA special-emphasis resources (e.g., spinal cord injury, blind rehabilitation, mental health, prosthetics, etc.). In areas for which VHA has special expertise, VHA should also play the role of enhancing care in the local communities by collaborating with community care providers to implement services that may not exist, focused on the needs of veterans (e.g., expansion of integrated primary care/mental health care).
- Networks should be built out in a well-planned, phased approach, overseen by the new governing board, which determines the criteria for the phases to ensure effective execution of the strategy.
- VHA should credential community providers. To qualify for participation in community networks, providers must be fully credentialed with appropriate education, training, and experience; provide veterans access that meets VHA standards; demonstrate high-quality clinical and utilization outcomes; demonstrate military cultural competency; and have capability for interoperable data exchange.
- Providers in the networks should be paid using the most contemporary payment approaches available to incentivize quality and appropriate utilization of health care services (i.e., using Medicare Access and CHIP Reauthorization Act of 2015 [MACRA] physician payment methodology being proposed by the Centers for Medicare and Medicaid Services).
- The highest priority access to the VHA Care System should be provided to service-connected veterans, and low-income veterans should also be of high priority.
- The current time and distance criteria for community care access (thirty days and forty miles) should be eliminated.
- Veterans choose a primary care provider from all credentialed primary care providers in the VHA Care System.
- All primary care providers in the VHA Care System coordinate care for veterans.
- The VHA Care System should provide overall health care coordination and navigation support for veterans.
- Veterans choose their specialty care providers from all credentialed specialty care providers in the VHA Care System with a referral from their primary care provider.

Many critics of the current system were stunned by the commission's recommendations, because it focused on fixing the VA's health care system instead of transforming it into a private network. Insiders, who expected a revolutionary change to the VA's current system, were pleasantly surprised. But the hard work of building a new system to solve the problems identified by Dennis Wagner and other investigators remained.

QUESTIONS TO CONSIDER

1. If you were a vet, would you prefer to go to a facility dedicated especially to deal with the problems of you and fellow vets—or would you prefer to go to a local health care provider?

2. Just what kind of promise should America make to its vets—and how best should it design a system to keep that promise?

3. Consider the basic strategic question here: private versus governmental delivery of health care for vets. What are the pros and cons of the two options?

4. What kind of system would you put in place to track progress in implementing the commission's recommendations, so the problems don't perpetuate themselves?

NOTES

1. "Timeline: The Road to VA Wait-Time Scandal," *Arizona Republic* (April 7, 2016), http://www.azcentral.com/story/news/arizona/politics/2014/05/10/timeline-road-va-wait-time-scandal/8932493/.

2. Michael D. Shear and Richard A. Oppel Jr., "V.A. Chief Resigns in Face of Furor on Delayed Care," *New York Times* (May 30, 2014), http://www.nytimes.com/2014/05/31/us/politics/eric-shinseki-resigns-as-veterans-affairs-head.html?_r=0.

3. U.S. Department of Veterans Affairs, "Veterans Health Administration," http://www.va.gov/health/findcare.asp.

4. Commission on Care, *Commission on Care: Final Report* (June 30, 2016), p. 24, https://commissiononcare.sites.usa.gov/files/2016/07/Commission-on-Care_Final-Report_063016_FOR-WEB.pdf.

KEY CONCEPTS

FOR FURTHER READING

Arnold, Peri E. *Making the Managerial Presidency: Comprehensive Reorganization Planning, 1905–1980.* Princeton, N.J.: Princeton University Press, 1986.

Campbell, Colin. *Managing the Presidency: Carter, Reagan, and the Search for Executive Harmony.* Pittsburgh: University of Pittsburgh Press, 1986.

Fesler, James W. *Area and Administration.* Tuscaloosa: University of Alabama Press, 2008.

Fountain, Jane E. *Building the Virtual State: Information Technology and Institutional Change.* Washington, D.C.: Brookings Institution, 2001.

Heclo, Hugh. *A Government of Strangers: Executive Politics in Washington.* Washington, D.C.: Brookings Institution, 1977.

Hess, Stephen, and James Pfiffner. *Organizing the Presidency.* Washington, D.C.: Brookings Institution, 2003.

Nathan, Richard P. *The Administrative Presidency.* New York: Wiley, 1983.

Perri 6. *E-Governance: Styles of Political Judgment in the Information Age Polity.* New York: Palgrave, 2004.

Seidman, Harold. *Politics, Position, and Power: The Dynamics of Federal Organization.* 5th ed. New York: Oxford University Press, 1998.

SUGGESTED WEBSITES

The National Academy of Public Administration conducts excellent research on the management of the executive branch and on management problems within individual agencies, making its reports available on its website, **www.napawash.org**. In addition, the Government Accountability Office, **www.gao.gov**, is an invaluable source for analysis of both management and policy issues.

For information about employment trends in the federal government, see the Office of Personnel Management's Federal Employment Statistics webpage, **www.opm.gov/ feddata**.

Moreover, the Partnership for Public Service produces a vast and invaluable reservoir of research on the management of the federal government, ranging from its "best places to work" study to analyses on the roles of agencies like OMB. See **https://ourpublicservice.org**.

There is an enormous amount of information about e-government available on the web. An excellent foundation for exploring the federal government's websites is the federal portal **www.usa.gov**. Most state and local governments have webpages and portals as well; among the very good ones are those for the Commonwealth of Virginia, **www.virginia.gov**, and for the city of Phoenix, **http://phoenix.gov**.

$SAGE edge™
for CQ Press

WANT A BETTER GRADE?

Get the tools you need to sharpen your study skills. Access practice quizzes, eFlashcards, video, and multimedia at **edge.sagepub.com/kettl7e.**

6
ORGANIZATION PROBLEMS

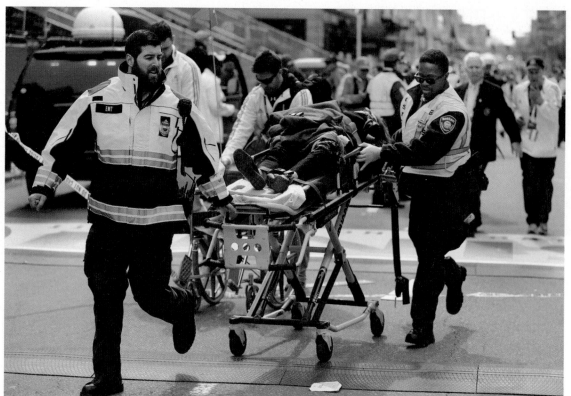

John Tlumacki/The Boston Globe via Getty Image

The response of emergency workers in the aftermath of the Boston Marathon bombing in 2013 proved remarkably effective. A massive manhunt, involving federal, state, and local law enforcement officials, tracked down the two bombers within days of the explosion.

If there's anything that most people think they know about public administration, it's that it just doesn't work well. News reports are full of tales ranging from overpayment for military equipment to excessive delays in responding to fire calls. *Fortune* began a story about city government by saying they "aren't exactly known for innovation. 'Get in line,' 'fill out this form' and 'you need a permit' are the bureaucracy's invariable responses to virtually any question."[1] Cynicism reigns.

In truth, most governmental programs work well most of the time. But Americans are never far from their revolutionary spirit and bureaucracy is often the target. Because their expectations about government are often very (sometimes impossibly) high, anything short of exceptional performance tends to disappoint. Tales of waste, fraud, and abuse only feed the worst fears of angry taxpayers. A sure-fire staple of television newsmagazines is the "can you believe your government did this?" story. There are far fewer stories reporting that "emergency responders risked lives to save citizens."

Of course, private-sector organizations are scarcely immune to waste. The U.S. Environmental Protection Agency, for example, estimates that Americans dispose of 35 million tons of food every year.[2] Behind every business is a collection of tales of mistakes, failed products, and miscalculations. Three U.S. airlines shut down in just one week in 2008: Skybus, ATA, and Aloha Airlines. Several large banks collapsed in the 2008–2009 economic meltdown, and one of the world's proudest, oldest, and largest investment banks, Lehman Brothers, disappeared almost overnight. Smaller miscalculations are simply buried in corporate balance sheets. Success comes to corporations that solve problems and make money. Those that don't will go under. In government, however, public administrators don't have the choice of going out of business—their missions exist by law, and the law requires them to administer their programs. The public expects high performance as a matter of routine, and government often ends up with jobs that the private sector will not or cannot do. Problems with—and complaints about—how government handles those chores are inevitable and are sometimes splashed across the headlines for everyone to see.

Many organizational problems have their roots in politics because, as Jack Knott and Gary Miller point out, the very choice of organizational structure itself "is inherently political; we must ask 'who gets what?' from any institutional arrangement."[3] Politics and performance become intertwined in charting what agencies do, how they do it, and how they might work better. These basic puzzles, as Herbert Kaufman recognized in a classic 1956 article, have long revolved around three basic organizational values: **neutral competence**, **executive leadership**, and **representativeness**.[4] The quest for *neutral competence* calls for the creation of a highly skilled bureaucracy insulated from the political interference that can undermine efficiency. This does not mean that

- Understand the sources of organizational performance problems

- Examine the strategies to improve coordination

- Chart the advantages and disadvantages of structural reorganization to solve organizational problems

bureaucracy is politically unaccountable or unresponsive; rather, it means that organizational designers must minimize political meddling in issues that address the technical parts of administration. The quest for *executive leadership* calls for a strong elected executive—president, governor, mayor—and strong and loyal department heads, all politically chosen. It also calls for a strong hierarchy that ensures the responsiveness of organizational units to the elected executive's policy priorities. The quest for *representativeness* calls for organizational arrangements that respond to legislative interests and to the clienteles most affected by agency decisions.

In American government, we have long professed strong allegiance to each of these values; we seek them all, simultaneously and enthusiastically. Because they obviously conflict, we never quite get what we want from bureaucracy. Therefore, bureaucracy can never give us all of the contradictory things we ask of it. As a result, we have a relentless need to tinker and reform. Sometimes we find a better solution, but often we simply substitute one set of values for another. One reform then sets the stage for the next round of political complaint and administrative reform.

THE SEARCH FOR EFFECTIVE ORGANIZATION

Why, despite eternal calls for better administration, do organizational problems recur? Consider the ongoing problem of coordinating emergency response in New York City. In 1988, the New York City police and fire commissioners nearly came to blows in the mayor's presence because of their departments' long rivalry over the handling of emergencies and rescues. In one case, police blocked fire department scuba divers from joining the search for survivors of a helicopter crash in a river. The police were jealously guarding an image as saviors, not just arresters. The city's firefighters, underemployed by a decade's 40 percent decrease in fires and fearing a loss of jobs, were seeking emergency responsibilities comparable to those of other cities' fire departments and, with time on their hands, promising a faster response to emergencies than that supplied by the police department. It took a detailed treaty in 1990, negotiated between commissioners appointed by a new mayor, to bring peace.[5]

That treaty did not solve the basic problem, however. On the morning of September 11, 2001, the NYPD's helicopter hovering above the World Trade Center towers had a better perspective on the buildings' condition than did the rescuers below, but the police helicopter crew had no way of telling firefighters that the towers were about to collapse. Meanwhile, fire commanders in the lobbies of the two buildings often lost radio and telephone contact with their firefighters on the upper floors. These communication problems, both technical and bureaucratic, had tragic consequences.[6] In the aftermath of the buildings' collapse, everyone promised that the problems would never recur. Years after the terrorist attacks, however, the two departments continued to tussle over who would be in charge of the new integrated command centers. Fire officials explained that they could not risk a command structure that put their forces under the control of other officials who did not really understand firefighting; police officials said the same thing. Each side had a point, but even high-level peace treaties failed to resolve the underlying conflict.

Administrators often find it reassuring to learn that the big issues with which they are struggling are new versions of very old problems. It can sometimes help to know that there are often no easy, good, or lasting solutions. Most often, the problems are new versions of the eternal

Government firefighters join to attack a fire in Santa Clarita, California. Such efforts often engage teams from local governments, the state, and even the federal government.

search for better **coordination**. The instinct to build strong functional competence often creates barriers to coordination across organizational boundaries. That, in turn, often makes elected officials and policy analysts very cynical. Unresolvable problems invite criticism, and their unresolvability invites political interference. Why insist on neutral competence if it seems to produce incompetence? American government tends to sort out these issues through four general approaches: (1) the choice among criteria of good organization, (2) interagency conflict, (3) interagency coordination, and (4) the role of staff in supporting and controlling operating activities.

Organizational Criteria

From the building blocks of organizational theory comes a handy checklist for assessing what makes for a good organization, as a federal task force concluded. The points are ageless; the checklist below comes from a 1974 report:

- *Public acceptance:* the amount of trust the public places in the integrity, fairness, and judiciousness of the information and decisions a system generates
- *Adaptability:* the ability of a system to react quickly and positively to changes in (a) technology, (b) major public policies, (c) international developments, (d) state-federal relationships, and (e) economic conditions
- *Consistency of decisions:* the degree to which a system promotes consistent policy decisions
- *Professional competence:* the degree to which a system makes it easy to recruit high-caliber professionals and makes effective use of their talents

- *Participation, representation, and diversity:* the degree to which a system provides for diverse public inputs to governmental decision making
- *Effective database:* the capacity of the system to generate, verify, and use reliable and complete information
- *Cost and timeliness:* the reasonableness of the expense and time required by a system to yield decisions
- *Promotion of private efficiency:* the extent to which a system avoids unintended pressures on private decision makers in their choices of technology, markets . . . , and other decisions
- *Accountability to the president:* the extent to which a system provides clear lines of executive authority
- *Accountability to Congress:* the extent to which a system provides clear data for congressional review and clear charters of responsibility for carrying out congressional mandates
- *Compatibility with state regulation:* the extent to which a system . . . fosters effective state-federal relationships[7]

Most important, the task force concluded,

Each criterion is important, but all cannot be satisfied at the same time. For example, it is unlikely that a system that yields the fastest decision and also entails the least administrative cost would rank among the best systems with respect to public credibility or public participation. In short, the design of any [organizational] system requires compromises and tradeoffs among desirable attributes.[8]

There is no formula to guide these tradeoffs, so the inevitable battles often prove very frustrating. But it would be foolish to abandon the quest for better answers because no answer works perfectly. Critics often want government to behave more like the private sector, but government often works with different problems, its leaders rarely have the control that private executives have, and private executives rarely have to work within the political constraints facing public executives. That makes resolving interagency conflict a top priority.

Interagency Conflict

The very choice of organizational structure for one agency often creates the foundations for conflict with others. Spotless windows were a rarity in Queen Victoria's nineteenth-century English palace, because their outside cleaning was under the control of the Woods and Forests department, their inside cleaning was the responsibility of Lord Chamberlain's department, and the work schedules of the two departments often did not match.[9] The queen could rarely view her kingdom through clean windows. Connecting the dots isn't a new problem.

The standard approach for solving coordination problems is to ask the official at the next step above the dispute to work out a solution. The more coordination problems there are, however, the heavier the burden on higher officials. No one wants two different agencies to waste resources doing the same thing—or to risk having important problems fall through the cracks between two agencies, who each assume the other will deal with the problem.

Coordination is a basic goal of complex organizations; making it happen is a basic problem. Coordination problems sometimes arise from a mismatch of organizational strategies. Classical organization theory suggests four different strategies: organization by purpose, process, clientele, and place. Agencies organized by one strategy can encounter coordination problems with agencies organized by another. In addition, there are often conflicts among organizations organized by function, when several agencies believe they each are primarily responsible for the same issue.

PURPOSE VERSUS CLIENTELE. The Department of Health and Human Services (HHS) is a purpose-based organization, and it serves the general population through welfare programs, health research and health system financing, and food and drug regulation, among other functions. The Department of Veterans Affairs (VA) and the Interior Department's Bureau of Indian Affairs (BIA) are clientele based. These single-clientele agencies perform or arrange for many services for their special groups that HHS would otherwise provide for them under its general, national programs. The VA, for example, runs the nation's single largest health and hospital care system, whereas the BIA has its own health clinics—and each operates independently of other health agencies organized by function at the federal, state, and local levels.

The different focus on purpose versus clientele inevitably creates tensions. HHS cannot claim to speak for a truly national health or welfare policy, nor can it assert coordinative authority to ensure equity and consistency in policy execution. Many of the horror stories of administration—two or three agencies building hospitals in a locality that needs only one, or agents of the purpose-based Federal Bureau of Investigation (FBI) being killed while serving warrants on an Indian reservation that is under the jurisdiction of the clientele-based BIA—are results of the crisscrossing of jurisdictions of purpose-based agencies and clientele-based agencies.

A reverse situation occurs when a clientele-based agency embraces inconsistent or even contradictory purposes. Many industry-based agencies seek both to promote and to regulate the industry they are assigned to monitor. For instance, the federal agencies regulating both atomic energy and mines tended to emphasize promotion over control in their respective spheres. Congress feared that the Atomic Energy Commission was neglecting protection of the public health and safety, so it moved that function to a new Nuclear Regulatory Commission and placed nuclear energy promotion in the new Department of Energy. The goal of the Interior Department's Bureau of Mines was "to stimulate private industry to produce a substantial share of the nation's mineral needs in ways that best protect the public interest,"[10] but it also was the agency charged with protection of the health and safety of coal miners through mine inspections and enforcement actions. Mine disasters and the resulting public outcry led Congress to transfer the protective function from the Interior Department to a new Mine Safety and Health Administration in the Department of Labor.

In both the nuclear energy case and the coal mining case, a single agency faced the incompatible tasks of fostering an industry while constraining it through health and safety standards. Similarly, state officials have often been criticized for trying to both control and promote gambling out of a single agency. State environment and parks agencies regularly find themselves caught up in battles between anglers and hunters, who want easy access to the best sporting spots, and environmentalists, who seek to protect scenic parks from snowmobilers and all-wheel-drive vehicles.

FUNCTION VERSUS AREA. Other conflicts often grow up within departments. Many departments, from local public works agencies to the federal Forest Service, are organized by both function and area. The State Department, for example, manages the nation's foreign policy, and its traditional internal organization is by region and country. Alongside the place-based offices are functional bureaus focused on politico-military affairs (e.g., arms control), human rights and humanitarian affairs, environmental and scientific affairs, economic and business affairs, refugee programs, and international organizations. No functional issue, whether managing the oceans or aiding refugees, stops at any nation's border. However, it is usually difficult to get action on any functional problem without dealing with individual nations, and that requires the department's traditional country-based structure. One of the secretary of state's most difficult internal management jobs is setting the ongoing balance between these conflicting—and inevitable—approaches.

Chapter 5 pointed out that, in contrast with some other countries, the U.S. government has no prefectoral, area-based officials to coordinate the field activities of the various departments and agencies within each of the country's regions. Each functional department has field offices, but coordination among the field offices of different departments in the same region occurs irregularly, at best. For decades, presidents have tried different approaches to this coordination problem, from creating uniform regions to establishing super-regions where high-level officials would have the power to pull related agencies together. The individual departments, not surprisingly, have always resisted the more aggressive efforts. Coordination of federal programs is always difficult in Washington, but it is often a tougher problem where agency officials face the job of managing programs.

CONFLICTS AMONG PURPOSE-BASED AGENCIES. Of course, conflicts also occur among purpose-based departments. The names of departments commonly identify a general field of activity; they do not necessarily convey a sharp sense of purpose. The nation's oldest federal departments—State, Treasury, Defense, and Justice—all have fuzzy missions that have evolved radically since these departments were first created. New issues emerge constantly, from the pressures of the Cold War following World War II, the fall of the Soviet Union, pressures on the dollar along with inflation, the rise of the European Union, and the sudden intrusion of terrorism on American soil. These departments, and many others, have worked to adapt their mission and their work, often with little structural change to match the shifting purposes.

Rather than have clear and constant purposes, departments focus on core activities that define the issues to which they—as well as their leaders and most important constituencies—pay the most attention. They do not have clear, constant purposes or firm jurisdictional boundaries. Rather, departments tend to focus on general fields of activity.[11] That's one reason why border warfare among departments is so common, because the boundaries cannot be precise. Policymakers are eternally tempted to solve these problems by overhauling organizational structure. Such reorganization can remap the terrain, but it cannot end departmental border wars. For the agencies involved, jurisdictional boundaries remain crucial.

For example, the commission investigating the September 11, 2001, attacks found substantial problems in the sharing of information among the nation's intelligence agencies. Indeed, some observers speculated that the attacks might have been prevented if the government had made better use of the information it had collected before the attacks. (Of course, the attacks were on a scale that most officials had not imagined, and the real meaning of

Seafood Safety

Americans love seafood. They're eating more and more of it, especially as more kinds of seafood have become available in stores and the price has come down. But most Americans don't know where most of the seafood they eat comes from—and they haven't stopped to think about the role they expect government to play in keeping that seafood safe.

The U.S. Food and Drug Administration, an organization within the U.S. Department of Agriculture, is the primary federal agency responsibile for seafood safety.

Pounds of fish and shellfish consumed by the average American in 2011:

15

Number of laws affecting food safety:

30

Sources of our seafood:

Wild-caught	Farm-raised	Imported
50%	50%	91%

Shrimp

Shrimp is the most popular seafood consumed in the U.S.

Top five shrimp exporters to the U.S.:

China
Mexico
Thailand
Ecuador
Indonesia

Percentage of our shrimp that's imported:

90%

Shrimp as a share of all seafood consumed:

30%

Salmon

Salmon is the third most popular seafood in the U.S. behind canned tuna and shrimp.

Pounds of salmon consumed by the average American in 2011:

2

Where we get our salmon:

Wild-caught	Farm-raised
67%	33%

Major sources of farm-raised salmon:

Norway
Canada
Chile

Pollock

Pollock is the fish used in McDonald's Filet-O-Fish sandwiches.

Pollock caught in Alaska:

100%

Source: NOAA Fisheries, "The Surprising Sources of Your Favorite Seafoods," at http://www.nmfs.noaa.gov/aquaculture/archive/09_13_12_top_seafood _consumed.html; and McDonald's, "What Type of Fish Do You Use in the Filet-O-Fish?," at http://www.mcdonalds.com/us/en/your_questions/our_food/what-type-of-fish-do-you-use-in-the-filet-o-fish.html.

QUESTIONS

1. Are you surprised by the share of imported seafood in the food chain?

2. Is there a problem with the fragmentation of the government's food safety oversight?

3. What challenges do you think are presented with American government agencies being responsible for the safety of seafood that arrives from foreign countries? What kinds of regulatory strategies are most likely to be effective to protect the food supply? Would it make more sense to have a single agency in charge of food safety regulations? What issues would that create?

4. Should the source of seafood products be labeled (e.g., on product labels or menus for food purchased in supermarkets or restaurants)?

much of that information became clear only in hindsight. Indeed, that is why the 9/11 Commission ascribed a large part of the problem to a "failure of imagination.") To reduce the likelihood of future attacks, Congress insisted on creating a new Department of Homeland Security that would answer the constant call to devise a better way of connecting the dots among any pieces of information that might be collected. When the new department emerged from Congress, however, it did not include any of the nation's key intelligence bureaus: the Central Intelligence Agency, the National Security Agency, the Defense Intelligence Agency, or the FBI. Each bureau had waged a fierce behind-the-scenes battle to retain its independence—contending that it had critical core activities that would be compromised through a merger—and each emerged victorious. So the department that had been prompted by the urgent need to connect the dots ended up leaving most of the dots where they were, with only relatively weak new interagency councils to strengthen information sharing among them.

Interagency Coordination

Conflict among agencies is inevitable. Conflict can undermine coordination, yet coordination is the core of administration. Executives therefore resort to a variety of methods to manage and moderate conflict among agencies.

Coordination is a *horizontal* activity: it seeks to draw related agencies together in a common purpose. Because no agency willingly surrenders control over its core activities to another, coordination rarely happens naturally or easily. Coordination requires a coordinator—it rarely happens spontaneously—and that requires a *vertical* activity. So to further complicate the problem, the horizontal and vertical dimensions themselves require coordination.

HORIZONTAL COOPERATION. Horizontal cooperation depends on the willingness of agencies to come to agreement with one another. Four methods stand out:

1. Thousands of **interagency agreements** ("treaties") have been negotiated between the concerned agencies to establish specific boundaries and, therefore, to clarify which

agency will do what without interference from the other. Most local governments, for example, have agreements on shared responses to emergencies, including who provides which equipment for 911 emergency calls.

2. Hundreds of **interagency committees** at the cabinet, subcabinet, and bureau levels exist to promote collaboration in jointly occupied areas. Officials at all levels complain about spending so much time in meetings, but these meetings provide the foundations for much horizontal cooperation.

3. Under the **lead agency formula**, one agency is designated to lead and attempt to coordinate all other agencies' activities in a particular area. Ironically, even though the lead agency formula does not work well in the federal government, federal agencies often require state and local governments to create lead agencies as a condition of federal grant programs. Most emergency response systems now designate one agency to take the lead when problems develop. After the Boston Marathon bombings in 2013, for example, the FBI became the lead investigative agency.

4. A **clearance procedure** links agencies horizontally by requiring that an agency's proposed decisions in a subject-matter area be reviewed, whether for comment or for formal approval or veto, by other interested agencies.[12]

There is vast experience with these mechanisms. Sometimes, as in the case of the Boston bombings, they work remarkably well. But important issues are often hard to solve and it's easy to dodge the tough decisions.

Narcotics-control efforts illustrate the common situation when neither horizontal cooperation nor vertical coordination seems likely. With the efforts split among many agencies, the Reagan administration's principal recourse in its "war on drugs" was creating multiagency committees.[13] Congress, disenchanted with this weak response, provided in the Anti-Drug Abuse Act of 1988 a "czar" for coordination of narcotics-control efforts, and President George H. W. Bush appointed the first such officer.[14] But if largely voluntary cooperation was no answer, neither, apparently, is a major shift to vertical coordination through a high-level antidrug director. Such directive power as the czar has over bureaus concerned with narcotics conflicts with department heads' authority over the same bureaus. Most of these bureaus—including the Coast Guard, FBI, Central Intelligence Agency, Customs and Border Protection, and Citizenship and Immigration Services—have core functions unrelated to narcotics control. Nonetheless, the czar idea is a popular one; it has been advanced, for example, as the cure for the bureaucratic fragmentation that impeded response to the AIDS crisis.[15] When Congress and President George W. Bush concluded that the White House Office of Homeland Security was not powerful enough to ensure the coordination needed in the area of domestic security, they abandoned the czar approach in favor of a more traditional department, but this arrangement was challenged when the 9/11 Commission countered that a cabinet-level intelligence czar was needed to bring the nation's disparate foreign intelligence together into a coherent picture. Chief executives can't resist naming czars when big problems surface. In the Obama administration, there was a cascading supply of czars for energy, urban issues, health care, and the economy, among others.

VERTICAL COORDINATION. A principal function of hierarchy is to provide vertical coordination of units with shared interests. Backed by both authority and structure, vertical coordination is relatively strong compared with the horizontal approach. The two patterns are very different. In the vertical coordination model, two warring agencies are brought together by the organizational superior of both, who has the formal authority to impose a decision and to monitor the agencies' compliance with it. Although their willingness to use authority may be limited by many influences, superiors are highly motivated to ensure that the programs under their responsibility proceed effectively.

The vertical dimension involves much more than arbitrating jurisdictional controversies. Superiors must constantly be on guard to protect themselves—including their time, energy, and political capital—against the eagerness of subordinates to push up the ladder tough decisions that they do not wish to make themselves. It can often be tempting for officials to pass along these "hot potato" issues, some of which may involve problems of coordination or may hinge on sharp political conflicts. But superiors who allow their subordinates to shirk responsibility in this way can soon find themselves swamped by decisions that they do not need to make. That can make it harder for them to focus on the matters that truly do require their time, and it can make effective coordination more difficult by allowing decisions to rise up above the level at which the issues need to be resolved. If lower-level officials pass the buck instead of working through the problems they encounter, those problems often remain unresolved and the superiors become overwhelmed.

Because the horizontal and vertical dimensions of the hierarchy interact, an eternal question emerges: What is the best number of cabinet-level departments? In brief, how many subordinate units can a superior adequately supervise? This is the "span of control" puzzle we saw earlier in the book. If the number is very large, three things are predictable. First, border disputes would multiply beyond the chief executive's capacity to arbitrate. Second, individual department and agency heads' access to the chief executive would be curtailed. Third, cabinet and subcabinet committees would be too large for effective discussion and decision (or advice to the chief executive). If the number is very small, the chief executive can lose contact with frontline operations and can struggle to hold cabinet officials accountable. There are more choke points to block the flow of information up the chain, which creates more potential for distortion; there are also more points at which the flow of instructions down the chain can be drained of clarity and force. A small span of control can also produce delays, because transmission and consideration of messages through a long series of offices takes longer than their passage through a short series.

The result is a search for a happy medium, which tends to settle to between ten and thirty departments.[16] A major exception is the New Zealand government's reforms in the 1980s, which actually increased the number of departments to almost forty as part of a strategy to streamline government. However, critics there soon began making the point that so many departments hindered the coordination of the government's programs. In searching for the best span of control, we confront a tradeoff for which there is no simple, good solution.

The Role of Staff

So far in this section we have focused mainly on *operating* agencies. That is, we have discussed people and units responsible for managing programs that directly serve or regulate the public. However, agencies also rely on other units to support their functions. The standard term for these support units is **staff activities**, compared with **line activities**, or operating activities. Of course, we often use the word **staff** to refer to all government employees. Strictly speaking, however, employees who manage the core functions of an agency are *line* officials. Those who support their work are *staff* officials.

There are, in fact, three different staff roles: **core staff**, which provides basic support to the agency's line activities; **auxiliary staff**, which provides a basic housekeeping function; and **control staff**, which helps top officials secure leverage over the organization. The first two roles facilitate operations, and because persons performing these activities assist in the organization's mission, classical theory prescribes that they should have no power to command the line officials. The third activity is quite different, for control necessarily imposes restraints on the freedom of line officials. This intersection of functions often creates deep conflict: staff activities can—and often do—conflict with line activities. We will return to that point shortly.

THE PURE-STAFF ROLE. Aides who work in the pure-staff role serve as the top manager's eyes, ears, and auxiliary brain. They assist the manager by originating ideas; gathering, screening, and appraising ideas from others; organizing information for decision making; and keeping track of how quickly relevant agencies execute decisions. In 1975, the Commission on Organization of the Government for the Conduct of Foreign Policy captured the staff function well by listing the appropriate tasks of the president's staff and then strictly defining the scope of the tasks:

- Identify issues likely to require presidential attention
- Structure those issues for efficient presidential understanding and decision making—ensuring that the relevant facts are available, a full set of alternatives are presented, and agency positions are placed in perspective
- Assure due process, permitting each interested department an opportunity to state its case
- Ensure that affected parties are clearly informed of decisions once taken, and that their own responsibilities respecting those decisions are specified
- Monitor the implementation of presidential decisions
- Assess the results of decisions taken, drawing from those assessments implications for future action

> The defining characteristic of these tasks is that they embody staff responsibilities rather than line authority. They provide assistance to the president, not direction to department officials other than to convey presidential instructions. There should be only one official with line responsibility in the White House, and that is the president himself.[17]

All top officials need strong staff assistance. The more complex the organization's mission and structure, the more these officials need help in gathering information, interpreting details, anticipating issues, weighing decisions, and following the process of implementation.

The staff function is so important that it often becomes institutionalized in an organizational unit. For example, presidents have aides in the White House to inform and advise. Department heads and bureau chiefs have not only "assistants to" themselves but also organizational units concerned with program analysis, planning, and research. At least at the departmental level, staff units abound, with such assignments as legislative affairs, international affairs, intergovernmental affairs, public affairs (media relations), civil rights and minority affairs, small business, and consumers. In some departments, all or most of the assistant secretaries have primarily staff roles cutting across the bureaus, instead of, as in other departments, being line officials, each supervising a group of bureaus. At the state and local levels, the pattern is precisely the same.

THE AUXILIARY ROLE. Organizations rely heavily on auxiliary activities to assist in accomplishing their mission. For example, most governments have central purchasing offices, building management offices, accounting offices, libraries, public affairs offices, and publications units. These jobs tend to be grouped together under the *administrative support* or housekeeping label. We often tend to ignore the importance of auxiliary staff support—until we try to obtain a job in the agency. Then the important role of the personnel staff becomes very, very clear.

THE CONTROL ROLE. Organizations rely on control activities to monitor performance and enforce compliance with standards and procedures. Federal departments, for example, have inspectors general, who are given broad authority to investigate and report to the secretary and to Congress on suspected fraud, waste, and other mismanagement. In addition, personnel and budget offices enforce civil service laws and regulations as well as appropriations acts and other restrictions on expenditures and programs. Technically, such control activities are not the same as the exercise of line authority. Technicalities aside, operating officials invariably resent the so-called meddling of controllers, particularly when the controllers divert the operators' energies from what they view as the vigorous implementation of programs to side issues, such as compliance with burdensome red-tape requirements.

POWER BUILDING. In practice, staff members often take on very strong power, even compared with line functions.[18] Many staff assistants have regular access to the chief of the unit, and this "face time" can powerfully shape the chief's decisions. Lower-level line officials, therefore, often try to cultivate the staff assistant, to find back doors into the decision-making process. On the other hand, top officials often face a large number of tough problems and are often tempted to trust staff assistants to handle problems. Persons with staff roles can therefore find themselves slipping into the chair of command. Indeed, cabinet officials regularly complain that the president's staff aides often take it upon themselves to issue orders and to filter information to the president. The growing role of the National Security Council, which we examined in the last chapter, is the leading example.

The problem of power building is aggravated by a tendency for staff, auxiliary, control, and command functions to second-guess operating units. A department's procurement office may be charged not only with supplying the operating units' needs for supplies (an auxiliary activity) but also with the authority to question operating officials' specifications of their requirements (a control and command activity). Line officials, of course, cannot be free to purchase whatever strikes their fancy, but function as a critical organizational problem. Few things annoy operating officials more than finding that purchasing-office employees, sitting far from the front lines of the agency's activities, have overruled their decisions on what supplies they need.

Staff activities thus differ from line (or operating) activities because their role is to assist, not to command, line officials. Although this line is neat, it's often breached in operation, because there is an irresistible temptation to give orders as well as advice. Because staff functions depend so critically on access to information, this can give staff officials a powerful additional source of leverage. It's little wonder that there is often friction between the line and staff roles.

SOLUTIONS? There are no easy solutions to these deep and lasting dilemmas. For staff officials, there is one obvious solution: provide a clear sense of the role of staff by those who serve in these positions. Staff persons need to practice self-restraint and resist the temptation to go into business for themselves as decision makers and order givers. Of course, such restraint is often in short supply—it is never easy to fade into the background while others take center stage, and it is hard to push away the temptations of power that the staff role offers. Although the staff-line distinction is not quite as simple as a difference between thinkers and doers, the cultures of most operating organizations tend to put those who "do" into a more valued position than those who "think," and those who think often believe they can do best.

Auxiliary units inevitably exercise specialized control functions, especially because top executives rarely want to invest their scarce time in housekeeping disputes. However, program administrators are often frustrated by the need to share control over the tools for their jobs with outside auxiliary units that are committed less to achieving program results than to managing the support apparatus, from personnel rules to purchasing standards. As we see in Chapter 8, substantial efforts have been made to give operating managers more control over their personnel systems.

REORGANIZATION

If so many problems are structural, why, some wonder, can't they be solved by reorganizing the structure? To be sure, executive restructuring efforts have regularly sought to rearrange the organizational building blocks to enhance symmetry, improve the logical grouping of activities, reduce the executive's span of control, and strengthen administrative coordination and efficiency. These efforts fall largely within the neutral competence approach to organization, and they have long been an important part of administrative strategy.[19]

Reorganizations have been a never-ending campaign for most government executives. For example, in his 2011 State of the Union address, President Obama took on the challenge of governmental organizations for salmon:

> There are 12 different agencies that deal with exports. There are at least five different agencies that deal with housing policy. Then there's my favorite example: The Interior Department is in charge of salmon while they're in fresh water, but the Commerce Department handles them when they're in saltwater. [Laughter.] I hear it gets even more complicated once they're smoked.[20]

Like all great stories, this one gets even better the more one pokes into the details. Interior is in charge of protecting natural resources in the nation's interior, which covers fresh water.

Larry Gerbrandt/Barcroft USALa/Getty Images

In his 2011 State of the Union address, President Obama joked about the multiple government agencies charged with regulating salmon. The quip led to an ongoing debate about how the federal government could improve its efficiency by restructuring its operations. Bears would be unaffected by any of the proposed changes for salmon.

Commerce seeks to promote business development through fisheries, and that takes the department into the saltwater, where many salmon swim freely. We've organized the government's policy toward salmon to manage the areas where they swim and the purposes—recreation or commercial fishing—to which those areas are put. We could simplify the situation by creating a "department of salmon," but then commercial fishermen might find the department of salmon's regulations conflicting with those of the departments of cod and haddock. Behind every complaint about governmental organization is a complex puzzle of policy, politics, and efficiency.

Reorganization is always about much more than efficiency, because reorganization is as much a political act as an administrative one. Structure determines which issues get priority. Structure also defines which constituencies get prime attention, strengthens government's ability to serve some of these constituencies, and sends a powerful message about who and what matter most. If a program is in an unsympathetic department, it is less likely that the secretary will fight for adequate financing and staffing; as a result, the program will likely be anemic. If a program is placed far down in the hierarchy, the director's access to the secretary will be impeded; recommendations about resources and policy will have to move through a chain of intermediaries, who may block or change them. When those in immediate charge of a program feel like orphans in their department, they will look elsewhere for support—for funds, staff, and program autonomy that enables them to ease the burdens of abandonment. All of these issues become folded into the value of representativeness that Herbert Kaufman identified as one of the basic approaches to organization.

For much of the past half-century, the president had statutory authority to propose to Congress reorganization plans creating, renaming, consolidating, and transferring whole

Do Americans Prefer State or Federal Power?
Theme: Politics

If Americans had the choice, at what level would they prefer to concentrate power? A Gallup poll provides an interesting answer: 55 percent of those surveyed prefer the state government, versus 37 percent at the federal level.

Gallup had asked the question twice before. In 1981, respondents had almost exactly the same preference for state governments (56 percent). The preference for the federal government was a bit lower, at 28 percent.

In 1936, by contrast, the preference for state government was 44 percent, compared with 56 percent for the federal government. That was in the middle of Franklin D. Roosevelt's "New Deal," a federal-led effort to revitalize the economy.

"Americans' preferences for how power is distributed in the U.S. have differed over the past century, and could change again as the politics of the country continue to shift," explained Gallup's analyst, Justin McCarthy.

Source: Bill Lucia, "Do More Americans Prefer State or Federal Power?" *Route Fifty* (July 12, 2016), http://www.routefifty.com/2016/07/gallup-poll-state-power/129850/?oref=rf-today-nl; and Justin McCarthy, "Majority in U.S. Prefer State over Federal Government Power," *Gallup* (July 11, 2016), http://www.gallup.com/poll/193595/majority-prefer-state-federal-government-power.aspx.

agencies (other than cabinet departments and independent regulatory commissions) and any of their component units. By means of an ingenious legislative veto arrangement, the president's plans automatically went into effect in sixty days if neither house adopted a resolution of disapproval. In 1983, however, the Supreme Court ruled unconstitutional the legislative veto provisions appearing in hundreds of statutes, including the Reorganization Act.[21] Now, for a president's reorganization plan to be effective, it must be approved by a joint resolution of the two houses passed within ninety days after receipt and signed by the president (or, if vetoed because of amendments, overridden by Congress).[22]

The president therefore has a choice of tactics in seeking to restructure. One option is to seek comprehensive reorganization of the executive branch through an act of Congress. This option is always tempting but, whatever the potential benefits, it always stirs opposition among the interest groups happy with the existing structure—or at least fearful that change might shrink their power and access. Alternatively, the president can focus reorganization efforts on a small handful of bureaus. Sometimes the opposition to such limited action can be just as fierce, however, and it always has a less sweeping impact. In fact, some bureaus have proven immovable despite long histories of recommendations for restructuring. Reformers have long sought to move the Forest Service and the civil works functions of the Army Corps of Engineers to the Interior Department, in order to bring natural resource functions together in a single department. Both bureaus—and the interest groups supporting them—have fought off every effort to move them.

Reorganization powers vary at the state and local levels of government, but rarely can chief executives remake the structure of the bureaucracy on their own. Most organizational changes require approval of the state legislature, county board, or city council.

Comprehensive Reorganization

Nearly every one of the presidents from Hoover through George W. Bush has supported some kind of sweeping overhaul of the executive branch. (The exceptions were Kennedy and Ford, because of their short tenures in office, and Reagan, who focused his efficiency efforts on privatization.[23]) Even conservatives like George W. Bush could not resist shuffling the organizational boxes. He championed the largest single government restructuring since the end of World War II with the creation of the Department of Homeland Security. Why, given the odds against them, do presidents bother? Some come into office trailing campaign promises to "straighten out the mess in Washington." Some—such as Hoover and Carter, who were engineers—are personally disposed to fix the machinery of government. Some seek popular credit for trying to improve administration, which may count for more politically than would actual achievement, to which they may devote little energy. Some—including former senators Truman, Nixon, and Johnson, who knew Washington well—may perceive existing executive branch organization as poorly serving the national interest and propose to invest political capital in structural reform.

But political capital is precious. It can quickly evaporate or shift to urgent policy initiatives. Nixon's ambitious plan (described below) failed to win congressional support, and the Watergate scandal then exhausted his political capital. In 1967–1968, Johnson, losing his political capital because of the Vietnam War, neither allowed publication nor advocated adoption of the recommendations of his Task Force on Government Organization. Of Roosevelt's far-reaching proposals, only two were initially approved by Congress.[24] Two joint congressional-presidential Commissions on Organization of the Executive Branch of the Government, each chaired by former president Herbert Hoover, reported in 1949 and 1955.[25] Over half of the First Hoover Commission's recommendations were adopted, mostly because of Truman's support and a massive public relations campaign. The Second Hoover Commission focused not on major reorganization but on procedural techniques and policy issues—especially how to reduce the government's competition with and regulation of private enterprise. Nevertheless, "not a single major permanent program resulting from the years of depression, recovery, war, and reform was abolished as a result of this prodigious inquiry."[26]

In 1971, President Nixon proposed a drastic reorganization of the executive branch.[27] The plan would have retained unchanged only the four departments whose heads had sat in George Washington's cabinet. Four departments—Commerce, Labor, Transportation, and Agriculture—would be abolished, most of their work being absorbed by a wholly new Department of Economic Affairs. Three newly named and reconstituted departments—Natural Resources, Human Resources, and Community Development—were to supersede the departments of the Interior; Health, Education, and Welfare; and Housing and Urban Development. But Congress refused to act.[28]

President Carter mounted a heavily staffed reorganization study in the Office of Management and Budget, but the results were modest compared with his ambitions; Carter's successes were establishment of the Department of Education (fulfilling a campaign pledge) and the Department of Energy, partition of the Civil Service Commission into two new agencies, and reorganization of the president's Executive Office.[29] President Reagan then futilely sought abolition of the new Education and Energy Departments he had inherited from Carter but proposed no overhaul of executive branch structure.[30] Reagan instead relied on his cabinet councils to harmonize interagency concerns, as well as on procedural changes, political appointments, and centralized control of agency behavior.[31] Congressional Republicans returned to the battle in 1995 and fought—yet failed—to eliminate the Commerce Department. The creation of the Department of Homeland Security in 2002 moved more agencies (twenty-two) and more employees than any restructuring since the creation of the Department of Defense, but critics continued to battle over the department's effectiveness.

Among state governments, comprehensive reorganizations have come in waves; a recent one centered in 1965–1978 when twenty-one states recast their executive branches. Usually the governor initiates the enterprise, and it is achieved through a constitutional amendment, statute, or both.[32] Yet the taste for reorganization has scarcely gone away, as shown by the massive 2004 proposal to restructure California's state government. That proposal spawned many more. The instinct to reorganize is eternal.

Obstacles to Reorganization

There is never a shortage of reorganization ideas, both because there are always ways of improving government's efficiency and because past reorganizations create the seeds for new ones. However, relatively few of these ideas are translated into action. Ideas that are adopted tend to be specifically focused in response to perceived performance failures that are seen as products of poor organization. In addition, the reforms either promise enough benefits to command political support or they seem minor enough to avoid creating political opposition. Some reform ideas eventually succeed because they have recurred so often over the years that objections lose credibility.[33]

Indeed, *stability*, not fluidity, characterizes the executive branch's organization.[34] How do we account for this? Most obviously, departments and bureaus resist the loss of functions—they seek to protect their turf. Moreover, although some agencies act imperialistically to expand their realms, protecting what they have tends to be more important.[35] How do agencies attract enough political support to discourage and even defeat reorganization initiatives by presidents and department heads? The answer is that congressional committees and powerful interest groups create intense counterpressures. Mustering their forces against a reorganization effort is not difficult; often the opposition springs to arms without much invitation.

Congressional committees have their own jurisdictions to protect. One reason that Congress failed to support Nixon's major reorganization effort was dissatisfaction with the impact it would have had on legislative committees: on average, over nine existing committees would have had fragmentary jurisdiction over each of the four new departments. The alternative would have been a reorganization of the committees' jurisdictions to match those of the departments—this prospect would not warm the hearts of the leading members of committees marked for abolition or loss of jurisdiction.

Interest groups that perceive potential harm to their members throw their lobbying strength against proposed reorganizations, allying themselves with the affected departments or bureaus and with sympathetic congressional committees. The result often is what some writers call an **iron triangle**, a closely linked network of interest groups, congressional committees, and public administrators that unite to protect their long-term relationships.

Indeed, a major study of government reorganization by Craig W. Thomas teaches several important lessons. First, although we are very long on rhetoric about reorganization, we are very short on evidence. We simply know relatively little about whether changes in government organization do in fact improve efficiency. Second, many efforts to improve government efficiency through reorganization have been disappointing: contracting out and creating government corporations can improve efficiency if the changes are well managed, but a common approach—centralizing authority—often does not improve efficiency. Third, despite the constant rhetoric about trying to reorganize government agencies to improve efficiency, "reorganizations are profoundly and unavoidably political and we should accept them as such."[36] If reformers promote reorganization to produce more efficient and more effective government, they cannot be sure of achieving the results they desire. But they can be sure of provoking deep political battles over the structure and symbols of governmental programs.

This strong array of forces against restructuring might be overcome more often if theory and experience pointed to one best way to organize the executive branch or a department or bureau. The difficulty is that when those knowledgeable about administration are asked how to organize, they are likely to answer, "It all depends." This does not mean that anything goes. It does mean, as we have seen, that there are persistent organizational problems and several alternative approaches to them, and a set of variables might carry different weights in one situation compared with another. Furthermore, any reorganization's potential for achieving its objectives is contingent on so many factors that neither theory nor experience can ensure that the potential will be fulfilled. Finally, the ultimate choice often depends more on political values than on administrative efficiency.

CONCLUSION

Responses to organization problems usually seek to promote one or another of the values of neutral competence, executive leadership, or representativeness. Such responses may be infused with politics, with concern for "who gets what?" This is true, even of responses in the neutral competence mode, because administrators, including careerists, prefer arrangements that protect their units' powers and that ensure their control of subordinate units.

Organization problems, we have discovered, are not chance or unique occurrences. Instead, they fall into patterns that not only persist or recur but that, more remarkably, also appear at all levels—presidential, departmental, bureau, and field service. The fact that conflict seems structurally embedded, that things go wrong even when neutral competence is the goal, stems from organizers' failure to take account of the salient criteria: incompatibilities among the organizational structures; the fuzziness of jurisdictional boundaries; the weakness of voluntary, horizontal cooperation; the limits of vertical, hierarchical coordination; and the frustrations that operating officials suffer because of the controls exercised by staff and auxiliary aides and units.

Although organizational structure seems passive, it should now be clear that it both results from and shapes the dynamics of organizational conflict. Those dynamics are political, and they reflect the claims of both the president and Congress to achieve the values of executive leadership and representativeness, respectively, as well the clash of interest groups.

As later chapters show, public organizations, however passive they appear in the abstract, come to life when perceived as sets of human beings, as both civil servants and political appointees, as wrestlers over policy issues and battlers for scarce budgetary resources, as agents attempting to implement service and regulatory programs that have ambitious and contradictory goals, and as bureaucrats adapting to the control efforts of executive, legislative, and judicial overseers. The next chapter examines those puzzles.

CASE 6.1

Sunset, the Golden Retriever: Governor Schwarzenegger and the Restructuring of California's Executive Branch

For Sunset, a golden retriever, the news from Sacramento wasn't good. Sunset was training to be a guide dog for the blind, and Sunset's instructor, Katryn Webster, was worried about the future of her organization, Guide Dogs of the Desert.[1] The Board of Guide Dogs for the Blind, the state government agency regulating Sunset's training and Webster's organization, was threatened with radical surgery as part of Governor Arnold Schwarzenegger's new reform agenda, the California Performance Review. Webster wasn't sure whether the performance review's recommendations would permanently change the way her organization worked and how effective it could be.

When he took office in January 2004, Schwarzenegger launched the performance review program to eliminate waste and inefficiency across state government, in part by reducing perceived duplication in "common functions and responsibilities."[2] The "Gubernator," as he quickly became known to fans of his action-hero movies, faced a huge budget deficit and a public tired of taxes. At his inauguration, Schwarzenegger told California's citizens that his performance review could help slash the state government's costs. "I plan a total review of government—its performance, its practices, its cost," he announced.[3]

Luckily for Sunset, when Schwarzenegger's task force made its recommendations in August 2004, it didn't suggest wiping out the guide dog program and the board that supervised it. Rather, it recommended moving the Board of Guide Dogs for the Blind to a new Department of Education and Workforce Preparation—along with similar changes for more than a hundred other boards and agencies that existed independent of the governor's cabinet agencies. But the board's supporters worried the move would weaken their work.

"Guide dogs take you into situations where it's life and death," explained board member Jane Brackman, "and if a dog isn't properly trained or a student isn't properly trained, people die."[4] Sheila Styron, president of Guide Dog Users, a national support organization, added, "Most people in California are pretty happy with the board." In fact, she said, "We would like it to become stronger."[5]

Eliminating the board, its supporters said, would not even save the state any money—Schwarzenegger's primary goal in launching the performance review—because license fees paid the board's $141,000 annual budget. (Blind persons received the dog and training for free; donations covered the $50,000-per-dog training cost, and the three dog-training academies that exist in California paid the state a license fee to be allowed to operate.) The board was scarcely a mega-bureaucracy soaking up taxpayer dollars; its seven members each received $100 (plus expenses) per day for the board's eight meetings per year.

Tough government rules were necessary, said the board's supporters, because some dog owners were taking unfair advantage of the special rules for guide dogs. Dog lovers with perfectly good eyesight, for example, were pretending their pets were guide dogs to be able to bring them into restaurants. The board performed important advocacy work as well, such as its effort to get an exemption for guide dogs from Hawaii's rule that dogs moving into the state had to be quarantined (to protect Hawaii from importing rabies). Moving the board into the new department, supporters feared, would make it harder to provide dogs for blind citizens. "You put a small entity like the state board into an overarching entity," explained Mitch Pomerantz, a disability law compliance officer for Los Angeles, "and it's going to get lost in the shuffle."[6]

Critics, however, wondered if the California Performance Review had gone far enough. "They did not go to the hard step and say, 'Do we really need to regulate guide dog trainers anymore?'" explained Julie D'Angelo Fellmeth, administrative director of the Center for Public Interest Law at the University of San Diego. "They're not shrinking government. They're just getting rid of multi-member boards and substituting bureaucrats."[7]

The battle over the Board of Guide Dogs for the Blind played itself out hundreds of times over. Schwarzenegger's task force recommended that a third of the state's 339 independent boards and commissions should be moved into executive departments, whose heads would report to the elected governor.

Three months after the California Performance Review issued its report, experts told a public hearing that any kind of reorganization would be difficult to implement. Every board had its own constituency, and every constituency feared its influence over policy would be watered down if the location of its organization was moved lower on the bureaucratic food chain. While searching for billions of dollars of savings, Schwarzenegger and his aides had to decide how far to take a reorganization battle that promised few budgetary savings.

On the other hand, if he were to step back from the reorganization battle, Schwarzenegger risked undermining his credibility. In his 2004 State of the State address, he had pledged to "blow up boxes" in restructuring the state's bureaucracy—eliminating those boxed entries that are so ubiquitous on organizational charts. Toward the end of his first year in office, however, a *San Francisco*

Chronicle editorial said his term so far had mostly been a "victory parade." His performance review offered 1,200 recommendations—ranging from improved electronic government to changing vehicle registration from once a year to once every two years—which would produce $32 billion in predicted savings. "Is he serious about government reform, or is the package for political show?" the newspaper asked.[8]

Schwarzenegger was vastly underrated when he took office. Critics laughed off his campaign as an ego-driven publicity stunt. But they had grossly underestimated the wily Austrian bodybuilder and chess player. In case after case, he proved a far more effective governor than his critics had expected. After a few months, "The only people who are still laughing at Governor Schwarzenegger," explained Jack Pitney, a Claremont McKenna political scientist, "are the people who don't know California."[9]

But his performance review remained a long-running battle. Schwarzenegger had called California's sprawling government bureaucracy "a mastodon frozen in time." He saw the job of restructuring the state bureaucracy—including the Board of Guide Dogs for the Blind—as a symbol to demonstrate his determination to transform the state government. He knew that the reorganization, in itself, would not save billions. But if he could prevail, it would strengthen his hand in controlling the state government apparatus and in enhancing his ability to win on even bigger policy battles later.

The battle had enormous implications, many observers of California politics believed. "To me, the jury's still out on whether he wants real, true structural reform," said Joe Canciamilla, a Democrat from the State Assembly. "If he's not willing to take that step, with the popularity he's had, the independence he's had, the public statements he's made—if this governor isn't willing to go there, it ain't gonna happen for several generations."[10]

The battle hinged on the supervision of Sunset, the golden retriever, and thousands of cases just like Sunset's throughout the state and its government.

QUESTIONS TO CONSIDER

1. Consider the case for moving independent boards and commissions into executive branch departments. What are the advantages and disadvantages of such a restructuring?

2. Government reformers often lose their appetite for the political battle over restructuring the executive branch when they discover that, in itself, it tends to save little money. Are there other reasons to consider such reorganization? Do these reasons make a strong enough case to make it worth the political fight, even if there are not big savings in tax dollars?

3. Consider the symbolic value of an organization's structure. What roles do such symbols play, on both sides of the reorganization battle?

4. Just how much do you believe that the *structure* of government bureaucracies really matters? If you were an adviser to Governor Schwarzenegger, how much of his political capital would you advise him to invest in the battle over eliminating so many quasi-independent boards and commissions?

NOTES

1. See the organization's website, http://www.guide-dogsofthedesert.org.

2. See the report of the *California Performance Review* (2004), http://www.cpr.ca.gov/CPR_Report/.

3. Ed Mendel, "Optimistic Governor Doesn't Pull Punches," *San Diego Union-Tribune*, January 7, 2004, A1.

4. Jordan Rau, "Guide Dog Board Threatened," *Los Angeles Times*, November 29, 2004, B1.

5. Ibid.

6. Ibid.

7. Ibid.

8. "Now, Governor's Second Act," editorial, *San Francisco Chronicle*, November 17, 2004, B10.

9. Alan Greenblatt, "Strong Governor," *Governing* (July 2004), http://www.governing.com/topics/politics/Strong-Governor.html.

10. Ibid.

CASE 6.2

Obama Launches Management Reform: New—or Recycled—Ideas?

It's become inevitable—presidents need to put their own distinctive mark on the executive branch by launching their own brand of management reform. At least since Truman, presidents have made new management strategies a signature of their administrations. When he succeeded Roosevelt, Truman asked a special commission to find ways of increasing the efficiency of the federal government. Eisenhower followed with a continuation of the effort, this time aimed at restructuring government. Kennedy sought the "best and the brightest" for government service, while Johnson brought "planning programming budgeting" to capture the full cost of a program in decisions about whether to launch or continue it. Nixon expanded that to a "management by objectives" approach. He also proposed a massive reorganization of the federal government, which foundered in the midst

 DATA.GOV   DATA   TOPICS ▾   IMPACT   APPLICATIONS   DEVELOPERS   CONTACT

The home of the U.S. Government's open data

Here you will find data, tools, and resources to conduct research, develop web and mobile applications, design data visualizations, and more.

GET STARTED
SEARCH OVER 186,099 DATASETS
▼

Monthly House Price Indexes

BROWSE TOPICS

Agriculture   Business   Climate   Consumer   Ecosystems   Education   Energy

Finance   Health   Local Government   Manufacturing   Ocean   Public Safety   Science & Research

The federal website, Data.gov, became a vast repository of information about the government's operations, as part of an extended commitment to open government.

of the impeachment battle. Ford stabilized government. Carter brought "zero-base budgeting," which wasn't exactly budgeting from a zero base but a way of bringing tough analysis to packages of spending beyond a specified floor (say, 80 percent of existing spending). Reagan launched broad privatization initiatives to contract out much of the federal government's work. Bush continued it. Clinton sought to "reinvent" government, aimed at making government work better and cost less. Bush (George W., that is) had his own management agenda, with a stoplight set of performance measures to assess the accomplishments of federal programs.

So how did Obama wish to transform the government? In July 2013, after the budget battles simmered down enough to put his second-term budget and personnel team into place, he laid out his three-part plan[1]:

- "Deliver the services that citizens expect in smarter, faster, and better ways." For example, following Hurricane Sandy's assault on the Northeast, citizens could apply for emergency assistance using mobile and web apps. Federal Emergency Management Agency workers, armed with iPads, checked in on citizens.
- Identify "new ways to reduce waste and save taxpayers money." For example, the administration estimated that it saved more than $2.5 billion by eliminating overlapping information technology systems.
- Open "huge amounts of government data to the American people." For example, at Data.gov, it's possible to look through 75,000 government datasets on everything from weather to what different hospitals charge for different procedures.

Obama said he had more he wanted to do. He asked Congress for broader authority to reorganize the federal government. He promised that new information systems would make it easier for citizens to choose the best health care coverage. He told citizens that it would be easier to fill out federal forms because the government's information systems would remember basic information for the next time and that citizens would be able to check the status of their applications for programs through online apps. He concluded by saying, "We've got to have the brightest minds to help solve our biggest challenges," with a simple goal: "deliver on the kind of 21st century government the American people want."

Some analysts were underwhelmed. Writing in *Government Executive*, Tom Shoop wondered if the reforms amounted to much. "Most of the specific recommendations Obama discussed today, such as getting reorganization authority from Congress to restructure agencies, already have been proposed and haven't gotten much traction," he said. Moreover, he wondered if many of the ideas relied on innovation from outside the government. Instead, Shoop argued, "what government needs is to unleash the creativity of its experienced managers and employees, who are the only ones with the savvy to know what can and can't be done within the system of laws, rules and regulations that govern all federal activity—and which aren't going away."[2] For better or worse, in the midst of the titanic battles with Congress, these initiatives represented the Obama administration's best plans for reforming the executive branch.

QUESTIONS TO CONSIDER

1. What do you think of the Obama administration's reform agenda? Do you agree with the president that it represents a plan for delivering the kind of government that the American people want? Or do you agree with Shoop that the plan represents old ideas and fails to harness the energy of federal workers?

2. Several commentators have noted the administration's heavy reliance on ideas and strategies from the private sector. What role do you think leading practices in the private sector can—and should—play in rethinking the federal government's own management strategy?

3. Suppose you had the responsibility of laying out a management reform agenda for the next four years. What would your plan be?

NOTES

1. "Remarks by the President Presenting New Management Agenda" (July 8, 2013), http://www.whitehouse.gov/the-press-office/2013/07/08/remarks-president-presenting-new-management-agenda.

2. Tom Shoop, "Obama on Management Reform: It's a Private Matter," *Government Executive* (July 8, 2013), http://www.govexec.com/federal-news/fedblog/2013/07/obama-management-reform-its-private-matter/66173.

 **CASE 6.3**

Naughty Aughties: Has American Government Become More Centralized?

What's happened to the balance of power between the federal, state, and local governments in the last fifteen years? Here is my list of the top ten game changers during the Naughty Aughties and beyond.

1. *Census (2000 and 2010).* Take the decennial count, add personal computers equipped with mapping software, and presto—there's a new game where incumbents can create safe legislative districts and permanently lock in their advantage. Reapportionment shrank the number of marginal seats and increased the level of conflict between increasingly polarized political parties. That made it harder for everyone to govern and for newcomers to run in elections.

2. *The September 11 attacks (2001).* Everyone conceded the need to do a far better job connecting the dots, but as the feds fought over who was in charge, state and local governments often found themselves alone on the front lines of first response. The government has done a lot better in pulling the emergency systems together, but too many of the dots remain unconnected.

3. *No Child Left Behind (2002).* The George W. Bush administration's signature domestic initiative had broad support. Who favored leaving children behind? But no one was very happy about the way the initiative worked out. Local school districts complained that the program imposed unfunded mandates. Attacking the program was one of the few things Democratic presidential candidates agreed on in 2008, but finding a fix is proving very hard without pumping in a lot more cash.

4. *John Roberts named chief justice (2005).* The William Rehnquist Court left behind a long string of decisions expanding the power of the states at the expense of the feds. Although it's still a bit early to determine the mark of the Roberts Court, the Rehnquist "federalism revolution" is ebbing in favor of a much more pragmatic approach. The Court, however, is just one vote away from sliding toward a new revolution in states' rights.

5. *Hurricane Katrina (2005).* The storm not only devastated the Gulf States, but it also left a major city in near-anarchy and made FEMA a dirty word. The feds concluded that they made a big mistake by trusting state and local officials to deal with really big problems. In the aftermath of the Hurricane Katrina fiasco, the feds have quietly decided they'll be quicker on the trigger with a mega-federal response the next time a big disaster occurs.

6. *Minneapolis bridge collapse (2007).* When the I-35W bridge came down in the Twin Cities, the nation got a stunning reminder of the crumbling state of its infrastructure. Cable failures on the San Francisco–Oakland Bay Bridge, the shutdown of I-95 in Philadelphia to repair a crumbling bridge, and the implosion of a major bridge connecting New York and Vermont underlined the emerging crisis. Great video, but little action.

7. *Ireland rejects European Union reform treaty (2008).* Voters decisively rejected the EU's plan to smooth out battles among its states, create a new president, and strengthen foreign policymaking. Kudos to James Madison and the gang from 1787—this federalism stuff is a lot harder to create and sustain than it looks.

8. *Economic meltdown (2009).* As the rest of the economy staggered back to its feet, state and local governments continue to battle the long-term effects of the Great Recession. At the end of 2009, state and local tax revenues were down 7 percent over the dismal previous year. Almost every state was looking at big deficits. Mayor Scott Smith of Mesa, Arizona, told the *Wall Street Journal* that he wasn't sure if his city's services would ever return to previous levels. "We are redefining what cities are going to be," he says.

9. *New transparency (2009).* What's not to like about tens of billions of dollars in stimulus money? The cash, though, came with lots of strings. Loads of information delivered through Recovery.gov became the new accountability, and it's a safe bet that this "new transparency" will endure long after the stimulus money is gone. Everyone agrees transparency is the answer. No one really knows what it is going to mean.

10. *Health reform (2009).* As the "public option" evaporated from the debate, the states became even bigger players in the national health care reform effort. A close reading of the proposed bills, however, revealed that the feds had taken to writing in state agencies as if they were agents of the federal government. In practice, of course, they long have been. The frantic drafting process of the health care reform bills simply stripped away the old pretense and laid bare the way Congress really thinks about the states.

Where does this leave the country as the new century grows into its teens? The United States has changed a lot since the 1990s, when the states were in the driver's seat of domestic policy and the governor's mansion was the proving ground for presidential candidates. Take away item No. 4—with the balance of the U.S. Supreme Court's views on federalism teetering on the next appointment—and the feds are steering the system.

It's hard to see concerns about terrorism ebbing away, and health care reform is likely to cement the federal government's preeminence. It will be hard for state and local governments to fight back when their coffers are dry and the feds can tip the game with vast infusions of cash borrowed from foreign investors.

QUESTIONS TO CONSIDER

1. As you assess the balance of centralization and decentralization in American government, what do you think have been the major events of the last fifteen years?
2. Is there a trend in this balance? Do you think we are becoming more centralized or decentralized? What are the forces shaping this trend, if there is one?
3. What difference do you think this makes, both for governance in America and for public administration?

Note: This case comes from my column in *Governing* (February 2010), http://www.governing.com/columns/potomac-chronicle/A-Decade-To-Remember.html.

CASE 6.4

Who's in Charge When Fires Strike?

U.S. Forest Service fire captain David Ruhl loved tackling big wildfires. So there was little surprise when he volunteered to leave his wife and two children behind in South Dakota's Black Hills to help California during its monstrous fire season. In late July 2015, while he was strategizing on how to fight a particularly nasty one in the Modoc National Forest, a wall of flames suddenly trapped him. Search teams found his body the next day.

Ruhl's death was a tragic reminder of the enormous toll taken by wildfires raging across the West in 2015. But it was also a reminder of the remarkable partnerships that have emerged to fight them. Joining Ruhl were other feds, including expert interagency "hotshot" teams. They worked closely with local firefighters and Air Force C-130 air tankers. Private contractors provided pilots and more aircraft, ranging from small helicopters to giant air tankers. Coordinating everyone was Cal Fire, the state's premier wildfire agency. It was a genuine mosaic of federalism, with the intricate boundaries lost amid the smoke of the worst fire season on record.

But this impressive show of collaboration was hard won. It represents decades of evolving strategies, from the 1950s, when fighting large-scale forest fires involved teams of hikers who drove to the scene in trucks, to today's firefighters, who are aided by aerial tankers that can drop 20,000 gallons—enough for 800 ten-minute showers—in a single attack.

The advances go beyond technique. Training has vastly improved and has become more standardized so that firefighters know what their colleagues know. Strategy has evolved to incorporate the "incident command system," so that leaders can coordinate the complex interagency, intergovernmental, and intersectoral teams that fighting these monster fires now requires. These changes have also shifted the Forest Service's budget. In 1995, fighting wildfires accounted for 18 percent of its spending. In 2015, this had grown to more than half the budget, and the agency now forecasts that firefighting will take 67 percent of its funds by 2025. "Instead of basically maintaining and restoring and making our forest more resilient," U.S. Agriculture Secretary Tom Vilsack, who supervises the Forest Service, told *NBC News*, the agency became "one large fire department." Some analysts even suggest—tongue only partly in cheek—that the U.S. Forest Service should be renamed the U.S. Fire Service.

As the drought in the West has worsened over the years, so too have fire seasons. Americans have grown used to watching dramatic footage of giant planes dropping water on raging, out-of-control fires, and they see those tankers as a sign of government action. Local residents increasingly expect a response that is federal and instant.

Nowhere was this more the case than during the 2011 Texas wildfires, which burned more than 3 million acres and devastated Bastrop County, near Austin. Texas Rep. Michael McCaul, who represents the area, hammered the U.S. Forest Service for failing to pre-position a giant DC-10 aerial tanker that the state could use whenever a wildfire should happen to erupt. When the Bastrop fire started, the Forest Service's contractor fleet was busy in California, fighting an outbreak of wildfires there. The Forest Service shifted a DC-10 to

Texas, but residents were infuriated as the plane sat idle for two days on a runway while Bastrop burned.

Why was the plane idle? The DC-10's crew had to adhere to mandatory rest requirements. Furthermore, ground crews had to build a facility to supply flame retardant for the plane. But all that missed a larger issue, according to Tom Harbour, the Forest Service's director of fire and aviation. At an oversight hearing that McCaul held in Austin after the disaster, Harbour pointed out that the Forest Service was only responsible for fighting the fires on its lands, which accounted for just 0.1 percent of all the land involved in the 2011 Texas fires. The agency had deployed its teams to help on nonfederal lands "because our friends in the Texas Forest Service asked us to help." And they needed that help because Gov. Rick Perry had cut funding for the state's own forest service.

But truthfully, the feds would have been in Texas no matter what. After all, firefighting has become an interagency, intergovernmental affair—that's why David Ruhl was 1,300 miles from home fighting fires.

And there's no doubt these interagency partnerships have vastly improved firefighting, but they have also blurred responsibilities, raised expectations for the federal government's help, and shifted local costs to the federal budget, even when the problems are caused by nature and the prime responsibility for attacking them rests in state and local hands. The strategy that so greatly improved the management of fires has, paradoxically, deeply confused who's really responsible for dealing with and paying for a huge problem that is only growing.

QUESTIONS TO CONSIDER

1. Who is responsible for fighting these kinds of fires?

2. How can firefighters coordinate their work to ensure the most effective strategy for dealing with the fires—and to make the most of limited resources?

3. How can—and should—administrators deal with the political expectations that they can solve tough problems all the time, even if elected officials sometimes aren't interested in providing support?

Note: This case comes from my column in *Governing* (October 2015), http://www.governing.com/columns/potomac-chronicle/gov-wildfire-paradox.html.

KEY CONCEPTS

auxiliary staff 155
clearance procedure 153
control staff 155
coordination 147
core staff 155
executive leadership 145
interagency agreements 152
interagency committees 153

iron triangle 161
lead agency formula 153
line activities 155
neutral competence 145
representativeness 145
staff 155
staff activities 155

FOR FURTHER READING

Arnold, Peri E. *Making the Managerial Presidency: Comprehensive Reorganization Planning, 1905–1980.* Princeton, N.J.: Princeton University Press, 1986.

Fesler, James W. *Area and Administration.* Tuscaloosa: University of Alabama Press, 2008.

Kaufman, Herbert. "Emerging Doctrines of Public Administration." *American Political Science Review* 50 (December 1956): 1059–1073.

Knott, Jack H., and Gary J. Miller. *Reforming Bureaucracy: The Politics of Institutional Choice.* Englewood Cliffs, N.J.: Prentice Hall, 1987.

Lee, Mordecai. *Nixon's Super-Secretaries: The Last Grand Presidential Reorganization Effort.* College Station: Texas A&M University Press, 2010.

National Commission on Terrorist Attacks upon the United States. *The 9/11 Commission Report.* New York: Norton, 2004.

Thomas, Craig W. "Reorganizing Public Organizations: Alternatives, Objectives, and Evidence." *Journal of Public Administration and Theory* 3 (1993): 457–486.

SUGGESTED WEBSITES

The federal government has moved its extensive guide to its organizational structure, the *U.S. Government Manual*, online to **www.usgovernmentmanual.gov**. This is an invaluable resource for understanding the structure and function of government agencies.

The California Performance Review, **www.cpr .ca.gov**, has assembled thorough background discussions about the organization of the state's government. It is a useful guide for understanding the structural issues faced by the nation's most populous state. Many other state and local governments regularly explore how best to improve their operations, and a web search will uncover the most recent initiatives they are taking.

for CQ Press

WANT A BETTER GRADE?

Get the tools you need to sharpen your study skills. Access practice quizzes, eFlashcards, video, and multimedia at **edge.sagepub.com/kettl7e.**

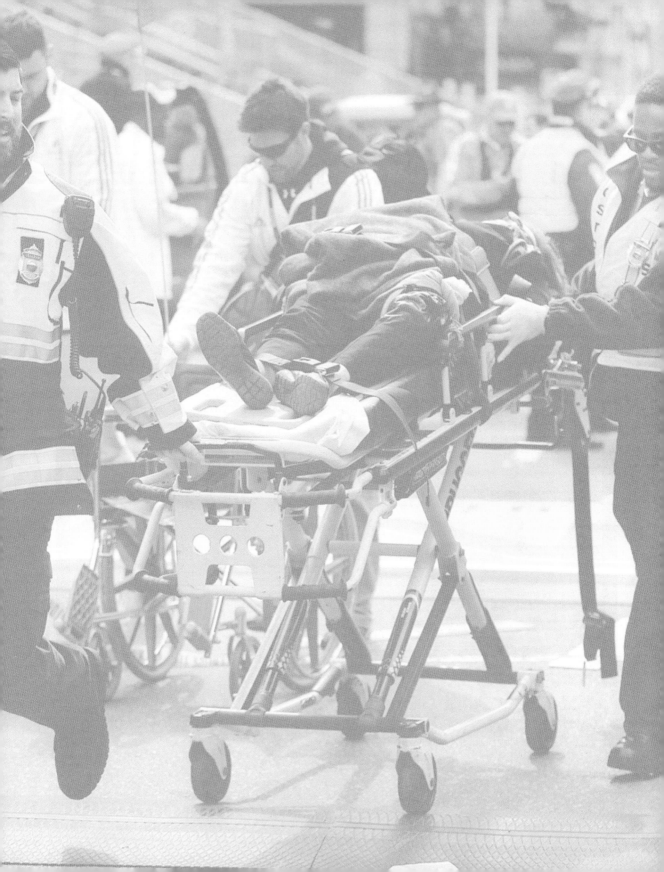

7

ADMINISTRATIVE REFORM

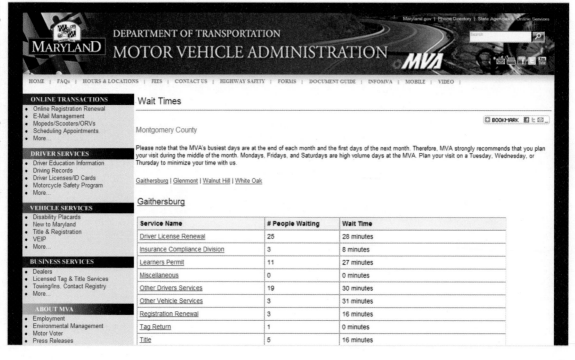

In many states, the Department of Motor Vehicles has used the Internet to connect better with citizens. The website in Maryland provides real-time information about the number of people in line and how long a wait there is to transact business.

n the administrative world, nothing has become more constant than change. In fact, administrative reform has become an imperative of modern management, both in the United States and abroad.[1] A 2001 report by the Organization of Economic Co-operation and Development, an association of the world's major industrialized nations, concluded,

> As society continues to change rapidly, the solutions of the past are no longer sufficient. Not only is there no "one size fits all" solution across countries, but countries should also learn to use reform to create institutions that can constantly adapt to changes in their own societies and to changing outside forces.[2]

In fact, Christopher Pollitt and Geert Bouckaert argue, public management reform "has become a key element in many [political] party manifestos, in many countries. It has internationalized. It has acquired a body of doctrine, and a set of competing models and approaches. In short, it has 'arrived.'"[3]

If reform has arrived, however, it has emerged in many different forms, with multiple personalities, often driven by very different political motives. But beyond the differences is a remarkably universal movement: virtually every government everywhere is deep in administrative reform, driven by a powerful imperative "to make government work better and cost less," as Vice President Al Gore's "reinventing government" movement put it in the 1990s. These bold promises, however, are extremely difficult for governments to achieve, because reform is tough, reforms often move in very different directions, and the underlying politics make it hard to build a stable base of support for very long. Despite these challenges, however, there is a powerful and inescapable truth. There often is relatively little upside political gain for success in improving government's performance. Voters rarely feel moved to reward administrators for doing their job better. That, after all, is what they believe they pay taxes for. But there can be deep, even brutal retribution for failure. Trust in government is low. Failure to perform can drive it lower. And unhappy voters are often quick to punish elected officials who do not perform as they expect. That's the core of the political motivation for reform. Doing better is good. Doing worse—failing to meet citizens' expectations—can be devastating. In an era of rising expectations and tighter budgets, that makes reform a big and inescapable imperative.

REFORM IN AMERICA

Three important truths characterize public management reform in the United States. First, America was born in revolution and, from its earliest days, has built on a movement for reform. The country began with a commitment to changing the way that government works, and it hasn't stopped since. Most presidents, governors, and mayors come into office pledging to make public programs work better. Donald Trump, for example, arrived in the White House with his own six-point "Contract with the American People." In fact, that frames a fundamental paradox of American public administration: there is an enduring sense that public bureaucracy is a large, immovable object, and there is a fundamental belief that top executives need to produce deep, constant change. Few elected officials champion the cause of public administration, per se, but no official can ignore the imperative to make public programs work.

Second, in the United States, the most innovative administrative thinking has often occurred in the private sector. Public managers anxious to save money and improve service delivery have looked for solutions wherever they could find them, and that search has often led them to corporate strategies and tactics. In part, this is because of the recurring, but often wrongheaded, belief that government would be better if it were managed more like the private sector. Private solutions and public problems are not often well matched, but public officials often try to borrow anything from the private sector that might prove a good idea. Occasionally, as in the Progressive Era of the late nineteenth century, public-sector theorizing has moved in advance of private management. However, the "make government work more like the private sector" approach has dominated, especially for most of the last century.

Finally, many American governmental reforms have tended to move up from the experiments of state and local governments, rather than move from the federal government down; the federal government has often been the last link in the chain. In playing catch-up, however, the federal government has often found that its programs, such as food stamps and Social Security, are poor matches for innovative solutions developed for some state and local programs such as garbage collection and park maintenance. Reform often needs a strong hand from the top, but many of the best ideas have bubbled up from the bottom.

American public administration's continued commitment to reform springs from a variety of sources. Some of it reflects a fundamental tension between great ideals and effective pragmatism in the American political character. Many reform ideas are drawn from settings that offer a much different context for the problems they are trying to solve: private-sector strategies applied to government, and state government strategies applied to the federal government. Furthermore, some of this commitment to reform derives from an ongoing dynamic: government has always tried to do very hard things, and reform has always been a coping strategy when results inevitably fall short of expectations. Finally, some of it simply demonstrates that Americans have always been tinkerers who love to tweak the way their government works.

CONFLICTING THEORIES

If the idea of reform has become virtually universal, its strategies and tactics have covered a remarkably broad scope. Moreover, the political context of reform differs widely. Some newly elected officials come into office determined to distinguish themselves as much as possible from their predecessor, especially if their predecessor was from the opposite party. Some arrive on the heels of a scandal or crisis, and they want to quickly bend the government in a new direction. Some officials are good-government types who want to expand and strengthen it. Some want to cut government and slash taxes.

These very different motivations can all lead to reform, but it's not surprising that reforms often take very different paths. Moreover, reforms vary with cultural, social, and political traditions. Utah has a long tradition of highly professionalized government based on a strong information technology backbone. Wyoming often gets high marks because of its relatively small population and careful attention to its budget. In Texas, state officials have worked hard to shrink government spending and manage the oil revenues that flow into the state's treasury. New York City and Baltimore have long traditions of using information about government performance to drive city administration. Chicago is developing new strategies for connecting social media with policy feedback. All have engaged in "reform," but because of the strategies of government officials and the settings in which they work, all are very different.

Reform movements have generally converged on three basic approaches: **downsizing**, **reengineering**, and **continuous improvement.** The terms speak to the aspirations of citizens and government officials alike. Cutting government is often appealing, so reformers resort to downsizing. When results fall short of expectations, reformers seek to reengineer organizations. Continuous improvement is continually attractive.

In Garland, Maine, Mary Adams campaigned in 2006 for a "Taxpayer Bill of Rights" to cut taxes and bring down government spending. The 68-year-old grandmother helped advance a movement that had spread from coast to coast.

There is a fundamental challenge behind these basic approaches. The old bureaucratic orthodoxy, founded on traditional authority and hierarchy, promised a clear, straightforward, and universal set of principles: delegation of authority on the basis of expertise, and democratic accountability through hierarchical control. The new ideas driving bureaucratic reform, however, are neither orthodox nor universal. Moreover, at their core are important—but often unrecognized—contradictions that threaten the success of reform efforts, as recent American experience illustrates.

Downsizing

Conservatives have long argued that government is too big and needs to be cut back. In 2010, Republican congressional candidates pledged to impose a freeze on hiring most federal employees and cutting "wasteful and duplicative programs" to "curb Washington's irresponsible spending habits and reduce the size of government."[4] In 2016, Republican primary candidates proposed which agencies they would eliminate if they were elected. It was a long list: the Environmental Protection Agency (EPA); the Departments of Education, Energy, and Housing and Urban Development; and the perennial target, the Internal Revenue Service, among others. But downsizing hasn't just been the province of conservative Republicans. In the 1990s, the Clinton administration dramatically reduced the size of the federal government's workforce as part of its "reinventing government" initiative, as we will shortly see.

The American downsizing movement began at the state and local levels, especially during the property tax reduction movement of the 1970s. New Jersey legislators in 1976 limited the growth of expenditures to the growth of per capita personal income. California voters fired the loudest shot in 1978 by approving an amendment to the state constitution, Proposition 13, which reduced property taxes to 1 percent of market value and limited future property tax growth to a 2 percent annual increase over the amount calculated from the 1975–1976 base. Massachusetts voters followed with Proposition 2½, which reduced property taxes by 15 percent per year until they reached 2½ percent of full market value, where they had to remain (hence the name applied to the proposition).[5] State legislators passed scores of other tax limitations or special tax breaks in the following decade.[6] Between 1976 and 1982, legislators and voters in nineteen states agreed to limit revenues or expenditures.[7]

The movement continued through the 1990s and 2000s, led by Colorado's passage in 1992 of a constitutional amendment to limit tax increases—christened the **Taxpayer Bill of Rights**, or TABOR for short—which spread to other states as well. The proposal passed with 54 percent of the vote; a decade later, almost three-fourths of Colorado residents favored its tough approach.[8] The Colorado effort sparked a string of copycats over the next decade. In 1994, Michigan voters agreed to shift a substantial amount of local property tax revenues for education to state taxes. Wisconsin legislators voted to replace most local property taxes for schools with state aid, to be financed by state government spending cuts. In both cases, state officials first committed themselves to the broad reform—property tax relief—without deciding how they would produce it. In both cases, the strategy provoked wild bargaining in the state legislatures to produce the promised aid.

According to public opinion surveys, it's not that citizens were unhappy with government services. They simply believed that their taxes were too high, and that government could easily provide the same services for less money.[9] In 2010, the Pew Center on the States and Public Policy surveyed residents of five of the nation's most financially distressed states. Two-thirds of survey respondents said that they never trust state government to do what is right, or they trust it only some of the time. They wanted major reforms, but the reforms that they wanted didn't align with the services they expected (see Table 7.1). Little has changed since.

Promising to cut the unholy trinity of "waste, fraud, and abuse" always resonates well with voters. For better or worse, both elected officials and voters have come to believe that government's inefficiency is so great that it's possible to cut spending without hurting the quality of services. E. S. Savas argued in 1982 that the public, "despairing of the ability or will of its elected government to reduce expenditures, has taken the matter directly into its hands and reduced revenue, like a parent rebuking his spendthrift child by cutting its allowance."[10] The basic strategy was clear. Government, critics believed, would spend whatever money it collected, and it wouldn't always spend it well. Cut revenues, and that would force government to be more efficient.

In the mid-1980s, led by President Ronald Reagan, the downsizing movement spilled into the federal government. In 1984, the President's **Private Sector Survey on Cost Control** (better known as the Grace Commission, after its chairman, J. Peter Grace) produced 2,478 recommendations that its report said would save $424.4 billion over three years. The commission concluded that the federal government was "suffering from a critical case of inefficient and ineffective management" and that only more businesslike practices and, in particular, huge cuts in governmental programs could reduce the deficit hemorrhage.[11] Academic critics argued that the report was built largely on an ideological, probusiness, antigovernment base; that it contained misrepresentations; and that following its recommendations could actually hurt the work of the federal government.[12] Suspicious Democrats, who controlled Congress, saw it as a partisan maneuver by Republican president Ronald Reagan, and the resulting partisan battles doomed almost all of the report's recommendations.

The Grace Commission report did, however, fuel a downsizing movement at the federal level, helping to promote in 1985 the **Balanced Budget and Emergency Deficit Control Act**, better known as the Gramm-Rudman Act, after two of its key sponsors, Senators

Table 7.1	**Distrust of State Governments: Survey of Residents in Five States**

States surveyed: Arizona, California, Florida, Illinois, and New York

1. **Government Performance Matters:** Residents are more likely to say their elected leaders are wasting their money and could deliver services more efficiently than to complain that state government is too big.

    Reality Check: About two out of three residents say their state government could spend less and still provide the same level of services. Of those, most residents think cuts of 10 percent to 20 percent or even more are possible. But experts who work closely with state budgets say that perception may not be realistic, especially given the steep spending reductions many states already have made since the recession started.

2. **Protect the Essentials:** In all five states, by a range of 63 percent to 71 percent, majorities say they would be willing to pay higher taxes to keep K–12 public schools at current funding levels. Fifty-two percent to 57 percent say they would pay higher taxes to preserve funding for health and human services.

    Reality Check: It will be extremely difficult, given the size of deficits in all five states, to fully protect K–12 education and health and human services, the biggest recipients of state dollars. Doing so would compel deeper cuts everywhere else, and even then may not be enough.

3. **Tax the Other Guy:** Residents would prefer to charge the other guy—particularly corporations, smokers, drinkers, and gamblers.

    Reality Check: The revenue raisers that residents are most widely willing to tolerate—hitting smokers, drinkers, gamblers, and corporations—would tap marginal revenue streams and likely would not be sufficient to address their state's budget shortfalls.

4. **No More Borrowing:** The public is tired of lawmakers borrowing and passing costs to future generations—they'd rather keep cutting and taxing than see states borrow. Given three choices to balance state budgets, more than two-thirds of residents in all five states pick spending cuts first; they prefer tax increases second and borrowing last.

    Reality Check: State and local government borrowing is on the rise. In many cases, debt plays a productive role in providing funding for infrastructure, services, and budget flexibility. Not all debt is bad debt, and borrowing is an important financial tool for state governments. But too much of any kind of debt is problematic.

5. **Lack of Trust—and Desire for Reform:** Across all five states, two-thirds or more of respondents report that they either never trust state government to do what is right or trust it only some of the time. Residents overwhelmingly believe their state should pursue major reforms to their budget processes, and pursue them now.

    Reality Check: Residents across the five states overwhelmingly believe their state should pursue major reforms to their budget processes, and pursue them now.

Source: Excerpt from Pew Center on the States, *Facing the Facts: How Residents in Five States View Fiscal Priorities for State Government* (2010), http://www.pewcenteronthestates.org/report_detail.aspx?id=60803.

Phil Gramm (R-Tex.) and Warren Rudman (R-N.H.). (The bill also had the support of Ernest Hollings [D-S.C.], but the "Gramm-Rudman" label stuck. Comedians suggested they had to cut here, too.) Among its many important effects, Gramm-Rudman forced both the president and Congress, Democrats and Republicans alike, to begin bringing the burgeoning federal deficit under control. Downsizing became an inescapable part of politics at all levels of American government. Gramm-Rudman and the TABOR movements intersected and reinforced each other.

Soon after taking office in 1993, President Bill Clinton named Vice President Al Gore to work on **reinventing government**, to make the federal government work better and cost less. The term came from a best-selling 1993 book, *Reinventing Government*, by David Osborne and Ted Gaebler.[13] Gore's campaign, the National Performance Review, promised voters $108 billion in savings by fiscal year 1999. Some of the savings were to come from reforms already underway, but most of the projected savings were from reducing the federal workforce by 12 percent over five years—a total cut of 252,000 positions—to leave the workforce at under 2 million for the first time since 1967. The vice president's report promised that the cuts would consist of pruning unnecessary layers of the federal bureaucracy.[14]

Federal Employees per Million Dollars in Federal Spending

There's a constant debate about the need to cut the number of government employees. They've often been the symbol of government growth. But has the number grown?

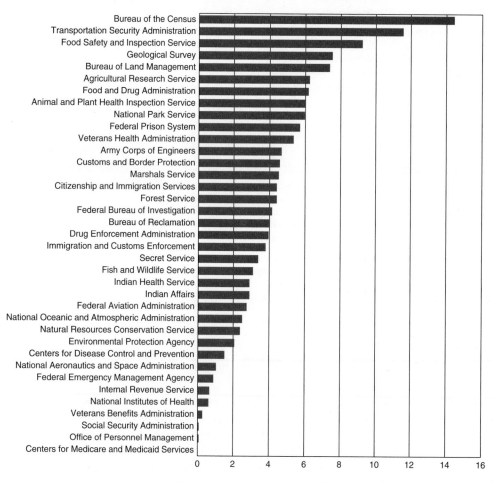

Source: U.S. Office of Management and Budget, *Budget of the United States Government, Analytical Perspectives: Fiscal Year 2015* (2014), Table 29.1, http://www .whitehouse.gov/sites/default/files/omb/budget/fy2015/assets/29_1.pdf; and U.S. Office of Personnel Management, "FedScope," https://www.fedscope.opm.gov.

QUESTIONS

1. How does the number of federal government employees vary by this selected group of agencies?

2. What would account for this variation?

3. What implications do you think this variation has for public administration?

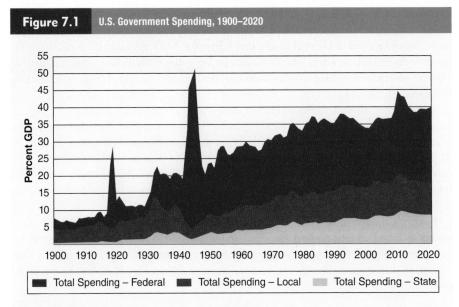

| **Figure 7.1** | **U.S. Government Spending, 1900–2020** |

Source: USGovernmentSpending.com, http://www.usgovernmentspending.com/spending_chart_1900_2020USp_17s2li0 181421_902cs_FOsFOIFOf_Federal_State_and_Local_Spending_In_20th_Century.

Gore's report asserted that the many reforms it proposed—from streamlining the procurement process to giving managers more flexibility to make decisions without endless cross-checking—would improve governmental efficiency, making it possible to eliminate functions and layers of the federal bureaucracy and, therefore, to save billions of dollars. In practice, the biggest changes came through downsizing the workforce. Most departments met their targets by offering employees buyout packages that included financial inducements for taking early retirement.[15] By 2001, the number of federal civilian employees had declined by 365,000 (17 percent). The workforce reduction was the biggest single impact of Gore's effort—but he barely mentioned it during his 2000 run for the White House.

The recurring battles over the size of the government workforce have raised important questions about the downsizing movement. First, the question of government's size has been disconnected from its function. Even in the Clinton-Gore reinventing government effort, the downsizing target had little or nothing to do with how many employees were needed to carry out government's job. Broad strategic decisions about how much government needed to be cut, rather than how many employees were needed to accomplish its missions, dominated the debate. As Congress's watchdog agency, the General Accounting Office (in 2004 it became the Government Accountability Office), concluded in 2002:

> Much of the downsizing was set in motion without sufficient planning for its effects on agencies' performance capacity. Across government, federal employers reduced or froze their hiring efforts for extended periods. . . . This helped reduce their numbers of employees, but it also reduced the influx of new people with new knowledge, new energy, and new ideas—the reservoir of future agency leaders and managers.[16]

Second, there were big ideas at the core of these downsizing initiatives, but they were very different big ideas. Conservatives tried to "starve the beast": if the "beast" they see as government cannot be killed in a frontal assault, they believed it could be weakened by denying it the tax revenues it needs to work. Liberals focused on big policy ideas without determining what capacity government needed to carry them out. Both ideologies helped support downsizing initiatives.

Third, despite these strategies and tactics, American government has continued to grow. As a share of the economy, total government spending has increased from 8 percent of the gross domestic product (the total of goods and services produced within the country) in 1900, to 22 percent in 1950, 34 percent in 2000, and a projected 41 percent in 2020 (see Figure 7.1). As we saw in Chapter 2, spending for governments in the United States ranks toward the bottom of government spending around the world. Government is not particularly large— and efforts to constrain its growth have not been particularly effective.

Fourth, although these strategies have not made government smaller, they have made it weaker, as John J. DiIulio pointed out.[17] By starving the beast, conservatives made it harder for government to have the capacity to work. By focusing more on creating new policies than on how to deliver them, liberals did the same. By very different roads, both sides weakened government's capacity.

Reengineering

At the same time that "reinventing government" caught fire in the 1990s, another reform movement emerged. In 1993, Michael Hammer and James Champy wrote *Reengineering the Corporation*, a tale of private companies faced not only with new challenges but also with threats to their very existence.[18] These authors claimed that business leaders needed to move past incremental improvements to a fundamental reexamination of their operations in order to succeed, or even to survive. Their case for creating completely new work processes soon spilled over into government.[19]

Reengineering, Hammer and Champy argue, begins by putting everything on the table. It "means starting all over, starting from scratch," through "discontinuous thinking."[20] They sought to bring fundamental changes to big organizations. By the 2010s, *disruptive innovation* had become the popular phrase. But the key remained the same: push aside incremental improvements in favor of big reforms, if organizations were to meet the equally big challenges of the information age. Reengineering focuses on radically redesigning work processes. Indeed, *process* is the fundamental building block of reengineering, with an eye to ensuring that organizations understand and meet their customers' needs. Central to the effort is the latest technology to wring extra efficiency out of their operations. Reengineers search for breakthrough strategies instead of incremental improvements—rather than trying to do a job 10 percent better, reengineers look for strategies that can work ten, or a hundred, times better.[21]

Public managers found the movement irresistible. Massachusetts, for example, reengineered its child support collection system. Previously, collection efforts began with complaints by the caregiving spouse against the nonsupporting spouse; caseworkers, through a labor-intensive system, then tried to track down scofflaws and intervene to try to win support. Under the new system, the state instead began relying on computers to find cases with similar characteristics, to search the database for parents who owed support, and to generate letters insisting on payment. After two years, according to one report, 85 percent of collections had occurred without a caseworker's intervention, the number of cases in which payments were collected had increased 30 percent, and the compliance rate had jumped from 59 percent to 76 percent. In Merced County, California, new software designed for individual workstations replaced mainframe-based programs for processing welfare eligibility claims; in the process, the time between the initial application and the interview decreased from four weeks to three days or less.[22] Texas, meanwhile, launched several major initiatives to improve the state's tax administration system, which supporters believed could produce an additional $51 million in revenues per year.[23] The reengineering program recommends focusing on the program's mission, identifying its customers, and rethinking how best to deliver services. The movement argues that more efficient services will follow. Even much-maligned state Department of Motor Vehicles (DMV) offices got a reengineering makeover. According to a 2014 survey, the best DMV offices were in Ohio, Illinois, and Indiana. Connecticut, South Carolina, and Oregon ranked at the bottom.[24]

The reengineering movement undoubtedly produced big improvements in government's delivery of services to citizens. But it also fueled a big debate over whether its premise—changing processes to improve customers' satisfaction—fit government. H. George Frederickson, for example, contends that "governments are not markets" and that "citizens are not the customers. They are the owners."[25] Critics add that the broader movement to make government more entrepreneurial is dangerous; even if entrepreneurial behavior were a good idea, they argue, the concept could never be applied to government because there frequently is little private competition in most public functions.[26] Nevertheless, the reengineers countered that energetic, problem-solving managers would perform far better than more traditional bureaucrats rooted in standard operating procedures and organizational structures.

Moreover, even though citizens quite clearly "own" their government, many reformers argue that governments could treat citizens better—as "customers" of governmental programs—without violating the fundamental premises of democratic government. Wisconsin's DMV, for example, installed new systems to make it much easier to obtain driver's licenses: take-a-number machines that tell citizens how long they can expect to wait, new strategies to minimize those waits, and satellite offices located in shopping malls and open evenings and weekends to give citizens wider access. The state's Department of Revenue developed a new quick-refund system that got taxpayers their income tax refund checks within two weeks. Maryland's DMV has a website that allows citizens to wait times—before they leave their homes. In Oregon, the state's driver's license bureau surveyed citizens to determine what problem they most wanted solved; the number one problem was the poor quality of the driver's license photographs that embarrassed citizens had to carry around for years. The state installed a new electronic system that allowed citizens to choose the photos that would grace their licenses, which made them much happier with the service. As computer programs like TurboTax and TaxCut have made it easier for individuals to prepare their tax returns at home, governments have worked hard to make it easier for taxpayers to file their taxes with a touch of a button. For many Americans, the IRS has an online tax filing service that's free.

There is nothing new about strategies to improve organizational processes. Process, in fact, was central to much organizational thinking in the 1930s, especially to the work of Henri Fayol.[27] Indeed, Luther Gulick's famous paper "Notes on the Theory of Organization," which was written for the Brownlow Committee and advised President Franklin Roosevelt on reorganization of his office, explicitly tackled the issue of "organization by major process." Along the way, Gulick noted the critical problem of process-based organization: "while organization by process thus puts great efficiency within our reach,

Rooting Out Sexual Harassment
Theme: Accountability

In July 2016, the *Washington Post* ran a series of stories pointing to an ongoing pattern of sexual harassment in the National Park Service. Departmental investigators at both the Grand Canyon National Park (in Arizona) and Canaveral National Seashore (in Florida) found that multiple women had been repeatedly pressured for sex and had been subjected to unwanted attention from supervisors.

Interior Secretary Sally Jewell said that the reports were probably "just the tip of the iceberg" and she pledged aggressive action. Jewell said she was "not proud" of the charges. "But I am proud of the fact that we are going to deal with it and deal with it immediately," she said on a national radio talk show.

Getting to the bottom of the problem and developing a strategy proved difficult. The department planned new face-to-face training, as well as a Park Service–wide survey to determine just how broad the problem was.

Rooting out the problem, Jewel said, was important. "What needs to change is really a function of leadership," she explained. "It's painting a picture of what is behavior that people aspire to be a part of and what is unacceptable behavior, so individuals will report, but the work group will stop it, nip it in the bud if they see something happening."

Source: Lisa Rein, "Interior Chief: 'Culture' of Sexual Harassment Probably Pervades the National Park Service," *Washington Post* (July 12, 2016), https://www.washingtonpost.com/news/powerpost/wp/2016/07/12/interior-chief-culture-of-sexual-harassment-likely-pervades-the-national-park-service/.

---

this efficiency cannot be realized unless the compensating structure of coordination is developed."[28]

In the decades after World War II, organizational theorists' (especially *public* organizational theorists) interest in organizational process diminished considerably. Most discussions of process revolved around *due process* and the guarantee of fair treatment for citizens.[29] James Q. Wilson's brilliant book *Bureaucracy*, however, talks about "procedural organizations" as ones where "managers can observe what their subordinates are doing but not the outcome (if any) that results from those efforts."[30] This limited perspective creates a stark tension: in a situation where they cannot determine what results subordinates produce, Wilson warns, government managers often cannot understand, let alone control, the results of their programs. The reengineers, in contrast, contend that controlling process to improve results is essential to better administration. Indeed, organizational process is implicit in the work of most modern public organization theorists, but it is central to almost nothing (except, as noted earlier, to securing fair treatment).[31] Reengineering seeks to reestablish organizational process in the minds of managers, and to elevate it above even the level it enjoyed in the prewar period.

The risks of reengineering lie in its potential: overpromising and underdelivering. But as the battles over taxes grow, managers continuously look for new strategies to squeeze more productivity from scarce dollars. This has made reengineering an inescapable imperative.

Motivation

Other administrative reformers have taken a very different approach, based on improving the motivation of employees to perform well. Instead of discontinuous, top-down, revolutionary change, as the reengineers recommended, the motivation-driven reformers have advocated a more gradual, continuous, bottom-up movement, grounded in the effort to motivate employees to produce better results. This approach has grown since the 1960s and has built on the work of W. Edwards Deming especially.[32] A fundamental theme is at the core: the quality of the work matters most and, with the right motivation, workers will produce better results.

Deming contends that costs decline as quality increases. "Better quality leads to lower costs and higher productivity," one admirer explains. "The consequences for an individual company are that increasing quality leads to higher productivity, lower costs, higher profits, higher share price, and greater security for everyone in the company—the managers, the workers, and the owners."[33] Employees dominated by the profit motive tend to be unhappy; employees pursuing quality take more satisfaction in what they do, feel more secure, and work more productively. A total commitment to quality—"**total quality management**," or TQM for short—is the key to managerial success.

The motivation approach builds on a long tradition of organizational theory rooted in the 1940s, beginning with Mary Parker Follett[34] and Abraham H. Maslow[35] and continuing on to more modern motivation-based theorists. This approach has not moved to the center of organization theory, in part because it does not promise the same fundamental transformation as reengineering and in part because (once launched) it is never finished. However, the motivation-based reformers argue that this is one of the movement's strengths: no level of quality is ever enough—and only the constant search for quality can keep an organization and its workers sharp.

From Vice President Gore's reinventing government task force to state and local government efforts, the movement has often found deep resonance in American government. Reinventing government promises to "put citizens first," with employees "empowered to get results." Indeed, the footnotes at the end of the report are littered with references to TQM. Similar customer-based, continuous processes have driven reforms at state and local levels as well, from state-based reinvention efforts in Minnesota to sweeping strategic planning in Oregon.[36] The EPA used the TQM technique to improve its management of a program dealing with leaking underground storage tanks. The Air Force Logistics Command used it to improve the readiness rate of its fighter planes from 40 percent to 76 percent. In the New York City sanitation department, TQM helped to resolve labor union problems. The U.S. Department of Veterans Affairs (VA) Philadelphia Regional Office used TQM to improve service to veterans applying for loans.[37] In fact, two students of the process concluded, "quality improvement projects have resulted in significant cost savings, improved services to agency customers and clients, and measurable improvements in employee morale and productivity."[38] The quality movement, compared with reengineering, has tended to focus more on people than on organizations, more on frontline workers than on top leadership, and more on the ability of individual workers to improve results than on the need to change structures and processes.

Finding new strategies to motivate public employees is a matter of utmost importance, because surveys across government show profound problems. Public employees are significantly less happy than private employees, according to a survey by the private consulting firm PricewaterhouseCoopers, by a margin of 43 to 32 percent. Fewer than half of public employees in Michigan believe that their "department leadership communicates openly and honestly with employees." In the city of San Antonio, 86 percent of employees agreed they were treated with dignity and respect, but only 54 percent said they "receive recognition for a job well done" (Figure 7.2).[39]

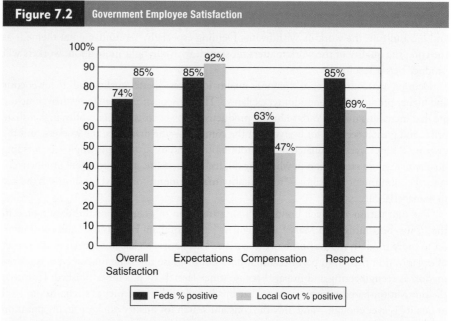

Figure 7.2 Government Employee Satisfaction

Source: Katherine Barrett and Richard Greene, "What Employee Surveys Reveal about Working in Government," *Governing* (June 9, 2016), http://www.governing.com/columns/smart-mgmt/gov-employee-surveys-state-local-government.html.

At the same time, however, government's system for assessing employee performance tends to rank almost all employees at the top of the scale. Minnesota humorist Garrison Keillor for decades closed his public radio monologue, based on his fictional hometown, with this: "Well, that's the news from Lake Wobegon, where all the women are strong, all the men are good looking, and all the children are above average." In government, according to a GAO survey, 99 percent of federal employees were ranked "fully successful" in 2013, and 60 percent were scored even higher (see Figure 7.3). The number was even higher for employees in the upper levels of the federal civil service: 78 percent.[40] The employee assessment system provides no real differentiation in employee performance. So there's a fundamental paradox here: many government employees feel they are not recognized for good work—and the system designed to assess their performance tends to conclude that just about everyone is doing great work.

What could be done about this? The results of a 2015 survey of federal government employees provide some useful clues. Five big themes emerge to help improve employee motivation and satisfaction[41]:

1. *Meaningful work.* Government employees want to go to work and accomplish something important. Few things could be more important than the missions that government takes on, from keeping the streets and the food supply safe to financing health care for the poor and cleaning the environment. But in day-to-day work, supervisors don't always communicate clearly to employees about how their work advances these important missions.

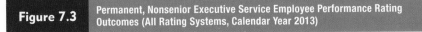

| Figure 7.3 | Permanent, Nonsenior Executive Service Employee Performance Rating Outcomes (All Rating Systems, Calendar Year 2013) |

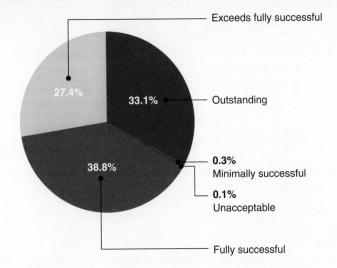

Source: U.S. Government Accountability Office, *Federal Workforce: Distribution of Performance Ratings across the Federal Government*, 2013 (May 9, 2016), http://www.gao.gov/products/GAO-16-520R.

Note: N = 1,171,400 permanent, Executive Service employees (rounded to nearest 100). Numbers may not add to 100 percent due to rounding.

2. *Hands-on management.* Effective managers don't micromanage, but they do provide strong coaching to help employees determine the best direction for their work.

3. *Positive work.* Regular recognition of employees who are making strong contributions can reinforce motivation.

4. *Growth opportunities.* No employee wants to get stuck in a job. Creating opportunities for promotion and advancement, including providing training to help employees conquer new challenges, often proves very important—especially for millennials.

5. *Trust in leadership.* Followers learn to lead by watching good leaders. If they see good leaders, they're likely to become better leaders themselves. And nothing is more fundamental to that process than leaders who are transparent about agency goals and procedures and who inspire workers to do their best.

Motivating employees has always been important. In an era of government bashing, it's never been more important—or challenging. But strong and effective leaders can help motivate their employees toward better and more fulfilling work. Strong leadership development, reinforced by good research about who is doing it well, has proven an important strategy for reform.

Delivery Framework

Many governments around the world are focusing on delivery, in an effort to concentrate on the outputs and outcomes of government agencies and to devise improved strategies, from the center of government, to make delivery work better. Sir Michael Barber pioneered this effort when he worked for British Prime Minister Tony Blair, and his approach has been followed in nations around the world.[42] Barber focused on what he calls "the most difficult thing in politics, which is to run a country." The challenge, he wrote, centers "on the difficulty of getting things done." He concluded that "The path to accountable government is that much easier to walk if governments succeed in delivering at least some of what they have promised."[43]

Barber's model builds on the following concise set of rules:

1. *Have an agenda.* It's impossible to do everything, and it's hard for leaders to do anything without a clear focus on what they want to do.

2. *Decide on your priorities.* Often, of course, the list is long. Getting things done requires deciding what has to be done first.

3. *Be unreasonable.* Many things that governments want to accomplish are hard and require hard choices. Political courage is central to the process.

4. *Set a small number of well-designed targets.* It's hard to be precise about where a leader wants to go without targets to provide a guide. Too many targets really mean there are no targets. So the key is driving results to a relatively manageable collection of targets.

5. *Apply science to target setting.* Benchmarks—targets with measures that track results—can tell readers how ambitious they can be, and at what pace.

6. *Check for perverse or unintended consequences.* Not everything that happens is good, and some things that happen haven't been foreseen. Smart leaders are constantly on the lookout for results that weren't anticipated.

7. *Consult without conceding on ambition.* Effective leadership requires learning as much as possible from clients and others in the field. Consulting can richly inform action but, Barber contends, it should not put a brake on action.

8. *Targets are important but not the point.* Moral purposes—the broader goals of governance—ultimately are most important.

9. *Review the capacity of your system to deliver the goals.* Sometimes doing ambitious things requires building new government capacity—new agencies or newly trained employees—to get them done.

10. *Set up a delivery unit.* This organization, a small unit close to the government's top leader, should organize and transmit these rules throughout the rest of the government.

Other rules followed (a total of fifty-seven in all), but the first ten guide his strategy. Barber used the rules to guide a fundamental reshaping of British government, and many nations have picked up the model, often with great impact.

In the United States, a variety of "stat" programs have followed Barber's general model. The CompStat strategy in New York City was the foundation. The police department created a central unit, set priorities for reducing crime, tracked crime trends, intervened aggressively, and followed up strongly. The model spread to other police departments across the country, based on four principles that reflect Barber's strategy:

- Accurate and timely intelligence (police commanders need to know what is happening),
- Effective tactics (they need to have a plan to respond),
- Rapid deployment (acting fast is key), and
- Relentless follow-up (as some experts have put it, "If it works, do more. If not, do something else").[44]

Martin O'Malley, during his two terms as mayor of Baltimore, brought the strategy to the entire city, and then he used it as two-term Maryland governor to transform state operations. This "stat" approach has been the most important application of the performance strategy in the United States.[45]

At the federal level, the VA used the "stat" strategy to sharply drive down homelessness among veterans. By 2014, the problem had become a national tragedy. The Office of Management and Budget (OMB) reported that veterans accounted for 9.3 percent of the American population, but 11.3 percent of homeless adults. On one January night in 2014, 49,933 veterans were homeless.[46] The VA launched a targeted program to reduce homelessness among vets, including close coordination with the U.S. Department of Housing and Urban Development. The VA set a target of finding permanent housing for 49,000 vets. In fact, it helped 64,902 vets find homes. The department used a series of metrics to track the program and drive its success (Figures 7.4 and 7.5).

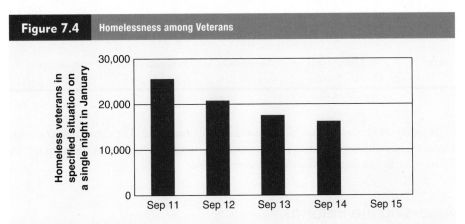

Figure 7.4   Homelessness among Veterans

Source: U.S. Office of Management and Budget, "End Veterans Homelessness," https://www.performance.gov/content/end-veterans-homelessness#indicators.

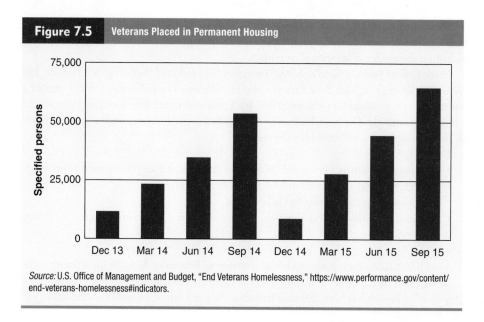

Source: U.S. Office of Management and Budget, "End Veterans Homelessness," https://www.performance.gov/content/end-veterans-homelessness#indicators.

Table 7.2	Administrative Reform Strategies in the United States			
	Downsizing	**Reengineering**	**Motivation**	**Delivery Framework**
Goal	Lower expenditures	Efficiency	Responsiveness	Outcomes
Direction	Outside-in	Top-down	Bottom-up	Top-down/bottom-up
Method	Blunt targets	Competition	Cooperation	Transparency
Central focus	Size	Process	Interpersonal relations	Information
Action	Discontinuous	Discontinuous	Continuous	Virtual, through Internet

We will explore these strategies in more detail in Chapter 12. The rise of delivery units, supported by performance indicators, has proven an especially important government reform initiative in the first decades of the twenty-first century.

Assessing the Reforms

A side-by-side comparison of the defining ideas of these three major administrative reforms—downsizing, reengineering, and continuous improvement—reveals stark differences. Table 7.2 displays the reforms according to the goals they seek, the directions in which they are implemented, the methods that characterize them, the central focus of managers following them, and the kinds of action that drive them. In brief, they may be described as follows:

- *Downsizing*, enforced from the outside in by angry citizens, seeks lower government expenditures. Its methods are blunt targets, driven by the assumption that there is ample waste in government to accommodate the cuts. Downsizers seek to shrink the size of government through strategic intervention, indeed, by firing a weapon of sufficient size to signal their fundamental disdain for existing policymakers and managers.
- *Reengineering* seeks greater organizational efficiency by pursuing a radical change in organizational process. Top leaders, with the broad strategic sense of where the organization needs to go, attempt to harness competition and the urge to serve customers and thereby to transform their organizations.
- *Motivation* seeks to improve the results of government by creating stronger incentives among employees for strong performance and by reinforcing positive work. It builds on the relationship between workers and their supervisors.
- *Delivery frameworks* seek to create structures and processes that focus crisply on defining the most important goals, developing strong metrics, and driving the system to meet them. **Delivery frameworks** have been adopted in other countries but haven't yet penetrated American government on a broad scale.

Assessing the conflicts among the driving ideas of these administrative reform approaches is itself an important problem. We simply don't know which one works best. More important, we don't know how to create and sustain a movement over the long haul, since many of these reforms have patterns of rising and falling in importance and interest. As reforms come and go, employees sometimes conclude that they are fads; the bigger a change they'd be required to make, the stronger an incentive they have to wait out a reform initiative—and to await the next one. But, as noted at the beginning of this chapter, reform and change have become the great constants in public administration. The challenges are so great that leaders reach for new ideas to help them carry out the change they need—and the promises they make to citizens. Change is indeed the great constant, including in the reforms that leaders advance. But the instinct toward reform is the even more fundamental constant.

These contradictions, however, have scarcely prevented both public managers and policymakers from embracing the basic ideas. The labels themselves have strong symbolic appeal, and the overall goals of each technique are unassailable. Citizens and elected officials alike find the promise of a smaller government alluring, engineered with better processes and devoted to greater responsiveness to citizens and quality. The contradictions of administrative reform ideas are both fundamentally unresolvable and politically unavoidable.

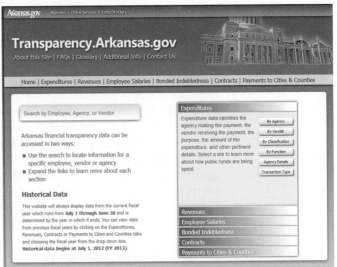

Citizens wanting to track government spending in Arkansas, from employees' salaries to aid to local governments, can easily find the data on a special website devoted to transparency in government.

ALL THE WORLD'S A STAGE

Around the globe, two undeniable truths about public administration are evident.[47] One is that administrative reform is a fixture of government everywhere—indeed, it may well be the feature that governments share more than any other. Nations that broke out of a generation of domination by the Soviet Union are struggling to catch up. They face tasks ranging from inventing a system of public law within which a new private sector can grow to revising a tax system in order to fund public programs better. Developing nations are rushing to modernize their economies, and reconstructing their governments is a critical part of that strategy.[48] More developed nations are seeking to reinvent themselves by wringing waste out of the public sector and making governmental programs more efficient. China is a management reform movement in a class by itself, as the country works quickly to both modernize a vast rural population and sustain world-class technology in other areas. But management reform is central to the country's ongoing transformation efforts.

The other truth is that, despite widespread reform, no single set of ideas is driving it. Reform of public administration is as varied as the nations attempting it. The number of basic ideas at the core of the reform movement is small, but they have come together in a remarkable array of combinations.

Downsizing carries a simple goal: shrink the public sector as much as possible, whether by selling off public enterprises, contracting out services that remain publicly provided, or imposing limits to future growth. However, although downsizing is one of the few government reforms that can quickly produce cost savings, it risks pushing government's management capacity out of sync with the job to be done. Downsizing is rarely accompanied by a restructuring of government's workforce; as a result, it is very easy to end up with too many of the wrong employees and not enough employees with the skills government needs most. Nevertheless, virtually every major government around the world has tried it, both to signal its determination to cut costs and to produce real savings.

The reengineering approaches employ both procedural and analytical tactics. Many countries have developed new processes to link operating units together better. For example, New Zealand is training top managers to develop new skills in administering programs that cut across agency boundaries. The French decentralization movement aims, in part, to bring together at the local level all those concerned with similar problems. Spain has introduced information technology to link governmental units, and **e-government** has spread around the globe. Meanwhile, a worldwide movement to reduce the number of government regulations, launched in the 1980s, is continuing. In addition, countries are relying on information and analysis to increase leverage over administrators' actions. Governments have also spent more than a decade developing **performance management** systems, in which operating managers are given greater discretion in return for accountability for performance measured against agreed-upon indicators. Many nations are linking such performance measurement with reform of financial management systems to promote planning and cost control. Australia, Finland, Iceland, New Zealand, the United Kingdom, and the United States have all moved (some much further and more eagerly than others) from cost toward accrual accounting to improve accountability. Overall, the result is a widely varied collection of strategies that fly loosely under the reengineering banner.

At the same time, many nations are relying on better measurement and training systems as they seek to change the culture of bureaucrats. Performance measurement systems are designed to focus managers on results and outputs instead of budgets and inputs. Countries are working to change expectations about career paths and to enhance managers' leadership ability. Both the Netherlands and the United States have committed to pushing decisions down to the lowest possible level. Many nations are also working to make public services more "customer centered." In Canada, for example, public officials are working to "co-locate" related services so that citizens needing public services can come to one place instead of having to run from one government office to another. Japan has launched a major movement to make its programs more consumer oriented and transparent to citizens. The United Kingdom has championed "joined-up government" to improve service coordination.

All the world unquestionably has become a stage for administrative reform in the public sector. Indeed, the past two decades have seen an unprecedented revolution, in both scale and breadth, in public administration. Not since the immediate post–World War II years have so many governments attempted so dramatic a reshaping of the way they do business. The postwar reforms focused principally on establishing the right structures, organized according to existing administrative orthodoxy to help governments manage their programs most efficiently; those reforms proved remarkably long-lasting. By the 1980s, however, it was clear that the postwar reforms had sowed the seeds of their own undoing. Earlier strategies to create strong bureaucracies for solving postwar problems had evolved into bureaucracies that too often seemed oversized, overbearing, and overcontrolling. Citizens around the world complained that the taxes they paid to governments were far higher than the benefits they received. Meanwhile, governments in less developed countries and in newly independent countries struggled to catch up. A new, global revolution in public administration sprang up and, as it quickly spread around the world, it often echoed many of the same notes.[49]

CONCLUSION

One overarching conclusion stands out sharply in this review of administrative reform in industrialized countries. Although many different ideas have driven administrative reform and some seem to have built-in contradictions, reformers have indiscriminately mixed and matched approaches with little regard for the contradictions. Moreover, because the mixtures tend to come together in very different forms, patterns rarely repeat. That makes it hard to determine whether the administrative reforms work, whether some ideas work better than others, and which work best where. Reformers can and do take credit for any positive change that happens on their watch. Reform theorists do likewise, quickly pointing to inadequate application of their theories to explain any problems.

It would, in fact, be possible to use this explanation to drive a broader, cynical conclusion that administrative reform is nothing but symbolic politics, cleverly practiced. Is there, under it all, anything real going on? The cynical challenge has merit, for the symbols have proven to have broad and lasting value, in the United States and around the world. Moreover, the reform movement is about vocabulary and prescription: developing a way to capture the unhappiness that so often surrounds government performance and a strategy for solving government's problems.

It would, however, be far too cynical to stop there, for three reasons. First, the reforms have genuinely produced significant effects. American efforts have had a deep, if uneven, impact.[50] In New Zealand, reforms have profoundly transformed the public sector.[51] Indeed, the reform movement has clearly proven that government *can* change, and many of these changes have made government more efficient and effective. Quite simply, management matters. It provides a symbolic language for understanding governmental activity and both strategies and tactics for improving results. This may not seem a very bold claim, but it is one that often is underestimated.

An equally important second conclusion is that management matters only to the degree to which it matters *politically*. It is unrealistic to expect that public administration can live a life independent of politics, or that its most fundamental meaning will be administrative rather than political. The internal theoretical contradictions of most administrative reform efforts matter far less than the fact that the contradictions themselves often seem to have important political value. It is the politics of the administrative process that matters most.

Third, many of the reforms have created big and sometimes unexpected new problems that demand careful attention. Downsizing has often created imbalances in the workforce. Growing reliance on contracts with the private sector has created problems in supervising those contracts and in ensuring the pursuit of the public interest. More attention to serving the needs of citizens as customers has flown directly into the teeth of a basic paradox: most citizens want more public services than they are willing to pay for. If government reforms have solved some problems, they have created new ones. These new issues too often have remained unexplored—and, of course, they thereby plant the seeds of a future round of reforms.

This dynamic suggests a pair of important implications. First, public managers themselves must be ready to accommodate conflicting and contradictory demands. Their lives would unquestionably be far simpler if they were allowed to pursue a single administrative approach. For that matter, their lives would be simpler yet if they were free to follow their own ideas independently of the policies established by elected officials or the needs of citizens. But that was not what they were hired to do. In democratic societies, the fundamental mission of public managers is to reconcile such fundamentally irreconcilable demands. As OMB frankly admitted in 2001:

> Though reform is badly needed, the obstacles are daunting—as previous generations of would-be reformers have repeatedly discovered. The work of reform is continually overwhelmed by the constant multiplication of hopeful new government programs, each of whose authors is certain that this particular idea will avoid the managerial problems to which all previous government programs have succumbed. Congress, the Executive Branch, and the media have all shown far greater interest in the launch of new initiatives than in following up to see if anything useful ever occurred.[52]

That pattern has repeated over the years.

The job in the twenty-first century has become harder because expectations have grown even as resources have shrunk. This means that the challenges for public managers have never been higher, nor has the need for good public managers ever been greater.

Second, administrative theorists have perhaps an even more daunting challenge. To a significant degree, the central ideas of *public* administration reform have tended to come from *private* managers. Administrative theory has significantly lagged behind these startling changes. The tasks and environment of public administration are so fundamentally different, however, that no matter how suggestive private-sector reforms may be, they are unlikely to provide very sure guides for the public sector. For example, the **customer service movement** has swept the Western world, but there simply has been little careful thought about who government's customers are, how governmental activities can be restructured to advance customer service, how to balance the often conflicting expectations of government's multiple customers, and what other important goals might be sacrificed in the process.

Moreover, administrative theorists face an equally imposing job of reconciling the contradictions that political realities impose on neat organizational theories. Too often, like public managers who complain that their jobs would be much easier if elected officials would stop interfering in their work, theorists complain about elected officials whose contradictory messages muddy neat theories. The problem is far more with the theory than with the practice. And the pace of administrative reform around the world demonstrates just how important it is to tackle these issues.

 # CASE 7.1

How Best to Contribute Public Good: Government or Nonprofit?

Cole Ledford was a sophomore at Ohio State and was majoring in political science. He was excited about the internship he got in the Ohio legislature—until he got to the capitol in Columbus. What he learned surprised him.

"I thought I wanted to be one of them," he told a reporter for *USA Today*. After his internship experience, however, he found "it was more that politics was a game they wanted to play, and it wasn't about the constituents." His goal was to "give back and influence the world." He's decided to do that by switching his major to nonprofit management and by focusing instead on working for a charitable organization.

Ledford isn't alone. A 2013 poll showed that Americans want to make a difference, but by a margin of more than two to one, they believe that the best way to do so is through charities and volunteer organizations, not through government. The gap is especially large for those under thirty. Just one in five of those surveyed said they trusted the government to do what's right most of the time. Among those surveyed, it was almost even about whether they saw government as an advocate (42 percent) or an adversary (38 percent) for them and their families.

John F. Kennedy, in his famous 1961 inaugural address, raised a clear call: "Ask not what your country can do for you—ask what you can do for your country." Many of today's Americans want to do something for their country. But as Kelsey Gallagher from Ohio State put it, "Working at a nonprofit or doing community service, you get more of a first-hand experience." She concluded, "You get to see the direct effects."

Government's leaders looked carefully at these findings and worried about where they were going to find the talented individuals they needed for the next generation of government leaders. The USA Today/Bipartisan Policy Center poll gave them pause.[1]

QUESTIONS TO CONSIDER

1. Where do you think that a college graduate can make the biggest impact on society—working for government or working in a nonprofit organization? Why?

2. Why do you think that the trend has developed toward lower trust in government and a greater tendency to think of government as an "adversary" to families?

3. What steps can be taken to reverse this trend? Is it a trend that can—or should—be reversed?

NOTE

1. The poll and quotes for this case come from Susan Page, "Poll: Public Service Valued; Politics—Not So Much," *USA Today* (July 22, 2013), http://www.usatoday.com/story/news/nation/2013/07/21/public-service-valued-politics—not-so-much/2573743.

Poking through the Luggage: At San Francisco Airport, Private Contractors (Not the TSA) Inspect Your Bags

For Samantha and Darrin, it had been a long and grueling trip back home. They finally snagged their luggage from the baggage claim carousel, dragged the bags to the car, and staggered up the stairs. "What a great trip that was!" Samantha told Darrin. "Imagine. Just a day ago—or was it two?—we were standing on top of the Great Wall of China. That's one more item on my bucket list."

Darrin was jet-lagged and found it hard to join the conversation. He unlocked the bags and started pulling out the clothing from their two-week trip. As Samantha started sorting through everything on the bed, she pulled out a paper tag. "What's this?" she asked. Darrin looked more carefully. They found a very polite "Thank you for flying from San Francisco International" printed tag inside—but the next line brought them up short. "Notification of Inspection" the tag continued. "To protect you and your fellow passengers, Covenant Aviation Security (CAS) is required by law to inspect all checked baggage." Who was Covenant? According to the tag, "CAS is a private company under contract with the Transportation Security Administration (TSA) to provide baggage and passenger screening at San Francisco International Airport."

One of Darrin's bags had been singled out for an inspection. He had been using one of the TSA-approved locks. Covenant used a special key, poked through the luggage, left behind the inspection tag, and resealed it. Neither Darrin nor Samantha had been present for the inspection. They had pulled their bags from the carousel in San Francisco, trudged through immigration and customs before reaching the domestic transfer desk, and piled their luggage on top of the growing mountain of bags waiting to be sorted onto connecting flights. At some point after they left their bags in San Francisco, Covenant employees gave the bag and its contents a close look.

Darrin was slightly incredulous that someone had gone through his stuff without his being present. He was too tired to care much that night, but in the next few days he started digging through the Internet.

Soon after the September 11, 2001, terrorist attacks, Congress and the Bush administration decided to federalize airport screeners. Analysts worried that the previous privately operated screening stations had allowed armed terrorists to board the aircraft, and policymakers concluded that the public would feel safer about flying again if federal workers conducted the screening. However, the law also contained a provision allowing individual airports to opt out of the federalized program if they hired private contractors who met tough national standards. San Francisco International Airport decided to go with Covenant.

Thank you for flying from San Francisco International, a world-class Airport dedicated to serving the "City by the Bay".

NOTIFICATION OF INSPECTION (NOI)

To protect you and your fellow passengers, Covenant Aviation Security (CAS) is required by law to inspect all checked baggage. CAS is a private company under contract with the Transportation Security Administration (TSA) to provide baggage and passenger screening at San Francisco International Airport.

As part of this process, your bag was identified for physical inspection. If your bag was locked using non-TSA recognized locks, CAS may have had to break the locks. If prohibited items, including Hazardous Materials, were discovered during an inspection, they were turned over to the appropriate authorities.

Furthermore, to ensure the highest quality of service, CAS employees are continuously monitored by either direct supervision or camera surveillance.

We appreciate your understanding and cooperation. For questions and packing tips that may assist you during your next trip, or to learn how to submit a claim, please visit us at _www.covenantclaims.com,_ or call us toll free at 1-800-764-8050.

Screener ID: _101/38_

Flight: _888_

At SFO, as the airport is known, the company holds an annual tournament where its employees can win big cash prizes for winning competitions. They are challenged to find explosives in carry-on bags, pick locks on luggage, and find disguised terrorists on videos. In one competition, Covenant's president, Gerald L. Berry, posed as a dangerous-looking character. Cash prizes range as high as $1,500. "The bonuses are pretty handsome," Berry explained. "We have to be good—equal or better than the feds. So we work at it, and we incentivize."[1]

So the card Darrin found inside his luggage was part of a far larger policy debate: deputizing private companies and their employees to open locked luggage and poke through an individual's private property. The debate grew even more heated toward the end of 2010, when John Tyner, a thirty-one-year-old software programmer, filmed his screening by federal TSA officials at San Diego's airport. He complained about the physical pat-down that one TSA employee gave him. "If you touch my junk," he said, "I'll have you arrested." The story—and his clandestine video—quickly went viral online (see http://johnnyedge.blogspot.com/2010/11/these-events-took-place-roughly-between.html). Rep. John L. Mica (R-Fla.) charged pointedly that TSA "was never intended to be an army of 67,000 employees."[2]

QUESTIONS TO CONSIDER

1. Would you be concerned if you found a note saying a private security guard had opened a locked piece of luggage and searched it, without you being present and without your knowledge or permission?

Or would you assume this action is part of the security procedures you submit yourself to when you fly these days?

2. Do you think there's any difference between using private security guards to check luggage versus having private security guards conduct private pat-downs in the airport security area?

3. What is the proper federal role in airport security? Should the federal government concentrate on setting standards and overseeing those who administer those standards, regardless of whether they are public or private employees? Or do steps like searching luggage and patting down flyers constitute the kind of use of police power that only government officials should be empowered to use?

4. This raises a broader question. Are there functions that are inherently governmental, which only the government should perform? How far should government reform go in turning public power over to the private sector?

NOTES

1. Derek Kravitz, "As Outrage over Screenings Rises, Sites Consider Replacing TSA," *Washington Post* (December 31, 2010), http://www.washingtonpost.com/wp-dyn/content/article/2010/12/30/AR2010123004986.html.

2. Ibid.

 # CASE 7.3

StateStat: Performance Management in Maryland State Government

In 2009, *Governing* magazine named Maryland Governor Martin O'Malley one of the nation's "public officials of the year." O'Malley had already made a national reputation as mayor of Baltimore, where he created CitiStat and brought numbers-based performance management to city government. When he was elected governor, he upped the ante with an even broader initiative, christened StateStat. He launched a sweeping website and used it to chart performance ranging from the state police and corrections to social services and juvenile justice.

He focused especially on efforts to improve the water quality in the Chesapeake Bay. Locals are fond of pointing out that the bay has more shoreline than the entire west coast of the United States, but over the years, pollution has seriously injured the bay and starkly reduced the crabs and oysters for which it has long been famous. The bay is

Chesapeake Bay Report Card, University of Maryland Institute of Marine and Environmental Technology

Improving Trends throughout the Bay

Bay Health Trends

- Significantly improving
- Slightly improving
- No change
- Slightly declining
- Significantly declining

C **Upper Western Shore**

Moderate ecosystem health. Improved the most in total nitrogen and aquatic grasses and had a perfect dissolved oxygen score. Over time, this region is showing a significantly improving trend.

2015 Chesapeake Bay Health:

D- **Patapsco and Back Rivers**

Poor ecosystem health. There were strong improvements in total phosphorus, benthic community, and aquatic grasses. Overall this region is showing a significantly improving trend.

Upper Bay **C**

Moderate ecosystem health. This area had improvement with gains in chlorophyll *a* and total nitrogen scores. Over time, this region is showing a significantly improving trend.

D **Lower Western Shore (MD)**

Poor ecosystem health. Large improvements in chlorophyll *a* and benthic community and slight increases or no change in other indicators led to better scores. Over time, this region is showing a slightly improving trend.

Upper Eastern Shore

Moderate ecosystem health. Improvements in six out of seven indicators. The aquatic grass score increased the most out of any region. However, this region is still very close to showing a slightly declining trend.

D **Patuxent River**

Poor ecosystem health. This region remains steady. While some indicators improved, others declined. This region had the lowest aquatic grass score.

Choptank River

Moderate ecosystem health. Overall health improved the most out of all regions due to increases in benthic community, aquatic grass, and chlorophyll a scores.

C- **Potomac River**

Moderately poor ecosystem health. This region's score remained steady from the previous year. Improvements in chlorophyll *a* were offset by declines in total phosphorus.

Lower Eastern Shore (Tangier)

Moderate ecosystem health. Health remained steady. While some indicators improved, others declined. Over time, this region is showing a significantly improving trend.

C **Rappahannock River**

Moderate ecosystem health. Scores improved from the previous year. There were large improvements in benthic community, total nitrogen, and chlorophyll *a*.

Mid Bay

Moderate ecosystem health. While water clarity had the highest score of all regions, dissolved oxygen was lowest. This region is very close to showing a slightly declining trend.

D+ **York River**

Poor ecosystem health. Declines in total phosphorus were balanced by strong increases in total nitrogen. Over time, this region is showing a slightly improving trend.

Lower Bay **B**

Moderately good ecosystem health. Continues to be the highest scoring region, especially for total nitrogen and total phosphorus. Chlorophyll *a* and water clarity also improved from the previous year.

C+ **James River**

Moderate ecosystem health. Improvements in chlorophyll *a* were balanced by declines in total phosphorus. This region is showing a significantly improving trend.

Elizabeth River **D+**

Poor ecosystem health. Health remained steady. The high benthic community score offset indicators that declined. This region is showing a significantly improving trend.

Map labels:
- Upper Western Shore **C**
- Patapsco and Back Rivers **D-**
- Lower Western Shore (MD) **D**
- Upper Bay **C**
- Upper Eastern Shore **C**
- Patuxent River **D**
- Potomac River **C-**
- Choptank River **C+**
- Mid Bay **C**
- Lower Eastern Shore (Tangier) **C**
- Rappahannock River **C**
- York River **D+**
- Lower Bay **B**
- James River **C+**
- Elizabeth River **D+**

Maryland's online performance system reports on a wide range of state issues, including this report card on the health of the Chesapeake Bay.

KEY CONCEPTS

Balanced Budget and Emergency Deficit Control Act 176
continuous improvement 175
customer service movement 192
delivery framework 189
downsizing 175
e-government 190

performance management 190
Private Sector Survey on Cost Control 176
reengineering 175
reinventing government 177
Taxpayer Bill of Rights (TABOR) 176
total quality management (TQM) 183

FOR FURTHER READING

Barber, Michael. *How to Run A Government: So That Citizens Benefit and Taxpayers Don't Go Crazy.* London: Allen Lane, 2015.

Kamarck, Elaine C. *The End of Government as We Know It: Making Public Policy Work.* Boulder, Colo.: Lynne Rienner, 2007.

Kettl, Donald F. *The Global Public Management Revolution: A Report on the Transformation of Governance.* Washington, D.C.: Brookings Institution, 2000.

Niskanen, William. *Bureaucracy and Representative Government.* Chicago: Aldine Atherton, 1971.

Osborne, David, and Ted Gaebler. *Reinventing Government: How the Entrepreneurial Spirit Is Transforming the Public Sector, from Schoolhouse to Statehouse, City Hall to the Pentagon.* Reading, Mass.: Addison-Wesley, 1993.

Osborne, David, and Peter Hutchinson. *The Price of Government: Getting the Results We Need in an Age of Permanent Fiscal Crisis.* New York: Basic Books, 2004.

Pollitt, Christopher, and Geert Bouckaert. *Public Management Reform: A Comparative Analysis—New Public Management, Governance, and the Neo-Weberian State.* Oxford: Oxford University Press, 2011.

Savas, E. S. *Privatizing the Public Sector: How to Shrink Government.* Chatham, N.J.: Chatham House, 1982.

Wilson, James Q. *Bureaucracy: What Government Agencies Do and Why They Do It.* New York: Basic Books, 1989.

SUGGESTED WEBSITES

The Office of Management and Budget website, **www.whitehouse.gov/omb**, contains the administration's most recent management reform initiatives. The congressional Government Accountability Office, **www.gao.gov**, conducts independent assessments of the effectiveness of government management. The best source for tracking government reform initiatives around the world is the Organization for Economic Co-operation and Development, **www.oecd.org**.

for CQ Press

WANT A BETTER GRADE?

Get the tools you need to sharpen your study skills. Access practice quizzes, eFlashcards, video, and multimedia at **edge.sagepub.com/kettl7e.**

Reasonable. Effective.
TAXPAYER
BILL OF RIGHTS

PART III

People in Government Organizations

The famous informal motto of the U.S. Postal Service, "Neither snow, nor rain, nor heat, nor gloom of night stays these couriers from the swift completion of their appointed rounds," has its roots in the Greek historian Herodotus. But Herodotus could not have foreseen the many demands placed upon postal workers—or their need to cope with challenges from UPS, FedEx, email, texts, Facebook, and Twitter. Nor could he have anticipated the rise of antigovernment campaigns. Despite all of the challenges the Postal Service faces, Herodotus would certainly recognize a fundamental truth: the organization's performance, as well as the performance of most public organizations, depends on the people who work for it.

Doing the public's work—and doing it well—requires finding, recruiting, and retaining good people; ensuring that they work according to the laws and norms of a democratic society; and creating incentives for the highest levels of performance. This section examines the foundations of the civil service system, the system of political leadership that guides it, and the efforts to reform it. The quality of the system's people determines the quality of the government's work, regardless of whether that work encounters snow, rain, heat, or gloom of night. And, as earlier chapters hinted, the relationship between the work of public administrators and the mission of administrative organizations is the keystone of accountability.

8

THE CIVIL SERVICE

As residents worried about the spread of Zika through infected mosquitos, Miami police officers James Bernat and Michelle Albelo distributed cans of insect repellent to the city's residents.

The first man to set foot on the moon, Neil Armstrong, was a civil servant, an employee of the National Aeronautics and Space Administration. The day was one of enormous national celebration, and President Richard Nixon designated the day of the moonwalk a holiday for the government's employees. Some employees had jobs that required them to work anyway, but civil servants working on holidays receive premium pay (twice their regular pay). Armstrong's work that day did not qualify, however. He was at the General Schedule level 16 (GS-16) in the federal civil service system, and Congress forbade provision of premium pay for workers above the GS-15 level. So despite the enormous personal risk Armstrong took with that "one small step for man," as he put it, providing him holiday pay would have been illegal—even though the eight-year Apollo moon-landing program had spent $25 billion to put him there.[1] He did receive the standard government per diem provided to employees on a travel assignment—$8 per day, although the government made deductions for accommodations, since he was provided a place to sleep in his moon lander (translating to the value of the dollar today, that works out to about $50 per day). His salary was about $17,000 per year.[2]

Armstrong's case illustrates four basic principles about government civil service systems. First, the government *hires employees by merit.* Armstrong went through a highly competitive process to qualify to be an astronaut. He got the job because of the match between his personal skills and the job requirements. Second, government workers receive *pay according to their position*, not their personal characteristics. Astronauts with Armstrong's level of training qualified for the GS-16 salary level. It was the job, not the person holding the job, that determined the pay. Third, once they are in the civil service system, workers receive many *protections from political interference and dismissal*, in exchange for their agreement to abide by laws and regulations. This safeguard stems from a long-held belief that there is not a Republican or a Democratic way to land on the moon or to perform most technical government jobs. Rather, there has long been a belief that there is a best way of doing the government's work—such as flying a moon lander—and the government's workers should do what is needed in the best way possible. The focus is on effectiveness, separated (in theory) by a wall from politics. Fourth, in doing their work, government's workers have an *obligation to accountability*, to administer the law to the best of their ability regardless of their personal views. For Armstrong and the nation's other government workers, this meant keeping the public interest paramount. There are many variations in details among the federal, state, and local governments, but these four basic principles guide the civil service system throughout American government.

The Pendleton Civil Service Act of 1883 established these principles in law. In the years since, however, the principles have been the focus of unending debate. The basic standard is to treat all employees the same, but government's work is so broad and complex that uniform treatment is

- Examine the work of public employees

- Understand the basic principles and practices of the civil service system, including strategies for hiring new employees

- Explore the ongoing issues surrounding the civil service

impossible—and unwise. It's important to motivate individual employees. Employees who feel trapped in a rigid system will never perform well, especially in dealing with government's most difficult puzzles; being treated as one cog among many, trapped in one wheel among thousands, can hinder employee performance. Balancing the system's need for basic rules with the individual's need for motivation is a central—and eternal—problem of the civil service.

Why is this civil service so important? The answer is clear: the quality of the government's performance depends heavily on the skill of its workers. Crime control hinges on how police officers on the front lines patrol the streets. The skill of firefighters determines whether fires are extinguished. One trained emergency medical technician can save someone's life. Moreover, because so much of government's work happens through third parties, such as private contractors, a very small number of government employees can leverage an enormous amount of government activity. Consider the federal government's Centers for Medicare and Medicaid Services (CMS). CMS is responsible for managing the Medicare program, which funds health care for senior citizens, and Medicaid, which funds health care for the poor. Together, these programs account for about 20 percent of all federal spending. There are just over 4,000 federal employees—0.2 percent of all federal employees—responsible for this money. On average, each CMS employee was responsible for more than $140 million (million!) in federal spending in 2016. The quality of government can only be as good as the quality of the people who work for it.

At the same time, simply trying to understand the civil service system's rules and procedures is amazingly complex. "For the unanointed," journalist Jonathan Walters explains, "no topic around public administration is considered more baffling—or stultifying—than civil service."[3] To be frank, most students look at the textbook chapter on the civil service with a sense of dread, because they are sure it will be hopelessly boring. They aren't alone. As David Osborne and Ted Gaebler argue in the best-seller *Reinventing Government*, "The only thing more destructive than a line item budget system is a personnel system built around civil service."[4]

But this is very far from the truth. The quality of government depends on the skills of its workers. Walking away from the details gives control of government over to those willing to master them. With only a quick look, it's clear that these issues are enormously fascinating. Without a system that selected a skilled astronaut like Neil Armstrong, and the thousands of workers who supported him, an American might not have walked on the moon. We often refer to the work of government employees as "public service," because so many workers are engaged in service to the public.

FUNDAMENTAL ELEMENTS OF THE CIVIL SERVICE SYSTEM

Suppose an individual wants to work for the government. What are the steps? First, of course, government must have an opening, and the tight economy and antigovernment sentiment have sometimes made openings scarce in recent years. The federal government provides a one-stop website for its vacancies at www.USAjobs.gov, which was updated in September 2016. Many state and local governments have produced their own job-hunting websites. For example, the city of Seattle lists its jobs at www.seattle.gov/personnel/employment. Job hunters can view positions in the Arizona state government at www.hr.az.gov/azstatejobs/.

In many civil service systems, the process gets vastly more complex from there. Most web-based systems invite applicants to file their materials online. Because the websites are open, job announcements can attract floods of applications, often far more than personnel officers can review. Many of the individuals trying to work through these systems come away frustrated and disappointed, since applications disappear into an online morass without any feedback. Even for those who successfully navigate the system, the delays and procedural hassles prove discouraging. As the federal government's chief performance officer, Jeffrey Zients, put it in May 2010,

> The current hiring system uses overly complex job descriptions, involves filling out lengthy forms and essays, and is a black hole, providing no feedback to applicants along the way. I know from my business experience that the best talent doesn't wait around for jobs, they find work elsewhere.[5]

One of the biggest challenges in government today is resolving the issue of civil service hiring: preserving the age-old principles of civil service protection while recruiting the top talent that government needs.

There are three fundamental elements of the **civil service system**: position classification rules, staffing rules, and compensation rules. There's a complex chain of issues and actions, for agencies and employees, in filling a government job (see Figure 8.1). Beyond that set of hurdles are policies outlining employee rights and obligations, which make government work so fundamentally different from private-sector jobs.

Position Classification

In civil service systems, as well as in most large corporations, each position is identified in terms of the special knowledge the job requires, its level of difficulty, and the responsibilities (including supervisory duties) that come with it. This process is known as **position classification**, and it is the foundation of the system. Each position is defined according to the occupation (e.g., policy analyst, civil engineer). The grade level captures the position's degree of difficulty and responsibility. In the federal civil service system, there are fifteen grades in the GS, which governs most employees. Civil service systems at the state and local levels generally operate in the same way.

Each position opening is thus described by GS level (or its equivalent in other personnel classification systems) and occupation, which in turn define the qualifications an applicant must meet to be considered for the position. Once an individual is hired, the position description details the duties and salary (see Table 8.1 for the grades and salary ranges as well as the various roles performed at each level). In the federal GS system, levels 1 through 8 tend to be clerical positions. College graduates often qualify for entry-level professional positions, beginning at the GS-5 level. With a master's degree, an applicant may qualify for placement at the GS-7 to GS-9 levels. Levels 10 and above tend to be managerial levels that require more experience.

Applicants who want to be considered for a position must demonstrate not only that they have the necessary skills but also that they are better qualified than other applicants. Over time, the government has devised a series of tests to judge an individual's qualifications. The most traditional test is for clerical positions, where applicants are tested for typing accuracy and speed—although with the spread of computers, there are far fewer individuals in this

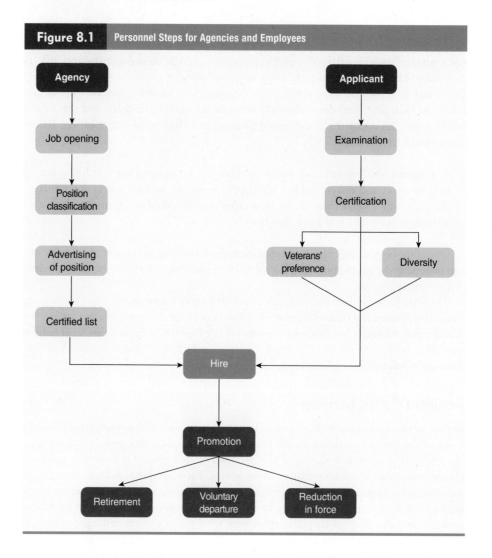

Figure 8.1 **Personnel Steps for Agencies and Employees**

classification. Firefighters and police officer candidates must pass both written exams and tests of strength and agility. In some local governments, these traditional tests have been the source of great controversy. As more women sought to move into firefighting positions, for example, critics argued that some strength tests did not match the actual skills required of firefighters and served only to exclude women from the workforce. For professional-level positions, other systems have been developed to test the applicant's skills; this chapter returns to that process later.

The goal of position classification is to choose employees based on *what* applicants know, not *whom* they know, but it is a process full of problems. First, no matter how hard government workers in the personnel offices try, the written descriptions rarely match the actual job. Supervisors constantly add to and subtract from the actual duties and responsibilities of their staff members. This mismatch means that the testing process may not produce the best person for the actual job because the actual job changes after the test is designed.

Table 8.1	General Schedule (GS) of the Federal Civil Service System		
GS Grade	Bottom Salary	Top Salary	Typical Roles
1	18,343	22,941	General entry-level and preprofessional
2	20,623	25,959	
3	22,502	29,252	
4	25,261	25,261	
5	28,262	36,740	Senior clerical and entry-level professional
6	31,504	40,954	and administrative
7	35,009	45,512	
8	38,771	50,399	Senior clerical
9	42,823	55,666	Intermediate professional or administrative
10	47,158	61,306	Full professional or administrative
11	51,811	67,354	
12	62,101	80,731	
13	73,846	96,004	
14	87,263	113,444	Executive
15	102,646	133,444	

Source: U.S. Office of Personnel Management, "Salary Table 2016-GS," https://www.opm.gov/policy-data-oversight/pay-leave/salaries-wages/salary-tables/pdf/2016/GS.pdf.

Second, the system creates strong incentives for **grade creep**: a tendency for agencies to multiply the number of high administrative positions, shift professional specialists to administrative roles, or seek higher classifications for existing positions. The higher the classification, the more supervisors can pay their employees, which makes it easier to hire the workers they want and to keep the good ones they have. Government supervisors worry constantly about losing their best employees to better-paying jobs in the private sector; within the civil service system, it is impossible simply to give the worker a salary increase, because it is the position, not the worker, that determines the salary level. Therefore, in order to increase the salary, the supervisor seeks to upgrade the position. To guard against such grade creep, government personnel offices employ classification specialists, whose job is to review every request for reclassification, looking carefully at the technical skills required and the number of persons supervised by the employee in question. But the review of reclassification requests only adds to the complexity of the system's rules.

Third, the changing nature of government work makes it hard to keep the system up to date. Information processing experts have replaced clerks and typists. Government sometimes needs experts with special skills—not just a mining engineer, but one especially knowledgeable in the shale oil being extracted in many states. The government needs the best experts, for sure—but sometimes agencies define a job so narrowly that only a handful of persons could possibly qualify. That, in turn, makes it tempting for hiring officials to define the job in a way that gives a special advantage to those they know well and thus defeats the purposes of competitive hiring. Government managers quickly respond that they want to make sure they get the employees that they need, and they can't afford to be handcuffed by arbitrary testing processes. Central personnel offices try to balance both sides of the argument. Not surprisingly, the tensions are an ongoing source of controversy in the personnel system.

Staffing

Online job systems have made it much easier to *search* for job openings. However, once an individual finds a job in which he or she is interested, it is usually necessary to qualify for the position through an examination or other means of demonstrating qualifications, and that process often proves extremely difficult to navigate.

The testing process is central to hiring new government employees. The federal government's long-standing regulations require

> open, competitive examinations for testing applicants for appointment in the competitive service which are practical in character and as far as possible relate to matters that fairly test the relative capacity and fitness of the applicants for the appointment sought. . . . An individual may be appointed in the competitive service only if he has passed an examination or is specifically excepted from examination.[6]

For many jobs, of course, there is no good standardized test. Even for these positions, the government has had to devise some alternative means of testing a candidate's qualifications to meet both the letter and spirit of the civil service system requirements. The debate over how best to choose government employees has spilled over into the states. In Wisconsin, for example, the state switched from its previous testing system to a résumé-based assessment in 2016 to select new government employees.

THE HIRING PROCESS. In recent years, the Office of Personnel Management (OPM) has given agencies much greater flexibility in devising the best tests for their potential employees, including moves to replace the old tests and Knowledge, Skills, and Abilities (KSAs) with detailed résumés. Through these changes, government agencies have come to rely far less on traditional exams. Over time, exceptions to the exam process have grown, including internships, special provisions for veterans, and flexibility for hiring in high-demand positions like airport screeners.[7] What are the implications? The long-standing principles that supported the merit system have eroded dramatically, and there is a risk that the multiple routes of entry could open the door to favoritism in hiring and a workforce that recruits disproportionately from some groups. With many baby boomers certain to retire in the coming years, these cracks in tradition worried some observers, who feared that the flexibilities would open the door to favoritism and a return to the patronage that the system was created to abolish.[8]

Suppose that an agency wishes to fill a vacant position. It may promote or transfer a civil servant already in the agency or elsewhere in the government. That individual must meet the qualifications for the new position, and the classification of the new position defines the new salary. If the agency wishes to consider outsiders, the process generally begins with a request to the personnel agency to certify the names of the top three qualified persons. Sometimes the personnel system operates very slowly and the agency's chosen person may already have accepted another position. The system therefore typically provides a process

**Job Categories of Federal
Civil Service Employees, 1975–2015**

I n recent years, some critics of the federal civil service system have criticized it for becoming more top-heavy. Along the way, the makeup of the civil service has changed markedly over time, as these data show.

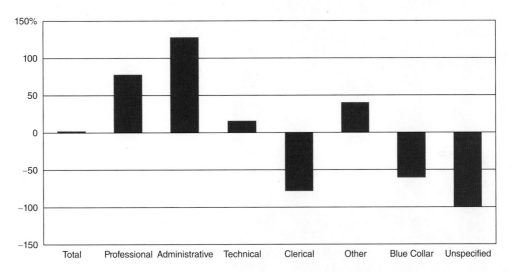

Source: U.S. Office of Personnel Management.

QUESTIONS

1. How much has total federal government employment changed over this period?
2. Which categories of federal government employment have risen most? Which ones have declined most?
3. Why do you think this has happened?
4. What implications does this have for the federal civil service?

for supplying additional names. Sometimes, the agency does not find any of the candidates acceptable, and agency officials may then simply keep the position vacant and hope for better candidates on the next try.

Agencies often find this "rule of three" annoying and many personnel reforms, as we will see in the next chapter, have sought to change it. Yet it remains one of the fundamental principles of most civil service systems. The examination and certification process reduces the hiring flexibility of agencies and can sometimes prove difficult, or even incomprehensible, for applicants. College placement officers sometimes wisely suggest that individuals who want to work for the government play an inside strategy, by finding someone within government who would like to

At a Rutgers University job fair, FBI Special Agent Debra Jean Aros recruited students for careers in the agency. With many senior workers scheduled to retire in the coming years, most government agencies work hard to bring in fresh talent.

hire them—and then allow that person to figure out how to help the candidate navigate the process. In recent years, however, turmoil in federal internship programs has complicated that strategy. The federal government has created three new "pathways" for entry into service: an internship program; a recent graduates program, to allow those who have just completed their degrees time to find a government position; and a revised Presidential Management Fellows program, a highly competitive opportunity to find federal jobs. All of these programs, however, require agencies to advertise open positions, and ongoing budget cuts have made this task difficult.

Beyond the complexities of the hiring process are two recruitment goals that the government also pursues: providing favorable treatment for veterans in federal employment and increasing the diversity of the workforce at all levels of government.

VETERANS' PREFERENCE. There has long been a principle that individuals who serve in the armed forces should get preference in the search for government jobs. In the federal system, veterans earn a five-point bonus; if they are disabled, they get a ten-point bonus. As a result, the names of veterans often rise to the top of the list, above nonveterans with much higher exam ratings. That, in turn, has led the federal government to hire large numbers of veterans—half of all new hires in 2014 were veterans, and a third of the federal workforce has military experience.[9]

Veterans' preference has sparked widespread debate. Some observers think that the nation's obligation to ensure employment opportunities for those who have fought its wars could be met by granting veterans' preference in governmental appointments during only the first few years after discharge from military service. Others suggest that veterans' preference could be employed at the last stage of the hiring process, after the testing and selection process identifies the top candidates by merit. However, veterans' organizations oppose any modification of lifelong preference, and Congress shares their view. The large number of veterans who served in the wars in Iraq and Afghanistan has vastly increased the number of young veterans seeking government employment, and that has squeezed out many other applicants for government service.

DIVERSITY. In many of the world's largest nations, including the United States, diversity among government employees has become increasingly important, to help "achieve

Table 8.2	Diversity and the Government Workforce (Percentage of Employees)	
	Federal Workforce	**U.S. Population**
Native Hawaiian/Pacific Islander	0.4	2.0
American Indian/Alaskan Native	1.7	1.2
Asian	5.6	5.4
White	64.7	77.4
Black	18.1	13.2
Hispanic	8.4	17.4
Female	43.2	50.8
Male	56.8	49.2
Lesbian, gay, bisexual, or transgender	2.8	3.4

Source: U.S. Office of Personnel Management, "Federal Workforce at a Glance" (2016), https://www.opm.gov/policy-data-oversight/diversity-and-inclusion/federal-workforce-at-a-glance/; U.S. Census Bureau, "QuickFacts" (2016), https://www.census.gov/quickfacts/table/PST045215/00; and U.S. Centers for Disease Control and Prevention, "Sexual Orientation and Health among U.S. Adults: National Health Interview Survey, 2013" (July 15, 2014), http://www.cdc.gov/nchs/data/nhsr/nhsr077.pdf.

political and social government objectives such as social mobility, equity, and quality in service delivery," as argued in a 2009 Organization for Economic Co-operation and Development (OECD) report. A more diverse government workforce can also "help to preserve core public service values such as fairness, transparency, impartiality and representativeness," OECD concluded.[10] The diversity argument embraces, in part, the recognition that government is about not only delivering services but also defining and promoting values. It is also about the debate between Friedrich and Finer that we saw in Chapter 1, on the question of whether a government whose employees mirror the citizens they serve is more likely to be accountable to those citizens. Governments at all levels have requirements that protect applicants against discrimination in hiring.

These policies have produced a remarkably diverse workforce (see Table 8.2). For example, the federal workforce is more diverse in many categories than the population as a whole. Pacific Islanders, Asians, and blacks are more represented in the federal workforce than in the population. Federal employment of Hispanics, women, and lesbian, gay, bisexual, or transgender individuals lags behind the population (but, in all likelihood, ahead of most other employers). Overall, the federal workforce is a remarkably diverse community—and the same is true of many state and local governments (although good figures on diversity among state and local employees are hard to come by).

PROMOTION. Employees who hold career positions advance principally by promotion and transfer. Here the operating agencies have great discretion, subject to the promoted or transferred employee's having at least the minimum educational and experience qualifications for the higher position. The employee need not be put in competition with possibly superior talent outside the government, and the agency does not need to

Changing Pay and Benefits for Government Employees
Theme: Politics

In its collection of policy proposals for the 2016 presidential campaign, the conservative-leaning Heritage Foundation focused squarely on the civil service system. The key recommendations in its report called for a smaller government, fewer government regulations, and less federal spending. Moreover, Heritage said, the federal government needed to rein in pay for federal employees, who "receive significantly higher compensation, on average, than private-sector employees receive." Heritage estimated that compensation is 30–40 percent higher in the federal government than in the private sector. It cited other studies pointing to a range of 16–61 percent. Other analysts disagreed strongly and contended that federal employees earned what they received.

Although policy analyses on the question produced an enormous range of results, Heritage and other conservative groups strongly argued that the system needed fundamental changes. Among their recommendations are the following:

- Reduce pay provided through the General Schedule to bring it in line with private-sector jobs.

- Emphasize pay based on performance rather than provide automatic pay increases.

- Reduce paid leave.

- Require employees to contribute more to their retirement benefits.

- Increase the probationary period for new employees from one to three years.

- Limit the appeals process for employees who are fired.

- Provide executives with more money to reward top performers.

The unions representing public employees predictably fought back. J. David Cox Sr., president of the American Federation of Government Employees, countered, "This report is a tedious restatement of Heritage's vicious old attacks on federal employees and the hardworking Americans they serve." His statement argued, "It is disgusting to advocate for cutting the pay for the people who care for our veterans, patrol our borders, and inspect our food, while showering the wealthy with billions in tax cuts."

Source: Kellie Lunney, "Are Federal Pay and Benefits Too Generous?" *Government Executive* (July 15, 2016), http://www.govexec .com/pay-benefits/2016/07/are-federal-pay-and-benefits-too- generous/129943/?oref=workforce_week_nl; and Heritage Foundation, *Blueprint for Reform: A Comprehensive Policy Agenda for a New Administration in 2017* (Washington, D.C.: Heritage Foundation, 2016), http://thf_media.s3.amazonaws.com/2016/BlueprintforReform.pdf.

look at all the employees in the government, department, or bureau who might be qualified for the position. Employees can break out of dead-end positions by shopping around to find a unit to which they can be transferred and promoted. The relative ease of transfer, in fact, may encourage individuals to accept a job at a lower level than they might be qualified for, in the hope that in relatively short order they can learn the system to find a better job at a higher salary.

The promotion system rests on the following four premises:

1. *Career service.* The initial recruitment of able candidates for entry to the public service is enhanced by prospects of long, possibly lifetime, careers with advancement by promotion. A mostly closed promotional system, without much lateral entry at higher levels by "outsiders," improves those prospects. Many employees, in fact, spend their entire careers within a single agency.

2. *Face-to-face assessment.* Important on-the-job characteristics, such as ability to meet and deal with others, cannot be accurately judged by initial or subsequent formal examinations. They can be accurately judged by an employee's supervisor and an agency promotional board.

3. *Flexibility.* Agency officials need to be accorded much discretion in choosing supervisory personnel and in rewarding demonstrated competence. Effective supervision and high morale depend on finding good matches between people and responsibilities, and the more flexibility managers have to promote from within, the more likely they are to produce high-performing programs.

4. *Chain reaction.* Promotion from within builds staff morale, because each promotion creates a vacancy, which can set off a series of promotions down the line.

Central personnel procedures are often cumbersome and time-consuming for managers and applicants alike. Both complain that the process too often makes it difficult to accomplish the twin goals: choosing the candidate who will do the best job and protecting the system from arbitrary actions tainted by favoritism. Moreover, a closed promotion system, in which most positions are hired from within, can keep out new ideas. Some systems, including those for officers of the armed services and in the foreign service, follow a tough up-or-out process: at a certain level, officers are either promoted or must leave the service; at each step up the hierarchy, there are fewer positions at the next level, so the up-or-out process tends to weed out employees along the way. Government managers sometimes complain that individuals who do not actively seek to get ahead can settle into their positions, produce merely adequate work, be impossible to remove for cause, and lower the overall performance of the organization. Some of the reforms we explore in the next chapter are designed to solve that problem.

SEPARATION. Government employees tend to sustain long careers in civil service: the average length of service of full-time federal employees is about fourteen years.[11] Relatively few government workers are fired. In fact, in the federal service, the number of employees terminated or removed has hovered around 0.5 percent of the workforce.[12] Most departures from government service come from retirements, typically at the of an employee's career, and from resignations, as employees take other jobs. Compared with the private sector, turnover of government employees is a bit less than half of turnover in the private sector.[13]

Despite the popular perception, all civil service systems make it possible to remove employees for cause, although the effort required to work through these challenges often discourages supervisors from doing so. Supervisors are often reluctant to remove employees; it is a long and complex process and, if unsuccessful, they may only find themselves saddled with disgruntled employees who can undermine morale. As a result, a supervisor may instead encourage an inferior employee to transfer elsewhere; indeed, the supervisor may be all too willing to provide a glowing recommendation of such an employee's qualifications—for another job.

Governments sometimes find that tight budgets require them to downsize their workforce. In economic downturns, state and local governments have relied on **reductions in force** (**RIFs**, or "riffing," for short). Governments reduced their personnel ceilings, thus triggering elaborate rules about which employees could be retained and which ones had to be riffed first. In general, lowest-seniority employees are the first to go. A higher-seniority employee whose unit shrinks in size generally can "**bump**" a lower-seniority employee, even from a job at a lower level than the one the higher-seniority employee originally occupied. That, in turn, can trigger further bumps, until the lowest-seniority employees must leave government service. Needless to say, such RIFs can devastate both an agency's capacity and employee morale. Governments also sometimes use **buyouts**, which provide employees with cash payments in exchange for a decision to leave public service. When the government needs to reduce its personnel costs because of short-term budget crises, it sometimes will impose a furlough, in which employees are told not to report to work for periods ranging from days to weeks and they do not receive their pay during that time. As governments navigated through the tough budget problems that followed the 2008 financial crisis—and as the federal government struggled to pass its budget—buyouts and furloughs became more common, to the detriment of employee morale.

Compensation

The government's capacity to attract and keep able people depends heavily on the salaries (and fringe benefits) it offers. Pay, to be sure, is not the only factor that a worker considers in seeking, accepting, or staying in a particular organization, and working in the public interest is an important motivating force. Still, government must compete in the labor market for competent people, and its employees, current and prospective, naturally weigh their pay in deciding where to work.

There often are wide differences in pay, both between government and the private sector and between governments. Teachers in Pittsburgh make more than twice as much as teachers in Newark after accounting for differences in the cost of living, according to a 2014 study by the National Council on Teacher Quality. In Boston, it takes teachers seven years on average to reach a salary of $75,000. In Wichita, it takes more than thirty years.[14]

In general, governmental policy provides that pay should be comparable between government and the private sector—and between women and men. Often, however, there is a gap for state and local government workers, with government workers earning less than their private-sector counterparts. A study shows that the pay gap between the private and public sectors tends to be greatest for those with the highest levels of education (like teachers) and lowest for those with the lowest levels of education (like police officers and firefighters).[15] The federal government has similar patterns, according to a study by the Congressional Budget Office (CBO). CBO found that, on average, federal workers have slightly higher salaries than their private-sector counterparts (by 2 percent). They had substantially higher benefits (by 48 percent) and 16 percent higher overall compensation. The comparisons vary greatly by employees' education, however. For employees with a high school education, federal workers had a big edge. Federal employees with a college education still had an advantage. But for employees with advanced degrees, private-sector employees earned 23 percent higher salaries (see Figure 8.2).[16] Because the federal government tends to employ relatively more workers with advanced degrees, this issue is important. However, not everyone agrees that there is a pay gap. An analyst at the Heritage Foundation, for example, contends that Americans are "overtaxed to overpay the civil service."[17] The hotter the issue has become, the harder it has been to determine who is right.

Beyond the numbers, however, is a debate about whether the federal government should compete with the private sector for the best employees. Terry Culler, a Reagan

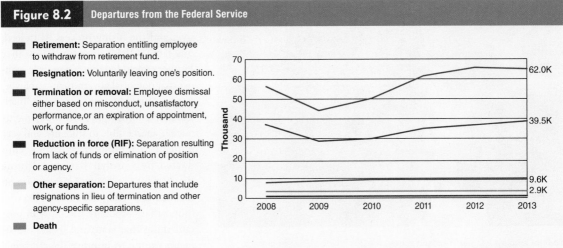

Figure 8.2 Departures from the Federal Service

- **Retirement:** Separation entitling employee to withdraw from retirement fund.
- **Resignation:** Voluntarily leaving one's position.
- **Termination or removal:** Employee dismissal either based on misconduct, unsatisfactory performance, or an expiration of appointment, work, or funds.
- **Reduction in force (RIF):** Separation resulting from lack of funds or elimination of position or agency.
- **Other separation:** Departures that include resignations in lieu of termination and other agency-specific separations.
- **Death**

Source: Partnership for Public Service, "Federal Departures" (August 14, 2014), https://ourpublicservice.org/publications/viewcontentdetails.php?id=352.

administration political appointee, concluded that "the federal government is able to hire the caliber of people it needs at current wage levels and could do so at even lower pay scales. It should be content to hire competent people, not the best and most talented people." The federal government, he wrote, does not "need laboratories full of Nobel laureates, legal offices full of the top graduates of the best schools, administrative offices staffed with MBAs from Wharton, or policy shops full of the brightest whatevers." Indeed, Culler stated that "the brightest and most talented people should work in the private sector."[18] In 2012, however, a U.S. Department of Commerce scientist, David Wineland, *did* win the Nobel Prize in physics, for his work in quantum mechanics. Wineland had worked at the department's National Institute of Standards and Technology for thirty-seven years and made breakthroughs that established the basis for super-fast computers in the future. When the federal government shut down in 2013 because of a budget battle between President Obama and the Republican Congress, three Nobel laureates found themselves furloughed, without their regular paycheck.[19]

THE NEED TO BUILD A QUALITY WORKFORCE. The public service can attract the best employees only by being competitive. That is partly a product of pay, promotional opportunities, and other conditions of work. It also depends on the perceptions of government as a place to work. Although elected officials have often talked about the importance of government service, bureaucrat bashing has become a popular sport. President Barack Obama put it crisply. In the midst of his 2008 campaign, he told a Columbia University audience that "Our campaign from the beginning has been about changing government." The goal, he said, was to "transform Washington" and "make government cool again."[20]

Despite such support, however, government has struggled to attract the high quality of recruits it needs.[21] As the National Advisory Council on the Public Service found, "the Federal government now has a confused and incomplete patchwork of recruiting programs. Potential applicants for Federal employment are discouraged by a perplexing and overly complicated

Federal employee David Wineland shared the 2012 Nobel Prize in physics. The award committee recognized Wineland, who worked for the National Institutes of Standards and Technology in Colorado, for his work in quantum physics, "measuring and manipulating individual particles . . . in ways that were previously thought unattainable."

process." In addition, "Too often, there is no link between the recruiting initiatives and the hiring process."[22] Indeed, one-time OPM director Constance Horner concluded that it was little wonder that potential government employees were confused by a process that is "intellectually confusing, procedurally nightmarish, inaccessible to students, and very difficult to administer."[23] A study conducted by Carolyn Ban and Norma Riccucci for the Winter Commission on the state and local public service likewise found that "probably the most important thing that state and local governments can do to improve the efficiency of their workforce is to improve the quality of the people they hire."[24]

EMPLOYEE RIGHTS AND OBLIGATIONS

For more than a century, public employees have organized to assert their rights, especially by joining unions and bargaining over their work conditions. However, there has been a major effort to weaken public employee unions in recent years, in part to reduce the costs of government and in part to change the political balance of power, since most unions have tended to lean toward the Democrats.

Unionization and Collective Bargaining

Across all levels of government, 39 percent of government employees are represented by unions, a decline of 3 percent since 2000. Union membership is much lower in the private sector, where just 7.4 percent of employees are represented by unions (see Table 8.3).

The issues posed by **unionization** of public employees run deep. For over fifty years, federal statutes have ensured that private-sector employees can organize, join unions, and bargain collectively through their unions about pay, fringe benefits, promotion, hours of work, and working conditions. Of course, the right to bargain collectively is effective only if unions have the ultimate weapon of the right to strike. However, the rules are very different in the public sector. The rules are even more different at the state and local levels, where laws and policies on public employees' rights to organize, join unions, and strike vary dramatically around the nation. Some states, including Georgia, have moved away from **collective bargaining**. In 2011, Wisconsin's Republican governor, Scott Walker, pushed a bill through the state legislature removing the right of public employees to collectively bargain, and union membership dropped sharply. Many state and local governments, moreover, are engaged in substantial reforms, and that process is further transforming the relationship between governments and their employees.

THE STRIKE. In general, government employees do not have the same right to strike as workers in the private sector. Citizens would consider it intolerable if they suddenly found

Table 8.3	Union Representation (Percentage of Employed Workers)	
	2000	**2015**
Private sector	9.8	7.4
Public sector	42.0	39.0
Federal government	36.7	32.3
State government	34.2	33.6
Local government	47.9	45.0

Source: U.S. Bureau of Labor Statistics, "Union Affiliation of Employed Wage and Salary Workers by Occupation and Industry, 2014–2015 Annual Averages" (January 28, 2016), http://www.bls.gov/news.release/union2.t03.htm; and U.S. Bureau of Labor Statistics, "Union Members in 2000" (January 18, 2001), http://www.bls.gov/news.release/history/union2_01182001.txt.

themselves without police and fire protection, air traffic control, schools, and garbage collection. And while Americans might not notice it immediately if the employees of the State, Treasury, or Defense Departments went on strike, the implications could be equally momentous.

But this rationale becomes strained when it is applied to less vital governmental services, such as cataloguers at the public library or assistants in a federal research lab. Yet no simple rule can sharply distinguish among the occupations of public employees in terms of the tolerability of strikes. A 1977 strike by only 2,500 cleaners and handymen forced New York City's 960 public schools to hold only half-day sessions for their more than 1 million pupils and deprived half a million of them, mostly from poor families, of free hot lunches.[25] In Philadelphia, transit police officers have the right to strike (and they exercised it in 2008), but city police officers do not.

Theory may not matter, however. Public employees do strike, and government officials usually decide that resorting to the courts is not a promising method in getting employees back to work. Firing the strikers, as President Reagan did to the 11,000 air traffic controllers in 1981, leads to a long process—over many years in the case of the Federal Aviation Administration (FAA)—of recruiting and training a new staff. Meanwhile, the government risks having a public function poorly performed. Even when the government denies employees the right to strike, that prohibition does not prevent employees from resorting to job actions that can tie public administration in knots. A "sick-in" by schoolteachers can shut down schools even while the teachers receive sick-leave pay. When air traffic controllers "work to the rule" (strictly adhering to prescribed procedures), they can cripple

Scott Olson/Getty Images

Teachers in Chicago's public schools, the third-largest district in the country, went on strike at the beginning of the 2012 school year for better compensation and job security.

the flow of landings and takeoffs under the guise of enforcing every safety regulation to the letter. A "slowdown" by postal clerks can build up mountains of unsorted and undelivered mail. Teaching assistants at state universities can grade final exams but refuse to turn the grades over to the registrar, leaving thousands of seniors without the credits they need to graduate.

WHO ARE THE BARGAINERS? The second difference is that the civil service system itself, along with budget decisions by elected policymakers, sets the basic conditions of work. As a result, no executive official can bargain over many of the issues about which the union is concerned. Managers cannot agree to pay increases or fundamental changes in working conditions. Since the main decisions are political, often the most that the unions can do is to build their political strength, which turns them into interest group lobbyists—a very different role from that of unions in the private sector. The president of the largest federal union says, "We've got no choice except to try to put pressure on enough congressmen and senators to see things our way. That's our bargaining table."[26]

These pressures can make executives quick to give in to union demands. Union members and their families have substantial voting strength in many legislators' districts and wards; those in local governments may actually be able to determine mayoral elections. The unions' voting strength, lobbying skill, and collective bargaining tactics reinforce one another. In addition, the public is often so angered by the loss of police, trash collection, or school services during a strike or slowdown that it puts pressure on government officials for a speedy settlement of the dispute. Public employee unions, of course, do not get all that they ask for, because government bargainers know that citizens dislike settlements that substantially raise taxes or that pay public employees more than others in the community who are doing comparable work. For the most part, government bargainers try to balance between protecting the merit principle and the civil service system and avoiding bargaining away government's ability to determine public policies and improve administrative performance.

There are two important lessons here. First, the civil service system and the supervisory arrangements it creates are one thing; labor-management relations often are quite different. At state, local, and federal levels, the result frequently is a dual personnel system.[27] Second, despite the frequently large gaps between top officials and frontline managers, management and labor, and supervisors and subordinates, many managers are coming to recognize the need for fresh alliances. One private-sector executive's conclusion speaks loudly to the public sector as well: "We have lots of team efforts with union involvement. The biggest lesson we have learned is that we are all in the same boat and we need to work together."[28]

THE SCOPE OF ISSUES. Finally, government differs from private enterprise in the scope of issues on which employees and their unions want to, or are able to, bargain. The line between employees' own conditions of work and the government's policies and programs seems a clear one—the former being the stuff of collective bargaining, the latter the responsibility of legislative bodies and political executives. But public employee unions have blurred the line. If a union blocks a mayor's effort to staff police patrol cars with one officer instead of two, or if it prevents reducing the number of firefighters on a fire truck, that may simply reflect the concern that all unions have about workers' safety and the loss of jobs. But what if the mayor wants to shift firefighting companies at night-time from the depopulated business districts to the most populous and fire-prone areas of the city? Should the size of school classes or the content of school programs be determined by government-union bargaining? Should the size of payments to welfare clients, or the location of welfare centers, be so determined? All these issues have in fact been the subjects of negotiation and strikes.[29]

In the federal government, the scope of negotiable issues is restricted. Bargaining cannot concern matters that are the subject of any law or government-wide rule or regulation, or any agency rule or regulation for which "a compelling need" exists (the Federal Labor Relations Authority [FLRA] settles disputes over compelling need). Furthermore, the Civil Service Reform Act of 1978 (which established the FLRA) preserves the authority of agency management officials "to determine the mission, budget, organization, number of employees, and internal security practices" of their agencies; to hire, assign, lay off, and retain employees; to remove or otherwise discipline employees; and to assign work and determine the personnel by which agency operations shall be conducted. The procedures for exercise of such authority are negotiable, however, as are grievance procedures for adversely affected employees.[30] An agency may choose to bargain about "the numbers, types, and grades of employees or positions assigned to any organizational subdivision, work project, or tour of duty, or on the technology, methods, and means of performing work."[31]

Given the statutory restrictions, what do agencies and unions bargain about? So far, it has been mostly about the assignment and scheduling of work (overtime, workweek definition, temporary assignments, shift hours, work breaks, meal periods), grievances and other procedures, safety, employee counseling, technological displacement, and the color of wall paint. Compared with the private sector and state and local governments, the federal bargaining table is a meager one: many highly significant issues relating to pay, job security, promotions, and fringe benefits that are accepted as negotiable in the private sector are precluded from bargaining at the federal level. On many issues, federal statutes accord unions the right to be consulted—but consultation is not bargaining.

In recent years, public employee unions have nervously eyed government officials who have battled the unions. President George W. Bush worked to limit the collective bargaining rights of employees in the new Department of Homeland Security. Many federal managers believe that unions have grown too powerful. FAA managers, for example, have complained that they have great difficulty in scheduling work shifts because union provisions allow air traffic controllers to come to work early or stay late; this practice allows them to accumulate credit hours, which they can use flexibly at a later time. At CMS, negotiations at one point became so tense that a union official said simply, "It's a war."[32] In some states, like Wisconsin, that war spilled out into open conflict involving tens of thousands of demonstrators in the state capitol and an open revolt of Democratic state senators, who left the state rather than vote on a plan to strip public employee unions of most of their bargaining rights. In 2016, following big problems in the Department of Veterans Affairs (VA), some members of Congress tried to remove most workplace protections from senior VA officials.

The Right to Privacy

After being hired by government, how much of a right to privacy do government employees retain? That question framed a major debate in the war on drugs in the 1980s.

In 1986, President Reagan signed an executive order requiring federal employees to refrain from the use of illegal drugs and declaring persons who use illegal drugs unsuitable for federal employment.[33] He authorized each agency to test any applicant for illegal drug use and, most important, directed federal agencies to "establish a program to test for the use of illegal drugs by employees in sensitive positions." Such positions include more than the term suggests. Among those affected are employees in positions designated sensitive by their agency, employees with access to classified information, presidential appointees, law enforcement officers, and employees in "other positions that the agency head determines involve law enforcement, national security, the protection of life and property, public health or safety, or other functions requiring a high degree of trust and confidence." In 2004, the federal government extended the testing to include hair, saliva, and sweat samples. Although many employees are required to submit to these tests, only about one-fourth of federal employees work in jobs covered by the tests.[34] Local governments have also instituted mandatory urinalysis for police, firefighters, schoolteachers, and other employees.

Employee unions oppose mandatory testing of urine for evidence of illegal drug use, if inclusive or random—without, therefore, reasonable grounds for suspicion of an individual employee—as an invasion of privacy and a violation of the Fourth Amendment's protection against unreasonable searches and seizures. In 1989, the Supreme Court (by a 5 to 4 vote) agreed on the applicability of the Fourth Amendment but ruled it was reasonable for the U.S. Customs Service to inclusively administer drug tests to newly hired and transferred employees whose duties included direct interception of drugs or carrying of firearms.[35] Although it granted the government's "compelling interest in protecting truly sensitive information," the Court deferred ruling on the reasonableness of testing those handling classified information, pending a lower court's inquiry into why baggage handlers, messengers, lawyers, and accountants were included in the testing.

AIDS testing also invokes the issue of privacy. The standard blood test identifies persons who have HIV antibodies, but that does not mean that they have AIDS or will get it,[36] and the danger of their infecting others is limited to sexual relations and intermixture of blood (e.g., when drug users inject with needles used by others). In 1987, the U.S. Foreign Service began to test its job applicants, officers, and their dependents for the AIDS virus, rejecting any applicants testing positive for HIV antibodies and restricting any persons in service abroad—the concerns being both adequacy of medical facilities at some foreign posts and foreign governments' attitudes toward receiving official representatives who have or may develop AIDS.[37]

Political Activity

Public employees, of course, are citizens and have basic rights. But how should employees' own political values and rights to free speech connect with their responsibilities to administer the law without political favoritism? The 2013 IRS scandal, in which investigators found that federal workers were subjecting conservative groups to additional scrutiny, provoked enormous outrage. Further investigation showed that liberal groups received additional checks as well. What standards should shape the political rights of employees and protect citizens from political bias in the administration of the law?

THE HATCH ACT. To address these issues at the federal level, Congress adopted "An Act to Prevent Pernicious Political Activities" in 1939, usually called the **Hatch Act** after its sponsor, Senator Carl Hatch of New Mexico. The key provision applicable to federal employees reads as follows:

> No officer or employee in the executive branch of the Federal Government, or any agency or department thereof, shall take part in political management or political campaigns. All such persons shall retain the right to vote as they may choose and to express their opinions on all political subjects.[38]

The act's restrictions extend to virtually all employees who are not in policymaking positions, whether in the merit system or not.[39]

Box 8.1	Hatch Act Rights and Restrictions for Federal Government Employees

Federal and D.C. employees *may*

- be candidates for public office in nonpartisan elections
- register and vote as they choose
- assist in voter registration drives
- express opinions about candidates and issues
- contribute money to political organizations
- attend political fundraising functions
- attend and be active at political rallies and meetings
- join and be active members of political parties or clubs
- sign nominating petitions
- campaign for or against referendum questions, constitutional amendments, or municipal ordinances
- campaign for or against candidates in partisan elections
- make campaign speeches for candidates in partisan elections
- distribute campaign literature in partisan elections
- hold office in political clubs or parties

Federal and D.C. employees *may not*

- use official authority or influence to interfere with an election
- solicit or discourage political activity by anyone with business before their agency
- solicit or receive political contributions (may be done in certain limited situations by federal labor or other employee organizations)
- be candidates for public office in partisan elections
- engage in political activity while
  - on duty
  - in a government office
  - wearing an official uniform
  - using a government vehicle
- wear partisan political buttons on duty

Source: U.S. Office of Special Counsel, "Hatch Act," https://osc.gov/pages/hatchact.aspx.

From 1940 to 1974, the Hatch Act's ban on political activity extended to state and local appointive officers and employees engaged primarily in any activity wholly or partly financed by federal loans or grants. In 1974, Congress shrank the ban to cover only candidacy for office in a partisan election and use of official authority or influence to affect others' voting or political contributions. The act was further amended in 1993 to allow most employees of the federal government to be more involved in political campaigns. Federal employees therefore have the right to be candidates for office, but only in nonpartisan elections. They can vote and assist in voter registration drives. As Box 8.1 shows, they can make political contributions and express opinions about political issues. (However, some federal employees, including those working for the CIA, the FBI, and the Secret Service, have greater limits on their political activity.) State government and local government employees are allowed a broader range of activities, with fewer restrictions (see Box 8.2). In general, government officials cannot run for office in a partisan election, campaign while on the job, or use their position to influence an election.

REVOLVING-DOOR RESTRICTIONS. Most governments also restrict activities of employees after they leave government service, for two reasons. First, the restrictions seek to prevent government officials from using their positions to set themselves up in lucrative jobs after their government employment. Many higher-level officials have the power to award contracts, and it would be tempting to use that power to steer contracts to a company and then jump to that company in a high-paying position to manage the work. Second, the restrictions seek to prevent government officials from joining a company and then using their vast network of government contracts to pull business to their new employer.

Box 8.2   Hatch Act Rights and Restrictions for State and Local Government Employees

State and local employees *may*

- run for public office in nonpartisan elections
- campaign for and hold office in political clubs and organizations
- actively campaign for candidates for public office in partisan and nonpartisan elections
- contribute money to political organizations and attend political fundraising functions

Covered state and local employees *may not*

- be candidates for public office in partisan elections
- use official authority or influence to interfere with or affect the results of an election or nomination
- directly or indirectly coerce contributions from subordinates in support of a political party or candidate

Source: U.S. Office of Special Counsel, "Hatch Act," https://osc.gov/pages/hatchact.aspx.

For example, in 2004 Boeing was fighting to win a large contract for 767 aircraft, which would be transformed into tankers to replace the Air Force's aging KC-135 models. The company's principal competition was Airbus, a European consortium that was the only other builder capable of producing a long-range tanker. The Air Force's second-highest civilian in charge of procurement, Darleen Druyun, was jailed for a deal she made: she favored Boeing in the competition and negotiated a new job with Boeing after she left the federal government. She received a nine-month prison sentence, plus seven months in-home (or halfway house) detention, a $5,000 fine, and orders to complete 150 hours of community service.

In her plea agreement, Druyun confessed that, as "a parting gift" to her new employer, she had supported a higher price than the deal required and that she had shared data about one of Boeing's competitors with the company. She also had favored Boeing on a $4 billion avionics contract, as well as on a $100 million North Atlantic Treaty Organization (NATO) contract in 2002, and she had pushed for a $412 million settlement with Boeing on a contract dispute between the company and the government in 2000. As a further incentive, Druyun's daughter and son-in-law had been Boeing employees either at the time of or shortly after each of those deals.[40] Congressional heat, including attacks from Senator John McCain (R-Ariz.), led the Air Force to call for a fresh competition for the contract. In 2008, the Air Force awarded the contract to Airbus, but GAO found that the Air Force had bungled the contract review, and the project went back to the drawing board yet again. In 2011, the Pentagon finally decided to grant the contract to Boeing.

Over the years, GAO carefully examined the issue of "the revolving door." In an analysis of 2,435 officials who had previously served in the government, GAO found

> There are acknowledged benefits to employing former government officials for both DOD [Department of Defense] and defense contractors; for example, former DOD officials bring with them the knowledge and skills in acquisition practices they have developed at DOD which also benefit DOD when communicating with these contractor personnel. However, a major concern with post-government employment has been that senior military and civilian officials and acquisition officials working for defense contractors immediately after leaving DOD could lead to conflicts of interest and affect public confidence in the government.[41]

Rules to prevent such problems vary with the level of government and typically are very complex. In general, however, former officials are permanently barred from joining a company and dealing with their former employer on issues for which they had direct responsibility. Most levels of governments impose "cooling-off periods," ranging from six months to several years, during which individuals may not contact their former employer on government issues. Despite the rules, GAO found that many former military officials had, in fact, worked on contracts related to their former work and some had even worked on the same contracts for which they had responsibility at the Pentagon.[42]

The revolving-door regulations are very complicated. Former employees often have a hard time deciphering the rules without hiring an attorney for guidance. There are many stories of individuals who turn down government jobs because of the restrictions they face on leaving public service. No one, of course, wants to allow government employees to trade on their service to line their own pockets. On the other hand, everyone wants the government to hire the most capable employees for the work to be done. The enduring challenge is determining how best to find the balance.

CONCLUSION

Getting high-quality workers is one of the most important issues in public administration. Indeed, perhaps the biggest lesson from the private sector for government management is that people are the most important resource, and that government's work depends on the quality of the government's employees. Because government employees exercise great power on behalf of the public, there is a strong public interest in ensuring that neither favoritism nor employees' own political values creep into administration. Discovering the best way to make that happen has long been the driving force of the government's civil service system.

The civil service *system* is actually a series of interlocking *subsystems*: one for position classification, one for hiring, and one for compensation. These subsystems are complex, largely because of the competing values the government seeks to balance. The rules that have grown up around the subsystems also help explain why so many of government's other problems regularly recur—from an impersonal style to a preoccupation with red tape. Even the most important goals, such as equity and merit, reinforce these tendencies. Indeed, as Patricia W. Ingraham pointed out, the system's "problems highlight the difficulties created by the long-term emphasis on *administering* procedures, rather than *managing* people and programs."[43]

The civil service system is complex because it brings together the basic challenges of the administrative process. It's about *effectiveness*, because the quality of government's people shapes the quality of its work. It's about *politics*, because it must balance the competing demands for employees' freedom and the need to protect the system from political favoritism. And it's about *accountability*, because the public rightly expects that they will get fair and impartial service from those entrusted with government's work. Balancing these values, however, has long been very difficult, because as a GAO study put it, "Federal employees have often been viewed as costs to be cut rather than as assets to be valued."[44]

If there's anything about which virtually everyone agrees, it's this: the government's civil service system is broken. Conservatives believe it creates inflexibility and inefficiency. Liberals believe it undercuts government's responsiveness. Nearly everyone agrees that civil service rules hinder the performance of public programs. Looking ahead, everyone knows that with large numbers of baby boomers retiring from government, the need to improve the civil service system will only increase if government is to work well.

That led the Obama administration to make hiring reform a top priority. In 2010, OPM Director John Berry said,

> Hiring process reform isn't the most exciting topic, but it's extremely important, because it affects everything government does. Yet for far too long, our HR systems have been a hindrance. We have great workers in government now in spite of the hiring process, not because of it. As they retire, it's tough to replace them when it takes five months on average to hire someone. Or when there are 40 steps to the process and 19 signatures.[45]

At the core of these issues is the basic question: How best to identify the skills that the government most needs and how to build them into government? In the midst of the contentious 2010 midterm elections, *Washington Post* writer Steven Pearlstein argued:

> You can't expect to support and finance political candidates who preach that government is menacing and wasteful, that public employees are incompetent and corrupt, that taxes are always too high and destroy jobs, and then turn around and expect that the government will respond to your demands to hold down the cost of health care, or fund basic research, or provide good schools, efficient courts and reliable transportation systems.[46]

We turn to those puzzles in the next chapter.

 CASE 8.1

Who Is More Efficient—Government Workers or Private Contractors?

Everyone knows that the private sector is more efficient than the public sector. A major case for privatizing public work, its proponents say, is that the private sector can do it better, cheaper, and smarter.

But is "everyone" right? Not if they look at the experience of Chesapeake, Virginia. In 1995, the city council told the public works director to get bids from private companies for collecting trash in the city's "Western Branch," the area collected on Mondays. The public works department responded with a "managed competition" model. "The bottom line cost to the citizens was the most important consideration," explained Thomas Westbrook, the department's assistant director.[1]

The city hired a private consultant to manage the competition process. Four bids for the job were received.

The winner? As Bill Davis, the city's purchasing director, announced, "the proposal submitted by the city's public works department, solid waste division, was the most responsive and responsible offer and represents the least expensive and most advantageous situation for the city."[2]

In short, the public sector outcompeted the private sector. How did this happen? Facing the heat of competition, the city's solid waste division found a way to change its waste-collection process: instead of using two different trucks, staffed by two different crews, to collect overflow garbage and yard waste, it could use a single truck with a single crew and with its capacity split between the two loads. Had it not been for the competition, the department's officials might not have devised this method, which contributed to a 39 percent savings over the previous arrangement. Facing the potential loss of their jobs, however, city workers came up with an innovative approach.

"We felt that we were as cheap as private industry and we wanted to be able to bid on that service as well," Westbrook explained.[3] His employees did so—and Westbrook was right.

In this effective bidding process, Chesapeake followed a model established by Phoenix, Arizona, which has been contracting out public services since 1979. In the first twenty years of the process, Phoenix city officials estimate that they saved more than $30 million. In six garbage-collection auctions, the city department won three of the competitions and it placed second in the others. Between 1979 and 1998, the cost of collecting a ton of garbage in Phoenix fell from $67.88 to $41.96, a 38 percent decrease. Moreover, analysts have determined that Phoenix's costs are less than those of similar cities.[4]

Phoenix established basic ground rules for all the competitors:

1. *Reserve rule.* Wanting to ensure that the city department remained viable in case service problems arose with the private contractors, Phoenix would not allow more than half of its households to be served by private contractors.

2. *Previous experience.* Bidders had to present evidence of garbage-collection work in similarly sized areas.

3. *Bonding.* Private bidders had to post a bond to guarantee that they would complete the work.

4. *Insurance.* Private contractors had to carry liability insurance in case their vehicles and workers caused property damage or injury.

5. *Medical benefits.* The city required private contractors to provide medical insurance that matched what city workers received.

6. *Displaced city workers.* Private contractors were required to offer employment to any city workers who lost their jobs as a result of the competition.

7. *Fleet restrictions.* Competitors could not use their vehicles for other purposes, and garbage pickup was not allowed on Wednesdays and Saturdays.

When some private competitors balked at these restrictions, city workers countered that private contractors should have to play by the same rules that the city observed. Accepting the ground rules would make it harder for those private companies to lowball bids, especially by not funding basic benefits to employees and by using equipment for other purposes. Indeed, public employees fought against any competition strategy that would allow private companies to win by providing their employees with fewer fringe benefits, in part because city employees believed that would be unfair and in part because they feared that it might increase pressure to lower their own benefits. Everyone agreed that competition helped lower costs, but determining how best to create a level playing field proved a deceptively difficult problem.

Analysts concluded that these cases demonstrate that the problem with governmental efficiency isn't government itself—or the people who work for it. Rather, it is the set of restrictions that limit government's flexibility and the lack of incentives to improve their productivity. Create a strong incentive—such as the potential loss of jobs—and city workers can produce remarkable efficiencies. Level the playing field, and they can even win out over the private sector. Private competitors countered that they could provide even cheaper service at lower cost if the city were to change its ground rules.

Beyond the procedural disputes, however, there's a surprising nugget of truth to be found in this mixed experience. What "everyone" knows—that the private sector is more efficient than the public sector—isn't true. Armed with the right incentives, government can outcompete the private sector.

QUESTIONS TO CONSIDER

1. What factors account for the cost savings in Chesapeake, Virginia, and Phoenix, Arizona?

2. Are there broader lessons that come from their experiences?

3. Should such competitions be extended to more cities? To more services? To more levels of government?

4. Are there public functions that should *not* be contracted out? Where would you draw the line?

5. Consider *who* does the public's work. How much does it matter if those providing public services are not public employees? Is there a value in having public employees provide public services? If so, how can we keep their work accountable, efficient, and effective?

NOTES

1. Rob Shapard, "Collection: City's Managed Competition Model Tops Private Sector," *Waste Age* (June 1, 1997), http://www.waste360.com/mag/waste_collection_citys_managed.

2. Ibid.

3. Ibid.

4. Robert Franciosi, *Garbage In, Garbage Out: An Examination of Private/Public Competition by the City of Phoenix*, Arizona Issue Analysis 148 (Phoenix: Goldwater Institute, 1998).

CASE 8.2

Federal Furloughs: Government Employees Suffer from Budget Battles

"Everyone's bracing for the impact," said Army Master Sergeant Trey Corrales. He wasn't talking about a fear his plane would crash. He had just listened to a speech by Defense Secretary Charles Hagel, who warned the troops and their civilian Department of Defense partners that more budget cuts and furloughs were coming.[1] (Furloughs are days when employees may not work and are not paid.) Members of the armed forces were exempt from the furloughs but civilian support workers, who provide everything from health care to equipment supply, took the cuts.

The good news was that the initial forecast of twenty-two furlough days had been reduced to eleven days in 2013 and then reduced again to six days as the department found new ways to stretch its tight budget. The bad news was that when the furlough days began in July, civilian workers lost a day's pay every week, the equivalent of a 20 percent pay cut for every week with a furlough day. The worse news, Hagel said, was that a failure by Congress to pass a new budget and restore the cuts imposed by sequestration, before the October 1 start of the new fiscal year, could lead to more budget reductions, layoffs of civilian workers, more furlough days, and more reductions in services by civilian support workers for the armed forces. Troops had already had extra pay eliminated for deployments to some danger spots. Training missions had been eliminated, and even the Navy's famous Blue Angels flight demonstration team had been grounded. When the rest of the nation celebrated Independence Day, fireworks on many military bases were eliminated in 2013.

One research manager at the Navy's air station in Jacksonville told Hagel, "I'm sure you realize how disruptive the furlough is to our productivity. So I'm hoping we're not going to do it again next year." Hagel's sober reply was that "there will be further cuts in personnel, make no mistake about it," if Congress failed to restore the cuts. "I don't have any choice." He sadly concluded, "There's no good news."[2]

In fact, Deputy Defense Secretary Ash Carter said there is "the possibility that this does become the new normal and that our budget is simply cut and stays low for a period of time." Carter told participants at the Aspen Security Forum in Colorado that furloughs are a "miserable way to treat people." In looking ahead to the new fiscal year, however, he said that more furloughs coupled with layoffs could continue in the next fiscal year.[3]

The furloughs were a bizarre side-product of the sequestration into which the federal government fell in early 2013. The original plan was to create budgetary consequences so severe that they would force the president and members of Congress to the bargaining table. However, those on the right found that they were getting—automatically—large cuts in government spending. Those on the left, including the president, found that they could not retreat from an automatic trigger to which they had agreed. In the end, there was no political means of escape, so the sequestration kicked in. The once-unimaginable cuts were automatic, affected all parts of the federal government except a handful of entitlements like Social Security and a small number of programs like veterans benefits, and were to be imposed uniformly down to the program and operational levels. (Exemptions were later added for meat inspectors and air traffic controllers, after fears that the food processing and airline industries would be crippled by the furloughs.) Managers had no discretion about shuffling their budgets to produce the same level of savings. So from park rangers in national parks to staffers supporting members of the military on their bases, the hammer fell—hard, but uniformly.

For so many federal employees, however, the problem wasn't only that the furloughs came. It was that the number of furlough days and their timing was so unpredictable. That made it hard for families to plan everything from vacations to payments for college tuition, and it made it difficult for the government to manage its operations.

QUESTIONS TO CONSIDER

1. What do you think of the strategy of using sequestration and furloughs as a strategy to manage budget cuts? Some analysts say it forces the government to make the hard cuts it's been avoiding for a long time. Others say that the across-the-board cuts bear no resemblance to mission and are the worst way to manage budget cuts.

2. How would you treat this situation if you were a manager overseeing employees who were subject to these furloughs and cuts?

3. How would you approach the problem of reducing the federal budget? Everyone agrees that spending cuts are needed. What kind of strategy could build enough political support to obtain the needed reductions?

NOTES

1. "Pentagon Chief Can't Offer Hope in Budget Cuts," *USA Today* (July 22, 2013), http://www.usatoday.com/story/news/nation/2013/07/21/defense-cuts/2573881.

2. Ibid.

3. Leada Gore, "Pentagon Says Sequestration and Furloughs Could Be Its 'New Normal,'" *All Alabama* (July 22, 2013), http://blog.al.com/wire/2013/07/pentagon_says_sequestration_an.html.

CASE 8.3

Keeping Volunteers Out of the Library? Battling the Teachers Union in Bridgewater, Massachusetts

In the middle of a hotly contested gubernatorial campaign in Massachusetts, Republican candidate Charlie Baker stopped in Bridgewater for a press conference. He was outraged that the local teachers union in this town south of Boston was trying to stop the use of volunteers in school libraries. "There are many examples of teachers unions making decisions based on the interests of adults rather than the kids." He continued, "It's outrageous that the union leadership is trying to block the students from the library."[1]

Baker found support from Merry Boegner, a mother of two preschoolers, who supported the candidate's position. "I think it's disgraceful," she argued. "We're in economic times where we need to be creative. We do the same at home with our families. Here, you have people willing to help out, and you don't want it."[2]

No volunteers in the library? No one to help kids find the joy of reading and to provide extra support in tough budget times?

Union officials explained that the story was much more complicated than the candidate's hot rhetoric suggested. As the local budget crisis worsened, the school district reduced the number of middle school librarians in Bridgewater and in neighboring Raynham. The money they saved went into hiring more teachers to reduce class size as more students flooded the schools. To keep the libraries open, the district recruited volunteers. The teachers union objected that volunteers were taking the place of paid teachers—and couldn't possibly provide high-quality service.

The president of the union, Anita Newman, told a reporter, "You're putting unqualified people into the library who are not certified." She explained, "We don't want to ruffle feathers, but you're responsible for the children. We don't use volunteers for recess or lunch either." For the union, the question was simple. "I love volunteers," she said, "but when they take the place of a teacher—and a librarian is a teacher—that's a violation of the contract."[3]

For Baker, it was a matter of raw politics. He charged the teachers union with attacking him at every campaign stop. They were afraid that, if Baker won, "it [wouldn't] be business as usual" in the state capital. The union, usually aligned with the Democrats in Boston, knew that "All bets are off in January" if he won.[4]

"I was hoping this wouldn't become a tempest in a teapot, but it did," Newman sadly concluded.

QUESTIONS TO CONSIDER

1. Unions work hard to protect the jobs of their members, so their opposition to the use of volunteer librarians is understandable. But do you think the school district, faced with tight budgets, made the right call in shifting paid librarian positions to the classroom and using volunteers to keep the libraries open?

2. Does the use of volunteer, uncertified librarians put the education of middle school children in jeopardy?

3. The majority of union members now work for government, as traditional trade unions have lost manufacturing jobs and unions have successfully organized more government workplaces. Do you think that the spread of public employee unions—focused on promoting job security, good working conditions, and generous benefits—is a good thing? Or do you think that the rise of public employee unions unwisely restricts the ability of elected government officials to make policy decisions that are responsive to voters' wishes?

NOTES

1. Christine Legere, "Baker Criticizes Teachers' Union for Objecting to Library Volunteers," *Boston Globe* (October 12, 2010), http://archive.boston.com/yourtown/budgetblues/2010/10/baker_criticizes_teachers_unio.html.

2. Ibid.

3. Ibid.

4. Elizabeth Moura, "Gov. Candidate Baker Weighs In on Bridgewater-Raynham Union Grievance" (October 13, 2010), http://www.wickedlocal.com/x1767883977/Gov-candidate-Baker-weighs-in-on-Bridgewater-Raynham-union-grievance.

CASE 8.4

What Do We Owe Vets?

The federal civil service has long required that returning veterans be given a preference in hiring. The case is simple. After having disrupted their lives to serve their country—after stepping out of the civilian job market, getting very different training, investing much personal time and energy in the military, and facing a sometimes-difficult transition back to civilian life—the argument was that veterans deserved a running start at a good government job.

In the 1990s and 2000s, however, several threads came together that created big challenges for veterans preference. The wars in Iraq and Afghanistan ranked among the longest-running military operations in American history, with millions of soldiers dispatched to the field. Many of them served several tours, and the country felt it owed a special debt to veterans for their service. At the same time, budget crises mounted and hiring of new federal employees tightened. When the economy weakened after the Great Recession, the Obama administration issued an executive order committing federal agencies to hire more vets into government, so that returning vets wouldn't find themselves unemployed.

That combination boosted the hiring of vets in the federal workforce. Vets accounted for almost half—47.4 percent—of new hires into full-time permanent jobs in 2014, a big increase from 39.2 percent in 2010. That boosted the percentage of federal employees who were veterans to 30.8 percent in 2014.[1] For returning vets, that made a huge difference in their ability to find jobs upon leaving the service.

But veterans preference also created substantial problems for federal policy. Within some agencies, tensions between vets and nonvets grew. Nonvets chafed at the deference to authority that former members of the armed services often showed. One technology specialist complained, "In meetings, you can't question anything." The attitude, he said, is: "You're my boss. You could be a complete lunatic, but I won't question you." Another federal employee said, "They're a little rough with their people skills." Vets, on the other hand, often felt their skills were unappreciated. There was a sense, some feared, that "most people think if you're a vet, you don't have to be qualified" because you can get the job through veterans preference. The cultural differences could sometimes be deep and profound.[2]

Moreover, vets have tended not to stay in their new jobs as long as nonveterans. In the Small Business Administration, for example, 62 percent of vets stayed at least two years, compared with 88 percent of nonveterans. In the Commerce Department, there were similar numbers, with 68 percent remaining for two years or more. For nonveterans, the number was 82 percent.[3] Experts weren't sure what explained the gap, but the issue compounded the tensions over veterans preference: more vets were hired, but fewer of them remained.

Veterans preference, in addition, was making it harder to manage the big generational transition in the federal government. In 2015, 13.5 percent of all federal employees were over the age of 60. Just 7.9 percent were under the age of 30, a big decline from 11.5 percent in 2009. In the population as a whole, however, the 20–30 age cohort is 13.9 percent of the American population. As federal human capital expert Jeff Neal argues,

> Young people are significantly underrepresented in the federal government workforce. The Congress and OPM need to take steps to address the problem. Simply telling agencies to do better will not make it happen. We need an easier and more effective way of doing college recruiting and hiring, along with more effective ways of hiring young Veterans (who have a far higher than average unemployment rate). It is in the government's interest to not bypass an entire generation of workers.[4]

Some analysts argued a connection: as more veterans took advantage of veterans preference and as the federal government hired fewer workers, it became harder for younger job-seekers to find federal jobs. That, in turn, made it harder for the federal government to bring in young talent to replace aging baby boomers. Some analysts, in fact, worried this might drive millennials even further away from government work.

QUESTIONS TO CONSIDER

1. What do you think about the policy of veterans preference? Is it a fair and important way of providing opportunity to veterans who served their country? Or should government seek to hire new employees solely on the basis of the qualifications of applicants?

2. To what degree should considerations other than merit—the goal of creating a workforce whose composition matches the American people, or that provides affirmative action for groups long neglected in society—influence government's hiring decisions?

3. If you are not a veteran, would veterans preference make you less likely to apply for a federal job?

4. What could the federal government do to be more successful in recruiting people like you into the federal workforce?

NOTES

1. U.S. Office of Personnel Management, *Employment of Veterans in the Federal Executive Branch, Fiscal Year 2014* (Washington, D.C.: OPM, July 2015), https://www.fedshirevets.gov/hire/hrp/reports/EmploymentOfVets-FY14.pdf.

2. Lisa Rein, "Obama Push to Hire Veterans into Federal Jobs Spurs Resentment," *Washington Post* (September 14, 2014), https://www.washingtonpost.com/politics/obama-push-to-hire-veterans-into-federal-jobs-spurs-resentment/2014/09/14/c576e592-2edc-11e4-bb9b-997ae96fad33_story.html?tid=a_inl.

3. Lisa Rein, "Record Numbers of veterans Are Getting Jobs in the Government—But a Lot of Them Quit," *Washington Post* (August 28, 2015), https://www.washingtonpost.com/news/federal-eye/wp/2015/08/28/record-numbers-of-veterans-are-getting-jobs-in-the-government-but-a-lot-of-them-arent-staying/?tid=a_inl.

4. Jeff Neal, "The Ticking Time Bomb in the Federal Workforce," *Federal News Radio* (March 2, 2016), http://federalnewsradio.com/commentary/2016/03/the-ticking-time-bomb-in-the-federal-workforce/.

KEY CONCEPTS

bump 214
buyouts 214
civil service system 205
collective bargaining 216
grade creep 207

Hatch Act 220
position classification 205
reductions in force (RIFs) 213
unionization 216

FOR FURTHER READING

Ingraham, Patricia Wallace. *The Foundation of Merit: Public Service in American Democracy.* Baltimore: Johns Hopkins University Press, 1995.

Johnson, Ronald N., and Gary D. Libecap. *The Federal Civil Service System and the Problem of Bureaucracy.* Chicago: University of Chicago Press, 1994.

Mosher, Frederick C. *Democracy and the Public Service.* 2nd ed. New York: Oxford University Press, 1982.

National Commission on the Public Service (the Volcker Commission). *Urgent Business for America: Revitalizing the Federal Government for the 21st Century,* January 2003. https://ourpublicservice.org/publications/viewcontentdetails.php?id=314.

Partnership for Public Service. *Building the Enterprise: A New Civil Service Framework.* Washington, D.C.: Partnership for Public Service, April 2014.

Perry, James L., and Ann Marie Thomson. *Civic Service: What Difference Does It Make?* Armonk, N.Y.: M. E. Sharpe, 2004.

SUGGESTED WEBSITES

The U.S. Census Bureau's "Public Employment and Payroll Data," **www.census.gov/govs/apes**, is an excellent source of comparative data on public employees at the federal, state, and local levels. At the federal level, the Office of Personnel Management's "Federal Employment Statistics," especially "The Fact Book," is a useful guide; see **www.opm.gov/feddata**.

Labor practices vary greatly from state to state; some prohibit collective bargaining, while others allow government employees a limited right to strike. The Legal Information Institute at Cornell University compiles state laws, and its website provides a source for exploring state-by-state variations; see **www.law.cornell.edu/wex/table_labor**.

In recent years, more information about working for government, including available positions and (in some cases) applications, has moved online. The federal government's source for job openings is USAJobs, **www.usajobs.gov**. Many state and local governments have similar systems. Pennsylvania, for example, has an integrated website that lists private- and public-sector jobs (at all levels of government); see **www.pa.gov**.

The National Academy of Public Administration periodically issues reports on the role and function of the civil service; NAPA's studies can be found at **www.napa wash.org**.

The Government Accountability Office, at **www.gao.gov**, consistently produces some of the most thorough analysis of human capital issues.

The Partnership for Public Service examines the policy issues in building a high-performing government workforce. Its studies and analyses can be found at **www.our publicservice.org**.

for CQ Press

WANT A BETTER GRADE?

Get the tools you need to sharpen your study skills. Access practice quizzes, eFlashcards, video, and multimedia at **edge.sagepub.com/kettl7e.**

HUMAN CAPITAL

At a breakfast meeting with community leaders in Millinocket, Maine, National Park Service Director Jonathan Jarvis listens carefully to citizens' views about a controversial plan to create a new national monument in the state's North Woods.

The quality of government depends on the quality of the people who work for it. But how good of a job is government doing in matching the job to be done with the people who need to do it? This is the issue of **human capital**: find the right people, for the right jobs, with the right skills, at the right time. It's a huge challenge. In 2003, the Government Accountability Office (GAO) concluded that "today's federal human capital strategies are not yet appropriately constituted to meet current and emerging challenges or to drive the needed transformation across the government." But, GAO concluded, "federal employees are not the problem." The real problem "is a set of policies that are viewed by many as outdated, overregulated, and not strategic."[1] Things have not changed much since then and, just as important, government is investing relatively little energy in trying to fix it. The government's human capital system is in disrepair. Meanwhile, important debates are reshaping the system.

The fundamental challenge lies in matching the skills of government's workers with the changing strategies and tactics of the government's operations. At all levels of government—but especially at the federal level—more of government's work depends on creating, managing, and leveraging partnerships with the many partners on which government depends to get its work done. More of government managers' work aims to focus these partnerships on solving problems, instead of simply managing agencies, which puts even more emphasis on interpersonal skills, information management, and other collaborative skills. Government's fundamental struggle is to identify, recruit, reinforce, and reward these skills. That in turn requires government to adapt and change a system that has been in place for more than 130 years, a system whose very rigidity was designed to prevent political interference in the professionalism of government. This change poses an enormous test.

Experts have long pointed to the rise of a "knowledge society," as management expert Peter Drucker explains:

> Knowledge workers, even though only a large minority of the work force, already give the emerging knowledge society its character, its leadership, its central challenges and its social profile. They may not be the *ruling* class of the knowledge society, but they already are its *leading* class.[2]

This description of the knowledge economy is even truer for government, whose work increasingly depends on managing information to leverage partnerships with other government agencies, other levels of government, the private and nonprofit sectors, and increasingly with other players around the globe as well. Indeed, many of the issues in future chapters, especially about implementation and regulation, revolve around tracking information and using it to improve performance. In this chapter, we explore the emerging issue of human capital, efforts to transform the civil service system, and strategies for strengthening leadership at the top of the bureaucracy.

CHAPTER OBJECTIVES

- Understand the meaning and importance of human capital for the performance of government

- Explore the alternatives for reforming the civil service and improving the government's human capital

- Examine the role of leadership in the public service

THE HUMAN CAPITAL CHALLENGE

In January 2001, GAO named human capital management as a high-risk area facing the entire government—and it's been on the list ever since. In fact, new challenges have arisen. As GAO's 2015 report concluded, "Mission-critical skills gaps in such occupations as cybersecurity and acquisition pose a high-risk to the nation."[3] The failure to build human capital, GAO worried, courted failure in the government's performance.

Building Human Capital

The challenge of building human capital revolves around four issues: (1) leadership, (2) strategic human capital planning, (3) acquiring, developing, and retaining talent, and (4) results-oriented culture.[4]

LEADERSHIP. Developing human capital begins at the top, with organizational leaders who focus on building a workforce with the capacity to accomplish the organization's goals. In part, this requires top managers to give sustained attention to management. Big policy issues—from scandals to political battles and new legislative proposals to congressional oversight hearings—often drive out a manager's focus on administrative issues. But whenever the urgent (as indeed these policy issues are) drives out the important (especially a long-term focus on organizational performance), governmental organizations risk spending their time fighting brush fires instead of accomplishing their overall missions.

For example, the Department of Homeland Security (DHS), created in 2002 to bring together more than twenty agencies and over 170,000 federal employees, presents a daunting administrative challenge. The department's secretary and top officials face a bewildering flood of terrorism warnings, intelligence analyses, logistical problems, and bureaucratic battles. Congress insists on regular briefings, and the secretary by necessity must invest a great deal of energy and time in working with the heads of other agencies charged with important pieces of the homeland security function, including the secretaries of defense and state and the heads of the Federal Bureau of Investigation (FBI) and the Central Intelligence Agency. It is very easy for these issues to become all-consuming, but if the big policy questions consume the leadership, there may well be little time and no senior officials left to address the critical long-term task of bringing the department's vast bureaucratic empire together into a smoothly functioning operation. The risk is that the department's top officials will busy themselves with policy puzzles but find they do not have the capacity to implement them effectively. Many of these challenges are rooted in human capital; there is no solution to the larger puzzles of homeland security without building a strong human capital system.

Doing so, in DHS and throughout government, is not only hard, but it also requires long-term effort. Deep organizational change takes sustained work over a long time—five to seven years or more, according to the private sector's experience. Yet high-level political appointees serve, on average, less than three years.[5] That pattern of transience at the top leaves much of the task of long-term transformation in the hands of senior career officials, but, as we will see later in this chapter, that part of the government's workforce is aging and many of the most experienced managers are nearing retirement. Leadership, therefore, requires not only sustained attention to management but also careful attention to the problem of building the next generation of leaders.[6]

STRATEGIC HUMAN CAPITAL PLANNING. Although government planning often gets a bad name, it is impossible for government to solve its human capital issues without

| Figure 9.1 | Average Age of Workers in the Federal and Private Sectors |

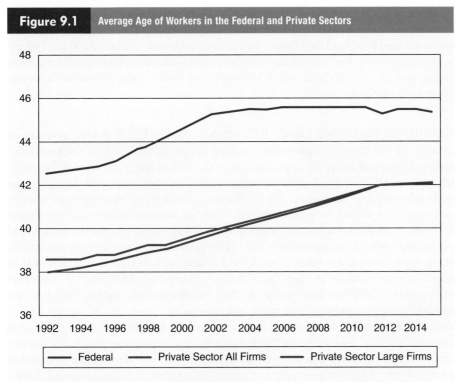

Source: U.S. Office of Management and Budget, *Budget of the United States Government, Fiscal Year 2017: Analytical Perspectives* (2016), Chart 8-4, https://www.whitehouse.gov/sites/default/files/omb/budget/fy2017/assets/ap_8_strengthening.pdf.

taking a longer-term view of its key strategies, fundamental missions, and needed capacity. Many government agencies, at all levels, face big turnover in their staffing. And as Gen Xers and millennials replace baby boomers, big challenges in the culture of government agencies lie ahead. The rise of Gen X, for example, has already brought fundamental changes in the way government agencies connect electronically with citizens. As today's college students move into the workforce, even bigger changes will follow, from the use of technology to debates about the role of government.[7] In the past, many government workers saw public employment as a lifetime career. Gen X and millennial workers seem to show far less attachment to their employers but even greater interest in finding impact through their work.

Meanwhile, the long-predicted baby boom retirement wave—the "silver tsunami"—has begun, analysts have found. "The looming talent crisis that we've been talking about for years is right on our doorstep," explained Elizabeth Kellar, president of the Center for State and Local Excellence. In Virginia, 37 percent of state government workers are eligible to retire by 2020. Nearly a third of Washington State employees are 55 years or older. Nevertheless, the coming retirement of millions of government-employed baby boomers will create substantial opportunities for younger people who want to work for government. At the federal level, for example, the workforce is on average much older than in the private sector (see Figure 9.1). The coming generational change is sure to transform government—and the way it relates to citizens.

That means governments will need to do a lot of hiring, and that raises two big challenges: attracting younger workers to government jobs, and planning for the skills for which governments will need to recruit.[8] One thing is for certain: government cannot move forward simply by replacing retiring workers with new employees, doing the same things in the same ways. Hiring workers with twentieth-century skills will never work to solve government's twenty-first-century problems.

HIRING, DEVELOPING, AND RETAINING TALENT. Of course, government agencies are not the only organizations seeking to operate effectively in the knowledge society. Private and nonprofit organizations, in the United States and around the world, are competing for the highly skilled workers needed for these tasks. Although there are many advantages to working for the government—from fringe benefits to the rewards that come from serving the public—in many cases government workers can find similar positions in the private sector, and many of these private-sector jobs involve work under the general umbrella of government rules. The government thus needs to compete in hiring top talent—and it needs to work hard to keep its best employees committed to public service. Indeed, as Kay Coles James, director of the Office of Personnel Management (OPM) in the George W. Bush administration, argued, "We have no problem attracting people." The crisis, she concluded, "is in the hiring process"—getting interested individuals in the door, as we saw in Chapter 8, is often the biggest problem.[9] In fact, an important 2014 report by the Partnership for Public Service concluded, "The world has changed dramatically, but the civil service system has remained stuck in the past, serving as a barrier rather than an aid to attracting, hiring and retaining highly skilled and educated employees needed to respond to today's domestic and global challenges."[10]

The problem of ensuring an adequate supply of skilled workers is common throughout government. In the Department of Housing and Urban Development (HUD), half of the staff members responsible for monitoring the performance of the contractors managing government housing programs were found to have no training in contract management. Even worse, HUD's procurement officials did not know of the gap.[11]

More broadly, government struggles with critical gaps between the workers it needs and the employees it has recruited. At the federal level, analysts have found the government especially needs information technology and cybersecurity specialists, acquisition specialists, economists, human resources specialists, auditors, and science/technology/engineering/math specialists who can make the connection to government policy.[12] Many state and local governments have similar gaps. Few governments have developed strong plans to fill the gaps they have.

RESULTS-ORIENTED CULTURE. Too often, as we saw in the previous chapter, government personnel processes become part of government's broader compliance culture (a tendency to focus on rules and procedures) rather than a performance culture (a focus on results). In the aftermath of the September 11, 2001, attacks, for example, the FBI discovered that the mismatch of rules and missions hindered the bureau's effectiveness. To resolve this problem, top FBI officials reorganized the bureau's structure to match its mission and worked to match the personnel system to the new priorities.

Ten-year-old Anna Ramsier (left) celebrates her sister Jill's success in using a penny and a washer to make a battery and illuminate a light held by University of Akron engineering student Kenton Lawson. Their experiment was part of a program sponsored by the U.S. Department of Defense to encourage young girls to explore science, technology, engineering, and math.

As American governments at all levels develop more aggressive performance management systems, it becomes easier to use those systems to drive the personnel system—and to reshape the personnel system to support the mission. Other nations have been pursuing such strategies. In Canada, the province of Ontario has redefined its system for measuring employee performance to capture how well its employees contribute to the organization's goals. A similar overhaul has occurred in the Tax Office in Australia. These governments have created a "line of sight" performance management system, designed "to clearly demonstrate how an individual's performance contributes to the overall goals of the organization as well as to broader government-wide priorities."[13] The idea is simple: measure each employee's performance, and connect that employee's work to the work of the organization. Strengthening the incentives for each employee improves the organization's ability to accomplish its mission.

Such an approach, of course, is both complex and difficult, but many analysts have concluded that this should be the foundation for reform in the United States.[14] As part of its broader reform effort, Barack Obama's administration launched a major performance improvement effort that focused on

- using performance information to lead, learn, and improve outcomes;
- communicating performance coherently and concisely for better results and transparency; and
- strengthening problem-solving networks, inside and outside government, to improve outcomes and performance management practices.

That effort, the administration said, would produce "unrelenting attention to achieve the ambitious, near-term performance goals" that agency leaders themselves identified as top-priority objectives.[15]

Box 9.1	Human Capital Standards

- *Strategic alignment:* connecting the mission and objectives with strategic plans and budgets

- *Leadership and knowledge management:* effectively leading employees to sustain a learning environment focused on continuous improvement

- *Results-oriented performance culture:* defining goals and providing incentives for employees to seek high levels of performance

- *Talent management:* identifying the skills that the agency needs, defining the gap between existing skills and those needed, and developing a strategy for closing the gap

- *Accountability:* using a data-driven performance system to ensure results

Source: U.S. Office of Personnel Management, "Human Capital Management," https://www.opm.gov/policy-data-oversight/human-capital-management/.

Government Reforms

OPM, GAO, and the Office of Management and Budget have all launched major human capital efforts. OPM has published human capital standards. Box 9.1 charts the connections between agency missions, human capital, program performance, and government's accountability. Former comptroller general David M. Walker concluded, "Strategic management of human capital should emphasize that people are the key to the success of our government transformation effort. As such, they should be treated more like assets instead of liabilities."[16] The Obama administration's reforms in performance and civil service advanced these notions one more step, and many state and local governments have explored related plans and strategies.

This strong convergence of rhetoric and ideas has begun to have an impact. During President Bill Clinton's administration, OPM wiped away two of the most notorious symbols of the troubled personnel system. Accompanied (literally) by a fife and drum corps, OPM Director James King dumped the *Federal Personnel Manual* into the trash. This multivolume set contained 10,000 pages of rules—including 900 pages of instructions for filling out just one federal form. As King explained, "It is written in such gobbledygook that it takes a team of Washington's finest attorneys to understand what is required to hire, fire, classify and reward employees."[17] The job of writing rules was instead turned over to federal agencies.

The Clinton administration then followed up that theatrical gesture by eliminating the much-hated SF-171, the federal government's standard résumé form, which often stretched six feet or more when completed. The form was replaced by a computerized system and by acceptance of more standard résumés. With the death of Knowledge, Skills, and Abilities essays in the Obama administration, the movement toward simplicity in the application process took another big step. Many state and local governments have likewise embraced the need for a strong human capital strategy as part of their efforts to build a government for the twenty-first century.

NEW FLEXIBILITY FOR THE PERSONNEL SYSTEM

In the late 1990s, new and more aggressive flexibilities began creeping into the personnel systems at all levels of government. Each was designed to link employee performance with agency missions and to enhance the ability of the government to do its job.

At all levels of government, managers complain that the personnel system has too many layers, with too many subcategories, which makes it difficult to classify employees and even more difficult to manage employees effectively. Because the nature of the job defines the personnel classification and the classification defines who can do the job, managers have a hard time moving employees to where they are most needed or into the jobs in which they might be able to produce the best results. Many state government personnel managers believe that their states have far too many job titles. The average state reported 1,802 titles that the personnel managers had to track, yet most of these titles covered very few employees—an average of just twenty-four each—which created groupings too small for broad policy. Moreover, the classification and pay systems were very old, averaging twenty-three years since their inception in the mid-1970s.[18] Government's functions and strategies had changed considerably in the meantime, but the personnel system had not.

In 2014, the Partnership for Public Service proposed a simple plan, with broad support, to improve the government's human capital system:

- *Principles.* Create a unified civil service, operating under core principles while providing agencies flexibility to meet the needs of their missions.
- *Job classification.* Collapse the fifteen levels of the current General Schedule into five work levels that match the knowledge federal employees perform, and allow them to advance by improvements in what they know rather than how many people they supervise.
- *Pay.* Create a pay system matched to occupations and markets to make government pay comparable with private-sector wages.
- *Performance management.* Improve the system for assessing employees' performance by awarding salary increases only to those who exceed expectations.
- *Hiring.* Increase agencies' hiring flexibility to make it easier to bring talented individuals into government.
- *Accountability.* Make it easier to hold workers accountable for their work and to discipline (or fire) workers for poor performance or misconduct.
- *Executives.* Simplify and strengthen the executive service, especially by focusing the top level on officials with interagency, intergovernmental, or intersector experience and by decreasing the number of political appointees in managerial positions.[19]

This approach has widespread support for reform at the federal, state, and local government levels. But the politics of changing the civil service system are intense. Despite the great power of these recommendations and the strong support they have received, little action has advanced.

Departmental Flexibilities

Many reformers have agreed on the need for an even more fundamental reform of the federal civil service system, but they disagree on how best to pursue it. Some reformers

Richard Hartog/Los Angeles Times via Getty Image

An air traffic controller works at New York's LaGuardia Airport, in one of the nation's most crowded air spaces. Recruiting new controllers to replace retiring workers is one of the air traffic control system's biggest challenges.

despaired of enacting a broad-based reform that would apply to the entire federal government after the power of public employee unions and a lack of congressional interest in such sweeping change paralyzed the effort. Faced with tough management problems, Congress has allowed some agencies exemptions from portions of the civil service law. That, in fact, was the keystone of reforms created to give the U.S. Department of Veterans Affairs (VA) more flexibility to deal with the crisis of reforming the agency following complaints beginning in 2014 that veterans were not being treated in a reasonable amount of time. Some reformers have worried that a series of ad hoc reforms would produce widespread inconsistency in federal personnel standards. Paul Volcker, the former Federal Reserve Board chairman who headed a series of civil service reform commissions, said that he sensed "something of a thread of incoherence" in the efforts of these agencies.[20] They struggled between doing what could be done, at the risk of undermining more than a century of uniform civil service policies, and seeking a broader reform, at the risk of inviting political conflicts that would make it impossible to do anything.

When air traffic controllers went on strike in 1981, President Ronald Reagan determined that they had broken the law and he fired them. For years afterward, the Federal Aviation Administration (FAA) struggled to rebuild the system. In 1996, however, Congress approved an agency-wide reform granting top managers more flexibility. The law gave the FAA a broadband pay system, requirements for more frequent feedback on employee performance and a linking of performance with pay, better workforce planning, and a competitive hiring practice that bypassed the federal government's central system. Following intensive hearings that produced charges of widespread mismanagement, Congress then gave similar personnel flexibility to the Internal Revenue Service (IRS) in 1998. However, these IRS personnel reforms did not—and, indeed, could not—solve the problems that had first prompted Congress to act. (See Box 9.2 for a comparison of the traditional civil service provisions and proposals for change in the new DHS.)

Box 9.2	Proposed Civil Service Rules for the Department of Homeland Security

Provisions Maintained	**Provisions Not Maintained**
Merit system principles	Employee appeal rights
Whistleblower protection	"Rule of three" hiring rule
Basic employment rules (e.g., veterans' preference)	Performance appraisal system
Senior Executive Service	Position classification
Reduction-in-force procedures	Pay rates and systems
Training rules	Labor-management relations
Incentive awards	Adverse action procedures
Personnel demonstration authority	Appeal rights
Payroll administration	
Travel rules	
Special allowances (e.g., for overseas duty)	
Attendance and leave standards	
Antidiscrimination	
Political activity limits	
Gift limits	
Drug-use policy	
Work life and safety services	
Injury compensation	
Insurance and retirement benefits	

Source: Brian Friel, "Homeland Security Leaders Win Broad Power over Civil Service Rules," *Government Executive* (November 21, 2002), http://www.govexec.com/dailyfed/1102/112102b1.htm.

These efforts sharpened a basic debate about the civil service system. Should there be a single system that applies to all government employees? Or, given the difficulty of passing legislation to improve the civil service, should reformers take advantage of opportunities where they find them, on an agency-by-agency basis, even if that means the system as a whole falls out of sync? This focuses the most basic question of all: What is the role and meaning of the nineteenth-century merit system in the twenty-first century?

Rethinking the Meaning of Merit

Over the past two decades, three states—Texas, Georgia, and Florida—have taken even bigger steps toward escaping the bounds of the current civil service system. They took the advice of Walter Broadnax, former director of the New York State civil service system and longtime analyst of the process, who, in frustration at the system's constraints, said simply, "Blow it up."[21] These three states followed just that course.

The Texas legislature led the way in 1985 by abolishing the Texas Merit Council, a body that did not have control over all the state's employees but did oversee ten agencies' compliance with federal law. The state legislature decided to eliminate the council and delegated responsibility for complying with federal civil service standards to the state agencies themselves. The agencies, in turn, were given complete flexibility in setting hiring and firing procedures for their employees. The state government, for example, cannot calculate how long it takes to hire new employees, since the agencies follow their own rules and the state does not keep centralized statistics. Indeed, Texas is the only state without a central personnel office.

Georgia followed in 1996 with an even more radical reform, which Republican Governor Zell Miller made a centerpiece of his effort to transform government management. When the state set up its civil service system in the 1940s, he said, creating "a professional workforce that was free of political cronyism" was important. But, he contended,

> too often in government, we pass laws to fix particular problems of the moment, and then we allow half a century to roll by without ever following up to see what the long-term consequences have been. Folks, the truth of the matter is that a solution in 1943 is a problem in 1996. The problem is governmental paralysis, because despite its name, our present Merit System is not about merit. It offers no reward to good workers. It only provides cover for bad workers.[22]

Miller won overwhelming support for his plan to abolish the state's merit system. Employees hired after July 1, 1996, would serve at will, which meant that they had no civil service protection and could be fired without benefit of the standard civil service procedures. The new employees would receive the same benefits as employees currently in the system, but they would not accrue seniority rights, so, in case of reductions in force, they could not protect their jobs by "bumping" less-senior employees (as described in Chapter 8). They would have no formal rights of appeal of disciplinary actions or performance assessments. Managers could promote, demote, transfer, or fire employees as they saw fit. The legislature also abolished the traditional grade-and-step process that set employees' wages.

Despite the worries of many advocates of the traditional civil service, Georgia's new system has been remarkably free of tales of abuse. Investigative reporters found little expansion of patronage. In fact, they determined that patronage in Georgia was little different than in states with tough civil service laws. Different employees doing similar jobs might receive different pay, which would not have occurred in the old system. And managers found that they had lost the ability to blame the system for being unable to respond to requests. As one senior state official put it, the buck stops with managers, who have to shoulder responsibility for their decisions.[23] The 2008 Government Performance Project (GPP) survey of state government management capacity found the state at the cutting edge, stating that "Georgia continues to push the envelope in workforce and human capital planning."[24]

In 2001, Florida made three fundamental changes in its civil service system. First, supervisors became **at-will employees**—top officials could hire and fire them without having to deal with civil service protections. Second, the state collapsed its existing pay structure into a broadband system. Finally, with a handful of exceptions for police officers, firefighters, and nurses, the state eliminated seniority protections for state employees. As journalist Jonathan Walters explained, "What lawmakers in Florida seemed to have decided was that if it's not possible to eliminate civil service coverage for all state employees outright, then the best thing to do was to drastically reengineer what that coverage amounts to."[25] The state continued to push ahead without a strategic workforce plan, however, and the GPP found the state drifting into growing trouble. Florida outsourced more of its administrative work and made one-fifth of its workforce at-will employees (that is, they could be fired at the will of their supervisors). Turnover rose, and the state's capacity to get its work done shrank.[26]

What effect did these reforms have? There has been little evidence of widespread abuse in any of the three states, either through hiring substandard workers or political interference in the hiring process. Few lawsuits alleging discrimination or other violations of the law have arisen. The basic principles for which the civil service system had been created a century before remained intact. Managers simply found it easier to manage: they had more flexibility and could act more quickly, and they had an easier time firing poor performers and, when necessary, shrinking the size of the government workforce.

It is hard to predict what would happen if such reforms were to be instituted in other states with stronger traditions of political patronage. As in the federal system, establishing good performance measurement systems has proven difficult, and none of the states has yet systematically assessed the impact of the reforms—with the devolution of responsibility came a hands-off policy on collecting data. However, it is clear that, faced with tension between the restrictions of the current civil service system and the needs of adapting government to fast-changing realities, more state and local governments will be exploring flexible personnel systems.[27]

Virginia's state government, in many ways, has become the national model. The GPP found that

> The commonwealth has a strategic plan for management of human resources (HR) that identifies current and future needs and is linked to the human capital plan. Virginia has readily available comprehensive data about its current and future workforce needs that it uses to make decisions involving human capital management. The commonwealth has evaluated and updated its classification, compensation and management systems and implemented emergency workforce planning.

Virginia developed innovative approaches to recruiting new employees, which included devising a strategy to give state service a special cachet and contracting with a private company to recruit foreign-born nurses to fill high-demand positions. The state has broadband pay ranges and flexible fringe benefits, along with a generous pay-for-performance system. Training and development are high priorities.[28] The state found that human capital development paid off, with higher performance for taxpayers and better jobs for state employees.

More broadly, fundamental changes to many of the civil service system's oldest features are emerging throughout the states. Florida's at-will system has expanded to Georgia and Indiana. In Arizona, new employees must agree to "uncovered" status, forgoing traditional civil service protections. North Carolina has expanded the number of employees exempt from civil service requirements, and Tennessee has eliminated "bumping." As North Carolina Governor Pat McCrory put it, "I've got a $20 billion operation I've got to run, and you can't run it with your managers' and your executives' hands tied."[29] In fact, Paul Verkuil found that at least twenty-eight states have moved to some version of at-will employment, which replaces civil service protections with a system far more like what exists in the private sector.[30] There is no agreement on the best civil service system for the twenty-first century—but there is a strong consensus that the current system is a poor match for today's governance challenges.

In fact, political scientist John DiIulio has advanced an even more radical idea. In his fascinating and important book, *Bring Back the Bureaucrats*, he contends that government ought to pull more of its work back in-house and hire more government workers to do it: this would mean a million more workers for the federal government by 2035. That, DiIulio explains, would help trim the size of government by paradoxically increasing it: the strategy would enhance government's ability to get things done.[31] Neither policymakers nor citizens have shown much appetite

Scott J. Ferrell/Congressional Quarterly/Getty Images

In the George W. Bush administration, the president's director of the White House Office of Faith-Based and Community Initiatives, John J. DiIulio Jr., took part in a rally on the floor of the U.S. House of Representatives. Along with House Republican Conference Chair J. C. Watts Jr. (R-Okla.), he celebrated the administration's partnerships with neighborhood organizations to improve social services.

for this eminently sensible and powerful idea. The problem, at the core, is that we tend to disconnect the broad debates about "bureaucracy" from the job that bureaucrats do. If we want high performance from government, we need enough government bureaucrats with the right skills

LEADERSHIP IN THE PUBLIC SERVICE

Among all these ideas, however, one is most important: high performance in government depends on strong leadership by top officials. No system for hiring, firing, promoting, and rewarding employees—whether it is a civil service system or not—can work without strong and sustained direction. Building and maintaining human capital begins with leadership.

Just as the government has grappled with how best to nurture its rank-and-file employees, it has long struggled with how best to recruit and reward its top leaders. In this section, we focus on leadership in the federal government. State and local governments often follow the same general pattern, but they can also present enormous variations.

Every modern government deals with the leadership task by creating a mix of political and administrative officials at the top. The fundamental puzzle is how to set that mix: political officials provide a larger measure of responsiveness, whereas career administrators bring a larger measure of professional competence. Methods for establishing the mix vary greatly. In Britain, a change of parties brings only about 120 members of Parliament into the executive part of the government, with such titles as minister, junior minister, and parliamentary secretary. In France, the government of the day has only 100 to 150 politicians, mostly ministers, secretaries of state, and their staff aides. In Germany, the strictly political echelon is thin—about forty members, including ministers and parliamentary secretaries. Denmark has perhaps the thinnest layer of political officials of any major democracy: the minister of each agency is a political official, but all officials below that level are careerists. The American federal government, of course, stands at the opposite extreme.

Political Leadership

In the American executive branch there are over 3,000 political positions, about 1,500 of which are at the higher levels.[32] Of these, approximately 1,000 are leadership positions, including cabinet secretaries, administrators of agencies such as NASA and the Small Business Administration, ambassadors to foreign nations, and regulatory positions in agencies such as the Federal Trade Commission and the Securities and Exchange Commission.[33] By any measure, the United States has a far larger number of political officials at the top of the bureaucracy than other Western democracies. Moreover, the number of executives at the top of the federal bureaucracy has steadily been increasing over the past forty years.

Why does the United States stand out? One explanation is that some presidents—notably Richard Nixon, Jimmy Carter, and Ronald Reagan—have entered office on campaigns vilifying "the bureaucracy" and, believing their own rhetoric, concluded that only a small army of their own selection could ensure agencies' responsiveness to presidential policy priorities.[34] Even presidents who have expressed more confidence in government—including Bill Clinton and both presidents Bush—find that political appointments can help build a trusted cadre of officials throughout the government.

More basically, however, the American separation of powers, in contrast to European systems, leaves the president less in command of administrative agencies than are European executives, who have more administrative freedom. In parliamentary systems, leaders can count on legislative support because their party or coalition has the most votes. The U.S. president, in contrast, faces a Congress that engages in active oversight and intervention in administrative agencies' affairs, and the president often confronts a situation in which the opposite party controls one or both houses. In addition, as Terry Moe has argued, the mismatch between the public's extravagant expectations of a president's performance and the limited resources available for satisfying those expectations makes the president seize on the tools readily at hand, namely politicization of appointments and centralization in the White House.[35]

No one doubts the need for having a layer of political positions and, immediately below that layer, for mixing political appointees and careerists. It is widely agreed that a president or department head needs people who share the same policy orientation; who will advocate the chosen policies to congressional committees, interest groups, and the public; who can serve as their superiors' loyal agents in bringing the permanent bureaucracy into effective service of those policies; and who have their superiors' confidence. The leader also needs officials who are expendable—who can readily be removed when they lose the president's or department head's confidence, resist policy directives, or become liabilities because they have antagonized relevant congressional committees or interest groups.[36] The question for debate is how deep into the bureaucracy this political appointment process should go.

As Paul C. Light, a leading scholar of the presidential appointments process, found in an important study of senior officials, the federal government has steadily "thickened" as the number of political appointees has risen. There are, Light discovered, "more layers of leaders" and "more leaders at each layer." The result has been an important transformation in government:

In the 1950s, the federal bureaucracy looked like a relatively flat bureaucratic pyramid, with few senior executives, a somewhat larger number of middle managers, and a very large number of frontline employees. By the 1970s, it was beginning to look like a circus tent, with a growing corps of senior political and career managers, a sizable bulge of middle managers and professionals, and a shrinking number of frontline employees.

In the 1980s and 1990s, the configuration began to resemble a pentagon, with even more political and career executives at the top and almost equal numbers of many middle-level and frontline employees.[37]

In his survey, Light found fifty-two potential managerial layers from top to bottom in the federal government. Some positions are held by political appointees, others are occupied by careerists. Not all departments have every position: only the Department of Energy, for example, has a principal associate deputy undersecretary. Moreover, the government is getting even thicker. Light also discovered that there were sixty-four different categories of supporting positions (chief of staff to the secretary, deputy chief of staff to the secretary, chief of staff to the undersecretary, and so on) in 2004, which was up from fifty-one in 1998 and thirty-three in 1992.[38]

Even amid the recent enthusiasm for downsizing the federal government, presidents have shown little inclination to reduce the number of layers or, especially, the number of political appointees who fill them. Every position is an opportunity to reward a valued campaign aide or a generous contributor. But the increase of governmental layers weakens accountability by making it harder to assign clear responsibility for results.

Recruitment

Filling the politically appointed positions is one of the most daunting problems facing a new president. After the election, a new president has only about ten weeks to assemble the team that will take over the executive branch on inauguration day. The president must rely heavily on top campaign staff to handle the flood of candidacies self-generated or proposed by political and interest group patrons. Campaign staff members are rarely qualified for the shift of focus from campaigning to governing, because the qualifications required for specific positions are poorly understood and often poorly match those of the chosen candidates.[39] After inauguration, the task shifts to the White House personnel office, and haste gives way to delay. By November of his first year, George H. W. Bush had not nominated candidates for 27 percent of departmental and other agency positions requiring Senate confirmation—a higher percentage than in the four preceding major transitions.[40] As Paul C. Light observed, "It now takes as long, on average, to get an appointee into office as it does to have a child."[41] It took the Obama administration more than a year to fill even 80 percent of its top politically appointed positions in the agencies.

The recruitment of political executives is so difficult that one must marvel that it works as well as it does. It succeeds best in the selection of cabinet members, a matter to which the president-elect gives personal attention. Most cabinet members have had federal government experience.[42] They are often generalists with prior service in other cabinet posts, at the subcabinet level, in Congress, or in the White House. Some have served at the state and local levels, especially those named to cabinet posts for such departments as Health and Human Services (HHS) and Transportation, which have a heavy state and local government connection. They are likely to be qualified for the processes of advocacy, negotiation, and compromise that dominate governmental policymaking, especially if they are lawyers, although this skill set is less likely to be found with corporate executives and academics and not at all with ideologues.[43]

The vast number of appointments below the cabinet level poses the biggest challenge, because it is virtually impossible for the president-elect to give the selections personal attention. Therefore, the president is dependent at first on the campaign staff and then on the personnel office at the White House. An initial impulse of some incoming presidents is to delegate to cabinet members the selection of their subordinates, but after the inauguration, subcabinet appointments are generally cleared or initiated in the White House personnel office.

Most political executives have solid educational backgrounds, and many have subject-matter knowledge relevant to their particular responsibilities. But there are two important problems. First, many political appointees have suffered from lack of experience in the federal executive branch. Former appointees without such prior experience express regret at how poorly prepared they were for the Washington setting of interest groups, congressional committees, and White House staff, as well as the goldfish-bowl exposure to the media, the budget process, and the permanent bureaucracy. A few appointees have even revealed defective appreciation of the Constitution, faithful execution of the laws, and the public service code of ethics. The contrast with Britain is striking. There the political officials are drawn from Parliament. A new cabinet typically consists of individuals who in opposition were members of a "shadow cabinet," each specializing in the affairs of a particular ministry. Often the ministers have had experience in one or more earlier governments when their party was in power.

Second, many political appointees arrive at their positions without extensive management experience.[44] Many come from law firms, university faculties, research institute staffs, interest group organizations, and congressional members' offices and committees. Such experience scarcely prepares them to run a bureau of 5,000 employees, let alone to operate effectively in one of the cabinet departments. In fact, the largest governmental organization Barack Obama had run before becoming president was his Senate office. Senate staffs average thirty-four persons. Recruits from business are more likely to have experience in large-scale management—although when Reagan appointed more businesspersons (a fifth of all his appointees) than any president since Eisenhower, his appointees did not exhibit significantly better performance. In 2008, G. Edward DeSeve laid out a set of competencies that political executives need to do their job, but progress in implementing these remained fleeting.[45]

Turnover

Political appointees serve only briefly in their posts. For decades, the median length of service for presidential appointees has been little more than two years; a third stayed a year and a half or less.[46] This rapid-fire **turnover** creates a host of problems, the most important of which is what Max Stier calls a lack of "continuity of focus."[47]

First, many presidential appointees leave after they have barely learned their jobs and adapted to the Washington environment. Analysts widely agree that appointees need at least a year to become productive performers in their government posts. Some, moreover, are aware that the second year may be their last. To initiate and see results from new projects, appointees will prefer those that are short range, even though significant achievements in the public interest require emphasis on long-range outcomes. Executives who do not pay attention to the likelihood that they will not be in the position very long may invest energy in substantial undertakings, but the job of carrying them through will be passed on to their successors, who may well push them aside to make way for a new set of priorities. An administration loses sustained focus through such a stop-and-go or go-and-stop process. One career civil servant, who became an assistant secretary of commerce, reported his experience this way:

> I don't know how many assistant secretaries I have helped break in. . . . And there is always a propensity for a new guy to come in and discover the wheel all over again. And then you have the classic case of a political officer who is going to make a name for himself, and therefore he is going to identify one golden chalice he is going after, and he will take the whole goddam energy of an organization to go after that golden chalice. He leaves after eighteen months, a new guy comes in, and his golden chalice is over here. "Hey guys, everybody, this way."[48]

Turnover at the cabinet level has similar costs. At the Department of Labor, the GAO reported, the then-serving secretary "demonstrated the strong leadership needed for a well-managed Organization, and his management system established a sound framework for strategic planning and management." Nevertheless, of nearly 200 Labor Department managers polled about this official's efficient system, "about 92 percent believed it should remain despite top-level turnover, whereas only about 35 percent believed it would."[49] Below the cabinet and assistant secretaries, the phenomenon repeats itself: between 1997 and 1987, the Social Security Administration had seven commissioners or acting commissioners. As the GAO found, "These short tenures, along with commissioners' differing priorities and management approaches, resulted in frequent changes of direction, diminished accountability, and little long-term operational planning."[50]

Second, despite frequent talk of a president's or department head's "team," rapid turnover undermines teamwork. In a department, the set of top executives is constantly changing, as the timing of individual departures is usually set by each official's choice. More broadly, because so many policies and programs involve interdepartmental collaboration, their shaping and constancy depend on interdepartmental networks of political executives sharing concerns with particular policy areas. Such networks, as Hugh Heclo has observed, require "relationships of confidence and trust."[51] But the chemistry of these interpersonal relations develops only over time, and subtraction and addition of new elements can upset the developed formula.

Third, civil servants' incentives to obey political superiors tend to fray when those superiors who are here today are likely to be gone tomorrow. Some high careerists patiently tutor one after another political executive to speed the learning process. But others, if in charge of bureaus and programs, mount defenses to minimize damage by ill-prepared and very temporary political executives.[52] Indeed, hardened top career officials have learned that there are two ways of embarrassing a new political appointee. One, they say, is to do nothing the new boss wants, on the assumption that the appointee will not be around long enough to notice. The other is to do *everything* the new boss wants, on the assumption that the appointee will quickly learn to depend more on the career staff to avoid the inevitable political problems that come from charging ahead too quickly.

Fourth, the high rate of turnover means that a new administration never completes its staffing. Departures constantly create vacancies that need filling, which produces both problems and opportunities. It often takes many months, and sometimes years, to recruit, nominate, and obtain Senate confirmation of successors to the vacant posts. On the eve of Reagan's second inauguration, HHS lacked three assistant secretaries, a general counsel, and two commissioners. Its Social Security Administration in early 1985 had an acting commissioner (who had served thus for sixteen months) and three acting deputy commissioners (two having served nineteen months).[53] At the beginning of 1986, one-sixth of the 176 cabinet department positions that required presidential nomination and Senate confirmation were either vacant or occupied by persons designated as only "acting" in their positions.[54] During the first years of

**The Number One Challenge
for State and Local Governments**
Theme: Performance

In October 2015, the Government Business Council and *Route Fifty*, an online news service sponsored by *Government Executive*, surveyed state and local government officials throughout the country. What was the biggest challenge they faced? Here are the results, in order:

1. Human capital and workforce issues
2. Budget planning process
3. Information technology and technology management
4. Collaboration
5. Data-driven decision making
6. Acquisition and procurement

Human capital was easily the most important issue. In fact, more than 90 percent of respondents identified it as a challenge and 37 percent ranked it as the single most important issue they faced.

One respondent explained, "Workforce aging and retirements across the board in key management positions [are] leaving a void in institutional knowledge." Another official pointed to the baby boom retirement surge and explained that many of these retirees "are not being replaced [and] the brain drain and loss of institutional memory is critical." The personpower of the workforce easily ranked as the most important issue facing state and local governments.

Source: Mark Lee, "2016 Top Management Challenges for State & Local Government," *Route Fifty* (2015), http://www.routefifty.com/feature/management-challenges-state-local-government/.

the George W. Bush administration, the Presidential Appointee Initiative tracked appointments and charted a constant lack of leadership at the top. When a position is vacant or held by a temporary designee, fresh initiatives are rarely taken, on the grounds that those should be left for the properly appointed successor. Thus, a yellow light for the long pause in filling vacancies is added to the red-and-green traffic light symbols of stop-and-go administration.

In 1998, Congress passed the Vacancies Reform Act, which required agencies to report to Congress and the GAO on vacant positions requiring Senate confirmation. The law also limited the service of acting administrators to 210 days. Many agencies, however, proved slow in reporting vacancies and sometimes did not report them at all. Many acting administrators served for longer than the 210-day limit.[55]

Finally, during the last year or eighteen months of a presidency there is likely to be a substantial exodus of political appointees, many intent on capitalizing on their government experience by obtaining remunerative employment in the private sector. As a presidency winds down, restaffing can be exceedingly difficult, because few qualified persons will take public office for a predictably brief period. Moreover, no president wants to risk a contentious confirmation battle when launching a reelection campaign. Both problems can lead to weak leadership—or no leadership—in the waning months of an administration.

This constellation of issues posed special problems for DHS. Turnover in the department was 8.4 percent in 2005, twice the government-wide average. Among airport screeners, attrition was more than 14 percent. As the Federal Emergency Management Agency within DHS struggled to respond to Hurricane Katrina in 2005, it had 500 vacancies and acting administrators headed eight of its ten regions—including the region overseeing Louisiana. Basic problems in staffing and leading federal agencies continued to pose big problems for performance. The result? In a Partnership for Public Service survey, DHS placed thirty-first out of thirty-three agencies.[56]

How Many Are Too Many?

Debate continues over whether the growing number of political appointees is a good thing for the administrative process. Chief executives, it is argued, need political appointees to ensure accountability of the bureaucracy. Two important questions remain: (1) How many political appointees are needed to achieve the objective? (2) At what point does the number of such appointees become so large as to frustrate the objective?

There are no precise answers to these questions, but political appointees themselves over the years have proposed some formulations. President Nixon's top political recruiter wrote:

> The solution to problems of rigidity and resistance to change in government is not to increase the number of appointive positions at the top, as so many politicians are wont to do. . . . An optimum balance between the number of career and noncareer appointments . . . should be struck in favor of fewer political appointees, not more. In many cases, the effectiveness of an agency would be improved and political appointments would be reduced by roughly 25 percent if line positions beneath the assistant secretary level were reserved for career officials.[57]

The Volcker Commission, which included fifteen former top political appointees, recommended in 1989 that "the growth in recent years in the number of presidential appointees, whether those subject to Senate confirmation, noncareer senior executives, or personal and confidential assistants, should be curtailed. . . . The commission is confident that a substantial cut is possible, and believes a cut from the current 3,000 to no more than 2,000 is a reasonable target." The commission also observed that

> excessive numbers of political appointees serving relatively brief periods may undermine the president's ability to govern, insulating the administration from needed dispassionate advice and institutional memory. The mere size of the political turnover almost guarantees management gaps and discontinuities, while the best of the career professionals will leave government if they do not have challenging opportunities at the sub-cabinet level.[58]

As we have seen, the 2014 Partnership for the Public Service recommendations strongly agreed. If the answers seem so clear, why has it been so hard to translate them into reality? There are two reasons: because Congress must act to transform political appointments to career staff and because presidents claim that they need these positions to steer the administration.

SENIOR EXECUTIVE LEADERSHIP

No matter how strong or problematic the bureaucracy's political leadership, effective performance depends on strong leadership from the bureaucracy's top career officials. Indeed, these executives serve as the critical "shock absorber" in the administrative system, connecting the expert bureaucracy with elected officials and ensuring that elected officials' policy is transmitted through the bureaucracy.

At the cornerstone of the Civil Service Reform Act of 1978 was the creation of the Senior Executive Service (SES), which was designed to provide this career leadership. The SES absorbed most of the previously GS-16 to GS-18 career and noncareer positions, together with some executive-level positions filled by the president without Senate confirmation. The SES consists of about 7,700 employees, most of whom are career officials but 575 are presidential appointees.

The 1978 reform act aimed to give agency heads greater flexibility in assigning members of this cadre among positions and tasks. Under the old system, the position occupied (tenure, grade, and salary) determined the status of a level GS-16 to GS-18 career official. Under the civil service rules, the agency could dislodge incumbents (apart from position abolition, firing, or forced resignation) only by promoting, demoting, or transferring them to a position at the same grade and matching their qualifications. It was often difficult to find a position for which a bureau chief or other high careerist had the requisite qualifications, let alone a position that was vacant or could be made so. Substituting an SES system of rank-in-person (with the salary set by the individual's qualifications) for the old one of rank-in-position (with the salary set by the requirements of the position) promised to remedy this problem. Even more important has been the definition of "executive core qualifications," which lists five skills that senior executives should possess:

- ECQ 1: Leading change
- ECQ 2: Leading people
- ECQ 3: Results driven
- ECQ 4: Business acumen
- ECQ 5: Building coalitions

These are not only the qualifications for senior federal executives, but they are also the core descriptions of the skills that senior government leaders need, across government, at every level and in every agency.

In addition to this new flexibility in staffing, reformers believed that the senior levels of government would be stronger if top officials could assemble their own management teams. Instead of encouraging long-term tunnel vision among executives who rose within their agencies and stayed there, the idea was to create a flexible cadre of skilled managers who would move around government to gain additional insights and expertise and would then lend that expertise to government management. In practice, however, the system has never quite worked the way it was originally intended.

In December 2015, Barack Obama signed an executive order that fundamentally changed the SES.[59] The key elements of this reform were as follows:

- *Performance awards.* Agencies were limited to awarding a total of 7.5 percent of senior executive salaries as performance awards, to avoid the problem that a very high number of executives received performance pay without being directly connected to superior performance on the job.
- *Pay.* Senior executives were to be paid more than the people they supervised. Pay compression had, in many cases, resulted in executives being paid less than managers below them in the hierarchy.
- *Hiring.* The executive order streamlined the application process for the SES, to reduce the burdens on both senior executives and agency personnel systems. The previous system was extremely complex and sometimes unpredictable, which made it hard to manage for everyone.
- *Rotations.* The executive order set a target of having 15 percent of the SES rotate for at least four months into other jobs, to give executives a broader perspective on government management. This was a goal in the original act, but rotations rarely happened.

DIVING INTO DATA

Millennials in the Workforce

A major challenge facing government, like all organizations, is making the generational transition, from retiring baby boomers to emerging millennials. An ongoing debate is just how different the millennial generation is from its predecessors. Data provide an interesting snapshot.

Additional data from Gallup, a major polling organization, show that 21 percent of millennials say they changed jobs in the previous year, more than three times higher than nonmillennials. Job turnover, Gallup estimates, costs the economy $30.5 billion each year.

Millennials are the Least Engaged Generation at Work

Engaged

Millennials	Gen Xers	Baby Boomers	Traditionalists
29%	32%	33%	45%

Not Engaged

Millennials	Gen Xers	Baby Boomers	Traditionalists
55%	50%	48%	41%

Actively Disengaged

Millennials	Gen Xers	Baby Boomers	Traditionalists
16%	18%	19%	14%

Source: Gallup, "How Millennials Want to Work and Live" (2016), http://www.gallup.com/reports/189830/millennials-work-live.aspx?.

QUESTIONS

1. The data show employee engagement in the workplace, ranging from the youngest workers (millennials) to the oldest (traditionalists). What is the relationship between age and employee engagement?

2. Do you see this as a problem?

3. Are these patterns likely to result from characteristics of each generation—or do the data reflect individual attitudes that change with age? What would you need to know to explore this question more thoroughly?

4. Do you feel it is necessary to increase employee engagement of millennials? If so, what would—and could—you do to accomplish this?

- *Development.* The government was required to improve training for senior executives, both in their first months and throughout their careers, to enhance their ability to serve as effective executives. Many executives previously started their new positions without much preparation and found little support as they worked their way through tough problems.
- *Talent.* The government was also required to create a stronger program to help executives learn about new job opportunities, rotations, and other career development methods. The program previously paid little attention to talent development once executives were placed.

These steps marked big changes from the SES's existing practice—but big steps back toward the original intent of the program. The SES plays a critical shock absorber role, between short-term political appointees at the top and long-term career staff throughout the bureaucracy. A strong executive leadership team is increasingly critical to improving government performance. In many ways, it is the foundation of an effective human capital system in government.

THE PROBLEM OF TOP-LEVEL LEADERSHIP

Despite recurring attempts to reform the system, leadership at the very top of the bureau-cracy remains one of government's most important and difficult problems. At the core is a dilemma that is hard to break. Elliot Richardson, who headed four cabinet departments at different points of his career, summed it up this way:

> The trouble is that all too many [new] political appointees . . . suspect . . . that senior civil servants lie awake at night scheming to sabotage the President's agenda and devising plans to promote their own. Having worked with most of the career services under five administrations, I can attest that this is not true. . . .
>
> Almost any job at the deputy assistant secretary level . . . is more responsible and has wider impact on the national interest than most senior corporate positions. . . .
>
> I have many friends who once held responsible but not necessarily prominent roles in government and who now occupy prestigious and well-paid positions in the private sector—some of them very prestigious and very well-paid. Not one finds his present occupation as rewarding as his government service. . . . Society treats public servants, together with teachers, ministers, and the practitioners of certain other honorable but low-paid callings, as the beneficiaries of a high level of psychic income. But the psychic income of public service is being steadily eroded.[60]

At the end of Ronald Reagan's second term, C. William Verity, his secretary of commerce and formerly chief executive officer of a large steel company, added,

> I had always felt that Government people were not motivated, because in industry you have various incentives where you can motivate people, and that perhaps Government people didn't work so hard because they weren't so highly motivated. Well, I was dead wrong.
>
> I find that in this department there [is] a tremendous cadre of professionals, highly motivated not by financial incentives but to serve their country. It's as simple as that.[61]

A proper balance between financial and psychic incomes in the higher public service varies roughly by rank. Attracting cabinet members is not a serious problem: most are well off and at an age when family responsibilities are not pressing, and they welcome high public status and the prospect of posthumous life in history books as a suitable culmination of successful careers. None of these conditions apply, however, to most of the potential candidates for noncareer, subcabinet posts—who are, in fact, a diverse group. Consider, first, the individuals accepting presidential appointments. Most suffer salary cuts in accepting a federal appointment. We know that people of high quality decline presidential appointments for financial reasons, forcing the White House to turn to less preferred candidates.

Many citizens express dismay at the salaries paid public officials. Imbued with the egali-tarian spirit of democracy, and sensitive to the disparity between their own incomes and those of high officials, citizens show little patience with arguments that government needs a fair share of the best educated and most skilled managers and professional specialists. They do not easily accept that this fair share must come from an elite pool whose members need incentives for high performance. Yet without some way of solving this problem, citizens will not get the level of performance they expect—and, indeed, deserve—as value for the taxes they pay.

THE CHANGING WORKFORCE

Special challenges are arising from the new workers about to enter government—and all workplaces. The emerging workforce was raised on the Internet and technology and is immersed in information unlike any previous generation, which presents very different human capital challenges. We know that a talent war for the top achievers in this new Internet-driven generation has already broken out. We also know that bringing these individuals into the workforce at a time when older workers have very different norms poses some big challenges.

How is the new generation different? It is distinctive—and large, even larger than the baby boomers who have dominated American society for the last generation. Analysts have identified eight norms that shape the lives of the new generation:

1. *Freedom*: setting priorities, especially to focus on time with family and friends

2. *Customization*: flexibility in jobs, benefits, and working conditions, with a preference for positions that will allow them the most choice

3. *Scrutinizers*: an instinct for quick, comparative analysis, especially about competing job opportunities

4. *Integrity*: a search for employers with a commitment to high ethical values

5. *Collaboration*: an expectation of collaboration on what to do and how to do it

6. *Entertainment*: a search for jobs that are fun and rewarding

7. *Speed*: a focus on speedy communication, including quick feedback on performance and rapid professional growth within the organization

8. *Innovation*: working hard to devise new ideas and devices to fit their needs and solve their problems[62]

The result, a government report suggests, is a new generation shaped by very different events and driven by fundamentally different values (see Table 9.1). Government's human capital managers believe that this will require the government to transform itself into a workplace with more flexibility in work schedules (including the ability to carry time over from week to week), workplaces (including telecommuting), and work environments (including making the job more fun). Government is not alone in facing these challenges. Yet if government cannot adapt at least as fast as other employers, it's likely to fall behind in the quest for the new generation's best workers—and the quality of the work done for the American people will inevitably suffer. Perhaps most fundamentally, government needs to rise to the challenge of matching its human capital system, based for generations on the idea of a career workforce, with a new generation of workers whose members don't assume they'll work for a single organization throughout their careers.

Table 9.1	Understanding the Generations through Life-Defining Events			
	Greatest Generation	Baby Boomers	Gen X	Millennials or Net-Gen
Age	Retired	Nearing retirement	Mid-life	Early career
Population	75 million	78 million	45 million	80 million
Key characteristics	Pragmatic Conservative Conformists	Value driven Priority on self-actualization	Cynical Media savvy Individualistic	Tech savvy and diverse Media saturated Fluid lifestyle
Defining events	Great Depression World War II Korean War	Berlin Wall up JFK, MLK, RFK shot Watergate Vietnam	Berlin Wall falls *Challenger* O. J. Simpson First Gulf war	Columbine, Virginia Tech shootings Oklahoma City and September 11, 2001 Wars in Iraq and Afghanistan Corporate scandals
Key values	Accountability Tradition Stability	Fulfillment Indulgence Balance Equality	Freedom Reality Self-reliance Work-life balance	Diversity Flexibility Empowerment Service oriented

Source: Chief Information Officers Council, *Netgeneration: Preparing for Change in the Federal Information Technology Workforce* (Washington, D.C.: Chief Information Officers Council, 2010), 45, Table 6-1, http://www.govexec.com/pdfs/042310ah1.pdf.

CONCLUSION

Our discussion of human capital identifies seven important issues. First, the importance of senior executives far exceeds their number. They are the managers of major federal programs, the advisers and often the decision makers on large policy questions, the interagency negotiators, the agents of the current administration in carrying out policy, the foundation of continuity of government, and the spokespersons for and bargainers with the elected chief executive, congressional committees, interest groups, and the general public. In short, these executives are essential for ensuring both the effectiveness of government and its accountability to elected officials and citizens.

Second, the number of political appointments at the top of the bureaucracy in the United States is far larger than in other countries.

Third, the top career officials are a highly specialized and high-performing group. However, recruiting and retaining them—and providing incentives for superior performance—is an enduring problem that remains unsolved.

Fourth, the careers of political appointees are short and those of careerists are long. This disparity makes for an uncomfortable relationship. Political superiors operate within a brief time frame, initiating ideas they often cannot see to completion or restricting themselves to short-run ventures for which they can get credit. Careerists, operating within an extended time frame, have a deep memory of what has and has not worked in the past, an awareness of the long lead time from a program's genesis to its maturation, and an institutional loyalty and interpersonal network within agency and government that are uncharacteristic of most of the strangers recruited for political posts. Government is like a repertory theater whose regular cast was there before and remains during and after the visit of each celebrity imported to star in plum lead roles for a short run.

Fifth, although strong support remains for protecting the civil service system from political interference, frustration is growing with the restrictions that have accumulated in the system over time. Reformers are eager to provide managers with more flexibility, but every reform raises twin problems: fears that the changes will uproot the nation's long and deep commitment to politically neutral administration, and worries that the reforms will not go far enough in ensuring government grows its capacity to meet big, tough problems.

Sixth, generational changes are bringing deep and sharp issues to which the government must adopt new and innovative approaches. These will rank among the biggest human capital challenges the government has faced in a very long time.

Seventh, all of these are deep, enduring, and critical issues. In his 2008 book *A Government Ill Executed*, Paul C. Light tracked the fundamental puzzles back to the debate between Thomas Jefferson and Alexander Hamilton on the nature of the American republic. Light found that although much of government works well, human capital problems cripple its ability to rise to fundamental challenges. He concluded that "the federal service is suffering its greatest crisis since it was founded in the first moments of the republic . . . running out of energy [and] unable to faithfully execute all the laws."[63] Only a fundamental and sweeping reform, Light argued, can help government rise to the challenges it faces. Solving government's most important and fundamental problems depends on resolution of these issues of human capital management—and on linking them to the broader puzzles of governmental decision making and implementation. Human capital is not an isolated topic in itself but one that is intimately connected to government's capacity to do what must be done. The next chapter turns to the issues raised in that connection of doing what must be done.

CASE 9.1

The Brain Train: Planning for the Coming Federal Retirement Boom

A careful study in 2013 by the Partnership for Public Service and the private consulting firm McKinsey & Company laid out a stark challenge. In the next five years, they estimated, two-thirds of the federal government's senior executives would be likely to retire. With government's problems growing, "The need for savvy, well-trained government leaders to fill executive positions will only become more acute." That, they pointed out, was a huge challenge, but "it also presents an opportunity to take a deliberate approach to developing talent and equipping future executives with the skills they will need." In turn, this frames the big challenge: "What exactly are agencies doing to ensure they have a healthy pipeline of leaders?"[1]

For years, human capital analysts had predicted a retirement boom, but it didn't seem to materialize. Some outsiders suspected that a weak economy, coupled with the stock market collapse, encouraged many employees to stay on the job until the situation improved. As the report appeared, however, there were two trends that seemed to suggest the retirement boom was likely to begin. The age distribution of the federal government was getting older. Employees might delay their retirement, but they were going to take it at *some* point. Moreover, the trend toward retirement was growing. In 2009, 5.8 percent of the members of the federal government's SES retired. By 2012, the number had grown to 8.3 percent. The retirement boom had come—and the challenge for restocking the government's brain train had begun.

The Partnership/McKinsey report laid out four big worries as the government prepared for this transition.[2]

1. "Each agency is responsible for preparing its own talent for executive positions, with little central oversight or accountability." The federal government is a vastly complicated place, of course, and no single strategy could fit every agency. OPM, moreover, has provided assistance to agencies on executive development and shares best practices with agency leaders. Nevertheless, "No federal entity holds agencies accountable for developing potential executives who can become government-wide assets. There's no standardized approach for preparing executives for the SES—and because every agency independently develops its executive pipeline, quality varies markedly and little attention is given to government-wide needs."

2. "Many federal agencies have strong elements of SES talent development in place, but these elements are seldom part of a cohesive strategy." Many employees take part in coaching, mentoring, and advanced education, but they "often are disconnected from one another rather than functioning as parts of a cohesive strategy." There are few checks to see whether the skills in which executives were trained are the skills that government needs." As one individual interviewed for the report pointed out, "There are people who were hired 20 years ago that have skills we don't need anymore."

3. "Many senior agency leaders pay insufficient attention to executive development." The report concluded that many senior agency leaders simply pay little attention to how best to identify, prepare, and retain the best executives. Political appointees have many demands on their time, and they often have very short time horizons. The result, the report concluded, was a "disconnect" between the talent the agency needed and the processes in place to produce it.

4. "Agencies show a strong preference for a pipeline of internal talent." It's not surprising that agencies prefer to promote from within, but that strategy hinders the opportunity to bring fresh skills and perspectives from other agencies. Not only do most senior leaders pay little attention to the problem—they tend to solve it in ways that reinforce existing patterns.

It was time, the report concluded, to pay serious attention to this issue. The collision of the retirement boom and the patterns of human capital development demanded action.

QUESTIONS TO CONSIDER

1. If you were the head of OPM, what steps would you take to address this issue?

2. As someone who has carefully studied the importance of human capital, what overall approach do you think would be most useful in creating a long-term strategy, not only for filling the vacancies coming in the next few years but also in preparing younger workers for the SES?

3. What steps would be most attractive to you as you consider the possibility of becoming a senior executive in the federal government at the height of your career?

NOTES

1. Partnership for Public Service and McKinsey & Company, *Building the Leadership Bench: Developing a Talent Pipeline for the Senior Executive Service* (Washington, D.C.: July 22, 2013), 5, https://ourpublicservice.org/publications/viewcontentdetails.php?id=29.

2. Ibid., 7–9.

Reining in the Unions? State Employees Targeted in Wisconsin, Ohio, and Beyond

Shortly before taking office as Wisconsin governor in 2011, Scott Walker fired a warning shot toward state employees. With multibillion-dollar deficits looming, Walker said, "We can no longer live in a society where the public employees are the haves and taxpayers who foot the bills are the have-nots." He went on, "The bottom line is that we are going to look at every legal means we have to try to put that balance more on the side of taxpayers."[1] Walker, a Republican, proposed taking away the right of government employees to collectively bargain over contracts and working conditions and making it much harder for unions to collect dues to support their operations.

He wasn't alone. In Ohio, Governor John Kasich proposed an end to the ability of child-care and home-care workers to unionize and to ban strikes by teachers. "If they want to strike, they should be fired," Kasich said. "They've got good jobs, they've got high pay, they get good benefits, a great retirement. What are they striking for?"[2] Elsewhere, attacks on public employee unions surfaced in Indiana, Maine, and Missouri. Even in California, with a Democratic governor, union power came under tough scrutiny. "We will have to look at our system of pensions and how to ensure that they are transparent and actuarially sound and fair—fair to the workers and fair to the taxpayers," Governor Jerry Brown said. The American Federation of Labor and Congress of Industrial Organizations (AFL-CIO) warned that this was part of a national battle to wipe unions out by eliminating their ability to collect dues from everyone in a bargaining unit. If each employee had to opt in to allow union dues to be used for political purposes, "it [would] cut them off at their knees" because the move would starve unions of the cash on which they relied.[3]

The political motivation was clear. Public employee unions had long been strong supporters of Democratic candidates, including at the state and local levels. Many Republican governors had to fight against union campaigns to win election, so their interest in disabling the unions was understandable. The *New York Times* estimated that unions had invested more than $200 million in campaigns against Republican candidates.[4] But the issue goes much deeper. Following the Great Recession, which started in 2008, many taxpayers resented the job security, pay increases, and generous pensions that many state and local government employees received, even as these employees had to dig ever deeper into their own pockets to pay for them. Republicans—and

some Democrats—asked whether government employees had become a privileged class of workers protected from the economic downturns that had savaged so many private-sector workers.

Moreover, even as some analysts argued that the economy had slowly begun getting back on its feet, state and local budgets remained deeply in the red. Unlike the federal government, which can borrow money to pay its bills, state and local governments must balance their budgets. In the early stages of the downturn, state officials had already used up most of the easy options to make do with less and economize, and they began moving to harder and harder decisions. As states looked into projections about future budgets, one item that loomed especially large was the share of state and local government spending accounted for by employee salaries and especially fringe benefits, including pensions. In many states, state and local government employees were entitled to a fixed monthly pension, called a "defined benefit" plan, based on their salary and years of service. Most of the private sector had long ago moved away from such plans to "defined contribution" plans, in which individuals invested their own money sometimes along with a company contribution, and the monthly payment was determined by the performance of the investments. Many individuals watched their retirement savings shrink after the 2008 stock market crash. However, those who had defined benefit plans didn't have to worry.

Analysts have projected that state and local governments will have increasing difficulty in meeting their pension obligations in the future. GAO estimates that state and local governments have hundreds of billions of dollars in unfunded pension obligations (commitments to pay pensions to employees without having enough money in place).[5] New governors—Republicans and Democrats alike—have come into office and had to confront these tough long-term projections. Many have concluded that they will not be able to balance their budgets without fundamentally restructuring their pension systems, perhaps by moving future employees to defined contribution systems or by reducing defined benefit programs for all employees. Public employee unions, of course, immediately objected to such plans, fearing that they would undermine one of the most important benefits the unions had negotiated for their workers. Some Republicans savored the opportunity for a fight against a group that had bankrolled their electoral opposition.

Nowhere was that battle more intense than in Wisconsin. For decades, the state's labor unions had invested heavily in issue ads during political campaigns. Business groups raised their own funds to counterattack, in what had become an escalating arms race. Governor Walker's proposals to restrict the unions' power were, in part, to help the state deal with its enormous budget deficit. Restrictions on fringe benefits for state employees, and requirements that employees contribute more to their health and retirement plans, would help the state stem the flood of red ink. The proposal went further, however, in limiting the unions' ability to raise money from members and the length of time for which the unions could bargain over working conditions. All of the state's Democratic senators fled to Illinois, which denied Republicans the quorum they needed to pass the measure—until the Republicans found a parliamentary measure that permitted a vote without a quorum. With the Democrats hiding out across the border, the Republicans pushed the bill through the legislature and the governor signed it, before the Democrats could react.

As the smoke settled after the fire, longtime political analyst Mordecai Lee sadly wrote, "While ideology and energy are welcome in Wisconsin politics, I can't help but think that the politics of political destruction are not."[6] Wisconsin's struggle over the future of public employee unions helped stoke other blazes around the nation. Public employee union leaders said they were determined not to give in. Those seeking to weaken their power were just as determined to use the budget battles to redefine the unions' role—in both public administration and the nation's politics. Governor Walker beat the drive to recall him. The protests continued, with a daily "Solidarity sing-along" at the capitol. One protester, Steven Bray, was arrested a half dozen times—but he vowed to keep coming back to sing.[7]

QUESTIONS TO CONSIDER

1. Do you think public employees should have the right to organize and be represented by unions? Do you believe that they should be able to bargain over the full range of issues—pay, fringe benefits, and working conditions? Should they have the ability to strike to support their demands? Do you think there should be limits on which employees can organize and what steps they can take?

2. Public employee unions have long argued that their members don't always receive the highest pay, and that their efforts to negotiate better benefits have helped them win the fringe benefits that have created a quality workforce. A new breed of politician has argued that the nation can no longer afford these benefits and that public employees shouldn't receive better protection or benefits than other workers. How do you weigh this battle?

3. What do you think about the role that public employee unions play in elections? Should they be allowed to assess dues on their members and use the money to support individual candidates, even if it risks having to work for elected officials whom they opposed?

4. A critical issue is the future role of public employee pensions. Should the public employee pension system be restructured to move public employees to defined contribution plans? How should this work, to be fair to employees who have spent their entire careers working for a pension and who wouldn't have time to build up their own individual savings plan to replace a government pension? The longer the transition to a new pension plan, of course, the longer it would take for state officials to realize budget savings from the change.

NOTES

1. Steven Greenhouse, "Strained States Turning to Laws to Curb Labor Unions," *New York Times* (January 3, 2011), http://www.nytimes.com/2011/01/04/business/04labor.html?pagewanted=all.

2. Ibid.

3. Ibid.

4. Ibid.

5. U.S. Government Accountability Office, *Government Pension Plans: Governance Practices and Long-term Investment Strategies Have Evolved Gradually as Plans Take on Increased Investment Risk*, GAO-10-754 (Washington, D.C.: Government Printing Office, 2010), http://www.gao.gov/new.items/d10754.pdf.

6. Mordecai Lee, "Welcome to Thunderdome Politics," *Milwaukee Journal Sentinel* (March 12, 2011), http://www.jsonline.com/news/opinion/117830143.html.

7. Marti Mikkelson, "Two Years On, Protesters Still Fighting Wisconsin Governor," *National Public Radio* (September 12, 2013), http://www.npr.org/2013/09/12/221084521/two-years-on-protesters-still-fighting-wisconsin-governor?sc=17&f=1001.

CASE 9.3

Who You Gonna Call? It's One Man Who Decides Who Gets How Much from the BP Oil Spill Compensation Fund

When America faces an impossible job, who does the president call? For a series of tough tasks, it was the phone of Kenneth Feinberg that rang.

After the September 11, 2001, terrorist attacks, for example, Congress created a fund to compensate the families of the nearly 3,000 people killed. That was a strong and generous national gesture. But how much should each family receive? One approach would have been to divvy the money up, with each family receiving the same amount. Some of those killed, however, were very high-level executives whose families had homes, educational expenses, and other expenses that depended on that income. Some of those killed earned close to the minimum wage. Some were very young; others were at or past retirement age. Was it fair to give everyone the same amount? Congress decided no—but left it up to the Bush administration to figure out how to divide the money fairly. President Bush put Kenneth Feinberg in charge.

That was an effort to put a small bandage on a gaping national wound. However, the 2010 BP oil spill dwarfed the number directly affected by the September 11, 2001, attacks. As the oil flowed across the Gulf, many thousands of Gulf residents (some boat captains, others oystermen and shrimpers, and others hotel and restaurant operators) lost their livelihoods for weeks or months, and some worried whether they would ever be able to regain their lives. BP put $20 billion in a compensation fund. But how were they to distribute the cash?

Those who believed they were injured had two choices. They could take their chances by filing suit in court, knowing that they were relatively small players up against one of the world's largest companies. Or they could make their case to Feinberg and accept what he believed was just. As Feinberg told CBS News's *60 Minutes*, "It's a free country. If you wanna come into the fund, with all the benefits of the fund, come on in. You're welcome. We'll give you a fair shake. We'll process your claim. We'll pay you what you're due. If you don't like what we're paying you, if you think we're nickel and diming you, if you think we're not being fair, opt out and go the other route [to court with a civil suit]." He had been down that road before, he explained. "Now, in 9/11, 97 percent of all eligible claimants entered the fund. Only 94 people out of 3,000 decided to litigate."[1]

His decisions for the September 11 fund involved payments to victims' families that, at the core, involved setting a value on human life. For the BP spill, the payments required Feinberg to determine the long-term impact on individuals' livelihoods. How many oysters in the future simply wouldn't be there to be harvested? How many hotels and restaurants

©iStock.com/lushik

might suffer permanent economic damage because of the lost business? How many boat captains might have to look for new ways of making a living?

"What these fishermen and others want to see are checks and compensation," he told *60 Minutes*. The average for each claim, in the first months of the program, had been $5,000, for six months of damages, one audience member at a public meeting pointed out. "And that, sir, is nothing to brag about." Morley Safer, the *60 Minutes* correspondent, noted, "They really go after you." Feinberg replied, "They do. They do, but it goes with the territory." He continued, "I mean, you go in there expecting that you're gonna receive that criticism. And woe be unto you if you hide. That is a mistake. You cannot hide."

It was a tough process—an emergency payment, for six months to help those affected meet short-term needs, followed by a final settlement. Feinberg found himself in the middle of constant, raucous town meetings, facing furious Gulf residents who had lost money and, in some cases, their livelihoods, from the BP spill. BP executives and representatives weren't there; Feinberg was, and he bore the brunt of their anger. His job was to listen, take it, weigh their claims, and make awards he believed were fair—awards that, in many cases, were less than residents thought they deserved.

"Do you believe what he's telling you?" Safer asked a group of fishermen.

One replied, "Absolutely not." Another said, "I think he's just another attorney talking his talk."

Safer replied, "But don't you think his record in dealing with 9/11 was an honest job?"

"To be honest with you, I could care less about 9/11," one said. "I care about the oil spill. And I could care less about anyone else's claims. I care about my claim. That's it."

QUESTIONS TO CONSIDER

1. What do you think of this policy—creating a fund to compensate individuals for losses from major national incidents, and then giving the power to decide compensation to one person, armed with a small staff?

2. What kind of person would you hire to perform such a function? Feinberg is not a permanent government employee. Rather, he's been appointed by the government as the "special master" for the September 11 victims' compensation fund and as the administrator for the BP compensation fund. This is a great deal of power to place in the hands of a single person. Do you think this is a good move?

3. Feinberg's background is as an attorney specially trained in mediation. He's taught extensively in law schools ranging from Columbia and Georgetown to Penn and Virginia. We're likely to encounter more

mega-issues like September 11 and the BP oil spill that require the government to deal with tough compensation decisions. One of the tasks of public administration is to grow smart leaders who can do hard jobs in predictably high-quality ways. In fact, public administration exists to make sure we don't have to trust to chance in trying to do hard things well. What recommendations would you have for improving our chances for having top government leaders for important jobs like this one?

NOTE

1. "BP's Victims Fund: Kenneth Feinberg's Tough Task," *60 Minutes* (September 30, 2010), http://www.cbsnews.com/stories/2010/09/30/60minutes/main6915445.shtml?tag=contentMain;contentBody.

CASE 9.4

Big Reform Ideas from House Republicans

In the last days before Congress recessed for the 2016 presidential conventions, the House of Representatives passed a bill bringing sweeping changes to the federal workforce. House Majority Leader Kevin McCarthy (R-Calif.) claimed that the legislation would "bring greater accountability to our nation's federal bureaucracy, making it easier to sanction poor performance and bad behavior by government employees." Prompted in part by charges that the IRS and the VA had not been serving citizens and taxpayers well, McCarthy said, "These reforms will make our federal workforce more efficient and accountable to the people they are supposed to be serving."[1]

Even before members of the House voted, however, the Obama administration threatened to veto the bill. The administration charged that the bill's changes "would weaken the rights of Federal employees, and be impractical and administratively burdensome to implement. They would also have harmful unintended consequences, while failing to address the issues they are designed to solve and while raising serious constitutional concerns."[2]

We've come to take the nation's civil service system for granted, with its basic principles of hiring based on merit and protection against firing, but it's easy to forget that the system grew out of violence and has always been politically

contentious. Congress created the original civil service system in 1883, christened the Pendleton Civil Service Reform Act after its sponsor, following the assassination of President James A. Garfield by Charles Guiteau, a political operative convinced he deserved a high-level position he didn't receive. In the years since, forces supporting public employees have argued that they needed political protection to prevent political interference in their work. Opponents have long argued that the protections tended to make the government inflexible and made employees focused more on protecting their jobs than on performing their work.

Several scandals rocked the system in the 2010s. A series of news stories contended that veterans died waiting for appointments at VA hospitals, and that VA workers then covered up the wait times. Critics savaged the IRS for what appeared to be partisan decisions in processing applications for tax-exempt status of political groups, with conservative-leaning organizations going to the back of the line. Republicans were furious at these cases and pointed squarely at the civil service system as the cause. Echoing McCarthy's charges, they said civil service protections had created the problem at the VA and made it impossible to clean up—and that IRS employees could not be sanctioned for the problems processing the forms.

Here's what the Republicans proposed in a bill that passed on a mostly party-line vote (241 to 181):

- *SES.* For the top-level career officials in government, the bill significantly reduced their rights of appeal to charges of poor performance. It shortened the time senior executives had to respond to charges, required that hearing officers make a decision within twenty-one days of the time a case is filed, and eliminated the right to appeal of the decision. Opponents argued that these steps would raise big constitutional questions by shrinking the due-process rights of the government's most senior career officials.
- *Official time.* Employees would be required to report annually on how they used "official time," as time spent on union duties was called. Government agencies would be required to collect information and report how much time their employees spent on official time, what they did at that time, and how much it cost the government. The intent was to discourage the government from paying employees to work on union business—and to discourage union representation of government workers.
- *Limits on rulemaking.* There would be restrictions on new regulations in presidential election years between the November elections and inauguration day, to prevent an outgoing administration from putting last-minute changes in place.
- *Pornography.* Employees would be prohibited from viewing pornography on government computers, except in the course of official investigations.
- *Probationary period.* The probationary period for new employees, during which they can be dismissed without going through the usual protections

afforded government workers, would be increased from one to two years.

Congress went into recess before the Senate acted, and the ultimate fate of the proposals was unknown. But the legislation represented some of the biggest challenges to the federal civil service system in a long time.

QUESTIONS TO CONSIDER

1. Consider the items in this legislation. Do you think some of them are good ideas? Do you oppose others? Which ones—and why?

2. Most of these proposals would create great political controversy. What political forces are likely to line up on which sides of these proposals?

3. There are undoubtedly big problems that we need to solve, in aligning the federal civil service system with the jobs government must do. What reforms would you recommend to make this work better?

NOTES

1. Eric Yoder, "House Approves Wide-Ranging Changes to Federal Personnel Policies," *Washington Post* (July 6, 2016), https://www.washingtonpost.com/news/powerpost/wp/2016/07/06/house-sets-vote-on-wide-ranging-changes-to-federal-personnel-policies/?hpid=hp_regional-hp-cards_rhp-card-fedgov%3Ahomepage%2Fcard.

2. Ibid.

KEY CONCEPTS

at-will employees 242
human capital 233

turnover 247

FOR FURTHER READING

DeSeve, G. Edward. *The Presidential Appointee's Handbook.* Washington, D.C.: Brookings Institution, 2016.

General Accounting Office (now the Government Accountability Office). *High-Risk Series: Strategic Human Capital Management,* GAO-03-120. Washington, D.C.: GAO, 2003.

Heclo, Hugh. *A Government of Strangers: Executive Politics in Washington.* Washington, D.C.: Brookings Institution, 1972.

Ingraham, Patricia W. "Striving for Balance: Reforms in Human Resource Management." In *Handbook of Comparative Administration,* edited by Laurence Lynn Jr. and Christopher Pollitt. Oxford: Oxford University Press, forthcoming.

Light, Paul C. *A Government Ill Executed: The Decline of Federal Service and How to Reverse It.* Cambridge, Mass.: Harvard University Press, 2008.

Light, Paul C. *Thickening Government: Federal Hierarchy and the Diffusion of Accountability.* Washington, D.C.: Brookings Institution, 1995.

Moe, Terry M. "The Politicized Presidency." In *The New Direction in American Politics,* edited by John E. Chubb and Paul E. Peterson, 235–271. Washington, D.C.: Brookings Institution, 1985.

Nathan, Richard P. *The Administrative Presidency.* New York: Wiley, 1983.

Radin, Beryl A. *The Accountable Juggler: The Art of Leadership in a Federal Agency.* Washington, D.C.: CQ Press, 2002.

Selden, Sally Coleman. *Human Capital: Tools and Strategies for the Public Sector.* Washington, D.C.: CQ Press, 2009.

SUGGESTED WEBSITES

The Government Accountability Office has carefully examined the problem of managing human capital for a long time; see its work at **www.gao.gov**. In addition, the Office of Personnel Management, **www.opm.gov**, is an important source for both data and analysis of the human capital issue. For independent studies of human capital in government, see the work of the National Academy of Public Administration, **www.napawash.org**.

for CQ Press

WANT A BETTER GRADE?

Get the tools you need to sharpen your study skills. Access practice quizzes, eFlashcards, video, and multimedia at **edge.sagepub.com/kettl7e.**

DISTILLED WATER

PART IV

Making and Implementing Government Decisions

If organizational structure is the *basic building block* of administration, decision making is the *central administrative act*. However, organizational theorists have long disagreed about how best to make administrative decisions—and which decisions are best. This section probes the competing theories of decision making and applies those theories to the most important of all administrative decisions: the budget. In any public administration, most decisions are hollow without money to back them up.

Making good decisions, however, is not enough. Decisions do not, in themselves, produce *results*. They require skillful management by effective managers if the bold promises embodied in public policy are not to end in disappointment. This section concludes by examining how to translate decisions into results.

10

DECISION MAKING: RATIONALITY AND RISK

Former Newark mayor Cory Booker won a huge audience on his Twitter account—more than 1.4 million followers. In 2012 he took up a Twitter challenge to live on food stamps for a week. During blizzards, he tweeted from the cab of a city snowplow. He used this at-the-front approach to service delivery to win a 2013 race for a seat in the U.S. Senate.

M ost early students of public administration concentrated on *structure* and how best to design it so it would function as efficiently as possible. Their contributions heavily shape Chapter 4 of this book. In 1945, however, Herbert A. Simon made a very different argument, based on decision making. He argued,

> The task of "deciding" pervades the entire administrative organization quite as much as does the task of "doing"—indeed, it is integrally tied up with the latter. A general theory of organization that will insure correct decision-making must include principles of organization that will include correct decision-making, just as it must include principles that will insure effective action.[1]

Simon thus established decision making as *the* foundation of public administration. There have been fierce arguments since about its role, but one thing is clear: It is impossible to understand administration without understanding administrative decision making.

Bureaucracies are complex organizations designed to do complicated things. Much of the doing depends on power delegated to administrators—and the expertise they use in exercising their discretion. Accountability depends on holding administrators accountable for how they do that. Therefore, the effectiveness and accountability of public administration both hinge on decision making. As Simon pointed out, doing is impossible without deciding. There have been many conflicts on what theory of decision making is best, both for describing how it *does* work and how it *should* work. These questions both lie at the foundation of the field.

This chapter first examines the basic problems that decision-making theories must answer and then probes competing approaches to decision making. It also examines the enduring problems of decision making and then focuses, in particular, on the challenges of risk in making good decisions. This chapter has twin themes: rationality (what a *good* decision is) and risk (how to make sure that decisions don't court *unintended problems* that undermine the effort to make good decisions).

BASIC PROBLEMS

Every approach to administrative decision making must tackle two issues. First, what *information* can decision makers use in reaching their judgments? Information is the basic raw material of decisions, and decision makers must acquire, weigh, and act on the data they collect. Second, how do political *values* affect decisions? The sheer complexity of public problems and the overwhelming volume of information force decision makers to simplify the context shaping their decisions. This inevitable simplification is the product of political values. Moreover, for a decision to stick, it must win enough support to prevent others from seeking to overturn it. Building support means finding a common base of values among those who could sustain the decision. Both information and values constantly intermingle as administrators seek to make decisions and as theorists seek to develop arguments about how the process does—and ought to—work.

Information

If decision making is the central administrative act, information is the lifeblood of decision making. Decisions, of course, can be made at whim or on the basis of strong opinions. But, as Max Weber pointed out long ago, administrators are hired not for their bias but for their expertise.[2] We expect administrators to use that expertise to make good decisions.

The problem, of course, is that information rarely is an abstract truth. Most often it's a matter of interpreting reality. No one ever knows everything. Not everyone knows the same things. And no one is sure that what they think they know is correct. Acquiring information is often expensive, and some participants have an advantage because they have greater resources to get more information. Moreover, participants sometimes have a vested interest in keeping information hidden from others. Two aspects of information thus critically affect decision making: who has what information and how they and others interpret the information they have.[3]

Values

Values matter in making decisions because of the complexity of the problems. "Most important decision puzzles are so complicated that it is impossible to analyze them completely," Robert D. Behn and James W. Vaupel argue. Furthermore, they contend, "Decisions depend upon judgments—judgments about the nature of the dilemma, the probabilities of events, and the desirability of consequences. Decision making is inherently subjective."[4] Any process that includes some questions but not others or weighs some outcomes as more important than others is, inevitably, a value-laden process. Therefore, decision-making theories must consider the question of how best to make such value judgments.

Furthermore, because value judgments are political judgments, no public policy decision, no matter how expertly reached, can endure if it does not command political support.[5] As Francis E. Rourke points out, political support for administrative decisions can come from two sources: an agency's decisions may enjoy a favorable opinion among the general public (what Rourke calls an agency's "mass public") or they may draw support from its "attentive publics" (groups that have a "salient interest in the agency"). Most effective agencies cultivate support from both.[6] The National Aeronautics and Space Administration (NASA), for example, works hard to promote the allure of space flight among the general public, while it labors to build support among its contractors for the unending battles on Capitol Hill over financing for its expensive programs.

As important as broad support is, however, political support from an agency's attentive publics typically is much more crucial. Few private citizens have the resources or time to follow or comprehend the intricate detail and complex trail that most public policy decisions follow. In most decisions, only individuals who have the strongest interest are willing to devote the time and money needed to understand and influence the issues. This means, of course, that most difficult administrative decisions are reached within a relatively closed world dominated by those with common and intense interests.[7] But that, in turn, raises a problem: seeking the support of an agency's attentive publics risks sacrificing the broader interests of the general public. Moreover, few public decisions are ever stable, because the political lineup of forces constantly changes. That makes decision making "inherently unstable," as Stone puts it, and the boundaries between the forces are "border wars waiting to happen."[8]

The complexity of decision making in bureaucracy has led to many different approaches. In this chapter, we explore four approaches and we examine how each deals with the fundamental problems of information and values: (1) the **rational approach**, which seeks to maximize efficiency; (2) the **bargaining approach**, which seeks to maximize political support; (3) the **participative decision-making approach**, which seeks to improve decisions by intimately involving those affected by them; and (4) the **public-choice approach**, which attempts to substitute market-like forces for other incentives that, its supporters argue, distort decisions.

RATIONAL DECISION MAKING

The most fundamental theory of decision making focuses on rationality: seeking the greatest return for any investment or, more simply, getting the biggest bank for the buck. **Rational decision making** builds on the work of microeconomists, who hold efficiency as the highest value. It seeks to produce the most output for a given level of inputs—or, to use the minimum amount of inputs needed to produce a given amount of output. In short, the goal is to find the most efficient decision. The theory is so simple that it's easy to understand why it's become a classic.

Basic Steps

The rational decision-making approach follows five basic steps:

1. *Define goals.* Rational decision making defines the problem we want to solve and the goal we want to achieve. For example, a policy analyst might seek to determine the best way to reduce automobile accident deaths by 10 percent, reduce costs of garbage collection by 5 percent, or reduce air pollution below dangerous limits.

2. *Identify alternatives.* Once we define the goal, the next step is to identify alternatives for achieving the goal. It might be possible to reduce highway deaths by installing new guard rails, encouraging safer car interiors, or making it impossible to text and drive at the same time.

3. *Calculate the consequences.* We then assess the alternatives by measuring the costs and benefits of each one, in dollar terms. We also consider indirect benefits and costs—often called **externalities** or **spillovers**—that relate to other goals. For example, a highway route that is best in terms of the stated transportation goal may destroy parks and increase downtown traffic congestion.

4. *Decide.* Once the analysis is finished, the decision maker chooses the alternative with the most favorable balance of benefits to costs.

5. *Begin again.* Systems analysis is not a once-and-done process. Instead, analysts see it as an iterative process. Every solution generates the next set of problems, and we always seek to learn from the past.

The rational approach appeals to common sense: any sensible person will choose the most rational (and efficient) route to his or her goal. Who, after all, wants to be irrational?[9]

Fighting Fraud in Health Care
Theme: Performance

Late June 2016 turned into very bad days for health care providers who had been stealing from the federal government's Medicare program. In a concentrated effort, a multiagency task force spearheaded by the Department of Justice and the Department of Health and Human Services (HHS) took down three hundred defendants who were charged with more than $900 million in fraud.

There's no bigger risk to taxpayers than individuals who create schemes to steal taxpayers' money. More than one in ten Medicare dollars, intended to provide medical care for older Americans, goes to improper payments. So the June 2016 arrests—involving pharmacists, physical therapists, nurses, and doctors who had submitted fraudulent bills, engaged in money laundering, and committed bribery—were a very big deal. In one big step, the task force arrested professionals who had improperly received nearly $1 billion in federal funds.

As Attorney General Loretta Lynch explained, "One group of defendants controlled a network of clinics in Brooklyn that they filled with patients through bribes and kickbacks. These patients then received medically unnecessary treatment, for which the clinic received over $38 million from Medicare and Medicaid—money that the conspirators subsequently laundered through more than 15 shell companies."

How did the feds identify the bad actors and develop strategies to prevent the problems from recurring? Under the leadership of a new information technology team, led by the HHS chief data officer, Caryl Brzymialkiewicz, federal officials developed new strategies of data analytics. They dove into the vast number of transactions in the program, fine-tuned their computers to look for suspicious patterns, and used those patterns to root out fraud. The strategy was a huge step from the painstaking case-by-case checks that investigators used previously. In one big step, data analytics helped to take three hundred criminals off the streets who had perpetrated $1 billion in fraud. "Data can be the unsung hero," Brzymialkiewicz explained.

Source: Charles S. Clark, "Interagency Task Force Completes Largest 'Takedown' of Medicare Fraud Yet," *Government Executive* (June 22, 2016), http://www.govexec.com/management/2016/06/interagency-task-force-completes-largest-takedown-medicare-fraud-yet/129318/; and Frank Konkel, "Better Data Just Saved Taxpayers $900 Million in Medicare Fraud," *Nextgov* (June 23, 2016), http://www.nextgov.com/big-data/2016/06/better-data-just-saved-taxpayers-900-million-medicare-fraud/129357/.

Appraisal

Because the rational approach to decision making seems so straightforward, it has a large following. Decision makers using the rational approach, however, must ensure they get enough good information and sort out competing values. An important part of this process is figuring out what "good enough" means.

INFORMATION. Rational decision making requires an extraordinary amount of information. Considering the full range of policy options is, of course, impossible. So, too, is understanding all their benefits and costs. In fact, some critics have argued that the information demands are so intense as to undermine the theory's power. As Charles E. Lindblom, perhaps the method's strongest critic, argues: "Men have always wanted to fly. Was the ambition to undertake unaided flight, devoid of any strategy for achieving it, ever a useful norm or ideal? . . . Achieving impossible feats of synopsis [comprehensive analysis] is a bootless, unproductive ideal."[10] Moreover, by trying to do the impossible, Lindblom worries, "they fall into worse patterns of analysis and decision." Even the cost, in time, energy, and money, of a nearly comprehensive search is extremely high, and the decision maker driven by comprehensiveness can never be sure what has been left out. The goal itself is impossible, the gaps are rarely defined, and the result is an uncharted gap in the analysis whose effects are unknown.[11]

In real life, of course, everyone knows it's impossible to be completely comprehensive. Decision makers instead simplify the process: (1) they screen out the silly options and minor ideas, and they restrict themselves to a few major alternatives, and (2) they stop searching for options when they come upon a satisfactory alternative, even if they believe that further searching might eventually turn up a better one. James G. March and Herbert A. Simon have called this approach **satisficing**.[12]

But that leaves us at a difficult place. If we are going to rely on something less than a full pursuit of rationality, how much is enough? If we're going to satisfice, how much searching is enough? Because, as human beings, we have intellectual limits, the model leaves us little choice. The rational model has great power in its simplicity, but there are big challenges in trying to figure out how best to follow it.

VALUES. Rational decision making also depends heavily on the values that decision makers and analysts choose. Because it is impossible to be completely rational, something has to be left out—and the choice of what to include and what to omit is, inevitably, a question of values. That is even more challenging because public administrators face their most difficult and important decisions in exercising discretion within the often-vague laws enacted by legislators. Consequently, rational decision makers are left with two choices: to make their best guess about what the legislature might have intended in passing a law (and risk being told they are wrong when, as is likely, someone disagrees), or to apply their own values in defining the goals (and risk undercutting the very objectivity at the core of rational decision making). In either case, values intrude into a process designed to be rational.

Of course, efficiency is not the *only* goal we seek. Equality, for example, is often a central objective in public programs. In fact, economist Arthur M. Okun calls the job of balancing equality and efficiency "the big tradeoff," stating that "We can't have our cake of market efficiency and share it equally."[13] Economist Murray Weidenbaum, who served in the Ronald Reagan administration as chairman of the Council of Economic Advisers, goes even further, observing that

> it is possible to develop government investment projects which meet the efficiency criterion (that is, the total benefits exceed the total costs) but which fail to meet the simplest standards of equity. . . . Unfortunately, there has been a tendency on the part of some economists to dismiss such "distributional" questions as subjective and political, and hence not within the proper concern of economic analysis.[14]

The rational approach is thus very attractive because it offers an elegant prescription for how to make the best decisions. In practice, however, this approach inevitably falls short. The elegance often tarnishes in practice. In fact, its advocates sometimes follow rational techniques only as long as it leads to their own personal preferences and feeds their own political ends. Rational decision making is a simple and powerful tool—until it is not.

Risk Management in Clackamas County, Oregon

Everyone wants the best decisions, but government's actual operations often raise a big collection of thorny questions. Consider these issues that local government officials in Clackamas County faced.

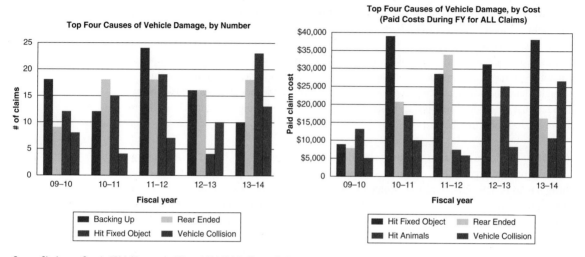

Top Four Causes of Vehicle Damage, by Number

Legend: Backing Up, Rear Ended, Hit Fixed Object, Vehicle Collision

Top Four Causes of Vehicle Damage, by Cost (Paid Costs During FY for ALL Claims)

Legend: Hit Fixed Object, Rear Ended, Hit Animals, Vehicle Collision

Source: Clackamas County, "Risk Management Report 2014," http://www.clackamas.us/des/risk2014.html.

QUESTIONS

1. These data show accidents for which county employees were at fault in Clackamas County, Oregon. What conclusions do you draw from these data?

2. Are there trends in the data? What might explain any trends?

3. Suppose you were the risk manager for the county. What advice would you give the county executive and department heads about how to reduce accidents that are the fault of county employees?

PUBLIC CHOICE

Spinning off the rational approach to decision making is a theory of both decisions and bureaucracy based on individuals. This has been labeled as *public choice*, *rational choice*, or *principal-agent theory*. This theory builds on the assumption that individuals are rational. Rational individuals seek to maximize whatever is important to them—what economists call utility. The most rational thing, according to the theory, is to promote one's self-interest.[15]

This theory of decision and bureaucratic action thus begins with the individual. If we can identify individuals' utility functions, we can predict their behavior. Such predictions are often quite sophisticated, including formal mathematical equations. Most often, the models assume that individuals want to maximize their power, budgets, and autonomy. The theory then builds by arguing that bureaucracy can be understood as a series of relationships between principals (individuals who want to get things done) and agents (individuals who are responsible to the principals for doing them).[16] If we can understand the goals—the utilities—of principals and agents as well as the complexities of their relationships, we can make predictions about how bureaucracies will behave.

As Christopher Pollitt pointed out in 2016, "Maximizing utility/satisfying preferences may sound like a beautifully simple proposition but it is actually very complicated." Pollitt argues that the following are some of the most important puzzles:

- *Utility.* Determining "utility" often turns out to be deceptively complex. Sometimes it might even include the pursuit of "other-regarding" issues, like altruism and loyalty. But often it focuses on "self-regarding," including maximizing things that are important to individuals, like income and power.
- *Stability.* The more stable these preferences are, the stronger the rational-choice models are. However, ongoing political battles and individuals' own circumstances often cause preferences to change. The more they change, the harder it is to make predictions.
- *Effects.* For the model to work, individuals need to be able to make good predictions about what results will come from the decisions they make. In practice, however, it's very hard to know enough, especially about the turbulent world of politics, to predict what consequences will flow from which decisions. Rational-choice theorists often tackle this problem by assuming limits on information or boundaries around rationality, but that can sacrifice theoretical precision for connection with a bureaucracy's operations.
- *Tests.* Because it's hard to know what the preferences of individuals actually are, it's often very hard to test whether the predictions of the rational-choice approach actually match operating reality.[17]

The public-choice theory has had enormous power. The theory has produced a vast and rich theoretical foundation for understanding the dimensions of public administration. It has helped counter the common critique that public administration is a collection of ideas without rigor. And it has fueled an important reform movement. If government bureaucrats seek to maximize their own power, then the key to improving government programs is to subject more of government to the discipline of private markets, which are designed to promote efficiency. Much of the privatization movement, in fact, flows from the basic assumptions shared with public-choice theory. As Stuart Butler, one of the movement's strongest voices, put it, **privatization** is a kind of "political guerrilla warfare" that directs demand away from government provision of services and reduces the demand for budget growth.[18]

Appraisal

Public choice has the great advantage of being a simple approach that leads to straightforward propositions. It's also led to policy prescriptions—to turn over as many public programs as possible to the private sector and, when that is impossible, to bring private-sector-style competition within the government. When Department of Veterans Affairs (VA) hospitals struggled to reduce the waiting time for appointments, a problem that exploded into a national crisis in 2014, critics argued that the VA's work ought to be transferred to private hospitals and clinics.[19] But underlying these debates are important issues about information and values.

INFORMATION. The attractiveness of the public-choice approach lies in its embrace of the market. As Pollitt points out, however, the approach also depends on information, and there are three problems in obtaining the information needed. One is **information asymmetry**. In complex systems, it is inevitable that some people will know more than others, and it's likely that subordinates (agents) will know more than their superiors (principals). Those working the day-to-day operations of government programs will almost always have better frontline information than those designing the programs. That can lead to **adverse selection**, where supervisors' decisions are not as good as they would be if the supervisors had better information. This can also produce a **moral hazard** problem. If supervisors cannot know enough about what their subordinates are doing, this can lead subordinates to do things that don't match the supervisors' goals. That, in turn, can allow the administration of government programs to drift off course, without the supervisors knowing it until small problems explode into big crises.

This constellation of issues can also lead to big policy problems. Many of the lending issues at the core of the 2008 financial crisis stemmed from information asymmetry and moral hazard. Some lenders engaged in unsafe practices, like providing mortgages for more than the home's worth to people who couldn't pay them back. Government regulators lacked enough information to determine what was happening until it was too late—and some lenders who made these loans were able to pass the costs off to others. The tangled story was captured in the 2015 movie *The Big Short*, which won an Oscar for its screenwriters.

VALUES. Critics have long argued that the simple assumptions of public-choice theory don't capture reality. As Steven Kelman contends, this approach is a caricature:

> It ignores the ability of ideas to defeat interests, and the role that public spirit plays in motivating the behavior of participants in the political process. The "public choice" argument is far worse than simply descriptively inaccurate. Achieving good public policy, I believe, requires . . . a norm of public spiritedness in the political action—a view that people should not simply be selfish in their political behavior. . . . The public choice school is part of the assault on this norm.[20]

The approach unquestionably has helped advance the theory of public administration. But it's proven more troublesome in providing prescriptions for government reform. Relying more on markets has brought a new collection of problems to government, as we will see in Chapter 12. Furthermore, the approach undervalues the power of public ideas and the public interest: the concept that some things are good for all of us and that decision makers seek to achieve those things.[21]

BARGAINING

An alternative to the rational approach to decision making is bargaining. Charles E. Lindblom argued that the rational approach is paradoxically less rational—and that it is more rational to bargain over a decision that can attract political support. Lindblom offers a simple prescription for the analysis of public decisions: incrementalism.[22] It is best, he says, to limit that analysis to a few alternatives instead of trying to judge them all; to weigh one's values along with the evidence instead of holding them separate, as the rational approach would suggest; and to concentrate on the immediate problems to be solved rather than the broader goals to be achieved. The great goals are almost always beyond reach, especially in the short run, and problems presented in smaller chunks are easier to define, diagnose, and solve. Furthermore, it is easier to build support for a series of incremental changes from the current situation and to correct any errors that might creep in.[23]

Decisions thus emerge as the product of bargains. In the bargaining game, the perspective of each player is shaped by the player's position: "where you stand depends on where you sit," as the saying goes.[24] Who wins depends on who has the strongest hand and who bargains most effectively.[25]

Appraisal

The bargaining approach has drawn withering fire from its critics, especially among proponents of the rational approach.

INFORMATION. Critics contend that the bargaining approach is dangerously incomplete and risks depriving decision makers of important information.[26] The political process, they contend, can be counted on to present decision makers with political opinions, but it is far less useful in identifying which alternatives are likely to be the most efficient. The result, critics suggest, is that scarce resources can be wasted. When money is tight, bargaining over public programs might produce common ground only by spreading money among the combatants. One economist, Charles Schultze, acknowledged that "it may, indeed, be necessary to guard against the naïveté of the systems analyst who ignores political constraints and believes that efficiency alone produces virtue." But in taking aim at the incrementalists, he concludes, "it is equally necessary to guard against the naïveté of the decision maker who ignores resource constraints and believes that virtue alone produces efficiency."[27] It is possible, Schultze argues, to take account of political realities while doing systems analysis.

Lindblom replies that systems analysis cannot be done and argues that his decision-making approach is indeed analysis. He suggests instead that limited, successive comparisons are better than trying to be comprehensive. The bargaining approach, however, does not really tell the analyst just how comprehensive to be and how much analysis to do. How large should an increment be? How many alternatives should a decision maker consider? The only answer is a circular one: the increments should be small enough and the alternatives few enough to produce political consensus. A decision maker knows that the approach is right if a consensus forms and wrong if it does not. While this formula may offer a useful description of many decisions, it provides a weak guide for officials trying to design a decision-making process.

VALUES. The bargaining approach is obviously at its strongest in *describing* how decisions are made and how decision makers build political support for their judgments. The political strength of different players in this approach, however, varies greatly, so some players have a

AP Photo

As tensions with the Soviet Union escalated in 1962, President John F. Kennedy met with his brother, Attorney General Robert F. Kennedy, on the portico outside the Oval Office. The government's decision-making strategies during that month's Cuban missile crisis became a much-studied case of how—and how not—to frame governmental policy.

far stronger advantage than others. Moreover, when insiders bargain over their differences, it is easy for the broad public interest to be forgotten. Those who follow an issue closely can shape decisions before the general public even knows that a major decision is on the table. Interests with enough money can have a disproportionate say in these decisions.

Bargaining thus provides a useful description of how many, but not all, administrative decisions are made. There are reasons why it can provide a useful model of how they should be made. But the playing field is never level: not everyone is represented equally around the table, and some interests may not even be invited. Nevertheless, the approach is important: it asserts the importance of values in decision making, in stark contrast with the rational model.

PARTICIPATIVE DECISION MAKING

Beyond the theory of incrementalism is another approach even more based on politics: involving those most affected by policy decisions in the process of making them. Who, after all, is most likely to know better what the best decision looks like? But this simple principle raises a host of questions.

First, what does *participation* mean? It may mean being consulted for advice by someone who has power to make a decision, or it may mean sharing decision-making power, as when those affected vote on a proposed decision and their vote settles whether the proposal is adopted or rejected. Second, just who should be entitled to participate in decision making? Four groups can make claims: (1) the employees of the organization making the decision; (2) the persons whom the organization serves or regulates (the clientele); (3) the taxpayers whose pocketbooks the decision will affect; and (4) the whole public, or at least the voting public.

Who could object to having the decisions be enlightened by the views of those who have to live with them? The problem, of course, is insiders often have different views than either policymakers or citizens. Moreover, there are often strong pressures to keep noisy, dangerous, or otherwise contentious programs "not in my backyard," or **NIMBY**, for short. Many citizens might resist having a drug treatment center located in their neighborhood, for example. And it can work in reverse. When shrinking populations leave neighborhoods with more schools or fire stations than makes economic sense, residents often fight to keep them, as Detroit's leaders found out.

With the rise of social media, many governments have created blogs and have conducted quick, if unscientific, online polls through tools like SurveyMonkey. Twitter and Facebook have quickly become governmental institutions, as public officials work to keep up with the torrent of virtual communication. More traditional neighborhood forums, like actual town hall meetings, continue to flourish. Nearly everyone finds these processes valuable, and nearly everyone has a way to participate in some form or another. The lasting question is what impact universal

D.C. Advisory Neighborhood Commission 3D. http://www.anc3d.org

In many communities, like Washington, D.C., advisory councils work on issues affecting their neighborhoods. These local governments consider a variety of policies and programs, like parking, trash collection, zoning, and street improvements.

participation has on decision making—and how this participation might improve the quality of the decisions made.

Appraisal

Since the mid-1970s, complaints have grown about too much decentralization to citizen groups. The trend gradually has been to centralize control and put more decision-making responsibility in the hands of elected officials. This trend underlines the recurring dilemmas of participative decision making.

INFORMATION. Few insights into the management of public programs are better than those of the persons who must administer them, and few observers of any program's effects have keener insights than the citizens most affected by them. The very wealth of this information is a problem, however, because it typically flows to decision makers as a large, undifferentiated mass, with no easy clues about which information is most important. Too much information can sometimes be as bad as too little. That can encourage decision makers to see only what they want to see.

VALUES. In sorting through the vast amount of information that the participative approach produces, decision makers must also confront important value questions. The approach spawns these recurring dilemmas:

1. *Self-interest versus no interest:* whether to serve a narrow clientele dedicated to protection of its own self-interest or a broad, mixed clientele with a less keen interest in the policy

Students at a Denver elementary school hold signs protesting cuts in funding for local schools. Reductions in spending led teachers and students to furlough days, in an effort to save money.

2. *Too much versus too little representation:* whether to allow direct participation in decision making by all members of the clientele who wish to participate—at the risk of assembling an impossibly large group to deal with—or direct participation only by those who get appointed or elected to committees, councils, or boards that are officially assumed to represent the clientele—but that may not be very representative

3. *Too much versus too little power:* whether to give formal or informal power to citizens for making governmental decisions—raising the problem of who looks out for the public interest—or have them simply provide advice (and demands) to public administrators who weigh those views with other considerations and make the actual decisions—but who may not take that advice seriously

These tradeoffs are hard, but they have big implications for responsive and effective policymaking. On the one hand, participative decision making has led to new public access to governmental decisions and to the creation of a new cadre of civic leaders. On the other hand, the system has created some avenues of patronage and new officials seeking to protect their own positions. The record is mixed.[28]

LIMITS ON DECISION MAKING

From this discussion, it is clear that no one approach offers a solution to the problems of making administrative decisions. Each approach has its own special virtues and its own idiosyncratic problems. Every approach, though, shares the fundamental complication that administrative decisions, after all, are made by collections of human beings, each of whom operates in a large organization full of complex pressures, contradictory information, and diverse advice. Even the theories of satisficing and incrementalism do not fully take account of the psychological environment in which government executives must operate. James Webb, who served for eight years as a NASA administrator, described the problem well:

> Executives within . . . a large-scale endeavor . . . have to work under unusual circumstances and in unusual ways. . . . The executive trained only in . . . traditional principles, able to operate only in accord with them and uncomfortable in their absence, would be of little use and could expect little satisfaction in a large complex endeavor. So too would the executive who has to be psychologically coddled in the fashion that the participative school of management advocates.
>
> In the large-scale endeavor the man himself must also be unusual; he must be knowledgeable in sound management doctrine and practice, but able to do a job without an exact definition of what it is or how it should be done; a man who can work effectively when lines of command crisscross and move in several directions rather than straight up and down; one who can work effectively in an unstable environment and can live with uncertainty and a high degree of personal insecurity; one willing to work for less of a monetary reward than he could insist on elsewhere; one who can blend public and private interests in organized participation for the benefit of both.[29]

Two social psychologists, Irving Janis and Leon Mann, make the point more poignantly. They see the human being "not as a cold fish but as a warm-blooded mammal," one "beset by conflict, doubts, and worry, struggling with incongruous longings, antipathies, and loyalties, and seeking relief by procrastination, rationalizing, or denying responsibility for his own choices."[30] All approaches to decision making share problems: the enormous uncertainty surrounding complex issues, bureaucratic pathologies that distort and block the flow of important information, and recurrent crises that deny the luxury of lengthy consideration.

Uncertainty

It is easy to underestimate how difficult it is for decision makers to know what results their decisions will produce, or even to get good information about the current state of the world. Congress, for example, has charged the Federal Reserve with making monetary policy, but it is deceptively difficult even to decide just what "money" is.[31] The Fed has developed various measures of money—including cash, checking accounts, savings accounts, and long-term certificates of deposit—but these measures have been changed over the years as Americans' banking practices have changed. To make things worse, the supply of money is really only an estimate, subject to constant revision.

Other important economic statistics share the same problems. It often takes months to get good numbers on the growth of the economy or the rate of inflation. What initially seemed to be good months can sometimes become bad months as more data emerge. Furthermore, it is sometimes hard to interpret the numbers: Is high economic growth, for instance, a sign of a healthy economy or of an inflationary trend that is starting to take off? There are lots of numbers, but Fed officials constantly struggle to obtain good, reliable, up-to-date information about the true state of the economy. Even worse, there are very few reliable models about what figures from the past may signal for the economy's future. Even if Fed officials could determine the health of the economy and where it is headed, it is even more difficult to determine how—and when—best to use its tools to steer the economy in a different direction. Moreover, even before the home mortgage market meltdown in 2007 and 2008, some analysts had predicted the impending collapse. Determining what to do, who should do it, and when to act, however, proved impossible—until the collapse forced the regulators' hands.

With increasing frequency, in areas ranging from space exploration to homeland security and from new telephone technologies to the risk of new diseases, decision makers must tackle issues on the edge of current knowledge, where experts disagree and the road ahead is uncertain. Indeed, risk is the first cousin to uncertainty, and the cost of being wrong can sometimes be catastrophic (as, for instance, in judging the risk of exposure to known cancer-causing chemicals).[32] Apart from political pressures, this uncertainty makes any one approach to decision making an inadequate guide—and the risk is all the more hazardous because many decisions, once made, are irreversible and offer no opportunity for the feedback and correction assumed in both the rational and bargaining approaches.

Despite uncertainty, decision makers ultimately must make decisions, from which there is no going back. That, in fact, is the lesson of Julius Caesar at the Rubicon River. Roman law forbade him from bringing his army back into Rome, for the Romans knew that armed emperors would be impossible to resist, and the Rubicon was the boundary. But as Caesar returned to Rome after a successful military campaign in 49 B.C., he decided to challenge the law and Rome's rulers. Once he crossed the boundary, the Rubicon River, with his army, conflict was inevitable. As Plutarch writes:

> [Caesar] wavered much in his mind . . . often changed his opinion one way and the other . . . discussed the matter with his friends who were about him . . . computing how many calamities his passing that river would bring upon mankind and what relation of it would be transmitted to posterity. At last, in a sort of passion, casting aside calculation, and abandoning himself to what might come, and using the proverb frequently in their mouths who enter upon dangerous and bold attempts, "The die is cast," with these words he took the river.[33]

In an age in which a detection system may incorrectly report an enemy's launching of an atomic attack, the few minutes afforded for decision on whether to launch a counterattack permit little computation and calculation, yet the decision is irreversible. The die will have been cast. (It's an old dilemma. The "die is cast" phrase actually comes from Julius Caesar. Roman generals were forbidden from bringing their armies into Rome. He decided to do so anyway and, once he made the move, there was no going back.)

Many decisions less momentous for the world are irreversible, or substantially so: drafting an individual into military service and assignment to a war zone, withholding of a license to practice a profession or operate a business, denial of a loan to prevent bankruptcy of a business or farm, refusal of a pardon to a prisoner scheduled for execution. Decisions often have a stubborn finality for those who suffer loss or risk of life and for those whose livelihoods are impaired. A decision maker doesn't know what results a decision will produce, and the burden of uncertainty weighs all the heavier on decisions that are irreversible.

Information Pathologies

The very structure of bureaucracy, furthermore, can distort the flow of information as it moves upward through the organization. Not all information collected at the bottom, of course, can be passed along to officials at the top—they would quickly become overwhelmed and uncertain about what is actually happening. Therefore, information must be condensed at each bureaucratic level. The process of *condensation*, however, often leads to *filtering*. Public officials, not surprisingly, tend to pass along the good news and suppress the bad. At best, this tendency can distort the information flow; at worst, it can completely block early warnings about emerging problems. Furthermore, officials' own professional training can attune them to some kinds of information more than others. An engineer, even one who has assumed a general managerial position, still may attend more carefully to engineering problems than to others that might be more pressing.[34]

Sometimes these information pathologies create continuing, nagging problems. In the Peace Corps, one former official discovered, "Training was usually inadequate in language, culture, and technical skills. Volunteers were selected who were not suited to their assignments." But upper-level officials were usually kept in the dark about this problem, he explained, because lower-level officials often worked "to prevent information, particularly of an unpleasant character, from rising to the top of the agency, where it may produce results unpleasant to the lower ranks."[35]

Sometimes these pathologies cause disasters. On the night before NASA's launch of the space shuttle *Challenger* in January 1986, for example, engineers for one NASA contractor argued furiously that the cold weather predicted for the launch site the next morning could be dangerous. Mid-level NASA managers rejected the advice and refused to pass it on to top launch officials. The engineers, however, proved tragically good prophets, and the shuttle exploded seventy-three seconds into the flight. Officials with the responsibility for giving the "go" for the launch did not learn about the worries the engineers had expressed that night until the investigation into the disaster began.[36] When the *Columbia* disintegrated on reentry in 2003, officials later discovered that similar worries expressed by engineers had never been communicated to top agency officials.[37]

Decision makers obviously cannot make good decisions without the right information, so they often create devices to avoid the pathologies. They can rely on outside sources, ranging from newspapers to advice from external experts. They can apply a counterbias, using their past knowledge about information sources to judge the reliability of the facts they receive. They can bypass hierarchical levels and go right to the source; some management experts, in fact, advocate "management by walking around," getting the manager out from behind the desk and onto the frontlines to avoid the "nobody ever tells me anything" problem.[38] They can develop precoded forms that avoid distortion as the forms move up through the ranks.[39] Many governmental forms and much red tape, in fact, are designed precisely to prevent uncertainty from creeping into the process ("what information should I pass along?") even if it creates additional headaches for administrators and citizens.

Nevertheless, attempts to rid the information chain of these pathologies can, paradoxically, create new problems:

- Improvements in incoming information may clog internal channels of information.
- Increasing the amount of information flow to decision makers and attempting to eliminate the fragmented features of decision making may simply overload top officials.
- Greater clarity and detail in the wording of decisions may overwhelm implementing officials.[40]

These paradoxes paint a disturbing but very real picture. Administrators are scarcely defenseless, however, because the problem often is not having too little information but having too much—and then trying to sort through it all to find the right combination of facts on which to make decisions. In fact, top NASA officials had been informed earlier of the problem that caused the *Challenger* disaster, "but always in a way that didn't communicate the seriousness of the problem," a House committee found.[41] Later, the same lack of urgency surfaced again to claim a second shuttle. The key to resolving such problems of information management is redundancy: creating multiple sources of feedback that allow decision makers to blend competing pieces of information together into a more coherent picture—without wasting scarce resources on too much redundant information. Decision makers therefore have needed to develop different approaches for dealing with values (see Table 10.1).

Crisis

Crises often precipitate decisions. The deaths of 119 men and 78 men in mine explosions in 1951 and 1968 led to the passage of national coal mine safety acts in 1952 and 1969, respectively. Catastrophic floods have time after time broken logjams that had obstructed major changes in national flood-control policy.[42] A 1979 accident in a Pennsylvania nuclear reactor, Three Mile Island, threatened the population for miles around and stimulated a fundamental reconsideration of governmental policy toward the nuclear power industry. The 2011 crisis at Japan's nuclear reactors rekindled all those debates. The *Challenger* explosion sped up redesign of the booster rocket and produced plans for a new emergency escape system, while the *Columbia* accident led to new launch procedures and improvements of many parts of the space shuttle. And Superstorm Sandy's horrific assault in late 2012 on the northeast prompted a fundamental rethinking of the nation's infrastructure and its zoning policies in flood plains.[43]

In addition to upsetting the normal sequences of decision making, crises increase the difficulty of many potential strategies: the comprehensive analyses that rational decision making requires, the trial and error of bargaining, the consultation of participative decision making, and the reliance on the private sector of public choice. Crises worsen uncertainty, especially in areas of technological complexity. Most important, they highlight an issue of decision making that is not well considered in most approaches: in the end, the public official is responsible for ascertaining and ensuring the public interest—a duty that always proves difficult.

Crises can be managed. In the private sector, the manufacturers of Tylenol were widely hailed for their aggressive action in dealing with the poisoning of their capsules in 1982. Furthermore, Irving L. Janis argues, "vigilant problem solving" can reduce the risks of crises, as managers aggressively seek to formulate the problem, collect available information, reformulate the situation, and frame the best options.[44] When Pennsylvania Governor Richard Thornburgh faced the potential of a nuclear disaster during the Three Mile Island nuclear power plant crisis in 1979, he had to follow precisely these steps in finding his way. Nevertheless, the sudden appearance of the unexpected coupled with high risk for wrong decisions poses enormous problems for decision makers.

MANAGING RISK

No matter how hard administrators try to make good decisions, problems can arise. Sometimes that's because administrators make the *wrong* decisions. That was the case with the Flint water system, where technical mistakes ended up poisoning citizens. Yet

Table 10.1	Approaches to Decision Making	
Approach	Information	Values
Rational	Collect comprehensive information to maximize rationality	Are assumed
Public choice	Use self-policing forces of the market	Use self-interest of players
Bargaining	Limited	Are struggled over
Participative	Acquired through those affected by decision	Focus on clients' values

sometimes it's because problems pile up behind the scenes, either because administrators never see them coming or because they don't have the capacity to solve them. Much of government consists of doing hard things. Hard things bring risks. And risks can create big costs.

Avoiding—or minimizing—those costs is the challenge of **risk management**. But we need to be frank. Most people, including many experienced professionals inside big agencies, find it boring. Risk management is often ignored or, when organizations do pay attention to it, is an afterthought toward the end of meetings, when participants find their minds drifting off to other problems. That, however, is a huge mistake. Disasters destroyed two NASA space shuttles, the *Challenger* in 1986 and the *Columbia* in 2003. Hurricane Katrina devastated the Gulf Coast in 2005. Neither the federal, state, nor local governments were prepared to respond. In 2010, a massive explosion on the *Deepwater Horizon*, an oil-drilling platform in the Gulf of Mexico, killed eleven workers, spilled tens of millions of gallons of oil, and caused billions of dollars in damage. (The story became a major movie in the fall of 2016.) The basic questions of risk management are as follows: Can we do a better job of anticipating such problems? Can we either prevent them or improve our ability to respond? And, more broadly, can better managing such large-scale risks improve the overall performance of government?

Many risks are *external* to the organization. They can range from cyberattacks to an aging workforce. Other risks are *internal*, such as inadequate financial controls or employee training. External and internal risks can combine to create a wide range of costs to organizations: *hazards*, such as fire and theft; *finances*, including cost overruns and credit damage; *operations*, including poor service and cybersecurity breaches; *strategy*, including shifting demographics and technology; and *reputation*, including perceptions of government mismanagement (see Table 10.2). These are all big problems. The challenge, Stephan Braig, Biniam Gebre, and Andrew Sellgren point out, is this: "By its nature, risk management comes under scrutiny only when it fails."[45] Needless to say, that kind of failure is bad—but if it truly were needless to say, the failures would not recur. Government needs a more effective risk management strategy.

Steps toward Effective Risk Management

What would such a system look like? A careful study of risk management by McKinsey in 2011 suggested five steps. Let's consider those steps and their broader implications.[46]

1. *Establish transparency.* Managing risks first requires understanding them. Organization managers need to begin by exploring and identifying the risks that could affect their

Table 10.2	**Examples of Risks That Organizations Face**

Examples of Types of External and Internal Risks Organizations Face

Hazard risks, such as:
- Liability suits (e.g., operational, products, environmental)
- Fire and other property damage
- Theft and other crime

Financial risks, such as:
- Price (e.g., interest rate, commodity)
- Liquidity (e.g., cash flow, opportunity costs)
- Credit (e.g., default by borrowers)

Operational risks, such as:
- Customer service
- Succession planning
- Cybersecurity

Strategic risks, such as:
- Demographic and social/cultural trends
- Technology innovations
- Political trends

Reputational risks, such as:
- Procedural and policy mistakes by staff
- Perceptions of misuse of government resources
- Fraud or contract mismanagement

Source: Douglas W. Webster and Thomas H. Stanton, *Improving Government Decision Making through Enterprise Risk Management* (Washington, D.C.: IBM Center for the Business of Government, 2015), p. 6, http://www.businessofgovernment.org/sites/default/files/Improving%20Government%20Decision%20Making%20through%20Enterprise%20Risk%20Management.pdf.

performance. They need to understand which risks matter most. And they need to communicate them, both internally (to other members of the organization) and externally (to key stakeholders, including those affected by the risks, like citizens, and those who make policy about the risks, like legislators and elected executives). The biggest consequences often come from risks that organizations don't anticipate—or risks they recognize but whose implications they don't fully grasp. The failure of a simple rubber insulation ring caused the explosion of the space shuttle *Challenger*. Engineers understood that the ring was not as flexible in colder weather. But neither they nor launch officials fully understood that temperatures below freezing could cause the ring to fail. The lack of transparency—their inability to see the risks and its implications—proved catastrophic.

2. *Create a risk constitution.* Once organization managers understand risks as well as they can, they need to understand who is in charge of them. The McKinsey authors call this a "risk constitution." Which risks should managers decide that they "own," that they are responsible for understanding and solving? Which risks should they work to transfer to others? What capacity do they need to deal with the risks in their portfolio? The key is to understand that someone must be responsible for every risk that matters, and that each person responsible must have the capacity to deal with it. It does no good to see a problem and to assume that someone else will solve it.

3. *Change what matters most.* A risky part of risk management is trying to fix *everything* connected with the underlying risk. Not only is that impossible. It can also undermine support for the risk management approach, since the more change it imposes, the more resistance it will generate. But, as the McKinsey team suggests, some fundamental processes are likely to be far more important than others in reducing the risks an organization faces. Identifying those core processes, and fixing them first, can substantially shrink risk. In many

cities, busy intersections near fire stations can increase the response time. Some cities have installed special systems on traffic lights at those intersections to turn them green until the firefighters have passed. That way they're not sitting in traffic as they've barely pulled out of the station.

4. *Make every risk management issue someone's business.* One lesson is that risk management must be everyone's business. But it's often the case that if something is everyone's job, it becomes no one's job—especially if stakeholders see the process as getting in the way of the day-to-day activities of their core mission. To be effective, risk management must be the concentrated focus for a unit within the government, both to make sure it's on everyone's agenda and to deal with the inevitable risks that cross over multiple organizations within the government. No one wants to see released prisoners return to jail. But ensuring that they don't return requires coordinated work by parole officers, job training programs, housing and welfare programs, and medical programs—a network of services to help released prisoners cope with and solve the often-difficult challenges they face, which often led them to prison to begin with.

5. *Build a risk culture.* Risk management is one of those organizational principles that attracts broad agreement and, sometimes, little action. Managers can easily come to see it as an add-on to their job, instead of a core part of it. In practice, risk management rarely works well unless it becomes part of everyone's business—part of the organization's culture. That, of course, lies at the core of local policing and Air Force pilots. They know that every time they go to work, they face life-and-death risks, and they do all they can to manage them, from checking their gear to maintaining constant awareness of their circumstances. Risk surrounds the work of most government employees—often not life or death, but important nonetheless, ranging from effective snow removal, to avoid putting drivers at risk, to processing Social Security payments, to ensure that retirees can pay their bills.

In this light, risk management isn't quite so boring after all. We create government programs, after all, because we collectively decide that we want to do something important. If we fail to do it—or fail to do it well—we not only waste money and often put lives on the line. We also undermine the faith and trust of citizens in their government. Risk management thus is about both organizational change and organizational fidelity: how to make public administration work as we expect.

Overcoming Barriers to Risk Management

If risk management is so important, why is it so hard? There are several reasons.

First, it's often difficult to sustain the attention of top managers.[47] So many big issues—both policy debates and immediate crises—crowd the desks of senior executives. It's little wonder that they spend their days fighting what's at the top of the list. However, what's most urgent isn't always the most important. The riskiest thing about risk management is that failures are often huge—and top managers never see them coming. It takes an effective risk management system to ensure the organization can prevent big problems or minimize their costs. Top managers might not spend a lot of time doing risk management themselves, but they need to spend enough time on it to make sure it gets done.

Second, organizational fragmentation can prevent a broad view. Analysts often see this as the result of organizational "silos"—tall structures often unconnected with the rest of the bureaucracy. Risks, however, often flow across government programs and organizations, and that makes it even harder for administrators to manage them. Moreover, as we will see in Chapter 12, some of government's most important risks flow from programs that cross organizational boundaries. It's especially easy, in such programs, for government's managers to violate the fourth principle above—making every risk management issue someone's business—because it's especially easy for managers to assume that someone else will be taking care of a problem. That often means no one is taking care of it—and risks can escalate.

Third, transparency on risks means identifying opportunities for political attack. Identifying risks—things that could go wrong—can open administrators up to political attack. Legislators and reporters can single out such problems and press on what more isn't being done to get ready for problems. If problems occur—and, in complicated programs, problems are inevitable—a paper trail documenting known risks in advance is sure to draw fierce fire. If administrators knew about the problem, why didn't they fix it when there was time? That was an especially important argument after Hurricane Katrina struck. After all, experts for years had warned that a big storm could swamp New Orleans. After Katrina hit, they asked why the city wasn't better prepared. One way to avoid such after-the-fact attacks is to ensure there is no paper trail to be found. Minimizing risk management means there is no risk analysis to be discovered later. That, of course, only ensures that the problems of risk grow even greater.

These puzzles get to the core of the problem of accountability, to which we'll return in Chapter 14. There is *always* politics in public administration, and competing political forces will *always* look for political advantage in any circumstance. The bigger the stakes, the more they're likely to seek bigger political advantage. In many ways, therefore, the biggest risk of risk management is that those inside the system will conclude that it's just too risky: that it unnecessarily exposes them to additional political attacks. However, as we saw at the beginning of Chapter 1, failing to consider the risks and consequences of big decisions can lead to enormous, even catastrophic, results. The Flint water crisis became a crisis because government officials made decisions without carefully exploring the possibilities and what could have been done to avoid them. When problems began appearing, they were blind to the risks and caught flat-footed in responding. Only when the problems began having catastrophic consequences for children did the government respond. This was a case where the risks were knowable in advance and discoverable along the way. The failure to look for—and act on—them made the problems worse: the political impact on government officials and the personal health for the citizens. That is as strong a case for risk management as one could imagine.

CONCLUSION

We have examined several approaches to administrative decision making: rational analysis, public choice, bargaining, and participative. Though in some measure all of these approaches have been put into practice, they all are expressions of theories—full of assumptions—which have tended to harden into dogmas. They also offer, as Table 10.1 shows, a wide range of tactics for dealing with the lasting problems of information and values.

The approaches share, in varying degrees, certain basic defects. This chapter discussed some oversights, especially uncertainty, information pathologies, and crisis, but there are others, such as how a problem or a need for a decision is discovered, formulated, and put on the agenda (most approaches start with a known and stated problem or need). Furthermore, nondecision—the decision not to decide or the avoidance of an issue altogether, whether conscious or unconscious—often has consequences as great as those of a decision itself. When senior Bush administration officials received the President's Daily Brief on August 6, 2001, that warned, "Bin Laden Determined to Strike in U.S.," no one took action. The brief was unclear about how or when, and it wasn't clear from the brief what the administration could or should do. But this was a case where a nondecision had catastrophic consequences just a month later.

More basic are two problems. First, each approach tends to focus on a single value, such as the focus of economists on efficiency in systems analysis, the attention of public choice advocates on private-sector competition, incrementalists' dedication to maximizing participation, and participative managers' commitment to full public voice in decisions. These are all important values. However, any approach focused on just one of them is sure to be inadequate for the complex reality of the political world.

Second, it can be difficult to understand what is required to make an approach succeed. Sometimes, as in systems analysis, the conditions may not exist in the real world, and the theorists do not explain very well how to adapt their approaches to reality. Often, however, the adaptations may drain the approach of its power. For example, attempts to adapt the rational decision-making approach by trying to absorb elusive policy goals, the shortage of sufficient quantitative data, the distortion that inevitably comes from converting qualitative goals or accomplishments into measurable terms, and the behavior of members of Congress may lead to so truncated a version of the rational approach that it is less useful than, say, the more reality-oriented incremental approach.

It is possible, of course, to identify which approaches work best for which problems.[48] The rational approach, for example, tends to work better for issues with clear objectives, quantitative measures, and minimal political pressures. However, even if we can somehow determine which approaches best fit which problems—itself a very tall order—we are left with the puzzle of how to put these different tactical systems to work as a coherent whole. These problems, of course, become even greater when put in the context of risk—programming and political—that always surrounds the tough questions of public administration.

Those puzzles come into the sharpest focus in the budgetary process, which we examine in Chapter 11. As the government's system-wide decision-making process, budgeting raises the difficult issues of how best to deal with the conflicting pressures toward comprehensive planning and incremental politics that lie at the core of decision making. Theorists and public officials alike have long struggled to manage an elusive marriage between the two so as to capture the value of each while avoiding the flaws of both.

Baltimore Battles the Banks

In 2012, Baltimore Mayor Stephanie Rawlings-Blake publicly savaged international bankers for taking money out of the pockets of city residents. The bankers, she told reporters, "are pretty much playing fast and loose with the people they are meant to protect." She added, "We are not afraid of a fight."

How did a mayor of a medium-sized city end up dueling with giant banks like Barclays, Bank of America, Citigroup, HSBC, JPMorgan Chase, and UBS? Like many state and local governments, Baltimore invested its cash in complex financial instruments, including interest-rate swaps. Rawlings-Blake and other litigants in a federal lawsuit charged that the banks set interest rates artificially low, which cut governments' investment returns and led to bigger spending cuts. No politician likes to slash programs or raise taxes. Politicians hate to discover they had to do so more than might have been necessary.

Because many state and local governments borrow at floating rates, investment returns can be highly unpredictable. So to smooth out the highs and lows, financial managers trade the floating bonds for fixed-rate investments. Most of the rates for floating bonds and swaps are pegged to "Libor," the London Interbank Offered Rate. Insiders know it as BBA Libor (for British Bankers' Association Libor), the product of a daily survey among bankers about the rates banks can get in the London market at 11 a.m. every business day, across a range of maturities. They toss out the highest and lowest rates, and the average of what's left determines the interest rates that just about everyone pays for just about everything. In fact, anyone can follow the results on Twitter: @BBALIBOR.

This is rather arcane stuff, but it worked well through gentlemen's agreements for decades until July 2012. In both the United States and the United Kingdom, government regulators found that traders working for one of London's most respected banks, Barclays, had been playing Libor games by misrepresenting the rates. Soon government regulators in Canada and Switzerland joined in the investigation, which spread to sixteen banks, including Bank of America, Citigroup, and JPMorgan Chase in the United States. Fallout quickly ensued when Barclays' high-flying chairman Marcus Agius was forced to resign.

The regulators probed whether the banks had colluded to keep interest rates artificially low, in part to make money on trades and in part to convey the impression that, even in the financial meltdown, they remained solid companies. (The riskier the company, the higher the rates it would have to pay. So lower rates both helped banks play the market better and signaled a rosy corporate picture.)

That takes us back to Baltimore and a quickly growing list of state and local governments filing legal action. Their claim: by artificially driving Libor down, the banks cheated them out of enormous investment returns at a time when their budgets were already badly damaged from the Great Recession and when every dollar of investment income was a dollar of services that didn't have to be cut.

The Libor scandal has exploded across the global financial scene. It's already cost the jobs of top bankers and has dragged many of the world's leading banks into a very harsh spotlight, just as they were trying to make the case for the return of financial stability. Mad-as-hell government officials, who concluded they slashed spending more than was necessary, are seeking compensation and retribution. Moreover, many state and local investment officials holding bonds with variable rates converted them to interest-rate swaps to stabilize their returns, but now they can't get out of them because in many cases the penalties are too high. So not only are their investment returns lower than they should be—they're stuck with them.

Perhaps most fundamentally, the foundations of much they had taken for granted have been shaken. It turns out that the key benchmark for most interest rates around the world was Libor, and that Libor wasn't the actual rates bankers charged but estimates that could be gamed. As blogger Darwin Bond-Graham sharply put it, "Libor was always a club of powerful banks inventing the price of money," and with Agius's resignation, the workings of that club came under investigation, including the threat of criminal rate-fixing charges. According to one government official, "It's hard to imagine a bigger case than Libor."

That all leads to two final questions. First, why didn't the feds step in sooner to help protect state and local governments? The Treasury had detected the problem a few years earlier and even managed to extract a $450 million settlement from Barclays. Some state and local officials have complained that federal regulators were not riding shotgun for them.

Second, how much of the problem came from state and local investment officials putting money into instruments whose risks they didn't really understand? As Jeffrey Gibbs, director of special investigations for Pennsylvania's auditor general, put it, swaps, derivatives, and other complex financial instruments are typically understood only by the people who sell them. It's another searing lesson of the risks of governing in a globalized world, with state and local leaders forced to navigate through seas they can't control and sometimes can't even see.

QUESTIONS TO CONSIDER

1. What lessons does Baltimore's Libor experience teach? What would you advise the mayor of your community about how to make decisions on such investments?

2. An important question about modern budgeting and complex financial instruments is the last point: only the people who sell them (and, sometimes, not even the salespersons) understand the important questions. A time-honored piece of investment advice is that investors should never put their money in something they don't understand. But is that realistic in today's global marketplace? If you have a savings account in your bank, do you really know where the money is going? How much information do you need to make good decisions?

3. What do you think you have to know to be a good steward of the public's money? How should a government build adequate capacity in its own agencies to ensure it manages the public's money well?

Note: This case comes from my column in *Governing* (October 2012), http://www.governing.com/columns/potomac-chronicle/col-global-libor-scandal-cost-states-localities-millions.html.

 # CASE 10.2

Pay to Spray? Fire Protection and the Free Rider Problem in South Fulton, Tennessee

Gene Cranick was devastated as he poked through the remains of his house. His grandson Lance had been clearing out trash and burning it in a barrel near the home. Lance went inside to take a shower and when he came back outside he found a shed in flames. His garden hose couldn't keep up with the spreading fire, which soon reached the house. The family lost everything, including three dogs and a cat and a lifetime's belongings.

The rural town of South Fulton, Tennessee, had a fire department. In fact, the fire department arrived at the scene—and watched as the home burned down. The town imposes an annual $75 fire protection fee, commonly known as "pay to spray," for citizens like Cranick who live outside the South Fulton city limits and who rely on South Fulton's fire department. "I just forgot to pay my $75," Gene Cranick explained later. "I did it last year, the year before.... It slipped my mind." The firefighters arrived when his neighbor, who had paid the fee, called 911. The trucks sprayed down the fence line separating the homes but refused to put out the fire at Cranick's house. As Jeff Vowell, South Fulton's city manager, later explained, "We have to follow the rules and the ordinances set forth to us, and that's exactly what we did."[1]

Cranick's neighbor had pleaded with the fire department to train the hoses next door. They begged firefighters to help the family, and Cranick offered to pay whatever it would cost for help. The firefighters responded that it was simply too late. The policy, in place for more than two decades, was clear: pay, in advance, to spray. "Anybody that's not inside the city limits of South Fulton, it's a service we offer. Either they accept it or they don't," South Fulton Mayor David Crocker said.[2]

The sad case led to a national debate over the decision of the firefighters to stand by and watch the home burn. Jacqueline Byers, at the National Association of Counties, explained, "If the city starts fighting fires in the homes of people outside the city who don't pay, why would anyone pay?"[3] It's a classic free rider problem, some experts said: allow others to pay the cost of municipal services, and then use the services when they're needed. But the president of the International Association of Fire Fighters said the policy was "incredibly irresponsible." He argued, "Professional, career firefighters shouldn't be forced to check a list before running out the door to see which homeowners have paid up." Instead, "They get in their trucks and go."[4]

Conservative commentator Glenn Beck said that the argument will go "nowhere if you go onto 'compassion, compassion, compassion, compassion.'" The fee, he said, is "to pay for the fire department to have people employed to put the fire out." He concluded that to use fire services without paying the fee "would be sponging off your neighbor's $75."[5] But another conservative commentator, Daniel Foster, countered with this argument: "I have no problem with this kind of opt-in government in principle—especially in rural areas where individual need for governmental services and available infrastructure vary so widely. But forget the politics: what moral theory allows these firefighters (admittedly acting under orders) to watch this house burn to the ground when (1) they have already responded to the scene; (2) they have the means to stop it ready at hand;

(3) they have a reasonable expectation to be compensated for their trouble?"[6]

QUESTIONS TO CONSIDER

1. Do you believe that the firefighters should have used their equipment to put out the fire, even though local policy explicitly told them not to?

2. Should Cranick have been able to pay on the spot for service, so the firefighters could save his house?

3. Do you think that a policy to opt-in for governmental programs—to pay in advance for basic municipal services—is a good one? Do you think there are some services where such a policy is appropriate and some where it is not? Consider, for example, a range of basic services including fire protection, police protection, garbage pickup, snow plowing, road repair, parks, recreation, and local schools. Are some services different from others—and, if so, how would you differentiate between them?

4. If local ordinances set clear policies for local administrators, under what circumstances might it be proper for these administrators to step over the policies? It must have been hard for the firefighters to watch a family grieve as all their possessions went up in flames. Then there is the free rider problem: If someone can plead his or her case in a crisis, why shouldn't everyone rely on their neighbors to pay for the cost of providing the service? Would it ever be permissible to go against policy in the case of need?

NOTES

1. Bradley Blackburn, "Family Misses Fee, Firefighters Let House Burn," *ABC News* (October 5, 2010), http://abcnews.go.com/m/story?id=11806407.

2. "No Pay, No Spray: Firefighters Let Home Burn," *NBC* (October 6, 2010).

3. Blackburn, "Family Misses Fee."

4. "No Pay, No Spray."

5. Evann Gastaldo, "Glenn Beck: Firefighters Right to Let Home Burn," *Newser* (October 6, 2010), http://www.newser.com/story/102300/glenn-beck-firefighters-right-to-let-home-burn.html.

6. Daniel Foster, "Pay-to-Spray Firefighters Watch as Home Burns," *National Review* (October 4, 2010), http://www.nationalreview.com/corner/248649/pay-spray-firefighters-watch-home-burns-daniel-foster.

 # CASE 10.3

Tweeting to the Rescue? How the Mayor of Newark Used Social Media to Improve Public Service Delivery

Some newswriters christened the 2010 Christmas weekend blizzard the Great Tsnownami or Snowmageddon. As nearly two feet of snow buried New York in deep drifts, in one of the five worst storms ever to hit the metropolitan region, thousands of flights were canceled and Amtrak was stalled for two days. Dozens of ambulances became stuck in drifts and even heavy front-loaders had to be tugged out of clogged city streets.

Local newspapers complained about the pace of snow removal. The website of the *New York Daily News* ran a photo of the Staten Island home of John Doherty, the sanitation commissioner. "Does your street look like this?" the website asked. That street, the *Daily News* said, "was plowed clean," but "the dead-end streets on either side of his block remained a snow-choked winter blunderland."[1]

New York Mayor Michael Bloomberg acknowledged that "many New Yorkers are suffering serious hardships." He also said, however, "The world has not come to an end." In fact, "The city is going fine. Broadway shows were full last night. There are lots of tourists here enjoying themselves. I think that the message is that the city goes on." A *New York Times* writer thought wryly of Bloomberg's comment as he was looking at two men trying to push a Cadillac Escalade out of a Brooklyn snowbank, with the smell of burning rubber from spinning tires in the air. Were they thinking of taking in a Broadway play, the writer asked? One of the men

trying to free the Escalade was incredulous. "Take in a play?" he asked. "What does the mayor suggest? Walking?" Times Square, after all, was a ten-mile hike or a half-hour drive, even in good traffic without snow.[2]

Across the Hudson River, Newark Mayor Cory Booker was camped on Twitter (http://twitter.com/corybooker) and was putting his own shoulder to the shovel. One woman said she was stuck and needed to get to a medical procedure. "I will dig you out. Where are you?" he Tweeted. One Twitter follower worried about how Booker's back was holding up. "Thanks 4 asking, back killing me," he responded. "Breakfast: Advil and Diet Coke."

Booker assured residents he was personally on the case. Two days after the storm ended, he Tweeted, "Stepping off streets for hour or so 2 take a meeting I couldn't cancel. We still have dozens of trucks & 100s of workers out clearing snow." When he got out of the meeting, he told a worried resident, "I'm on my way to Treamont Ave now to help dig your mom out." Then a Tweet arrived: "don't forget brunswick street by astor." He was quickly back in touch. "Thanks for the heads up. I'm sending a crew. It will be there in a bit." From a worried resident, about Booker's trademark look: "Saw u out there on S Orange. Put a hat on that head. Us baldies can't be going commando out there." The reply: "No need I've got a hot head."

Snow removal has a long history of causing officials heartburn, both political and administrative. Chicago Mayor Michael Bilandic lost a primary election in 1979 because, most local political analysts believed, local voters punished him for failing to respond quickly enough to a major blizzard. In 1969, another New York blizzard so politically crippled Mayor John Lindsay that he never recovered. When he visited Queens, residents scorned him. "You should be ashamed of yourself," screamed one angry woman. Another said, "Get away, you bum."[3]

Booker was determined to avoid that fate. A Tweet arrived: "quitman/spruce need plowing. noone has touch those streets—becoming dangerous." He shot back, "We r on it. DM me ur # if u want 2 talk."

QUESTIONS TO CONSIDER

1. Compare the two strategies: Bloomberg and Booker. Consider the differences in scale between the two cities. Think about the differences in communication. Which do you believe was most effective?

2. How has the rise of social media, like Twitter and Facebook, changed the decision-making landscape, both in how officials make decisions and how they are *seen* to make decisions? How do social media affect the way accountability for public decisions might work?

3. Voters and citizens expect good results from their public officials. They expect to hold them accountable for their decisions and, as the Chicago and New York examples show, they can do so at the ballot box. On the other hand, is there a risk in a decision maker becoming too personally identified with individual actions on the frontlines? Is there a risk that having a mayor shovel out the car of one resident himself might take him away from command decisions that affect opening up the streets for everyone? How should decision makers sort out the question of who makes which decisions?

NOTES

1. Edgar Sandoval and Larry McShane, "Sanitation Boss John Doherty's Street Plowed Clean, but Nearby Streets Remain Winter Blunderland," *New York Daily News* (December 29, 2010), http://www.nydailynews.com/ny_local/2010/12/29/2010-12-29_a_madhouse_out_there_but_not_for_boss.html.

2. Michael Powell, "For a Snow-Crippled City, a Morsel of Humble Pie from the Mayor," *New York Times* (December 28, 2010), http://www.nytimes.com/2010/12/29/nyregion/29about.html.

3. Sewall Chan, "Remembering a Snowstorm That Paralyzed the City," *New York Times* (February 10, 2009), http://cityroom.blogs.nytimes.com/2009/02/10/remembering-a-snowstorm-that-paralyzed-the-city.

CASE 10.4

What Are You Eating for Breakfast?

Most Americans eat breakfast, surveys find. In fact, on average Americans ate breakfast 361 days a year in 2016, an increase from 350 days a year in 2010. That's been especially good news for fast-food restaurants, where breakfast-time stops increased 8 percent from 2014 to 2016.[1] Americans love breakfast—and increasingly they like it to be portable, in everything from sandwiches to yogurt to granola bars. Some food chains, like McDonald's, rose to the challenge by offering breakfast all day.

But this has been bad news for cereal manufacturers. Breakfast meals eaten at home fell from 31 percent in 2009 to 27 percent in 2015. Cereal sales dropped 9 percent in the four years from 2011 to 2015. In fact, the cereal industry suffered a bigger hit than did any other business selling packaged food.[2]

A large part of this trend is younger Americans' declining interest in eating cereal. For example, Ashley Peters, who works in Minneapolis, explained that she grew up eating Cheerios and Cap'n Crunch but now eats a granola bar on the job. "It's just easier to do," she explained. "I don't have time for milk at work."[3]

All companies are chasing millennial consumers, who now are the largest demographic in the country—larger even than baby boomers. That goes for cereal companies, too, who know they need to appeal to millennials if they are to stop the slide in sales. But a *New York Times* story caught national attention when its author pointed to one survey that said 40 percent of millennials didn't like cereal because it "was an inconvenient breakfast choice because they had to clean up after eating it."[4] Organic products and brands perceived as healthful are selling well, but sales in the overall cereal market are decreasing. Convenient on-the-run snacks are doing better. Sales of food bars, especially granola bars, have been surging, especially because they're convenient and consumers view them as healthy.

The problem, however, is that often these granola bars are not healthy. A *New York Times* study showed that 71 percent of the public thinks that granola bars are healthy, but only 28 percent of nutritionists agree. Although granola bars sound healthy, with ingredients such as oats and other grains, some are full of sugar. A Twix candy bar, in fact, has about as much sugar and as many calories as a typical granola bar.[5] In fact, consider those foods where the gap between what consumers *think* is healthy and what nutritionists have concluded is greatest.[6]

Foods Considered Healthier by the Public Than by Experts

Percent Describing a Food as "Healthy"	Nutritionists	Public	Difference
Granola bar	28	71	43
Coconut oil	37	72	35
Frozen yogurt	32	66	34
Granola	47	80	33
SlimFast shake	21	47	26
Orange juice	62	78	16
American cheese	24	39	15

Then there are foods that cut the other way, where experts believe items are healthier than consumers think:

Foods Considered Healthier by Experts Than by the Public

Percent Describing a Food as "Healthy"	Nutritionists	Public	Difference
Quinoa	89	58	31
Tofu	85	57	28
Sushi	75	49	26
Hummus	90	66	24
Wine	70	52	18
Shrimp	85	69	16

Then there are foods that both consumers and experts agree are healthy—and not.

Foods That Both Groups Think Are Healthy

Percent Describing a Food as "Healthy"	Nutritionists	Public	Difference
Apples	99	96	3
Oranges	99	96	3
Oatmeal	97	92	5
Chicken	91	91	0
Turkey	91	90	1
Peanut butter	81	79	2
Baked potatoes	72	71	1

Foods That Both Groups Think Are Unhealthy

Percent Describing a Food as "Healthy"	Nutritionists	Public	Difference
Hamburgers	28	29	1
Beef jerky	23	27	4
Diet soda	18	16	2
White bread	15	18	3
Chocolate chip cookies	6	10	4

Nutritionists are always urging us to eat healthier food. But there are big, sometimes remarkable, differences between what ordinary consumers *think* is healthy and what experts believe. This affects not only the sales of cereals and granola bars. What consumers think is good and what experts believe often don't connect, both for breakfast and in many other decisions we make about our food throughout the day.

QUESTIONS TO CONSIDER

1. Are you surprised by the findings of this analysis?
2. For the food items where you are surprised, what is the source of your beliefs?

3. What explains the difference between what experts think and what consumers believe—and do you believe the experts?

4. What are the implications for decision making, where there so often are big gaps between citizens' perceptions and what experts believe? Do such gaps lead to bad or dangerous decisions?

5. Could—and should—the process be improved, so we make more decisions on the basis of better evidence? What steps would be most likely to be most effective?

NOTES

1. Martha C. White, "Here's What Americans Are Eating for Breakfast," *Money* (May 18, 2016), http://time.com/money/4339331/breakfast-habits-morning-snacks/; and Brad Tuttle, "How Fast Food Players Are Battling Back against McDonald's All Day Breakfast," *Money* (February 29, 2016), http://time.com/money/4239505/fast-food-mcdonalds-all-day-breakfast/.

2. "Cereal-makers Try to Get Millennials Back to Table," *The Gazette* (May 24, 2016), http://www.thegazette.com/subject/news/business/cereal-makers-try-to-get-millennials-back-to-table-20160524.

3. Ibid.

4. Kim Severson, "Cereal, a Taste of Nostalgia, Looks for Its Next Chapter," *New York Times* (February 22, 2016), http://www.nytimes.com/2016/02/24/dining/breakfast-cereal.html.

5. Kristine Lockwood, "Dangerfood: Granola Bars" (October 11, 2011), http://greatist.com/health/dangerfood-granola-bars.

6. Kevin Quealy and Margot Sanger-Katz, "Confused about Quinoa and Nutrition? So Are Other Americans" (July 6, 2016), http://www.nytimes.com/2016/07/07/upshot/confused-about-quinoa-and-nutrition-so-are-other-americans.html.

KEY CONCEPTS

adverse selection 274

bargaining approach 269

externalities 269

information asymmetry 274

moral hazard 274

NIMBY phenomenon 276

participative decision-making approach 269

privatization 273

public-choice approach 269

rational approach 269

rational decision making 269

risk management 283

satisficing 271

spillovers 269

FOR FURTHER READING

Allison, Graham T. *Essence of Decision: Explaining the Cuban Missile Crisis.* Boston: Little, Brown, 1971.

Cohen, Michael, James March, and Johan Olsen. "A Garbage Can Model of Organizational Choice." *Administrative Science Quarterly* 17 (March 1972): 1–25.

Downs, Anthony. *An Economic Theory of Democracy.* New York: Harper and Row, 1957.

Etzioni, Amitai. "Mixed Scanning: A Third Approach to Decision-Making." *Public Administration Review* 27 (December 1967): 385–392.

Lindblom, Charles E. "The Science of 'Muddling Through.'" *Public Administration Review* 19 (Spring 1959): 79–88.

Pollitt, Christopher. *Public Management and Administration.* Cheltenham, U.K.: Edward Elgar, 2016.

Simon, Herbert A. *Administrative Behavior: A Study of Decision-Making Processes in Administrative Organization.* 3rd ed. New York: Free Press, 1945, 1976.

SUGGESTED WEBSITES

The study and practice of decision making has produced a vast array of approaches to this important and complex field. Many areas of public policy have developed new methods of decision making, for instance, in the environmental arena (see the Global Development Research Center, **www.gdrc.org/decision**). In health care, many practitioners have argued for an approach to the field that is based far more on the application of evidence, including work at websites like **www.evidencebased.net**. Moreover, the Federal Executive Institute's training programs for the federal government's top managers contains a wide-ranging collection of courses on decision making (see **www.leadership.opm.gov**).

The Society for Judgment and Decision Making has prepared a useful website, which contains links to a wide spectrum of work in the field (see **www.sjdm.org/links.html**). In addition, the *International Journal of Information Technology and Decision Making*, **www.worldscinet .com/ijitdm/ijitdm.shtml**, regularly reviews cutting-edge thinking on the subject.

$SAGE edge™

for CQ Press

WANT A BETTER GRADE?

Get the tools you need to sharpen your study skills. Access practice quizzes, eFlashcards, video, and multimedia at **edge.sagepub.com/kettl7e.**

11

BUDGETING

In 2013, Richard Trott of the National Park Service posted a sign at the Lincoln Memorial telling visitors that the monument was closed because of the government shutdown. Congress had failed to approve new funding for many federal programs, which forced them to close until it passed new appropriations.

I
f decision making is the central administrative act, budgeting is the
fundamental administrative decision. Big policy ideas are important,
but ideas are nothing without the money to back them up. Budgets set
the basic priorities. To know what an organization—or a government—
truly values, look at how the money is spent. Likewise, to change an organization's priorities, change the budget. According to an old saying,
attributed to many insiders, "Grab them by their budgets, and their hearts
and minds will follow." Most of the big battles in government—and in
public administration—sooner or later become budgeting battles. That,
in turn, makes budget making perhaps the most central political act in
public administration.

Budget decisions are both important and political because they frame the
focus on three central questions that have recurred throughout history.[1]

First, *what should government do?* Budgeting is, at its core, the fundamental
decision about the use of scarce resources from the people. There are always
more good ideas than there is money to fund them. Just how big should government be? Which public programs most deserve the public's support: Highways
or health care, weapons or welfare? More police officers and firefighters or
more teachers and social workers? Budgetary politics is enmeshed in perpetual
conflict because it involves the toughest, most central questions that societies
must answer.

Second, *who in government should decide these questions?* Throughout U.S.
history, the balance of financial power has shifted between the national and
subnational governments, and between the legislature and the executive. The
budgetary arena has been the continuing forum for broad policy disputes and
pitched battles over not only who should benefit from governmental programs
but also who should decide the fate of those programs. Charting the *who* of
budgets also provides a strong guide to sources of real governmental power.

Finally, *how should citizens and public officials make these decisions?* In 1940,
political scientist V. O. Key Jr. framed the classic problem: "On what basis shall
it be decided to allocate x dollars to activity A instead of activity B?"[2] Budgeting
is about scarcity. There are always more claims on budget dollars than there is
money to spend. Budget makers always face the challenge of deciding which
claims are funded—and which are not. Addressing this challenge is about process, analysis and what defines the best way of making decisions (as we saw in
Chapter 10), politics and the battles over the public's money, and basic values
about how decisions should be made. In fact, note how often the word *should*
appears in discussions about budgeting. That provides a hint about the big
value debates that are never far from any budgetary discussion.

This chapter explores these questions in sorting out the functions and processes of budgeting. It begins with an examination of the far-reaching economic
and political roles of the budget. It continues by probing the basic parts of the
budgetary process: budget making, budget appropriation, and budget execution. Finally, this chapter concludes by reviewing the relationship between

- Understand the twin roles of budgeting: steering the economy and making political choices

- Chart the steps in the budgetary process

- Explore the challenges to budgeting

- Compare federal versus state and local government budgeting

budgetary politics and public administration. State and local governments vary tremendously in the way they budget and account for their money, and trying to describe the full range of their practices would fill another book this size. So this chapter will focus heavily on the federal government's budget strategies and tactics to explore the basic challenges that stretch across the budgetary issues for all governments.

THE BUDGET'S TWIN ROLES

All budgets are about financial decisions. At the federal level, the budget plays an additional role because of how it shapes the national economy—and how the economy shapes the budget. Because these decisions affect the allocation of resources among competing claimants, the budget has important political effects as well. After exploring these broad economic features, we'll turn to the issues affecting budgets at the federal, state, and local levels.

The Economic Role

The very size of the government's financial activity inevitably makes it a strong player in the national economy.[3] That role is reciprocal: the budget has enormous impact on the economy, and the economy plays a strong role in shaping the budget. That leads, not surprisingly, to the conclusion that because the budget *can* be used to steer the economy, it *should* do so.

THE BUDGET'S EFFECT ON THE ECONOMY. Let's start with the basics. Governments do their accounting by their budget calendar, known as the **fiscal year**. They can run a **surplus** (where revenues exceed expenditures) or a **deficit** (where expenditures exceed revenues). Governments can borrow money in the short term and repay it in the long term. This is **debt**. At the federal level, the government borrows money to finance deficits, and the accumulated deficits over time produce the **national debt**. Federal surpluses have been relatively rare, so most of the debate hinges on the role of deficits and the management of the national debt.

It is important to remember that state and local governments cannot run deficits, often because their constitutions forbid it—and always because of basic principles of public finance. These principles hold that state and local governments ought to borrow only to pay for items that have long lives and only for the life of the project. For example, if a state wants to build a bridge that will last twenty-five years, it would borrow money by issuing a twenty-five-year bond. If a local government wants to buy a new school building that will last twenty years, it would issue a twenty-year bond. Sound practices, and in many cases the law, prohibit state and local governments from borrowing money for long periods to fund short-term expenses, like salaries and program expenses. They should not borrow money to cover a gap between spending and revenues.

At least since the Great Depression in the 1930s, economists and government officials have recognized that government taxation and spending, known as **fiscal policy**, affect the economy. (The word *fiscal* is Old French in origin and appears to have roots in the Latin word for "treasury" or "basket," terms that, put together, sum up the topic well.) British economist John Maynard Keynes argued that government can—and should—use the budget to steer the economy: to boost employment, to cut inflation, to improve the nation's balance of trade abroad, and to keep the value of the dollar secure.[4] That theory has grown into the cornerstone of macroeconomics and the study of the broad interactions between government's economic activity and the behavior of the economy. Belief in the power of fiscal policy to steer the economy reached its zenith with the Kennedy tax cut, passed in 1964 after John F. Kennedy's assassination, to spur economic growth.[5] Since then, presidents and economists alike have tangled over the relationship between taxes, spending, and the economy, and what combination would produce the best long-run economic growth.

Economists have long recognized that the economy goes through cycles of growth and recession. Keynesian economics preaches that the government can use its taxing and spending powers to moderate those cycles, to offset the dangers of both too-rapid growth (inflation) and recession (unemployment). The theory suggests that in good times, the government ought to run a surplus to keep the economy from expanding too quickly; in bad times, it should run a deficit to keep the economy from becoming sluggish. Because state and local budgets must be balanced, and because no individual state or local budget is big enough to steer the national economy, this is a tool exclusive to the federal budget. And it inevitably creates temptations to use the budget's steering forces for political advantage.[6]

Although the basic Keynesian model retains a strong hold on economists and budgeters, in practice it has lost most of its power. The federal government has fallen into an overwhelming pattern of deficits. Since 1973, the federal budget has been in surplus only four times, between 1998 and 2001. In fact, deficits have been the rule for most of our recent history. Using the budget to steer the economy requires making decisions that can shift the budget from surplus to deficit and back again. The overwhelming sea of red ink has the budget's engines stuck in one direction, constantly pumping stimulus into the economy. That, in turn, has left most of the work of steering the economy to the Federal Reserve, which has used its power to manage interest rates and the money supply (called **monetary policy**).[7] As deficits have become a near-permanent condition of fiscal policy, the Fed and its monetary policy have become the only game in town. In fact, when the collapse of the financial markets crippled the national—and the global—economy in 2008, it was the Fed and its central bank partners around the world that provided most of the tools to cushion the fall.

Most economists agree that continued huge deficits are unsupportable. The more money the government borrows, the less there is left for private investment (and thus to feed future growth). They argue that big deficits over the long run make inflation worse than it would otherwise be. Economists contend that large deficits would tie the federal government's hands in fighting future recessions, since there would be limited ability to increase spending and thus stimulate the economy. Finally, they conclude that deficits over the long run would worsen the nation's international trading position by eroding the value of the dollar. In the short run, deficits can help the government negotiate through difficult economic problems, but budget deficits over the long run are dangerous. The larger the deficit, the more the federal budget must be devoted simply to paying interest. The more money paid in interest, the less money that is available for the things (from new roads to new weapons) that public officials really want to spend money on.

Economists do not necessarily argue that the federal budget must be balanced all the time. Rather, the consensus among most economists is two-fold: that it's important not to constantly grow the debt to the point that rising interest payments make it hard to pay for other government services on which citizens depend, or that the tax burden drains the private sector's ability to grow jobs and create a high quality of life.

Over the years, the share of the budget devoted to interest has dropped, from more than 15 percent in 1996 to 6 percent in 2015. Even the smaller percentage in 2015, however, amounted to $223 billion that could not be spent on other programs. Moreover, large interest payments give elected officials little maneuvering room, since interest must always be the first expense paid from a government budget. (Why? If governments miss interest payments, no one will want to lend to them in the future, and no government can survive for long without the ability to borrow.)

THE ECONOMY'S EFFECT ON THE BUDGET. If the budget has become a less useful tool in managing the economy, the economy's performance has become a much more important force in shaping the budget. In general, a strong economy helps lower the budget deficit by increasing revenues. In the first part of 2013, for example, the projected federal deficit shrank by $200 billion—not because any federal official did anything different but because the economy performed better than expected, which increased federal tax collections. Budget officials can often find their estimates swinging by enormous amounts without changing anything. In general, a strong economy shrinks deficits, as revenues go up (a product of better economic growth) and expenditures go down (with fewer individuals receiving benefits tied to income). A weaker economy drives deficits up.

Budget making, at all government levels, depends critically on estimating the likely levels of economic growth, unemployment, inflation, and interest rates. Minor errors in the estimates can have huge effects. Very small errors in economic forecasts can have huge effects on the deficit. Moreover, these effects tend to build on themselves over time, with relatively modest forecasting errors swamping painful political compromises. Imagine, for example, making a decision to increase taxes or cut spending by $200 billion in a single year, only to have changes in the economy swamp these decisions. That in turn tempts budget analysts to choose economic forecasts that make their job easier. As Rudolph G. Penner, former head of the Congressional Budget Office, and Alan J. Abramson explain,

> Changing a deficit estimate by $10 billion by changing an economic forecast is a minor statistical event. Changing policies sufficiently to alter a deficit estimate by $10 billion is a significant political event. This asymmetry creates an enormous temptation to achieve a given target deficit reduction by adopting optimistic economic assumptions rather than by cutting programs or raising taxes.[8]

That can make it possible for deficits to shrink or even evaporate in the long run. It also helps explain why that hopeful long-run day never seems to arrive. As former Citicorp president Walter Wriston put it, "A government budget deficit is the intersection of two wild guesses [on expenditures and revenues] a year from now."[9]

These crosscurrents—the effect of the budget on the economy and vice versa—have become more important through the years. The federal budget is far greater than the sum of the government's expenditures and revenues: it is a statement of the government's relationship with the rest of the economy and of political officials' attempts to influence economic performance. The crosscurrents have also affected the way the budget is made. The technique and politics of forecasting have taken on a far larger role, and this in turn has opened a new arena in which fundamental budget battles are fought. Finally, the crosscurrents have enhanced the role of the staff members who run the computer models that produce the economic estimates.[10]

The Political Development of the Budgetary Process

Budgeting is, of course, much more than an economic decision about how to allocate citizens' wealth among governmental programs. Budgeting embodies fundamental political choices, both about values—which programs get funded and which do not—and institutions, especially the relative sway of the legislative and executive branches of government.

Forecasts of low economic growth, or even a recession, can prove especially difficult for policymakers. A slow economy drives up spending, shrinks tax revenue, and increases the deficit. Therefore, it is little wonder that top officials shy away from forecasts of a slow economy, which make budgeting even more painful. In the Carter administration, Alfred Kahn, adviser on inflation and later chairman of the Council on Wage and Price Stability, got into trouble with the president's political advisers for talking too much about the risks of a recession. He continued to insist on speaking his mind, but he changed his language. In briefings, he substituted the word *banana* for *recession*—and then talked in detail about the possibility that the economy might encounter a banana. For politicians, as Clinton political strategist James Carville was fond of pointing out, "It's the economy, stupid." The economy always has enormous political implications for political campaigns—and big effects on the budget. It's little wonder that the economics and politics of the budget are so closely intertwined.

THE BUDGET AND POLITICS. Americans have always had deep distrust for how public officials dealt with their money. After all, the American Revolution was, in part, about a dispute between the colonists and King George about taxes, and the tensions bubbled over during the Boston Tea Party. When the new country came to life, there were big debates about how best to organize the country's financial operations. Alexander Hamilton worked hard to build a strong financial system, but the tensions were so fierce that Vice President Aaron Burr killed him in a duel—and set the stage for *Hamilton*, a Broadway rap-based musical that won a Grammy Award and a Pulitzer Prize and received a record-breaking sixteen Tony Award nominations.

The early debates were huge. Congress quickly decided that the Departments of State and War would each be headed by a single secretary, but it considered putting the Treasury under the control of a board (so that no single person could become too powerful) and keeping the board under its own tight control (so that the legislative branch could closely oversee how the executive spent money). Although the Constitution clearly granted the executive branch the power to wage war and make treaties, it gave Congress the power to coin money, levy taxes, and appropriate money. The Constitution explicitly requires that all tax measures originate in the House of Representatives, the body that the founders believed would be the "people's house," to make sure that citizens had a voice in their own taxation. Ever since, budgetary politics has been a forum for sharp competition between the president and Congress.[11] Two different national banks collapsed under populist pressure—and the Internal Revenue Service has long been one of Americans' least favorite agencies. The dispute over whether the federal government should assume the Revolutionary War–era debts of the state governments became one of the most heated battles between Hamilton, who argued that was the essential foundation for the new nation's stability, and Thomas Jefferson, who feared it would lead to a more centralized government. That battle shaped the nation's financial future. It also led to some of the most powerful scenes in *Hamilton*.

For America's first century, federal budgeting was mostly a congressional function. In fact, the executive budget was little more than the Treasury Department's assembly of agency and departmental requests. Congress was the central force in budgeting.

RIPPED FROM THE HEADLINES

Can State Governments Stop Earthquakes?
Theme: Performance

Scientists were perplexed at a string of 2015 earthquakes that plagued the central and eastern parts of the United States. The outbreak seemed highest in Oklahoma, Kansas, Texas, Colorado, New Mexico, and Arkansas, with 7 million residents at risk.

For a nation long focused on watching for the Big One in California, the outbreak of earthquakes seemed bizarre. What was causing them? And could government stop them? To the surprise of many observers, the answer to the second question seemed to be: yes.

Scientists investigating the phenomenon zeroed in on oil drilling—not the drilling process itself, but what happens in the aftermath. New drilling techniques involve injection of water thousands of feet underground to extract oil and gas. The process increases the pressure on deep geological formations and, in some cases, actually causes faults to move.

In some states, officials imposed drilling restrictions, and there were dramatic results. Oklahoma, which had experienced six earthquakes a day in 2015, saw the number drop to two per day. In Kansas, the prevalence of earthquakes dropped to one-fourth the previous levels.

The restrictions were a hot political issue. Drilling brought both jobs and badly needed state revenue. Nobody wanted to do without either, but nobody wanted to subject citizens to damaged buildings or rattled nerves. Oklahoma Governor Mary Fallin, a Republican, was not sure about the connection between the disposal of waste water from the drilling and the earthquakes. But after feeling her own walls shake, she decided she need to act. Fallin spent $1.4 million of state emergency funds to improve the state's research and monitoring of the quakes. "I'm committed to funding seismic research, bringing on line advanced technology and more staff to fully support our regulators as they take meaningful action on earthquakes," she said. Better research, she concluded, would provide the evidence the state needed to determine the best steps for promoting—and regulating—oil production in Oklahoma.

Source: Jen Fifield, Pew Charitable Trusts, "Can States Stop Man-Made Earthquakes?" *Route Fifty* (July 14, 2016), http://www.routefifty.com/2016/07/states-stop-man-made-earthquakes/129918/?oref=govexec_today_nl.

THE RISE OF PRESIDENTIAL POWER. At the beginning of the twentieth century, the Progressive movement increased citizens' concern about the management of government at all levels. Budgetary reform swept state and local government as part of the broader trend toward strengthened executive powers.[12] By the end of World War I, the congressionally dominated system had proved inadequate for managing the federal government's vastly expanded fiscal functions, and the budget-reform movement launched in the states and cities bubbled up to the federal level.

The culmination of this movement was passage of the Budget and Accounting Act in 1921, which revolutionized federal budgeting. For the first time, the president was to submit an annual budget to Congress. A Bureau of the Budget was created in the Treasury Department (and later moved to the president's own executive office) to assemble and adjust, if necessary, the department's requests to conform to the president's program.[13] Meanwhile, the Treasury Department's auditing functions were transferred to Congress's new General Accounting Office (GAO, which was renamed the Government Accountability Office in 2004). By gaining the authority to produce their own budget, presidents acquired leverage over both the executive branch departments and agencies—which first had to bargain with the president before having their requests sent to Congress—and Congress itself, because the document submitted by the president would frame the terms of debate.

The Budget and Accounting Act of 1921 thus divided the traditional budget functions into areas of executive and legislative supremacy: budget preparation and execution in the executive branch, budget appropriation and postaudit in the legislative branch, and shared executive-legislative authority over budget control.[14] The division has always been sloppy, but the act nevertheless put the president into a position of preeminence not previously known.

The 1921 act proved a significant advance in presidential power—in many ways, it marked the emergence of the modern presidency. It was the beginning of fifty years of steadily growing presidential dominance over Congress in the budgetary process. While Congress has tried, especially since the mid-1970s, to regain its earlier preeminence in the budgetary process, the president has held the upper hand over most of the years since then.[15] These struggles between the branches have played themselves out in the arenas of budget making, budget appropriation, and budget execution. (Chapter 14 deals with a related part of the budgetary process, postaudit and performance measurement.)

BUDGET PREPARATION

We now turn to the basic steps for budgeting, which all levels of government share. The first step is preparation of the budget: a set of spending and revenue plans combined in a single document.[16] While the details vary around the country, the process typically includes both top-down and bottom-up features.[17]

Budget Targets: Top-Down

A government's budget is not simply a collection of agencies' spending requests. Instead, each government's executive—whether mayor, city manager, county administrator, governor, or president—sets broad targets for overall spending and revenues. Executives naturally want to shape taxing and spending to meet their basic policy goals, so early in the year, they work with their budget staffs to define those targets and to send them to the operating agencies. These targets flow from estimates made by the executive's budget staff: how expected changes in the economy will affect revenues and expenditures (will the economy's growth bring more tax collection, or will its slump put higher demands on welfare?), how demographic changes are likely to affect existing programs (will more school-age children require the school board to hire more teachers?), and what new initiatives the executive wants to launch (how much money will a new mass-transit upgrade cost?).[18]

Budget preparation focuses on producing a budget by the start of the fiscal year. (At the federal level, the fiscal year begins on October 1. Most state and local governments have a July 1 start for their fiscal years.) Well before the beginning of the fiscal year, economic forecasters estimate the revenue that will likely be available. They also calculate the likely costs of past decisions, such as a multiyear legislation (a five-year job training program that might be in year two) and automatic programs (such as spending for pensions, which are based on formulas). This produces a three-part package of spending, revenue, and economic estimates, which form the basis for the executive's initial decisions. These decisions produce targets that go out to agency heads, who then break down the targets for their operating units. Budget proposals, including requests for new money for new programs, then flow back up the chain to the budget director. Final appeals go to the executive in the weeks before the budget is officially submitted to the legislature (Congress, state legislature, county board, or city council) for review and action.

Preparing the federal budget thus begins nearly a full year before the finished document is submitted to Congress, more than a year and a half before the fiscal year begins, and two and a half years before the fiscal year ends. Getting the numbers right requires an especially good crystal ball. It also makes constant tinkering inevitable. At any given time, administrators must deal with three different budget years: executing the current fiscal year's budget, defending the next year's requests before the legislature, and making budget estimates for the year after that. Any year's budget battle is thus actually part of interlocking skirmishes that stretch over many years.[19]

Budgets and Incrementalism: Bottom-Up

The top-down snapshot is the big picture, full of worries about the size of the budget deficit, the budget's role in macroeconomic policy, and large-scale policy changes such as the introduction of new defense systems, schools, or highways. However, the picture is much different from the lower-level administrators' point of view.

The central theory (both descriptively and prescriptively) of bottom-up budgeting is **incrementalism**, originally put forth by Aaron Wildavsky. It builds on the theory of incremental decision making explored in Chapter 10 and captures the twin threads of that theory. Incrementalism, Wildavsky argues, is both the best description of how budgeting works and the best prescription for how it *should* work. How much should an agency official request in the budget preparation process? How should it answer V. O. Key's basic question about how resources are to be allocated? Wildavsky's answer was that officials do, and should, begin with their budget base and ask for a "fair-share" increase (or, in bad times, protecting the budget against more than their fair share of cuts). "The base is the general expectation among the participants that programs will be carried on at close to the going level of expenditures," Wildavsky explained. The increments are relatively small increases over the existing base that reflect the agency's share of changes in the budgetary pie.[20]

In budgeting, incrementalism has two important implications. First, no one really considers every amount for every item in the budget. The details are far too many for anyone to examine everything, so it is far easier and, Wildavsky argues, more rational to focus on *changes*. Second, the real political battles focus on the changes. Budgeting is a battle fought on the margins, with the sharpest struggles focused on changes in the distribution of the government's pie.

Incremental theory, both as a description of how budgeting operates and as a primer on how agency officials should behave, has dominated the budgeting debate since the first publication of Wildavsky's work in 1966.[21] Many theorists have taken sharp issue with his view, for three reasons. First, incremental budgeting begins with the budget base, but the definition of that concept is anything but clear. The budget base can be the current estimate of spending in the previous year, although that estimate constantly changes as legislators act on the budget and agencies carry out their programs. It can be the cost of continuing current activities at the same level, which includes increases for inflation and population shifts and decreases for improved productivity. Finally, it can be a spending level set by law, which often can be a different amount from the first two.

Second, budget experts do not always make changes from the existing level of spending in small increments. On average, budgeting does appear incremental, but the averages hide the rich politics of budgeting: aggressive program managers seeking to build budgets, budget officials seeking to keep a ceiling on total spending, and executives and their staffs seeking to pursue new initiatives.[22] Big, nonincremental changes sometimes do occur. In the turbulent weeks after the September 11, 2001, terrorist attacks, the Bush administration led the campaign to make all airport screeners federal employees in an enormous new federal agency, the Transportation Security Administration.

Third, the real focus of budgetary politics is not changes in the budgets for agencies but in the budgets for their programs. The competitive success of alternative programs, not changes in the budgets of agencies, occupies budget makers. In that arena, policy entrepreneurs have the power to build the strongest political case for their ideas.[23]

Although the incrementalism model has many shortcomings, from areas such as fair-share increases to the budget base, it nevertheless continues to have a very powerful force on budgeting. Most budgeters tend to think about their budgets as a search for increases over their base. Most reporters focus on those debates. Most reformers seek to find some way to break the incremental pattern. Incrementalism tends to capture the way most people think about budgeting. It also captures how it most often works—and even how many people think it *ought* to work.

BREAKING THE INCREMENTAL PATTERN. Especially since the mid-1960s, chief executives have experimented with reforms to break the incremental pattern. Most notable was Lyndon Johnson's **Planning-Programming-Budgeting System (PPBS)**, which aimed to bring a rational, planning-based approach to budgeting. In 1961, Secretary of Defense Robert McNamara introduced PPBS in the Pentagon.[24] The technique involved three phases: (1) planning, in which top-level managers developed five-year strategies for defense activities; (2) programming, in which the strategies were transformed into detailed descriptions of the department's needs, including which weapons systems had to be purchased on what schedule; and (3) budgeting, in which officials transformed the program into year-by-year budget requests. The basic idea was to link the annual budgetary process with long-range plans instead of making haphazard requests. Furthermore, each branch of the service was to budget by program instead of by organizational unit. The Pentagon, for example, would decide whether the nation's strategic needs required a new jet fighter and, if so, what capabilities it ought to have. Program budgeting, McNamara hoped, would drive down the cost of buying weapons systems by reducing competition among the services for their own individually tailored weapons systems.

President Johnson was so pleased with the results in the Department of Defense that he extended the technique in 1965 to almost all federal civilian departments and agencies. Each agency submitted its budget to the Bureau of the Budget (now the Office of Management and Budget, or OMB) by program.[25] The program budgets were, in turn, supported by massive memoranda that considered "all relevant outputs, costs, and financing needs" as well as the "benefits and costs of alternative approaches" to solving problems. Each agency also prepared a five-year projection of its future programs and financial requirements. The plans, however, were often "lengthy wish lists of what the agencies would like to spend on their programs if no fiscal constraints were imposed." The connection between PPBS paperwork and what agencies actually planned to do was often amorphous. Since Congress continued to run its appropriations process the old way, the link between PPBS and congressional decisions was fuzzy indeed.[26]

In terms of its original objectives, PPBS was a failure. It never transformed the base of government planning or linked budgets—government's inputs—to its outputs. In the foreign governments and nearly all state and local governments that have tried PPBS, it has produced similar results.[27] Nevertheless, PPBS's long-term impact was substantial. It brought into the government a number of able analysts, many of whom remained.[28] It acquainted a large number of top executives and career civil servants with a new style of analysis, emphasizing clear objectives, alternative ways to meet goals, and quantification of benefits and costs. The regular budgetary process now transmits multiyear projections. Moreover, the Pentagon still actively operates a modified PPBS. Defense officials continue to develop long-range plans, translate those plans into programs, and develop the programs into budgets.

The important lessons here are these. Budgetary problems are huge and fundamental. Chief executives constantly want to improve their control over budgetary decisions. There is an irresistible yearning to study more, analyze more, and know more about the budget—and all important public policy decisions—in the hope that better analysis will produce better decisions. In fact, more and better analysis *does* improve decisions. But because these decisions capture the most fundamental political judgments, politics—and political games—inevitably intrude. Big analytical reforms tend to erode over time, as their warts become more clear, but they never go away. Instead, they leave important residue that continues to shape budgetary decisions.[29] New strategies to improve the budget pop up, prompted by the same instincts, and the pattern repeats itself. Cynics point to this as a case of politicians failing to learn the central lessons of politics. Optimists point to the improvements that have been made over time. One thing is certain: this pattern will not end any time soon.

The lessons continued with the Nixon administration, when OMB attempted a different strategy, **management by objectives (MBO)**, intended to strengthen the ability of managers to manage. Agency heads and their principal executives would focus on quantified objectives to be attained in the coming year and then break down each objective into targets for achievement in, say, each quarter year; this process would then be repeated in turn for each subordinate. MBO had a mixed record: it made a significant contribution in some departments and bureaus, but it failed and was quickly abandoned in many others. As with PPBS, there has been "a noticeable disenchantment with MBO as a panacea in the government."[30]

When Jimmy Carter took office in 1977, he brought with him the **zero-base budgeting (ZBB)** approach that he had used as governor of Georgia. Despite its name, ZBB was not budgeting from a zero base. Instead, budgeters began from a certain level of spending (say, 80 percent of current expenditures). They then assembled "decision packages" (consisting of different ways of increasing the level of services) and ranked them. In this way, decision makers could set priorities for spending increases.[31] ZBB seemed attractive at first. It pushed away the assumptions of incrementalism—political battles over increments to the base—and substituted focused analysis on spending. It's no surprise, however, that politics soon overtook ZBB. Agency officials discovered how to game the process. For example, they sometimes ranked very low a project they knew would never be cut, and they ranked high projects they favored but worried might be vulnerable. ZBB, moreover, was an enormous burden of analysis and paperwork for budget makers, which undermined support for ZBB at the federal level. At the state and local levels, however, many governments continued to find the process helpful for making choices within their smaller budgets.[32]

Executives have since tried a variety of performance-based tools to get greater leverage over the budgetary process. Bill Clinton had his **National Performance Review**, which managers used to devise strategies for improving government operations while setting top-down targets

| Figure 11.1 | Changes in the Composition of Federal Spending, 1962–2012 |

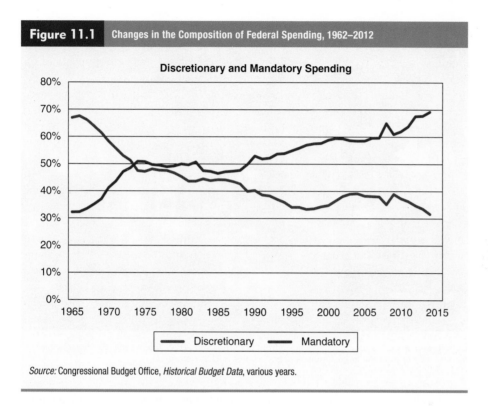

Discretionary and Mandatory Spending

Source: Congressional Budget Office, *Historical Budget Data*, various years.

for reducing the number of government employees. George W. Bush instituted a new **Program Assessment Rating Tool (PART)** and sought to integrate measures of agency performance with budgetary decisions. Barack Obama used a more decentralized management agenda designed to improve the crossboundary management of government programs. Similar strategies have emerged at the state and local levels of government.

From this ongoing cauldron of innovation, three conclusions have emerged. First, every chief executive now feels obliged to launch a major reform in analysis and management to improve control over the budget. Second, few of these reforms endure, because they rarely give executives real leverage over decisions that are inevitably political. Third, the impulse toward reform leads new administrations to try new changes, all in the hope of getting better control over the most fundamental decisions that governments make.

THE RISE OF THE UNCONTROLLABLES. Even more important, more government spending has become dictated by past policy decisions, especially at the federal level. At the federal level, budgeters encounter the stark reality of **uncontrollable expenditures,** which are dictated by mandatory formulas for programs like Social Security and Medicare. As Figure 11.1 shows, discretionary spending—the share of the budget not locked in by these mandatory formulas or by interest in the debt—fell from 67 percent in 1966 to 32 percent in 2015. At the same time, mandatory spending (including entitlement programs, like Social Security and Medicare, where recipients are entitled to benefits by law) grew from 32 percent to 69 percent. Even with "discretionary" programs, however, government officials often have little real discretion. Having signed contracts for new weapons

Laura McDermott/Bloomberg via Getty Images

Detroit residents celebrated the city's move from bankruptcy in 2014. Tough fiscal decisions helped the city recover from the largest municipal bankruptcy in U.S. history.

systems, defense planners don't want to walk away from their investment. We count on airport screeners to get us through airports and Social Security workers to process payments for retirees. We don't want to shut down federal prisons and national parks, and no one wants to send the armed forces home without pay. In any given year, the share of the budget over which the president and Congress have any real control is thus very, very small—just a few percent of the total spending. It's little wonder, then, that budgetary politics has become more intense, with tougher battles over smaller pots of money.

State and local governments do not tend to measure uncontrollables as explicitly as the federal government does. But many state governments find that formula-based spending for many programs, from aid to local schools to money for highways, takes up a growing share of their budgets. Moreover, years of tight budgets and taxpayer resistance to higher taxes have dramatically reduced the flexibility of state and local officials for reshaping their budget decisions. Although they are not constrained by entitlements in the same way as the federal budget, the political implications for state and local budgets are much the same.

APPROPRIATION BY THE LEGISLATURE

Although the submission of the executive budget is always an event of great theater, the budget is ultimately only a set of estimates and recommendations. In the American system of government, however, the executive proposes the budget and the legislative branch must approve taxes and spending.[33] That affects the executive's proposal in two ways. First, executives behave according to the **rule of anticipated reactions**—they shape their recommendations according to how they think legislators will react to them.[34] A budget maker who expects legislators to cut the agency's spending by 10 percent may submit a request 15 or 20 percent higher. Legislators, of course, understand this classic ruse. They estimate how much padding they think has been built into the budget and cut accordingly. The result is an intricate chess match.

Second, when the economy is weak, tax revenues suffer and executives conclude that cuts are inevitable. They sometimes propose cuts—but in areas with strong political support, betting that legislators won't dare cut them. This is a maneuver so classic that it even has a name: the **Washington Monument ploy**. When pressed to make tough budget decisions, agencies offer to cut their most popular programs (which, for the National Park Service, would be closing the Washington Monument), with full knowledge that legislators will never allow such cuts to take effect (see Case Study 11.2 for the background on the Washington Monument ploy and for a recent example of how budgeters have actually used it). The executive may also propose new taxes to bring the budget into balance, and then leave to legislators the tough decision to reject the taxes or risk a deficit.[35] Very experienced budgeting officials have a vast collection of games they're especially skilled at playing.

Congressional Budget Reforms

To gain better control of the federal budget process, Congress passed the Congressional Budget Act in 1974.[36] The act shifted the start of the fiscal year from July 1 to October 1 to give Congress more time to complete its work on the budget. The act also mandated that the president must present a "current services budget" projection each year, which is an estimate of the cost of continuing all of the previous year's programs in the new fiscal year at the same level and without policy changes. That, members of Congress hoped, would allow them to focus attention on changes in existing programs. The act also created new budget committees in each house and instituted the following three-part legislative process to accompany them:

1. *Setting the totals.* For the first time, Congress obligated itself to prepare a **legislative budget**: an estimate of total expenditures and revenues—and thus of the deficit. To do the job, the 1974 act established a new Committee on the Budget in each house, charged with creating a single resolution that combined all spending proposals.

2. *Authorizing programs.* Next, the subject-area committees create **authorizations** for programs under their purview. These authorizations, approved by both houses of Congress and signed by the president, can be for one year (including much of the government's routine operations), for several years (including many defense programs), or for permanent programs (including Social Security), which remain in effect until the basic law is changed. These authorizations set ceilings on the money that Congress can spend on programs or, in the case of permanent authorizations, define the standards by which benefits are to be paid.

3. *Appropriating money.* While authorizations create the programs, **appropriations** provide the money to fund them. Congress can authorize a program without providing any appropriations for it, and it often authorizes higher spending than can be covered by the appropriations it is willing to provide. The reverse, of course, does not happen, since appropriations cannot exceed the original authorization. Like authorizations, appropriations can last for varying lengths of time. The appropriations committees in each house decide how much money should actually be spent by recommending **budget authority.**

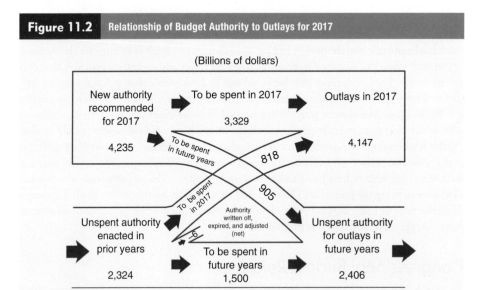

Figure 11.2 Relationship of Budget Authority to Outlays for 2017

(Billions of dollars)

Source: U.S. Office of Management and Budget, *Budget of the United States Government: Fiscal Year 2017, Analytical Perspectives* (Washington, D.C.: OMB, 2016), 110, https://www.whitehouse.gov/sites/default/files/omb/budget/fy2017/assets/spec.pdf.

This three-step process, however, does not precisely define the issue that gets the most attention: how much money the government actually spends, and how large the deficit might be. The total of spending—known as **outlays**—is an estimate of how much money federal agencies will also spend during the coming fiscal year. The projected deficit is the result of subtracting outlays from estimated revenues.

As Figure 11.2 shows, estimating outlays (and, therefore, the deficit) is an extremely complicated process. Analysts must determine how much budget authority from past years will be used in a given fiscal year, how much new budget authority will be created and spent, how much previous budget authority will expire at the end of its time limit, and how much budget authority will be carried over into subsequent years. For some uncontrollable spending such as Medicare, the outlays depend on how many people get sick and what kinds of treatment they require. Outlays can vary according to many factors, such as the unemployment rate, the progress in building a new fighter at an aircraft plant, or how many natural disasters strike. Thus, no matter how close a watch Congress keeps on its books, it has only a loose rein on outlays in any given year. Hard-fought congressional deficit battles, which revolve around budget authority levels, can be undone when outlay totals do not cooperate—if, for example, economic growth proves sluggish, interest rates rise, or unemployment surges.

Bumps in the Federal Budget Process

The budget process has always been difficult, but problems have grown to the breaking point in recent years. There are several reasons.

First, a large part of the budget is classified, and this **black budget** does not receive the same oversight as other kinds of federal spending. The only people in government who know what or how much is in this black budget cannot tell, and the size and scale of these secret projects are hidden from all but a handful of members of Congress. Some projects have secret code names, such as "Tractor Rose" or "Retract Larch," while others are funded by vague appropriations that do not describe what the money buys. The black budget hides the size of the Central Intelligence Agency's budget, spy satellites, research and development of top-secret defense programs, and the operation of at least some of the military's drone programs as part of the war on terror. Officials who work in the programs often sport embroidered patches. One for "Project Zipper" shows a smiling face with sunglasses and a zipped mouth and the motto "We make threats not promises." Another has a mushroom on a dark background—mushrooms are grown in the dark—and the motto *Semper en Obscurus* ("Always in the dark"). A third quotes the first-century Roman emperor Caligula with *Oderint Dum Metuant*, which means "Let them hate so long as they fear."[37] Following Edward Snowden's leak in 2013 of an enormous quantity of classified information, including reports on the black budget itself, the entire process came under much tougher scrutiny—but not more transparency.

Officials who work on classified black budget programs within the Department of Defense sometimes wear embroidered arm patches, like the one pictured here.

Second, although the shift in the start of the federal fiscal year from July 1 to October 1 was designed to give Congress more time to finish its work, Congress has fallen further and further behind in its schedule. As noted budget expert Philip G. Joyce has found, Congress managed to get its work done on time just three times since 1977 (in fiscal years 1989, 1995, and 1997).[38] When Congress can't complete its work, it has resorted to passing **continuing resolutions**, which allow the government to continue operating until Congress passes a budget—or another continuing resolution. Sometimes (as in 1979) Congress has operated the entire year on a single continuing resolution. At other times, it has passed a flurry of continuing resolutions, with the record at twenty-one in 2001, Joyce found. Over time, Congress has proven less able to pass budgets. The strengthening of Congress's budgetary role, envisioned in the 1974 reforms, has gradually fallen apart.

Third, the consequences of Congress's procedural failures have become larger. If Congress fails to pass appropriations, no federal agency can spend money, except for emergency operations. In 1995, that led to a five-day shutdown in November, because of fierce battles between the Clinton administration and Republican House Speaker Newt Gingrich. Continuing skirmishes led to a twenty-one-day shutdown from late December 1995 through early January 1996, which was then capped by an epic blizzard that further crippled the capital. In the Obama administration, a shutdown ran more than two weeks in 2013. During such shutdowns, essential employees (like air traffic controllers and federal prison guards) can continue to work, but other employees must go home and not be paid, a process known as **furloughs**. (Many state and local governments, facing big budget crises in the late 2000s, likewise relied on furloughs for budget savings.)

In the 2013 shutdown, "essential" federal employees, like air traffic controllers, border patrol agents, the Secret Service, and the Capitol Police, were told to continue to come to work. Other employees, including employees at the Environmental Protection Agency, the National Aeronautics and Space Administration (NASA), and the Library of Congress, stayed home, and they were told they could not even use their government-issued BlackBerry smartphones or check their government email accounts. At first, the Pentagon announced that the football teams at the service academies could not play their scheduled games but, after days of derisive laughter, top officials ruled that the Navy, Army, and Air Force could play after all. Most of the Pentagon's civilian workers were originally told to stay home, but they were told part way through the shutdown that they were essential enough they could come to work. Over time, more functions have been declared "essential" and Congress has tended to provide back pay to federal employees thrown out of work. The result has been a growth of procedural chaos without a real impact on budget policy—except increasing the uncertainty of those who manage and rely on government programs.

Fourth, Congress passed a law in 2001 that required automatic budget cuts—**sequestration**, in the budget's arcane language—if it did not pass a budget that kept the budget under deficit targets. No one really expected the automatic cuts would take place. Members of Congress saw it as a tool to create implications so unthinkable that they would have no choice but to agree on a budget. In practice, this has not worked well and has led to even more uncertainty in the budgetary process—although it has helped restrain the growth of federal spending.

Several headline-grabbing stories demonstrated the tensions of the 2013 government shutdown. Three days into the shutdown, the Secret Service and the Capitol Police found themselves in a tense car chase. A dental hygienist from Stamford, Connecticut, tried to ram her car into barriers protecting the White House, struck a Secret Service agent, and then raced her car at speeds of eighty miles per hour down Pennsylvania Avenue to the Capitol. She led federal officers on a wild chase around the building until they cornered her car against a barricade and then shot her when she tried to bolt from the car. Nervous members of Congress were caught inside the Capitol as the building was locked down. In guarding the White House and the Capitol, the Secret Service and the Capitol Police were surely essential employees—and they put their lives on the line even though they weren't being paid. Meanwhile, hundreds of miles above them, the International Space Station was circling with two American astronauts on board. Not only were they not being paid, Karen Nyberg and Mike Hopkins couldn't share what they saw with Americans below because NASA's website was dark because of the shutdown. Nyberg and Hopkins sent back some remarkable photos, but they had to use their personal Twitter accounts.[39] (The NASA workers and contractors ensuring their safety, of course, were "essential.")

The 2013 shutdown ricocheted around the nation and around the world. Visitors to the American cemetery in France, where soldiers stormed the Normandy beaches during World War II, discovered that the gate was locked and the American flag wasn't flying. The scenic roads through the Great Smoky Mountains National Park in Tennessee were closed, at the peak autumn foliage season. The Tennessee state government, along with two county governments that had seen tourist income evaporate, provided their own funds to get the park reopened. The New York state government paid to reopen the Statue of Liberty. The families of four soldiers killed in action in Afghanistan were told that the government could not pay for their funerals or provide death benefits, until the Pentagon worked out a deal with the Fisher House Foundation to make the payments until the government could reimburse them later. As the

When Congress and President Obama failed to agree on a plan to fund the federal government in 2013, many parts of the federal government shut down. Some agencies, like the Department of Agriculture, simply had their websites go blank.

shutdown stretched into a second week, such stories continued to accumulate. Public disgust, directed especially at members of Congress, soared.

The 2013 government shutdown reminded us, yet again, that tough politics inevitably surrounds big decisions—and few decisions are bigger than those about taxing and spending. The shutdown also seriously damaged the congressional budget process, and close observers wondered whether the federal budget process had broken down completely. Lurching from one crisis to the next, with funding supplied through short-term continuing resolutions, was making it increasingly difficult for federal managers to plan anything. They were spending an inordinate amount of time trying to understand and cope with the uncertainties, for their own paychecks and for the operations they were responsible for managing. The real decisions on the budget were becoming increasingly disconnected from the formal process of submitting, debating, and approving it, and the short-term battles were increasingly separate from the fundamental long-term budgetary issues. Critics complained that the budgetary process was no longer accountable to the public—or to anyone else, for that matter. Even the most optimistic Washington observers concluded that budgeting had run amok.

One analyst warned of a budgetary "ice age"—with the process locked in "a frozen mass of spending priorities that no one has really chosen and that no one really likes."[40] Proposals surfaced to reform the budget, including creating a budget that would last two years instead of one and passing a constitutional amendment to require a balanced budget. None of the procedural fixes, however, offered much hope for resolving what, at their core, were political problems. In 1987, Senator Mark O. Hatfield (R-Ore.) captured the problem with an analysis that still rings true: "We are not going to work our way out of federal deficit difficulties with procedural gimmicks. There is nothing wrong with our present system if we summon the will to make it work. And if we do not have will, no new procedures will work any better." Carol G. Cox, president of the Committee for a Responsible Federal Budget, agreed: "These are not economic problems. They are not analytical problems. They are political problems."[41]

Of course, budget battles between the president and Congress are as old as the Republic, but the battles have unquestionably become fiercer since the mid-1960s. Divided party control of the executive and legislative branches accounts for some of the conflict. So too does the rise of entitlements, which focus more political attention on a smaller share of the budget. Even more fundamentally, the nation is in the midst of profound debate about how big government ought to be and what it ought to do. These big questions shape the process and the politics of the federal budgetary process.

For state and local governments, the issues are just as sharp—and just as grounded in politics. Governors in Kansas and Louisiana made big cuts in state spending on the promise of creating strong economic growth, but the promises went unmet. From 2015 to 2016, Illinois went without a state budget or an education plan for a year because legislators could not agree on spending. A 2015 study by the Volcker Alliance pointed to even more fundamental problems in state budgeting. Many states use one-time-only revenues to pay for recurring expenditures, which means they are always struggling to fill budget holes. It's tempting to postpone decisions into the future, which means that officials are always hopeful the economic situation will make it easier to solve budget problems—although it never does. Many states underfund maintenance of infrastructure, such as highways, bridges, and water systems (like the one in Flint), which means that the bills eventually become due—only at higher costs. And many states are underfunding their pension systems, which means they will have to dig deeper when employees retire—either by raising taxes, cutting spending, or both.[42]

BUDGET EXECUTION

Once the executive and legislature agree on a budget, the challenge falls to the executive to, well, execute the spending plan. While the importance of this stage of the budgetary process might seem obvious, Allen Schick has noted that these practices are a "dark continent" of budgeting.[43] The budget execution process is a delicate balance between ensuring that a program's legislative goals are served and providing adequate flexibility for administrators to do their work.

For legislators, it's a dual problem: making sure that executive branch officials do not exceed their authority to spend money and making sure that they implement the programs that legislators have approved. Either problem—doing more than the legislature approved or not doing all that the legislature expects—proves enormously frustrating to legislators. For executives, it's a matter of matching the resources they get with the laws they are charged with administering, and the appetite for results always exceeds the money available.

A critical piece of budget execution is management control, and "follow the money" is its basic commandment. The flow of money throughout the bureaucracy provides a valuable tool for controlling the implementation of governmental programs, and it provides important leverage on administrators' activities.[44] First, the money trail demonstrates who is doing what. The flow of cash doesn't tell us much about the quality of an agency's work, but it does tell us whether work is taking place. Overseeing the flow of cash is also very helpful in tracking the work of contractors and grantees who produce much of government's work.

Second, by controlling the flow of money, the executive can control the direction and pace of governmental activity. Managers sometimes presume that everyone within an organization is working toward the same goal, only to be surprised later by employees' actions that are grossly out of line with the organization's goals. The flow of money signals the goals an organization considers important. It is important managerially because it helps to secure a match between the organization's broader goals and the workers' individual goals.

Finally, the flow of money is important for reporting and evaluating an agency's performance. It can help managers to identify the "hot spots" that need attention, either because a unit is spending too much money too quickly (will the budget run out before the year is done?) or, paradoxically, because it is spending too little (does the unit have enough expertise to know how to manage the program?). More broadly, it provides important raw materials for program evaluation. By measuring what the money goes for, managers can take a first step toward determining a program's, and thus an agency's, efficiency and effectiveness.

Management control builds on the financial structure, Robert N. Anthony and David W. Young explain.[45] The financial structure, in turn, is constructed with the building blocks of accounts. Each function or agency, and each of their subunits, generally has an account code. Account number 3-45983-6803, for example, might identify precisely the source and use of the money: the first 3 might mean that the money comes from a particular funding source, such as an excise tax on gasoline. The 45983 might mean that the money is allocated to the field unit in charge of repairing roads in the southern part of the state. The 6803 might mean that the money is going to purchase asphalt patching material. Computerized reports allow managers to track the flow of money, monitor activities, and report back to the legislature about the results of the programs they've funded.

Weak accounting systems can cost the government vast amounts of money. GAO, for example, discovered that eighteen federal agencies paid 25 percent of their bills late, costing the government millions of dollars in penalties. Another 25 percent of the bills were paid too early, which meant that the government often had to borrow money, costing it $350 million annually in interest. The Department of Defense, meanwhile, could not account for over $600 million that foreign customers had forwarded for the purchase of weapons.[46]

Different governments operate by different systems, but they all rely on management control systems built on accounts.[47] While the intricacies of such fund accounting often seem boring to those worrying over broad legislative-executive conflicts and the politics of deficit reduction, they are anything but: fund accounting provides critical information about what government does and what happens to taxpayers' money. Management control gives executive branch officials important information about the behavior of those who implement governmental policies, both within and outside government. Through routine auditing functions, it provides the mechanism for discovering problems and correcting them before they become large. Most important, effective management control provides important leverage over the activities of government officials, contractors, and grantees and thus improves the chances for effective and efficient provision of public services.

BUDGETING FOR STATE AND LOCAL GOVERNMENTS

State and local governments face special budgeting challenges, just as the federal government does. Because of the vast array of subnational governments, there are many different state and local issues but they share several common features.

First, unlike the federal budget, state and local governments must balance their budgets. The federal government can print money and engage in long-term borrowing to cover its operating deficits. State and local governments cannot, often by law and constitution and always by accepted practice. If state and local governments suffer a temporary shortage, they can slide deficits over into the next fiscal year, dip into rainy day funds, or engage in short-term borrowing, but they cannot engage in the long-term patterns of debt that shape so much of

DIVING INTO DATA

Few topics in American government attract fiercer debate than the size of the federal government and the battles over how best to cut government spending. To understand those battles, it's important to begin with a look at the actual trends in federal spending.

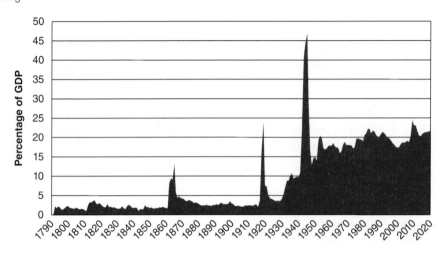

Source: USGovernmentSpending.com, http://www.usgovernmentspending.com/spending_chart_1792_2020USp_16s1li011mcn_F0t.

QUESTIONS

1. The data show total federal government spending as a percentage of gross domestic product (GDP), the total of goods and services produced in the domestic economy. Why is this a better measure of long-term spending trends than simply showing total spending?

2. How would you explain the large spikes in spending that occur periodically throughout the country's history?

3. What is the overall trend of spending? What explanation would you have for this?

federal budgeting. A steady pattern of such borrowing, however, can dig them into deep holes, and they don't have the federal government's tools for getting out.

Second, state and local governments draw fundamental distinctions between their operating budget (to cover the cost of day-to-day functions) and **capital budgets** (to cover the cost of long-term expenses for equipment and facilities). In general, state and local governments borrow to fund capital expenditures. The basic principle of capital budgeting is that the term of the loan ought to match the life of the equipment or facility. A state or local government might issue a twenty-year bond to pay for a sewage treatment plant expected to last two decades or a ten-year bond for a new fire engine. Taxes pay for operating expenses, like the salaries of firefighters and police officers. The federal government operates on a cash basis, and a dollar spent for a long-range bomber that flies fifty years or more (like the famous B-52, older than most of the pilots flying it) is counted the same as a dollar spent on a piece of paper used to scribble a quick note.

Third, budget practice varies widely on what happens if the legislature cannot pass a budget. In some states, like Wisconsin, state activities continue automatically at the same level if the budget isn't passed. In most states, failing to pass a budget means that the authority to spend money expires and shutdowns, from closing state campgrounds to laying off employees, are both fiscal reality and political theater. In the recent economic downturn, many state and local government employees found themselves subject to furloughs as their governments struggled to balance their budgets. In Detroit, the accumulation of a generation of budget problems and a shrinking economy led the city to declare bankruptcy in 2013, the largest municipal bankruptcy in the nation's history. The bankruptcy filing led to debates on questions ranging from whether the city could walk away from its pension obligations to retired employees to whether it should sell works of art by masters like Matisse that were owned by the Detroit Art Museum. Deep budget problems led the state to send managers to oversee many local governments, and it was a state manager who approved the decision in Flint to switch over the source of its water supply—and ultimately subjected city residents to the risks of lead poisoning.

In the long run, the federal government and state and local governments face many of the same big budget questions. Health care expenditures and pension costs are rising rapidly, and they will strain state and local finances for the next half-century.

However, the long-term fiscal picture for state and local governments raises many of the same big budget questions facing the federal government. Health care expenditures are rising rapidly and, GAO projects, will equal all other state expenditures by 2060.[48] The rise of these expenditures, coupled with the ongoing struggle to modernize tax systems to fit the twenty-first-century economy, threatens to drive state and local government budgets deeper into the red. These challenges will strain the budgets of state and local governments—and their budgetary policies and politics. The long-run picture will create fundamental decisions for state and local government officials in future decades.

CONCLUSION

Budgeting is central to the politics of the administrative process and is at the core of many issues, including the effect of government taxing and spending on the economy, the effect of the economy on the budget, the use of the budgetary arena for fighting (if not always resolving) battles between the legislative and executive branches, and ultimately the role of government in society. Budgeting is the arena that most fundamentally shapes public policy decisions and is responsible for carrying them out. By putting dollars together with often ambitious, and sometimes conflicting, goals, policymakers provide the resources needed to bring programs to life. Although the budgetary process varies greatly at all levels of government, the basic issues remain. V. O. Key's basic question is at the very center: "On what basis shall it be decided to allocate x dollars to activity A instead of activity B?"

The decision-making models discussed in Chapter 10 laid out the basic issues. The current chapter demonstrates the challenges of resolving them. It is one thing to discuss the basic models of decision making. It is another to breathe life into them, and that happens through the budget.

The next question, of course, is how to bring that breath fully to life: How does the administrative process adapt, refine, and sometimes even reshape the results of the legislative-executive battles? This is the process we call *implementation*, which we turn to in Chapter 12.

CASE 11.1

The movie *Zero Dark Thirty* won an Oscar for its portrayal of the daring raid on terrorist mastermind Osama bin Laden in 2011. The movie peels back just a bit of the secret intelligence world that made the raid possible. But the reality is a far larger and more sophisticated world than most Americans—in fact, most members of Congress—realized. For example, as SEAL Team Six was on the ground, they had help from incredibly sophisticated satellites overhead that picked up intelligence as the commandos broke into the compound. Before the SEAL team hit the ground, the federal National Reconnaissance Office had collected more than 387 high-resolution images of the compound, and a special outfit called the Tailored Access Operations group installed spyware and tracking devices on phones and computers used inside the al Qaeda network. A special stealth drone, the RQ-170, flew over Pakistan to pick up information. All this helped intelligence analysts determine they had zeroed in on their target. Afterward, managers managed to dig up an extra $2.5 million in money for overtime and extra computers to sift through all the intelligence that the SEALs brought out with them on their helicopters.[1]

All this came out of the federal government's "black budget," hidden in super-secret compartments of the national security budget. Only a handful of members of Congress know the details of what's inside the "black" part of the defense budget and, until very recently, almost no one outside the intelligence community even knew how large it was. Until, that is, former National Security Agency (NSA) analyst Edward Snowden leaked top-secret documents to the *Washington Post* and Britain's *Guardian* newspapers. From those materials came a first-ever portrait of the government's clandestine world.

As Figure 11.3 shows, the "black budget" was $52.6 billion in fiscal year 2013, with the CIA receiving the largest share. Close behind was the NSA, which intercepts foreign electronic signals to analyze intelligence, and the National Reconnaissance Office, which operates reconnaissance satellites. Two smaller operations rounded out the top five of the "black" world: the National Geospatial Intelligence Program, which develops imagery and mapping, and the General Defense Intelligence Program, which assesses foreign intelligence and capabilities. Together these five agencies accounted for over 85 percent of total "black budget" spending.

And who works inside this secret world? The leaked documents revealed that the intelligence community has almost 84,000 civilian employees, in the United States

---

Figure 11.3 **Top Five Recipients of Black Budget Spending**

Central Intelligence Agency

National Security Agency

National Reconnaissance Office

National Geospatial Intelligence Program

General Defense Intelligence Program

$0 $2 $4 $6 $8 $10 $12 $14 $16

Billions of U.S. Dollars (2013)

Source: Washington Post, http://www.washingtonpost.com/wp-srv/special/national/black-budget.

Note: The top five recipients amounted to approximately $45.1 billion of a total $52.6 billion (about 85.7%) in black budget spending. The remaining recipients included the Department of Justice, Office of the Director of National Intelligence, Specialized Reconnaissance Programs, Department of Defense Foreign Counter-Intelligence Program, Department of Homeland Security, and Department of Energy.

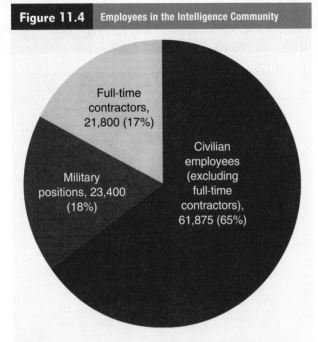

Figure 11.4 Employees in the Intelligence Community

Full-time contractors, 21,800 (17%)

Military positions, 23,400 (18%)

Civilian employees (excluding full-time contractors), 61,875 (65%)

Source: Washington Post, http://www.washingtonpost.com/wp-srv/special/national/black-budget.

and abroad (with the CIA accounting for the largest share, at more than 21,000). Military officials accounted for 23,400 employees, two-thirds of whom were in the NSA. As Figure 11.4 shows, about 17 percent of the total (21,800) are full-time contractors—like Edward Snowden (who worked for the NSA in Hawaii, after receiving his security clearance after a review by employees working under contract).

The bin Laden raid was only part of the huge "black" world. In 2011, the *Post* learned, the intelligence community undertook 231 offensive cybersecurity operations. In an operation under the code name GENIE, American experts hacked into foreign computers to allow the government to monitor their operations and control them from afar. Special targets were China, Iran, North Korea, and Russia, the top-secret documents said. And in an elite operation known as "the ROC" (short for the Remote Operations Center), elite NSA hackers ran a sophisticated effort to discover and exploit defenses in foreign computers.[2]

These "black" operations might not make for the blockbuster drama of a midnight raid by Navy SEALs. But that raid wouldn't have been possible without these "black" operatives—and the operatives define a vast new part of the nation's intelligence operations that had been largely invisible before Edward Snowden leaked the documents.

QUESTIONS TO CONSIDER

1. Are you surprised by the dimensions of the "black budget" and the people paid by it? What, if anything, surprises you most?

2. Consider the issues of accountability. Given the competing demands for transparency and oversight, do you believe that the "black budget" is sufficiently accountable?

3. Now consider the future of cybersecurity and "black ops" programs. They're sure to increase, as pressures mount about information security and terrorism. No intelligence official will want to manage programs through the pages of the *Washington Post* or the *Guardian*. What would you recommend for the future of budgeting for these programs?

NOTES

1. Craig Whitlock and Barton Gellman, "To Hunt Osama bin Laden, Satellites Watched over Abbottabad, Pakistan, and Navy SEALs," *Washington Post* (August 29, 2013), http://www.washingtonpost.com/world/national-security/to-hunt-osama-bin-laden-satellites-watched-over-abbottabad-pakistan-and-navy-seals/2013/08/29/8d32c1d6-10d5-11e3-b4cb-fd7ce041d814_story.html?wpisrc=al_national.

2. Barton Gellman and Ellen Nakashima, "U.S. Spy Agencies Mounted 231 Offensive Cyber-Operations in 2011, Documents Show," *Washington Post* (August 30, 2013), http://www.washingtonpost.com/world/national-security/us-spy-agencies-mounted-231-offensive-cyber-operations-in-2011-documents-show/2013/08/30/d090a6ae-119e-11e3-b4cb-fd7ce041d814_story.html.

From the Front Lines of Budgeting: Funding SEPTA

As a Southeastern Pennsylvania Transportation Authority (SEPTA) bus passed Independence Hall in Philadelphia, negotiators haggled over how best to support the mass-transit system. SEPTA daily carried half a million people throughout the region.

For years, customers of Philadelphia's mass-transit system could hardly get through their daily commute without bumping into a sign advertising the system's motto: "We're getting there." Disgruntled commuters asked, "When?"

Cynics couldn't help but point out a double meaning: "We're getting there" was meant to suggest progress, but it also implied that SEPTA[1] had a long, long way to go. Full buses often drove right past impatient commuters waiting at the stops. Long delays left trolley riders fuming. Fares continued to rise, and patrons continued to complain about the service.

By many measures, SEPTA's troubles shouldn't even have existed. Philadelphia has one of the nation's best mass-transit systems, due in large part to its long history and its prime location along the busy New York–Washington corridor. In contrast to cities such as Washington, D.C., which have squeezed their mass-transit lines into already fast-growing suburbs, Philadelphia's suburbs grew up along preexisting mass-transit routes. Despite those advantages, SEPTA has faced chronic budget deficits, and those deficits in turn have created bigger and bigger service problems.

Toward the end of 2004, the system faced a $62 million budget deficit, which SEPTA officials said could lead to a 25 percent fare hike, a 20 percent reduction in service (including the elimination of all weekend service), and a cut of 1,400 jobs. One plan even raised the possibility of boosting the $2 fare to $3, which would have resulted in one of the highest fares in the nation. "This is the worst crisis to face SEPTA in its 36-year history," system chairman Pasquale T. Deon Sr. said. SEPTA's general manager, Faye Moore, added, "The impact of these measures on the lives of our customers, businesses in the region, as well as my fellow SEPTA employees, would be devastating."[2]

In November of that year, the system's budget woes exploded into a statewide issue. SEPTA organized busloads of riders, system managers, and union members for a bus trip to the state capitol in Harrisburg to lobby for state help. These activists pleaded with the governor for aid, and they warned state legislators of the economic crisis that would befall the region if the aid did not arrive in time.

Those who followed Pennsylvania politics recognized that a SEPTA budget crisis was a recurring drama. Every two years, as its budget came up for debate in the state legislature, SEPTA presented a forecast full of red ink. Every two years, it warned riders and employees that, without more

In Philadelphia in June 2008, a striking transit police officer distributes flyers to pedestrians shortly after his union declared a strike against SEPTA, the regional transportation authority. The prospect of inadequate security in the city's subway system led to a quick settlement.

state support, the system would face big cutbacks. Every two years, the state provided additional support. And then, by the next year, the whole process began again.

The recurring budget crises made some state officials, both Democrats and Republicans, suspect that the threats of service cuts were SEPTA's version of the "Washington Monument ploy." This was a strategy invented by George B. Hartzog, who directed the National Park Service during the Nixon years. In 1969, the administration cut the service's budget. Hartzog responded by closing all national parks, including the Washington Monument and Grand Canyon, for two days each week. "It was unheard of," he recalled later. "Even my own staff thought I was crazy."[3] He complied with the letter of the policy but created such a political storm that Congress and the administration soon restored the funding. Other leaders copied his lesson and responded to threats of budget cuts by offering up cuts that were politically unacceptable. But it also made policymakers cynical and suspicious, for it became difficult to tell which problems were real and which were just clever budget tricks. In SEPTA's case, a spokesperson for House Majority Leader Samuel

H. Smith suggested that "SEPTA creates these budgets to create a crisis."

But the head of the Pennsylvania Public Transportation Association, Michael Imbrogno, insisted that the 2004 crisis was real. The implications, he warned, could stretch from Philadelphia to Pittsburgh, which had the state's other large mass-transit system, and from there to "nearly all the systems, including community services that impact senior citizens, the disabled and transit-dependent workers."[4] The system's advocates contended that the spillover effects on the state's economy would be huge, since so many people without cars relied on the system and that, without a good system, traffic in key transportation corridors would become hopelessly clogged. The chairman of the SEPTA board put it more bluntly, warning that if the agency did not get state help, "The ship is really going down this time."[5]

Whether real or manufactured, SEPTA's critics concluded, the transit system's perpetual crisis was in large part a symptom of deeply rooted management problems. Providing more aid each year gave the system no incentive to fix them. If the state caved in again, they warned, SEPTA would only learn once again just how well its budget strategy worked.

For their part, SEPTA officials claimed that the deepening budget problems were a symptom of the state's failure to provide a firm foundation for the system's financial operations. They never knew how the budget battles would come out, so they could never plan ahead. Because the state provided inadequate support, these officials argued, they had little choice but to divert funds intended to build the system's future to pay for this year's emergency maintenance. As a result, they were forced to delay maintenance that needed to be done and to squeeze riders with higher fares, less service, and more unpredictable trains, buses, and trolleys.

SEPTA officials argued that the problem could be fixed once and for all if the state would provide a predictable flow of revenue to the system from a dedicated funding stream (that is, a revenue source whose proceeds would flow automatically to SEPTA). They suggested that a higher gasoline tax would do the trick: it would keep money within the transportation system, it would nudge the cost of gas higher and thus create incentives for riders to switch to more fuel-efficient mass transit, it would get SEPTA out of the battle for other state revenues, and it would allow system officials to make long-term plans for a more reliable system.

Unfortunately, that proposal was not very popular in Harrisburg, where the Republicans who controlled both houses of the legislature were not eager to drive up the price of gasoline for their constituents and then ship the revenues off to Democratic Philadelphia. That city's legislators tried to build a broader coalition with the moderate Republicans who represented the suburbs around the city, but raising taxes was never an easy sell for them. The Philadelphia legislators also hoped for help from Governor Ed Rendell, a Democrat

who had previously been mayor of Philadelphia, but he had no love for SEPTA, and other battles he needed to fight with the Republican legislators made him wary about engaging them on this front.

The Republicans, for their part, saw real value in the biennial fight to save SEPTA. It was a must-win issue for their Democratic colleagues from Philadelphia—and every must-win issue created opportunities to extract votes from them on other issues that mattered to legislators elsewhere in the state.

No one really wanted SEPTA to go down the drain—or even to eliminate weekend service—but no one was sure exactly how to fix its chronic problems. Meanwhile, keeping the budget game going worked, sometimes in subtle ways, for many of the players in the state budgetary process. But the fix didn't last long—many of the same issues resurfaced in SEPTA's 2016 strike.

QUESTIONS TO CONSIDER

1. How does the "Washington Monument ploy" work? Do you believe it is likely to be an effective strategy? Will players in the process catch on after an agency has tried it once or twice?

2. How does the regular nature of SEPTA's budget battles affect its ability to plan and operate in the long term?

3. What lessons does the biennial budget game teach about the incentives for those who play it?

4. What options might policymakers consider for "fixing" SEPTA? What would you recommend?

NOTES

1. See the system's website: http://www.septa.org.

2. "SEPTA Proposes Drastic Actions to Deal with Deficit," press release (September 9, 2004), http://groups .yahoo.com/neo/groups/nwgreens/conversations/ topics/176.

3. Matt Schudel, "George B. Hartzog Jr., 88: Expanded Nation's Park System," *Washington Post*, July 6, 2008, C6.

4. "Fund a System in Need," editorial, *Philadelphia Inquirer*, November 11, 2004, A18.

5. Jere Downs, "SEPTA Details Proposed Cuts," *Philadelphia Inquirer*, November 12, 2004, B8.

CASE 11.3

Performing under Fire: Budget Constraints Force Fire Departments to Better Manage Resources

Jonathan Walters is a longtime journalist and a veteran firefighter. He's president of Ghent Fire Company Number One in upstate New York. He's a Class A interior-attack qualified firefighter, which means that if your home or building catches fire, he's trained to come inside and save you. He's been a volunteer for fifteen years in his fire company and, as he jokes, he's used "to things getting hot around me."[1]

He's also an expert on performance management in government. He worries about basic questions: "in the face of constrained budgets, is my fire company amassing and deploying resources in the smartest, most sophisticated way possible?" His conclusion, he says, "is that we in the fire service have a long way to go when it comes to using performance metrics to drive what we do. We like to talk about our annual run rate, response times, crew sizes, etc., but not about how many of our calls are real, or what they consist of, or how we performed once we got to the scene. As I tell my guys all the time, our image as local heroes isn't going to inoculate us forever from tough questions about what we cost versus what we do."[2]

Firefighters do have an image as local heroes. Which of us, after all, would stir from a sound sleep, leap onto a truck, and run into a burning building that could collapse around us? But as local budgets across the country suffered hard hits in the Great Recession, calls have come for wage give-backs and cuts in pensions. "Painting firefighters as something of a pampered class," he wrote, "would have been unheard of just a few years ago. Today, it's a widespread practice."[3] Lowell, Massachusetts, relies on mutual aid from surrounding communities in case of big fires. Baltimore firefighters faced the tough choice of five to eight furlough days—days off, without pay—or losing 100 positions. San Diego officials created "rolling brownouts," which closed firehouses on a rotating basis to save money. As Tom Wieczorek, director of the International City/County Management Association's Center for Public Safety Management, noted, "It's one of the most challenging times I've ever seen."[4]

As local fire departments are facing these realities, they're also being forced to confront the nature of their work. In many communities, fire departments respond both to fires and to medical emergencies. In the typical community where the department handles both, 80 percent of the calls are for emergency medical services and just 20 percent are for fires. Many fire calls are for small fires or false alarms. In San Jose, a call for a medical emergency gets a response with a pumper and four firefighters. In Fargo, North Dakota, the chief says the department has moved away from that approach. Fire trucks are dispatched, says Chief Bruce Hoover, if "there's bleeding, breathing complications, or

trauma." That, in turn, has "cut our run count back by 1,000 a year, and has kept apparatus and manpower in place for real emergencies."[5]

That step, however, is a big one for most local governments, where that shift would challenge long-standing practice. The alternative, Wieczorek says, could be far worse. "Don't get caught up in the hysteria trap of believing that if you pursue things like brownouts and budget cuts that children are going to die and senior citizens will burn up," he argued. "That might happen, but only if we keep doing business in the same old ways."[6]

QUESTIONS TO CONSIDER

1. What do you make of Walters's argument that fire departments need to move to better performance measures as a strategy for dealing with tight budgets?

2. If you agree with this approach, what barriers do you see standing in the way? What would you do to break these barriers? If you disagree, what alternatives would you suggest?

3. Consider Wieczorek's argument that the real threat to public safety lies not in restructuring fire departments but in failing to do so—and risking that tight budgets will lead to larger and harder-to-manage budget cuts. Do you agree?

4. This is an issue that always provokes sharp public debate. How would you deal with citizens as such a debate catches fire?

NOTES

1. Jonathan Walters, "Firefighting through a Performance Management Lens," *Governing* (January 10, 2011), http://www.governing.com/blogs/view/Firefighting-Through-a-Performance-Management-Lens.html.

2. Ibid.

3. Jonathan Walters, "Firefighters Feel the Squeeze of Shrinking Budgets," *Governing* (January 2011), http://www.governing.com/topics/public-workforce/firefighters-feel-squeeze-shrinking-budgets.html.

4. Ibid.

5. Ibid.

6. Ibid.

Lessons on Budgeting from *House of Cards*

If you marathoned a recent season of *House of Cards* on Netflix, you know that one major plot line hinges on a federal disaster-relief law—the Stafford Act of 1988, which authorizes the use of federal money to respond to hurricanes and other natural disasters. In the show, President Frank Underwood, played by Kevin Spacey, battles his foes in Congress over implementation of the law and just what constitutes a "disaster."

It's a testament not only to the political machinations that drive *House of Cards* but also to the increasing importance of federal emergency funding. We've gone more than ten years since Hurricane Katrina savaged the Gulf Coast. Retrospectives on the storm instantly bring back the searing images of a drowned city, especially New Orleans, the tales of unimaginable chaos inside the Superdome shelter, and the misuse of police power in trying to regain control.

Behind the retrospectives, though, are some big questions. How much should we spend on disaster relief? Who ought to pay for it? And when calamity strikes, who should be in charge? Since Katrina, new answers to these questions have emerged—and they've quietly but dramatically shifted the balance of intergovernmental power.

Disaster spending is up in part because disasters themselves are becoming more frequent. In the nine-year period from 1997 through 2005, according to the Federal Emergency Management Agency (FEMA), there were 470 such events. In the following nine-year period from 2006 through 2014, there were 583. The National Oceanic and Atmospheric Administration found that the number of severe weather events—those causing more than $1 billion in damage—averaged two per year in the 1980s, but more than ten per year since 2010. Many scientists suspect that climate change has made us more vulnerable to big storms. And, quite simply, there are more of us living in harm's way, concentrated on the coasts and on floodplains, and where forest fires strike and earthquakes threaten.

Not only is spending on the rise, but the feds account for more of it. According to a 2012 report by the Federal Reserve Bank of New York, the federal government on average paid about 26 percent of the damage costs for major hurricanes from 1989 to 2004. Since Katrina, that's increased to 69 percent, along with a rising expectation that the feds will pick up the tab for large-scale multistate cataclysmic events. After all, Congress has an easier political road than state and local governments in getting money for disaster relief.

But there's no consensus on what restrictions the feds ought to place on postdisaster rebuilding in exchange for providing this greater level of aid. In the past, federal aid programs often encouraged disaster victims to rebuild in the very spots that had suffered damage. Since Katrina, that has started to change, with requirements that homes rebuilt in New Orleans be raised above typical flood levels. Following Superstorm Sandy, some local governments on the East Coast forbade any rebuilding in low-lying areas. FEMA issued a policy that took effect in March 2016 requiring states to address climate change before they can become eligible for disaster relief.

Federal restrictions on local choices, however, often don't go down well, especially if they come through FEMA. The agency is so despised in Texas, for example, that, before this spring's epic floods there, citizens debated how to protect themselves from FEMA setting up detention camps as part of a martial-law takeover. (Nothing of the sort was afoot, of course.) Then, after the floods, victims urgently waited for FEMA's help. No one really wants the government to tell them where they can live and how they must build their homes, even if the regulations reduce death and damage in future disasters. But when disaster strikes, government help can't come fast enough.

Katrina's other major legacy, the dispute over who's in charge at the moment of impact, is equally tricky. Behind the scenes there's been an enormous shift in whether and when the feds need to pull the trigger.

The government of New Orleans all but collapsed during Katrina. The Bush administration was also politically embarrassed by FEMA's problems. In fact, after the storm the president's political negatives rose sharply and never really returned to their previous levels.

Within FEMA and the Department of Homeland Security, a quiet consensus has emerged: there will never be another Katrina, at least in political terms. If a disaster threatens public order, the federal government will hit fast and hard.

All in all, Katrina's legacy marks a permanent change in relations among federal, state, and local governments. It shifted more of the cost of natural disasters to Washington, and it's gradually pushed the feds deeper into what had long been mostly local decisions. More subtly, it's also reset the trigger for federal intervention in other state and local functions, including fundamental ones such as public safety and criminal justice. Hints of these changes have sharply heightened simmering tensions about the federal government's role, with an expectation of instant relief but an unwillingness to accept Washington's efforts to control the costs of future disasters.

These shifts have taken place deep inside the corridors of government, without attracting much attention among Americans at large. It took President Underwood to give the general public a hint about what's really happened in the decade since the storm.

QUESTIONS TO CONSIDER

1. What obligation do you think government has to provide assistance to those physically hurt or financially harmed by natural disasters? After all, it is possible to buy private insurance to cover loss and damage. But many individuals cannot afford to buy insurance—or fail to take advantage of the opportunity.

2. To the degree you think government has an obligation to help, how much of the burden should be borne by state and local governments? How much by the federal government? The cost of disasters can often outstrip the financial capacity of state and local governments. But the federal government does not want to provide aid without setting conditions. How should we set that balance?

3. With more natural disasters occurring, with rising political expectations that government will provide aid, and with the federal government shouldering more of the cost, are you comfortable with the implication that this could lead to a growing concentration of power in the federal government?

4. Consider *House of Cards* and the political story here: to what role can—should—and will—issues of partisan politics enter into the basic budgetary decisions shaping disaster relief?

Note: This case comes from my column in *Governing* (August 2015), http://www.governing.com/columns/potomac-chronicle/gov-hurricane-katrina-disaster-spending.html.

KEY CONCEPTS

appropriations 309
authorizations 309
black budget 310
budget authority 309
capital budgets 316
continuing resolutions 311
debt 298
deficit 298
fiscal policy 298
fiscal year 298
furloughs 311
incrementalism 304
legislative budget 309

management by objectives (MBO) 306
monetary policy 299
national debt 298
National Performance Review 306
outlays 310
Planning-Programming-Budgeting System (PPBS) 305
Program Assessment Rating Tool (PART) 307
rule of anticipated reactions 308
sequestration 312
surplus 298
uncontrollable expenditures 307
Washington Monument ploy 309
zero-base budgeting (ZBB) 306

FOR FURTHER READING

Arnold, H. Douglas. *Congress and the Bureaucracy: A Theory of Influence.* New Haven, Conn.: Yale University Press, 1979.

Key, V. O., Jr. "The Lack of a Budgetary Theory." *American Political Science Review* 34 (December 1940): 1237–1240.

Rubin, Irene S. *The Politics of Public Budgeting.* 4th ed. New York: Chatham House, 2000.

Tufte, Edward R. *Political Control of the Economy.* Princeton, N.J.: Princeton University Press, 1978.

Webber, Carolyn, and Aaron Wildavsky. *A History of Taxation and Expenditures in the Western World.* New York: Simon and Schuster, 1986.

Wildavsky, Aaron, and Naomi Caiden. *The New Politics of the Budgetary Process.* 5th ed. New York: Pearson/Longman, 2004.

SUGGESTED WEBSITES

A rich amount of information about the federal budget is available on the Internet. An excellent place to start is the Office of Management and Budget (OMB) website, **www.whitehouse.gov/omb**, which contains each year's budget as proposed by the president, voluminous supporting information, and historical tables to track the budget's long-term trends. Several databases can be downloaded from this website into spreadsheet programs, which makes analysis and charting easy.

The Congressional Budget Office's website, **www.cbo.gov**, contains a wide variety of studies and analyses. In addition, its historical tables provide useful information that often breaks down government spending and income differently than OMB's data, which often can be useful in considering long-term trends, especially for entitlement, discretionary, and uncontrollable spending.

The president's Council of Economic Advisers publishes analyses at **www.whitehouse.gov/cea**, as does the Board of Governors of the Federal Reserve System at **www.federalreserve.gov**.

WANT A BETTER GRADE?

Get the tools you need to sharpen your study skills. Access practice quizzes, eFlashcards, video, and multimedia at **edge.sagepub.com/kettl7e.**

12

IMPLEMENTATION AND PERFORMANCE

For many observers, one of the biggest surprises of Edward J. Snowden's release of classified documents in 2013 was the discovery of how many private contractors are working in the world of highly classified intelligence. This photo shows Booz Allen Hamilton's cybersecurity center in Maryland, near the National Security Agency. Snowden worked for Booz Allen, which had a contract with the NSA, but he lived in Hawaii and did his work through the Internet. He held a security clearance, but a different private contractor was responsible for processing that clearance for a different federal agency, the U.S. Office of Personnel Management.

Of course, making good decisions means nothing unless they produce good results. More than 125 years ago, Woodrow Wilson—then a professor at Princeton University before his days as U.S. president—wrote that "it is getting harder to *run* a constitution than to frame one."[1] To Wilson's observation, add this: it is easier to *write* laws than to *execute* them.

Concerns about the execution of laws gave birth in the 1970s to a field of study called **implementation**. Some traditional public administration scholars asked what was really new about studying the execution of laws. But the distinctive contribution of implementation lay in its focus. Traditional public administration concentrated on government *agencies*, with the goal of understanding how they operated and how they could work better. Implementation, in contrast, concentrates on *programs* and why, too often, their results seem to disappoint. It's not a happy tale, public opinion polls have found. A 2015 Pew survey showed that just 20 percent of Americans thought that the federal government was doing an "excellent" or "good" job running its programs, down from 25 percent in 1997. Republicans had an even more negative view, with just 10 percent believing that the federal government was doing at least a good job (see Figure 12.1). However, when questioned in detail about individual programs, Americans said they thought the federal government did more "good" than "bad" in all areas except helping people get out of poverty and managing the immigration system (see Figure 12.2).[2] Hillary Clinton talked about the former in her 2016 presidential campaign. Donald Trump made immigration the centerpiece of his.

The Pew survey reinforces a basic and troubling finding. Americans don't trust government much or believe it generally performs well. But they like and appreciate much of what it does. There's a large gap between views of government in general and perspectives on government programs in particular. And that frames our basic problem of implementation. How should we look at the issue? And what can we do to make implementation work better?

Every citizen—and taxpayer—is entitled to ask straightforward questions about the administration of governmental programs. Which programs are successful and should be continued? Which are failures and should be ended? What changes make the most difference in improving the efficiency and responsiveness of governmental programs? Which of these changes can be made by program administrators themselves, and which require action by elected legislators or executives?

The questions are straightforward, but straightforward answers are hard to come by. It is hard even to define what success and failure are, let alone to learn how to achieve success while avoiding failure. This chapter explores the rocky terrain of implementation in several ways: by considering how to judge a program's success or failure; by studying the special implementation problems of

CHAPTER OBJECTIVES

- Understand the forces that contribute to success and failure in program implementation

- Explore the role of state and local governments and the private sector as partners in implementing government programs

- Examine the role of evaluation and information in improving program implementation

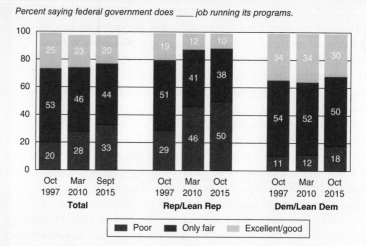

Figure 12.1 Public Attitudes about Federal Government Performance

Percent saying federal government does _____ job running its programs.

Source: Pew Research Center, *Beyond Distrust: How Americans View Their Government* (November 23, 2015), http://www.people-press.org/2015/11/23/2-general-opinions-about-the-federal-government/.

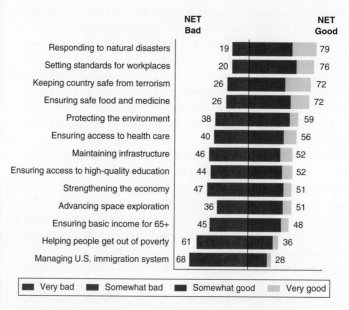

Figure 12.2 Public Attitudes about the Performance of Specific Federal Government Programs

How is the federal government doing in each area? (%)

Source: Pew Research Center, *Beyond Distrust: How Americans View Their Government* (November 23, 2015), http://www.people-press.org/2015/11/23/2-general-opinions-about-the-federal-government/.

administering governmental programs through the American intergovernmental system, as well as through private contractors; and, finally, by examining case studies that demonstrate that failure is not inevitable—and that success requires great skill in both politics and administration.

JUDGING PROGRAM SUCCESS AND FAILURE

This process called "implementation" can be a bit confusing: Isn't the entire public administration field about the management of government programs, and thus about implementation? In broad terms, the answer, of course, is yes. As long as people have been engaged in the administration of government, from the earliest days of human civilization, they have been worried about translating policy decisions into implementation. The book of Exodus in the Bible says that Moses shattered the first version of the Ten Commandments because, as he came down from the mountain, he discovered that his people were already violating the new rules they had agreed to follow.

However, the study of implementation as a discrete process in administration is more recent. In 1973, Jeffrey L. Pressman and Aaron B. Wildavsky sparked great interest with their book, *Implementation.* The book's subtitle ranks as one of the greatest in the field's history: *How Great Expectations in Washington Are Dashed in Oakland; Or, Why It's Amazing That Federal Programs Work at All, This Being a Saga of the Economic Development Administration as Told by Two Sympathetic Observers Who Seek to Build Morals on a Foundation of Ruined Hopes.*[3] Their worry: too many programs start with overly ambitious promises, which lead to disappointing results. In fact, Pressman and Wildavsky argued, implementation analysis concentrates on the *results* of administrative action, not just on its *process.* Pressman and Wildavsky believed that results too often fall short of promise because the "seamless web" of programs tends to become very complex—and the greater the complexity, the greater the chance of failure.[4]

Implementation studies have often been depressing reading. After Pressman and Wildavsky's book came a long collection of failure stories. One study concludes, "Domestic programs virtually never achieve all that is expected of them."[5] Others see the process as "an uphill battle from start to finish."[6] Some scholars of implementation look on themselves as physicians seeking to diagnose the many diseases afflicting governmental programs.[7] The field is the very embodiment of Murphy's Law: "If anything can go wrong, it will." Indeed, the presumption of failure seems endemic to the study of implementation.[8] It is mostly a collection of programs that go wrong and promises that disappoint.

This argument, however, builds on a wobbly foundation. Problems are more interesting, but focusing on them provides a distorted view of reality. Successes rarely attract attention. Newspapers never feature banner headlines declaring "Mail Delivered Yet Again Today," "Thousands of Flights Land Safely Because of Air Traffic Control System," "Fire Department Successfully Puts Out Four-Alarm Fire," or "Rescue Squad Saves Life of Accident Victim." Of course, bad news deserves attention, because taxpayers and policymakers alike deserve to know when programs fail and why. But it would be a mistake to use news coverage and the speeches of public officials as evidence of how well public programs work. Successes are often ignored, and failures dominate the headlines. In fact, from the quick response of emergency medical technicians to the backwoods work of forest rangers, most governmental programs work pretty well most of the time. The trick is determining what works well, what does not, and how to transform the latter into the former.

What Are Success and Failure?

Judging whether a program works requires comparing its results with its goals. In practice, however, knowing what a program seeks to do is often very difficult. Legislative objectives are often unclear. There frequently are many of them, sometimes they conflict, and they almost always change over time. In the Johnson administration's War on Poverty, for example, the law required local communities to provide "maximum feasible participation" for the poor in making spending decisions. This was a classic example of fuzziness. What did "participation" mean? Just how much was the "maximum," especially when put through the filter of what was "feasible"? A leading expert on the program, and later a U.S. senator, Daniel Patrick Moynihan, said that the law produced only "maximum feasible misunderstanding."[9]

Legislative goals are often vague because that's typically what it takes to win the votes necessary to pass a law. It's usually easier to put together a coalition if there are fewer things for legislators to object to, so vague—even conflicting—goals are often the product of the legislative process.[10] It's no surprise that the debate about what a program is supposed to accomplish—and whether it's been a "success" or "failure"—becomes a continuation of the struggles that shaped the program to begin with.

Moreover, goals can change over time. In New Haven, Connecticut, for example, local officials created a youth employment program. The original goal was to place program participants in union jobs, but a slowdown in building construction made that difficult, so the officials broadened their goals to include nonunion placements. When they found that the sixteen-year-olds in the program were too young to work in some construction jobs, they recruited older participants than the program was first designed to recruit. And when the officials discovered that most participants lacked the high school degree that many apprenticeship programs required, the director of the program taught an evening General Educational Development class to help participants qualify for apprenticeships.[11]

No matter how fuzzy, however, goals and objectives are critical for shaping how administrators manage their programs. Donald Rumsfeld, who served twice as secretary of defense (for Presidents Gerald Ford and George W. Bush) and once as chief of staff (for President Ford), collected a series of axioms outlining the problem. He called them "Rumsfeld's Rules" and quoted World War II General George Marshall as saying, "If you get the objectives right, even a lieutenant can write the strategy." To that he added, "When you're skiing, if you're not falling you're not trying."[12] Clear objectives make implementation much easier. Government often works on hard problems that the private sector cannot or will not take on. Many of government's programs—and many newspaper stories—demonstrate how hard it is to turn Rumsfeld's simple rules into effectively administered programs. Government constantly risks falling down the slopes because it contends with some of society's slipperiest challenges.

Moreover, implementation is rarely a straight-line start-to-finish process. Most of the time, it's part of a complex system where each event affects the next. It is often a highly political process. The rich dynamics of American politics play themselves out in administrative struggles, just as they do through legislative, judicial, and executive decisions.[13]

PROBLEMS OF PERFORMANCE

Five issues resurface, over and over again, in the struggle of government agencies to perform well: (1) uncertainty about how to reach a program's goals; (2) inadequate resources to get the job done; (3) organizational problems that interfere with an agency's handling of its programs; (4) uneven leadership in guiding bureaucracies through difficult issues; and (5) growing dependence on others, whether at other levels of government or in the private sector, through a complex of networked government.

Uncertainty

Difficult problems may have no known solutions—and tough problems tend to end up at government's doorstep. After all, the reason why many problems become governmental problems is that the private sector cannot, or will not, solve them. That realization often leads policymakers to embrace the merely plausible, the currently fashionable, or the most powerfully supported program. One local official once described this to me as the "nifty idea, I'm for that!" approach to problem solving. Elliot Richardson, a member of President Richard Nixon's cabinet, wrote in more detail:

> Our impatience toward delays in curing social ills reinforces the "don't just stand there, do something" impulse. [This syndrome] encourages . . . the illusion that we know how to cure alcoholism, treat heroin addiction, and rehabilitate criminal offenders. In fact, we do not. The state of the art in these areas is about where the treatment of fevers was in George Washington's day.[14]

In fact, George Washington's wife, Martha, died of a fever. Washington himself was bled for a fever he contracted, and the treatment contributed to his death. Fashion often shapes strategies, but the strategies very often build on uncertainty.

Even when the uncertainty is technological, formidable challenges often remain. The Soviet nuclear disaster in Chernobyl, near Kiev, in 1986 and the tragic disintegration in February 2003 of the space shuttle *Columbia* all too vividly demonstrate the tremendous difficulty of attempting complex engineering tasks in never-before-attempted systems. Engineers designed Japanese nuclear reactors to survive a massive earthquake—which they did when a 9.0 temblor hit in March 2011. The resulting tsunami, however, swamped the seawalls protecting the reactors and knocked out the cooling systems. When the problem is social instead of technological, as with welfare programs, the uncertainty about how to deal with complexity is different, though just as troubling.

Knowledge is always imperfect, and that makes it hard to devise strategies to solve complex problems, and solutions that sometimes look smart can lead to unintended consequences. Programs intended to reduce the oversupply of major agricultural crops have offered subsidies to farmers for taking some of their acreage out of production, and farmers sometimes have removed their poorest-yield acres from production. The ingenuity of taxpayers seeking loopholes in the Internal Revenue Service's (IRS) voluminous regulations is legendary. IRS managers struggle to keep up with the inventiveness of thousands, or millions, of clever attorneys, accountants, and other experts who make it their business to find loopholes and save their clients money.

Uncertainty thus often handicaps program implementation. Complex technologies, from space shuttles to nuclear reactors, from the Internet to electronic commerce, produce problems that are hard to predict. Interactions between people, and between citizens and their government, are even harder to forecast and influence: people often do not know what they want done, not just in government but in many aspects of an intricate society—and even when they do know, they often do not know how to do it. All these uncertainties can hurt the performance of governmental programs.

Next Steps in Government Procurement
Theme: Performance

Anne Rung took over the Office of Federal Procurement Policy (OFPP) in the Office of Management and Budget in 2014. It's one of the least-known offices in the federal government. Many people think it's boring. But the agency focuses on some of the government's most important issues, including how best to manage the acquisition of nearly half a trillion dollars' worth of goods and services the government buys through contracts every year.

"We have a great opportunity to create a new model for federal contracting to drive greater innovation and performance, and generate savings," Rung said. How did she plan to do that?

First, Rung promised a major initiative on "category management," in which the federal government would bundle together goods and services into categories, like travel or computers. OFPP would then work with federal agencies to develop sophisticated strategies for negotiating a good deal on those products—and for developing plans for working more effectively with the private suppliers who provided those products. That, she expected, would both save the government money and provide better service to taxpayers.

Second, Rung developed a training program for those in charge of buying products for the government. The federal government did not have the talent needed to manage some of the acquisitions well, especially in digital services (computers and the software that drives them). The training program would fill the gap.

Third, she launched a program to make the federal government a better customer for private suppliers to work with. Rung said that the goal was to create a "Yelp" for contracting operations in federal agencies, to provide better feedback on what works—and what the federal government could do better.

"We are piloting these ideas and really trying to test the marketplace, and tweak it, and re-tweak it and build on it over time as we develop and are more thoughtful about these great ideas," Rung explained.

Source: Jason Miller, "OFPP's Rung Rolls Out 3-Pronged Acquisition Improvement Plan," *Federal News Radio* (December 4, 2014), http://federalnewsradio.com/defense/2014/12/ofpps-rung-rolls-out-3-pronged-acquisition-improvement-plan/.

Inadequate Resources

The resources, in both budgets and skilled personnel, often aren't adequate to implement the ambitious programs created by legislatures. Cynics, of course, argue that government is full of unnecessary bureaucrats, but in fact there's often a large gap between government's capacity and the job to be done.

When he was secretary of the Department of Health, Education, and Welfare (later split into the Department of Health and Human Services and the Department of Education), Elliot Richardson discovered that the $100 million Congress had approved for a new elderly nutrition program would reach only 5 percent of those who were eligible, and the Community Health Program would reach only 20 percent of the intended beneficiaries. When Richardson asked his staff to estimate the cost in fiscal year 1972 of having all the department's programs reach every eligible person, they told him that the amount needed was $250 billion—more than the total federal budget at that time. He concluded that "all too often, new legislation merely publicizes a need without creating either the means or the resources for meeting it."[15] And sometimes, as was the case with the Flint water crisis, the investment of relatively small amounts of money could prevent enormous problems—if only policymakers had examined the risks and assessed the consequences before making decisions.

Sometimes, too, problems of implementation come from simply not having enough government employees to manage programs. Critics savaged the IRS in the mid-2010s for failing to answer taxpayers' phone calls looking for help. But congressional funding cuts made it impossible to put enough experts on the phone to answer those calls.

Organizational Pathologies

Sometimes an agency's internal problems damage implementation. Some agencies have an open culture and are extremely friendly toward new programs, whereas others treat new ventures as unwanted children. Common organizational problems often turn out to be central.

First, it is risky to mix missions. For example, the core mission of the U.S. Department of Veterans Affairs (VA) is to provide health care and benefits to vets. Its struggles to build a new VA hospital in Denver led to a $1.1 billion cost overrun.

Second, it is risky to place a program in an agency whose staff is unsympathetic to the program.[16] In the early years of the Reagan administration, for example, top Environmental Protection Agency (EPA) officials had a negative attitude toward government regulation of business, and many environmental programs suffered. Many critics blamed the move of the Federal Emergency Management Agency from independent status to part of the new Department of Homeland Security for its failure in 2005 to move more swiftly to deal with the many disasters that Hurricane Katrina produced.

Third, it is risky to assign *closely related* programs to *different* agencies. The program manager's strategy may then depend on the strategies and actions of his or her rivals, and bureaucratic objectives may tend to replace public policy objectives. In the competition for "customers," the manager may overserve or underregulate the clientele shared with other programs. Classic examples include the competition between the Army Corps of Engineers (in the Defense Department) and the Bureau of Reclamation (in the Interior Department) to build dams, and local governments' shopping around among the four federal agencies (the Departments of Agriculture, Commerce, and Housing and Urban Development, as well as the EPA) that can make sewage treatment construction grants. In the regulatory arena, three federal agencies oversee banks: the Comptroller of the Currency (in the Treasury Department) as well as the Board of Governors of the Federal Reserve System and the Federal Deposit Insurance Corporation (both independent regulatory agencies). The result, said one Federal Reserve chairman, is "a jurisdictional tangle that boggles the mind" and fosters "competition in laxity, sometimes to relax constraints, sometimes to delay corrective measures. Agencies sometimes are played off against one another."[17] That tangle vastly complicated efforts in the late 1980s to solve the savings-and-loan crisis and created even worse problems in managing the recovery from the 2008 financial collapse.

Inconsistent Leadership

As Ralph Waldo Emerson put it, "an institution is the lengthened shadow of one man."[18] In the bureaucratic world, an exceptional administrator can make the difference in a program's success. For a generation, the Federal Bureau of Investigation was indeed the lengthened shadow of director J. Edgar Hoover. The early success of the Peace Corps owed much to the energetic leadership of Sargent Shriver, and James E. Webb managed NASA's remarkable drive to the moon in the 1960s. Tom Ridge guided the first uncertain steps of the federal government's homeland security operations. At the state and local levels, great leaders have often dominated individual agencies. Bureaucratic entrepreneurs have radically transformed government agencies with the force of their ideas and energy.[19]

However, poor leaders can lead to poor results. As James Q. Wilson has pointed out, however, "the supply of able, experienced executives is not increasing nearly as fast as the number of problems being addressed by public policy." And, he continued,

> the government—at least publicly—seems to act as if the supply of able political executives were infinitely elastic, though people setting up new agencies will often admit privately that they are so frustrated and appalled by the shortage of talent that the only wonder is why disaster is so long in coming.[20]

We often fall short of what we seek to accomplish because our government agencies fall short of the leadership talent they need.

Networked Government

As I've noted in earlier chapters, more of government is interwoven—between different agencies, between levels of government, between sectors of society, and between nations. That's led to some of the complexity that Pressman and Wildavsky pointed to. And it's led to growing challenges in building the capacity government needs to manage its programs well.

The fundamental problem is that different organizations have different purposes, and the people who work for them naturally pursue different goals. Whenever the government relies on a proxy to produce a service, it faces the task of trying to impose its goals on the often very different objectives of the proxy. Conflict is the least problematic outcome that can result from such a process. Deflection of the government's goals toward those of its proxy is the most problematic outcome. The two varieties of this proxy implementation strategy raise particular concerns within their separate spheres of operation: relations with different levels of government, and contracts with the private sector.

The chain of implementation increasingly is not a hierarchical set of linkages structured by authority but, rather, a collection of organizations working—often loosely—to collaborate with each other. These continuing interactions shape and reshape policy implementation.[21] Managers often do not manage their agencies so much as they manage the *partnerships* that define their agencies' success. They also can make the implementation process exceptionally challenging.

Consider, for example, evidence from the list prepared by the U.S. Government Accountability Office (GAO) identifying the thirty-two "high-risk" programs—federal programs especially prone to waste, fraud, abuse, and mismanagement. Among the problems that put these programs on the high-risk list, three stand out.[22] All are rooted in the challenges of managing an interwoven government:

- The inability of agencies to effectively *work across organizational stovepipes.*
- The inability to *track performance* and use information to make timely decisions.
- The challenge of *updating inadequate and aging legacy information systems.*

For example, fifteen agencies share responsibility for coordinating national policy and administering thirty different laws to prevent food-borne illnesses—and the federal government relies on state agencies to investigate food-borne outbreaks. In the case of national flood insurance, local governments have a large role in determining what can be built in flood plains, and state governments have important roles as well. The effectiveness of the national flood insurance program depends on building strong coordination among all three levels of government.

But GAO has found that many agencies are making substantial progress in cracking the problems that put their programs on the list. The following are among the most effective solutions:

- *Improvements to legacy information systems.* Aging legacy information technology systems, and ineffective efforts to modernize them, have been a stumbling block for many agencies. Successful leaders make fundamental management changes to bring together technology, contracting, and program management skills. For example, GAO in 2013 removed the IRS's Business Systems Modernization Program because it successfully installed its new taxpayer information system, the Customer Account Data Engine 2.
- *Strengthened financial management systems to control resources.* At their core, most high-risk programs are on the list because they pose big financial costs for taxpayers. Managers need to know where the money is going and how to redirect it. Better financial management of the Defense Department's supply chain resulted in the department's directing billions of dollars more closely to forecasts of needed spare parts. That produced big cost savings. In the case of the Department of the Interior's oil and gas leasing programs, better financial management led to significant improvements in the collection of revenues from leases.
- *Strengthened contract management to ensure contractors aligned with mission needs.* The federal government relies heavily on contractors but often struggles to draft good contracts and manage them well. That's the case for the Medicare program, which has been on the GAO high-risk list since its inception in 1990. However, GAO has recognized the Centers for Medicare and Medicaid Services for putting in place stronger competitive bidding procedures for products, like durable medical equipment (including wheelchairs) and stronger auditing and contract review processes. Taxpayers have saved substantial money as a result.

In short, it's possible to assess failure, GAO found, in terms of whether a program met its mission and whether an agency's implementation of a program exposes it to fraud, waste, abuse, and mismanagement. It's possible to make progress by attacking these problems. And it's possible to achieve success. From 1990 to 2015, GAO removed twenty-three programs from the list. Failure by no means is inevitable. Success depends on managing the increasing complexity of an ever-more-interwoven government.

INTERWEAVING THROUGH FEDERALISM

That's especially the case for intergovernmental programs, which increasingly shape the implementation of domestic programs. In the case with which we began this book, Flint's water policy built on complex intergovernmental connections: the federal government delegated responsibility for overseeing national water standards to Michigan's environmental quality agency. State officials oversaw the operation of Flint's local government. The same

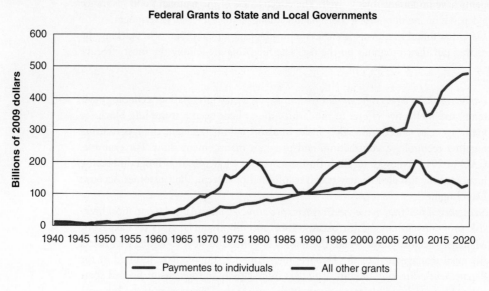

Federal Grants to State and Local Governments

Source: U.S. Office of Management and Budget, *Budget of the United States Government, Fiscal Year 2017: Historical Tables* (2016), Table 6.1.

holds for much of the nation's regulation of food safety, where state governments have increasingly taken over responsibility for investigating the causes of food-safety problems, as they oversee national policy. Under the Affordable Care Act, the Obama administration's signature health insurance program, state governments are on the front lines, responsible for ensuring that citizens have quality health insurance to buy—except in those states that have opted out of the program, and where the federal government therefore has had to step in. This kind of intergovernmental interweaving creates a fabric of sometimes unimaginable complexity.

The states, moreover, have become the key administrators for the Medicaid program, which provides health care for low-income citizens—mostly children, poor families, and the elderly who have outlived their savings. Medicaid has grown rapidly since its creation in 1965. Over time, Medicaid and other programs providing payments to individuals have become a far larger part of federal aid to state and local governments, squeezing out more traditional grants for programs like bridges, highways, community development, and job training. That, in turn, has vastly complicated the administrative structure of key domestic programs—and it's drawn state governments, in particular, into the interwoven system that's increasingly characterized the federal government.

The grant system has also pulled state and local governments into regulatory policy. Each grant program brings with it a package of regulations and **mandates** that further spreads federal influence over state and local governmental activities. By reserving to the states any powers that are not otherwise given to the federal government, the Tenth Amendment to the Constitution prohibits the federal government from directly ordering states to engage in many activities. In the irresistible lure of grants, however, the federal government has found a way around this constitutional impediment: by making the money available, but subject to certain conditions, it can get state and local governments to do what they otherwise might not be inclined to do.[23]

Every program carries its own special rules. Potential Medicaid recipients must meet certain income guidelines, and federal highway funds can be spent only on certain kinds of projects. In addition, the federal government has promulgated a remarkable range of crosscutting rules that apply across the board, to all grant programs. Recipients must, of course, properly account for how they spend their money, but they must also survey the environmental effects of any program they plan, they must not discriminate in how the money is spent, they must preserve the historical aspects of federally funded projects, and they must make projects accessible to the disabled, among many other things.

Furthermore, state and local recipients must comply with **crossover sanctions**: failure to meet one program's standard can produce a punishment in another program. For example, during the energy crisis of the 1970s, Congress forbade the secretary of transportation from approving any highway construction project in a state posting a speed limit of more than fifty-five miles per hour. Since many states, especially in the west, had speed limits of sixty-five miles per hour on highways, they had the choice of lowering the limits or losing the money. The choice was obvious.[24] From automobile pollution inspection to a minimum drinking age of twenty-one, such crossover sanctions are a favorite instrument for inducing uniform national standards.

The federal government sometimes employs a mixed regulatory strategy, called **partial pre-emption**.[25] A federal agency sets standards that state and local governments must follow—for example, legislation mandating minimum water quality standards—and if the subnational government does not meet those standards, the federal government steps in to administer the program itself. Thus, in some states, a program will be run by a state or local official. In others, federal field officials will administer it. For example, the Occupational Safety and Health Administration conducts inspections and enforces regulations in thirty states while only approving and monitoring programs run by twenty state governments. The financial structure of such a mixed-level program can be equally complicated.

Attacking the mandates was easy; devising a solution was far tougher. Most reforms would not roll back existing mandates but would only make it harder to impose new ones. Estimating the costs of mandates before they are imposed, however, is an extremely difficult technical problem. Moreover, many interest groups find it far easier to organize in Washington to press for a uniform policy to be applied across the country than to fight fifty separate battles in the state capitols. Many businesses worried about trying to accommodate fifty separate sets of laws and standards may also find uniform standards, enacted in Washington, much more desirable.

Intergovernmental administration of government programs thus has become a central cornerstone of implementation. The system is exceptionally complex, but state and local governments are natural, if sometimes reluctant, administrative partners in federal programs. By relying on them, the federal government promotes the principles of responsive self-government that date from the nation's earliest days.[26] After all, the federal government is the creation of the states, and we've chosen to call ourselves the *united states* in the continent of America. The intergovernmental system often strains under the weight of its burdens, and it's struggled with budget cuts, but the strategy of interwoven responsibility through federalism is here to stay.

INTERWEAVING THROUGH CONTRACTING

Contracting in America is older than American government itself. As commander of the Continental army, George Washington constantly struggled with his private suppliers, who schemed to make a quick profit at the expense of his soldiers.[27] Contracting issues, in fact, go back thousands of years. Julius Caesar had his own troubles in dealing with the private merchants on which he relied for supplies during his foreign campaigns.

Contracting now stretches into virtually every nook and cranny, and every level, of American government. Governments have long relied on for-profit contractors to build roads. Minneapolis hired a private organization to manage its schools and linked its pay to performance on educational goals. Contractors administer Florida's child welfare program. The city of Los Angeles decided to contract out the management of its convention facility. The Texas Department of Transportation moved most of its information technology workers to a private company, in a search for greater productivity. Most state governments rely on their counties to administer social service programs, and many of these programs are administered through nonprofit organizations that serve as contractors. It's hard to find any area of government at any level that has not joined the march to greater contracting out.

The federal government obtains a substantial amount of goods and services for its operations through **contracts** with private companies, research institutions, and individual consultants. In fiscal year 2015, federal spending on contracts totaled $439 billion, about 12 percent of all federal spending.[28] The Department of Defense accounted for most of the contracting, followed by the Departments of Energy, Health and Human Services, and NASA. Aggressive efforts to rein in contracting during the Obama administration produced a substantial slowdown from the growth of federal contracting that had characterized federal spending for decades, and the administration celebrated "this bending of the procurement spending curve."[29]

Despite this slowdown, the federal government contracts out for a remarkable range of activities. Traditionally, contracts have dealt with such needs as the purchase of supplies and equipment and the lease of buildings, but now contractors also provide research and development of everything from new weapons systems to new treatments for bioterrorism. Contractors do much of the work of the space program; indeed, 90 percent of NASA's budget goes to contracts. Contracting has spread far into the defense and intelligence services, including what P. W. Singer calls the rise of a new "privatized military industry" in which hundreds of companies, thousands of employees, and billions of dollars work to support the armed forces.[30] In the wars in Afghanistan and Iraq, contractors provided most of the logistical support, from trucking in gasoline to cooking the meals. The contractors trained the Iraqi police force and guarded military convoys. When American administrator Paul Bremer traveled around Iraq, he flew in a helicopter operated by a private security company, which also provided his personal bodyguards. And in 2004, when investigators learned that American soldiers had been caught on camera torturing Iraqi prisoners, they also discovered that the prison personnel included security officers and interrogators who were private contractor employees. In the end, there were as many contractor employees as soldiers in Iraq. As Singer concluded,

> the problem is that not all those involved were U.S. soldiers. While the military has established structures to investigate, prosecute, and punish soldiers who commit crimes, the legal status of contractors in war zones is murky. Soldiers are accountable to the military code of justice wherever they are located, but contractors are civilians—not part of the chain of command.[31]

American soldiers in Afghanistan depended heavily on MRAPs (Mine Resistant Ambush Protected vehicles) to shield them from roadside bombs. Most of the work in constructing and repairing the MRAPs, however, was done by private contractors, like Hal Moore from AC first company, who is working here in Afghanistan's Khost province.

Advantages of Contracting

Contracting out has several important advantages.

FLEXIBILITY. Because contractors are not permanent government organizations, staffed by permanent government employees, contracting out provides government with greater flexibility, especially in coping with surge demands, like gearing up to support a war or a new highway program. Government managers often value the ability to bring new teams in fast to deal with new problems, and reliance on contractors makes that easier. Once relationships are created, however, it can be hard to end them; it's easier to contract out than to end the contracts. But contracting out provides much-valued additional flexibility. For short-term projects, it's often attractive to avoid setting up permanent bureaucratic units for temporary problems.

COST SAVINGS. Many proponents argue that contracting out saves money. During the Reagan administration, for example, a presidential commission concluded that "privatization" of many goods and services would improve them and that it would be better to have government "provide services without producing them"—that is, by contracting out.[32] Analyses of cost savings, however, vary widely. Public employee unions often complain that private contractors don't pay their employees equivalent benefits, like health care and vacation time, or that they lowball their cost estimates only to have

Implementation—Contractors and Soldiers

We tend to think about defense contractors, building tanks and ships and planes, as a relatively new part of the governmental system. In fact, since the very beginning—including the Revolutionary War—the country has relied on contractors. The patterns, though, have changed greatly over time.

This chart shows the estimated presence of contractor personnel compared to military personnel during U.S. military operations.

(In thousands):

Conflict	Contractor[a]	Military	Contractor-to-Military Ratio
Revolutionary War	2	9	1 to 6
Mexican-American War	6	33	1 to 6
Civil War	200	1,000	1 to 5
World War I	85	2,000	1 to 24
World War II	734	5,400	1 to 7
Korea	156	393	1 to 2.5
Vietnam	70	359	1 to 5
Gulf War	9[b]	500	1 to 55
Balkans	20	20	1 to 1
Iraq theater[c]	190	200	1 to 1

Source: Congressional Budget Office, based on data from William W. Epley, "Civilian Support of Field Armies," *Army Logistician,* vol. 22 (November/December 1990), 30–35; Steven J. Zamparelli, "Contractors on the Battlefield: What Have We Signed Up For?" *Air Force Journal of Logistics,* vol. 23, no. 3 (Fall 1999), 10–19; Department of Defense, *Report on DoD Program for Planning, Managing, and Accounting* for *Contractor Services and Contractor Personnel during Contingency Operations* (October 2007), 12.

a. For some conflicts, the estimated number of contractor personnel includes civilians employed by the U.S. government. However, because most civilians present during military operations are contractor personnel, the inclusion of government civilians should not significantly affect the calculated ratio of contractor personnel to military personnel.

b. The government of Saudi Arabia provided significant amounts of products and services during Operations Desert Shield and Desert Storm. Personnel associated with those provisions are not included in the data or the ratio.

c. For this study, the Congressional Budget Office considers the following countries to be part of the Iraq theater: Iraq, Bahrain, Jordan, Kuwait, Oman, Qatar, Saudi Arabia, Turkey, and the United Arab Emirates. Figures are based from data in early 2008.

QUESTIONS

1. Are you surprised by the role that private contractors played in early American wars, like the Revolutionary War and the Civil War?

2. How has the government's reliance on contractors to fight wars changed over the course of American history?

3. What implications do you think these changes have, both on implementation (including strategies for war-fighting) and on broader policy (including the political stakes that contractors have in national defense)?

costs increase over time. Cost comparisons between public and private provision of services are always a matter of fierce contest.

SPECIAL EXPERTISE. Contracts enable the government to obtain the services of outside specialists. An agency may not have workers with the needed skills, or its employees with those skills may be fully occupied with their regular duties. For some assignments, the most competent specialists may be found outside government either because the pay is better or because they favor the work environment in universities, research institutes, and private companies.

REDUCING RED TAPE. Contracting also tends to bypass the bureaucratic syndrome that handicaps large government agencies: the very bureaucratic rules designed to promote fairness, competence, and accountability can prevent quick and effective action on problems. An independent organization can sometimes assemble an integrated team to study multidimensional problems. Within government, such efforts often encounter all the difficulties of interbureau and interdepartmental coordination.

BODY COUNTS. Contracting is often attractive because contractors' staff members are not counted as government employees and are not subject to regulations governing the civil service. Budget constraints sometimes put ceilings on the number of government employees, and elected officials sometimes look to the number of government employees as a measure of agency size. Government agencies can rely on contractors to expand their capacity without growing the number of employees.

Problems with Contracting

Contracting out can also pose problems, often the mirror images of their advantages. Consider these issues.

CHOICE OF CONTRACTORS. Governments deal with a vast variety of contractors. Some are operated for profit, while others (such as universities) are nonprofit organizations. Some do most of their business with government, while government is only a relatively small share of their work. Some are very large organizations, while others are small—and government has long had an explicit policy of encouraging work with small and minority-owned contractors.

The theory of contracting is that competition among contractors will produce lower costs and higher value. But many large contracts have few potential bidders. One of the richest contracts in federal government history, a $4.5 billion competition for a new government telephone system, drew sustained interest from only two groups of bidders—and the contract was so complicated that even AT&T did not tackle the project on its own.[33] Because only two American companies are equipped to build submarines, the Pentagon believes that it is in the national interest to keep both companies in the business, so it often splits or alternates contract awards to ensure that both companies survive. Only one American company can build aerial refueling tankers for the Pentagon. Government is limited in how tough it can be in the oversight of contracts once they are signed because it has few—if any alternative—suppliers. The theory of market competition sometimes doesn't work in practice.

OVERSPECIFICATION. Government contracting, especially for weapons, tends to prescribe "ultra" features to outperform any potential threat or surpass any potential problem. In defense and space programs, the risks of failure can be catastrophic, so it's understandable that government sets tough specifications. During the Clinton administration, however, Vice President Al Gore frequently complained that the telephones on Navy ships were designed to continue working even if the ship itself sank, a process known as "goldplating."[34] Then there's the problem of complexity. The specifications for one military aircraft ranged over 24,000 documents, one of which, for electronic parts, referred to 235 other documents, which in turn referred to 1,374 more, of which half were more than ten years old. To follow the rules precisely meant installing obsolete components into frontline equipment.[35]

There have been strong pressures to move the government to buy more off-the-shelf supplies and equipment, from computers to cars. New technologies, including new printing technologies, could lead those who buy goods for governments to reduce supplies in their warehouses and replace them with three-dimensional printers, to produce spare parts on demand. That is leading to fresh debates: Can printer-produced spare parts for airplanes be trusted in supersonic jets?

UNDERPERFORMANCE. The American Federation of State, County, and Municipal Employees (AFSCME), worried that the growth of contracting would eliminate the jobs of government employees who were union members, compiled an extensive catalog of contract abuses. AFSCME found, for example, that 30 percent of school lunch "meal packs" served by contractors were deficient in basic nutrients:

> It would appear that a child eating these meal packs—especially with the usual amount of plate waste—would not be receiving iron and Vitamin A in adequate amounts. Here, it is essentially critical to remember that iron deficiency anemia is the most common of our [nutritional] deficiency diseases.

Of thirty-four meals served by one contractor, fourteen were hamburgers, "variously adorned," and eight were hot dogs. Children were served vegetables only six times in a two-month period.[36]

GAO surveyed contracts issued by the General Services Administration (GSA) over three years and found that the government had awarded more than $1 billion in contracts to vendors who repeatedly had failed to meet contract specifications and delivery schedules. Despite the problems, "GSA has continued to do business with repeat poor performing vendors." GAO found two reasons for this laxity. First, GSA's managers often had little good information on vendors' past performance. Managers could not avoid poor vendors if they did not know who they were. Second, GSA had not always emphasized product quality in making decisions. "Poor performance on GSA supply contracts has been a long-standing problem," GAO concluded.[37] Just because a good or service comes from a private contractor doesn't necessarily mean it's of high quality.

INADEQUATE SUPERVISION. Without adequate supervision, contracts—and their contractors—can draw the government into deep trouble. In 2010, a Senate committee discovered that contractors hired to provide security for American forces in Afghanistan were, in some cases, secretly members of the Taliban, the very group that the soldiers were deployed in Afghanistan to root out.[38] If government is to rely heavily on contractors, it needs to make sure they're doing the job well—and doing the job they were hired to accomplish.

OVERREGULATION. Contractors face a bewildering array of regulations with which they must comply. It is not unusual for the attachments to a small contract simply listing all these rules to be longer than the stipulations of the contract itself. So in addition to having to deliver goods and services that often are tailor-made to the government's specifications, contractors also must comply with a host of procedural standards, from financial recordkeeping to hiring principles, that can often prove expensive and time-consuming. Contractors often complain that government regulations make it hard for them to do their job.

CORRUPTION. Public contracts have always been a tempting way for the unscrupulous to make a quick profit at the government's expense—and for government officials to make money on the side for steering business to those with whom they're connected. As the AFSCME study put it, "Government contracting and corruption are old friends."[39] Corruption in state and local contracts has a rich history, as contractors have long paid government officials kickbacks and bribes to win contracts, and contractors have colluded among themselves to fix bids and thus share the government's contract bounty. In New York State, for example, ten road construction companies were indicted for bid rigging: arranging among themselves who would bid how much on which contracts, thus boosting their profits on more than $100 million in contracts over eight years.[40] "You make more money rigging bids than robbing banks—more than you could dealing drugs," one federal attorney explained.[41] At the federal level, corruption laid the foundation for the movie *American Hustle*, which was nominated for ten Oscars in 2014.

The recurring lessons of corruption in contracting are, first, that contracting is not an automatic, easy solution to the problems of implementing programs directly through government agencies. Instead, it replaces one set of administrative problems with another. Second, to be managed well, contracting requires a sophisticated collection of different administrative tools, which need to be tailored to the special implementation problems of contracting.[42] It requires incorruptible and highly competent government officials to manage the contracts.

INHERENTLY GOVERNMENTAL FUNCTIONS. Governmental policy has long required that government itself make government policy—that is, it should be responsible for "inherently governmental functions."[43] Federal regulations, for example, prohibit the government from contracting out the prosecution of criminal cases, the command of the armed forces, the conduct of foreign relations, and the decisions about agency policy and budgets.

The dividing line separating these core functions and activities that can be contracted out, however, is anything but clear. In 2013, intelligence analyst Edward Snowden stunned Americans—and most of the rest of the world—by revealing that the secret National Security Agency (NSA) was monitoring vast amounts of telephone and email communication in the search for clues about possible terrorist plots. Insiders were not surprised. The activities were reviewed by select members of Congress and approved by a special, secret federal Foreign Intelligence Surveillance Court. Investigations revealed that Snowden himself was not working for the NSA but for a private contractor, Booz Allen Hamilton. Snowden had a top-level security clearance to do the work, and a private contractor did the background check that produced the clearance. That is, a private contractor reviewed the qualifications of another private contractor to have access to private communications of American citizens. In fact, of the nearly 5 million Americans who held "top secret" security clearances, more than 20 percent worked for private contractors.[44] Everything about this story seemed completely legal, except for Snowden's decision to disclose highly classified information. But the under-story raised profound questions about the role of private contractors in some of the most sensitive issues in American public administration.

PERFORMANCE MANAGEMENT

As we saw at the beginning of this chapter, making good decisions means nothing unless they produce good results. Deciding isn't doing. And doing doesn't necessarily mean good things happen. The problem, as Herbert Kaufman explained, is this: "When managers die and go to heaven, they may find themselves in charge of organizations in which subordinates invariably, cheerfully, and fully do as they are bid. Not here on earth."[45]

Decision makers want to make sure their decisions produce actions, that the actions they produce track with what decision makers wanted, to make sure that these actions are as efficient and effective as possible, and to provide enough feedback to detect and correct any problems while they are small and fixable instead of becoming huge and expensive. All of these steps require good systems for obtaining feedback. There not only are informal systems of collecting information. Governments have also long relied on sophisticated program evaluations. Many governments have devised new strategies for short-term feedback assessments of performance, as we will see shortly. Put together, this feedback has become increasingly important for improving program implementation.

Citizen Feedback

Elected officials and top managers are always getting feedback from citizens—and from their own observations. Citizens are rarely shy about complaining about problems they see. Many cities have set up 311 call-in numbers, so citizens can register complaints and officials can tag them for followup. In New York City, the most common complaint in 2014 was noise.[46] In Chicago, these were the most-requested city services in 2016:

- Street lights—all/out
- Graffiti removal
- Garbage cart black
- Rodent baiting/rat complaint
- Shelter request
- Building violation
- Pot hole in street
- Abandoned vehicle complaint[47]

In many cities, including Kansas City, citizens can file a complaint online, get a tracking number, and keep an eye on the city's response. The city government then maps all the open service requests, and any citizen can check online to follow complaints in any neighborhood.[48]

Governments have come a very long way from the days when citizens could do little more than grumble about problems or call their city council members to complain. Many city and state governments have transformed citizen complaints into a strategy for collecting feedback about their operations.

Formal Program Evaluation

At the other extreme, governments have long relied on formal program evaluations to assess the results of their programs. "With objective information on the outcomes of programs, wise decisions can be made on budget allocations and program planning. Programs that yield good results will be expanded; those that make poor showings will be abandoned or drastically modified," as Carol H. Weiss argues.[49] The work is the province of policy analysts, who use sophisticated methods and controlled experiments to determine whether programs have impact—and what impacts they have.

A team of current and former government officials have called on the government to invest far more in creating—and using—good program evaluations. They point to the general manager of the Oakland Athletics, Bill Beane, who used sharp-eyed analysis to vastly improve the long-suffering baseball team. Sports writer Michael Lewis called the approach "moneyball," which became a best-selling book in 2003 and a movie starring Brad Pitt in 2011.[50] The approach led Republican Jim Nussle, President George W. Bush's former director of the Office of Management and Budget (OMB), and Democrat Peter Orszag, Barack Obama's former OMB director, to ask, "Can data, evidence, and evaluation similarly revolutionize American government?" Their answer: "a resounding yes." They argued that "less than one dollar out of every hundred dollars the federal government spends is backed by even the most basic evidence." The problem, Nussle and Orszag worried, was that "it is the relatively rare case when we actually have the evidence to tell us a program is working as intended and it's the most effective way to achieve the outcome we desire."[51]

It's hard to contest Nussle and Orszag's case that more and better program evaluations would significantly improve the administration of government programs. It would help us do more of what works and less of what doesn't. It would make us smarter in designing programs to begin with. But behind their powerful argument lie several big issues that have long plagued program evaluations.

First, evaluations cost money, and program advocates often contend that evaluation money would be far better spent on programs themselves than on studies. For advocates who believe in programs—and believe that they work—every penny spent on an evaluation is a penny not spent on doing good. Of course, that argument rests on the advocates' confidence that the programs work, and the point of evaluations is to determine whether they are right. The case for evaluation, however, often runs headlong into the political case that supported the program to begin with.

Second, the strongest evaluations require **randomized controlled trials**, and such evaluations are very hard to do. A randomized controlled trial is the gold standard of program evaluation. It requires program analysts to randomly assign participants to either (1) a treatment group that receives the program or intervention or (2) a control group that does not but is otherwise as much like the treatment group as possible. Analysts then use sophisticated statistical techniques to determine whether there is a significant difference in outcomes between the two groups—and whether the program's intervention was responsible for it. The Food and Drug Administration (FDA) assesses results of this approach to determine whether new drugs are "safe and effective," which is the standard for approving those drugs.

Both the politics and practicality of new programs, however, can make it hard to use randomized controlled trials. If proponents believe they have a great new idea for a program, it's challenging to work hard for passage and then deny the program to those who believe they'd benefit from it. If a town buys a new high-tech snow plow, it can be infuriating watching other streets get plowed better and faster if some residents live in a "control" neighborhood.

Moreover, urgent problems can sometimes make controlled experimentation difficult. For example, the Ebola virus outbreak reached the United States in late 2014. U.S. public health specialists treated ten individuals with Ebola, many of whom were missionaries or health care workers who contracted the disease from their patients. In addition to supportive care, seven Ebola-infected individuals received an experimental drug (ZMapp) that had not been tested for safety and efficacy in humans, had not received FDA approval, and had a very limited supply.[52] Because Ebola is often fatal and there were no approved treatment options, public health experts faced a very difficult question—would the experimental drug, with all of its unknowns, give patients the best chance for survival? Fortunately, five of the ZMapp-treated patients recovered and the FDA granted the drug "fast track" status in 2015 for further research and development. In such cases, it's pragmatically difficult, politically painful, and morally worrisome to assign individuals randomly to experimental and control groups.

Third, such randomized controlled trials are expensive because they require high levels of data collection and analysis, and they are lengthy because good analysis can take many years to produce definitive results. No manager wants to transform a program, based on a year's data, only to discover that the results came from a quirk—such as weather patterns for snow removal, patient behavior for drugs, or economic fluctuations for job training programs. Analysts need to conduct long-term analyses to root out these factors. But that can require elected officials to commit to a sophisticated study whose results won't be known until after they are out of office. That can make it even harder for officials to invest tight budget dollars in studies that will never help them politically—or help them improve programs during their term in office.

Fourth, it's surely not the case that we have even basic evidence on just 1 percent of federal programs. We don't have a large reservoir of randomized controlled trials, but we do have flight tests for Air Force jets, field tests of new NASA rockets, feedback on the success of VA treatments, data on the long-term stability of highway bridges, and experience in which forest firefighting techniques seem to work best—and politicians keep their ears constantly tuned for what their constituents think about what the government does. Thus, we have at least *some* feedback on almost every government program. We just don't have randomized controlled trials for many of them.

Still, one thing is certain. Nussle and Orszag are right: more and better evaluations of public programs would undoubtedly help us implement programs better.

Results-Based Management

Especially since the 1990s, many governments have developed results-based management systems to improve their program implementation. The approach is similar to formal program evaluation in some respects, especially requiring government managers to increase their commitment to using more information to sharpen their management of programs. But it is different in important ways.

First, the emphasis is on getting feedback in the very short term. Instead of waiting several years to determine the results of a program, these performance systems focus on learning what is happening on a daily, weekly, or monthly basis. This is a crucial step in picking up early signals about what problems are happening—and in fixing them fast. Second, that is because these performance systems focus on policy implementation, instead of policy design. The goal is to determine what works as programs are being administered, not what policy decisions to make. Third, these performance systems concentrate on program interventions. They seek to adjust program implementation quickly—and then determine whether the adjustments are moving the program in the direction managers want to go.

THE COMPSTAT MODEL. The prototype for these efforts is the New York Police Department's CompStat process. Soon after taking office in 1994, New York Mayor Rudolph Giuliani committed his administration to reducing crime in the city. His police commissioner, William Bratton, announced that he would seek to reduce crime by 40 percent in three years—a target three times higher than the city's improvement over the previous three years—and he devolved substantial operating decisions to the city's precinct commanders. To help them focus their actions, Bratton then launched CompStat. A special unit produced weekly reports on crime in each precinct. Bratton and his senior staff focused on these reports in twice-weekly staff meetings. The centerpiece of these sessions was an array of three eight-by-eight-foot screens, which mapped crime patterns on precinct-based street grids. This **geographic information system** (GIS) provided an instant snapshot of where crime was occurring. For example, if the data showed that a cluster of robberies had occurred in a particular neighborhood over the previous week, the precinct commander could devise a strategy for deploying police officers to break that pattern—and the CompStat team could track whether the precinct commander's strategy had reduced the number of robberies.

Police departments, of course, had always tracked the number of crimes. What was distinctive about CompStat was its focus on rapid collection of data, quick response, and tracking of effectiveness. Crime fell dramatically—by 12 percent overall, compared with a 1.1 percent decline nationwide.[53] NYPD has continued to use the CompStat system aggressively, and the program has led to further dramatic declines in crime. Some critics have suggested that complaints about police misconduct rose at the same time, perhaps because the new police strategy encouraged police officers to be more aggressive. Other critics contend that the CompStat approach leads police commanders to **gaming**, distortions in police behavior to make the numbers look good. For example, an investigation by the *Village Voice* captured complaints by police officers that they were pressured to record robberies as petty larcenies and to reduce the estimated value of property stolen in residential burglary claims, both of which created the appearance of a smaller number of more serious crimes.[54] These charges have led to recurring complaints about high-stakes performance measures: the more top officials pay attention to them, the more lower-level officials distort the information to make results look good and to hide problems. Precisely that kind of gaming helped produce the VA scandal in 2014, in which schedulers manipulated the wait times for appointments to make it look like the department was providing quick service, when in fact some vets had long waits that jeopardized their health. Early performance management systems in the federal government, Donald Moynihan and Stéphane Lavertu contended, often led to few positive results because leaders often didn't effectively use the data collected.[55]

Nevertheless, it was impossible to escape the fact that New York's results-based management approach had led to a dramatic decline in crime. Many other cities have picked up the approach, on a broader basis and for more programs, often supported by a stronger management commitment, to deal with the problems Moynihan and Lavertu found. After becoming Baltimore mayor in 1999, for example, Martin O'Malley created a CitiStat process. O'Malley converted the city's indicators of performance for programs, from sanitation to housing, to maps of the city. He and his senior leaders held regular meetings with department heads to identify problems and track progress.

For example, city officials tracked the location of fires to identify whether the arson prevention task force was effective, monitored the trail of the city's cleanup program, and evaluated efforts to eradicate rats. Other GIS displays showed the status of solid waste problems, graffiti cleanup, and filled potholes. Like many other cities, Baltimore also created a separate 311 call center, which allows citizens to telephone city officials to report nonemergency problems and to get information about city services. Baltimore created extensive mapping capabilities on its website (http://citistat.baltimorecity.gov) to allow citizens to track the progress of 311 calls as well as other city services. In one initiative, for example, the city created a "Rat Rubout" program whose goal was to eradicate rats, which can carry disease. Citizens could use the 311 system to report rat problems, and the city then deployed teams to remove garbage and set poison to wipe out problem areas. Map-based statistics allowed program managers to determine which neighborhoods had the largest rat problems and to concentrate their energies where they would do the most good.

When he became Maryland governor, O'Malley expanded the CitiStat process to state programs and to a new system to reduce pollution in the Chesapeake Bay. This BayStat system provides monitoring of the Bay's health, as well as ongoing tracking of the government programs designed to scrub pollution from its waters. The system produces a regular report card that tracks pollution sources around the Bay's shoreline.

These "stat" processes share four basic tenets that Bratton first developed:

- Accurate and timely intelligence
- Effective tactics and strategies
- Rapid deployment of resources
- Relentless follow-up and assessment

OPEN DATA AND PERFORMANCE ANALYTICS. Other states, especially Utah, Virginia, and Washington, have created similar efforts. Former New York City mayor

Michael Bloomberg funded an effort to bring **open data** to cities around the country. Open data focuses on collecting and analyzing the vast quantity of information governments are already collecting. For example, in June 2016, Chicago released a database containing 52 million rows of information about its bikeshare program, Divvy.[56] New York City posts its 311 citizen complaint data on the Internet, within a few days of the complaint arriving, and anyone can research underlying patterns. On June 15, 2016, for example, the system received complaints about paint and plaster in a Manhattan building, a rodent complaint in Manhattan, and noise problems in Staten Island and Brooklyn neighborhoods.[57] Montgomery County, Maryland, posts its restaurant inspection reports online.[58] Yelp began posting data from local restaurant inspections, to allow customers to check for problems before dining—and Chicago began using Yelp restaurant reviews to predict which restaurants were most likely to have problems that required in-depth inspections.[59] A growing part of such initiatives is **data visualization**, which allows managers to transfer their data to maps and use the maps to look for geographical concentrations of problems—and solutions.

Louisville has launched an especially wide-ranging performance management program, driven by an aggressive effort to couple open data with performance analytics. The city's website contains a wealth of information about government performance, including real-time information about snow routes, bike routes, traffic updates, property condition, and air quality. Its goal is not only to track the performance of city programs but also to create a broad portrait of the quality of life in the city, from the citizen's point of view.

The federal government has used similar initiatives, including a notable effort to reduce crime on Native American reservations (see Case 12.4). Some reservations faced soaring problems, with crime rates 2.5 times higher than the national average. As part of the Obama administration's performance agenda, the Bureau of Indian Affairs (BIA) committed to bringing violent crime down by 5 percent in 2010 and 2011. BIA worked with its tribal, state, and local partners in an aggressive effort to measure where crime was occurring and when it happened. They developed an intergovernmental team to attack crime—and brought rates down on four reservations by 35 percent.

These strategies set the stage for what Bloomberg's effort at the Johns Hopkins University Center for Government Excellence called performance analytics:

> Performance analytics is the practice of using data and technology to study how your government is performing to continuously make it better. By linking data to overarching priorities, collecting and analyzing data and evidence, and determining the desired outputs and outcomes, local government leaders can use performance analytics to best administer policies and programs to the benefit of their community and residents.[60]

ASSESSING DATA ANALYTICS. These initiatives certainly don't—and can't—replace more traditional program evaluations. Managers need solid, data-based analyses of which programs work best, both so they know how to guide their budget spending and so other decision makers know what bets to place on which policy strategies. Since the 1990s, "stat"-based reforms, coupled with improved data analytics and data visualization, have provided program managers with far stronger tools to improve policy implementation. There are important advantages. First, much of the data are already being collected, so the system allows managers to make more use of what they have. Second, the system provides quick feedback, both on problems and solutions, so managers can know more quickly what impact their actions have. Third, the open-data connection allows citizens to conduct their own analyses. Even if few actually do so—and the data analysis burdens can be quite substantial—the very fact that the government makes it possible creates more transparency and opportunities for strengthening trust. Fourth, by focusing on problems rather than agencies, the process helps encourage the cross-agency coordination that an increasingly interwoven system requires. Finally, the process creates new strategies for accountability, with more reliance on information in the information age.

The initiatives, however, bring big challenges. Making them work requires a strong leadership commitment, which must be sustained over time. When Martin O'Malley's terms as mayor of Baltimore and then as governor of Maryland ended, the next administration did not continue his "stat" processes with the same vigor. The process is time-consuming for agency officials and requires a profound change in culture, and that is unlikely to take root unless top leaders drive the process consistently. Moreover, the process requires high levels of analytical talent and the investment of significant resources, of both time and money. Such analytical talent is very different from the traditional policy analysis skills used in program evaluation, and graduate programs are just beginning to train graduates in the skills needed. Moreover, since "stat" meetings are often held weekly, they require a heavy commitment of top managers' time.

Finally, as we've seen, there is a dilemma built into these initiatives. If the measures become truly important, such high-stakes systems create strong incentives for those involved to game the system, feeding good information and trying to disguise bad news. If the measures are not heavily used, there's less of an incentive for gaming—but there's also a smaller incentive to invest in the systems and people to produce good measures. Still, for the reasons that Nussle and Orszag pointed out in *Moneyball*, we often know too little about the results of what government does. Improving the odds for successful implementation requires more investment in the information needed to make it happen.

Moreover, Donald P. Moynihan and Alexander Kroll have found that the more such systems become embedded in government operations, the more managers tend to use them. Routines, once well established, reinforce the use of good performance information. In addition, the higher the quality of information, the more managers are likely to use it.[61] These conclusions are reassuring. More information and better information tend to be more and better used. And more and better use leads to better implementation of public programs. These data systems are thus a very long way from the worries about disappointing results, which Pressman and Wildavsky wrote about in *Implementation*. And they reinforce a basic point of implementation made by Texas's chief information officer, Carolyn Purcell: "The complexity is in the relationships, not really in the technology itself."[62]

CONCLUSION

The story of implementation all too often is not a happy one. One study by the World Bank indicated that nearly a quarter of all World Bank projects around the world failed. In construction and high-tech projects, the failure rate sometimes rises to 60 percent. Things go wrong, the authors found, because a program might have been poorly designed, had weak top-level support, encountered bottlenecks, and didn't have feedback hard-wired in to help managers learn.[63]

However, the World Bank team—Jody Zall Kusek, Marelize Gorgens Prestidge, and Billy C. Hamilton—argue that five simple rules can greatly improve the odds of success[64]:

1. *Make it about the how.* Figuring out what managers are trying to accomplish, how much the program will cost, and who is in charge of doing what are essential first steps.

2. *Keep your champions close but your critics closer.* The World Bank team learned their lesson from *The Godfather Part II*, when Michael Corleone shared this wisdom with the members of his Mafia family. Some have attributed the quote to the Chinese general Sun Tzu or the Italian philosopher Niccolò Machiavelli, but the point is clear: managing stakeholders, both friends and opponents, is critical to maintaining political support for moving forward.

3. *Informed networks matter; work with them.* No one organization can control everything it touches. Both the formal and informal networks connected with a program can play a powerful role in shaping success.

4. *Unclog the pipes.* Success often comes from anticipating problems before they happen and acting quickly to sweep bottlenecks away.

5. *Build the ship as it sails.* No one gets everything right the first time, and it's impossible to anticipate and solve all problems in advance. Effective programs build in a system to learn from problems, even failures. They build from a small scale, learn where the problems lie, and move to scale once managers know how best to solve or avoid the problems that lurk around the corner.

Too often, there's a sense of dread that surrounds government management because of the expectation that programs will fail. The World Bank team has seen plenty of failure. But they underline a very important point: failure isn't inevitable, and charting the right steps can vastly shrink the odds of problems and greatly enhance the chances for success.

The media tend to focus on failure stories because they attract more readers and viewers. But behind the headlines are important and enduring examples of success. Much of government works very well much of the time. Many of the biggest problems can be solved, as GAO found in its analysis of the federal government's "high-risk" programs. Still, enduring problems remain. That's often because government often tries to do very hard things, because it does them through very complex systems, and because the implementation of its programs becomes wrapped in very contentious politics.

Behind these big debates are important and enduring themes. First, many problems we label "implementation" actually reflect far larger administrative issues. What we call failure may be the product of goals that policymakers do not agree on and results that they do not like. Many alleged failures turn out not to be breakdowns in the actual process of implementation but the consequence of poor policy choices, impossibly high hopes announced at a program's conception, or misjudgments in legislative prescription of implementation strategies. Sometimes, in fact, the more efficient the implementation of a bad policy, a poor program, or a legislatively mandated faulty strategy, the more conspicuous the failure will be. So-called implementation failures thus often reflect deep and enduring problems in other parts of the policy process.

Second, our principal focus has been on implementation by American governments. But wallowing in government failure stories can make it easy to forget that the private sector's record is scarcely clean. Anyone who has ever worked for a private organization can vouch for substantial waste of materials, inefficient ways of processing paperwork, and problems of bureaucracy that match those of the public sector. Millions of automobiles have been recalled for defects; drugs have been introduced and later found to cause fatal injuries and serious birth defects; computers fail and their software crashes; and other problems in workmanship, services, and materials abound. The point here is not to compound our misery but to emphasize that poor performance is not a purely public-sector problem. In fact, most of the outrageous fraud, waste, and abuse stories about government itself involve intricate programs whose implementation is deeply interwoven with government's nongovernmental partners.

Finally, many implementation problems arise out of the increasing complexity of American society instead of government's fundamental failure. The more the boundaries blur—between the public and private sectors, among federal, state, and local governments—the more dependent programs become on the interrelationship of all of these organizations and the more difficult it is to achieve true success.

These mitigating considerations do not mean that implementation by American governments is what it should be. On the contrary, the evidence shows not only that implementation is often unsatisfactory but also that its improvement has been neglected—by Congress, by the president, by operating agencies, and by the research community. Improving performance requires correcting that neglect.[65]

CASE 12.1

Crashing to Earth: Obama's Signature Health Insurance Program Stumbles

In late September 2013, Senator Ted Cruz (R-Tex.) was determined to bring back the great tradition of the filibuster, when members of the Senate would talk on the floor for endless hours to delay consideration of an issue they opposed. For Cruz, the issue was President Barack Obama's signature health insurance program, the Affordable Care Act (also commonly referred to as "Obamacare"). The program required all Americans to sign up for health insurance if they didn't already have it, and Cruz was determined to shut down the federal government, if necessary, to stop the launch of the program on October 1, 2013. And talk he did, for twenty-one hours straight, complete with a reading of Dr. Seuss's *Green Eggs and Ham* and an impression of Darth Vader from *Star Wars.* He failed to stop funding for Obamacare, but his speech helped galvanize Republican opposition to the program. True to their threats, Republicans refused to continue funding the government if the funding included money for the president's program. And that led to a limited shutdown of the federal government on October 1.

But in one of the biggest ironies in American history, the program actually started up just as much of the rest of the government shut down. Obamacare launched with funding independent of the annual congressional appropriations, so it was unaffected by the shutdown, and the Democrats gleefully watched Republicans take the heat for closing many government operations—except for the very one at which they aimed. Political pressures rose, with the public blaming Republicans most for the shutdown. As the country neared the ceiling on the national debt on October 17, congressional Republicans caved in. They agreed to reopen the government without defunding Obamacare, and the Democrats celebrated.

For the most part, Obamacare wasn't government-funded health care. It wasn't even government-funded health insurance. It was a government-created marketplace, called an "exchange," where citizens could shop among private health insurance plans and decide what to buy. Citizens who already had health insurance didn't need to do anything.

Citizens without health insurance were required to buy it, with escalating penalties over time if they did not. The poor were aided by federal subsidies to help them afford the insurance. Democrats looked forward to signing up millions of uninsured Americans and locking in support from happy consumers so Republicans could never uproot the program.

For citizens, the exchange was really a website, HealthCare.gov, where they could shop and sign up for coverage. In the first days of October, there were early signs the website wasn't working well. Some consumers complained that they couldn't access the site, that it crashed, or that it lost their personal information after they began entering it. Administration officials pointed to the technical glitches as a sign of the program's success. It was so popular, they said, that huge demand crashed the site. "Americans are excited to look at their options for health coverage, with record demand in the first days of the marketplaces," said an administration release announcing that there would soon be fixes to the information technology problems.[1]

But the reports of problems escalated—that the website was crashing or was simply unavailable, and that it would fail to capture the information that citizens entered. As soon as the government shutdown ended, reporters began turning to the website story, and they found complaints wherever they looked. At its launch, the site featured a smiling woman who seemed thrilled to be signing up for health insurance. As the problems mounted, the government took down her picture and replaced it with four icons suggesting ways to sign up: computer, phone, an in-person visit with a counselor (called a "navigator"), and an old-fashioned paper form.

The administration brought in Jeffrey Zients, former acting director of the Office of Management and Budget, to troubleshoot the site, and Zients promised quick action. "We're confident by the end of November, HealthCare.gov will be smooth for a vast majority of users," he said.[2] The website gradually became more reliable and reports began surfacing of citizens who had successfully signed up for coverage, but progress was slow.

As the website improved, however, many citizens who held existing insurance policies began to receive notices that their policies were being canceled. Estimates of the number of citizens who would lose existing policies ran into the millions. That produced outrage, since one of the bedrock promises of Obamacare had been "if you like your plan, you can keep it." In fact, he said it at least thirty-four times, in some version, during the debate on the bill's passage and in the months that followed.[3] Obama was forced to apologize, saying, "I am sorry that they, you know, are finding themselves in this situation, based on assurances they got from me." He reassured Americans that "I've assigned my team to see what we can do to close some of the holes and gaps in the law."[4] And he pointed out that the insurance most Americans would get under his plan would be better than the insurance it replaced. Republicans seized on the problem as evidence that they were right from the beginning: that Obamacare was a bad idea that should be repealed or defunded. One critic labeled it a sample of the "half-baked liberalism that has been popular among many Democrats for several decades."[5]

As investigating reporters started digging, the problems tumbled out. In the law, the states had primary responsibility for the exchanges and the websites, and the federal site was a fallback for states that could not—or would not—participate. Many Republican governors decided they wanted nothing to do with Obamacare, and some other governors decided it would be easier to let the feds figure out how to launch the program. So instead of HealthCare.gov covering just a handful of states, it was ultimately responsible at the program's launch for citizens in thirty-six states. That, in turn, made the job far larger than the administration originally anticipated.

Building the information system also proved very complicated—more complex, one state health official said, than the Manhattan Project, the program that was responsible for the first atomic bomb in the 1940s.[6] The information technology managers had to pull together information from insurance companies, provide citizens a chance to submit their own personal information, create computer matches for the options available for citizens with certain characteristics in each state, calculate the subsidy that lower-income citizens would receive under the program, and allow citizens to shop for coverage and then sign up. That was a very large number of simultaneously moving parts, and many of the pieces came together just in the last weeks before the October 1 launch.

That left very little time for careful testing—and no time at all to stress-test the system as a whole under the demand of millions of citizens expected to visit the HealthCare.gov site. By mid-November, the first numbers emerged on how many citizens managed to navigate the system—fewer than 27,000 people, of the perhaps 40 million uninsured, signed up under the federal government's portion of the program.[7] The signup period stretched until March 31, 2014, and administration officials had always expected that most individuals would sign up close to the finish line. The administration had been hoping for a first-month signup of ten times that size. The low numbers embarrassed the administration and reinforced the sense of chaos surrounding the program.

The website issues revealed deeper implementation problems. The federal government itself didn't build the website. Rather, the feds built a large private network of at least forty-seven different contractors to construct different parts of the system, according to a survey conducted by the Sunlight Foundation. The collection included some consulting giants, like Booz Allen Hamilton and Deloitte; a relatively unknown company called CGI Federal, which relied on contracts for almost all its business; and even a private university, George Washington University.[8] The feds had no effective "systems integrator" to supervise the effort and to pull the pieces together, so it was little wonder that, while individual pieces seemed to work well enough, the system failed when launched as a whole. And, to insulate what was essentially a startup venture from political scrutiny, the Obama administration pushed much of the work out from the Department of Health and Human Services into one of its small and relatively little-known agencies, the Centers for Medicare and Medicaid Services (CMS). CMS manages the two giant programs that compose its name, but its officials had no experience in managing a startup or in leveraging private insurance companies.

Obama's popularity slid throughout the debacle to the lowest point to date in his administration, with more citizens disapproving than approving of his job performance. He suffered especially among independents, who had been so important to his reelection in 2012.[9] Democrats and Republicans fiercely debated whether the problems were the natural growing pains of a large and complex new program or a sign of a fatal overreach. Former president Bill Clinton said "we're better off with this law than without it," but House Speaker John Boehner (R-Ohio) countered "that Americans were misled when they were promised that they could keep their coverage under President Obama's health care law. The entire health care law is a train wreck that needs to go."[10] This certainly wasn't the start Obama had been hoping for in the program he intended to be his most important legacy.

QUESTIONS TO CONSIDER

1. Do you think that the Obamacare problems in October 2013 were simply the result of launching a very complicated program? Or were they the result of a serious overreach by the Obama administration? Think about the administrative implications—not whether you believe that Obamacare is a good policy.

2. In retrospect, what steps do you think that the Obama administration should have taken, from the beginning, to avoid the problems it encountered?

3. How many of the problems came from the basic design of the program—that is, from policymaking—and how many came from the way it worked—that is, from program implementation? What lessons do you see in this case for the links needed between policymaking and implementation?

4. Step back and consider how the government communicates expectations to citizens. Policymakers want to claim credit for big ideas. But the bigger the idea, the harder it is to pull off. The government could promise less and exceed expectations—or make big promises and risk falling short. The government could also tell citizens that big change is hard and will take time to produce big results. How should policymakers deal with the challenge of communicating about big ideas and hard problems?

NOTES

1. *CBS News*, "Obamacare Website Goes Down for Repairs" (October 4, 2013), http://www.cbsnews.com/8301-201_162-57606175/.

2. Jason Millman, "Zients: HealthCare.gov to Work Soon," *Politico* (October 25, 2013), http://www.politico.com/story/2013/10/jeff-zients-healthcaregov-working-by-end-of-november-98850.html#ixzz2k0CK5oGo.

3. Aaron Sharockman, "Sorting Out the Real Story on 'If You Like Your Plan, You Can Keep It'" (November 6, 2013), http://www.politifact.com/truth-o-meter/article/2013/nov/06/sorting-out-truth-if-you-your-plan-you-can-keep/.

4. Juliet Eilperin, "President Obama Apologizes to Americans Who Are Losing Their Health Insurance," *Washington Post* (November 7, 2013), http://www.washingtonpost.com/politics/president-obama-apologizes-to-americans-who-are-losing-their-health-insurance/2013/11/07/2306818e-4803-11e3-a196-3544a03c2351_story.html.

5. Julian Zelizer, "Obamacare and the Failure of Half-Baked Liberalism," *CNN Opinion* (November 11, 2013), http://www.cnn.com/2013/11/11/opinion/zelizer-obamacare-liberalism/.

6. Interview with the author.

7. Amy Goldstein and Paul Kane, "Administration: 106,000 Enrolled in Health Insurance in First Month of HealthCare.gov," *Washington Post* (November 13, 2013), http://www.washingtonpost.com/politics/house-committee-hears-from-technology-officials-on-health-care-exchanges/2013/11/13/91d0bc5a-4c6e-11e3-9890-a1e0997fb0c0_story.html?hpid=z1.

8. Bill Allison, "Good Enough for Government Work? The Contractors Building Obamacare," *Sunlight Foundation* (October 9, 2013), http://reporting.sunlightfoundation.com/2013/aca-contractors/.

9. David Lauter, "Obama's Approval Ratings Continue to Slide, New Poll Shows," *Los Angeles Times* (November 8, 2013), http://www.latimes.com/nation/politics/politicsnow/la-pn-obama-approval-ratings-slide-20131108,0,1519711.story#axzz2kRulymTo.

10. Juliet Eilperin, "Bill Clinton Identifies 3 Big Problems with the Obamacare Rollout," *Washington Post* (November 12, 2013), http://www.washingtonpost.com/blogs/post-politics/wp/2013/11/12/bill-clinton-identifies-3-big-problems-with-the-obamacare-rollout/?hpid=z3.

CASE 12.2

On top of everything else you can blame aging baby boomers for, add millions of dollars for new street signs. The Federal Highway Administration (FHWA) has issued new regulations on street signs. Gone are old signs with street names in ALL CAPS. In are street signs in Upper and Lower Case. Why? Experts say that the mixed lettering is easier to read.

"As drivers get older, we want to make sure they're able to read the signs," explained FHWA Administrator Victor Mendez. "Research shows that older drivers are better able to read signs when they're written in both capital and small letters. It's really driven by safety."[1] In addition, new FHWA regulations (http://mutcd.fhwa.dot.gov) require communities to make their road signs easier to see at night, making them more reflective so drivers can see stop, yield, and railroad crossing signs better.

"I think it's ridiculous," complained Milwaukee Alderman Bob Donovan. His city will have to spend $1.4 million to meet the new sign standards. "Our street signs have worked perfectly well for 100 years or more. I think it's just the federal government run amok. If they don't have far more important things to deal with, they're not doing their job." In Canyon, Texas, the cost to the town would be nearly 2,000 signs at $100 each. City manager Randy Criswell said he had aging parents: "They think this is silly."[2] Critics pointed out that the feds require the new signs—but aren't providing any money to pay for them.

The regulations are very detailed. If a community installs a sign so the speed limit can be changed, the light-emitting diodes on the sign must be white.[3] Wisconsin signmakers can't use a picture of a lake to signify the exit to get to the lake.[4] In Washington State, the agency said communities couldn't use signs whose bottoms were too low (two feet instead of five feet above ground level).[5]

Then there's the answer to a question from the assistant township engineer in Wayne Township, New Jersey. FHWA tells him that the standard for signs warning of curves ahead is:

> In advance of horizontal curves on freeways, on expressways, and on roadways . . . that are functionally classified as arterials or collectors, horizontal alignment warning signs shall be used . . . based on the speed differential between the roadway's posted or statutory speed limit of 85th-percentile speed, whichever is higher, or the prevailing speed on the approach to the curve, and the horizontal curve's advisory speed.[6]

That, at least, was what the federal agency wrote in an attempt to clarify the policy.

QUESTIONS TO CONSIDER

1. What do you make of the criticisms from local officials of the new federal road sign requirements? Do you think that the federal government went too far? Or are the regulations an attempt to make sure that older drivers—a group that is getting larger in number every day—can more easily see the signs on the road?

2. What's the case for allowing local officials to design their own signs, free from federal supervision and interference? What's the case for ensuring national standards for signs everywhere in the country?

3. Consider the last explanation of federal standards for warning sides of a curve ahead. Does it make sense to you? (*Hint:* The idea is that wherever drivers are in the country, they ought to get about the same warning of which way the road is going, and that the faster that they are driving, the farther in advance they ought to get a warning. The trick is how to translate that idea into placing the sign—and how to compensate for the fact that drivers don't always travel at the speed limit.)

NOTES

1. Larry Capeland, "ALL CAPS? Not OK on Road Signs, Federal Government Says," *USA Today* (October 21, 2010), http://www.usatoday.com/news/nation/2010-10-21-road-signs-all-caps-lowercase_N.htm.

2. Ibid.

3. http://mutcd.fhwa.dot.gov/resources/interpretations/pdf/2_09_3.pdf.

4. http://mutcd.fhwa.dot.gov/resources/interpretations/pdf/2_646.pdf.

5. http://mutcd.fhwa.dot/gov/resources/interpretations/pdf/2_660.pdf.

6. http://mutcd.fhwa.dot.gov/resources/interpretations/pdf/2_09_2.pdf.

CASE 12.3

A century ago, whooping cough spread dread across the country, causing more than 5,000 deaths a year. But after scientists discovered that the pertussis bacteria caused the awful respiratory disease, with its characteristic "whoop" sound, researchers produced an enormously effective vaccine. Then they went a step further and combined that vaccine and the antibodies to diphtheria and tetanus into a single shot (DPT), putting an end to the three diseases that had terrorized kids for decades.

But by the 1970s, parents were growing increasingly suspicious of the DPT vaccine, particularly that it was causing brain damage, including encephalopathy, a condition that can produce personality changes, tremors, and seizures. After a 1982 NBC documentary won an Emmy Award for its tale of children said to be injured by the vaccine, an antivaccination epidemic was born, spurred further by a 1998 study that suggested the measles, mumps, and rubella vaccine caused autism. (In 2010, that study was retracted by the journal that had published it.)

Today, untold thousands of children have never received these vaccinations. As a result, the dreaded diseases of the early 1900s are making a comeback. In May 2013, Washington State public health officials declared a health emergency as whooping cough galloped across the state. In just the first month, the disease infected more than 2,500 Washingtonians, with children ages ten to thirteen hit especially hard. Other states, including California and Wisconsin, have had outbreaks as well, but in Washington the infection rose to an epidemic.

How could a disease we thought we had licked have spread so fast? Part of the explanation comes from Washington parents who took advantage of a new law allowing them to opt out of vaccinations for their kids. Another part comes as a result of a new DPT vaccine designed in the 1990s to cause fewer side effects, but which declined in effectiveness over time, leaving adults with lower levels of protection.

Perhaps the biggest part of the problem, however, comes from underinvestment in public health. Financially strapped states, including Washington, have been struggling to support programs to immunize kids, advertise the benefits of the dreaded shots, track the spread of diseases of all kinds, and manage the consequences. Becky Neff, a registered nurse in Skagit County, along the Puget Sound near the Canadian border, told a reporter, "It's the largest epidemic I've ever seen." How large? No one really knows, she explained, because the county has just two nurses compiling disease reports, compared with five just a few years ago. The nurses who are left "don't have time to call and say who's positive and negative."

The economic downturn left a trail of debris in its wake, and public health has been especially hard hit. Rhode Island's free breast and cervical cancer screening programs were suspended. In Washtenaw County, Michigan, budget cuts forced the government to suspend new enrollment in a health coverage program for low-income residents who didn't qualify for Medicaid. In 2010 and 2011, the local public health workforce dropped 15 percent, according to the National Association of County and City Health Officials.

Public health workers are usually the last noticed of the first responders. The public tends to dismiss them as disease-counters and shot-givers—until killer tomatoes strike (with a salmonella outbreak in 2008) or anthrax threatens (after the 9/11 terrorist attacks).

The recent whooping cough outbreak shows how fast disease can spread. The 1918 Spanish flu pandemic, which killed more than 50 million people around the world, showed just how serious that can be. And in today's super-linked world, any disease anywhere can deposit itself on anyone's doorstep in just hours. In fact, just one airplane passenger from Hong Kong brought severe acute respiratory syndrome (SARS) to Toronto in 2003. The resulting outbreak virtually shut the city down and killed forty-four people.

The Washington whooping cough emergency, fortunately, didn't rise to that scale. But it does raise two very worrisome points. First, disinvesting in public health now can pose serious consequences down the road. Whether we can accurately count the number of preteens struggling with whooping cough might not seem like a big deal, but if we suddenly have to track and manage the spread of a SARS-like disease, the lack of capacity would aggravate a grade-A crisis.

Second, if nervous parents push opt-out provisions on state policymakers, and if individual states loosen the requirements for vaccinations and other public health strategies, the individual decisions can quickly create far broader ripples. Many public health programs rely on the inelegantly named "herd" strategy. If almost everyone is immunized, a single whooping cough victim can easily be isolated. If large numbers of kids haven't been vaccinated, or if vaccines for their parents begin to wear off, one cough can quickly spread across the population.

Individual parents' decisions about vaccinating their kids might seem limited to their own families, but nothing could be further from the truth. It's no exaggeration to say that such parental decisions, sanctioned by individual states and repeated many times over, can have national consequences. Couple that with budget cuts at the heart of the nation's public health capacity. We see evidence everywhere of the huge consequences of the Great Recession, but Washington's whooping cough outbreak shows an important break in our first-response lines of defense.

QUESTIONS TO CONSIDER

1. How strong a stand should public health officials play in encouraging parents to vaccinate their children against whooping cough? Should aggressive regulations, like banning children from school, be part of the strategy?

2. What should be the public role of public health workers? What media briefing would you design in such a case?

3. What does this case say about the broader problem of homeland security, especially creating enough capacity in public health to deal with possible problems? Should the government invest more in state and local public health officials? How should they make that tradeoff?

Note: This case comes from my column in *Governing* (August 2012), http://www.governing.com/columns/potomac-chronicle/col-whooping-cough-comeback-raises-troubling-questions.html.

CASE 12.4

Better Numbers, Lower Crime

For residents of the Standing Rock Indian Reservation, which stretches across a large swath of the central Dakotas, crime was an enormous problem a few years back. By mid-2008, violence on the 3,500-square-mile reservation was six times the national average. Residents had so little confidence in the federal Bureau of Indian Affairs (BIA) to do anything about it that they often didn't even bother to report crimes.

It was part of a much bigger problem. According to data collected by BIA and the U.S. Department of Justice, there are 1.9 million American Indians and Alaska natives in the country. There are 566 federally recognized American Indian and Alaska Native tribes, on 310 reservations stretching across 55 million acres of land. And violent crime is 2.5 times higher on reservations than the national average.

Arnold Schott, both a mayor and coroner on the reservation, said at the time, "I can look out my door [and see] our little kids, 8, 9, 10 or younger" being lured into the drug trade. The director of the tribal health administration, Randy Bear Ribs, agreed that the crime problem was linked to drug and alcohol abuse. The reservation's chairman, Ron His Horse Is Thunder, added that soaring crime was fueling "a sense of hopelessness."

But the BIA didn't have any money to help, and they knew just throwing money at the problem wouldn't solve it, anyway. So along with the Department of the Interior, the BIA hatched a plan to take advantage of the Obama administration's management agenda, which challenged federal

leaders to set high-priority performance goals and seek big impacts. The Office of Management and Budget (OMB), which is leading the management program, required agencies not only to define goals but to develop metrics to gauge success—and hopefully produce real breakthroughs.

To get started, the Department of the Interior focused on reducing violent crime on four reservations: the Sioux Standing Rock Reservation in North Dakota and South Dakota, the Chippewa-Cree Tribe's Rocky Boy's Reservation in Montana, the Mescalero Apache Tribe's Reservation in New Mexico, and the Shoshone and Arapaho Tribes' Wind River Reservation in Wyoming. Given the big run-up in crime, any reduction looked like a very heavy lift, so the Interior initially set a very low crime-reduction target. OMB countered that if this goal really was a high priority, then the agency ought to aim for a significant cut. As a result, the Interior agreed to shoot for a 5 percent reduction in violent crime in 2010 and 2011.

Bending the crime curve was a hard enough problem. Making the job even tougher was the notorious short-staffing of the BIA's teams. Despite those huge hurdles, the BIA busted past its 5 percent target. In fact, the four reservations achieved an astounding 35 percent cut in crime. The Mescalero Reservation saw a whopping 68 percent reduction. Crime in Standing Rock dropped 27 percent; in Rocky Boy, the drop was 40 percent. Originally, the story wasn't as good in Wind River. Trust in the system was so bad that many citizens just didn't bother to report many crimes. The reservation was also the most underpoliced of the four and it took longer to gear up. But in the second year, after the program began to hit its stride, crime dropped 30 percent.

So how did they do it? This would be a huge story for any government program. But given the fed's long-troubled relations with Native American tribes, it's off the charts. Part of the improvement came from strategic investment—not to saturate the streets with cops but simply to bring staffing levels up to the national averages. (It's a sign of the nation's long-term neglect of the tribes that simply hitting the staffing norms can bring such a huge return.)

The central part of the story, however, was the careful work of Charles Addington, the BIA's associate director for field operations, whose crime-fighting strategy made him a finalist for a Partnership for Public Service Sammie award—what one writer called "the Oscars for federal employees." When Addington first took up the project, he knew he needed a crime statistics baseline. But the data were so bad that he had to begin by putting experts to work hand counting three years' worth of crime reports. He then used these data collections to compare where crime fighters were deployed and where crimes were happening. He adopted predictive-policing methods—which rely on using advanced technological tools and data analysis to take proactive measures to "preempt" crime—to position cops in advance where crime was likely to occur.

As BIA Assistant Director Jason Thompson told the Partnership for Public Service, "Charlie analyzed data to determine, based on time of day, location and other intelligence information, where the crime was going to be and how he could be on the preventive side, stopping it before it happened, rather than the reactive side where officers would be responding to calls." He worked closely with local communities to bring in a wide range of local support services to root out the causes of crime. And perhaps most important, he worked hard with tribal leaders to break down the long-standing barriers of distrust—and to make the tribal police an integrated team with BIA's crime fighters.

A bit more money unquestionably helped. But the real innovation here was tying the money to performance data, using the data to drive real-time policing decisions, and driving the system to rebuild frayed relationships. Better numbers built stronger partnerships and helped put a dent in one of the nation's nastiest problems, in ways neither the tribes nor the BIA imagined possible.

QUESTIONS TO CONSIDER

1. Given the long history of administrative challenges and problems with crime on the reservations, what performance target would you have set? Too high, and you risk falling short. Too low, and you don't look serious.

2. What lessons does the data strategy developed by the BIA teach?

3. Are there implications for implementation and leadership that come from Addington's role?

4. One of the big challenges is ensuring that the progress continues. What steps would you take to prevent the big steps forward from slipping back?

Note: This case comes from my column in *Governing* (February 2014), http://www.governing.com/columns/potomac-chronicle/gov-fighting-crime-on-the-rez.html.

KEY CONCEPTS

contracts 338

crossover sanctions 337

data visualization 349

gaming 347

geographic information systems 347

implementation 327

mandates 336

open data 349

partial preemption 337

randomized controlled trials 346

FOR FURTHER READING

Behn, Robert D. *The PerformanceStat Potential.* Washington, D.C.: Brookings Institution, 2014.

Beland, Daniel, Philip Rocco, and Alex Waddan. *Obamacare Wars: Federalism, State Politics, and the Affordable Care Act.* Lawrence: University Press of Kansas, 2016.

Derthick, Martha. *New Towns In-Town.* Washington, D.C.: Urban Institute, 1972.

Hogwood, Brian H., and B. Guy Peters. *The Pathology of Public Policy.* Oxford: Clarendon Press, 1985.

Kusek, Jody Zall, Marelize Goergens Prestidge, and Billy C. Hamilton. *Fail-Safe Management: Five Rules to Avoid Project Failure.* Washington, D.C.: World Bank, 2013.

Mead, Lawrence M. *Government Matters: Welfare Reform in Wisconsin.* Princeton, N.J.: Princeton University Press, 2004.

Nussle, Jim, and Peter Orszag, eds. *Moneyball for Government.* Washington, D.C.: Disruption Books, 2014.

Pressman, Jeffrey L., and Aaron B. Wildavsky. *Implementation.* Berkeley: University of California Press, 1973.

Wholey, Joseph S., Harry P. Hatry, and Kathryn E. Newcomer, eds. *Handbook of Practical Program Evaluation.* San Francisco: Jossey-Bass, 1994.

Wilson, James Q. *Bureaucracy: What Government Agencies Do and Why They Do It.* New York: Basic Books, 1989.

SUGGESTED WEBSITES

The Internet is full of the new initiatives in the area of program implementation. For New York City's performance management system, see **www.nyc.gov/html/ops/cpr/html/home/home.shtml**. Information about Baltimore's CitiStat program can be found at **www.baltimorecity.gov/Government/AgenciesDepartments/CitiStat.aspx**.

For case studies on implementation problems, see the report of the study committee that investigated the

Columbia space shuttle accident (**www.nasa.gov/columbia/home/index.html**), the special report on emergency response in New York on the morning of September 11, 2001 (**www.nyc.gov/html/fdny/html/mck_report/index.shtml**), and the report of the Arlington County September 11, 2001, response at the Pentagon (**www.co.arlington.va.us/Departments/Fire/edu/about/FireEduAboutAfterReport.aspx**).

for CQ Press

WANT A BETTER GRADE?

Get the tools you need to sharpen your study skills. Access practice quizzes, eFlashcards, video, and multimedia at **edge.sagepub.com/kettl7e**.

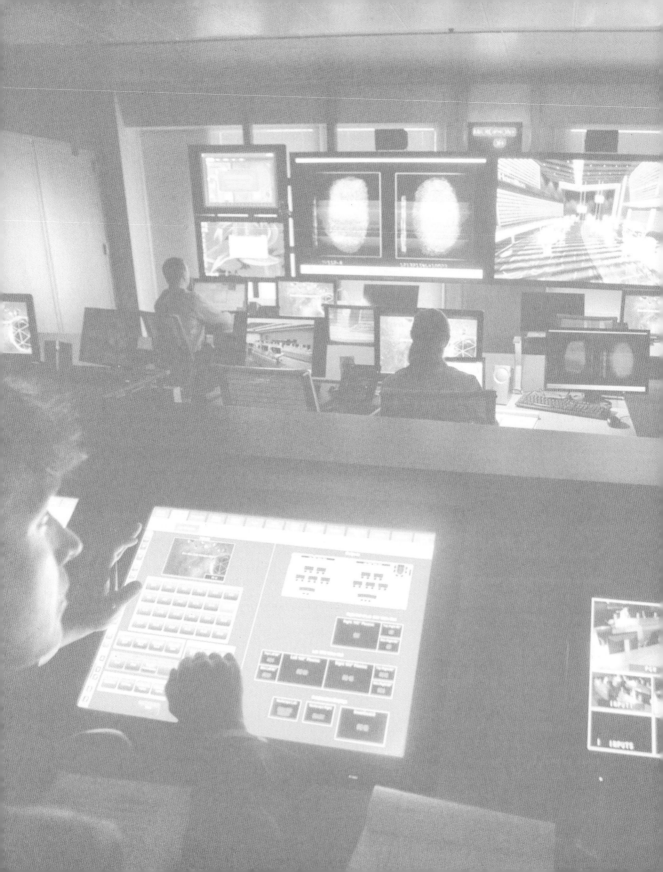

PART V

Administration in a Democracy

Running a bureaucracy in a democracy creates two sets of issues. As we saw in Chapter 1, we want to see programs managed efficiently and effectively—and we also want the bureaucracy to be responsive and accountable. And as we have seen throughout this book, the quest for accountability and effectiveness is, at its core, a political journey. This section examines the dynamics of bureaucracy's relationship with the larger political and economic system, especially the exercise of administrative power through regulation. We also examine the methods that legislatures can use in controlling the way administrators exercise the power delegated to them.

The core of administrative ethics in the public sector lies in balancing the competing goals of efficiency and accountability. We want administrators to be efficient and accountable, but crosscutting political forces make it hard to achieve either goal, let alone accomplish both. We conclude the book by circling back to the big questions with which we began: with a careful look at how the competing forces of accountability, effectiveness, and politics affect administration in a democracy.

13

REGULATION AND THE COURTS

As the New York Yankees finished their 2008 baseball season, a new stadium rose next door. For nostalgic fans, it was a difficult transition. Babe Ruth had christened the old stadium with a home run on its opening day in 1923. The new stadium promised luxury boxes and a martini bar.

Major League Baseball held its 2008 All-Star Game at venerable Yankee Stadium. As baseball commissioner Bud Selig explained, "When you think of Yankee Stadium, it is the most famous cathedral in baseball, and, I think, the most famous stadium in the world." And the 2008 season was also the stadium's last, "So we really believe that this is the way we can honor the cathedral that has meant so much to this sport for so long."[1] Baseball fans everywhere knew it as "the house that Ruth built," an enduring homage to one of the game's most famous sluggers and a tribute to legions of fans who cheered on the championships. But it was also a reminder to Yankees' fans of the culture shock coming their way. As a new stadium rose next door, officials were planning to demolish the old relic and convert the site into a park.

During the new stadium's construction, however, city officials discovered a big problem. Local government regulations required a check on the quality of the concrete poured in construction projects—faulty concrete could cause buildings to collapse. At the stadium and at other projects in New York City, including the new building rising at the World Trade Center, city investigators found that a private company, Testwell Laboratories, failed to properly test the concrete. It then falsely certified the tests. When asked why a company might do that, an official explained, "I guess it keeps your overhead and costs down if you don't actually do the tests."[2] That, of course, does nothing to ensure the safety of the building.

Tough concrete standards are important. After all, the collapse of part of the concrete ceiling in Boston's "Big Dig" tunnel killed a driver in July 2006. To get the job done, the regulatory chain was complex: the city wrote the rules, and it hired a private contractor to check on whether other private contractors were complying with the standards. As we saw in Chapter 12, layers of contractors are part of the implementation process. They are just as essential to government regulation. Regulation, of course, is a core element of government's work. It defines how government officials exercise their discretion, and how private companies connect with the public, from the safety of the foods we eat to the security of our bank deposits. Decisions might be the central governmental act, and budgets provide what administrators need to carry out those decisions, but regulations are the central nervous system of government.

REGULATION AS A FOUNDATION FOR GOVERNMENT'S WORK

Laws prescribe what government administrators do. Regulation defines *how* they do it. It translates complex tax laws into the forms that taxpayers love to hate, and it sets the rules that keep planes safely in the air.

CHAPTER OBJECTIVES

- Understand the role of regulation in public administration

- Explore the kinds of regulation

- Examine the steps in regulatory procedure

- Probe the ways in which regulators are held accountable

Regulations specify the size of reflectors on bicycle wheels and ensure the accessibility of public buildings. Rules both empower and limit government employees. They define how far government administrators can push into the lives of ordinary citizens, and thereby restrict their freedom. Rules limit how far government administrators can push their control, and thereby protect citizens. Government regulates the vitamin pills we take and the therapeutic claims that go on our toothpaste tubes. It controls the safety of our prescription drugs and our cars. It oversees the maintenance of airplanes and buses and sets the standards for highway guardrails and interstate buses. It is literally impossible to get out of bed in the morning without encountering a government regulation, since the government regulates the bedding on which we sleep and, famously, the tags on the pillows on which we rest our heads. (It *is* legal to cut away the tags on pillows—but only consumers can use the scissors, after they take the pillows home. The tags protect consumers by providing information about what materials are inside the pillow, which the consumer can't see.) If public administration revolves around the balance of power and accountability, regulation defines how public administrators balance individual freedom and government control.

Some government regulation exists to promote public health and safety. There are rules restricting the sale of tobacco and requiring warning labels on packages. There is consumer information on prescription drugs and even more information supplied to doctors. In 1997, the Food and Drug Administration (FDA) ordered the popular diet pill Fen-Phen (short for the combination of fenfluramine and phentermine) be taken off the market because of evidence that it had caused fatal side effects. Applying for a credit card or a student loan brings pages of disclosure information. In recent years, government has continually revised the rules to provide more protection while making the disclosures easier to read.

Three issues are central to this work. One is the *source of regulatory authority*: the law vests administrative discretion in agencies, and it specifies how that discretion can be exercised. A second is the *amount of resources* that legislatures and the executive make available to the agencies for performance of their regulatory responsibilities: regardless of what the laws or regulations say, administrators cannot enforce the rules unless they have the resources—people, computers, and travel funds, among others—to do so. An ageless part of the regulatory game is to write a law but handcuff the regulation, especially by denying agencies the resources they need to manage the rules. A third feature is *regulatory procedure*: the interplay between responsibility for regulating private behavior and the rules that the legislature, the chief executive, and the courts establish to govern the behavior of regulating agencies and employees. These three issues form the core of this chapter.

Government regulations range broadly. At one extreme are speed limits and stoplights, which govern ordinary behavior in daily life. At the other extreme are fundamental restrictions on liberty, and sometimes government intrusion into individual privacy. An individual cannot practice medicine or law without a state license. Some states regulate hairdressers and dog groomers as well. In most cities, local governments set the fares that taxicab drivers can charge and whether Uber drivers must be fingerprinted. In New York State, dentists battled state rules over who could regulate the state's dentists and what role the regulators can play. Many citizens were surprised to learn in 2013 the scope of the National Security Agency's surveillance of citizens' phone calls and email traffic. To truly understand government—and even more fundamentally, to truly understand public administration—one must understand government regulation.

The Roots of Regulation

Regulation goes back millennia. The Ten Commandments, after all, were part of God's compact with the Israelites after their release from Pharaoh's bondage and an entire book of the Bible—Ecclesiastes—is devoted to regulations. In the United States, regulation goes back to the beginning of the nation. The Constitution in 1789 gave Congress the power "to promote the progress of science and useful arts by securing for limited times to authors and inventors the exclusive right to their respective writings and discoveries."[3] This textbook is protected against plagiarism by a certificate issued by the U.S. Copyright Office, which administers a statute based on that provision. But this same constitutional grant of power has had far broader impact. In 1988, administering a statute under the same clause, the Patent and Trademark Office awarded the world's first animal-invention patent to Harvard University, whose scientists had transformed a mouse through genetic manipulation.[4]

Just *how far* government's regulatory power should go, of course, is a fundamental question of government. In this book, we focus on *how* the executive branch administers regulation. But the nonstop *how far* political controversy inevitably spills over into the *how* question. Regulation is grounded in law, but it's shaped by politics.[5] Trump began his administration by promising to peel rules back.

The public certainly has mixed feelings about regulation. Many critics complain that government regulation of business usually does more harm than good, that there are too many government regulations, and that too many rules make too little sense.[6] Yet most people do not favor rolling back government regulations that protect their workplace, safeguard the environment in their neighborhood, ensure the safety of the airplanes on which they fly, or set standards for the security of their bank accounts. Individuals do not like the idea of a big government interfering in their freedom, but they clearly expect government to protect them from danger, even if that means interfering in someone else's freedom. Indeed, the standard reaction to problems ranging from plane crashes to poisoned food is to interview government regulators. Why, reporters ask, did government not write a rule to prevent the problem from happening, even if the problem was the result of mistakes made by private companies?

Regulation is inevitably a matter of balancing its costs with its benefits, but it's just as much a matter of determining *who* pays the costs and *who* receives the benefits. America's approach to regulation is unique, David Vogel finds, because of both the way the process works and the level of the conflict it creates:

> The American system of regulation is distinctive in the degree of oversight exercised by the judiciary and the national legislature, in the formality of its rulemaking and enforcement process, in its reliance on prosecution, in the amount of information made available to the public, and in the extent of the opportunities provided for participation by non-industry constituencies. . . . The restrictions the United States has placed on corporate conduct affecting public health, safety, and amenity are at least as strict as and in many cases stricter than those adopted by other capitalist nations. As a result, in no other nation have the relations between the regulated and the regulators been so consistently strained.[7]

THE JOB OF REGULATION

Regulatory agencies vary in the kinds of regulation they administer.[8] Administrators are typically more expert in the issues than the legislators who write the laws and the courts who interpret them, but all three branches of government play major roles in regulation.

However, the most important issue is this: regulations not only define the power of government administrators, but they also shape the ways in which administrators exercise their discretion. Regulation is about creating and constraining government power.

Kinds of Regulations

Government regulation focuses on two kinds of problems: economic and social. The expansion of **economic regulation** began in the states, but in the federal government it dates from 1887, when the Interstate Commerce Commission was established to regulate the railroads.[9] It was the dominant form of regulation until the 1960s. Economic regulation has two characteristics. First, it has long sought to ensure competition by preventing monopolies and unfair methods of competition (including deception of consumers). These **antitrust laws** embrace all industries where such evils may appear and are administered by the Justice Department and the Federal Trade Commission. Second, in the effort to ensure fair and quality markets, the federal government has regulated the following aspects of economic activity: (1) entry to a business (by issuance or denial of "certificates of convenience and necessity," which are licenses to do business and serve certain routes or areas); (2) prices (by fixing maximum and, in some cases, minimum rates to be charged); (3) safety; and (4) standards of service.

At both the state and federal levels, government has typically lodged responsibility in independent regulatory commissions. These bodies tend to be separate from cabinet agencies and headed by boards. In most cases, the law ensures a balance on the boards between the political parties (although the party in power can often appoint the chair and secure a majority of commission votes). Each commission regulates a single industry or handful of industries, such as public utilities (gas, water, electric, and telephone companies), taxicabs, and airlines. The single-industry focus gives the regulatory commission special expertise, but it also increases the chance that the commission will fall under the domination of the industry it is supposed to regulate. Analysts have long worried about the **capture** of regulators by the organizations they regulate.[10] As oil was spewing from BP's well in the Gulf of Mexico, for example, critics charged that the chief regulator, the Minerals Management Service, had not paid enough attention to safety issues because it was preoccupied with helping oil producers expand production.

Social regulation began growing in importance early in the twentieth century, through restrictions on child labor and drugs, and then expanded enormously in the 1960s and 1970s. It focuses on the quality of life by seeking to safeguard the environment, protect workers' health and safety, ensure the safety and quality of consumer products, and prohibit discrimination on grounds of race, color, sex, age, or disability. Responsibility for achieving social regulation is mostly lodged not in independent commissions but in bureaus within departments or, as with the U.S. Environmental Protection Agency (EPA), in an independent agency with a single leader instead of a board. The jurisdictions of these bureaus and agencies are not confined to single industries but cover all industries where threats to health, safety, fair employment, and the environment may occur. Although social regulation seeks to improve the quality of life rather than counter economic imperfections of the market, it can also have substantial market effects—by reducing a business firm's freedom to act purely in its own self-interest and, more important, by often increasing costs.

Defense of the government's power of intervention rests on the economic concept of externalities, sometimes called spillover effects (discussed in Chapter 10). If a paper mill discharges pollutants into a river, downstream communities must pay the costs of cleaning up the river or purifying their intake to ensure safe drinking water for their citizens, while downstream swimmers, fishermen, and boaters pay the price in pleasures forgone. Dumping pollutants into the water is often cheaper than cleaning it up—and it's often a better deal for companies to pass the problems downstream. Economists would compare the manufacturer's savings to the downstream costs and would justify regulatory action to return the costs to the polluter if the value of the benefits accrued downstream were high enough. Thus, government could make an economic case for forcing the paper mill to internalize the externalities.[11]

Economic regulation and social regulation are not two sides of a single coin. In the political world, at least, they are two quite distinct coins. Although they retreat from extensive regulation of trucking, airlines, telecommunication, and financial services,[12] the Carter and Reagan administrations placed more elaborate protections on the environment, workers' health and safety, and consumers' products. The underlying politics were complex: economists of both liberal and conservative stripes succeeded in convincing both the president and members of Congress that economic deregulation would promote lower prices, better services, and stronger consumer choice. Meanwhile, however, the consumer and environmental movements were growing, building pressure for stronger social regulation.

There are very different political and administrative implications for economic and social regulation. In economic regulation, the regulatory agency often must consider just how much a stronger regulation might hinder market competition and increase costs. Local taxi commissions, for example, regularly debate whether they should mandate how clean a taxi should be, how the taxis are maintained, and whether taxi drivers must accept credit cards. Taxi companies often fight back on each of these rules by arguing that they would increase their costs—and the fares they must charge customers. New forms of public transport, like Uber and Lyft, both challenge the existing industry and pose big new regulatory challenges, like whether social-media-based systems should be regulated the same as taxis and how the relationship between the rideshare companies and their drivers should be regulated—if at all.

On the other hand, social regulatory agencies must often act to enforce strong, nonnegotiable standards. For example, the law requires the FDA to act immediately when a food or drug on the market is found to cause death or serious disease—and the procedural niceties must follow, rather than precede, an order to remove the product from store shelves. Sometimes regulatory action simply demands disclosure of information, such as the law requiring the labeling of health hazards on cigarette labels, or the EPA's standards for companies' disclosure of toxic materials they release into the environment. Regulated industries often fight back against proposed rules, but sometimes they actually welcome them. A single federal rule can replace a confusing collection of state and local standards. Tough rules can sometimes reassure customers and, thus, protect a company's sales.

Government agencies have many techniques for measuring a company's compliance with regulations. Some rules set technical standards, such as installing a guard around moving machine parts or installing bicycle reflectors of a certain size. Others set performance standards, such as an allowable level of pollution a facility can release. The company can then choose the method it prefers to reach the goal. The federal government has gone even further by creating a regulatory market to regulate some pollutants. In the effort to reduce acid rain, companies can buy and sell the *right to pollute* on the Chicago Board of Trade, in yet another case in which one private company—the Board of Trade—assists the government in the regulation of other companies. This system gives companies economic incentives to reduce their emissions, with the strongest incentives for the companies that can do so most cheaply. As a result, pollution

In 2015, Los Angeles became the largest city in the country to allow Uber and Lyft to operate side by side with the taxis at the city's airport.

has been dramatically reduced, acid rain levels have declined, and companies have won the flexibility to determine how best to reach the legislative goal.[13]

In addition to market incentives, regulatory information provides other pressures on companies' behavior. Crash tests by the federal government's National Highway Traffic Safety Administration and by private groups such as the Insurance Institute for Highway Safety have created strong inducements for automobile manufacturers to build safer cars. Federal research on medical errors has led to consumer scorecards of hospitals. Government inspections of nursing homes and restaurants often lead either to adverse publicity for poor performers or to certificates of approval that high performers can proudly hang on their walls.[14] Other agencies rely on companies' self-reporting of workers' accidents and health impairments, although owners' incentives for accurate reporting in this area are slight.[15]

State and Local Regulations

Regulation is also a major activity of state and local governments, such as New York City's efforts to ensure that concrete for the city's construction is safe and its campaign to force fast-food restaurants to list the nutritional information of the items they sell. A campaign to improve food safety in New York's restaurants led to a regulation requiring restaurants to post their inspection grades in the window, in large letters. A grade of less than an "A" invited potential customers to keep walking.

Their regulatory work is of two kinds. Some state regulation is independent of federal rules. State governments have created public utility commissions to control intrastate rates and services, banking departments to regulate state-chartered banks, and "lemon laws" to impose disclosure and warranty requirements on used-car dealers. State governments also have minimum-wage and antidiscrimination laws, bottle-deposit and recycling laws, and health and safety laws and regulations that cover a wide range of enterprises—from factory conditions to nursing homes to restaurants and bars to farmers' use of pesticides. Some states impose a five-cent deposit on recyclable beverage containers; in Michigan, it's ten cents. The states, not the federal government, regulate insurance companies, even though many insurance companies operate nationally. State regulation of health insurance created a huge challenge for the Obama administration's Affordable Care Act. Creating its national system of health insurance required the administration to dangle incentives for the states. Because of state dominance of health insurance regulation, the federal government could not directly intrude. Local governments also regulate broadly, sharing in the assurance of health and safety protections and the honesty of weights and measures (such as grocery scales and gas pumps). They administer land-use zoning, which seeks to control the location, structural features, and uses of buildings.

About 800 occupations are regulated in the United States. Some, such as attorneys, physicians, pharmacists, barbers, cosmetologists, and real estate agents, are regulated in every state.[16] Over half the states regulate funeral directors, chauffeurs, plumbers, and hearing-aid dealers, to cite only a few. Typically, licensing laws, which restrict entry to the professions and some other occupations, derive from lobbying by professional associations. These associations generally want to keep the number of competitors down and their own prices up. The rules are often administered by substantially autonomous licensing boards whose members are effectively nominated by the associations. Though rationalized as social regulation, necessary to protect the health and safety of consumers of such services, the licensing systems actually tend to produce economic regulation, limiting competition by restricting entry. State licensing of tattoo parlors, part a question of economics and part of consumer safety, varies widely. For example, tattoo parlors are regulated in Maryland by the state Board of Cosmetology, but not at all in New Mexico and North Dakota.

The second regulatory role of state and local governments is administration of national regulatory programs.[17] Congress has the power to preempt much state regulatory activity, displacing it with programs executed directly by federal officials. In some cases, like environmental protection and food safety, federal regulators contract with state agencies to administer national standards. In fact, that's just what happened in Flint: the city's water system was subject to national regulations, but the federal EPA had an agreement with the state's environmental agency, and the state agency was responsible for oversight of national standards. The state failed, and EPA failed to catch it.

Such interweaving is now a prominent part of the regulatory system, allowing some adaptation to local circumstances and letting individual state governments choose their roles in a regulatory system. It has the advantage of permitting a state to adopt more rigorous standards than those of the national laws and regulations, which would not be possible under full national preemption. It has the disadvantage shared by all farming out of the implementation of national policies—the weakness of federal sanctions against third-party noncompliance with national directives.[18]

In some cases, moreover, state governments set the standard that other states and even the federal government will eventually follow. California was the first state to require the installation of catalytic converters in cars, which reduce air pollution. No automaker could afford to ignore the huge California market or to build cars just for sale in California, so the catalytic converter soon became a national standard. Even though the George W. Bush administration had backed away from worldwide standards on global warming, California in 2002 passed a bill requiring that all cars sold in the state after 2009 meet tough standards for greenhouse gases, the carbon-based emissions that scientists believe promote global warming. California

DIVING INTO DATA

Tiny Houses in Portland

Who would have thought that television networks could make a hit series featuring homebuyers trying to squeeze into itsy-bitsy homes, both to save money and to reduce their environmental footprint? But the regulatory policy issues are deceptively complex.

The "tiny house" movement has become a national phenomenon, with a series of television shows featuring people who have decided to build and move into "tiny houses."

A "tiny house" is typically defined as a home of less than 400 square feet (for example, 20 feet by 20 feet), and are typically built on trailers.

Standards to ensure that that the plumbing won't flood the tiny house*: **Zero**

Standards to ensure that the internal electrical wiring won't catch fire*: **Zero**

*Unless the owner seeks to certify the tiny house as a recreational vehicle.

Federal Department of Transportation maximum dimensions for tiny houses on roads:

Height: 13.5 feet

Length: 40 feet

Width: 8.5 feet

You can park your tiny house and trailer in your back yard or on private property.

You can only park it on public roads or front yards for:

4 hours

State highway restrictions can vary, so the ability to pull a tiny house across state lines might be limited.

Trailers on which tiny houses sit must meet National Highway Safety Standards, including taillights, tires, and axels (so the trailer will not collapse on the road or be a hazard to other traffic).

Source: Portland Alternative Dwellings, at https://padtinyhouses.com/work-shop-follow-up-codes-and-tiny-houses.

QUESTIONS

1. Do these regulations seem reasonable for those who want to join the "tiny house" movement?

2. Chart the regulatory responsibility for these tiny houses. Which governments are responsible for which issues?

3. Do you think there ought to be more governmental regulatory flexibility to encourage people to build tiny houses?

4. Are you concerned that existing government regulations do not provide enough protection for those who build these homes?

5. Do these regulations provide enough protection for others who might be affected by the tiny houses—on the road and in neighborhoods?

has tough standards for flammability of office chairs and sets its own standards in a host of areas. In many policies, the state has led the way toward tougher rules.

Local governments, of course, issue regulations of their own. Most communities create zoning laws to determine where buildings can be constructed and how their owners can use them. Housing construction is impossible without water and sewage permits, and decisions about where to put water and sewer lines are the closest thing many communities have to an overall economic development plan. Some communities have even set their own minimum wages.

Expertise

An important part of the regulatory process is the concentration of technical expertise. Over time, doing so much work in a particular area means that the regulatory agency's staff often becomes highly expert. That can be very helpful in judging the safety of airbags in cars or the causes of airplane crashes. But a specialized agency can also develop a myopia that hardens its commitment to a single way of achieving statutory goals and to one set of procedures for obtaining input from affected interests. Such commitment can also reinforce its relationships with its most important clientele—a regulated interest, a public interest group, or a professional association—which has determined how best to play the game.

An especially important form of expertise is **cost-benefit analysis**, which has come to play a large role in regulatory programs. The idea is simple: government ought not impose new regulations whose benefits exceed the costs of complying with them. The idea has wide support, and applying that analysis has increased the importance of having experts in the agency. But it's also taken on a strongly ideological flavor, with conservatives seeking to use it to rein in regulations and the power of regulatory agencies. Forcing regulations to meet the cost-benefit standard, they believe, will result in fewer and less intrusive regulations.

There's great value in the ideas that the benefits of a regulation should exceed its costs. Underlying this notion, however, is a tough problem. Most costs are relatively straightforward to express in dollar terms. Many benefits, however, are subjective and hard to quantify. How much should reducing risk to health and safety be worth? What is the value of a life saved? What is the value of a Grand Canyon view free of noisy, low-flying airplanes, of fishable and swimmable streams, or of nondiscriminatory employment?[19] Translating these values into dollar figures becomes what Supreme Court Justice Oliver Wendell Holmes called, in another connection, "delusive exactitude," but it has a powerful impact on public policy. In July 2008, EPA quietly changed the value of a human life. Each of us might well believe we are priceless, but government regulators routinely set a dollar value on human lives. They then use that value to determine whether imposing new regulations is cost-effective, since policymakers have long held that the cost of regulations should not exceed their benefits. EPA had previously used a value of $8.04 million for each human life, but top officials decided in 2008 to cut that value to $7.22 million. That is still a lot of money, but the lower value makes it that much harder to make an economic case for tougher federal rules: the benefits of a new government regulation would have to be that much greater to make the rules worthwhile. Following the September 11, 2001, terrorist attacks and then after the *Deepwater Horizon* oil spill, attorney Kenneth Feinberg led an effort to determine reasonable compensation from disaster funds for the victims of the spill.

In one case, the Consumer Product Safety Commission (CPSC) faced a decision on whether to make mattresses less flammable. One proposal would require the industry to pay an extra $343 in manufacturing costs, but CPSC analysts expected the change to save 270 lives. The agency used a value of $5 million for a human life, which produced a benefit of $1.3 billion. That big margin for benefits over costs, agency officials concluded, made the new rule economically sensible.[20] Most people get uncomfortable with such calculations, but government has to use *some* standard for deciding which rules make sense and which do not. If policymakers do not explicitly set a value on human life, implicit judgments about what regulations are worthwhile will be made anyway. If the value is explicit, citizens and policymakers can debate it. But that does not make the debate any easier—and making the value explicit often draws fierce attack, as was the case with EPA's 2008 decision, because critics believed EPA was using the change to block new regulations.

Indeed, in a powerful critique of the application of cost-benefit analysis to government regulation, Frank Ackerman and Lisa Heinzerling contend,

> There is no reason to think that the right answers will emerge from the strange process of assigning dollar values to human life, human health, and nature itself, and then crunching the numbers. Indeed, in pursuing this approach, formal cost-benefit analysis often hurts more than it helps: it muddies rather than clarifies fundamental clashes about values. By proceeding as if its assumptions are scientific and by speaking a language all its own, economic analysis too easily conceals the basic human questions that lie at its heart and excludes the voices of people untrained in the field. Again and again, economic theory gives us opaque and technical reasons to do the obviously wrong thing.[21]

Risk assessment has taken its place alongside cost-benefit analysis as an approach to regulation. (It is closely connected with the risk management issues we examined in Chapter 10. In this case, however, the government analysts assess risk in deciding how to regulate industry.) We are all constantly exposed to risks. Some risks are more serious than others, and some persons are more exposed to risks than others. Some risks are a necessary cost of progress, even of progress toward greater safety.[22] Which risks should government try to eliminate or diminish and which should it leave unregulated? As with cost-benefit analysis, measurements and trade-offs are supposed to provide answers. Adequate reporting systems should tell us which industries and occupations have the highest rates of worker injuries and deaths, or how many children are strangled by crib toys or hurt by lawn darts. With ingenuity, we can compare risks, suggesting, for example, that (1) traveling the same route by automobile as by a scheduled airline flight increases the likelihood of death by a factor of seventy and (2) death is equally probable from one chest X-ray, a thousand-mile scheduled air flight, and living for fifty years within five miles of a nuclear reactor. A nagging problem, though, is that the public's perception of relative degrees of risk often does not fit the risk assessments by agencies' expert staffs. The agendas of both EPA and CPSC have given priority to citizens' concerns rather than to their staffs' top risk-rated concerns.[23]

Many citizens have distorted perceptions of risk: one airline accident killing two hundred people will get far more attention, from journalists and government regulators alike, than three hundred traffic accidents across the country that kill twice as many people. More people have been killed by traditional power plants than by nuclear plants, but the potentially catastrophic nature of nuclear accidents attracts far more concern. In the aftermath of Hurricane Katrina, analysts found that many homeowners had not purchased flood insurance because they believed they did not need it or could not afford it. Following Superstorm Sandy's assault of the northeast in 2012, many homeowners found their homes destroyed, but some found they could not rebuild because standards for elevating the home to prevent another catastrophe proved more than they could afford. Risk is in part a matter of statistics, but it is also a matter of perception—and perception shapes the political strategy for dealing with regulatory problems. Government inevitably finds itself stepping in to regulate risk—and to pay the costs of risk behavior.

At a congressional hearing on defective Takata airbags in 2014, U.S. Senator Bill Nelson (D-Fla.) showed holes in a device meant to protect car occupants. The airbag defects led to the largest recalls in American history.

JIM WATSON/AFP/Getty Images

Regulatory agencies, regardless of their expertise, are caught between detailed statutory mandates, including often unrealistic deadlines for action, and the uncertainties stemming from inadequate scientific, technological, and economic knowledge. Agencies face heavy pressures to consider benefits, costs, and risks, yet political pressure can force them away from such technical standards. Congress tends to focus on a difficult mix of cutting back on regulations its members dislike, reining in the regulatory apparatus to cut government's reach, but insisting on new rules when headline-grabbing problems surface. In 2016, the National Highway Traffic Safety Administration (NHTSA) discovered that airbags manufactured by a private company, Takata, were causing death and serious injuries in cars. The problem lay in Takata's design. But some members of Congress pointed blame at NHTSA and demanded to know why the agency didn't act sooner.

REGULATORY PROCEDURE

At the core of the debates about government regulation, there is an important principle. No government employee can come to work and decide that a problem deserves a regulation. Regulators can regulate only when the legislature allows them to do so, through an explicit grant of power in law. Regulators in government bureaucracies have great power, but they can only exercise their power within the limits of the discretion the law provides them. All regulations thus have their roots in law.

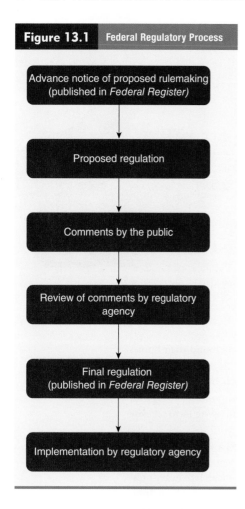

Figure 13.1 Federal Regulatory Process

Advance notice of proposed rulemaking (published in *Federal Register*)

Proposed regulation

Comments by the public

Review of comments by regulatory agency

Final regulation (published in *Federal Register*)

Implementation by regulatory agency

Moreover, the Constitution provides protections in how regulators can regulate. The Fifth and Fourteenth Amendments to the Constitution prohibit the government, at all levels, from depriving any person of life, liberty, or property without due process of law. These amendments protect not only individuals but corporations as well, since the Constitution has long been interpreted to apply the rights of individuals to private corporations. There are two principles here. First, regulators must follow *fair procedures* before taking action that could be viewed as depriving anyone of liberty. Second, any deprivation of property must be *reasonable* in the eyes of the courts. The basic standard is usually the law and the procedures it establishes: fair to citizens and consistent with constitutional requirements.

The fundamental steps for regulation, at the federal level, are found in the Administrative Procedure Act of 1946 (APA), as amended by the Freedom of Information Act and the Government in the Sunshine Act.[24] Specific legislation establishing an agency and its programs provide the rest of the legal foundation for regulation. The other is the organic statute establishing an agency and assigning its functions, together with other statutes on individual programs. State and local governments typically operate under similar standards, with a collection of basic regulatory standards and specific grants of authority through laws passed by the legislature.

These standards have led to two basic regulatory approaches by administrative agencies. One is **administrative rulemaking**, in which the agency sets forth broad standards that apply to all persons and organizations meeting certain guidelines. For example, the Department of Transportation might spell out the standards for reflectors on bicycles or the lights on eighteen-wheel trucks. The other is **adjudication**, in which administrative law judges within the agencies hear individual cases. Over time, these cases accumulate into a body of rules that individuals and organizations must follow. Because administrative rulemaking is far more prevalent and has become far more important in shaping regulatory policy, we'll concentrate on that approach.

Administrative Rulemaking

The core of administrative rulemaking lies in the legislature's delegation of power to administrators. And how should administrators exercise this power? At the federal level, most rulemaking moves through several steps. First, the agency publishes a notice of proposed rulemaking in the *Federal Register*, the daily online journal containing all rules and notices affecting the public.[25] Second, the notice gives interested parties the time and opportunity to submit written comments to the regulator. Third, after the regulator considers the comments, the final rule is published, together with an explanation of the basis and purpose of the rule (see Figure 13.1).

These steps are a relatively recent development. In the past, most economic regulatory agencies tended to proceed on a case-by-case basis, in which there were formal court-like decisions.

But as the government's regulatory reach grew, such adjudicatory steps became increasingly cumbersome. It was far easier for government to expand its decisions through the issuance of far-reaching rules.

THE COURTS' REGULATION OF THE REGULATORS

Rules can be—and often are—challenged in court. In fact, some EPA officials have candidly explained that they write *every* rule with the expectation that someone will challenge it in court. Judicial review of regulation tends to revolve around whether agencies have followed the proper procedures in issuing their rules, not whether the rules themselves are substantively valid.

Court challenges begin with a litigant who claims damage from a regulation: an environmental group claiming that the air will be made dirtier by the failure to write a tougher rule, or a company arguing its compliance costs will be unfairly high. The courts hear the cases based on documents filed by litigants and the agency's own explanation, based on the written record it's compiled. (That's part of the reason why agencies collect comments on proposed rules: it can not only review the arguments on both sides of a new regulation but also establish a record that the agency has been fair to all of the parties.)

Courts regulate the regulatory system in many ways. Often, they arbitrate appeals from parties complaining about specific agency rules and specific decisions. A party who believes it's been disadvantaged by a new rule—say, a company facing large costs for compliance—might file suit to block a regulation. At other times, courts deal with suits filed against agencies to require the issuance of rules mandated or implied in statutes. This has often been done by environmental interest groups, which fight in the courts to force tougher standards. Note the paradox here: some lawsuits are brought to stop a regulation, but other suits are filed to force the creation of one. Sometimes, an agency sues a company, seeking to punish noncompliance with a rule or order by obtaining a court order requiring compliance.

The process can be lively, at all levels of government. Consider a set of simultaneous cases—all within the metropolitan area of New York City—involving the regulation of asbestos (a harmful air pollutant that can cause cancer and lung disease, though the effects may not appear for many years). In November 1987, about two hundred employees sued the Consolidated Edison Company, seeking millions of dollars in damages because of asbestos exposure. In January 1988, EPA filed a civil suit against Consolidated Edison, seeking civil penalties of over $1 million and a court order requiring the company's full compliance with the Clean Air Act. The violations charged were failure to follow prescribed asbestos-removal procedures and failure to inform EPA fully and promptly of the removal operations. A few days earlier, the government had filed a criminal suit against officials of twenty-three companies removing asbestos materials. They were charged with bribing a federal inspector to overlook violations of federal regulations.[26] Here are three suits—a civil suit for damages brought by private citizens, a civil suit brought by the government, and a criminal suit brought by the government. All relate to EPA and its regulations.

Access to the Courts

The courts have an important role in regulation. Just as regulators cannot on their own decide which issues deserve new regulations, courts cannot decide to issue rulings in a particular area. Rather, it can only hear cases brought before it (although, in the appeals process, the volume of cases is so large that a court can not only pick which issues it wants to hear but which cases present the issues on which it wants to decide). To bring a case, a party must claim that it has a clear and direct interest in the outcome. That is known as the **standing to sue**. In recent times, the role of the courts has substantially grown because they have taken a broader view of just who has standing.

The right to sue has changed greatly over time. Many laws provide potential litigants the opportunity to seek judicial review of administrators' actions. In addition, the APA offers a blanket authorization: "A person suffering legal wrong because of agency action, or adversely affected or aggrieved by agency action within the meaning of a relevant statute, is entitled to judicial review thereof." A disagreement with an agency's action does not establish a right to sue. Rather, an individual must have suffered a "legal wrong," in the eyes of the courts—a specific damage to the individual as a result of the agency's actions.

CLASS-ACTION SUITS. One way that this right to sue has expanded is through the use of class-action lawsuits. In some cases involving a number of citizens, individuals might each suffer a loss. The loss might be so small individually that it's not worth hiring an attorney, but it could prove substantial cumulatively. A **class action** is a private lawsuit for money damages, usually brought against a private person or corporation. The principal plaintiff is typically only one or a few of the persons damaged, who are sufficiently indignant and well off to afford the lawyer. The suit is filed on behalf of all the affected individuals. Plaintiffs can bring suit to reinforce the regulatory work of a government agency, or sometimes to force action where agencies have not acted. Although these cases can be litigated through full-scale trials, they are often settled out of court. Corporations-as-defendants sometimes view such actions as "legalized blackmail," but class-action lawsuits can prove powerful tools to force changes in behavior, both to conform to the law and to avoid future suits. Since the 1970s, class-action suits have gained popularity, and the courts have been inclined to grant more litigants standing to bring such actions.

One of the most dramatic class-action suits was brought against seven corporations, on behalf of over 15,000 named persons following the Vietnam War. They claimed they had suffered severe illnesses, or that their children had suffered birth defects, as a result of exposure to an herbicide, Agent Orange, that had been used by the army. In 1985, the case ended with a settlement, which to that date, was the largest in history: $180 million plus interest.[27] In 1998, an even bigger settlement was reached. Years earlier, the Mississippi attorney general had begun a long legal campaign against the tobacco companies, seeking to recover damages to the state and its taxpayers that, he said, had been caused by smoking. This legal action snowballed into an action eventually involving all the states, promising to pay them an estimated $246 billion over twenty-five years and imposing new restrictions on the advertising of tobacco products. By cleverly claiming standing to sue the tobacco companies on the grounds of their need to recover Medicaid costs incurred in the treatment of smokers, the states won an enormous settlement and forced a major change in tobacco companies' business practices. Martha Derthick, however, raises serious questions about whether this entrepreneurial litigation circumvented constitutional practice by inserting executive branch officials in a province of policymaking that should have been left to the legislature.[28] Class actions have continued, nevertheless. In 2016, a federal judge approved a $20 billion settlement for those harmed by the BP *Deepwater Horizon* spill in the Gulf of Mexico.

More generally, citizens often seek to file suit against government agencies for damages they believe that government actions have caused. Such suits against the government are difficult to win, because of a long-standing principle from English common law that held that "the king can do no wrong" and could not be sued without his consent. However, government *employees* can be sued for how they exercise their discretion on the job. Schoolteachers, police officers, and FBI and narcotics agents are frequent targets of tort suits. In 2014, a Pittsburgh jury awarded a black art student $119,000 in damages for false arrest, after he sued the police department for a beating he received at the hands of officers. A Baltimore resident won $70,000 in 2016 on a similar suit. The courts—and juries—have become more open to suits against public officials—and to monetary damages when citizens demonstrate misconduct.

In general, the principle is that the government is not liable for an act or omission when the government employee is "exercising due care, in the execution of a statute or regulation, whether or not such statute or regulation be valid," or when he or she is performing or failing to perform "a discretionary function or duty on the part of a federal agency or an employee . . . whether or not the discretion involved be abused." The government is liable only to the extent that a private individual would be liable under the relevant state's law (though some government actions have no private counterpart). Federal officials tend to have immunity from suits when performing duties committed by law to their control or supervision.[29] There is, however, a major exception, introduced in the 1970s: officials are liable for violation of constitutional rights if they knew or reasonably should have known that they were violating them.[30] It is presumed that an official should know the rights protected by the Constitution, although the presumption has been criticized on grounds that every such right has been and continues to be interpreted through court decisions, which an official cannot be expected to have mastered. In 1988, the Supreme Court held that federal employees could be held personally liable for damages caused by negligent performance or omission of nondiscretionary conduct (such as, in this case, negligence in handling and storing hazardous material). Congress responded by passing a statute that makes the government, rather than the employee, the defendant in such suits.[31]

State governments, under the Eleventh Amendment, are immune from damage suits in federal courts, but local governments are not immune. State and local officials are liable under an 1871 act that provides: "Every person who, under color of any statute [or] regulation . . . of any State, subjects . . . any citizen . . . to the deprivation of any rights, privileges, or immunities secured by the Constitution and laws, shall be liable to the party injured in an action at law."[32] This provision is known as Section 1983 (from its location in the *U.S. Code of Federal Regulations*). Beginning in 1961, the federal courts experienced a great increase in Section 1983 tort actions, consistent with the Supreme Court's narrowing of officials' defenses. The principal defense is now lack of knowledge or presumptive knowledge of relevant provisions of the Constitution and laws.

Underlying these issues is a dilemma. On one hand, citizens have the right to monetary compensation for damages done them by overzealous, negligent, or malicious government officials and employees. These financial damages also create deterrence for other government bureaucrats in similar cases. On the other hand, it is important for administrators to execute the law and regulations promptly and efficiently. That calls for considerable discretion in exercising their duties. If they spend too much time second-guessing the consequences, this can lead to big problems in performance. That, in fact, is an argument often made by those defending police officers who face instant life-and-death decisions on the streets. It's important that those who suffer from a government employee's misbehavior have the right to be compensated. It's also important that government employees have the

Before the 2001 terrorist attacks, the CIA said it was looking to sign a contract with an expert. The agency had "the need for someone familiar with conducting applied research in high-risk operational settings," its plan said. It wanted to hire a consultant to "help guide and shape the future" of a research project described only as something "in the area of counter-terrorism and special operations."

The CIA decided to work with a psychologist, James E. Mitchell. The contract expanded over time into an $81 million arrangement, which was responsible for development of the agency's water boarding, sleep deprivation, and other techniques used against "high-value" individuals at secret facilities around the world—but not in the United States.

Mitchell was an expert in putting together psychological profiles. He had no experience in interrogation. But after September 11, 2001, the CIA worked with him to transform his project into tactics to extract information from detainees.

The work gradually expanded, as Mitchell worked with colleagues to create a company that won a contract that paid nearly $100 million.

The use of such interrogation techniques was uncharted territory. It was led by someone with no experience in using the techniques to get valuable information. And, in the end, one of the government's most turbulent policy issues of the 2000s was led by a private contractor, hired by an "agency eager to outsource the interrogation work," as *Washington Post* reporter Greg Miller put it.

Source: Greg Miller, "How a Modest Contract for 'Applied Research' Morphed into the CIA's Brutal Interrogation Program," *Washington Post* (July 13, 2016), https://www.washingtonpost.com/news/checkpoint/wp/2016/07/13/how-a-modest-contract-for-applied-research-morphed-into-the-cias-brutal-interrogation-program/?hpid=hp_rhp-top-table-main_checkpoint-cia-330pm%3Ahomepage%2Fstory.

flexibility to do their job well. It's a difficult tradeoff, made all the more difficult by the importance of "street-level bureaucrats"[33] and the huge expansion in the legislature's delegation of discretionary powers.[34]

Systems and Values

The question of access to the courts leads to some more fundamental issues: How much should courts intervene in the regulatory decisions of government agencies? How aggressively should the courts themselves work to open the doors for judicial redress of grievances? And who has access to these processes—is the playing field level for those who think they have been treated unfairly? These questions raise two issues: (1) the difference between the judicial system and the administrative system in which regulatory agencies operate and (2) the array of public values that everyone—citizens and policymakers alike—wants to see in the regulation of private affairs. How one balances these considerations has much to do with the balance between the regulatory agencies and the courts.

THE JUDICIAL AND ADMINISTRATIVE SYSTEMS. In regulatory administration, courts and agencies make strange partners. The two institutions have different traditions and are staffed with very different kinds of people.[35] Courts are passive; they cannot act on their own but, instead, depend on parties to bring cases before them. They don't issue broad policy decisions but, instead, rule on one case at a time. Because different courts might rule on different cases in the same general policy area, inconsistent decisions can emerge. With few exceptions (the federal district and appeals courts in the District of Columbia), neither the judges nor their clerks have deep expertise in regulatory issues, so they must rely instead on evidence and analysis offered by lawyers for the two sides.

The most important feature of the role of the courts is this: judges focus on the single case before them. Because courts cannot, on their own, reach beyond the case to make broader law, they focus on the reasonableness of a single agency's decision, made at a single point in time and affecting a single individual, corporation, or group. The court's judgment fits in a setting of legal doctrine and precedents, but it largely ignores how the particular agency's decision fits with the agency's full responsibility for achieving program objectives with limited funds and staff. Instead, a court may require the agency to respond to the particular case before it, without considering how this requirement may subtract from the resources supporting the agency's other programs. Courts therefore don't make policy. There's no doubt, however, that their decisions individually can have big impact on administrators. The Supreme Court's 1954 decision in *Brown v. Board of Education* was a milestone in the fight to end segregation in the schools. And the cumulative effect of judicial decisions undoubtedly transforms the way agencies carry out policy.

By contrast, most agencies are *active*—each one develops an agenda of priorities that balances its resources against relative opportunities for a significant impact. An agency makes decisions through time, linking each one with others to create coherence both in technical foundations and in program effectiveness. Within that agenda and continuity of focus, the agency's staff gathers facts, analyzes problems, and consults with interested persons and organizations, all as a basis for framing regulatory rules and orders. In sharp contrast to the courts, agencies specialize in their assigned subjects, and they have career staffs expert in economics, science, and engineering, as well as in law. Except for agency lawyers, the judges and agency staff members march to different drummers.[36] It would be a wonder if the two sides kept in step—and they rarely do.

Two strategies have emerged to accommodate these differences.[37] First, the courts have pressed the agencies to widen the participation of interested citizens and groups in the formulation of rules. The courts' broader rules of standing, moreover, have increased access to the courts for political players.[38] Second, courts' decisions can have broad impact, not only through decisions and orders but also interpreting legislative intent—sometimes in ways agencies did not anticipate.[39] The agencies generally regard these strategies as helpful: increased participation has favored environmental and other public interest groups whose efforts support the agencies' missions. In giving statutory weight to program activities not clearly specified in statutes, the courts have expanded the jurisdictions of the agencies.[40]

VALUES: CONFLICT OR HARMONY?. Regulatory administration revolves around three basic values: procedural fairness, substantive correctness of decisions, and achievement of public policy goals. Everyone agrees that the process leading up to agency issuance (or nonissuance) of a rule or individual order should be *fair*. But it is tempting for courts to say, "Why can't administrative agencies behave more like us?" In fact, the APA and many agency-specific statutes, as we have seen, support the courts' view, requiring notice, oral hearings, and cross-examination of witnesses. To be sure, these procedures are less rigorous in the rulemaking setting than in ordinary court cases, but they are, nonetheless, enough alike that lawyers play the leading roles, paperwork mounts, and tactics of delay are practiced by companies facing regulatory action. Despite these similarities, however, the trend in regulation is away from formal toward informal rulemaking—away from the procedures that are more judicial and toward those that the courts find troublesome.

The second value is not procedural, but substantive: the *correctness* of the decision reached. Theoretically, what the system should ensure is a correct decision, and if the agency does not make one, the court should. But neither agency nor court can ensure that a decision is correct or, for that matter, be sure they know what "correct" is. There are vast scientific and technological uncertainties in many policy issues, and even when there is relative clarity on the technical issues, different political judgments can muddy any sense about which decision is the right one. That, of course, was the lesson of Chapter 10. Both the agency subsystem and the court system provide opportunities for appeal to higher levels, but even in the judicial branch there is no certainty that the highest court's decision will be correct. The possibility of appeal can often simply create new arenas for political interests to continue—and to try to change—policy debates. At best, the courts can hope to limit error to a low, but not zero, tolerance level. Judges' self-restraint, reinforced by deference to agency expertise, permits agency discretion to operate in accord with this objective.

Of course, many issues turn out to be such a mixture of fact and law that a court cannot decide the legal question without also deciding a factual question. Appellate courts have historically often capitalized on this mixed focus to substitute their judgment for that of lower courts, by treating as a question of law whether the evidence was sufficient to support the lower court's decision. Appellate court doctrines have varied on whether they were merely looking to determine if there was "substantial" evidence on the winning side to warrant the decision, or whether they were completely second-guessing the lower court by weighing the evidence on both sides. In the latter case, disagreement about the preponderance of evidence can lead to overturning the lower court's decision. In reviewing agency decisions, the courts have applied the substantial-evidence test, but they take "a hard look."

The third value is achievement of public policy *goals*. Here lurks a very real danger: two very different institutions—judicial and administrative—can find the way they operate to be in conflict. Too many formal procedures can tie administrative regulation in knots—causing delay, absorbing budgetary and staff resources, increasing red tape, and inviting passivity in agency pursuit of policy goals. The prospect of finding their regulations challenged in court can lead administrators to regulate defensively. Many regulators, in fact, spend a very long time writing rules, trying to anticipate and counter objections that could arise later in court. Moreover, on most major issues, regulators simply assume that they will face a lawsuit on *every* regulation they write. Those who oppose a new regulation simply assume they'll continue policy battles in the courts. That often begins by carefully studying the rulings of judges in districts around the country—and shopping for a case in a jurisdiction in which they think a judge is most likely to rule in their favor.

Some agencies react to the risk of judicial reversal by adopting even more cumbersome procedures than courts are likely to demand; others seek to demonstrate the evidence behind a decision with massive accumulations of documents. Even in rulemaking, courts insist that an agency respond to every significant objection filed by individuals, groups, and companies. That imposes a significant burden on agencies—and it makes it hard for them to guess in advance which objections are most likely to be most important when a regulation gets to court. Meanwhile, as an agency spends time to try to figure that out, it can run afoul of legislators' expectations that administrators will implement the law quickly and smoothly. It's a tough dilemma.

The administrative tasks of some agencies are enormous, and their huge burden makes court-like procedures inappropriate. In the Department of Homeland Security, charged with reviewing applications for immigration and naturalization, the backlog of cases in 2004 was more than 6 million and growing. As T. Alexander Aleinikoff concluded, "If the process is not improved, millions of people will continue to wait many years for naturalization and immigration benefits to which they are entitled as a matter of law."[41] A hidden side effect of this backlog was that Homeland Security officials were lagging behind the effort to determine whether any of those on the list might be members of terrorist sleeper cells, quietly preparing for a new attack. That, in turn, played into Trump's pledge to deport illegal aliens.

The three values of regulatory administration—fair procedures, sound decisions, and policy goals—are interlinked and in conflict. Each is important in its own right, but to make one more important than the others is to invite trouble. Fairness in regulatory procedure may be enough to reassure everyone, including the courts, about the correctness of the decision reached. Relaxation of the expectation that regulatory procedures mimic that of courts may promote effective implementation of policy objectives. In the end, the courts have tended to reconcile these issues through the doctrine of judicial deferral to agencies' expertise. However, this is not an ideal formula. Courts differ on how much deferral is appropriate, how expert agencies really are, and whether in a particular decision the claim of expertise covers other issues on which the courts might weigh in. It is little wonder, then, that the courts' relationship with regulators is full of tension, and that it continues to evolve.

REGULATION OF THE REGULATORS

Elected chief executives, of course, seek to control regulatory agencies. These agencies are central to policymaking and administration—and the executives inevitably find themselves accountable for the actions the agencies take. There often are several interrelated goals at play. Executives want to ensure that the agencies' actions are consistent with their overall policy goals. They want to coordinate their actions, so that the actions are consistent with each other. And they often want to control—sometimes restrain—the costs the regulations impose on citizens, companies, and the economy. The costs are substantial. One 2016 study by the Mercatus Center contended that federal regulations had cost the economy $4 trillion in lost economic growth since 1980.[42]

At the federal level, this has led the president, especially in Republican administrations, to impose tough review over proposed new regulations, although all presidents have sought to shape regulations to fit their policy. The Reagan administration created a system in the Office of Management and Budget (OMB) to assess the benefits and costs of new regulations, and the George W. Bush administration expanded the review through a broader role for OMB. Democrats complained that these actions were designed to frustrate the implementation of legislation passed by Congress.

The regulatory management process has thus provoked much friction.[43] Over time, OMB has gained more review authority not only over the final stages of rulemaking but also over such early stages as initiation of research studies meant to contribute to agency consideration of whether to start rulemaking proceedings.[44] That sometimes has produced delays of months, even years, in the issuance of regulations, which opponents sometimes suggested was precisely the point. OMB's Office of Information and Regulatory Affairs, a small but powerful staff of economists, attorneys, and public policy experts, has become especially important in these reviews.

Since regulation is such an important part of policy implementation, such friction is inevitable. Regulation is the continuation of the policymaking and policy implementation processes, with all the politics, in a different forum. Executives want to control the bureaucracy and its actions. Interest groups want to win battles they might have lost in other arenas, or ensure that the battles they had won stay won. Members of the legislature know that their laws take on meaning only in the regulations written to implement them. So the political battles, sometimes over the most arcane regulations, are often very intense.

CONCLUSION

Regulation of the behavior of private individuals and corporations to protect others from harm is a central responsibility of government. The scope and methods of such regulation are disputed issues of public policy. However those issues are resolved, there is no doubt that some regulatory agencies must have considerable discretion, that this discretion can be abused, and that those who have a complaint are increasingly likely to challenge these decisions in court. Legislatures, courts, and chief executives all seek to reduce these problems, but in doing so they often see this as another opportunity to advance their own policy preferences. The steps they create can often, unintentionally or not, make it harder to write and enforce good regulations.

The balance between effective and ineffective regulation shifts from time to time, largely reflecting public opinion, elections, and appointments and attitudes of administrators and judges. As we move deeper into the twenty-first century, it's clear that government regulations have had huge impact. The air is cleaner, air travel is safer, and workplace safety is higher. But there are also big problems, like water quality in Flint. There is also a growing sense that, even though we want small government, government ought to step in to protect us from risks we face, from tainted food to exploding airbags. These underlying tensions are inevitable—and they are important signs of the underlying politics of government regulation.

Administrative discretion is tolerable only when not misused, and that shapes a major problem. One distinguished scholar of the legal aspects of public administration, Phillip Cooper, puts it this way:

> Just how we ensure that the public interest is served and that administrative power is not abused is the problem of administrative responsibility. . . . [While] the formal legal constraints have received the most attention . . . there is a risk that excessive concern with avoiding suits will cause us to ignore many aspects of the responsibility question of equal or greater significance.[45]

The next chapter addresses those very important aspects.

Judge Vaughn Walker struck down California's Proposition 8, which banned same-sex marriages. In his opinion, Walker wrote that "Proposition 8 fails to advance any rational basis in singling out gay men and lesbians for denial of a marriage license." California Governor Arnold Schwarzenegger applauded the decision, but legal observers wondered whether proponents of same-sex marriage would be able to find five votes if the case reached SCOTUS. Schwarzenegger was partially right—when the Court decided the case in 2013, it ruled 5–4 that the state's ban was illegal as it was drawn, but the Court stopped short of ruling that same-sex couples could marry.

We all know about the separation of powers from our high school civics and college public administration courses. We learned that the framers gave the courts independent power because they didn't fully trust democratic rule. When monumental decisions like those discussed here come down, however, they always strike like lightning bolts at the center of the typical battles between elected legislators and executives.

And we all know that the judiciary is independent of politics. But the lightning bolts are always political—they are launched by judges who bring to each case their own reading of the Constitution and the law, and the judges were put in place by elected officials who hoped that those readings were the right ones.

Before Obama, Republicans held the White House for twenty-eight of the previous forty years, and their lifetime appointments of federal judges have made a deep mark on the federal bench. Obama's election sent shivers through those who closely follow the federal lower courts, for they knew that Obama would have a large number of appointments to make. One judge, J. Harvie Wilkinson III of the Fourth Circuit Court of Appeals, appointed by President Reagan to a circuit viewed as the nation's most conservative, warned in a *Washington Post* op-ed in January 2009 that Obama's election would bring a "takeover" of the lower courts. In the Senate, some Republican senators have been sitting on Obama's nominations for the lower courts to try to prevent this from happening.

In one recent study, Washington attorney Eric R. Haren wrote that conservatives held the majority on most of the dozen federal courts of appeals, but he argued that "these courts are up for grabs, and Obama's impact on them could be sweeping." Some analysts have concluded that Obama had already tipped two appellate courts to a majority appointed by Democrats. That could bring an impact even larger and more lasting than whatever will happen on SCOTUS.

Huge policy battles with deep implications continue to brew in the states. We surely haven't seen the last of cases on issues like offshore drilling, immigration, and same-sex marriage. With the lower courts the last stop for more than 99 percent of all cases, whoever shapes the judiciary beyond SCOTUS could well make it the most quiet but lasting legacy.

QUESTIONS TO CONSIDER

1. Compare the roles of the U.S. Supreme Court and the lower federal courts. How would you assess their relative contributions to public administration?

2. Suppose you wanted to maximize your impact on policy and administration. Where would you invest most of your energy? (*Trick question:* You'd want to focus on both the Supreme Court and lower courts, but weigh how to balance the headline-grabbing potential of the Supreme Court with the fact that the lower courts decide most of the judicial questions.)

Note: This case comes from my column in *Governing* (October 2010), http://www.governing.com/columns/potomac-chronicle/why-states-localities-are-watching-lower-federal-courts.html.

CASE 13.3

Profile in ICE? Local Officials Opt Out of Federal Program They Worry Could Lead to Racial Profiling

Arlington County, Virginia, found itself in a scrap with the U.S. Immigration and Customs Enforcement agency (ICE, for short). Local officials opted out of a federal program that requires police to send the fingerprints of those arrested to ICE for a check against the FBI database and against Homeland Security records.

Officials in Arlington worried that the information would be used for racial profiling. J. Walter Trejeada, a member of the Arlington County Board, pointed out that one-fourth of the county's residents were born outside the United States and that one-third of the residents were multiracial. Bringing the federal immigration database together with the local arrest records, he feared, could lead to a dangerous blurring of responsibilities. John Morton, director of ICE, countered that local officials simply weren't responsible for federal policy. "No one in the Department of Corrections, no one in Arlington County, no one in the other jurisdictions in Virginia is being asked to enforce federal immigration law."[1]

The battle erupted out of requirements in the federal Secure Communities program, administered by ICE. The program's website noted that

> ICE is committed to protecting civil rights and civil liberties, and is serious about responding to complaints or allegations of racial profiling as a result of Secure Communities. Individuals and organizations should report allegations of racial profiling, due process violations or other violations of civil rights or civil liberties related to the use of this capability.[2]

But critics wondered if trading fingerprints was really advancing homeland security. One study concluded that "DHS's track record on prioritizing violent criminals is far from stellar, leaving much doubt about ICE's compliance with the stated intentions of the Secure Communities program."[3]

In New York, demonstrators picketed the governor's New York City office. "We were basically asking Governor Paterson to rescind the agreement involving S-Comm. The program is going to further terrorize our community and tear our families apart," Manisha Vaze, a representative of Families for Freedom, argued. "I think it's important that people know that the name Secure Communities does the opposite of what its name implies. It is masked as something that will benefit our community when in reality people don't know what the program is all about . . . mass deportation." A spokesman for ICE countered, "People are going to be arrested regardless." He defended the program by arguing that it was whether an individual committed a crime, and not his or her appearance, that prompted the program. "Of course you don't expect to be arrested because of how you look, whether it's Asian, Hispanic, Indian or whatever. If you commit a crime then you

can start to worry. S-Comm will simply provide more tools to find out arrestees' criminal and immigration histories."[4]

In Virginia, Attorney General Ken Cuccinelli welcomed the program as an important tool in crime prevention and homeland security. He pointed out that state law requires local governments to submit fingerprints to the state police, who in turn check them with the FBI database. "It's not a situation where Arlington's fingerprints can be treated differently," he argued.[5]

QUESTIONS TO CONSIDER

1. Map the regulatory chain for this program. Who's involved, and who's doing what?

2. Do you believe that communities ought to have the right to opt out of such national programs? If they can do so, can a national program truly be national? If you don't believe they should be able to do so, is there any place to draw the line in federal rules on local policing?

3. One of the issues prompting the Safe Communities program was the painful lesson taught by the September 11, 2001, terrorist attacks. One of the hijackers was stopped by a police officer for a routine traffic check, but the hijacker didn't trigger any alarms. The Safe Communities program applies only to people who are arrested, but federal policymakers were haunted by the possibility that a local government might have a potential terrorist in jail but fail to connect the dots with the federal FBI and immigration databases before an attack. Does the program make sense in this context?

NOTES

1. Dena Potter, "ICE: No Opt-Out for Program Checking Legal Status," *Associated Press* (October 8, 2010), http://www.sandiegouniontribune.com/sdut-ice-no-opt-out-for-program-checking-legal-status-2010oct08-story.html.

2. See https://www.ice.gov/secure-communities#tab1.

3. Immigration Policy Center, *The Secure Communities Program: Unanswered Questions and Continuing Concerns* (November 4, 2010), http://www.immigrationpolicy.org/special-reports/secure-communities-program-unanswered-questions-and-continuing-concerns.

4. Daysi Calavia-Lopez, "Rally against the Secure Communities Program," *Queens Courier*, December 22, 2010.

5. Potter, "ICE."

CASE 13.4

What a Box of Honey Nut Cheerios Says about Today's Politics

Honey Nut Cheerios—America's best-selling cereal—won't be the same anymore. Thanks to an epic battle in Vermont, every box of the friendly oats from General Mills contains a new label confirming the presence of genetically modified organisms (GMOs).

Outside Vermont, General Mills doesn't have to include the GMO label. But Jeff Harmening, the company's chief operating officer for U.S. retail, told a reporter that "having one system for Vermont and one for everywhere else is untenable." So, as Vermont goes, so goes the nation.

In fact, so went Congress, at least in a limited way. In mid-July 2016, both the House and Senate addressed the subject by passing legislation that would require some form of GMO identification on products sold in stores. But the new federal law will be much weaker than the one in Vermont, so it's likely Vermont's will be the one that many companies choose to follow.

That law, which went into effect on July 1, generated one of the biggest regulatory battles in recent memory. Supporters of the law said they simply wanted to give consumers enough information to make informed choices in the grocery store. Other supporters said they worried about the health effects of eating GMOs and thought that the labels would allow consumers to buy different products—or force manufacturers to use GMO-free ingredients. In Europe, Cheerios don't contain GMOs.

But getting GMOs out of the American food chain would be very tough. More than 90 percent of the corn, soybean, sugar beets, and canola raised in this country comes from crops genetically modified to produce sturdier grains that are more resistant to insects and drought. What's more, most government regulators have concluded that GMOs are safe, including the World Health Organization, the European Food Safety Agency, the United Nations Food and Agricultural Organization, and the U.S. Food and Drug Administration.

The public, however, isn't so sure. In a 2015 survey, just 37 percent thought that food with GMOs was safe to eat.

For producers, that has raised two options. One is shifting to more natural components, which is expensive. Ben & Jerry's, the quintessential Vermont institution in many people's minds, spent three years taking GMOs out of its caramel and cookie dough ice cream flavors—forcing prices to rise 11 percent. But removing GMOs caused the disappearance of a few popular flavors. Heath Bar Crunch had to go because the candy bar, manufactured by Hershey, contains GMOs. The other option, a push for substitutes that often don't undergo the same level of safety testing, hasn't proved very appealing.

The great GMO debate isn't just affecting cereal and ice cream. Campbell's Soups announced that, because of the Vermont law, it too would include GMO labels on all of its cans. Through a quirk in the nation's patchwork of laws, Campbell's SpaghettiOs need GMO disclosure, but not SpaghettiOs with meatballs. A food product in which meat makes up more than 2 percent of the weight is regulated by the U.S. Department of Agriculture, whose rules don't require GMO labeling and supersede those of the states. Campbell's didn't want to have

SpaghettiO varieties sitting on the shelves next to each other with different labels. It pulled out of the battle against state-by-state regulation and called for mandatory national labeling standards from the federal government.

General Mills, Campbell's Soups, and Mars Inc. candy stopped fighting and accepted the Vermont standards as well. But others in the food industry didn't give up. They used the new Vermont law to put enormous pressure on Congress. Two weeks after the Vermont policy took effect, Congress passed its own law to preempt it. The federal legislation gave manufacturers three options: the Vermont plan, with text describing GMO content; a QR code that consumers could scan with their smartphones to learn what was inside; or a symbol to be designed later.

In the end, Congress pushed aside Vermont's simpler and more immediate policy. But one small state—the nation's second-least populous—effectively forced a change in national standards.

It's not new, of course, for a state innovation to transform the nation. The catalytic converter, which dramatically reduced automobile engine emissions, got its start in a California law. That state's market was too big for car manufacturers to ignore, so it set the national standard.

Vermont is no California, but Capitol Hill gridlock gave it California-like leverage. Vermont transformed GMO labeling despite its small size because, in an increasingly interconnected food chain, the lowest—or highest—common denominator rules. Given the frequent gridlock in Washington, policy initiative flows to the states—even little ones. And the more these initiatives lay bare the peculiarities of the nation's regulatory system, the more feasible it is for any state to preempt federal rules. Just consider SpaghettiOs with meatballs.

So your next bowl of Honey Nut Cheerios—or even a morning with Cap'n Crunch—will be more than just a way to start your day. It will be a sign of how Washington's immobility is offering a new kind of leverage to states that want to shape national policy.

QUESTIONS TO CONSIDER

1. Consider the strategy used by the interests who wanted to expand labeling of food sources. What lessons does this case teach?

2. How does labeling encourage or discourage sales of a product?

3. Are you surprised that a small state could reshape national policy?

Note: This case comes from my column in *Governing* (August 2016), http://www.governing.com/columns/potomac-chronicle/gov-cheerios-gmo-vermont.html.

KEY CONCEPTS

adjudication 374

administrative rulemaking 374

antitrust laws 366

capture 366

class action 376

cost-benefit analysis 371

economic regulation 366

risk assessment 372

social regulation 366

standing to sue 376

FOR FURTHER READING

Ackerman, Frank, and Lisa Heinzerling. *Priceless: On Knowing the Price of Everything and the Value of Nothing.* New York: New Press, 2004.

Bardach, Eugene, and Robert A. Kagan. *Going by the Book: The Problem of Regulatory Unreasonableness. A Twentieth Century Fund Report.* Philadelphia: Temple University Press, 1982.

Cooper, Phillip J. *Governing by Contract: Challenges and Opportunities for Public Managers.* Washington, D.C.: CQ Press, 2002.

Derthick, Martha A. *Up in Smoke: From Legislation to Litigation in Tobacco Politics.* 2nd ed. Washington, D.C.: CQ Press, 2005.

Howard, Phillip K. *The Death of Common Sense.* New York: Random House, 1994.

Skowronek, Stephen. *Building a New American State: The Expansion of National Administrative Capacities, 1877–1920.* New York: Cambridge University Press, 1982.

Wilson, James Q., ed. *The Politics of Regulation.* New York: Basic Books, 1980.

SUGGESTED WEBSITES

The issues of government regulation provide rich puzzles for Internet-based research. Many complex public policy questions have played out through studies and analyses, which can easily be found through web search engines.

The federal government's catalog of regulations can be found on the U.S. Government Printing Office website, **www.gpo.gov/fdsys/search/home.action**. GPO publishes the Code of Federal Regulations, as well as the daily changes to federal regulations that are published in the *Federal Register*.

The National Academy of Public Administration has conducted an exhaustive study of federal clean air regulations. See the 2003 report *A Breath of Fresh Air: Reviving*

the New Source Review Program, which is available at **www.napawash.org**. In addition, the Government Accountability Office, **www.gao.gov**, regularly reviews regulatory issues through its studies.

Moreover, many government regulatory agencies have their own websites, which are invaluable for tracking policy issues. See, for example, the website for the National Highway Traffic Safety Administration, **www.nhtsa.gov**, for information about the safety of cars and trucks; the Food and Drug Administration, **www.fda.gov**, for the safety of prescription and over-the-counter drugs; and the Environmental Protection Agency, **www.epa.gov**, for clean air and water regulations.

$SAGE edge™

for CQ Press

WANT A BETTER GRADE?

Get the tools you need to sharpen your study skills. Access practice quizzes, eFlashcards, video, and multimedia at **edge.sagepub.com/kettl7e.**

14

ACCOUNTABILITY AND POLITICS

Chip Somodevilla/Getty Images

Before testifying before the House Veterans' Affairs Committee, Government Accountability Office Health Care Director Debra Draper, Assistant Deputy Veterans Affairs Undersecretary for Health for Administrative Operations Philip Matkovsky, Acting VA Inspector General Richard Griffin, and Assistant VA Inspector General for Audits and Evaluations Linda Halliday were sworn in. In an ongoing scandal, critics charged the VA with long delays in treating vets—a scandal that forced the department's secretary, Eric Shinseki, to resign.

Accountability is the core of this book. And for many Americans—policymakers, journalists, and citizens—accountability is a distinctly negative concept. There's an underlying sense that government doesn't work well. There's an assumption that this is because of poor performance by government bureaucrats. There's an inescapable impetus to identify those responsible and fire them. And, if that doesn't work, then fire more bureaucrats. Indeed, a major part of the government reform movement, at all levels of government, is to make more government employees "at will," without civil service protections, so they can be fired if they don't perform well. More than half of state governments have moved to such a system, as we saw in Chapter 9, and those ideas have in turn powerfully shaped the national debate on fixing the troubled federal Department of Veterans Affairs. For months, members of Congress and representatives of veterans groups complained bitterly that the problems at the Phoenix VA hospital, where the problems were first discovered, had resulted in little disciplinary action and only one person being fired. The VA fired three more employees in June 2016, which Senator John McCain (R-Ariz.) called "a long-overdue step toward bringing justice and accountability." McCain continued, "We have a long way to go to reform this agency and ensure its leaders are able to swiftly fire any employee who denies or delays life-saving medical treatment to our veterans." From the other side of the aisle, Rep. Ann Kirkpatrick (D-Ariz.) said that the fact it had taken two years to fire these employees showed that "something is very wrong." She promised to stay on the case. "We cannot rest until these problems are rooted out," she concluded.[1]

Violence erupted in Ferguson, Missouri, in 2014 after a police officer shot a black teenager, Michael Brown. The incident cost the police chief, Thomas Jackson, his job. The new chief, Delrish Moss, took a tough stand. "If you work hard, if you stay honest and committed, if you maintain respect for the community and do your job well, we will get along just fine," he told his officers. And then he continued: "If you fall short of that, and it's through a mistake of the head, we will work to correct that. But if you do it with malice, if you do the job in a way that disrespects the badge that you hold, I will see to it that you are either removed from police service, or further prosecuted."[2] Moss knew he had to work hard to change the culture of the city's police force—and to regain the trust of the community. Harsh eyes, from around the country, watched every step he made.

Is this what accountability means? A deep suspicion of government, with a focus on firing? These questions raise a series of tough issues.

First, it's impossible to deny that trust in government—and in government's ability to perform—is at a historic low. Citizens are suspicious, and reporters can't resist a fraud-waste-abuse story. In fact, this helps reinforce citizens' suspicions and the media's instincts—citizens pay attention to these stories, and

CHAPTER OBJECTIVES

- Understand the role of public administration in an environment of separation of powers

- Explore the role and function of legislative oversight of administration

- Examine the implications of performance information to promote accountability

- Take a final look at the challenges for accountability in modern public administration

reporters can't resist writing them. When problems occur, as they inevitably do in any large, complex system, they demand attention. And when administrators are at fault, they ought to be fired. So it's very easy to understand the foundation for the public debates about accountability.

Second, it's easy to understand the frustration of citizens and elected officials when it seems to take so long to fire bureaucrats accused of misbehavior. In the case of the VA, in fact, even Deputy Secretary Sloan Gibson was frustrated, and he admitted that "this process took far too long."[3] The delays tend to make the bureaucracy look even more rigid, unresponsive, and unaccountable. The reasons, of course, are far more complex than the headlines. Government employees have substantial due-process protections, deeply rooted in more than a century of the civil service, precisely because the system's founders wanted to make it hard for political officials to fire career bureaucrats. Otherwise, they worried, the bad old days of political pressure and patronage would creep back into the system. In the VA's case, the delays came from the time it took to carefully investigate the case and to work through the complex procedures on firing. The instinct to fire bureaucrats has to be balanced against the need to protect careerists against political pressure. We have never been comfortable with that tradeoff. However, as trust in government has declined and media coverage has become intense, anger at these tradeoffs has vastly increased.

Third, although the instinct to fire poor performers is strong, pinning specific blame for particular problems on individual administrators turns out to be very hard. As we have seen in this book, American public administration has become ever more interwoven, with responsibility for management of government programs shared among multiple agencies, multiple levels of government, multiple sectors, and even multiple nations. We have created such an interwoven system for reasons of pragmatism, which gives us more administrative flexibility, and of politics, which allows us to expand government's reach without expanding the number of government employees (especially at the federal level). But a direct consequence of these changes is that responsibility for implementation has become more broadly shared, and that makes it hard to identify single individuals responsible for poor performance. Firing VA managers proved difficult because the department's problems were deep-seated, connected to the department's culture and its vast complexity. No matter how strong the instinct to fire, it's hard to do so if it's hard to identify clearly who is responsible for problems.

Fourth, the question of firing bureaucrats is always a political as well as an administrative act. It represents a decision about the values of the agency and of the people doing the firing. And it almost always generates an enormous debate. Inside the VA, employees argued that it was unfair to single out a handful of employees as scapegoats. In fact, they argued that many of the problems came from a lack of funding, so they were especially angry at members of Congress who called for the firing of managers without providing them with the money to do their jobs. In many of the police departments where police officers were involved in the deaths of citizens, there have been fierce debates about the difficulty of the police officer's job, with the need for instant life-or-death decisions, and the need to protect citizens from excessive use of force. In these debates, the question of firing quickly becomes the core of a much broader—and hard-to-resolve—debate.

These four issues point to a fifth important point: no matter how unhappy we might be about government performance, we can't fire our way to success or accountability. The processes of public administration are far too complex for that to work. The irony is that problems of performance have led to an instinct to solve them by firing bureaucrats. Firing bureaucrats, however, often only undermines the ability of government to perform, because good work ultimately depends on good people who are strongly motivated to do well. That is the puzzle of accountability we'll explore in this chapter, beginning with a look at the principle of separation of powers that is the foundation of our political system.

THE SEPARATION OF POWERS

The classical view of the policy process—and the foundation of accountability—begins with a clear line between the legislative and executive branches: the legislature makes policy and the executive branch implements it. In reality, the roles are far more complex and the lines much more blurred. In much of the American system, the Constitution creates elaborate checks and balances, not just a separation of powers, which means that political responsibility is shared, not separated. Furthermore, as one scholar of congressional oversight has pointed out, "oversight is in many respects a continuation of preenactment politics."[4] The political battles of the legislative process continue to play out in the administrative process. Political forces that lose in the legislature often try to regain the advantage as administrators take over, and the forces that win the early battle must continue to struggle to make sure they retain their edge. Laws must be translated into rules; rules must be supported by budgets. And in the richly textured system of American federalism, few decisions rest at a single level of government.[5] That quickly focuses the question of political control of administration on the role of legislative oversight. Much of the analysis about legislative oversight focuses on Congress, but most of the issues apply just as sharply to oversight by state legislators, county boards, and city councils.

The Paradox of Oversight

At the core of legislative oversight is a profound paradox: although much of what legislatures do is oversight, in one form or another, oversight tends to rank low among legislative priorities. Nevertheless, oversight is essential to effective administration because, as Chapter 12 discussed, policy has little meaning except in its implementation.

As one panel of experts has pointed out, "oversight permeates the activities of Congress."[6] Many congressional actions involve some form of supervision of administrative actions, from the enactment of laws and budgets to committee hearings to program reviews by congressional staff agencies, such as the Government Accountability Office (GAO) and the Congressional Budget Office. Variations in the level of oversight can be quite remarkable, from investigation of a program's overall performance to probes of the most detailed of program activities. Nothing the federal government does lies beyond the reach of legislative oversight. In fact, critics have blamed congressional micromanagement for problems in many defense systems. In 1985, for example, the Pentagon submitted 24,000 pages of documentation to Congress in order to comply with 458 different reporting requirements established in previous legislation. The number of these reports, Department of Defense officials estimated, increased 1,000 percent in the decade and a half after 1970.[7] Such a penchant for particulars, moreover, imposes a heavy burden on top administrative officials. Former secretaries of state Henry Kissinger and Cyrus Vance, for example, have complained: "Surely there are better ways for the executive and legislative branches to consult than having the secretaries of state and defense spend more than a quarter of their time on repetitive congressional testimony."[8] As the federal government tried to strengthen its homeland security system in the aftermath of September 11, 2001, investigators found that many of the worst problems originated in the Immigration and Naturalization Service. They discovered that the agency was allowing too many security breaches and struggling to cope with a rising paperwork backlog. One critic felt that congressional micromanagement had caused many of the agency's problems. What Congress most needed to do, the expert concluded, was to make up its mind and then get out of the way.[9]

Despite the enormous power that oversight can bring, oversight usually is a low priority for legislators. Routine oversight does little to enhance a member's reputation back in the district. What matters most is passing legislation, taking stands on issues, and tending to constituents' needs through casework to solve constituents' problems.[10] Members are typically more interested in shaping the immediate future than in investigating what has gone wrong in the past—that is, unless, past events offer the opportunity for media coverage. An old joke in Washington is that the most dangerous place on Capitol Hill is between a member of Congress and a television camera. Immigration hearings rarely attract much public or media attention, but a 2010 immigration hearing featuring celebrity comedian Stephen Colbert packed the congressional hearing room and led to committee members sparring for the limelight. When Transportation Security Administration lines became hours long in 2016, many members of Congress were on television demanding a fix—which came quickly, given the glare of TV lights.

The important policy problems always involve difficult and detailed issues, and legislators rarely want to spend time learning them. They've found that constituents often care much more about help in getting Social Security and disability benefits, Medicare reimbursements, admission to a veterans' hospital, emergency home leave from military service, or a flag that flew over the Capitol. For state legislators, there is a cascade of complaints about motor vehicle licensing or highway signs. In fact, many state legislators get calls from constituents trying to sort out their federal Social Security checks. They've learned that it never makes sense to send them elsewhere—and that they get credit for helping solve a problem, even if it's not one of theirs. Legislators also pay a great deal of attention to fighting for projects in their districts—roads, dams, job training programs, and money for schools.

This frames the paradox of oversight: while nearly all legislative activities are a form of oversight, the kinds of activities in which legislators are most likely to be involved are least likely to provide good information about or leverage over administrative problems. When there's a chance to embarrass executives of the opposite party, the taste for oversight grows.[11] Most of the time, however, oversight is likely to be unsystematic, sporadic, episodic, erratic, haphazard, ad hoc, and based on a crisis.[12] Long-term improvement of implementation requires systematic, sustained attention. Legislators' incentives are often very different from what's required to improve policy implementation.

Mathew D. McCubbins and Thomas Schwartz have christened this approach **fire alarm oversight**, in which legislators focus their oversight on problems, as they arise. McCubbins and Schwartz contrast this to what they call **police patrol oversight**, in which legislators conduct routine patrols exploring the implementation of programs. They contend that the approach produces oversight that is much more effective: through periodic interventions sparked by apparent problems, members of Congress can more clearly define the goals they have in mind. Moreover, they contend, responding to problems as they arise is much more likely to detect troubles than is maintaining a regular police-patrol style.[13] There's much debate on this proposition. Opponents suggest that the fire-alarm style misses the opportunity to fix little problems before they become big ones and that it encourages legislators to play for the issues most likely to attract the cameras. At the very least, however, the debate makes an important point: oversight is a much more subtle process than the formal checks-and-balances system might suggest.

The Purposes of Oversight

Even if it is intermittent and ad hoc, oversight nevertheless serves a number of important purposes for legislators.[14]

- *Assurance that administrators follow legislative intent.* Legislators naturally wish to ensure that administrators' actions are consistent with what legislators intended in passing legislation. That intent is sometimes hard to determine, of course, because legislation is notoriously imprecise. Often, in fact, legislators do not know what they want until they see what they get. In these cases, oversight provides an opportunity for communicating more clearly, if often informally, to administrators just what results legislators expect.
- *Investigation of instances of fraud, waste, and abuse.* This unholy trinity is a frequent target of legislative investigations. From stories of overpriced hammers purchased by the Pentagon to suggestions of irregularities by contractors serving Native American reservations to problems with the parking authority, allegations of inefficiencies and illegalities frequently fuel the kind of press attention that draws legislators, which often sparks oversight.
- *Collection of information.* Since many programs must be reauthorized, oversight gives legislators and their staffs the opportunity to obtain basic data that will help them determine how laws ought to be changed and which new laws should be enacted.
- *Evaluation of program effectiveness.* Oversight can also provide legislators with information about how well a program is performing. This information can help legislators determine how best to improve an agency's effectiveness.
- *Protection of legislative prerogatives.* Legislators also sometimes use oversight to protect what they view as their constitutional rights and privileges from encroachment by the executive branch. The checks-and-balances system often breeds boundary-line disputes, and oversight gives legislators an opportunity to defend their points of view.
- *Personal advocacy.* Oversight frequently gives legislators their own "bully pulpits" from which to advance programs of interest and to attract publicity. Some legislators have built their reputations by championing particular causes, while others have used televised hearings to promote their careers.
- *Reversal of unpopular actions.* Finally, oversight provides members with leverage to force agencies to reverse unpopular decisions. Through veiled threats and direct confrontation, legislators can signal administrators about what activities are unacceptable and what can be done to address members' concerns.

Legislative oversight occurs through several channels, which this chapter investigates. We will focus especially on the work of Congress, which provides a model for how many state and local legislators operate. We will examine in particular the work of legislative committees and their staffs and the role of legislative support agencies, like GAO.

The Rise of Federal Tax Expenditures

We often think of government programs as spending. But to a growing degree, especially at the federal level, government advances its agenda through "tax expenditures"—tax breaks that allow individuals or corporations to deduct the cost of activities from their income or to take a credit against taxes they owe. Such programs can provide enormous incentives for action, with the government footing the bill by giving up tax revenues.

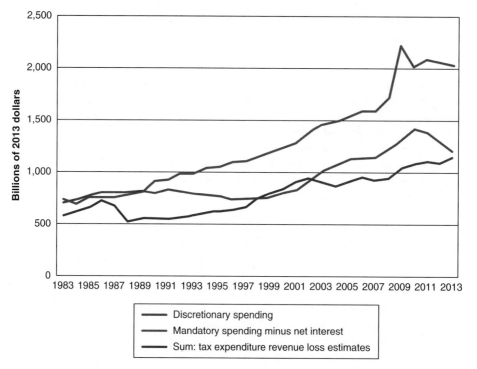

Source: U.S. Government Accountability Office, http://www.gao.gov/assets/670/664913.txt.

QUESTIONS

1. The chart shows the budget implications for several items, expressed in billions of 2013 dollars. Is it useful to use this "constant dollar" figure to make long-term comparisons? Why or why not?

2. The chart compares mandatory spending (for entitlements), discretionary spending (which requires congressional approval), and tax expenditures (the revenue lost each year by special tax breaks, including tax deductions and credits). What are the trends for each?

3. Discretionary spending requires congressional approval. Tax expenditures, once enacted, do not. What are the implications for oversight and accountability of government's operations, of this difference, given the trends?

COMMITTEE OVERSIGHT OF ADMINISTRATION

Even more than is the case with its legislative work, Congress depends heavily on its committees for monitoring administrative agencies and their implementation of programs. Indeed, the connection between congressional committees and administrative agencies is one of the most important in government.[15] The old saying "Congress at work is Congress in committee" applies especially to the executive-legislative relationship. Committee members write the legislation and fund the programs that bureaucrats must implement; the bureaucrats' decisions affect the members' abilities to claim credit for governmental action. It is an exchange relationship: "The ability of each to attain his goals is at least partially dependent on the actions of the other," R. Douglas Arnold writes.[16] For state and local government legislators, where elected officials often have much less staff help, these issues are often even more important.

Legislators have powerful sanctions in their arsenal, but their use of these tools varies. Some committees engage more frequently in oversight, especially those watching over agencies that must receive annual appropriations. Some committees are far tougher in approving budgets than others. Furthermore, some committees tend to be largely populated by members whose goal is constituency service and, in providing that service, bureaucrats can gain powerful allies. However, oversight may be harsher when a committee has a broad national agenda (such as education or labor), instead of a narrow constituency focus.[17] Nevertheless, "committees in both houses tend to give more attention to investigations of broad policy questions than to inquiries into agency implementation of programs."[18]

Varieties of Committee Review

Three sets of standing committees have responsibility for **legislative review** (the official term for legislative oversight): regular legislative committees (usually known as **authorizing committees**, because they prepare the laws that authorize programs), **appropriations committees**, and committees on government operations.

Authorizing committees can initiate, review, and report out bills and resolutions in particular subject-matter areas (such as labor, commerce, education, and foreign affairs). Each has the oversight responsibility to review the administration of laws within its jurisdiction. While some legislative committees have conducted extensive oversight, the overall tendency is for these subject-area committees to concentrate more on the passage of new laws than on review of the execution of existing ones. Further decreasing the frequency of oversight here is the growth in the number of programs receiving permanent authorizations (mandatory programs, especially entitlements, as we saw in Chapter 11). When program managers do not need to appear regularly to request continuation of their programs, the likelihood of oversight diminishes. Some committees are also moving toward longer reauthorizations to help reduce their workload, which has further reduced the opportunities for oversight.[19] Furthermore, some legislative committees (and subcommittees) are so close to agencies and the programs under their purview that they are not eager to launch deep probes into administrative mismanagement or program ineffectiveness.

Appropriations committees have the most impressive credentials for control of administration: prestige, broad scope, power, and competence. Appropriations committee members, and especially their staffs, typically command knowledge of agencies and programs rivaling that of career administrators and surpassing that of political executives. Yet Congress cannot rely

For most Americans, few public administrators are more important than those who answer 911 calls—especially when they're in desperate need of help. But 911 operators get a truly remarkable array of requests, as this survey from Reddit shows.

1. "9-1-1. [W]hat's your emergency?"

   Breathless, panicky voice: "How do I get the cranberry sauce out of the can without it coming out in chunks?"

   "Open the other end and slide it out on a plate."

   "OH! THANK YOU! You are brilliant!"

2. A panicked phone call arrived from a girl in gym class at the local high school. The emergency? There was a squirrel at the top of a telephone pole and it wasn't coming down.

3. Deer emergency

   Caller: A deer just swam across the river behind my house.

   Dispatcher: Okay?

   Caller: Well I am worried it might be cold.

   Dispatcher: . . . Well there is nothing we can do about a deer being cold. Didn't it run off after swimming the river?

   Caller: Yes.

   Dispatcher: Well ma'am it's a wild animal and I'd guess it's going to be fine.

   Caller: [Okay].

4. We had an old woman call in and say there were two guys dress[ed] in blue trying to break in her house and assault her. So we send about 6 cops over to her house. It turns out it was the gas company reading her gas meter.

5. A resident lived in a rooming house where the common area had a microwave—until one night he went looking for it, and it wasn't there.

   Dispatcher: You called 911 because a microwave you don't even own is missing? Did you ask your landlord if he took it?

   Guy: Uh, no.

   Dispatcher: Well, that's not an emergency, sir.

   Guy: But I'm really hungry.

6. One dispatcher said, "I've done this for a while. Do people abuse the system? Sure. But for the most part I'm happy with how our children are taught to only use 911 if it's a life or death emergency or if there's a crime in progress."

If you're in desperate need, there's nothing more important to government's performance, accountability, and politics than getting help there fast, and that's what 911 operators do.

Source: Reddit, https://m.reddit.com/r/AskReddit/comments/52to0o/911_operators_whats_the_dumbest_call_youve_ever_/?utm_source=mweb_redirect&compact=true.

mainly on the appropriations committees for the oversight function, because the members of these committees are already heavily burdened by their primary responsibility: they operate under the time pressure of the annual appropriations process, and their focus is on dollar figures and incremental changes from the previous year. The House Appropriations Committee's oversight, a staff member has said, is wide but not deep, whereas legislative committees' oversight is deep but not wide.[20] Moreover, with the rise of mandatory programs and reconciliation legislation discussed in Chapter 11, the influence of the appropriations committees, on both budgeting and congressional oversight, has decreased. In the early 2010s, Congress banned the use of "earmarks"—targeted spending on particular projects, favored by one or two members of Congress—in an effort to bring spending under control. But that in turn has diminished the leverage of the appropriations committees over the process and made it harder to put together deals to get legislation passed on time.

The Senate Committee on Homeland Security and Government Affairs and the House Committee on Oversight and Government Reform have the broadest responsibility and strongest powers for overseeing administrative activities. (After September 11, 2001, Congress rolled the new homeland security mission into governmental affairs to create a more unified look at governmental operations.) Since the early 1800s, Congress has used such committees to go beyond the usual grasp of legislative and appropriations committees. They are *the* oversight committees of Congress, and their jurisdiction is not constrained by the usual departmental or committee boundaries.[21]

While their potential for effective oversight is great, these committees have traditionally ranked relatively low in prestige.[22] One consequence is that the committees' members focus their primary interest elsewhere: members serve on multiple committees, and their other committee assignments often offer more of what they need for reelection. The oversight committees rarely have adopted any strategy to guide their work in monitoring administrative agencies, and the subject-area committees have jealously guarded their jurisdictions from review. When investigations promise big headlines, other committees are quick to seize the agenda. Both houses' oversight committees have been highly selective and episodic in the choice of the administrative activities to be reviewed, generally reflecting their own specific areas of legislative jurisdiction (e.g., executive reorganization, intergovernmental relations), reacting to public scandals, or registering the special concerns of leading committee members. They rarely have been able to pursue sustained investigations, however, because they receive only modest funding.[23] When major issues surface, such as the conduct of the second Bush administration's war in Iraq or decisions about licensing a new drug, the authorizing committees tend to take center stage.

Oversight and Redundancy

The problem of legislative control, at all levels of government, is clearly not a shortage of committees with oversight responsibilities and opportunities. Indeed, the multiplicity of committees and the overlaps among their jurisdictions provide many different avenues for legislative influence on administrative activities. In Congress, the increasingly decentralized system has expanded the points of access and the number of hearings, but "it has at the same time weakened the ability of Congress to conduct serious oversight and administrative control." The growing complexity of administrative activities, the difficulty of developing good information about program performance, and the counterbalancing power of interest groups all combine to lessen Congress's direct leverage over the executive branch.[24] As experts debated the creation of the new Department of Homeland Security in 2002, congressional scholar Norman J. Ornstein counted thirteen House and Senate committees with at least some jurisdiction over the issue, and there were more than sixty subcommittees sharing jurisdiction—with a total of eighty-eight committees and subcommittees in all.[25] After

September 11, 2001, anyone who could assert jurisdiction over a piece of the action did so. For top officials at the Department of Homeland Security, the situation is even worse. More than eighty congressional committees and subcommittees oversee the department's vast operations. The drive from the department's temporary headquarters in far northwest Washington to Capitol Hill is a tortuous one through the capital's clogged traffic. Constant congressional hearings, which are essential for accountability, make it hard to get the department's work done.

Such redundancy has magnified Congress's oversight problem. Changes in the budget process have duplicated the number of reviews to which agencies are subjected and have blurred the question of who is in charge of what. As one Georgetown University study on defense oversight argued, "redundancy in the congressional review process seriously aggravates the oversight problem." The redundant steps mean that "Congress rarely takes conclusive action on any issue," as a Senate Armed Services Committee staff report concluded.[26] One estimate is that assistant secretaries must spend as much as 40 percent of their time preparing for congressional testimony and responding to inquiries by members of Congress.[27] Thus, congressional committee structures and operating rules hinder rather than help in the oversight of administration. The multiplicity of committees overseeing the Department of Homeland Security led to constant complaints by senior officials, who said they needed to spend so much time tending their congressional relationships that they had little time left for their work. In 2008, Stephen R. Heifetz, the department's deputy assistant secretary for policy development, argued that "Congress should step back, streamline the number of committees with responsibility for homeland security—and give us room to do our job."[28] Congressional committees might reply that there was nothing more important in doing the job than ensuring accountability to Congress.

Congress's ability to monitor administrative activities effectively depends on its access to information, most of it generated in the executive branch. On the one hand, there are significant barriers to obtaining information about what is happening in the executive branch; on the other hand, legislators typically are awash in data. Effective oversight requires separating the truly useful information from the huge volumes of paper that flood Washington—as well as state capitals and city halls. Distilling the key issues from the mass of detailed data evokes the classic problem of trying "to distinguish the forest from the trees."

Barriers to Information Flow

Since Congress depends heavily on outside forces for the information needed to drive oversight, barriers in the way of the flow of information have a huge impact on the quality of oversight. Several kinds of barriers, both institutional and political, can effectively impede the flow of information.

SECRECY. Secrecy, particularly in the conduct of foreign affairs, the planning of military strategy and tactics, and the pursuit of intelligence activities, is the most formidable barrier.[29] Few would argue that these matters should be carried on in full view of the public or, for that matter, of the 535 members of Congress. The problem is that under the guise of national security, it is possible for administrators to classify documents—and classification, once done, is difficult to undo. During World War II, for example, documents often received security classifications simply because classified documents were delivered more quickly. In the Defense Department, even newspaper clippings have been stamped "secret," and a memorandum urging less use of the top secret classification was itself classified top secret.[30]

Forty years after the end of World War II, the Tower Commission, investigating the Reagan administration's elaborate plan to sell arms to Iran to secure the release of Americans held hostage there, and then to divert the arms-sales profits to aid the Contras in Nicaragua, concluded that "concern for preserving the secrecy of the initiative provided an excuse for abandoning sound process."[31] Almost fifteen years later, members of Congress continued to complain that they had not received timely information from the Pentagon about problems with the war in Iraq, especially about abusive treatment of Iraqi prisoners by American soldiers. Senator Carl Levin (D-Mich.) sternly admonished Defense Secretary Donald Rumsfeld in 2004 that consultation with Congress "is not supposed to be an option but a long-standing and fundamental responsibility" of administration officials.[32] Members of Congress continually complain that they have a hard time getting the information they want to oversee administrative actions. Administrators sometimes solve this problem by providing classified information to a few selected committees in executive session, closed to the press and the public (usually the House and Senate Intelligence Committees), or just to the chairpersons and ranking minority members of such committees. When news broke in 2013 (through leaks of classified information by Edward Snowden, an employee of a contractor for the National Security Agency) that the NSA was collecting massive amounts of information on the phone calls of Americans, many members of Congress were outraged. But both the Bush and Obama administrations had kept select members of Congress informed on the details, and the NSA argued it had acted legally. There was legislative oversight. But it did not involve most members of Congress.

How open can intelligence be and still be effective? At what point does secrecy pose a threat to democratic values?

©iStock.com/elnavegante

EXECUTIVE PRIVILEGE. A second barrier to the flow of information is **executive privilege**—a prerogative never mentioned in the Constitution but now a right that presidents have asserted to be inherent in their powers. In the government, the doctrine has most powerfully been invoked to protect the confidentiality of oral and written communication between the president and White House aides, especially during the Nixon administration's Watergate affair. The question of executive privilege has continued to resurface ever since, however, constricting the ability of courts and Congress to elicit information in incidents ranging from Bill Clinton's appearance before a grand jury investigating his personal conduct in office to George W. Bush's testimony before a commission investigating the September 11, 2001, attacks. Senior Bush aide Karl Rove claimed executive privilege as a defense against testifying before Congress on the leak of the identity of the name of a CIA spy to the media.

ADMINISTRATIVE CONFIDENTIALITY. A third barrier to legislative access to information is **administrative confidentiality**, which covers two distinct practices. One is the protection of private information: individuals' tax returns, completed census forms, possibly derogatory personal details collected in investigative agencies' files, and trade secrets and financial data from businesses. Such information is normally collected by government agencies under pledges of confidentiality, and administrators argue they

Gen. Keith B. Alexander, director of the National Security Agency and head of the U.S. Cyber Command, faced tough questions from congressional investigators in 2013. Following the leak of secrets through British and American newspapers by an NSA contractor, members of Congress probed the scope of the agency's surveillance of Americans' telephone and Internet communications.

cannot disclose such information. Doing so, they say, would impair the government's ability to obtain full and accurate information.

The other claim to administrative confidentiality relates to drafts, memoranda, and other internal records bearing on policy issues. Agency officials contend that if such internal records were released too soon, it would make it harder for administrators to give full and frank views on complicated issues. Releasing internal memos, moreover, could create a sense that an agency is about ready to make a large, formal step on a big issue, when in fact the agency might only be looking at a wide range of options. But that only whets the appetites of legislative committees, which often can't resist the urge to dig deeply into internal debates.

FINDING THE BALANCE. Secrecy, executive privilege, and administrative confidentiality are all part of deep and lasting disputes rooted in the principles of separation of powers and the checks-and-balances system. There are deep moral and practical considerations, on one side, in favor of limiting the flow of information. There are political and constitutional principles, on the other, in favor of greater transparency. On one side are citizens' stake in the confidentiality of personal information in government files, the president's and department heads' need for candid advice from their immediate assistants, the effects of disclosure of preliminary proposals, and the special need for secrecy in matters affecting defense and the conduct of foreign affairs. On the other side are the often deplorable results of official activities cloaked in secrecy; the people's right to know so that they can participate in democratic government; the legislature's oversight responsibilities as creator, authorizer, and financier of agencies and their programs; and its role as investigator and exposer of corrupt, illegal, and unethical behavior in the executive branch. With so many considerations in conflict, no formula, however complex, can provide an easy solution to this dilemma of administrative accountability.

Staffing

There's a paradox in sorting through these issues. Legislatures never think they have all the right information they need. On the other hand, they're inevitably swamped by massive amounts of information from the agencies. There are regular reports, background studies, supporting details for budget requests, and the growing amount of performance data (as we saw in Chapter 12). Legislators ask for more and struggle to digest what they get. The Environmental Protection Agency, for example, reported that it had to respond to more

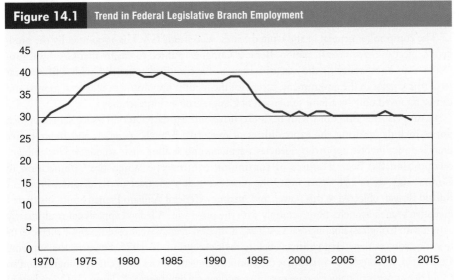

| **Figure 14.1** | **Trend in Federal Legislative Branch Employment** |

Source: U.S. Office of Personnel Management, *Federal Civilian Workforce Statistics—Employment and Trends,* various years.

than 4,000 letters per year from Congress requesting information.[33] On the other hand, agencies learned long ago that one way to fend off legislative investigation is to bury the investigators in more information than they can manage. The increasingly scientific and technological character of many fields of governmental activity has further complicated the problem.[34]

For years, Congress dealt with the problem of information overload by increasing the size of its own staff. With the rise of budget cuts in the mid-1990s, however, Congress has tried to set a model for cuts elsewhere in government by shrinking its own staff (see Figure 14.1). In fact, legislative branch employment at the federal level fell by 25 percent from 1993 to 2013, including not only committee staffs and the personal staffs of members of Congress but also the support staffs in agencies like GAO, the Congressional Research Service, and the Congressional Budget Office. These cuts have made it more difficult for Congress to keep up with the information overload.

THE GOVERNMENT ACCOUNTABILITY OFFICE

In helping Congress deal with the administrative challenges of government, GAO is the most important support agency. GAO has a rich history. In 1921, Congress transferred the government's auditing functions from the Treasury Department, where they had been based since 1789, to a new agency, called the General Accounting Office.[35] GAO originally was an agency wholly devoted to accounting: its staff reviewed all of the federal government's spending, and employees wearing green eyeshades processed piles of paper. That role has changed radically over the years. GAO now is Congress's chief arm for examining the performance of governmental programs. That's reflected in the change in the agency's name from *accounting* to *accountability* in 2004.

The comptroller general of the United States, who heads GAO, is appointed by the president subject to Senate confirmation. Because Congress wanted to ensure that GAO was protected from interference by the executive branch, the comptroller general holds a fifteen-year term (the longest in the government, except for the lifetime appointment of federal judges) and can be removed only by a joint resolution of Congress or by impeachment.

GAO performs functions with both executive and legislative roots. Its legislative branch duties include auditing the expenditures of executive branch agencies, and its executive branch duties involve approving agencies' payments and settling their accounts. This ambiguous position has been a source of continuing controversy. When the Competition in Contracting Act of 1984 gave GAO the power to halt a contract under dispute, President Ronald Reagan objected to this power, and Attorney General William French Smith instructed executive branch agencies not to comply with the provision. A federal appeals court ultimately agreed with Congress, holding that GAO was a "hybrid agency" that could exercise such executive functions as reviewing contracts before their execution. In 1986, however, the Supreme Court held, in *Bowsher v. Synar*, that the comptroller general was an agent of Congress and so could not constitutionally exercise executive budget-cutting powers.[36] Thus, GAO is a hybrid whose constitutional position is a vague one.

Changes in GAO's Strategy

In GAO's early years, it focused its work on auditing federal transactions: tracking expenditures to ensure that they were legal and matched the requirements for the mission. Vouchers for all federal transactions were transported from across the world to Washington for review by GAO. If it disapproved any expenditure, the public official who had approved the expenditure would, by law, be personally responsible for the difference.[37] The risk of such personal liability was so threatening that spending officers often asked GAO for advance opinions, and GAO increasingly preaudited expenditures before they were made. As a result, GAO not only delayed actions but became less an after-the-fact auditor than an active participant in the very transactions it was supposed to audit later. But that soon became unwieldy—and new issues of performance arose as well. That led to a fundamental shift in GAO's role.

Although GAO still has power to, and occasionally does, audit some individual transactions, it now relies more on agencies' internal audit and financial control systems. It's moved from cost accounting to program auditing, from examining the money trail to measuring program performance. Its reports on cost overruns in weapons procurement have often created sensations. But in more routine audits of agencies, GAO uses statistical sampling and other strategies to test the effectiveness of internal control systems, thus again removing itself from the burden of second-guessing every transaction. GAO has also begun identifying and tracking "high-risk programs," federal activities that have an unusually high threat for waste, fraud, and abuse. Most audits are now done in federal agencies and their field offices, so freight-car loads of vouchers (or gigabytes of electronic files) no longer are sent to GAO in Washington. These and other changes have reduced GAO staff numbers from 15,000 in 1946 to 3,000 today.

GAO's reviews are remarkable for both their detail and their variety, as a sample of report titles shows:

- "Defense Inventory: Further Analysis and Enhanced Metrics Could Improve Service Supply and Depot Operations"
- "Low-Income Housing Tax Credit: Some Agency Practices Raise Concerns and IRS Could Improve Noncompliance Reporting and Data Collection"
- "Aviation Security: TSA Is Taking Steps to Improve Expedited Screening Effectiveness, but Improvements in Screener Oversight Are Needed"
- "VA's Health Care Budget: In Response to a Projected Funding Gap in Fiscal Year 2015, VA Has Made Efforts to Better Manage Future Budgets"
- "Visa Waiver Program: DHS Should Take Steps to Ensure Timeliness of Information Needed to Protect U.S. National Security"

In addition, GAO has also begun producing a transition series, providing advice to members of Congress and newly elected presidents and their team on topics ranging from the budget deficit and the public service to NASA and national defense. It also produces reports on the high-risk programs especially susceptible to waste and abuse. Those reports have had great impact.[38]

As a direct congressional agent exercising delegated control authority over administrative agencies, GAO occupies a powerful position. In addition, it has a substantial, skilled investigative and analytical staff that aids congressional committees in their oversight of agency performance and sometimes conducts reviews on its own initiative.

However, GAO has two handicaps that make it hard for the agency to focus public attention on its work.[39] The first is its "green eyeshade" image, but that has changed as the agency has increasingly hired public administration experts, economists, and other social scientists, engineers, and computer and information specialists. Students often now view GAO as one of the most exciting places to work in government.

The second handicap is the time required to investigate and audit programs. This stems largely from GAO's commitment to accuracy, thoroughness, and objectivity, but the result is that its reports often lack timeliness for Congress's agenda. Nevertheless, GAO's reports—and their handy "highlights" page that summarize key findings—are staples at congressional hearings and in news reports of governmental activities. In the 1980s, GAO's computer experts provided much of the data used to track down the secret financial transfers used by Reagan aide Oliver North to channel arms-sale profits to Central American guerrillas. Its work was a centerpiece of Congress's investigation of problems at the VA.

State and Local Legislative Control

GAO's influence has spilled over into the states, where many legislatures have established their own "mini-GAOs" to conduct evaluations of state programs. They often have arcane titles, such as the Virginia Joint Legislative Audit and Review Commission, California's State Joint Legislative Audit Committee, and Wisconsin's Joint Committee on Audit, but their work is just as important and far-reaching. State legislators struggle with the same problems of information mismatch as members of Congress. In states where legislative service is part time, the problem is even greater. These state-level versions of GAO are typically small but highly professional, and their work often makes headlines.

In local governments, legislators (members of city councils and county boards) rarely have a separate GAO-style staff. They tend to rely on their own staffs. In small communities, such support is often meager, but in larger communities, legislators often have personal staffs that rival those of members of Congress.

AN ASSESSMENT OF LEGISLATIVE CONTROL

Legislative control of administration is based on the proposition that legislators as well as executives have a responsibility to see "that the laws be faithfully executed." Legislators create the programs that administrators manage. They have the power to fix problems by amending the law and appropriating money. They can oversee administration and provide a political nudge. Legislators, in short, have enormous power over the administration of law—and over the accountability of administrators. While the process is often confusing, the jurisdictions are often muddled, and legislative attention often erratic, the whole system provides an impressive range of information and leverage, both formal and informal, for legislative influence on administrative activities.

We have, however, discovered two major problems in legislative oversight and control. One is that legislators often have limited interest and modest capacity for oversight.[40] Oversight efforts are at best intermittent, and sustained legislative attention to major administrative issues is rare.

The other problem is the danger that legislators (especially in committees and subcommittees) will intrude excessively into the executive function, sometimes to promote their own self-interest.[41] It's dangerous if legislators seek to become, in effect, co-administrators of agencies and programs. A longtime chairman of the House Naval Affairs Committee, for example, was dubbed "the Secretary of the Navy," for his tireless interest in the Navy's activities. The involvement of judges in administration raises similar risks, as we saw in the previous chapter.

HOW DOES ACCOUNTABILITY WORK?

All these puzzles bring us back to the central problem of public administration, as discussed in Chapter 1: how to give administrators enough power to accomplish the work that policymakers want done, without having them exercise that power in a way that threatens democracy and liberty. Accountability, at its core, is *who is responsible to whom for what, through what means.* It is a relationship more than a process. It is dynamic rather than static. And it is the most important question of public administration.

Elements of Accountability

Systems for holding public administrators accountable have at least four elements: voluntary compliance, standard setting, monitoring, and sanctions.

The foundation of accountability is *voluntary compliance.* Even though people are not saints, people most of the time voluntarily comply with most of the significant constraints on their behavior. They do so for a variety of reasons, ranging from high moral standards to indifference to self-interest. As Max Weber stressed, they often do so because they believe in the legitimacy of the system of authority. Were it unrealistic to rely on substantial voluntary compliance, the scope and intensity of control systems would be unbearable.

The second element, *standard setting*—crafting rules to guide administrative discretion—sets boundaries, incentives, and penalties. It tells administrators what they are supposed to do (and what behavior they will be punished for). Some standards are obvious: few people need to be told that stealing is wrong, although petty theft—from pilfering government office supplies to using government photocopy machines to duplicate favorite recipes—is common. (And that's before the debate about using government computers at lunchtime to place online orders.) At the other extreme, some standards are so complicated that no one can know all of the rules that apply to their actions: the question of how—and how much—to pay government's contractors fills thick manuals. Frontline administrators rarely understand all the rules, and they rely on agency lawyers, procurement specialists, and masters of accounting regulations to raise a red flag about potential problems. Observing the standards, however, can become mechanical and trivial; nearly everyone has had experience in dealing with administrators so obsessed with rules and forms that the basic mission of public service becomes lost. The key to effective administration lies in ensuring that attention to the details does not undermine effective pursuit of the broader policy.

Third, an effective accountability system must *monitor* whether the standards are met. Sometimes that happens in advance—an administrator may need to get an action approved in advance. Some state governments, for example, require advance approval of all administrative rules before they become effective. Sometimes, before it becomes final, an action must "incubate"—lie in a legislative committee for a fixed period (say, sixty days), during which time committee members may (or may not) seek to persuade the agency to abort the action. Other forms of monitoring call for reviewing actions already completed. For example, monitors often conduct postaudits of financial transactions and review the error rate in payments to welfare clients. The auditors can criticize any improprieties they find and demand that the administrative agency mend its ways in the future.

Should policymakers use monitoring to identify, prevent, or correct all possible errors?[42] It is tempting to answer yes, but, in fact, that can make programs more expensive and less effective. An effort by the Internal Revenue Service to wring out every last nickel of taxes owed by every citizen would cost far more (in the time of revenue agents) than it would collect. A heavy-handed approach would infuriate taxpayers. So, instead, overseers selectively review administrators' actions, often in response to complaints by citizens, members of the press, congressional committees, or employees.[43] They may use sampling—by examining, say, every fifth case or by reviewing all of the cases in an agency unit in one out of five years; the sampling process shifts the focus from correcting individual errors to identifying those agencies or units that have so poor a pattern of actions that they need fundamental change. Or they may concentrate on areas (such as the awarding of government contracts or the operation of lottery programs) that might be especially prone to problems, or on programs in which government officials (such as inspectors, social workers, police officers, and other "street-level bureaucrats") frequently must make quick decisions or exercise broad discretion, which present special problems of accountability.

Finally, to be credible, an accountability system needs the ability to impose *sanctions*; if overseers find problems, there must be consequences. The delicate task here is to devise sanctions strong enough to be taken seriously by administrators but not so strong as to disrupt an agency's mission. They cannot be so punitive as to be impossible to enforce or so repressive as to require an impossible burden of proof. Sanctions can sometimes be too tough, such as when a federal agency offends Congress and Congress responds with a sharp budget cut, forcing the curtailment of important public services. Sometimes sanctions may be too mild or too poorly directed to serve as adequate punishment or deterrent, such as when a congressional investigation produces only a critical report—but no change in law or budget—so the agency may simply ignore the proceeding.

Principles to Make Accountability Work

Accountability is thus a matter of balancing internal norms with external processes. The external processes can be within the agency or from oversight bodies in both the executive and legislative branches. If the nation's founders created a separation-of-powers system to restrain government's power, American public administration has over time evolved a complex and layered system for holding administrators accountable.

The process relies on two principles to make this layered accountability system work. One is *independence*: making each control agency autonomous and insulated from those individuals and forces that might corrupt or restrain it. Independence helps ensure integrity by insulating it from the cross-pressures that often engulf elected institutions. For example, GAO is designed to be independent of the executive departments and is separate from Congress's own day-to-day work. The other answer is *redundancy*: multiplying the control agencies and overlapping their functions.[44] If one control agency misses a problem, having other control agencies with overlapping jurisdictions can increase the chances of catching it. Furthermore, competition among control agencies may stimulate energy in all of them. Inspectors general are likely to be more vigilant because they know that GAO, the Office of Management and Budget, and congressional watchdog committees may catch anything they miss—and possibly embarrass them for having missed it.

Redundancy, of course, can itself be a problem. Multiple control agencies can make conflicting demands. For example, until the 1950s, GAO, the Treasury Department, and the Bureau of the Budget separately prescribed the kinds of information that agencies' accounting systems had to produce. On the other hand, when several control agencies have jurisdiction over an especially troublesome case, each may await another's move—and in the end, nothing may happen. Finally, redundancy has one very obvious drawback: duplication of oversight is expensive, and at some point the costs may overwhelm the advantages produced. The trick lies in getting the watchdogs to bark loudly enough to alert policymakers to problems but not so obsessively that they become a distracting nuisance.

Consider the case of Gina Gray, appointed by the Pentagon as public affairs director of Arlington National Cemetery in early 2008. She discovered that top Department of Defense officials were imposing limits on media coverage of the burial of soldiers killed in Iraq. After poking through the regulations, she found no regulation against media coverage. If families approved the coverage, she allowed it. But just ten days into the job, she found that a senior cemetery official moved the media fifty yards from the service, which made it impossible for reporters to hear or photograph the service. Her supervisors took away her BlackBerry smartphone, demoted her, and ultimately fired her. "Had I not put my foot down, had I just gone along with it and not said regulations were being violated, I'm sure I'd still be there," Gray told a *Washington Post* reporter. "It's about doing the right thing."[45]

The "right thing," of course, was precisely what the issue was about. Who should make policy? What obligations do government officials have in following it? What should they do if they believe that the decisions of their supervisors violate policy or ethical standards? In a close call, should the decisions of supervisors or an official's internal norms rule? Gray decided that the rules did not forbid media coverage of the funerals and she was fired for her stand. In her termination letter, Gray's supervisor said she had "been disrespectful to me as your supervisor and failed to act in an inappropriate manner." It was an unusual typo—a double negative that created profound irony. The *Washington Post* reporter concluded, "Only at Arlington National Cemetery could it be considered a firing offense to act appropriately."[46]

Accountability, in the end, is about doing the right thing: administering the law in a way that delivers the most value to taxpayers, that advances the goals the legislature creates in law, and that builds trust in the process of governance. It's a tall order. But it's one that lies at the very core of today's government, as it has been at the center of debates about government for thousands of years.

BIG QUESTIONS

If the search for accountability is an eternal question in public administration, the field faces fascinating puzzles on the cutting edge. Consider these big, emerging questions that will shape debate about public administration in the years to come.

Gina Gray, public information officer at Arlington National Cemetery, was fired for disagreeing with the restrictions placed on the media's coverage of the burials of soldiers killed in Iraq and Afghanistan. The case touched off a national debate on the responsibilities of government administrators to balance the privacy of families with freedom of the press.

- *Decay.* Political scientist Francis Fukuyama has argued that government in general—and government in the United States in particular—is in decay.[47] The problem, he says, comes from the rising tide of interest groups, whose power threatens to subvert the effectiveness of government and citizens' trust in the way it works. Are the problems of trust and competence in government getting worse? Or are we simply in the midst of the kind of periodic reassessment that has often transformed government in the past?
- *Evidence.* Reformers have called for much more policy analysis to improve government. Many current and former government officials, for example, have argued for a form of "moneyball" to bring sharper analytics to public decisions.[48] On the other hand, there isn't much evidence that policymakers—and those who oversee administration—pay much attention to the evidence we produce. Can more and better information improve public administration? If so, what forms of information are most likely to be most powerful?
- *Narrow slices.* Some scholars, like Robert F. Durant and David Rosenbloom, have argued that the field of public administration is becoming "hollowed out": that the academic study of public administration has increasingly focused on narrow questions and that its ability to improve the practice of public administration has become weaker.[49]
- *Interweaving.* In my book *Escaping Jurassic Government*, I argue that American administrative strategies have become so interwoven with other governmental bureaucracies, other levels of government, other sectors, and other nations' administrative structures that it's become increasingly hard to hold the system accountable and to make it work well.[50] Can we change this basic system of interweaving? Or are there some strategies most likely to make it work better?
- *Administrative law.* Administrative law was once the cornerstone of public administration: a system for understanding how the rule of law structures administrative actions and holds them accountable. It's fallen on hard times—and, with the rise of

interweaving, private law has often pushed it aside. Should we devise a strategy for bringing administrative law back into the center of the field?

- *Federalism.* It's hard to imagine any domestic program that doesn't depend heavily on partnerships between the levels of government. From the administration of food safety to the financing of government health care programs, federalism is central. Indeed, the case with which we began this book—the Flint water crisis—is at its core a federalism problem. But the study of federalism has shrunk in the last generation. Is it time to bring it back, with a fresh foundation built from twenty-first-century challenges?

- *Strategic human capital.* An enduring theme of this book is that people—government administrators—matter. A lot. The quality of government depends heavily on the quality of people who work for it. However, there's little attention to this issue inside government, and human capital attracts little research among scholars. Would public administration be stronger if we paid more attention to these puzzles?

We could put together a longer list. But even these items reinforce one fundamentally important issue: the field of public administration is one of enormous importance and fundamental change. It's an area sure to attract the keen interest of scholars and to provide unmatched opportunities for young professionals. Public administration is one of the oldest disciplines, with roots stretching back to biblical times. The fundamental questions are not going away, and the new puzzles are making the fundamentals even more important, with accountability at the core.

CONCLUSION: ETHICS AND THE PUBLIC SERVICE

No matter how many layers of accountability policymakers build, the responsiveness and effectiveness of public administration depend ultimately on the ethics of individual public administrators. One implication of Michael Lipsky's theory of street-level bureaucrats, mentioned in Chapter 13, is that many administrators operate far from the view of elected officials and top policymakers. They have broad discretion on how they do their jobs, they have a big impact on the lives of citizens, and there are few watchdogs on hand to catch misdeeds. Roving television news helicopters might occasionally catch an unusual event, and investigative reporters are always on the prowl for a good story. The inescapable fact, however, is that the quality—as well as accountability—of the administrative system depends critically on the decisions that individual administrators make and the values they hold in making them.

Debates flourish over whether ethics can be taught. Researchers of child development constantly remind us that the values of most children are formed by the age of three years. Moreover, debates constantly swirl over whether ethics can be reliably enforced. No amount of oversight can fully control the uncountable numbers of individual decisions that administrators make every day to make public administration work.

The surest course to an ethical public administration is a careful balance. It requires a balance between the individual values of public administrators and the professional training they bring to the job. It requires a balance between the cultures of their agencies and the oversight of external forces. Most of all, it requires a strong relationship between public administrators and the citizens to whom they ultimately are responsible, for the effective use of public power and for the responsible protection of individual freedom. It would be hard to imagine a fundamentally more important issue than this.

CASE 14.1

The Department of Expectation Management

At a conference not long ago of homeland security experts from both the private sector and government, one of the participants said we needed a new government agency: the "Department of Expectation Management." The comment got big laughs from the audience—and some knowing smiles that suggested it wasn't such a bad idea. For many of the audience members, managing expectations was an enormous part of their lives. People don't think much about homeland security, they confided, unless something happens—a terrorist stages an attack, a tornado strikes a town, a hurricane floods a city—and then citizens expect instant and effective action.

Of course, the problem of managing expectations stretches much further than homeland security. One analyst joked that the perfect local bus service is one that picks up residents at their home, takes them directly to where they want to go, and costs a dollar. When it snows, citizens expect that their street will see the plow first. And for anyone who's taken ill, the wait for an ambulance can feel like an eternity as the siren gets louder.

Part of public administration is delivering high-quality services to citizens at a low cost. Just as much a part of public administration is defining what "high-quality" and "low" mean. Most public administrators, if they can quietly confide their own dreams, would wish for a Department of Expectation Management to help them.

QUESTIONS TO CONSIDER

1. Suppose you were appointed to head the mythical, magical Department of Expectation Management for your community. How would you approach your job? What steps would you take? Do you think you could succeed?

2. What does the discussion at the conference tell you about the puzzles of public administration—and the jobs of public administrators?

3. How much do you think that public administrators ought to care about what the public expects? After all, it might be impossible to meet the public's expectations, no matter what they do. And some would argue that it's the job of public administrators to administer the law—nothing more, nothing less—and that it's the job of elected officials to deal with what the public wants.

CASE 14.2

Scary Words: Governments Must Start "Doing More with Less"

Ronald Reagan famously said, "The nine most terrifying words in the English language are: I'm from the government and I'm here to help." The words are so famous that, decades later, it's possible to buy T-shirts with the words proudly displayed.

But columnist Bill Bott says there are four words even scarier: "Doing more with less." No saying, he argued, "strikes fear into the work place like 'doing more with less' because we all know what we're really saying is you are about to get a whole lot less." For government employees, it means, "A whole lot less people, a whole lot less money, a whole lot less support, and a whole lot less enthusiasm for doing the work we love."[1]

The saying has been around for a long time. Vice President Al Gore used it to champion his "reinventing government" movement. The idea was simple: provide incentives for government workers to be more productive; government can produce more and better services while saving taxpayers money. In practice, the idea proved terribly hard to achieve. It was easy to cut programs to save money. It was possible to invest strategically to make service better. But it proved very, very hard to make government work better *and* cost less at the same time.

Bott has hope. It begins, he argues, with a change of philosophy. He says that "we need to lose the words accountability, blame and fault. We need to stop thinking of errors as a people mistake, or a mistake at all. An error is simply what happens when something didn't go down the quickest path the first time." Cut down handoffs of officials-to-officials-to-more-officials and focus on results, Bott says. Then cut down the time that citizens have to spend in line transacting business with government. The key, he says, is to "reduce the number of handoffs and subsequent CYA measures." By doing this, he said that the State of Washington's Department of Social and Health Services cut down waiting times for visits from three to four weeks to five to forty-five minutes. The average time to process benefits shrank from fourteen to eighteen days to four to eight days, with increased accuracy. That allowed the department to deal with a 40 percent increase in customer demand while absorbing a 24 percent budget cut.

That scenario might not fit Reagan's quip. But Bott suggests that citizens are in no mood for fewer services, and government has little choice but to improve its productivity if it is to meet the challenge of twenty-first-century government.

QUESTIONS TO CONSIDER

1. What do you think about the "doing more with less" line? Does it capture the reality of twenty-first-century government?

2. Which do you think fits public perception better: Reagan's quip or Gore's motto?

3. Now consider Bott's argument to move away from accountability, which suggests the effort to identify and root out error, and to move toward a system that focuses squarely on trying to streamline the process, to learn from mistakes, and to focus government more on serving citizens better. Is that a better meaning for accountability? Or are there things that this approach might miss?

NOTE

1. Bill Bott, "The Scariest Four Words in Government," *Governing* (October 25, 2010), http://www.governing.com/blogs/public-great/Scariest-Four-Words-in-Government.html.

CASE 14.3

Will We Drink to That? The Florida Board of Education's War on Chocolate Milk

As he prepared to take over as Florida's agriculture commissioner, Adam Putnam stopped a budding statewide movement. Over several years, Florida's Board of Education had championed efforts to take chocolate milk off school lunch menus.[1]

For kids, the dispute had already produced a big battle. The state had eliminated sugared sodas and cut down on desserts. The next target was chocolate milk. The problem, nutritionists said, wasn't the flavor—it was the extra sugar that came with it. Vanilla- and strawberry-flavored milk each had 30 grams of sugar in an eight-ounce serving. Regular milk has just 13 grams. The American Heart Association recommends that children aged four to eight limit their sugar intake to 12 grams of sugar per day.

Most kids remember chocolate milk from their grade school days. Some of us enjoyed it during kindergarten snack breaks. But officials like state Board of Education member John Padget took a close look at the nutrition guidelines and concluded that the chocolate milk had to go.

Putnam called a time-out to give analysts at the state Department of Agriculture and Consumer Services time to consult with officials from the state Department of Education. Critics charged that Putnam was trying to pull the decision out from the Education Department and into the Agriculture Department because industry lobbyists thought they'd get a better hearing there. Putnam denied that there was any industry pressure. He described it as "Let's hit the pause button, and let's begin a new type of conversation and an unprecedented collaboration between the source of our food and one of the biggest providers of children's food—that being the school system." At the bottom, many political analysts suspected, was an effort to move the management of school lunches from the Education Department to the Agriculture Department. That shift, some critics said, was Putnam's move to satisfy the dairy industry, which had contributed to his campaign. According to some sources, only New Jersey and Texas have a similar structure.

The decision had big implications. In the 2010 school year, just the four largest school districts spent a total of $13 million on flavored milk, as students consumed 49 million half-pints of chocolate milk.

Some experts argued that the state ought to go far past chocolate milk to look at other items on school menus that had lots of sugar. Salad dressings, for example, often contain added sugar. Lora Gilbert, head of Orange County's cafeterias, concluded, "Rather than center on one food, really it's the whole diet you have to look at."

QUESTIONS TO CONSIDER

1. Do you think that government and its administrative agencies ought to get involved with the decision of which products to regulate?

2. The main mission of the Education Department is to produce a high-quality education for Florida's students. The main mission of the Agriculture Department is to promote agriculture and food safety. Which do you think would be the better home for resolving this question? Do you think it makes a difference which agency handles the question?

3. What implications does this debate have for accountability in government? There are crosscutting issues, multiple stakeholders, competing goals, and many government players. What is the public interest question in providing chocolate milk to school children? How should we sort it out?

NOTE

1. Denise-Marie Balona, "Next Agriculture Chief Stops State's Push to Bar Flavored Milk in Schools," *Orlando Sentinel* (December 25, 2010), http://www .orlandosentinel.com/health/os-fla-schools-ban-chocolate-milk—20101225,0,678391.story.

CASE 14.4

Lobbying for EpiPens and Uber

Shelly LeGere, a grieving mother from Elmhurst, Illinois, is an unlikely symbol of the changing face of lobbying in America. Her thirteen-year-old daughter, Annie, died from anaphylactic shock, most likely from something she ate. When a police officer arrived, LeGere asked, "Don't you have anything? What can we do?"

First responders rushed Annie to the hospital. But they weren't equipped with an epinephrine injector, most commonly known as an EpiPen, and she didn't get treatment fast enough. Annie died nine days later. To try to save other victims, LeGere launched a campaign to equip first responders with EpiPens. In doing so, she became part of a national effort spearheaded by the manufacturer of the EpiPen, Mylan Inc.

The injectors aren't cheap. A two-dose pack costs more than $500, and that quickly adds up for cash-strapped local governments. It's also made lobbying for the EpiPen into big business. Mylan is working around the country to require local schools to stock the injector, which can prevent life-threatening reactions in children like Annie who suffer from severe allergies. In 2010, the company had lobbyists in nine states; by 2014 they were up to forty-five states.

This is just a tiny glimpse into the fundamental shift underway in lobbying, as interest groups switch their focus from Washington to the states. According to a study by the nonpartisan Center for Public Integrity, the number of organizations with lobbyists in the nation's capital declined by 25 percent from 2010 to 2014. In state capitals, the number rose by 10 percent. Battles once fought in a single, massive Washington campaign are now being contested in dozens of states.

The reason, says Lee Drutman, author of *The Business of America Is Lobbying*, is simple. Thanks to gridlock, "not a lot is happening in Washington." The more partisanship clogs the capital's gears, the more "you start looking to the states."

That's especially true for the regulation of pharmaceuticals, an issue that's still being fought vehemently in Washington as well. Take, for example, the status of biologic drugs, new formulations that come from cutting-edge biotech research. In many states, pharmacists can prescribe the cheaper biologics, just as they can substitute less expensive generic drugs for brand-name products. But to protect their immensely profitable businesses, many pharmaceutical makers have launched fierce campaigns in state capitals to make it harder to dispense the substitutes. They want to require pharmacists to obtain a doctor's consent or to keep extra records before using the less expensive substitutes.

Lobbyists for the drugmakers claim that the manufacture of biologics is extra tricky, so substituting cheaper versions could be extra risky. New rulemaking is underway in Washington to determine just what kind of substitutions are safe. But state-based lobbyists are still working feverishly to protect their market.

Not all of the increase in drug lobbying is the direct work of corporations. There's the effort to equip first responders with naloxone—the quick-acting and remarkably effective treatment for heroin overdoses, which can bring patients back from death's door in less than two minutes. Public health workers and the World Health Organization have led the campaign to make naloxone available to frontline emergency workers. That's lobbying in the public interest, but the fact is there's a lot of money at stake for naloxone's manufacturers. The politics can also be radioactive, as the manufacturer discovered when Congress launched an investigation in late 2016 of why the price for EpiPens had doubled.

Meanwhile, in a much different field, Uber has mounted an intense state-level lobbying campaign to protect and expand its business. California legislators and regulators have been juggling mega-issues, like whether the company must treat its drivers as employees and give them benefits, and whether it needs to give the state data on every Uber ride. To fight off the rules, the tech startup has become one of the state's biggest lobbyists. In California, Uber now outspends lobbyists for Wells Fargo, Bank of America, and the country's biggest company, Walmart.

This spurt of lobbying hasn't just been at the state level. Uber invested millions in a failed effort to stop an Austin plan that would require fingerprinting its drivers.

What these campaigns have in common is the growing effort to promote policy change one state at a time. It's become easier to fight fifty different battles than to launch a single Washington campaign—and it's created an enormous growth industry for state-based lobbyists. In 1997, University of Iowa political scientists couldn't find a single lobbyist registered to do business in every state. By 2014, according to the Center for Public Integrity, at least nine interest groups and companies had set up shop in every state capital: AARP, the American Heart Association, AstraZeneca, AT&T, Express Scripts, the National Federation of Independent Business, the National Rifle Association, Pfizer, and PhRMA.

Reinforcing their campaigns are the state-based efforts of conservative groups such as the American Legislative Exchange Council, whose model bills have provided a blueprint for successful beachheads that would be hard to establish in Washington. Major changes in the federal civil service laws are on the table in large part because state-by-state campaigns have led to more flexible employment rules in twenty-eight states.

For a generation, the criticism of Washington-based lobbyists has itself been a cottage industry. Most of the 2016 presidential candidates campaigned to shrink the power of the Washington lobby and to send decisions back to the states. If they manage to do that, they'll discover that the lobbyists have beaten them to it.

QUESTIONS TO CONSIDER

1. The EpiPen has been proven to save lives. Having more EpiPens in stock would save more lives. But its manufacturer, of course, would make money from the broader distribution of the drug. Does the manufacturer's lobbying to spread the use of the EpiPen concern you? Or does it seem a matter of smart public policy?

2. EpiPens have a fixed shelf-life. When the medicine is no longer effective, the EpiPen has to be replaced (and the manufacturer makes another sale). What steps should state and local administrators take to determine how often they need to replace the EpiPens? If they do it too often, they are wasting taxpayers' dollars. If they don't do it often enough, they risk putting the lives of citizens at risk.

3. Does it make a difference *where*—at what level of government—policy decisions are made?

4. How does this affect the implementation strategies of public administrators?

———————————————

Note: This case comes from my column in *Governing* (June 2016), http://www.governing.com/columns/potomac-chronicle/gov-lobbying-states-washington.html.

KEY CONCEPTS

administrative confidentiality 401
appropriations committees 397
authorizing committees 397
executive privilege 401

fire alarm oversight 394
legislative review 397
police patrol oversight 394

FOR FURTHER READING

Aberbach, Joel D. *Keeping a Watchful Eye: The Politics of Congressional Oversight.* Washington, D.C.: Brookings Institution, 1990.

Arnold, R. Douglas. *Congress and the Bureaucracy: A Theory of Influence.* New Haven, Conn.: Yale University Press, 1979.

Behn, Robert D. *The PerformanceStat Potential: A Leadership Strategy for Producing Results.* Washington, D.C.: Brookings Institution, 2014.

Dodd, Lawrence C., and Richard L. Schott. *Congress and the Administrative State.* New York: Wiley, 1979.

Foreman, Christopher H., Jr. *Signals from the Hill: Congressional Oversight and the Challenge of Social Regulation.* New Haven, Conn.: Yale University Press, 1988.

Heclo, Hugh. "Issue Networks and the Executive Establishment." In *The New Political System,* ed. Anthony King. Washington, D.C.: American Enterprise Institute, 1978, 87–124.

Mayhew, David R. *Congress: The Electoral Connection.* New Haven, Conn.: Yale University Press, 1974.

Mosher, Frederick C. *The GAO: The Quest for Accountability in American Government.* Boulder, Colo.: Westview Press, 1979.

Scher, Seymour. "Conditions for Legislative Control." *Journal of Politics* 25 (August 1963): 526–551.

SUGGESTED WEBSITES

Each federal agency annually publishes the reports required by the Government Performance and Results Act, which are available at **www.performance.gov/agencies**.

The Government Accountability Office website, **www.gao.gov**, is a treasure trove of reports on the performance of government agencies.

Finally, the Office of Management and Budget website, **www.whitehouse.gov/omb**, contains a great deal of useful information on the performance of government agencies, including the reports OMB requires in support of the annual budgetary process.

for CQ Press

WANT A BETTER GRADE?

Get the tools you need to sharpen your study skills. Access practice quizzes, eFlashcards, video, and multimedia at **edge.sagepub.com/kettl7e.**

NOTES

1. ACCOUNTABILITY

1. Jessica Meyers, "Bill Gates Lambasts D.C. Dysfunction," *Politico* (March 13, 2013), http://www.politico.com/story/2013/03/bill-gates-on-dc-you-dont-run-a-business-like-this-088830.

2. Lenny Bernstein and Joby Warrick, "Michigan Gov. Snyder Confronts the Perils of Running Government Like a Business," *Washington Post* (March 13, 2016), https://www.washingtonpost.com/national/health-science/michigan-gov-snyder-confronts-the-perils-of-running-government-like-a-business/2016/03/13/29d0256c-e705-11e5-b0fd-073d5930a7b7_story.html.

3. Ron Fournier, "Snyder Concedes Flint Is His 'Katrina,' a Failure of Leadership," *National Journal* (January 18, 2016).

4. Laura Wagner and Merrit Kennedy, "Michigan Gov. Rick Snyder: 'We All Failed the Families of Flint,'" *National Public Radio* (March 17, 2016), http://www.npr.org/sections/thetwo-way/2016/03/17/470792212/watch-michigan-gov-rick-snyder-testifies-on-the-flint-water-crisis.

5. Thomas E. Mann and Norman J. Ornstein, *It's Even Worse Than It Looks* (New York: Basic Books, 2012).

6. Rob Moore, "Flood, Rebuild, Repeat: The Need for Flood Insurance Reforms" (National Resources Defense Council, August 11, 2016), https://www.nrdc.org/experts/rob-moore/flood-rebuild-repeat-need-flood-insurance-reforms.

7. Douglas A. Blackmon, Vanessa O'Connell, Alexandra Berzon, and Ana Campoy, "There Was 'Nobody in Charge,'" *Wall Street Journal* (May 27, 2010), http://online.wsj.com/article/SB10001424052748704113504575264721101985024.html.

8. Jacqui Goddard, "Embattled BP Chief: I Want My Life Back," *The Times* (London, May 31, 2010), http://www.thetimes.co.uk/tto/news/article2534734.ece.

9. Bobby Jindal, "Obama's Woes Flow out of Big Government Philosophy," CNN.com (May 24, 2013), http://www.cnn.com/2013/05/24/opinion/jindal-obama-big-government/index.html.

10. Sewell Chan, "Remembering a Snowstorm That Paralyzed the City," *New York Times* (February 10, 2009), http://cityroom.blogs.nytimes.com/2009/02/10/remembering-a-snowstorm-that-paralyzed-the-city.

11. Peter Self, *Administrative Theories and Politics* (London: Allen and Unwin, 1972), 277–278. (Emphasis in original.)

12. Juvenal, *Satires*, line 347. Our free translation communicates more immediately and less ambiguously than the standard translations, such as "Who will be guarding the guards?" "Who is to keep guard over the guards?" and "Who will watch the warders"—particularly as Juvenal describes distrusting the guards of a harem.

13. "The need for operative ideas on how to make accountability a reality under modern conditions is urgent, but it must be admitted that there is a remarkable dearth of such ideas despite great dissatisfaction with the present state of affairs and with the older . . . notions of accountability." *The Dilemma of Accountability in Modern Government*, ed. Bruce L. R. Smith and D. C. Hague (New York: St. Martin's, 1971), 28.

14. Ben Zimmer, "The Epithet Nader Made Respectable," *Wall Street Journal* (July 12, 2013), http://online.wsj.com/article/SB100014241278873233368704578596083294221030.html.

15. Joseph R. Strayer, *On the Medieval Origins of the Modern State* (Princeton, N.J.: Princeton University Press, 1970).

16. David Clark, "The Many Meanings of the Rule of Law," *Law, Capitalism, and Power in Asia: The Rule of Law and Legal Institutions*, ed. Kanishka Jayasuriya (Oxford: Routledge, 1999), 28–43.

17. Barry R. Weingast, "The Political Foundations of Democracy and the Rule of Law," *American Political Science Review* 91, no. 2 (1997): 245–263; and Judith N. Shklar, "Political Theory and the Rule of Law," in *The Rule of Law: Ideal or Ideology*, ed. Allan C. Hutchinson and Patrick Moynihan (Toronto: Carswell, 1987), 1–16.

18. Guillermo O'Donnell, "Why the Rule of Law Matters," *Journal of Democracy* 15, no. 4 (2004): 32–46.

19. Woodrow Wilson, "The Study of Administration," *Political Science Quarterly* 2 (June 1887): 220.

20. Frank J. Goodnow, *Politics and Administration* (New York: Russell and Russell, 1900).

21. John M. Gaus, "Trends in the Theory of Public Administration," *Public Administration Review* 10 (1950): 168.

22. John M. Gaus, "The Responsibility of Public Administration," in *Frontiers of Public Administration*, ed. John M. Gaus, Leonard D. White, and Marshall E. Dimock (Chicago: University of Chicago Press, 1936), 27.

23. Ibid., 31.

24. See H. George Frederickson, "The Repositioning of American Public Administration," *PS: Political Science & Politics* (December 1999): 701–711; and David H. Rosenbloom, "Whose Bureaucracy Is This, Anyway? Congress's 1946 Answer," *PS: Political Science & Politics* (December 2001): 773–777.

25. Carl J. Friedrich, "Public Policy and the Nature of Administrative Responsibility," in *Public Policy*, ed. Carl J. Friedrich and Edward S. Mason (Cambridge, Mass.: Harvard University Press, 1940), 3–24; and Herman Finer, "Administrative Responsibility in Democratic Government," *Public Administration Review* no. 1 (1941): 355–350.

26. Gaus, "The Responsibility of Public Administration," 37.

27. Smith and Hague, *Dilemma of Accountability*, 29.

28. "$16 Muffin Included Coffee, Tea, Event Space," *Politifact* (October 4, 2011), http://www.politifact.com/truth-o-meter/statements/2011/oct/04/bill-oreilly/16-muffin-included-coffee-tea-event-space.

29. We should not be interpreted as going so far as one scholar: "Bureaucrats ought not determine which of several competing demands they should follow, nor should they themselves 'scale down' impossibly high expectations. They should, however, refuse to be 'passed the buck,' and they should encourage higher authorities to make proper decisions." And "Bureaucrats incur responsibilities to make sure that policy makers provide the resources necessary to their policy tasks." John P. Burke, *Bureaucratic Responsibility* (Baltimore: Johns Hopkins University Press, 1988), 51, 82.

30. Albert O. Hirschman, *Exit, Voice, and Loyalty: Responses to Decline in Firms, Organizations, and States* (Cambridge, Mass.: Harvard University Press, 1970).

31. Ethical breakdowns in the 1980s partly account for growth of the literature about governmental ethics. See John A. Rohr, *Ethics for Bureaucrats: An Essay on Law and Values*, 2nd ed. (New York: Marcel Dekker, 1989); James S. Bowman and Frederick A. Elliston, eds., *Ethics, Government, and Public Policy: A Reference Guide* (Westport, Conn.: Greenwood Press, 1988); and Robert N. Roberts, *White House Ethics: The History of the Politics of Conflict of Interest Regulation* (Westport, Conn.: Greenwood Press, 1988).

32. G. Calvin Mackenzie, "'If You Want to Play, You've Got to Pay': Ethics Regulation and the Presidential Appointments System, 1964–1984," in *The In-and-Outers: Presidential Appointees and Transient Government in Washington*, ed. G. Calvin Mackenzie (Baltimore: Johns Hopkins University Press, 1987), 77.

33. Michael A. Nutter, "Inaugural Address," January 7, 2008, http://media.philly.com/documents/NutterInauguralSpeechFinal.pdf.

34. Preamble to the Constitution of the United States.

35. "Remarks to the Members of the Senior Executive Service," January 26, 1989, *Weekly Compilation of Presidential Documents* 25 (Washington, D.C.: Government Printing Office, 1989), 117–119.

36. Rick Stengel, "Q&A: Obama Talks with Rick Stengel," *Time* (November 29, 2007), http://content.time.com/time/magazine/article/0,9171,1689228,00.html.

2. WHAT GOVERNMENT DOES— AND HOW IT DOES IT

1. Dwight Waldo, *The Administrative State: A Study of the Political Theory of American Public Administration* (New York: Ronald Press, 1948).

2. See, for example, *A Centennial History of the American Administrative State*, ed. Ralph Clark Chandler (New York: Free Press, 1987); John A. Rohr, *To Run a Constitution: The Legitimacy of the Administrative State* (Lawrence: University Press of Kansas, 1986); Lawrence C. Dodd and Richard L. Schott, *Congress and the Administrative State* (New York: Wiley, 1979); Emmette S. Redford, *Democracy and the Administrative State* (New York: Oxford University Press, 1969); and David H. Rosenbloom, *Building a Legislative-Centered Public Administration: Congress and the Administrative State, 1946–1999* (Tuscaloosa: University of Alabama Press, 2000).

3. Ronald Reagan, "Inaugural Address" (January 21, 1981), http://www.presidency.ucsb.edu/ws/?pid=43130.

4. U.S. Government Accountability Office, *High-Risk Series: An Update*, GAO-15-290 (February 2015), http://www.gao.gov/assets/670/668415.pdf.

5. "Districts," *Last Week Tonight with John Oliver* (March 6, 2016), https://www.youtube.com/watch?v=3saU5racsGE.

6. Adam H. Edelen, *Ghost Government: A Report on Special Districts in Kentucky* (Frankfort, Ky.: Auditor

of Public Accounts, 2012), http://apps.auditor.ky.gov/Public/Audit_Reports/Archive/2012GhostGovernmentSpecialDistrictsreport.pdf.

7. Paul C. Light, *The True Size of Government* (Washington, D.C.: Brookings Institution, 1999).

8. U.S. Bureau of the Census; U.S. Office of Management and Budget, *Budget of the United States Government: Historical Tables.*

9. Social Security Administration, "Social Security Basic Facts," https://www.ssa.gov/news/press/factsheets/basicfact-alt.pdf.

10. *Wall Street Journal*, March 17, 1989, A1.

11. Philip Shenon, "Chilean Fruit Pulled from Shelves as U.S. Widens Inquiry on Poison," *New York Times*, March 15, 1989, http://www.nytimes.com/1989/03/15/us/chilean-fruit-pulled-from-shelves-as-us-widens-inquiry-on-poison.html.

12. Fire Department of the City of New York, "Citywide Performance Indicators" (2016), http://www.nyc.gov/html/fdny/pdf/stats/2016/fire/cw/fire_cwsum_0116.pdf.

13. Port of Los Angeles, "Facts and Figures," https://www.portoflosangeles.org/about/facts.asp.

14. Christopher C. Hood, *The Tools of Government* (Chatham, N.J.: Chatham House, 1983), 2.

15. See Donald F. Kettl, *The Next Government of the United States: Why Our Institutions Fail Us and How to Fix Them* (New York: Norton, 2009), 109–110.

16. See Donald F. Kettl, *Government by Proxy: (Mis?)Managing Federal Programs* (Washington, D.C.: CQ Press, 1988); and Lester M. Salamon, ed., *Beyond Privatization: The Tools of Government Action* (Washington, D.C.: Urban Institute, 1989).

17. Moshe Schwartz and Jennifer Church, *Department of Defense's Use of Contractors to Support Military Operations: Background, Analysis, and Issues for Congress* (Washington, D.C.: Congressional Research Service, May 17, 2013), http://www.fas.org/sgp/crs/natsec/R43074.pdf.

18. Donald Haider, "Grants as a Tool of Public Policy," in Salamon, *Beyond Privatization*, 93.

19. U.S. Office of Management and *Budget, Budget of the United States Government, Fiscal Year 2017:* Special Analyses, Table 14-3.

20. For a review of tax expenditures, see Stanley S. Surrey and Paul R. McDaniel, *Tax Expenditures* (Cambridge, Mass.: Harvard University Press, 1985); John F. Witte, *The Politics and Development of the Federal Income Tax* (Madison: University of Wisconsin Press, 1985); and Paul R. McDaniel, "Tax Expenditures as Tools of Government Action," in Salamon, *Beyond Privatization*, 167–196.

21. Lester M. Salamon, "Rethinking Public Management: Third-Party Government and the Changing Forms of Government Action," *Public Policy* 29 (Summer 1981): 260.

22. Ted Kolderie, "The Two Different Concepts of Privatization," *Public Administration Review* 46 (July–August 1986): 285–291.

23. Pew Research Center for People and the Press, "Public Trust in Government: 1958–2015" (November 23, 2015), http://www.people-press.org/2015/11/23/1-trust-in-government-1958-2015/.

24. Samantha Smith, "6 Key Takeaways about How Americans View Their Government" (November 23, 2015), http://www.pewresearch.org/fact-tank/2015/11/23/6-key-takeaways-about-how-americans-view-their-government/.

25. Dan Balz, "Republicans Ride the Tea Party Tiger," *Washington Post* (September 15, 2010), http://www.washingtonpost.com/wp-dyn/content/article/2010/09/15/AR2010091503387.html.

3. WHAT IS PUBLIC ADMINISTRATION?

1. Honoré de Balzac, *Les Employés*. English translations carry various titles (e.g., *The Civil Service, Bureaucracy*, and *The Government Clerks*).

2. These and other meanings of the term *bureaucracy* are fully analyzed in Martin Albrow, *Bureaucracy* (New York: Holt, Rinehart and Winston, 1971).

3. Nikolai I. Ryzhkov, speaking to the seventeenth Communist Party Congress, quoted in Philip Taubman, "Soviet Premier, in Congress Talk, Criticizes Economy," *New York Times*, March 4, 1986; Zhao Ziyang (later named general secretary of China's Communist Party), quoted in Edward A. Gargan, "More Change Due in China's Economy," *New York Times*, October 26, 1987.

4. For example, see Donald F. Kettl, *The Global Public Management Revolution: A Report on the Transformation of Governance* (Washington, D.C.: Brookings Institution, 2000).

5. For a well-documented and well-argued case explaining and defending bureaucracy, see Charles T. Goodsell, *The Case for Bureaucracy: A Public Administration Polemic*, 4th ed. (Washington, D.C.: CQ Press, 2004).

6. For a thorough exploration of the definitional problem, see Andrew Dunsire, *Administration: The Word and the Science* (New York: Wiley, 1973).

7. Dwight Waldo, *The Study of Public Administration* (Garden City, N.Y.: Doubleday, 1955), 5–6; and Herbert A. Simon, *Administrative Behavior* (New York: Macmillan, 1947; 3rd ed., New York: Free Press, 1976), 72–73. Ascertaining what the goals are and relating rational action to them is a difficult problem, recognized by both Waldo and Simon, as is determining the nonrational dimension of human behavior.

8. For a review of these arguments, see Harold F. Gortner, Julianne Mahler, and Jeanne Bell Nicholson, *Organization Theory: A Public Perspective* (Chicago: Dorsey Press, 1987), 16; and Gary L. Wamsley and Mayer N. Zald, *The Political Economy of Public Organizations: A Critique and Approach to the Study of Public Administration* (Bloomington: Indiana University Press, 1973), 4.

9. Douglas Yates Jr., *The Politics of Management* (San Francisco: Jossey-Bass, 1985), 7.

10. Barry Bozeman, *All Organizations Are Public: Bridging Public and Private Organization Theories* (San Francisco: Jossey-Bass, 1987), 83–85.

11. William A. Robson, "The Managing of Organizations," *Public Administration* (London) 44 (Autumn 1966): 276.

12. Dwight Waldo, *The Enterprise of Public Administration: A Summary View* (Novato, Calif.: Chandler and Sharp, 1980), 164. Compare Bozeman, *All Organizations Are Public*, 5; and Hal G. Rainey, Robert W. Backoff, and Charles H. Levine, "Comparing Public and Private Organizations," *Public Administration Review* 36 (March–April 1976): 234.

13. See Graham T. Allison Jr., "Public and Private Management: Are They Fundamentally Alike in All Unimportant Respects?" in *Current Issues in Public Administration*, 3rd ed., ed. Frederick S. Lane (New York: St. Martin's, 1986), 184–200.

14. Some theorists, for example, argue that the distinction is based on who benefits; public agencies are those whose prime beneficiary is the public. See Peter M. Blau and W. Richard Scott, *Formal Organizations: A Comparative Approach* (San Francisco: Chandler, 1962), 42–43. Others have argued that they are distinctive because of who owns and funds them; public agencies are those "owned" by the state. See Wamsley and Zald, *Political Economy of Public Organizations*, 8.

15. Gortner, Mahler, and Nicholson, *Organization Theory*, 26.

16. Steven Kelman, presentation to Seventeenth Intergovernmental Audit Forum (Philadelphia: May 22, 2008).

17. These distinctions are based on comparisons developed by John T. Dunlop and summarized in Allison, "Public and Private Management," 17–18. See also Ralph Clark Chandler, "Epilogue," in Ralph Clark Chandler, ed., *Centennial History* (New York: Free Press, 1987), 580–586; and Rainey, Backoff, and Levine, "Comparing Public and Private Organizations."

18. Anthony Downs, *Inside Bureaucracy* (Boston: Little, Brown, 1967), 30.

19. Arthur Okun, *Equality and Efficiency: The Big Tradeoff* (Washington, D.C.: Brookings Institution, 1975).

20. See Marver H. Bernstein, *The Job of the Federal Government Executive* (Washington, D.C.: Brookings Institution, 1958), 26–28; and James W. Fesler et al., *Industrial Mobilization for War* (Washington, D.C.: Government Printing Office, 1947), 971–972. The "goldfish-bowl" phenomenon applies specifically to the United States, rather than to public administration everywhere. See Harold L. Wilensky, *Organizational Intelligence* (New York: Basic Books, 1967), 116–118.

21. U.S. Code 31, § 1341.

22. There are, of course, requirements for private officials and their organizations to comply with governmental standards. But, in general, the point applies: in the private sector, officials and their organizations are free to follow their own judgment except as the law applies.

23. Wallace Sayre, "The Unhappy Bureaucrats: Views Ironic, Helpful, Indignant," *Public Administration Review* 10 (Summer 1958): 245.

24. See *Revitalizing Federal Management: Managers and Their Overburdened Systems: A Panel Report* (Washington, D.C.: National Academy of Public Administration, 1983); and *Urgent Business for America: Revitalizing the Federal Government for the 21st Century* (Washington, D.C.: National Commission on the Public Service, 2003), http://www.brookings.edu/events/2003/01/07governance.

25. For example, see Anne M. Khademian, *Working with Culture: How the Job Gets Done in Public Programs* (Washington, D.C.: CQ Press, 2002).

26. For the variety of approaches, see *Public Administration: The State of the Discipline*, ed. Naomi B. Lynn and Aaron Wildavsky (Chatham, N.J.: Chatham House, 1990); and Chandler, *Centennial History*.

27. Dwight Waldo, "Politics and Administration: On Thinking about a Complex Relationship," in Chandler, *Centennial History*, 89–112, at 96–104.

28. See Frank J. Goodnow, *Politics and Administration* (New York: Macmillan, 1900). Wilson is discussed later in this chapter.

29. Nicholas Henry, "The Emergence of Public Administration as a Field of Study," in Chandler, *Centennial History*, 37–85. See also *American Public Administration:*

Past, Present, and Future, ed. Frederick C. Mosher (Tuscaloosa: University of Alabama Press, 1975).

30. Luther Gulick, "Time and Public Administration," *Public Administration Review* 47 (January–February 1987): 115–119.

31. Carl J. Friedrich, *Man and His Government* (New York: McGraw-Hill, 1963), 464–483. The remarkable and lasting innovations in British and French administrative institutions and methods in the twelfth to fourteenth centuries are treated in James W. Fesler, "The Presence of the Administrative Past," in *American Public Administration: Patterns of the Past*, ed. James W. Fesler (Washington, D.C.: American Society for Public Administration, 1982), 1–27, at 3–16. A comprehensive administrative history, much broader than its title, is Carolyn Webber and Aaron Wildavsky, *A History of Taxation and Expenditure in the Western World* (New York: Simon and Schuster, 1986).

32. Alexis de Tocqueville, *Democracy in America* (New York: Knopf, 1945), 1:211–212; paperback ed. (New York: Vintage Books, 1954), 1:219–220.

33. All quotations of Woodrow Wilson are from his "The Study of Administration," *Political Science Quarterly* 2 (June 1887), as reprinted in *Political Science Quarterly* 56 (December 1941): 481–506. As the first scholarly article urging attention to public administration, Wilson's treatise is often described as "seminal"; however, the article was not widely read until its reprinting in 1941. For a full canvass of Wilson's significance, see *Politics and Administration: Woodrow Wilson and American Public Administration*, ed. Jack Rabin and James S. Bowman (New York: Marcel Dekker, 1984); and Daniel W. Martin, "The Fading Legacy of Woodrow Wilson," *Public Administration Review* 48 (March–April 1988): 631–636.

34. Fesler, *American Public Administration.* An excellent starting point is Stephen Skowronek, *Building a New American State: The Expansion of National Administrative Capacities, 1877–1920* (New York: Cambridge University Press, 1982).

35. Christopher Pollitt, *Time, Policy, Management: Governing with the Past* (Oxford: Oxford University Press, 2008), 2.

36. The list is not exhaustive. See James G. March, "How We Talk and How We Act: Administrative Theory and Administrative Life," in *Leadership and Organization Culture: New Perspectives on Administrative Theory and Practice*, ed. Thomas J. Sergiovanni and John E. Corbally (Urbana: University of Illinois Press, 1984, 1986), 18–35, esp. 21.

37. For a broad critique, see Charles Perrow, *Complex Organizations*, 3rd ed. (New York: Random House, 1986).

38. The concept of overlays is presented in John M. Pfiffner and Frank R. Sherwood, *Administrative Organization* (Englewood Cliffs, N.J.: Prentice Hall, 1960), 16–32. They propose a basic sheet portraying the formal structure of authority, with five overlays: sociometric ("contacts people have with each other because of personal attraction"); functional (arising out of "the relationships created by technical experts" and the authority they exercise "because of their superior knowledge and skills"); decisional; power; and communication.

4. ORGANIZATIONAL THEORY

1. For an exceptionally thoughtful review of organizational theory, see H. George Frederickson and Kevin B. Smith, *Public Administration Theory Primer* (Boulder, Colo.: Westview Press, 2003).

2. Daniel Katz and Robert L. Kahn, *The Social Psychology of Organizations*, 2nd ed. (New York: Wiley, 1978), 188, 196. Note, however, the caveat: "Role expectations are by no means restricted to the job description as it might be given by the head of the organization or prepared by some specialist in personnel, although these individuals are likely to be influential members of the role set of many persons in the organization" (p. 190).

3. This description merely lays the groundwork for the structural approach to governmental administration. For more substantial analysis of the complex issue of authority, see, for example, Carl J. Friedrich, *Man and His Government* (New York: McGraw-Hill, 1963); and Charles E. Lindblom, *Politics and Markets* (New York: Basic Books, 1977), 17–32.

4. Luther Gulick, "Notes on the Theory of Organization," in *Papers on the Science of Administration*, ed. Luther Gulick and L. Urwick (New York: Institute of Public Administration, 1937), 1–45. For an attack on that essay, see Herbert Simon, *Administrative Behavior* (New York: Macmillan, 1947, and later editions), 20–44. For reviews of the controversy, see Alan A. Altshuler, "The Study of Administration," in *The Politics of the Federal Bureaucracy*, 2nd ed., ed. Alan A. Altshuler and Norman C. Thomas (New York: Harper and Row, 1977), 2–17; Vincent Ostrom, *The Intellectual Crisis in Public Administration* (Tuscaloosa: University of Alabama Press, 1973), 36–47; Brian R. Fry, *Mastering Public Administration: From Max Weber to Dwight Waldo* (Chatham, N.J.: Chatham House, 1989), 73–97; and Thomas H. Hammond, "In Defense of Luther Gulick's 'Notes on

the Theory of Organization,'" *Public Administration* (London) 58 (Summer 1990).

5. Weber's views became accessible to American readers through two translations of portions of his works, which appeared in 1946 and 1947 and were reprinted in the following paperback editions: *From Max Weber: Essays in Sociology*, trans. and ed. H. H. Gerth and C. Wright Mills (New York: Oxford University Press, 1958); and *The Theory of Social and Economic Organization*, trans. A. M. Henderson and Talcott Parsons (New York: Free Press, 1964).

6. Weber, *Theory of Social and Economic Organization*, 328.

7. Weber, *From Max Weber*, 209.

8. Weber, *Theory of Social and Economic Organization*, 330.

9. Ibid., 337.

10. Weber, *From Max Weber*, 196–197.

11. Ibid., 228.

12. See Talcott Parsons's introduction to Weber, *Theory of Social and Economic Organization*, 56, 58–60n.

13. Systems theory and its organizational derivatives are more fully treated in Katz and Kahn, *Social Psychology of Organizations*, 17–34; and Chadwick J. Haberstroh, "Organization Design and Systems Analysis," in *Handbook of Organizations*, ed. James G. March (Chicago: Rand McNally, 1965), 1171–1211.

14. For a trenchant argument that an organization's survival is the lucky result of natural selection processes rather than of efforts to achieve that objective, see Herbert Kaufman, *Time, Chance, and Organizations: Natural Selection in a Perilous Environment* (Chatham, N.J.: Chatham House, 1985).

15. Sir Eric (later Lord) Ashby, *Technology and the Academics* (New York: Macmillan, 1958), 67–68.

16. Systems theories vary in attentiveness to authority. For a work that does incorporate authority and its hierarchical structuring in a systems framework, see Katz and Kahn, *Social Psychology of Organizations*, esp. 199–222.

17. Frederick Winslow Taylor, *The Principles of Scientific Management* (New York: Harper and Brothers, 1911; Mineola, N.Y.: Dover, 1998). See Fry, *Mastering Public Administration*, 47–72.

18. Taylor, *Principles of Scientific Management*, 28.

19. An early canvass of this literature is in James G. March and Herbert Simon, *Organizations* (New York: Wiley, 1957), although it is puzzling that the findings were not brought to bear on the book's later concerns with organizational structure and processes.

20. For reports of the research and reappraisals of the findings, see George C. Homans, *The Human Group* (New York: Harcourt Brace Jovanovich, 1950); and H. M. Persons, "What Happened at Hawthorne?" *Science* 183 (March 8, 1974): 922–932.

21. "Group members tend to feel better satisfied under moderate degrees of structure than under overly structured or totally unstructured situations. But they prefer too much structure over none at all. Groups tend to be more productive and more cohesive in structured rather than unstructured situations. Formal structure does not necessarily block satisfaction of needs for autonomy and self-actualization. Some degree of structure is necessary for the satisfaction of follower needs." Bernard M. Bass, *Stogdill's Handbook of Leadership: A Survey of Theory and Research*, rev. and exp. ed. (New York: Free Press, 1981), 588–589.

22. Edwin A. Locke, "The Nature and Causes of Job Satisfaction," in *Handbook of Industrial and Organizational Psychology*, ed. Marvin D. Dunnette (Chicago: Rand McNally, 1976), 1297–1349, at 1332. As Locke points out, the human relationists' causal arrow may point the wrong way; that is, high productivity may be a cause of high satisfaction.

23. Joe Pinsker, "Why Aren't Intelligent People Happier?" *GovExec.com* (April 26, 2016), http://www.govexec.com/excellence/promising-practices/2016/04/why-arent-intelligent-people-happier/127796/?oref=govexec_today_nl.

24. Chris Argyris, "Being Human and Being Organized," *Transaction* 2 (July 1964): 5. See also his "Some Limits of Rational Man Organization Theory," *Public Administration Review* 33 (May–June 1973): 253–267, esp. 253–254, 263–265.

25. For a full description and critique of the human relations model, see Charles Perrow, *Complex Organizations*, 3rd ed. (New York: Random House, 1986), 79–118. See also H. Roy Kaplan and Curt Tausky, "Humanism in Organizations: A Critical Appraisal," *Public Administration Review* 37 (March–April 1977): 171–180.

26. Douglas McGregor, *The Human Side of Enterprise* (New York: McGraw-Hill, 1960), 33–57.

27. Lawrence B. Mohr, *Explaining Organizational Behavior: The Limits and Possibilities of Theory and Research* (San Francisco: Jossey-Bass, 1982), 125–153; and Bass, *Stogdill's Handbook of Leadership*, passim.

28. Abraham H. Maslow, "The Superior Person," *Transaction* 1 (May 1964): 12–13. For a major test of "the participation hypothesis" in public administration, see *Government Reorganizations: Cases and Commentary*, ed. Frederick C. Mosher (Indianapolis: Bobbs-Merrill, 1967).

29. Francis Fukuyama, *Political Order and Political Decay* (New York: Farrar Straus, 2014).

30. Among the many writings illustrative of the pluralistic approach to public administration, three classics are David B. Truman, *The Governmental Process*, 2nd ed. (New York: Knopf, 1971), esp. 395–478; J. Leiper Freeman, *The Political Process: Executive Bureau–Legislative Committee Relations*, rev. ed. (New York: Random House, 1965); and Francis E. Rourke, *Bureaucracy, Politics, and Public Policy*, 3rd ed. (Boston: Little, Brown, 1984).

31. Rourke, *Bureaucracy, Politics, and Public Policy*. See also Carl E. Van Horn, William T. Gormley Jr., and Donald C. Baumer, *Politics and Public Policy*, 3rd ed. (Washington, D.C.: CQ Press, 2001).

32. A good introduction is J. Steven Ott, *The Organizational Culture Perspective* (Chicago: Dorsey Press, 1989). See also Edgar H. Schein, *Organizational Culture and Leadership* (San Francisco: Jossey-Bass, 1987); Michel Crozier, *The Bureaucratic Phenomenon* (Chicago: University of Chicago Press, 1964); and Anne Khademian, *Working with Culture: The Way the Job Gets Done in Public Programs* (Washington, D.C.: CQ Press, 2002).

33. Spatial relations are rarely treated in the literature. For a valuable exception, see Frederick C. Mosher, *A Tale of Two Agencies: A Comparative Analysis of the General Accounting Office and the Office of Management and Budget* (Baton Rouge: Louisiana State University Press, 1984), 87–98. The whole book usefully contrasts the organizational cultures of the two agencies.

34. Harold Seidman and Robert Gilmour, *Politics, Position, and Power: From the Positive to the Regulatory State*, 4th ed. (New York: Oxford University Press, 1986), 167. See pages 166–194, on "The Executive Establishment, Culture and Personality."

35. Donald F. Kettl, *Leadership at the Fed* (New Haven, Conn.: Yale University Press, 1986). The dominance issue is treated at pages 30–32 and 85–88.

36. "Firefighter, EMT Siblings Charged in Fistfight with Cops: Reports," *NBC News Channel 4, New York* (August 24, 2015), http://www.nbcnewyork.com/news/local/FDNY-Firefighter-EMT-Siblings-Arrested-Fist-Fight-Cops-322659741.html.

37. National Aeronautics and Space Administration, *Assessment and Plan for Organizational Culture Change at NASA* (Washington, D.C.: NASA, 2004), 4.

38. Warren E. Leary, "Better Communication Is NASA's Next Frontier," *New York Times* (April 14, 2004), A22.

39. The section that follows is adapted from Donald F. Kettl, *The Transformation of Governance: Public Administration for the 21st Century* (Baltimore: Johns Hopkins University Press, 2002), 88–90.

40. See Harrison C. White, "Agency as Control," in *Principals and Agents: The Structure of Business*, ed. John W. Pratt and Richard J. Zeckhauser (Boston: Harvard Business School Press, 1985), 187–212.

41. See Ronald H. Coase, "The Nature of the Firm," *Economica* 4 (1937): 386–405; and Oliver E. Williamson, *Markets and Hierarchies: Analysis and Antitrust Implications* (New York: Free Press, 1975).

42. See B. Dan Wood and Richard W. Waterman, "The Dynamics of Political Control of the Bureaucracy," *American Political Science Review* 85 (1991): 801–828.

43. Charles Perrow, "Economic Theories of Organization," *Theory and Society* 15 (1986): 41.

44. Terry M. Moe, "The New Economics of Organization," *American Journal of Political Science* 28 (1984): 739–777; and "An Assessment of the Positive Theory of 'Congressional Dominance,'" *Legislative Studies Quarterly* 12 (1987): 475–520.

45. See Donald F. Kettl, *The Next Government of the United States: Why Our Institutions Fail Us and How to Fix Them* (New York: Norton, 2009).

46. Donald F. Kettl, *Escaping Jurassic Government: How to Recover America's Lost Commitment to Competence* (Washington, D.C.: Brookings Institution, 2016). See also Frederick C. Mosher, "The Changing Responsibilities and Tactics of the Federal Government," in *American Public Administration: Patterns of the Past*, ed. James W. Fesler (Washington, D.C.: American Society for Public Administration, 1982), 198–212, quoted passage at 201. See also Lester M. Salamon, "Rethinking Public Management: Third-Party Government and the Changing Forms of Government Action," *Public Policy* 29 (Summer 1981): 259–278; and Lester H. Salamon, ed., *The Tools of Government: A Guide to the New Governance* (New York: Oxford University Press, 2002).

47. See, for example, Howard Aldrich and David A. Whettan, "Organization-Sets, Action-Sets, and Networks: Making the Most of Simplicity," in *Handbook of Organizational Design*, vol. 1, *Adapting Organizations to Their Environments*, ed. Paul C. Nystrom and William H. Starbuck (New York: Oxford University Press, 1981), 385–408; W. W. Powell, "Neither Market nor Hierarchy: Network Forms of Organization," in *Research in Organizational Behavior*, ed. B. Staw and L. L. Cummings (Greenwich, Conn.: JAI Press, 1990), 295–336; Robert Agranoff, "Human Services Integration: Past and Present Challenges in Public Administration," *Public Administration Review* 51 (1991): 533–542; H. Brinton Milward and Keith G. Provan, "Services Integration and Outcome Effectiveness: An Empirical Test of an Implicit Theory," paper presented at the annual

conference of the Association for Public Policy Analysis and Management, 1993; Fritz W. Scharpf, "Coordination in Hierarchies and Networks," in *Games in Hierarchies and Networks: Analytical and Empirical Approaches to the Study of Governance and Institutions*, ed. Fritz W. Scharpf (Boulder, Colo.: Westview Press, 1993), 125–165; and Eugene Bardach, "Generic Models in the Study of Public Management," paper presented at the annual conference of the Association for Public Policy Analysis and Management, 1993.

48. Eugene Bardach, "But Can Networks Produce?" paper prepared for the conference on "Network Analysis and Innovations in Public Programs," La Follette Institute of Public Affairs, University of Wisconsin–Madison, 1994, 2.

49. Rosemary O'Leary, Lisa Blomgren Bingham, and Catherine Gerard, guest eds., "Special Issue on Collaborative Public Management," *Public Administration Review* 66 (2007); and Stephen Goldsmith and Donald F. Kettl, eds., *The Power of Networks: Keys to High-Performance Government* (Washington, D.C.: Brookings Institution, 2009).

50. For a comprehensive review of theories we have discussed—and many more that reinforce the impression of disparity—see Jeffrey Pfeffer, "Organizations and Organization Theory," in *Handbook of Social Psychology*, vol. 1, ed. Gardner Lindzey and Elliot Aronson (New York: Random House, 1985), 379–435.

5. THE EXECUTIVE BRANCH

1. Rufus E. Miles, "The Origin and Meaning of Miles' Law," *Public Administration Review* 38 (September–October 1978): 399–403.

2. Donald F. Kettl, *The Next Government of the United States: Why Our Institutions Fail Us and How to Fix Them* (New York: Norton, 2009).

3. Harold Seidman, *Politics, Position, and Power: The Dynamics of Federal Organization* (New York: Oxford University Press, 1998), 142.

4. California Performance Review, *Form Follows Function*, 2004, chap. 1, http://www.cpr.ca.gov/CPR_Report/pdf/Vol_2_FormFolFunct.pdf.

5. The War Department is treated here as the antecedent of the Department of Defense, established in 1949; the War Department included naval concerns until establishment of the Navy Department in 1798.

6. See "The Independent Status of the Regulatory Commissions," in U.S. Senate Committee on Governmental Affairs, *Study on Federal Regulation*, vol. 5, *Regulatory Organization* (Washington, D.C.: Government Printing Office, 1977), 25–81.

7. Because no accepted definition of government corporations exists, counts differ. The figures cited are respectively from Ronald C. Moe, *Administering Public Functions at the Margin of Government: The Case of Federal Corporations*, Report No. 83–236 GOV, processed (Washington, D.C.: Congressional Research Service, December 1, 1983); and General Accounting Office, *Congress Should Consider Revising Basic Corporate Control Laws* (Washington, D.C.: Government Printing Office, 1983). Both reports are valuable reviews of the status and problems of government corporations.

8. For organizational history to 1922, see Lloyd M. Short, *The Development of National Administrative Organization in the United States* (Baltimore: Johns Hopkins University Press, 1923).

9. See Walter Isaacson, *Benjamin Franklin: An American Life* (New York: Simon and Schuster, 2003).

10. The contrasting problems of the functional and areal systems are explored and contrasted in James W. Fesler, "The Basic Theoretical Question: How to Relate Area and Function," in *The Administration of the New Federalism*, ed. Leigh E. Grosenick (Washington, D.C.: American Society for Public Administration, 1973), 4–14.

11. In France, as elsewhere, functional pressures by central departments force departures from the model, followed periodically by efforts to reestablish the model's purity.

12. See Donald F. Kettl, *System under Stress: Homeland Security and American Politics* (Washington, D.C.: CQ Press, 2004); and The Century Foundation, *The Department of Homeland Security's First-Year Report Card* (New York: Century Foundation, 2004).

13. The general problem is reviewed in James W. Fesler, *Area and Administration* (Tuscaloosa: University of Alabama Press, 1949, 1964).

14. Molly Ivins, Shrub: *The Short but Happy Political Life of George W. Bush* (New York: Vintage Books, 2000).

15. See Peri E. Arnold, *Making the Managerial Presidency: Comprehensive Reorganization Planning, 1905–1980* (Princeton, N.J.: Princeton University Press, 1986), 361–364; and, more generally, Richard P. Nathan, *The Administrative Presidency* (New York: Wiley, 1983); and Colin Campbell, *Managing the Presidency: Carter, Reagan, and the Search for Executive Harmony* (Pittsburgh: University of Pittsburgh Press, 1986).

16. *Leadership in Jeopardy: The Fraying of the Presidential Appointments System* (Washington, D.C.: National Academy of Public Administration, 1985), 4–5.

17. Kareem Fahim and Colin Moynihan, "An Emergency Call Brings So Much Help a Scuffle Breaks Out," *New York Times*, September 3, 2005, B1.

18. President's Committee on Administrative Management, *Report with Special Studies* (Washington, D.C.: Government Printing Office, 1937), 40.

19. Herbert Emmerich, *Federal Organization and Administrative Management* (Tuscaloosa: University of Alabama Press, 1971), 199; and U.S. Bureau of the Census, *Statistical Abstract of the United States*, various years. Here and later in this section, official data are presented; however, their accuracy has often been questioned. For the varying counts, see John Hart, *The Presidential Branch*, 2nd ed. (Chatham, N.J.: Chatham House, 1995), 42–46, 112–125; Gary King and Lyn Ragsdale, *The Elusive Executive* (Washington, D.C.: CQ Press, 1990), Tables 4.1 and 4.2; Office of Personnel Management, *Employment and Trends;* and Office of Administration, Executive Office of the President, "Aggregate Report on Personnel Pursuant to Title 3," *U.S. Code of Federal Regulations*, sec. 113 (annual), processed; and Office of Personnel Management, "Employment and Trends" (2013), https://www.opm.gov/policy-data-oversight/data-analysis-documentation/federal-employment-reports/employment-trends-data/2013/september/table-2/.

20. General Accounting Office, *Personnel Practices: Detailing of Federal Employees to the White House* (Washington, D.C.: Government Printing Office, July 1987); and *Personnel Practices: Federal Employees Detailed from DOD to the White House* (Washington, D.C.: Government Printing Office, March 1988).

21. Thomas E. Cronin, "The Swelling of the Presidency: Can Anyone Reverse the Tide?" in *American Government: Readings and Cases*, 9th ed., ed. Peter Woll (Boston: Little, Brown, 1984), 345–360.

22. President's Committee on Administrative Management, *Report with Special Studies*, 5.

23. Samuel Kernell, "The Creed and Reality of Modern White House Management," in *Chief of Staff: Twenty-five Years of Managing the Presidency*, ed. Samuel Kernell and Samuel L. Popkin (Berkeley: University of California Press, 1986), 193–222.

24. For a full and admiring description of the White House staff, see Bradley H. Patterson Jr., *The Ring of Power: The White House Staff and Its Expanding Role in Government* (New York: Basic Books, 1988).

25. Greg Schneiders, "My Turn: Goodbye to All That," *Newsweek*, September 24, 1979, 23. cf. "Even when working a seventy-hour week the President does not see most of his White House Office staff, or most of his Cabinet." Carter devoted a third of his time to seeing senior staff members and a sixth to seeing cabinet and other officials. Richard Rose, *The Postmodern President: The White House Meets the World* (Chatham, N.J.: Chatham House, 1988), 151–152.

26. Samuel Kernell, "The Evolution of the White House Staff," in *Can the Government Govern?* ed. John E. Chubb and Paul E. Peterson (Washington, D.C.: Brookings Institution, 1989), 235.

27. The best comprehensive review of the OMB is U.S. Senate Committee on Governmental Affairs, *Office of Management and Budget: Evolving Roles and Future Issues*, 99th Cong., 2nd. sess., February 1986, S. Rpt. 99–134 (Washington, D.C.: Government Printing Office, 1986). For OMB's and the Budget Bureau's history, see also Larry Berman, *The Office of Management and Budget and the Presidency, 1921–1979* (Princeton, N.J.: Princeton University Press, 1979); and Frederick C. Mosher, *A Tale of Two Agencies: A Comparative Analysis of the General Accounting Office and the Office of Management and Budget* (Baton Rouge: Louisiana State University Press, 1984).

28. Hugh Heclo, "OMB and the Presidency—The Problem of 'Neutral Competence,'" *Public Interest* 38 (Winter 1975): 80–98.

29. This will seem unimportant only to those who have not observed the frequency with which "new" ideas are enthusiastically advanced and acted on by newly recruited high officials who are unaware that the same idea, or a near analog, was earlier introduced and failed.

30. Hugh Heclo, *A Government of Strangers: Executive Politics in Washington* (Washington, D.C.: Brookings Institution, 1977), 80–81.

31. See David A. Stockman, *The Triumph of Politics: The Inside Story of the Reagan Revolution* (New York: Harper and Row, 1986; paperback ed., New York: Avon Books, 1987).

32. Ronald C. Moe, "Assessment of Organizational Policy and Planning Function in OMB," in U.S. Senate Committee on Governmental Affairs, *Office of Management and Budget*, 147–167, at 163. See also General Accounting Office, *Managing the Government: Revised Approach Could Improve OMB's Effectiveness* (Washington, D.C.: Government Printing Office, 1989).

33. *Revitalizing Federal Management: Managers and Their Overburdened Systems* (Washington, D.C.: National Academy of Public Administration, 1983), 10–13.

34. 50 U.S. Code 401. Reorganization Plan No. 4 of 1949 placed the NSC in the Executive Office of the President.

35. Attendance was expanded by President Reagan to include the attorney general, the secretary of the

Treasury, the director of OMB, and the chief delegate to the United Nations.

36. For details on the interagency committee structure and national security advisers' conceptions of their role before and after the Iran-Contra scandal of 1985–1986, see Robert C. McFarlane, Richard Saunders, and Thomas C. Shull, "The National Security Council: Organization for Policy Making," in *The Presidency and National Security Policy*, ed. R. Gordon Hoxie et al. (New York: Center for the Study of the Presidency, 1984), 261–273; and Colin L. Powell, "The NSC System in the Last Two Years of the Reagan Administration," in *The Presidency in Transition*, ed. James P. Pfiffner, R. Gordon Hoxie, et al. (New York: Center for the Study of the Presidency, 1989), 204–218. (McFarlane and Powell were national security advisers.) The first Bush administration simplified the interagency committee structure; see Bernard Weinraub, "Bush Backs Plan to Enhance Role of Security Staff," *New York Times*, February 2, 1989.

37. Bert Rockman, "America's Departments of State: Irregular and Regular Syndromes of Policy Making," *American Political Science Review* 75 (December 1981): 911–927.

38. "Fight Looms over Size of White House National Security Staff," *Roll Call* (April 26, 2016), http://www.rollcall.com/news/policy/fight-looms-size-white-house-national-security-staff-2; and Kathleen J. McInnis, "'Right-Sizing' the National Security Council Staff?" *CRS Insight* (June 30, 2016), https://www.fas.org/sgp/crs/natsec/IN10521.pdf.

39. Karen DeYoung, "How the Obama White House Runs Foreign Policy," *Washington Post* (August 4, 2015), https://www.washingtonpost.com/world/national-security/how-the-obama-white-house-runs-foreign-policy/2015/08/04/2befb960-2fd7-11e5-8353-1215475949f4_story.html; efile.com, "U.S. Taxpayers efiled More Than 128 Million Returns in 2015" (2016), http://www.efile.com/efile-tax-return-direct-deposit-statistics/.

40. See, for example, Perri 6, *E-Governance: Styles of Political Judgment in the Information Age Polity* (New York: Palgrave, 2004); Jane E. Fountain, *Building the Virtual State: Information Technology and Institutional Change* (Washington, D.C.: Brookings Institution, 2001); and Organization for Economic Co-operation and Development, *The E-Government Imperative* (Paris: OECD, 2003).

41. Kathryn Zickuhr and Aaron Smith, *Digital Differences* (Washington, D.C.: Pew Research Center's Internet & American Life Project, April 13, 2012), http://www.pewinternet.org/~/media//Files/Reports/2012/PIP_Digital_differences_041312.pdf; and Thom File and Camille Ryan,

"Computer and Internet Use in the United States: 2013" (U.S. Census Bureau, November 2014), https://www.census.gov/history/pdf/2013computeruse.pdf.

42. Fountain, *Building the Virtual State*, 205–206.

43. John B. Horrigan, *How Americans Get in Touch with Government* (Washington, D.C.: Pew Internet and American Life Project, May 24, 2004), http://www.pewinternet.org/Reports/2004/How-Americans-Get-in-Touch-With-Government.aspx.

6. ORGANIZATION PROBLEMS

1. Verne Kopytoff, "Move over Mr. Mayor, Cities Are Getting Chief Innovation Officers," *Fortune/CNN Money* (May 22, 2013), http://fortune.com/2013/05/22/move-over-mr-mayor-cities-are-getting-chief-innovation-officers/.

2. U.S. Environmental Protection Agency, "Food Recovery Challenge," https://www.epa.gov/sustainable-management-food/food-recovery-challenge-frc.

3. Jack H. Knott and Gary J. Miller, *Reforming Bureaucracy: The Politics of Institutional Choice* (Englewood Cliffs, N.J.: Prentice Hall, 1987), 274.

4. Herbert Kaufman, "Emerging Doctrines of Public Administration," *American Political Science Review* 50 (December 1956): 1059–1073. He assigns the relative dominance of these doctrines historically in this sequence: representativeness, neutral competence, and executive leadership.

5. Todd S. Purdom, "Scuba Feud Pits Idled Bravest against Prideful Finest," *New York Times*, May 5, 1988; and Ari L. Goldman, "New Rules Set for Handling Emergencies," *New York Times*, July 5, 1990.

6. For an analysis, see National Commission on Terrorist Attacks upon the United States, *The 9/11 Commission Report* (New York: Norton, 2004), chap. 9.

7. Federal Regulation Study Team, *Federal Energy Regulation: An Organizational Study* (Washington, D.C.: Government Printing Office, April 1974), appendix D, D1–D2.

8. Ibid., D2.

9. E. S. Turner, *The Court of St. James's* (London: Michael Joseph, 1959), 305–306.

10. *United States Government Organization Manual, 1977–1978*, 312.

11. The concept of core activities is akin to the concept of organizational essence in Morton H. Halperin, *Bureaucratic Politics and Foreign Policy* (Washington, D.C.: Brookings Institution, 1974), 28–40. Halperin soundly argues that an organization must vigorously protect its organizational core or essence.

12. See Allen Schick, "The Coordination Option," in *Federal Reorganization: What Have We Learned?* ed. Peter Szanton (Chatham, N.J.: Chatham House, 1981), 85–113, esp. 95–99.

13. For details on interagency strife in narcotics control, see W. John Moore, "No Quick Fix," *National Journal* 20 (November 21, 1987): 2954–2959; and "Turf Wars in the Federal Bureaucracy," *Newsweek*, April 20, 1989, 4–6.

14. 102 U.S. Statutes 4181. The czar is formally the director of National Drug Control Policy.

15. Sandra Panem, *The AIDS Bureaucracy* (Cambridge, Mass.: Harvard University Press, 1988).

16. See Jean Blondel, *The Organization of Governments: A Comparative Analysis of Government Structures* (Beverly Hills, Calif.: SAGE, 1982).

17. Commission on the Organization of the Government for the Conduct of Foreign Policy, Report (Washington, D.C.: Government Printing Office, 1975), 32–33.

18. Robert T. Golembiewski, *Organizing Men and Power: Patterns of Behavior and Line-Staff Models* (Chicago: Rand McNally, 1967), 62. Pages 60–89 provide the definitive analysis of the tensions between line and staff-auxiliary-control activities.

19. For major critiques of the neutral competence approach, see Knott and Miller, *Reforming Bureaucracy*; and *Organizing Governance and Governing Organizations*, ed. Colin Campbell and B. Guy Peters (Pittsburgh: University of Pittsburgh Press, 1988). See also Harold Seidman and Robert Gilmour, *Politics, Position, and Power: From the Positive to the Regulatory State*, 4th ed. (New York: Oxford University Press, 1986); James G. March and Johan P. Olsen, "Organizing Political Life: What Administrative Reorganization Tells Us about Government," *American Political Science Review* 77 (June 1983): 281–296; and Terry M. Moe, "The Politics of Bureaucratic Structure," in *Can the Government Govern?* ed. John E. Chubb and Paul E. Peterson (Washington, D.C.: Brookings Institution, 1989), 267–329.

20. "Remarks by the President in State of the Union Address" (January 25, 2011), http://www.whitehouse.gov/the-press-office/2011/01/25/remarks-president-state-union-address.

21. *Immigration and Naturalization Service v. Chadha*, 462 U.S. 919 (1983). See Barbara Hinkson Craig, *Chadha: The Story of an Epic Constitutional Struggle* (New York: Oxford University Press, 1988; paperback ed., Berkeley: University of California Press, 1990).

22. 98 U.S. Statutes 3192 (November 8, 1984). The president cannot use this method to propose creating a new agency outside a department or existing agency.

23. See Peri E. Arnold, *Making the Managerial Presidency: Comprehensive Reorganization Planning, 1905–1980* (Princeton, N.J.: Princeton University Press, 1986).

24. Others, however, led to later reforms. See James W. Fesler, "The Brownlow Committee Fifty Years Later," *Public Administration Review* 47 (July–August 1987): 291–296.

25. See Ronald C. Moe, *The Hoover Commissions Revisited* (Boulder, Colo.: Westview, 1982).

26. Herbert Emmerich, *Federal Organization and Administrative Management* (Tuscaloosa: University of Alabama Press, 1971), 127.

27. Office of Management and Budget, *Papers Relating to the President's Departmental Reorganization Program, March 1971* (Washington, D.C.: Government Printing Office, 1971). See also the revised edition of February 1972.

28. Frustrated by Congress's failure to act, Nixon set out in 1973 to do by fiat what Congress would not let him do by law: four cabinet members were additionally given White House posts as counselors to the president, each with powers over the existing departments in the fields of the proposed departments. In May 1973, with Watergate unraveling, Nixon abandoned this scheme of "supersecretaries."

29. The major success claimed was reform of the civil service, but this was mostly nonorganizational.

30. Reagan supported creation of the Department of Veterans Affairs, but its success in Congress was already assured.

31. The success of Reagan's strategy is assessed in *The Reagan Legacy: Promise and Performance*, ed. Charles O. Jones (Chatham, N.J.: Chatham House, 1988), esp. chaps. 1 and 4.

32. James K. Conant, "In the Shadow of Wilson and Brownlow: Executive Branch Reorganization in the States, 1965 to 1987," *Public Administration Review* 48 (September–October 1988): 892–902. One state, Iowa, reorganized in 1985–1986.

33. March and Olsen, "Organizing Political Life," 288, 292.

34. See Herbert Kaufman, *The Limits of Organizational Change* (Montgomery: University of Alabama Press, 1971); and *Are Government Organizations Immortal?* (Washington, D.C.: Brookings Institution, 1976).

35. For a classic analysis of the expansive tendencies, see Matthew Holden Jr., "'Imperialism' in Bureaucracy," *American Political Science Review* 60 (December 1966): 943–951.

36. Craig W. Thomas, "Reorganizing Public Organizations: Alternatives, Objectives, and Evidence," *Journal of Public Administration and Theory* 3 (1993): 457–486.

7. ADMINISTRATIVE REFORM

1. Portions of this chapter were originally presented at a conference in Brisbane, Australia, sponsored by the Australian Fulbright Symposium on Public Sector Reform. The conference, "New Ideas, Better Government," was held June 23–24, 1994, and was organized by the Griffith University Centre for Australian Public Sector Management. We are grateful to the conference organizers, Glyn Davis and Patrick Weller, for their support of the research and for their permission to use the material developed for the conference in this chapter.

2. Organization for Economic Co-operation and Development, *Government of the Future* (Paris: OECD, 2001), 15.

3. Christopher Pollitt and Geert Bouckaert, *Public Management Reform: A Comparative Analysis—New Public Management, Governance, and the Neo-Weberian State*, 3rd ed. (Oxford: Oxford University Press, 2011), p. 9

4. *A Pledge to America* (2010), 6, http://pledge.gop.gov/resources/library/documents/pledge/a-pledge-to-america.pdf.

5. Roy Bahl, *Financing State and Local Governments in the 1980s* (New York: Oxford University Press, 1984), 184–185.

6. Irene Rubin, *The Politics of Public Budgeting: Getting and Spending, Borrowing and Balancing*, 2nd ed. (Chatham, N.J.: Chatham House, 1993), 51–52.

7. J. Richard Aronson and John Hilley, *Financing State and Local Governments*, 4th ed. (Washington, D.C.: Brookings Institution, 1986), 223–224.

8. Ciruli Associates, "Coloradans Support TABOR Amendment Limits on Taxes and Government Spending," February 19, 2003, http://www.ciruli.com/polls/tabor03.htm.

9. See Bahl, *Financing State and Local Government.*

10. E. S. Savas, *Privatizing the Public Sector: How to Shrink Government* (Chatham, N.J.: Chatham House, 1982), 16–17.

11. President's Private Sector Survey on Cost Control (Grace Commission), *A Report to the President* (Washington, D.C.: Government Printing Office, 1984), II-1.

12. Charles Goodsell, "The Grace Commission: Seeking Efficiency for the Whole People," *Public Administration Review* 44 (May–June 1984): 196–204.

13. David Osborne and Ted Gaebler, *Reinventing Government: How the Entrepreneurial Spirit Is Transforming the Public Sector, from Schoolhouse to Statehouse, City Hall to the Pentagon* (Reading, Mass.: Addison-Wesley, 1993).

14. Al Gore, *From Red Tape to Results: Creating a Government That Works Better and Costs Less* (Washington, D.C.: Government Printing Office, 1993), iii–iv.

15. General Accounting Office, *Federal Employment: The Results to Date of the Fiscal Year 1994 Buyouts at Non-Defense Agencies*, GGD-94–214, September 1994.

16. General Accounting Office, *High Risk Series: An Update*, GAO-01–263, January 2002, 73.

17. John J. DiIulio Jr., *Bring Back the Bureaucrats* (West Conshohocken, Pa.: Templeton Press, 2014).

18. Michael Hammer and James Champy, *Reengineering the Corporation: A Manifesto for Business Revolution* (New York: Harper Business, 1993).

19. Jerry Mechling, "Reengineering Part of Your Game Plan? A Guide for Public Managers," *Governing* 7 (February 1994): 41–52; Russell M. Linden, *Seamless Government: A Practical Guide to Re-Engineering in the Public Sector* (San Francisco: Jossey-Bass, 1994); and Sharon L. Caudle, *Reengineering for Results* (Washington, D.C.: National Academy of Public Administration, 1994).

20. Hammer and Champy, *Reengineering the Corporation*, 2, 3.

21. Ibid., 47–49.

22. Mechling, "Reengineering Part of Your Game Plan?"

23. General Accounting Office, *Management Reforms: Examples of Public and Private Innovations to Improve Service Delivery*, AIMD/GGD-94–9, 1994, 37–38.

24. "DMV Satisfaction Survey: The Best and Worst DMVs in America" (2014), https://www.dmv.com/blog/best-worst-customer-satisfaction-520701.

25. H. George Frederickson, "Painting Bull's Eyes around Bullet Holes," *Governing* 5 (October 1992): 13.

26. Ronald C. Moe, Edward Davis, Frederick Pauls, and Harold Relyca, *Analysis of the Budget and Management Proposals in the Report of the National Performance Review* (Washington, D.C.: Congressional Research Service, September 1993, photocopied), 4.

27. Henri Fayol, *General and Industrial Management* (London: Pitman and Sons, 1925).

28. Luther Gulick, "The Theory of Organization," in ibid., 25.

29. Michael M. Harmon and Richard T. Mayer, *Organization Theory for Public Administration* (Boston: Little, Brown, 1986), 42–47.

30. James Q. Wilson, *Bureaucracy: What Government Agencies Do and Why They Do It* (New York: Basic Books, 1989), 163.

31. For an excellent survey, see James L. Perry, ed., *Handbook of Public Administration* (San Francisco: Jossey-Bass, 1989).

32. See W. Edwards Deming, *Out of Crisis* (Cambridge, Mass.: Massachusetts Institute of Technology Center for Advanced Engineering Study, 1986); and Rafael Aguayo, *Dr. Deming: The American Who Taught the Japanese about Quality* (New York: Simon and Schuster, 1990).

33. Aguayo, *Dr. Deming*, 19.

34. H. Metcalf and L. Urwick, *Dynamic Administration: The Collected Papers of Mary Parker Follett* (New York: Harper & Brothers, 1942).

35. Abraham Maslow, "A Theory of Human Motivation," *Psychological Review* 50 (July 1943): 370–396.

36. See, for example, Michael Barzelay with Babak J. Armajani, *Breaking through Bureaucracy: A New Vision for Managing in Government* (Berkeley: University of California Press, 1992); and Harry P. Hatry and John J. Kirlin, *An Assessment of the Oregon Benchmarks: A Report to the Oregon Progress Board* (June 1994, photocopied).

37. Cohen and Brand, *Total Quality Management in Government,* 175–197.

38. Ibid., 197.

39. Katherine Barrett and Richard Greene, "What Employee Surveys Reveal about Working in Government," *Governing* (June 9, 2016), http://www.governing.com/columns/smart-mgmt/gov-employee-surveys-state-local-government.html.

40. U.S. Government Accountability Office, *Federal Workforce: Distribution of Performance Ratings across the Federal Government, 2013*, GAO-16-520R (May 9, 2016), http://www.gao.gov/products/GAO-16-520R.

41. Liam Ackland, "The Five Factors That Drive Employee Satisfaction," *GovExec.com* (June 3, 2016).

42. See Michael Barber, *Instruction to Deliver: Fighting to Transform Britain's Public Services* (London: Methuen Publishing, 2008); and *How to Run a Government: So That Citizens Benefit and Taxpayers Don't Go Crazy* (London: Penguin, 2016).

43. Barber, *How to Run a Government*, xvii, xxiv.

44. Jeff Godown, "The CompStat Process: Four Principles for Managing Crime Reduction," *Police Chief* (June 2016), http://www.policechiefmagazine.org/magazine/index.cfm?fuseaction=display&article_id=1859&issue_id=82009.

45. For an analysis, see Robert D. Behn, *The Performance-Stat Potential: A Leadership Strategy for Producing Results* (Washington, D.C.: Brookings. 2014).

46. U.S. Office of Management and Budget, "End Veterans Homelessness," https://www.performance.gov/content/end-veterans-homelessness.

47. For two excellent surveys of administrative issues around the world, see Randall Baker, ed., *Comparative Public Management: Putting U.S. Public Policy and Implementation in Context* (New York: Praeger, 1994); and B. Guy Peters, *The Future of Governing: Four Emerging Models*, 2nd ed., rev. (Lawrence: University of Kansas Press, 2001). The Organization of Economic Co-operation and Development also publishes regular updates on reforms in public administration; see http://www.oecd.org.

48. An important commentary on reform in the developing world is Allen Schick, "Why Most Developing Countries Should Not Try New Zealand Reforms," *World Bank Research Observer* 13 (February 1998): 123–131.

49. For a broad discussion, see Peter Aucoin, "Administrative Reform in Public Management: Paradigms, Principles, Paradoxes and Pendulums," *Governance* 3 (1990), 115–137; and Christopher Pollitt and Geert Bouckaert, *Public Management Reform: A Comparative Analysis—New Public Management, Governance, and the Neo-Weberian State* (Oxford: Oxford University Press, 2011).

50. See Donald F. Kettl and John J. DiIulio Jr., eds., *Inside the Reinvention Machine: Appraising the National Performance Review* (Washington, D.C.: Brookings Institution, 1995).

51. Allen Schick, *The Spirit of Reform: Managing the New Zealand State Sector in a Time of Change* (Wellington, N.Z.: State Services Commission, 1996).

52. Office of Management and Budget, *The President's Management Agenda: Fiscal Year 2002* (Washington, D.C.: Government Printing Office, 2001), 3.

8. THE CIVIL SERVICE

1. Associated Press dispatch, *New Haven Register*, July 18, 1969; and 5 U.S. Code of Federal Regulations, 5546, 5547.

2. See Megan Garber, "Apollo 11's Astronauts Received an $8 Per Diem for the Mission to the Moon," *The Atlantic* (August 28, 2012), http://www.govexec.com/technology/2012/08/apollo-11s-astronauts-received-8-diem-mission-moon/57698/?oref=govexec_today_nl.

3. Jonathan Walters, *Life after Civil Service Reform: The Texas, Georgia, and Florida Experiences* (Washington, D.C.: IBM Endowment for the Business of Government, 2002), 7.

4. David Osborne and Ted Gaebler, *Reinventing Government* (Reading, Mass.: Addison-Wesley, 1992).

5. Max Cacas, "OPM Hosts CHCO Hiring Reforms Summit Today," *Federal News Radio* (May 12, 2010), http://www.federalnewsradio.com/?nid=35&sid=1954833.

6. 5 U.S. Code of Federal Regulations 3304(a). The substance and much of the language date from the Pendleton Civil Service Act of 1883.

7. U.S. Merit Systems Protection Board, *Federal Appointment Authorities: Cutting through the Confusion* (Washington, D.C.: MSPB, 2008), http://www.mspb.gov/MSPBSEARCH/viewdocs.aspx?docnumber=350930&version=351511&application=ACROBAT.

8. Brittany R. Ballenstedt, "MSPB: Competitive Hiring on the Decline," *Government Executive* (July 29, 2008), http://www.govexec.com/story_page.cfm?articleid=40577& dcn=e_gvet.

9. U.S. Office of Personnel Management, *Employment of Veterans in the Federal Executive Branch: Fiscal Year 2014* (July 2015), https://www.fedshirevets.gov/hire/hrp/reports/EmploymentOfVets-FY14.pdf.

10. Organization for Economic Co-operation and Development, *Fostering Diversity in the Public Service* (2009), 5, http://www.oecd.org/dataoecd/44/21/44860884.pdf.

11. U.S. Office of Personnel Management, "Profile of Federal Civilian Non-Postal Employees" (2013), https://www.opm.gov/policy-data-oversight/data-analysis-documentation/federal-employment-reports/reports-publications/profile-of-federal-civilian-non-postal-employees/.

12. Partnership for Public Service, "Federal Departures" (August 14, 2014), https://ourpublicservice.org/publications/viewcontentdetails.php?id=352.

13. Bureau of Labor Statistics, "Table 3. Total Separation Levels and Rates by Industry and Region, Seasonally Adjusted," http://www.bls.gov/news.release/jolts.t03.htm.

14. National Council on Teacher Quality, "National Council on Teacher Quality Releases Study Finding Teachers Must Work 24 Years, on Average, to Reach $75,000 Salary" (December 3, 2014), http://www.nctq.org/dmsView/Press_Release_-_Salary_range_Study_final.

15. David Lewin, Jeffrey H. Keefe, and Thomas Kochan, "The New Great Debate about Unionism and Collective Bargaining in U.S. State and Local Governments," *ILRR Review* 65 (2012): 749–778.

16. Congressional Budget Office, "Comparing the Compensation of Federal and Private-Sector Employees" (January 30, 2012), http://www.cbo.gov/publication/42921.

17. James Sherk, *Inflated Federal Pay: How Americans Are Overtaxed to Overpay the Civil Service*, Report CDA10-05 (Washington, D.C.: Heritage Foundation, 2010), http://thf_media.s3.amazonaws.com/2010/pdf/CDA10-05.pdf.

18. Terry W. Culler, "Most Federal Workers Need Only Be Competent," *Wall Street Journal*, May 21, 1986.

19. Eric Mack, "Meet Three Currently Furloughed Nobel Prize Winners," *Forbes* (October 14, 2013), http://www.forbes.com/sites/ericmack/2013/10/14/meet-three-currently-furloughed-nobel-prize-winners/#bdaf93e1880e.

20. Ben Smith, "Obama Plans to 'Make Government Cool Again,'" *Politico* (September 11, 2008), http://www.politico.com/blogs/bensmith/0908/Obama_plans_to_make_government_cool_again.html.

21. See Merit Systems Protection Board, Attracting College Graduates to the Federal Government: A View of College Recruiting (Washington, D.C.: Government Printing Office, 1988); Leadership for America Report, 3–4, 24; and Task Force Reports, 84–88.

22. National Advisory Council on the Public Service, *Ensuring the Highest Quality National Public Service* (Washington, D.C.: National Advisory Council on the Public Service, 1993), 20.

23. Constance Horner, OPM director, as quoted in Judith Havemann, "U.S. Plans New System for Hiring," *Washington Post*, June 23, 1988. Ms. Horner announced a new student recruitment program, but its realization depended on its appeal to her successor under the Bush administration. See Office of Personnel Management, "New Program to Fill GS-5 and GS-7 Entry-Level Jobs" (June 23, 1988), processed.

24. Carolyn Ban and Norma Riccucci, "Personnel Systems and Labor Relations: Steps toward a Quiet Revitalization," in *Revitalizing State and Local Public Service: Strengthening Performance, Accountability, and Citizen Confidence*, ed. Frank J. Thompson (San Francisco: Jossey-Bass, 1993), 83.

25. Leonard Buder, "Walkout Is Hobbling Schools in New York," *New York Times*, February 24, 1977.

26. Quoted in Frank Swoboda, "AFGE's Optimistic Organizer," *Washington Post*, January 21, 1988.

27. Joel M. Douglas, "State Civil Service and Collective Bargaining Systems," *Public Administration Review* 52 (January–February 1992): 162–171.

28. Quoted in National Academy of Public Administration, *Leading People in Change: Empowerment, Commitment, Accountability* (Washington, D.C.: NAPA, 1993), 10.

29. Ibid., 89–111; and Steven M. Goldschmidt and Leland E. Stuart, "The Extent and Impact of Educational Policy Bargaining," *Industrial and Labor Relations Review* 39 (April 1986): 350–360.

30. For the Federal Labor Relations Authority's interpretations of "compelling need" and "procedures," see Sar Levitan and Alexandra Noden, *Working for the Sovereign: Employee Relations in the Federal Government* (Baltimore: Johns Hopkins University Press, 1983), 36–40; and annual reports of the FLRA.

31. 5 U.S. Code, Part III, Subpart F, Chapter 71, Subchapter I, Section 7106.

32. Brian Friel, "Labor Pains," *Government Executive* (October 1, 2002), http://www.govexec.com/magazine/2002/10/labor-pains/12518/.

33. Executive Order 12564, September 15, 1986. For its implementation, see General Accounting Office, *Drug Testing: Federal Agency Plans for Testing Employees* (Washington, D.C.: Government Printing Office, 1989); and *Drug Testing: Action by Certain Agencies When Employees Test Positive for Illegal Drugs* (Washington, D.C.: Government Printing Office, 1990).

34. Amelia Gruber, "New Policy Would Broaden Drug-Testing Methods," *Government Executive* (April 6, 2004), http://www.govexec.com/dailyfed/0404/040604a1.htm.

35. *National Treasury Employees v. Von Raab*, 109 S. Ct. 1384 (1989).

36. The relationship between the presence of HIV antibodies and the likelihood of having AIDS is a matter of dispute. For technical discussion, see "The Cause of AIDS," *Science* 242 (November 18, 1988): 997–998.

37. Richard L. Berke, "State Department to Begin AIDS Testing," *New York Times*, November 29, 1986.

38. 5 U.S. Code of Federal Regulations 7324–7327. For specifically permissible activities and prohibited activities, see 5 U.S. Code of Federal Regulations 733.111 to 733.122. Exceptions to the ban exist (1) for nonpartisan elections and with regard to questions (such as constitutional amendments and referenda) not specifically identified with a national or state political party and (2) in certain local communities near Washington, D.C., and elsewhere (designated by OPM) where federal employees are a majority of voters. OPM restricts activity in such communities' partisan elections to candidacy as, or advocacy or opposition to, an independent candidate.

39. Those free of the restrictions are the president and vice president, aides paid from appropriations for the president's office, heads and assistant heads of executive departments, and officers who are appointed by the president, by and with the advice and consent of the Senate, and who determine policies to be pursued by the United States.

40. George Cahlink, "Ex-Procurement Chief Gets Jail Time," *Government Executive* (October 1, 2004), http://www.govexec.com/dailyfed/1004/100104g1.htm. The plea agreement can be found at this link.

41. Government Accountability Office, Defense Contracting: Post-Government Employment of Former DOD Officials Needs Greater Transparency, Report GAO-08-485 (2008), 6.

42. Ibid.

43. Patricia Wallace Ingraham, *The Foundation of Merit: Public Service in American Democracy* (Baltimore: Johns Hopkins University Press, 1995), 74. Emphasis in original.

44. Government Accountability Office, *High-Risk Series: Strategic Human Capital Management*, Report GAO-03-120 (2003), 7.

45. John Berry, "Launch of Hiring Reform Initiative" (May 11, 2010), http://www.opm.gov/news/speeches-remarks/launch-of-hiring-reform-initiative.

46. Steven Pearlstein, "Can Business Afford Jim DeMint?" *Washington Post* (September 29, 2010), http://www.washingtonpost.com/wp-dyn/content/article/2010/09/28/AR2010092806308.html.

9. HUMAN CAPITAL

1. General Accounting Office, *High-Risk Series: Strategic Human Capital Management*, GAO-03-120 (Washington, D.C.: Government Printing Office, 2003), 3–4. For a broad examination of the issues, see Jonathan D. Breul and Nicole Willenz Gardner, eds., *Human Capital 2004* (Lanham, Md.: Rowman and Littlefield, 2004).

2. Peter Drucker, "Knowledge Work and Knowledge Society: The Social Transformations of This Century," *1994 Godkin Lecture* (Cambridge, Mass.: John F. Kennedy School of Government, Harvard University, 1994).

3. U.S. Government Accountability Office, "Strategic Human Capital Management" (2015), http://www.gao.gov/highrisk/strategic_human_management/why_did_study.

4. GAO, High-Risk Series, 8–21.

5. Ibid., 10.

6. For a discussion of these issues, see Donna D. Beecher, "The Next Wave of Civil Service Reform," *Public Personnel Management* 32 (Winter 2003): 457–474.

7. Rob Gurwitt, "How Generation X Is Shaping Government," *Governing* (May 2013), http://www.governing.com/topics/mgmt/gov-how-generation-x-shaping-government.html.

8. Mike Maciag, "The 'Silver Tsunami' Has Arrived in Government," *Governing* (May 31, 2016), http://www.governing.com/topics/mgmt/gov-government-retirement-survey-center-state-local.html.

9. David McGlinchey, "Unwieldy Hiring Process Can Be Fixed, Top Personnel Official Says," *Government Executive* (June 8, 2004), http://www.govexec.com/dailyfed/0604/060804d1.htm. See also General Accounting Office, *Human Capital: Status of Efforts to*

Improve Federal Hiring, GAO-04-796T (Washington, D.C.: Government Printing Office, 2004).

10. Partnership for Public Service, *Building the Enterprise: A New Civil Service Framework* (Washington, D.C.: Partnership for Public Service, 2014), 7, http://ourpublic-service.org/publications/viewcontentdetails.php?id=18.

11. General Accounting Office, *HUD Management: Actions Needed to Improve Acquisitions Management,* GAO-03-157 (Washington, D.C.: Government Printing Office, 2002).

12. U.S. Office of Management and Budget, *Budget of the United States Government—Fiscal 2017: Analytical Perspectives,* 92, https://www.whitehouse.gov/sites/default/files/omb/budget/fy2017/assets/ap_8_strengthening.pdf.

13. General Accounting Office, Results-Oriented Cultures: Insights for U.S. Agencies from Other Countries' Performance Management Initiatives, GAO-02-862 (Washington, D.C.: Government Printing Office, 2002), 4.

14. For an excellent analysis of human resource reform, see Patricia W. Ingraham, "Striving for Balance: Reforms in Human Resource Management," in *Handbook of Comparative Administration,* ed. Laurence Lynn Jr. and Christopher Pollitt (Oxford: Oxford University Press, forthcoming).

15. Shelley Metzenbaum, "Performance Improvement Guidance: Management Responsibilities and Government Performance and Results Act Documents," *Memorandum for Executive Departments and Agencies* (June 25, 2010), http://www.whitehouse.gov/sites/default/files/omb/assets/memoranda_2010/m10-24.pdf.

16. Keynote address by David M. Walker, "Comptroller General of the United States, Joint Financial Management Improvement Program," 32nd Annual Financial Management Conference (March 11, 2003), http://www.gao.gov/cghome/jfmip32.pdf.

17. Stephen Barr, "OPM Turns over 10,000 New Leaves," *Washington Post,* January 28, 1994, A21.

18. American Federation of State, County, and Municipal Employees, "Broadbanding" (Spring 1997), http://www.afscmestaff.org/cbr/cbr297_1.htm.

19. Partnership for Public Service, *A New Civil Service Framework* (April 1, 2014), 10–11, http://ourpublicser-vice.org/publications/viewcontentdetails.php?id=18.

20. Quoted in Stephen Barr, "Is Road to Chaos Paved with 'Ad Hoc' Reform?" *Washington Post,* February 22, 2004, C2.

21. Quoted in Jonathan Walters, *Life after Civil Service Reform: The Texas, Georgia, and Florida Experiences* (Washington, D.C.: IBM Endowment for the Business of Government, 2002), 7. The discussion that follows draws heavily on Walters's analysis of the civil service reforms in these three states.

22. Ibid., 22.

23. Ibid., 28.

24. See http://www.pewtrusts.org/en/places.

25. Ibid., 30.

26. See http://www.pewtrusts.org/en/places.

27. For a broad assessment, see Jerrell D. Coggburn, "Personnel Deregulation: Exploring Differences in the American States," *Journal of Public Administration Research and Theory* 11 (2000): 223–244; Sally Coleman Selden, Patricia Wallace Ingraham, and Willow Jacobson, "Human Resource Practices in State Government: Findings from a National Survey," *Public Administration Review* 61 (September–October 2002), 598–607; and J. Edward Kellough and Sally Coleman Selden, "The Reinvention of Public Personnel Administration: An Analysis of the Diffusion of Personnel Management Reforms in the States," *Public Administration Review* 63 (March–April 2003): 165–176.

28. See http://www.pewstates.org/states/virginia-328052.

29. Melissa Maynard, "States Overhaul Civil Service Rules," *Stateline* (August 27, 2013), http://www.pewstates.org/projects/stateline/headlines/states-overhaul-civil-service-rules-85899500482.

30. Paul Verkuil, "Deprofessionalizing State Governments: The Rise of Public At-Will Employment," *Public Administration Review* 75 (March/April 2015), 188–189.

31. John J. DiIulio Jr., *Bring Back the Bureaucrats* (West Conshohocken, Pa.: Templeton Press, 2014).

32. I have interpreted "higher levels" strictly (i.e., at Executive Schedule levels, in the Senior Executive Service, at GS-16 to GS-18, or serving in the White House, or serving as ambassadors and ministers). About 1,650 persons are political appointees under Schedule C ("positions of a confidential or policy-determining character") at the GS-15 level and below; as noted earlier, about 1,000 of them are at GS-13 to GS-15 levels.

33. The Presidential Appointee Initiative, *A Survivor's Guide for Presidential Nominees* (Washington, D.C.: Brookings Institution, 2000), http://www.brookings.edu/research/papers/2000/11/15governance.

34. On Nixon and Reagan, see Richard P. Nathan, *The Administrative Presidency* (New York: Wiley, 1983).

35. Terry M. Moe, "The Politicized Presidency," in *The New Direction in American Politics,* ed. John E. Chubb and Paul E. Peterson (Washington, D.C.: Brookings Institution, 1985), 235–271.

36. Expendability is impaired when, as is often the case, a political appointee is the darling of a congressional committee, interest group, or both.

37. Paul C. Light, "How Thick Is Government?" *American Enterprise* 5 (November–December 1994): 60–61. See also the book based on his study, *Thickening Government: Federal Hierarchy and the Diffusion of Accountability* (Washington, D.C.: Brookings Institution, 1995).

38. Paul C. Light, "Fact Sheet on the Continued Thickening of Government" (July 23, 2003), http://www .brookings.edu/research/papers/2004/07/23governance-light.

39. For qualifications needed to perform well in one set of political posts, see John H. Trattner, *The Prune Book: The 100 Toughest Management and Policy-Making Jobs in Washington* (Lanham, Md.: Madison Books, 1988).

40. G. Calvin Mackenzie, "Appointing Mr. (or Ms.) Right," *Government Executive* 22 (April 1990): 30–35; the transitions exclude Johnson's and Ford's rises from the vice presidency. cf. Burt Solomon, "Bush's Laggard Appointment Pace . . . May Not Matter All That Much," *National Journal* 21 (December 2, 1989): 2952–2953. Through 1989 and often beyond, the Consumer Products Safety Commission lacked a quorum; only four of eighteen top Energy Department officials were in place, as was true of six of eleven assistant secretaries of labor; the Census Bureau's director had not been appointed, although the 1990 census was soon to start; and in Health and Human Services, the headships of the National Institutes of Health, Food and Drug Administration, and Health Care Financing Administration were unfilled.

41. Quoted in Christopher Lee, "Bush Slow to Fill Top Federal Posts," *Washington Post*, October 18, 2002, A35.

42. From 1953 to 1976, 55 percent of the initial appointees and 85 percent of appointees had had such experience. James J. Best, "Presidential Cabinet Appointments: 1953–1976," *Presidential Studies Quarterly* 11 (Winter 1981): 62–66.

43. This and later paragraphs draw on James W. Fesler, "Politics, Policy, and Bureaucracy at the Top," *Annals of the American Academy of Political and Social Science* 466 (March 1983): 23–41, and sources cited there.

44. For informative analyses of political officials who had such capability, see Jameson W. Doig and Erwin C. Hargrove, eds., *Leadership and Innovation: A Biographical Perspective on Entrepreneurs in Government* (Baltimore: Johns Hopkins University Press, 1987).

45. G. Edward DeSeve, *The Presidential Appointee's Handbook* (Washington, D.C.: Brookings Institution, 2008).

46. *Leadership in Jeopardy: The Fraying of the Presidential Appointments System* (Washington, D.C.: National Academy of Public Administration, 1985), 4–5. Regulatory commissioners, who have fixed terms and are removable only "for cause," are excluded from the figures we use. The figures measure tenure in specific positions; appointees' median service within the same agency was 3 years, and within the government 4.3 years.

47. Charles S. Clark, "Low Morale at DHS Linked to Heavy Turnover, Weak Training," *Government Executive* (March 22, 2012), http://www.govexec.com/defense/2012/03/low-morale-dhs-linked-heavy-turnover-weak-training/41549.

48. For details, see Linda L. Fisher, "Fifty Years of Presidential Appointments," in *The In-and-Outers: Presidential Appointees and Transient Government in Washington*, ed. G. Calvin Mackenzie (Baltimore: Johns Hopkins University Press, 1987), 21–26; Carl Brauer, "Tenure, Turnover, and Post-government Employment Trends of Presidential Appointees," in Mackenzie, *In-and-Outers*, 174–194; and Trattner, *Prune Book*. See also General Accounting Office, *Political Appointees: Turnover Rates in Executive Schedule Positions Requiring Senate Confirmation*, GGD-94-115 FS (Washington, D.C.: Government Printing Office, 1994).

49. Robert Thalon Hall, quoted in Brauer, "Tenure, Turnover, and Post-government Employment," 178–179.

50. General Accounting Office, *Department of Labor: Assessment of Management Improvement Efforts* (Washington, D.C.: Government Printing Office, 1986).

51. General Accounting Office, *Social Security Administration: Stable Leadership and Better Management Needed to Improve Effectiveness* (Washington, D.C.: Government Printing Office, 1987), 3.

52. Hugh Heclo, *A Government of Strangers: Executive Politics in Washington* (Washington, D.C.: Brookings Institution, 1972), 158 and passim.

53. For an entertaining fictional account of the comparable interplay between a British minister and his ministry's permanent secretary, see *The Complete "Yes, Minister": The Diaries of a Cabinet Minister by the Right Hon. James Hacker MP*, ed. Jonathan Lynn and Anton Jay (Topsfield, Mass.: Salem House, 1987).

54. HHS (including SSA) data from Robert Pear, "Many Policy Jobs Vacant on Eve of Second Term," *New York Times*, January 14, 1985. In 1987, when five Central American countries proposed a regional peace plan, the United States had ambassadors in only two of those countries; lesser-ranked diplomats represented the United States in the other three. Neil A. Lewis, "U.S. Envoys Told to Convey Doubt over Latin Plan," *New York Times*, August 18, 1987. The president's special envoy for Central America had also resigned.

55. U.S. Government Accountability Office, *Federal Vacancies Reform Act: Key Elements for Agency Procedures for Complying with the Act*, GAO-03-806 (Washington, D.C.: Government Printing Office, 2003), http://www.gao.gov/new.items/d03806.pdf.

56. Clark, "Low Morale at DHS."

57. General Accounting Office, Temporary Appointments: Extended Temporary Appointments to Positions Requiring Senate Confirmation (Washington, D.C.: Government Printing Office, 1986), appendix 1.

58. Frederick V. Malek, *Washington's Hidden Tragedy* (New York: Macmillan, 1978), 102–103.

59. Barack Obama, "Executive Order—Strengthening the Senior Executive Service" (December 15, 2015), https://www.whitehouse.gov/the-press-office/2015/12/15/executive-order-strengthening-senior-executive-service.

60. Frank P. Sherwood and Lee J. Breyer, "Executive Personnel Systems in the States," *Public Administration Review* 47 (September–October 1987): 410–416.

61. Elliot L. Richardson, "Civil Servants: Why Not the Best?" *Wall Street Journal*, November 20, 1987. In the Nixon period, he was undersecretary of state and then headed the Health, Education, and Welfare, Defense, and Justice Departments; under Ford, he was ambassador to the Court of St. James's and secretary of commerce; under Carter, he was ambassador-at-large.

62. See Don Tapscott, *Grown up Digital* (New York: McGraw-Hill, 2009); and Chief Information Officers Council, *Netgeneration: Preparing for Change in the Federal Information Technology Workforce* (Washington, D.C.: Chief Information Officers Council, 2010), 38–39, http://www.govexec.com/pdfs/042310ah1.pdf.

63. Paul C. Light, *A Government Ill Executed: The Decline of the Federal Service and How to Reverse It* (Cambridge, Mass.: Harvard University Press, 2008), 4.

10. DECISION MAKING: RATIONALITY AND RISK

1. Herbert A. Simon, *Administrative Behavior: A Study of Decision-Making Processes in Administrative Organization*, 3rd ed. (New York: Free Press, 1945, 1976). A few years earlier, Chester I. Barnard had also argued the importance of decision making; see *The Functions of the Executive* (Cambridge, Mass.: Harvard University Press, 1938). Simon's work, however, has proved more influential.

2. Max Weber, "Bureaucracy," in *From Max Weber: Essays in Sociology,* trans. and ed. H. H. Gerth and C. Wright Mills (New York: Oxford University Press, 1946), 196–244. Francis E. Rourke discusses this point more generally in *Bureaucracy, Politics, and Public Policy*, 3rd ed. (Boston: Little, Brown, 1984).

3. Deborah A. Stone, *Policy Paradox and Political Reason* (Glenview, Ill.: Scott Foresman, 1988), 21.

4. Robert D. Behn and James W. Vaupel, *Quick Analysis for Busy Decision Makers* (New York: Basic Books, 1982), 19, 20.

5. See Charles O. Jones, *An Introduction to the Study of Public Policy*, 3rd ed. (Monterey, Calif.: Brooks/Cole, 1984), esp. chap. 6.

6. Rourke, *Bureaucracy, Politics, and Public Policy*, 49–50.

7. This follows Hugh Heclo's argument in "Issue Networks and the Executive Establishment," in *The New American Political System*, ed. Anthony King (Washington, D.C.: American Enterprise Institute, 1978), 87–124.

8. Stone, *Policy Paradox and Political Reason*, 309.

9. Donald W. Taylor, "Decision Making and Problem Solving," in *Handbook of Organizations,* ed. James G. March (Chicago: Rand McNally, 1965), 70.

10. Charles E. Lindblom, "Still Muddling, Not Yet Through," *Public Administration Review* 39 (November–December 1979): 518. Lindblom himself has been subjected to vigorous counterattack.

11. To make matters worse, "rational decision makers" never use all the information they get, yet continue to seek even more. See Martha S. Feldman and James G. March, "Information in Organizations and Signal and Symbol," *Administrative Science Quarterly* 26 (1981): 171–186.

12. James G. March and Herbert A. Simon, *Organizations* (New York: Wiley, 1958), 140–141.

13. Arthur M. Okun, *Equality and Efficiency: The Big Tradeoff* (Washington, D.C.: Brookings Institution, 1975), 2.

14. Murray Weidenbaum, *The Modern Public Sector* (New York: Basic Books, 1969), 178.

15. For the roots of the theory, see Anthony Downs, *An Economic Theory of Democracy* (New York: Harper and Row, 1957); James M. Buchanan and Gordon Tullock, *The Calculus of Consent* (Ann Arbor: University of Michigan Press, 1962); Gordon Tullock, *The Politics of Bureaucracy* (Washington, D.C.: Public Affairs Press, 1965); Anthony Downs, *Inside Bureaucracy* (Boston: Little, Brown, 1967); and William A. Niskanen, *Bureaucracy and Representative Government* (Chicago: Aldine-Atherton, 1971).

16. Sytse Douma and Hein Schreuder, *Economic Approaches to Organizations*, 2nd ed. (London and New York: Prentice Hall, 1998).

17. Christopher Pollitt, *Public Management and Administration* (Cheltenham, U.K.: Edward Elgar, 2016), 39–40.

18. Stuart Butler, *Privatizing Federal Spending* (New York: Universe Books, 1985), 58, 166.

19. Alicia Mundy, "The VA Isn't Broken—Yet," *Washington Monthly* (March/April/May 2016), http://www.washingtonmonthly.com/magazine/marchaprilmay_2016/features/the_va_isnt_broken_yet059847.php?page=all.

20. Steven Kelman, "'Public Choice' and Public Spirit," *Public Interest* 87 (Spring 1987): 81.

21. See Robert B. Reich, ed., *The Power of Public Ideas* (Cambridge, Mass.: Ballinger, 1988).

22. The most persuasive and comprehensive descriptions and defenses of the incremental decision-making model are by Charles E. Lindblom. A good, brief statement is his "The Science of 'Muddling Through,'" *Public Administration Review* 19 (Spring 1959): 79–88. The model is further elaborated in *The Intelligence of Democracy: Decision Making through Mutual Adjustment* (New York: Free Press, 1965); *Politics and Markets: The World's Political-Economic Systems* (New York: Basic Books, 1977), 314–324; and *The Policy-Making Process*, 2nd ed. (Englewood Cliffs, N.J.: Prentice Hall, 1980). He responds to criticisms of the model in "Still Muddling, Not Yet Through."

23. The incremental approach, moreover, has not been limited to politics. For applications to business decision making, see James Brian Quinn, "Strategic Change: 'Logical Incrementalism,'" *Sloan Management Review* (Fall 1978): 7–21; "Strategic Goals: Process and Politics," *Sloan Management Review* (Fall 1977): 21–37; and "Managing Strategic Change," *Sloan Management Review* (Summer 1980): 3–20, in which Quinn promotes Lindblom's "muddling-through" approach.

24. The aphorism, first discussed in Chapter 5, is credited to Rufus Miles and is often known as "Miles's Law." See Rufus E. Miles, "The Origin and Meaning of Miles' Law," *Public Administration Review* 38 (September–October 1978): 399–403. See also Allison, *Essence of Decision*, 176.

25. For another case study of bargaining in decision making, see the study by two *Wall Street Journal* reporters of the passage of the tax reform act of 1986: Jeffrey H. Birnbaum and Alan S. Murray, *Showdown at Gucci Gulch: Lawmaking, Lobbyists, and the Unlikely Triumph of Tax Reform* (New York: Random House, 1987).

26. See Charles L. Schultze, *The Politics and Economics of Public Spending* (Washington, D.C.: Brookings Institution, 1968).

27. Ibid., 76.

28. The most comprehensive survey, covering 269 case studies of decentralization in urban areas, is Robert K. Yin and Douglas Yates, *Street-Level Governments* (Lexington, Mass.: Lexington Books, 1975). For private interest groups' participation in national and state administration, McConnell's *Private Power and American Democracy* is the classic source.

29. James E. Webb, *Space Age Management: The Large-Scale Approach* (New York: McGraw-Hill, 1969), 136–137.

30. Irving L. Janis and Leon Mann, *Decision Making: A Psychological Analysis of Conflict, Choice, and Commitment* (New York: Free Press, 1977), 15.

31. See Donald F. Kettl, *Leadership at the Fed* (New Haven, Conn.: Yale University Press, 1986), 7–8.

32. *Science* 236 (April 17, 1987): 267–300, contains a useful symposium on the problems of risk and uncertainty in public policy; see R. Wilson and E. A. C. Crouch, "Risk Assessment and Comparisons: An Introduction"; B. N. Ames, R. Magaw, and L. S. Gold, "Ranking Possible Carcinogenic Hazards"; P. Slovic, "Perception of Risk"; M. Russell and M. Gruber, "Risk Assessment in Environmental Policy Making"; L. B. Lave, "Health and Safety Risk Analyses: Information for Better Decisions"; and D. Okrent, "The Safety Goals of the U.S. Nuclear Regulatory Commission."

33. Plutarch, *The Lives of the Noble Grecians and Romans* (New York: Modern Library, n.d.), 874.

34. See Peter M. Blau and W. Richard Scott, *Formal Organizations* (San Francisco: Chandler, 1962); Tullock, *Politics of Bureaucracy*, 137–141; Downs, *Inside Bureaucracy*, chap. 10; Harold L. Wilensky, *Organizational Intelligence* (New York: Basic Books, 1967), chap. 3; and Brian W. Hogwood and B. Guy Peters, *The Pathology of Public Policy* (Oxford: Oxford University Press, 1985), chap. 4.

35. Charles Peters, "From Ouagadougou to Cape Canaveral: Why the Bad News Doesn't Travel Up," *Washington Monthly*, April 1986, 27.

36. See Presidential Commission on the Space Shuttle *Challenger* Accident [Rogers Commission], *Report to the President* (Washington, D.C.: Government Printing Office, 1986).

37. See *Columbia* Accident Investigation Board, *Final Report* (2003), http://www.nasa.gov/columbia/home/CAIB_Vol1.html.

38. Thomas J. Peters and Robert H. Waterman Jr., *In Search of Excellence* (New York: Warner Books, 1982).

39. See Downs, *Inside Bureaucracy*, 118–127, for a discussion of antidistortion factors.

40. Hogwood and Peters, *Pathology of Public Policy*, 85.

41. House Committee on Science and Technology, *Investigation of the* Challenger *Accident,* Report, 99th Cong., 2nd sess., 1986, 172.

42. Senate Report No. 91–411, *Federal Coal Mine Health and Safety Act of 1969,* 91st Cong., 1st sess., September 17, 1969, 5–6; Henry C. Hart, "Crisis, Community, and Consent in Water Politics," *Law and Contemporary Problems* 22 (Summer 1957): 510–537.

43. All rational (in the broad sense) models assume that crisis decisions made under severe time pressures are usually worse than those affording more time for data assemblage, specialists' advice, and deliberation. For the view that "a 'hasty' decision made under pressure may on average be better than a less urgent one," see Wilensky, *Organizational Intelligence*, 75–77. A full treatment of decision-making behavior under stress of crisis and shortness of time is provided by Janis and Mann, *Decision Making*, 45–67.

44. Irving L. Janis, *Crucial Decisions: Leadership in Policymaking and Crisis Management* (New York: Free Press, 1989).

45. Stephan Braig, Biniam Gebre, and Andrew Sellgren, *Strengthening Risk Management in the U.S. Public Sector* (Washington, D.C.: McKinsey & Company, May 2011), p. 1, https://www.mckinsey.com/~/media/mckinsey/dotcom/client_service/Risk/Working%20papers/28_WP_Risk_management_in_the_US_public_sector.ashx.

46. Ibid., especially Exhibit 1.

47. Webster and Stanton, *Improving Government Decision Making through Enterprise Risk Management*, 18.

48. See Amitai Etzioni, "Mixed Scanning: A Third Approach to Decision-Making," *Public Administration Review* 27 (December 1967): 385–392.

11. BUDGETING

1. For a broad look at the history of budgeting, see Carolyn Webber and Aaron Wildavsky, *A History of Taxation and Expenditures in the Western World* (New York: Simon and Schuster, 1986). On what questions a theory of budgeting must answer, see V. O. Key Jr., "The Lack of a Budgetary Theory," *American Political Science Review* 34 (December 1940): 1237–1240; and Verne Lewis, "Toward a Theory of Budgeting," *Public Administration Review* 12 (Winter 1952): 42–54.

2. Key, "Lack of a Budgetary Theory," 1237.

3. See, for example, Herbert Stein, *Governing the $5 Trillion Economy* (New York: Basic Books, 1989).

4. Keynes is best known for *The General Theory of Employment, Interest, and Money* (1936; repr. New York: Harcourt Brace Jovanovich, 1964). On compensatory economics in the Roosevelt administration, see Donald F. Kettl, "Marriner Eccles and Leadership in the Federal Reserve System," in *Leadership and Innovation: A Biographical Perspective on Entrepreneurs in Government*, ed. Jameson W. Doig and Erwin C. Hargrove (Baltimore: Johns Hopkins University Press, 1987), 318–342.

5. See Herbert Stein, *The Fiscal Revolution in America* (Chicago: University of Chicago Press, 1969); and James E. Alt and K. Alec Chrystal, *Political Economics* (Berkeley: University of California Press, 1983), 54–77.

6. See Edward R. Tufte, *Political Control of the Economy* (Princeton, N.J.: Princeton University Press, 1978).

7. The Federal Reserve operates through three principal policy tools: fixing reserve requirements that banks must hold against deposits (the higher the reserves required, the less money banks can lend out, and thus the higher interest rates become and the more economic growth is slowed), setting the discount rate (the rate at which the Fed lends to banks, which then affects interest rates across the nation), and managing open-market operations (in which the Fed purchases government securities to increase the money supply—thus lowering interest rates and fueling economic growth—and buys securities to decrease the money supply—thus raising interest rates and slowing economic growth). The classic treatment of the history of monetary policy is Milton Friedman and Anna Jacobson Schwartz, *A Monetary History of the United States, 1867–1960* (Princeton, N.J.: Princeton University Press, 1963). For a favorable account of the Volcker era, see Donald F. Kettl, *Leadership at the Fed* (New Haven, Conn.: Yale University Press, 1986), chap. 7. William Greider, in *Secrets of the Temple: How the Federal Reserve Runs the Country* (New York: Simon and Schuster, 1987), takes a far more critical view.

8. Rudolph G. Penner and Alan J. Abramson, *Broken Purse Strings: Congressional Budgeting, 1974–88* (Washington, D.C.: Urban Institute Press, 1989), 99.

9. *Wall Street Journal*, August 21, 1986, 22.

10. An excellent survey of the federal budget process is Allen Schick, *The Federal Budget: Politics, Policy, Process* (Washington, D.C.: Brookings Institution, 1995).

11. For a history of these issues, see Leonard D. White, *The Federalists* (New York: Macmillan, 1956), 116–127; Frederick C. Mosher, *A Tale of Two Agencies: A Comparative Analysis of the General Accounting Office and the Office of Management and Budget* (Baton Rouge: Louisiana State University Press, 1984), 13–34;

and Jerry L. McCaffery, "The Development of Public Budgeting in the United States," in *A Centennial History of the American Administrative State*, ed. Ralph Clark Chandler (New York: Free Press, 1987), 345–377.

12. See William F. Willoughby, *The Movement for Budgetary Reform in the States* (New York: Appleton, 1918).

13. In the wake of the Brownlow Committee's report (1937), the Bureau of the Budget was transferred from the Treasury Department to the newly established Executive Office of the President.

14. Mosher, *Tale of Two Agencies*, 32.

15. See Howard E. Shuman, *Politics and the Budget: The Struggle between the President and the Congress* (Englewood Cliffs, N.J.: Prentice Hall, 1984).

16. The federal budget is a two-inch-thick volume, the size of a large city's telephone directory, printed on very thin paper with tiny type. The task of publishing such a huge volume of information, in the quantities needed by members of Congress, the press, and interested members of the general public, preoccupies the Government Printing Office for more than a month each year. Copies of the budget are available at nearly all college and university libraries, usually in the government documents section.

17. See Lance T. LeLoup, "From Microbudgeting to Macrobudgeting: Evolution in Theory and Practice," in *New Directions in Budget Theory*, ed. Irene S. Rubin (Albany: State University of New York Press, 1988), 19–42.

18. On forecasting, see, for example, Larry D. Schroeder, "Forecasting Revenues and Expenditures," in *Management Policies in Local Government Finance*, ed. J. Richard Aronson and Eli Schwartz (Washington, D.C.: International City Management Association, 1981), 66–90. On the problems of forecasting the federal budget, see "Uncertainty and Bias in Budget Projections," in Congressional Budget Office, *The Economic and Budget Outlook: An Update* (Washington, D.C.: Government Printing Office, 1987), 63–86.

19. R. Douglas Arnold argues, for example, that congressional decisions may be used "partly as rewards for past support, partly as payments for support during the current year, and partly to create a favorable climate for future years." Arnold, *Congress and the Bureaucracy: A Theory of Influence* (New Haven, Conn.: Yale University Press, 1979), 56.

20. Aaron Wildavsky, *The New Politics of the Budgetary Process* (Glenview, Ill.: Scott Foresman, 1988), 83.

21. Wildavsky's work received support at the federal level by Otto A. Davis, M. A. H. Dempster, and Aaron Wildavsky, "A Theory of the Budgetary Process," *American Political Science Review* 60 (September 1966): 529–547; and at the state level by Ira Sharkansky, "Agency Requests, Gubernatorial Support and Budget Success in State Legislatures," *American Political Science Review* 62 (December 1968): 1220–1231. In his later work, Wildavsky moved away from incrementalism. For a discussion, see Irene Rubin, "Aaron Wildavsky and the Demise of Incrementalism," *Public Administration Review* 49 (January–February 1989): 78–81.

22. Lance T. LeLoup and William B. Moreland, "Agency Strategies and Executive Review: The Hidden Politics of Budgeting," *Public Administration Review* 38 (May–June 1978): 232–239; see also Peter B. Natchez and Irwin C. Bupp, "Policy and Priority in the Budgetary Process," *American Political Science Review* 67 (September 1973): 951–963.

23. Natchez and Bupp, "Policy and Priority in the Budgetary Process," 956, and, more generally, 951–963. On the role of entrepreneurs in building support for their programs, see *Leadership and Innovation: A Biographical Perspective*, ed. Doig and Hargrove.

24. For sympathetic accounts of PPBS in the Department of Defense, written by those in charge of its application, see Charles J. Hitch, *Decision Making for Defense* (Berkeley: University of California Press, 1965); and Alain C. Enthoven and K. Wayne Smith, *How Much Is Enough? Shaping the Defense Program, 1961–1969* (New York: Harper and Row, 1971). Compare James R. Schlesinger, "Uses and Abuses of Analysis," in Senate Committee on Government Operations, *Planning, Programming, Budgeting: Inquiry*, 91st Cong., 2nd sess., 1970, 125–136; and Blue Ribbon Defense Panel (Gilbert W. Fitzhugh, chair), *Report to the President and the Secretary of Defense on the Department of Defense* (Washington, D.C.: Government Printing Office, 1970), 112–118, which reports, "the PPBS does not contribute significantly to the decision-making process for consideration of programs which center on major weapons systems" (114).

25. Bureau of the Budget, *Bulletin No. 68–69*, April 12, 1968. All descriptive, but no evaluative quotations are from this text.

26. Jack W. Carlson (assistant director for program evaluation, Bureau of the Budget), "The Status and Next Steps for Planning, Programming, and Budgeting," in U.S. Congress, Joint Economic Committee, *The Analysis and Evaluation of Public Expenditures: The PPB System*, 91st Cong., 1st sess., 1969, 2: 613–634; and his testimony in U.S. Congress, Joint Economic Committee, *Economic Analysis and the Efficiency of Government*, Hearings, 91st Cong., 2nd sess., 1970, Pt. 3, 694–706.

27. Allen Schick, *Budget Innovation in the States* (Washington, D.C.: Brookings Institution, 1971); Aaron Wildavsky, *Budgeting: A Comparative Theory of Budgetary Processes* (Boston: Little, Brown, 1975), 335–352; Jack Rabin, "State and Local PPBS," in *Public Budgeting and Finance,* 2nd ed., ed. Robert T. Golembiewski and Jack Rabin (Itasca, Ill.: Peacock, 1975), 427–447. The most searching critiques of PPBS's inherent defects are in Aaron Wildavsky, *The New Politics of the Budgetary Process* (Glenview, Ill.: Scott Foresman, 1987), 416–420; idem, *The Revolt against the Masses* (New York: Basic Books, 1971); and Leonard Merewitz and Stephen H. Sosnick, *The Budget's New Clothes: A Critique of Planning-Programming-Budgeting and Benefit-Cost Analysis* (Chicago: Markham, 1971). See also Ida R. Hoos, *Systems Analysis in Public Policy: A Critique* (Berkeley: University of California Press, 1972).

28. For an illuminating study of these and other analysts (mostly oriented to economics), see Arnold J. Meltsner, *Policy Analysts in the Bureaucracy* (Berkeley: University of California Press, 1976).

29. Consider Richard Rose, "Implementation and Evaporation: The Record of MBO," *Public Administration Review* 37:1 (January–February, 1977): 64–71.

30. Frank P. Sherwood and William J. Page Jr., "MBO and Public Management," *Public Administration Review* 36 (January–February 1976): 11. The Office of Management and Budget agrees; see Clifford W. Graves and Stefan A. Halper, "Federal Program Evaluation: The Perspective from OMB," in Senate Committee on Government Operations, *Legislative Oversight and Program Evaluation*, committee print, 94th Cong., 2nd sess., 1976, 266–267. The MBO experience is perceptively analyzed in James A. Swiss, "Implementing Federal Programs: Administrative Systems and Organization Effectiveness" (PhD diss., Yale University, 1976). See also Richard Rose, *Managing Presidential Objectives* (New York: Free Press, 1976).

31. Peter A. Pyrrh introduced the system at Texas Instruments and helped Carter install it in Georgia. See his *Zero-Base Budgeting: A Practical Tool for Evaluating Expenses* (New York: Wiley, 1973). More broadly, see "Forum: ZBB Revisited," *Bureaucrat* 7 (Spring 1978): 3–70; Thomas P. Lauth, "Zero-Base Budgeting in Georgia State Government: Myth and Reality," *Public Administration Review* 38 (September–October 1978): 420–430; and George Samuel Minmier, *An Evaluation of the Zero-Base Budgeting System in Governmental Institutions* (Atlanta: School of Business Administration, Georgia State University, 1975), excerpted in Senate Committee on Government Operations, Subcommittee on Intergovernmental Relations, *Compendium of Materials on Zero-Base Budgeting,* committee print, 95th Cong., 1st sess., 1977.

32. Stanley B. Botner discusses the spread of PPBS, MBO, and ZBB, among other tools, in "The Use of Budgeting/Management Tools by State Governments," *Public Administration Review* 45 (September–October 1985): 616–620.

33. For an analysis of how congressional and presidential policies have differed, see Mark S. Kamlet and David C. Mowery, "Influences on Executive and Congressional Budgetary Priorities, 1955–1981," *American Political Science Review* 81 (March 1987): 155–178.

34. Carl J. Friedrich, *Man and His Government* (New York: McGraw-Hill, 1963), 199–215.

35. For a catalog of the many strategies used in the budget game, see Wildavsky, *New Politics of the Budgetary Process*, 21–62.

36. *Congressional Budget and Impoundment Control Act of 1974*, Public Law 93-344, 88 Stat. 337. For an analysis of the act's effects on Congress, see Dennis S. Ippolito, *Congressional Spending* (Ithaca, N.Y.: Cornell University Press, 1981); and Allen Schick, *Congress and Money: Budgeting, Spending, and Taxes* (Washington, D.C.: Urban Institute Press, 1980).

37. William J. Broad, "Inside the Black Budget," *New York Times* (April 1, 2008), http://www.nytimes.com/2008/04/01/science/01patc.html?pagewanted=all&_r=0.

38. Philip G. Joyce, *The Costs of Budget Uncertainty: Analyzing the Impact of Late Appropriations* (Washington, D.C.: IBM Center for the Business of Government, 2012), 12, http://www.businessofgovernment.org/report/costs-budget-uncertainty-analyzing-impact-late-appropriations.

39. These photographs can be viewed at http://newswatch.nationalgeographic.com/2013/10/16/nasa-shutdown-unleashes-beautiful-astronaut-photos-on-twitter/.

40. Jonathan Rauch, "The Fiscal Ice Age," *National Journal*, January 10, 1987, 58. For an appraisal of the process, see Donald F. Kettl, *Deficit Politics: The Search for Balance in American Politics*, 2nd ed. (New York: Longman, 2003); Wildavsky, *New Politics of the Budgetary Process*; Schick, *Congress and Money*; Allen Schick, ed., *Making Economic Policy in Congress* (Washington, D.C.: American Enterprise Institute, 1983); and Allen Schick, *The Capacity to Budget* (Washington, D.C.: Urban Institute Press, 1990).

41. Lawrence J. Haas, "If All Else Fails, Reform," *National Journal*, July 4, 1987, 1713.

42. Katherine Barrett and Richard Green, "Beyond the Basics: Best Practices in State Budget Transparency"

(New York: Volcker Alliance, 2015), https://www.volcker alliance.org/sites/default/files/attachments/Beyond% 20the%20Basics%20-%20The%20Volcker%20 Alliance.pdf.

43. House Committee on the Budget, *Congressional Control of Expenditures*, report prepared by Allen Schick, committee print, 95th Cong., 1st sess., 1977, 126.

44. This discussion draws on Robert N. Anthony and David W. Young, *Management Control in Nonprofit Organizations*, 4th ed. (Homewood, Ill.: Irwin, 1988), esp. 3–49.

45. Ibid., 21. (Emphasis in the original omitted.)

46. U.S. Comptroller General, Financial Integrity Act: Continuing Efforts Needed to Improve Internal Control and Accounting Systems (Washington, D.C.: General Accounting Office, 1987). See also these other GAO reports: Financial Management: Examples of Weaknesses (Washington, D.C.: GAO, 1988); and Managing the Cost of Government: Building an Effective Financial Management Structure (Washington, D.C.: GAO, 1985).

47. For an examination of these issues, see Leo Herbert, Larry N. Killough, and Alan Walter Steiss, *Governmental Accounting and Control* (Monterey, Calif.: Brooks/ Cole, 1984); and Leon E. Hay, *Accounting for Governmental and Nonprofit Entities*, 8th ed. (Homewood, Ill.: Irwin, 1989).

48. U.S. Government Accountability Office, *State and Local Governments' Fiscal Outlook: 2015 Update*, GAO-16-260SP (2015), http://www.gao.gov/assets/680/674 205.pdf.

12. IMPLEMENTATION AND PERFORMANCE

1. Woodrow Wilson, "The Study of Administration," *Political Science Quarterly* 2 (June 1887): 212.

2. Pew Research Center, *Beyond Distrust: How Americans View Their Government* (November 23, 2105), http:// www.people-press.org/2015/11/23/2-general-opinions-about-the-federal-government/.

3. Jeffrey L. Pressman and Aaron B. Wildavsky, *Implementation* (Berkeley: University of California Press, 1973). They cite their debt to an earlier work on implementation by Martha Derthick, *New Towns In-Town* (Washington, D.C.: Urban Institute, 1972).

4. Pressman and Wildavsky, *Implementation*, xv.

5. Randall B. Ripley and Grace A. Franklin, *Policy Implementation and Bureaucracy*, 2nd ed. (Chicago: Dorsey Press, 1986), 2.

6. Daniel A. Mazmanian and Paul A. Sabatier, *Implementation and Public Policy* (Glenview, Ill.: Scott Foresman, 1983), 277. See also Eugene Bardach, *The Implementation Game: What Happens after a Bill Becomes a Law* (Cambridge, Mass.: MIT Press, 1977).

7. Brian W. Hogwood and B. Guy Peters, *The Pathology of Public Policy* (Oxford: Clarendon Press, 1985).

8. For a spirited rebuttal to the literature of failure, see Sar A. Levitan and Robert Taggart, *The Promise of Greatness* (Cambridge, Mass.: Harvard University Press, 1976). See also Henry J. Aaron, *Politics and the Professors: The Great Society in Perspective* (Washington, D.C.: Brookings Institution, 1978); Robert H. Haveman, ed., *A Decade of Federal Antipoverty Programs: Achievements, Failures, and Lessons* (New York: Academic Press, 1977); and Malcolm L. Goggin, Ann O. Bowman, James P. Lester, and Laurence J. O'Toole, *Implementation Theory and Practice: Toward a Third Generation* (Glenview, Ill.: Scott Foresman/Little, Brown, 1990).

9. See Daniel P. Moynihan, *Maximum Feasible Misunderstanding: Community Action in the War on Poverty* (New York: Free Press, 1970).

10. Ripley and Franklin, *Policy Implementation and Bureaucracy*, 22–23.

11. Martin A. Levin and Barbara Ferman, *The Political Hand: Policy Implementation and Youth Employment Programs* (New York: Pergamon Press, 1985), 72–73.

12. See Ross Douthat, "Rumsfeld's Rules Revisited," *The Atlantic* (September 1, 2004), http://www.theatlantic. com/magazine/archive/2004/09/rumsfeld-s-rules-revisited/303425. For an examination of these rules, see Jeffrey A. Krames, *The Rumsfeld Way: The Leadership Wisdom of a Battle-Hardened Maverick* (New York: McGraw-Hill, 2002).

13. See Giandomenico Majone and Aaron Wildavsky, "Implementation as Evolution," in Jeffrey L. Pressman and Aaron Wildavsky, *Implementation*, 3rd ed. (Berkeley: University of California Press, 1984), 163–180.

14. Elliot Richardson, *The Creative Balance* (New York: Holt, Rinehart and Winston, 1976), 128.

15. Richardson, *Creative Balance*, 130, 132–134.

16. See Mazmanian and Sabatier, *Implementation and Public Policy*, 24.

17. Quoted in Louis M. Kohlmeier, "Banking Reform Chances Grow Dimmer," *National Journal*, September 20, 1975, 1341.

18. Ralph Waldo Emerson, "Self-Reliance," in *Essays*, Emerson (Boston: Houghton Mifflin, 1865, 1876, 1883), 62.

19. See Jameson W. Doig and Erwin C. Hargrove, eds., *Leadership and Innovation* (Baltimore: Johns Hopkins

University Press, 1987); John Kingdon, *Agendas, Alternatives, and Public Policies* (Boston: Little, Brown, 1984), 129–130; Eugene Bardach, *Implementation Game*, 274–275. See also Levin and Ferman, *Political Hand*, 5.

20. James Q. Wilson, "The Bureaucracy Problem," *Public Interest* 6 (Spring 1967): 7. See also his *Bureaucracy: What Government Agencies Do and Why They Do It* (New York: Basic Books, 1989).

21. Paul Berman, "The Study of Macro- and Micro-Implementation," *Public Policy* 26 (Spring 1978): 165.

22. Donald F. Kettl, *Managing Risk, Improving Results: Lessons for Improving Government Management from GAO's High Risk List* (Washington, D.C.: IBM Center for the Business of Government, 2016).

23. See, for example, Donald F. Kettl, *The Regulation of American Federalism* (Baltimore: Johns Hopkins University Press, 1987); Advisory Commission on Intergovernmental Relations, *Regulatory Federalism: Policy, Process, Impact and Reform* (Washington, D.C.: Government Printing Office, 1984); and Edward I. Koch, "The Mandate Millstone," *Public Interest* 61 (Fall 1980): 42–57.

24. Congress reversed itself in 1996 and allowed states to increase the speed limit back to sixty-five miles per hour.

25. For an examination, see Joseph F. Zimmerman, *Federal Preemption: The Silent Revolution* (Ames: Iowa State University Press, 1991).

26. Robert P. Stoker, *Reluctant Partners: Implementing Federal Policy* (Pittsburgh: University of Pittsburgh Press, 1991).

27. See John D. Hanrahan, *Government by Contract* (New York: Norton, 1983), esp. chap. 3.

28. USAspending.gov (2016), https://www.usaspending.gov/Pages/default.aspx.

29. Danny Werfel, Controller of the Office of Federal Financial Management, The White House, "Contracting Smarter, Saving More" (February 24, 2012), http://www.whitehouse.gov/blog/2012/02/24/contracting-smarter-saving-more.

30. P. W. Singer, *Corporate Warriors: The Rise of the Privatized Military Industry* (Ithaca, N.Y.: Cornell University Press, 2003).

31. Peter W. Singer, "Beyond the Law," *Guardian* (May 2, 2004), http://www.guardian.co.uk/comment/story/0,3604,1208237,00.html.

32. James Risen, "Afghans Linked to the Taliban Guard U.S. Bases," *New York Times* (October 7, 2010), http://www.nytimes.com/2010/10/08/world/asia/08contractor.html?_r=2. See also Congressional Research Service, *Department of Defense Contractors in Iraq and Afghanistan:* *Background and Analysis* (Washington, D.C.: Congressional Research Service, 2010), http://www.fas.org/sgp/crs/natsec/R40764.pdf.

33. President's Private Sector Survey on Cost Control, *Report on Privatization* (Washington, D.C.: Government Printing Office, 1983), 1. Compare President's Commission on Privatization, *Privatization: Toward More Effective Government* (Washington, D.C.: Government Printing Office, 1988).

34. Steve Coll and Judith Havemann, "Dispute Threatens U.S. Phone Contract," *Washington Post*, July 31, 1987, B1. See also Donald F. Kettl, *Sharing Power: Public Governance and Private Markets* (Washington, D.C.: Brookings Institution, 1993), chap. 4.

35. Senate Armed Services Committee, *Defense Organization: The Need for Change*, staff report, 99th Cong., 1st sess., 1985, 558. For one example, see Nick Kotz, *Wild Blue Yonder: Money, Politics, and the B-1 Bomber* (New York: Pantheon, 1988).

36. *New York Times*, June 15, 1986, sec. 3, 4.

37. American Federation of State, County, and Municipal Employees, *Passing the Bucks* (Washington, D.C.: AFSCME, 1983), 38.

38. General Accounting Office, General Services Administration: Actions Needed to Stop Buying Supplies from Poor-Performing Vendors, GGD-93-34 (January 1993), 2, 4.

39. AFSCME, Passing the Bucks, 69.

40. Selwyn Raab, "U.S. Indicts Ten Road Contractors on Bids," *New York Times*, June 26, 1987, B1.

41. AFSCME, *Passing the Bucks*, 69–70.

42. Effective contracting requires careful management. For a discussion of this problem, see John A. Rehfuss, *Contracting Out in Government: A Guide to Working with Outside Contractors to Supply Public Services* (San Francisco: Jossey-Bass, 1989).

43. Office of Management and Budget, Circular No. A-76, revised March 29, 1979.

44. Sean Reilly, "Report: 4.9 Million Feds, Contractors Hold Security Clearances," *Federal Times*, June 23, 2012.

45. Herbert Kaufman, *Administrative Feedback: Monitoring Subordinates' Behavior* (Washington, D.C.: Brookings Institution, 1973), 2.

46. Michael Lentin, "Most Common 311 Complaint," *Citiquiet* (February 28, 2014), https://citiquiet.com/most-common-311-complaint/.

47. City of Chicago, "311 City Services" (2016), http://www.cityofchicago.org/city/en/depts/311/supp_info/faq.html.

48. See http://maps.kcmo.org/apps/311ServiceRequest/.

49. Carol H. Weiss, *Evaluation Research: Methods of Assessing Program Effectiveness* (Englewood Cliffs, N.J.: Prentice Hall, 1972), 2.

50. Michael Lewis, *Moneyball: The Art of Winning an Unfair Game* (New York: Norton, 2003).

51. Jim Nussle and Peter Orszag, "Let's Play Moneyball," in Jim Nussle and Peter Orszag, eds., *Moneyball for Government* (Washington, D.C.: Disruption Books, 2014), 3, 4.

52. Sanjay Gupta and Danielle Dellorto, "Experimental Drug Likely Saved Ebola Patients," *CNN* (August 5, 2014), http://www.cnn.com/2014/08/04/health/experimental-ebola-serum/; Michael McCarthy, "US Signs Contract with ZMapp Maker to Accelerate Development of the Ebola Drug," *BMJ* (September 4, 2014), http://www.bmj.com/content/349/bmj.g5488; U.S. Centers for Disease Control and Prevention, "Ebola (Ebola Virus Disease): Treatment" (July 22, 2015), http://www.cdc.gov/vhf/ebola/treatment/; Jacque Wilson, "U.S. Ebola Survivors: Where Are They Now?" *CNN* (September 2, 2015), http://www.cnn.com/2015/09/02/health/ebola-outbreak-survivors-rewind/; Mapp Biopharmaceutical, Inc., "ZMapp Is Granted Fast Track Status by the FDA" (September 17, 2015), http://mappbio.com/zmapp-is-granted-fast-track-status-by-the-fda/.

53. An excellent summary of CompStat is *Assertive Policing, Plummeting Crime: The NYPD Takes on Crime*, C16-99-1530.0 (Cambridge, Mass.: Kennedy School of Government Case Program, Harvard University, 1999).

54. Graham Rayman, "The NYPD Tapes: Inside Bed-Stuy's 81st Precinct," *Village Voice* (May 4, 2010), http://www.villagevoice.com/news/the-nypd-tapes-inside-bed-stuys-81st-precinct-6429434.

55. Donald Moynihan and Stéphane Lavertu, "Do Performance Reforms Change How Federal Managers Manage?" *Issues in Governance Studies* 52 (Washington, D.C.: Brookings Institution, 2012).

56. Bill Lucia, "Chicago Just Released a Massive Amount of Bike-Sharing Data," *RouteFifty* (June 15, 2016), http://www.routefifty.com/2016/06/chicago-open-data-divvy-bikeshare/129135/?oref=rf-today-nl.

57. NYC OpenData, "311 Service Requests from 2010 to Present," https://nycopendata.socrata.com/Social-Services/311-Service-Requests-from-2010-to-Present/erm2-nwe9.

58. Montgomery County Government, "dataMontgomery," https://data.montgomerycountymd.gov/Health-and-Human-Services/Food-Inspection/5pue-gfbe.

59. Kathleen Hickey, "Cities Tap Yelp to Improve Health Inspection Process," *GCN* (March 2, 2015), https://gcn.com/articles/2015/03/02/yelp-city-restaurant-inspections.aspx.

60. Johns Hopkins University Center for Government Excellence, "GovEx" (2016), http://govex.jhu.edu/qa/.

61. Donald P. Moynihan and Alexander Kroll, "Performance Management Routines That Work? An Early Assessment of the GPRA Modernization Act," *Public Administration Review* 76 (March/April 2016): 314–323.

62. Quoted in Melissa Conradi, "Leadership, Process, and People," *Governing*, July10, 2003.

63. Jody Zall Kusek, Marelize Gorgens Prestidge, and Billy C. Hamilton, *Fail-Safe Management: Five Rules to Avoid Project Failure* (Washington, D.C.: World Bank, 2013), 2.

64. Ibid., 10–11.

65. For one effort, see James D. Carroll, "Public Administration in the Third Century of the Constitution: Supply-Side Management, Privatization, or Public Investment?" *Public Administration Review* 47 (January–February 1987): 106–114.

13. REGULATION AND THE COURTS

1. Jack Curry, "Yankee Stadium Gets One Last All-Star Game," *New York Times* (February 1, 2007), http://www.nytimes.com/2007/02/01/sports/baseball/01base.ready.html.

2. William K. Rashbaum, "Company Hired to Test Concrete Faces Scrutiny," *New York Times* (June 21, 2008), http://www.nytimes.com/2008/06/21/nyregion/21concrete.html?scp=2&sq=concrete&st=nyt.

3. U.S. Constitution, Art. 1, § 8, cl. 8. The current statute permits "fair use" of copyrighted material; the term's reach is judicially determined in individual cases.

4. Keith Schneider, "Biotechnology Advances Make Life Hard for Patent Office," *New York Times*, April 17, 1988.

5. For a more developed analysis, see *The Politics of Regulation*, ed. James Q. Wilson (New York: Basic Books, 1980), 364–372.

6. See Philip K. Howard, *The Death of Common Sense* (New York: Random House, 1994).

7. David Vogel, *National Styles of Regulation: Environmental Policy in Great Britain and the United States* (Ithaca, N.Y.: Cornell University Press, 1986), 267.

8. The best guide to each regulatory agency's activities, including problems encountered, is the *Federal Regulatory Directory*, 17th ed. (Washington, D.C.: CQ Press, 2016). In particular, see the section on the regulatory process.

9. For the development of Interstate Commerce Commission railroad regulation to 1920, see Stephen

Skowronek, *Building a New American State: The Expansion of National Administrative Capacities, 1877–1920* (New York: Cambridge University Press, 1982), 248–284.

10. The classic work on the capture phenomenon is Marver H. Bernstein, *Regulating Business by Independent Commission* (Princeton, N.J.: Princeton University Press, 1955).

11. Our treatment draws on Michael D. Reagan, *Regulation: The Politics of Policy* (Boston: Little, Brown, 1987), 38–40.

12. For an insightful account and analysis of the deregulation movement, see Martha Derthick and Paul Quirk, *The Politics of Deregulation* (Washington, D.C.: Brookings Institution, 1985).

13. See National Academy of Public Administration, *A Breath of Fresh Air: Reviving the New Source Review Program* (Washington, D.C.: NAPA, 2003).

14. Regulatory inspectors' roles and performance are a major subject of Eugene Bardach and Robert A. Kagan, *Going by the Book: The Problem of Regulatory Unreasonableness*, a Twentieth Century Fund report (Philadelphia: Temple University Press, 1982).

15. See General Accounting Office, *Occupational Safety and Health: Assuring Accuracy in Employer Injury and Illness Records* (Washington, D.C.: Government Printing Office, 1988).

16. See Reagan, *Regulation*, 203–204; and Kenneth J. Meier, *Regulation: Politics, Bureaucracy, and Economics* (New York: St. Martin's Press, 1985), esp. 175–201, on occupational licensing.

17. See, especially, Reagan, *Regulation*, 178–202; Donald F. Kettl, *The Regulation of American Federalism* (Baton Rouge: Louisiana State University Press, 1983); and Advisory Commission on Intergovernmental Relations (ACIR), *Regulatory Federalism: Policy, Process, Impact and Reform* (Washington, D.C.: Government Printing Office, 1984).

18. However, individuals claiming entitlement to benefits under federal statutes that a state fails to provide may sue to obtain the benefits for themselves and others with like entitlements. *Maine v. Thiboutot*, 448 U.S. 1 (1979).

19. For a detailed critique, see Reagan, *Regulation*, 123–131.

20. David A. Fahrenthold, "Cosmic Markdown: EPA Says Life Is Worth Less," *New York Times*, July 19, 2008, A1.

21. Frank Ackerman and Lisa Heinzerling, *Priceless: On Knowing the Price of Everything and the Value of Nothing* (New York: New Press, 2004), 9.

22. One of many provocative points made by Aaron Wildavsky, *Searching for Safety* (New Brunswick, N.J.: Transaction, 1988). The risk assessment literature is large. Entry to it and the issues may be pursued through ibid.; Charles Perrow, *Normal Accidents: Living with High-Risk Technologies* (New York: Basic Books, 1984); and Leroy C. Gould et al., *Perceptions of Technological Risks and Benefits* (New York: Russell Sage Foundation, 1988).

23. Peter Passell, "Life's Risks: Balancing Fear against Reality of Statistics," *New York Times*, May 8, 1989, and "Making a Risky Life Bearable: Better Data, Clearer Choices," *New York Times*, May 8 and 9, 1989; Adam Clymer, "Polls Show Contrasts in How Public and EPA View Environment," *New York Times*, May 22, 1989; and Cathy Marie Johnson, "New Agencies: What They Do and Why They Do It—The Case of the Consumer Product Safety Commission," paper prepared for the 84th annual meeting of the American Political Science Association, September 1–4, 1988.

24. 5 U.S. Code of Federal Regulations, 551–559; and 702–706 (judicial review).

25. See Office of the Federal Register, National Archives and Records Administration, *The Federal Register: What It Is and How to Use It*, rev. ed. (Washington, D.C.: Government Printing Office, 1985).

26. Leonard Buder, "U.S. Is Suing Con Edison over Asbestos," *New York Times*, January 8, 1988.

27. See Peter H. Schuck, *Agent Orange on Trial: Mass Toxic Disasters in the Courts* (Cambridge, Mass.: Harvard University Press, 1986). In 1989, the Department of Veterans Affairs abided by, instead of appealing, a federal court decision that could result in government payments to up to 35,000 veterans who claimed disabilities from Agent Orange. Charles Mohr, "U.S. Not Appealing Agent Orange Case," *New York Times*, May 12, 1989.

28. For an analysis of this story, see Martha A. Derthick, *Up in Smoke: From Legislation to Litigation in Tobacco Politics*, 2nd ed. (Washington, D.C.: CQ Press, 2005).

29. The leading case is *Barr v. Matteo*, 360 U.S. 564 (1959).

30. *Bivens v. Six Unknown Named Agents of the Federal Bureau of Narcotics*, 403 U.S. 388 (1971), and *Wood v. Strickland*, 420 U.S. 308 (1975). Curiously, absolute immunity continues to protect judges, administrative law judges, and prosecutors from tort actions (though not from criminal prosecution). The Supreme Court's reasoning, seemingly serving the self-interest of its branch's members and associates, has been criticized as indistinguishable from the reasoning that would ensure executive officials' risk-free exercise of discretionary judgment.

31. *Westfall v. Erwin*, 108 Supreme Court Reporter 580 (1988). Federal Employee Liability and Tort Compensation Act, 102 U.S. Statutes 4563. The key question

becomes whether the employee was acting "within the scope" of his or her official duties, not whether the duties were discretionary or nondiscretionary.

32. 42 U.S. Code 1983.

33. See Michael Lipsky, *Street-Level Bureaucracy: The Dilemmas of the Individual in Public Services* (New York: Russell Sage Foundation, 1980).

34. For an exploration of the issues of administrative law, see Phillip J. Cooper, *Governing by Contract: Challenges and Opportunities for Public Managers* (Washington, D.C.: CQ Press, 2002).

35. For further development of the contrasts, see Donald L. Horowitz, *The Courts and Social Policy* (Washington, D.C.: Brookings Institution, 1977).

36. So do agency lawyers and those in the Department of Justice, which claims (not always successfully) a monopoly of litigating authority. For the conflicting attitudes, see Donald L. Horowitz, *The Jurocracy: Government Lawyers, Agency Programs, and Judicial Decisions* (Lexington, Mass.: Lexington Books, 1977). For agency lawyers' attributes and incentives, see Eve Spangler, *Lawyers for Hire* (New Haven, Conn.: Yale University Press, 1986), 107–143.

37. See Phillip J. Cooper, "Conflict or Constructive Tension: The Changing Relationship of Judges and Administrators," *Public Administration Review* 45 (Special Issue, November 1985): 643–652.

38. The classic analysis of the courts' emphasis on wide participation in agency proceedings is Richard B. Stewart, "The Reformation of American Administrative Law," *Harvard Law Review* 88 (June 1975): 1667–1813.

39. The courts derive such intentions from the legislative history of a statute. For an argument that this has unhappily magnified the role of congressional subcommittees and their staffs, which compile the legislative history (reports, floor statements, and hearings), see R. Shep Melnick, "The Politics of Partnership," *Public Administration Review* 45 (Special Issue, November 1985): 651–660.

40. See Melnick, *Regulation and the Courts*, 379. Melnick's book is an admirable review of the throes of developing policies in a court-monitored setting. See also Jerry Mashaw, *Due Process in the Administrative State* (New Haven, Conn.: Yale University Press, 1985), 160–161. The shifting attitudes are well traced and appraised in this work. For greater detail, see Mashaw and Merrill, *Administrative Law*.

41. T. Alexander Aleinikoff, "Immigration," in *The Department of Homeland Security's First Year: A Report Card*, ed. Donald F. Kettl (Washington, D.C.: Brookings Institution, 2004), 94.

42. Bentley Coffey, Patrick A. McLaughlin, and Pietro Peretto, *The Cumulative Cost of Regulations* (Arlington, Va.: George Mason University Press, 2016).

43. Major assessments are Morton Rosenberg, "Regulatory Management, in U.S. Senate Committee on Governmental Affairs," *Office of Management and Budget: Evolving Roles and Future Issues*, 98th Cong., 2nd sess., Senate print 99–134 (February 1986), 185–233; *Presidential Management of Rulemaking in Regulatory Agencies: A Report by a Panel of the National Academy of Public Administration* (Washington, D.C.: National Academy of Public Administration, January 1987); and William J. Pielsticker, "Presidential Control of Administrative Rule Making: Its Potential and Its Limits," paper delivered at the 1988 annual meeting of the American Political Science Association, Washington, D.C., September 1–4, 1988. See also General Accounting Office, *Regulatory Review: Information on OMB's Review Process* (Washington, D.C.: Government Printing Office, 1989).

44. This is reinforced by OMB's power, under the Paperwork Act of 1980, to review and disapprove agencies' proposals to collect information. But the Supreme Court overturned OMB's use of the act to block agencies' regulations that require private parties such as employers to disclose information (e.g., exposure to hazardous substances) to other private parties such as employees. *Dole v. U.S. Steelworkers of America*, 110 Supreme Court Reporter 929 (1990).

45. Cooper, *Public Law and Public Administration*, 398–399.

14. ACCOUNTABILITY AND POLITICS

1. Dennis Wagner, "Three More Phoenix VA Officials Fired in Aftermath of Wait-Time, Retaliation Probes," *Arizona Republic* (June 8, 2016), http://www.azcentral.com/story/news/local/arizona-investigations/2016/06/08/three-more-phoenix-va-officials-fired-after-wait-time-scandal/85614056/.

2. Stephen Deere, "Ferguson's New Police Chief Has a Warning for Cops," *Governing* (May 10, 2016), http://www.governing.com/topics/public-justice-safety/tns-delrish-moss-ferguson-police.html.

3. Quoted by Wagner, "Three More Phoenix Officials Fired."

4. Christopher H. Foreman Jr., *Signals from the Hill: Congressional Oversight and the Challenge of Social Regulation* (New Haven, Conn.: Yale University Press, 1988), 12. For a thorough and careful look at oversight, see Joel D. Aberbach, *Keeping a Watchful Eye: The Politics of*

Congressional Oversight (Washington, D.C.: Brookings Institution, 1990).

5. See Richard E. Neustadt, "Politicians and Bureaucrats," in *The Congress and America's Future*, 2nd ed., ed. David B. Truman (Englewood Cliffs, N.J.: Prentice Hall, 1973), 119. For a history of congressional-administrative relations, see James L. Sundquist, "Congress as Public Administrator," in *A Centennial History of American Public Administration*, ed. Ralph Clark Chandler (New York: Free Press, 1987), 261–289.

6. National Academy of Public Administration, *Congressional Oversight of Regulatory Agencies: The Need to Strike a Balance and Focus on Performance* (Washington, D.C.: NAPA, 1988), 1.

7. J. Ronald Fox with James L. Field, *The Defense Management Challenge: Weapons Acquisition* (Boston: Harvard Business School Press, 1988), 76. See also David C. Hendrickson, *Reforming Defense: The State of American Civil-Military Relations* (Baltimore: Johns Hopkins University Press, 1988), 30–34. More broadly, see Louis Fisher, "Micromanagement by Congress: Reality and Mythology," in *The Fettered Presidency: Legal Constraints on the Executive Branch*, ed. L. Gordon Crovitz and Jeremy A. Rabkin (Washington, D.C.: American Enterprise Institute, 1989), 139–157.

8. Henry Kissinger and Cyrus Vance, "Bipartisan Objectives for American Foreign Policy," *Foreign Affairs* 66 (Summer 1988): 901.

9. Siobhan Gorman, "Experts Say INS Restructuring Won't Solve Management Problems," *Government Executive*, May 3, 2002.

10. See David R. Mayhew, *Congress: The Electoral Connection* (New Haven, Conn.: Yale University Press, 1974). See also Seymour Scher, "Conditions for Legislative Control," *Journal of Politics* 25 (August 1963): 526–551.

11. Ibid., 527.

12. These and similar terms are scattered throughout Senate Committee on Government Operations, *Study on Federal Regulation*, vol. 2, *Congressional Oversight of Regulatory Agencies*, committee print, 95th Cong., 1st sess., 1977. Despite the restrictive title, this volume is one of the best reviews of performance and problems of oversight of both regulatory and nonregulatory agencies by both the House and the Senate. See also NAPA, *Congressional Oversight of Regulatory Agencies*, which reached similar conclusions.

13. Mathew D. McCubbins and Thomas Schwartz, "Congressional Oversight Overlooked: Police Patrols versus Fire Alarms," *American Journal of Political Science* 28 (Fall 1984): 169, 172.

14. This list comes from NAPA, *Congressional Oversight of Regulatory Agencies*, 7–9.

15. See Hugh Heclo, "Issue Networks and the Executive Establishment," in *The New Political System,* ed. Anthony King (Washington, D.C.: American Enterprise Institute, 1978), 87–124.

16. R. Douglas Arnold, *Congress and the Bureaucracy: A Theory of Influence* (New Haven, Conn.: Yale University Press, 1979), 35.

17. Ibid., 67–68.

18. Lawrence C. Dodd and Richard L. Schott, *Congress and the Administrative State* (New York: Wiley, 1979), 170. More generally, see Morris S. Ogul, *Congress Oversees the Bureaucracy: Studies in Legislative Supervision* (Pittsburgh, Pa.: University of Pittsburgh Press, 1976).

19. NAPA, *Congressional Oversight of Regulatory Agencies*, 9.

20. See Foreman, *Signals from the Hill*, chap. 4.

21. Dodd and Schott, *Congress and the Administrative State*, 166.

22. On the basis of members' shifts to and from other committees prior to 1973, the House Government Operations Committee ranked eighteenth in prestige among the twenty standing committees, and its Senate counterpart ranked thirteenth among the sixteen standing committees. See Leroy N. Rieselbach, *Congressional Politics* (New York: McGraw-Hill, 1973), 60–61n.

23. Dodd and Schott, *Congress and the Administrative State*, 168.

24. Ibid., 173–184.

25. Norman J. Ornstein, "Perspectives on House Reform of Homeland Security," testimony before the Subcommittee on Rules, Select Committee on Homeland Security, U.S. House of Representatives, May 19, 2003, https://www.aei.org/publication/perspectives-on-house-reform-of-homeland-security/.

26. Senate Committee on Armed Services, Staff Report, *Defense Organization: The Need for Change*, committee print, 99th Cong., 1st sess., 1985, 581–582. The Georgetown University study is quoted in this report.

27. Thomas P. Murphy, "Political Executive Roles, Policymaking, and Interface with the Career Bureaucracy," *Bureaucrat* 6 (Summer 1977): 107.

28. Stephen R. Heifetz, "The Risk of Too Much Oversight," *New York Times* (July 21, 2008), http://www.nytimes.com/2008/07/21/opinion/21heifetz.html.

29. For one interest group's discussion of these issues, see Stephen L. Katz, *Government: Decisions without Democracy* (Washington, D.C.: People for the American Way, 1987).

30. Improper classification and other issues are reviewed in House Committee on Government Operations, *Executive Classification of Information . . . Third Report*, House Rpt. 93–221, 1973.

31. Summary of the board's findings by Edmund S. Muskie, in John Tower, Edmund Muskie, and Brent Scowcroft, *The Tower Commission Report* (New York: Bantam Books, 1987), xvii.

32. Pauline Jelinek, "Rumsfeld Apologizes for Iraq Prison Abuse," *Miami Herald*, May 7, 2004.

33. NAPA, *Congressional Oversight of Regulatory Agencies*, 24.

34. Excellent treatments of earlier congressional efforts to cope with scientific and technological issues are Thomas P. Jahnige, "The Congressional Committee System and the Oversight Process: Congress and NASA," *Western Political Quarterly* 21 (June 1968): 227–239; and House Committee on Science and Aeronautics, Subcommittee on Science, Research, and Development, *Technological Information for Congress*, 92nd Cong., 1st sess., 1971.

35. For a study of the history, development, and role of the General Accounting Office, see Frederick C. Mosher, *The GAO: The Quest for Accountability in American Government* (Boulder, Colo.: Westview, 1979).

36. See Louis Fisher, *The Politics of Shared Power: Congress and the Executive*, 2nd ed. (Washington, D.C.: CQ Press, 1987), 125–129; and *Bowsher v. Synar*, 106 S. Ct. 3181 (1986).

37. These officials could then attempt to collect disallowed payments from the recipients; failing that, they might seek passage of congressional acts reimbursing them. In the 1940s, about a million federal employees paid almost $2 million annually to insurance companies to cover any liabilities for disallowed payments of public funds. Finally, in 1955, Congress authorized agencies themselves to purchase blanket surety bonds for their employees. See Senate Committee on Government Operations, *Financial Management in the Federal Government*, 92nd Cong., 1st sess., 1971, 2:233–238.

38. See Government Accountability Office, "High Risk List," http://www.gao.gov/highrisk/overview.

39. These and other problems are treated by Joseph Pois and Ernest S. Griffith in Senate Commission on the Operation of the Senate, *Congressional Support Agencies*, 31–54, 126–133; Joseph Pois, "Trends in General Accounting Office Audits," and Ira Sharkansky, "The Politics of Auditing," in *The New Political Economy: The Public Use of the Private Sector*, ed. Bruce L. R. Smith (New York: Wiley, 1975), 245–318; and John T. Rourke, "The GAO: An Evolving Role," *Public Administration Review* 38 (September–October 1978): 453–457. A full history and analysis is Mosher, *The GAO*.

40. Complicating Congress's role is the era of divided government, with different parties in control of Congress and the presidency, for nearly all of the post-Vietnam period. See James L. Sundquist, "Needed: A Political Theory for the New Era of Coalition Government in the United States," *Political Science Quarterly* 103 (Winter 1988–1989): 613–635.

41. Judith E. Gruber, *Controlling Bureaucracies: Dilemmas in Democratic Governance* (Berkeley: University of California Press, 1987), 57.

42. See Chapter 12's discussion of "Performance Management."

43. For the prevalence and the inadequacy of this approach to internal control, see U.S. Comptroller General, *Federal Agencies Can and Should Do More to Combat Fraud in Government Programs* (Washington, D.C.: Government Printing Office, 1978); and Jerome B. McKinney and Michael Johnston, eds., *Fraud, Waste, and Abuse in Government: Causes, Consequences, and Cures* (Philadelphia: Institute for the Study of Human Issues, 1986).

44. The classic argument for redundancy in administrative organization and process is Martin Landau, "Redundancy, Rationality, and the Problem of Duplication and Overlap," *Public Administration Review* 29 (July–August 1969): 346–358.

45. Dana Milbank, "Putting Her Foot Down and Getting the Boot," *Washington Post*, July 10, 2008, A3.

46. Ibid.

47. Francis Fukuyama, *Political Order and Political Decay* (New York: Farrar, Straus and Giroux, 2014).

48. Jim Nussle and Peter Orszag, eds., *Moneyball for Government* (Washington, D.C.: Disruption Books, 2014).

49. Robert F. Durant and David Rosenbloom, "The Hollowing of American Public Administration," *American Review of Public Administration* (2016): 1–25.

50. Donald F. Kettl, *Escaping Jurassic Government: How to Recover America's Lost Commitment to Competence* (Washington, D.C.: Brookings Institution, 2016).

GLOSSARY OF KEY CONCEPTS

accountability: the process of holding administrators responsible for their actions, especially their compliance with the law and their effectiveness in managing programs.

adjudication: one of two basic regulatory approaches used by administrative agencies wherein administrative law judges within agencies hear individual cases and develop a body of rules.

administrative confidentiality: privacy protections afforded by government to individuals and organizations; and restrictions of access to internal records collected by governmental organizations.

administrative responsibility: the process of holding specific individuals responsible, within the bureaucracy, for specific actions.

administrative rulemaking: one of two basic regulatory approaches used by administrative agencies wherein public managers write regulations that apply to all persons and organizations meeting certain guidelines.

administrative state: Dwight Waldo's term to describe the rising importance and power of bureaucracy in American democracy.

adverse selection: because, in some cases, subordinates have information their superiors do not—or vice versa—distortions in behavior and problems of accountability can result.

agencies: the generic term for public bureaucracies, which carry out public programs on behalf of policymakers.

agents: those who carry out policies on behalf of superiors (known as principals).

Antideficiency Act: the federal law that forbids government officials from spending money not specifically appropriated for a purpose. The act limits the discretion of administrators.

antitrust laws: legislation intended to promote free competition by eliminating the power of monopolies.

appropriations: legislation that commits money to be spent (compare authorizations).

appropriations committees: standing committees that manage the annual appropriations process.

areal (or prefectoral) system: an approach to government that structures its organizations by a particular geographic region.

at-will employees: employees in an at-will employment system, in which they can be fired at the discretion of managers.

authority: the basic skeleton of bureaucracy, through which a government, an agency, or an individual is vested with the rightful power to make decisions within constitutionally defined limits with the expectation of widespread compliance.

authorizations: legislation that creates programs and puts a limit on the money to be spent managing them (compare appropriations).

authorizing committees: standing committees that can initiate, review, and report out bills and resolutions in particular subject-matter areas.

auxiliary staff: the staff of an agency that provides basic housekeeping functions, including management of the personnel and budgetary processes.

Balanced Budget and Emergency Deficit Control Act: an act sponsored by Senators Phil Gramm, Warren Rudman, and Ernest Hollings and passed in 1985, which set automatic spending cuts if Congress and the president could not agree on budget reductions. Its goal was to eliminate the federal deficit by 1990. Also known as the Gramm-Rudman Act.

bargaining approach: a method of making decisions in which parties negotiate their differences. This approach seeks to maximize political support.

black budget: the spending authorized for secret government activities.

budget authority: legislative approval of programs and the ability to spend money, which must be supported by an appropriation.

bump: the practice whereby a higher-seniority government employee can force out a lower-seniority employee.

bureaucratic model: the traditional approach to bureaucracy, based on hierarchy and authority.

bureaus: the basic building blocks of governmental organizations.

buyouts: offers of lump-sum payments to government employees in exchange for their agreement to retire from government service.

cabinet: the collection of administrative departments, as well as those additional offices that the chief executive (such as the president) raises to that rank.

capital budgets: the portion of the budget for items with long useful lives, like roads and fire trucks.

capture: the use of political influence by interest groups to shape the decisions of administrators.

chain of command: the line of authority from top policymakers through the hierarchy, which is used to define who is responsible for doing what.

charismatic authority: an approach to authority that relies on the personal magnetism of the leader.

civil service system: the collection of rules and procedures that govern the employees who work in career positions in government.

class action: legal action taken by a small group of individuals on behalf of a far larger group of people who share the same complaint.

classical theory: typically refers to organizations that operate through hierarchies structured with authority.

clearance procedure: a method of cooperation among agencies that entails that an agency's proposed decisions in a subject-matter area be reviewed, whether for comment or for formal approval or veto, by other interested agencies.

closed-system theorists: an approach to systems theory that focuses on the internal workings of the system.

collective bargaining: negotiation by members of a union over employee rights and compensation.

continuing resolutions: Congressional actions that continue the level of spending after the fiscal year at its current level while Congress and the president negotiate the details of a new budget.

continuous improvement: a management strategy devoted to developing ongoing feedback about an organization's results to enhance its success.

contracts: legal agreement in which a seller agrees to provide a good or service to a buyer for a mutually agreeable price. Government has increasingly relied on contracts with private-sector experts and outside organizations for the delivery of public services.

control staff: the staff of an agency that helps top officials maintain a check on the behavior of other agency employees.

coordination: the process of orienting the activities of individuals and organizations so they are mutually supportive.

core staff: the staff of an agency that provides basic support to the agency's line activities.

cost-benefit analysis: a comparison of the expenditures required for a program with the gains it produces. An example is risk assessment.

crossover sanctions: punishments incurred in a program that were caused by failures to meet another program's standards.

customer service movement: a management strategy devoted to focusing an organization's efforts on improving the satisfaction of its "customers"—those who benefit from its goods and services.

data visualization: a collection of strategies to translate data into graphs and charts to communicate them more clearly.

debt: money borrowed by the government in the short term and repaid in the long term.

deficit: the excess of expenditures over revenues in any given fiscal year (compare surplus).

delivery framework: a strategy for translating an elected executive's policies into results, usually supported by performance data.

direct administration: the provision of government goods and services by government organizations themselves, as compared with indirect administration, in which goods and services are provided through grants, contracts, tax incentives, or other multiorganizational/multisectoral policy strategies.

direct tools: instruments of government action through which government agencies themselves provide government goods and services.

downsizing: a focus on reducing the size and cost of government operations, especially through reductions in the workforce.

economic regulation: the portion of public-sector rulemaking that affects the behavior of private markets (compare social regulation).

efficiency: a measure of the level of inputs required to produce a given level of outputs.

e-government: a strategy of using information technology, especially the Internet and the World Wide Web, to make it easier for citizens to interact with government.

entitlements: governmental programs through which an individual is automatically guaranteed services—typically, a payment—because the individual meets requirements set in law.

ethical behavior: the adherence to moral standards and avoidance of even the appearance of unethical actions.

executive leadership: strategic direction provided by the top officials of an organization.

executive privilege: the claim by presidents that communication with aides is protected from outside scrutiny, including investigation by Congress.

exit: the decision by members of an organization to leave, especially because they disagree with policies and programs.

externalities: an economic term referring to indirect benefits and costs beyond the direct costs and benefits of a project. Also called spillovers.

federal grants: transfer of money from the federal government to state and local governments in pursuit of national objectives.

feedback loop: an element of systems theory that connects the outputs an organization produces to its inputs.

fire alarm oversight: a strategy of legislative oversight of bureaucracy based on instigation and response to crises and problems. Compare "police patrol oversight."

fiscal accountability: a method of accountability that focuses on the flow of money through an organization.

fiscal policy: decisions about government spending and taxing, and their effect on the economy's performance (compare monetary policy).

fiscal year: the government's budget year (starting October 1 for the federal government, and July 1 for many state and local governments).

formal approach: a theory of bureaucracy that relies on a rigorous model of the relationships between actors, especially between principals and agents.

function: the specific role or duty performed by a part of an organization.

furloughs: days off without pay for federal employees.

gaming: a tendency of performance measures to create incentives for managers and citizens to change their behavior to get good scores, without necessarily improving the overall result.

geographic information system: a tool for charting important variables, such as the levels of pollution or numbers of crimes.

government by proxy: the rise of government's use of indirect tools of public action (including contracts, grants, regulations, and special tax provisions) to pursue public goals.

government-by-proxy approach: an approach to organizations that notes that government delegates authority to other governments, to private organizations, and to mixed public-private enterprises as well as within its own organizational structure.

government corporations: organizations that perform public functions but that are organized—and operate—like private companies, with a profit-and-loss bottom line (including Amtrak and the Federal Deposit Insurance Corporation).

grade creep: the tendency for agencies to increase over time the number of top administrative positions and to seek higher classifications for existing positions.

Hatch Act: federal legislation passed in 1939 restricting political activity by government employees. Also called "An Act to Prevent Pernicious Political Activities."

hierarchy: the relationship between levels of a bureaucracy.

human capital: an approach to management that focuses on identifying the skills employees need to accomplish an organization's work and in developing those skills to ensure that they produce strong and effective governmental programs.

human relations movement: an approach to organizations that holds that the relationships among individuals, especially in motivating employees, are the most important element of organizational theory. Also called the humanist approach.

humanist approach: a strategy of management that builds on interpersonal relationships and that relies on motivating individuals toward high performance.

implementation: the process of transforming policy goals into results.

incrementalism: an approach to budgeting focused on the base of spending, plus fair-share increases.

independent agencies: governmental organizations that exist separately from the cabinet departments.

indirect tools: the provision of public goods and services by nongovernmental partners (and partners outside the level of government creating a program), through instruments like grants, contracts, regulations, and special tax provisions.

information asymmetry: subordinates sometimes know more about important issues than their superiors, which can create challenges to holding them accountable.

inputs: the resources, especially money and employees, that organizations use in producing outputs.

interagency agreements: mutual understandings reached by several organizations, which detail the contributions each organization will make to a common goal.

interagency committees: committees that exist to promote collaboration between jointly occupied areas at the cabinet, subcabinet, and bureau levels.

interweaving: the interconnection of the public, private, and nonprofit sectors in partnership to produce publicly funded services.

iron triangle: a theory that suggests agency managers, congressional committees and subcommittees, and interest groups work closely to shape policy, and that their shared work is more important than other forces on the process.

lead agency formula: a method of cooperation wherein one agency is designated to lead and attempt to coordinate all agencies' activities in a particular area.

legislative budget: fiscal policy decisions framed by the actions of the legislature, compared with budget recommendations made by the executive branch.

legislative review: the official term for legislative oversight.

line activities: those actions that contribute directly to the mission of an organization (compare staff activities). Also called operating activities.

loan programs: an indirect tool of government that seeks to fund public goals by making credit available to individuals and organizations, either by the government making a direct loan or by the government guaranteeing the repayment of a loan made by a private organization.

management by objectives (MBO): a strategy in which managers chart quantitative objectives for a program to accomplish in the coming year, which in turn determines the budget required for the program.

mandates: requirements that must be met as a condition of aid.

monetary policy: decisions by the Federal Reserve on interest rates and the money supply, and their effect on the economy's performance (compare fiscal policy).

moral hazard: the tendency to take more risks when someone else bears the costs.

national debt: the net deficit that accumulates over time.

National Performance Review: used during the Clinton administration by managers to devise strategies for improving government operations while setting top-down targets for reducing the number of government employees.

National Security Council: an organization within the Executive Office of the President, established in 1947, to advise the president on matters of foreign and military policy.

network analysis: an approach to organizational theory that focuses on the relationships among organizations in sharing responsibility for programs.

neutral competence: the public administration principle that administrators ought to perform their jobs to the highest possible level, without political favoritism.

neutrality doctrine: the principle that public administrators ought to manage programs without political favoritism.

NIMBY phenomenon: the aversion of citizens for projects they perceive will have a direct negative effect on them and their local area (short for "not in my backyard").

nonprofit: society's third sector, in addition to the public and private sectors. Some nonprofits charge fees, some receive grants and contracts from the public and private sectors, and others receive voluntary contributions; many operate under a combination of all three revenue sources. Nonprofits exist to serve social purposes, instead of making profits (like private organizations). They operate outside the public sector, but often help implement governmental goals.

Office of Management and Budget: an organization within the Executive Office of the President, to advise the president on budgetary and management policies. Initially established in 1921 in the Treasury Department, it came under the purview of the Executive Office in 1939.

open data: the commitment of government to make the data it collects available in their basic, unprocessed form, to allow citizens and analysts to use the data and create their own analyses of public programs.

open-system theorists: those who advocate an approach to systems theory that focuses on the relationship of the system with the environment.

organizational cultures: the ethos and philosophy that shape the behavior of individuals within an organization.

organizational structure: the arrangement of elements within an organization.

organizational theory: the collection of concepts that seeks to describe and predict the way that organizations—and the people within them—act.

outlays: expenditures that occur within any given fiscal year.

outputs: the goods and services that an organization produces.

oversight: review of the behavior of individuals within organizations, and organizations themselves, by those with authority over them. In public administration, the term is used most commonly to refer to the review of administrative acts by legislatures.

partial preemption: the decision by a higher level of government that, if a lower government does not meet predetermined standards, the higher level of government will step in and administer the program itself.

participative decision-making approach: a strategy of decision making that attempts to build support for decisions by including those affected in the decision-making process.

performance management: a strategy of using metrics to track the implementation of public programs, with the goal of improving results.

performance measures: assessments of success, of organizations and individuals, in achieving the goals set for them.

Planning-Programming-Budgeting System (PPBS): a budgeting system first introduced in the federal government in the early 1960s, which seeks rational decisions through the identification of goals, developing those goals into programs, and translating the programs into a long-term budget plan.

pluralist approach: an approach to organizations that focuses on the interaction of political forces in shaping organizational behavior.

police patrol oversight: a strategy of legislative oversight of bureaucracy based on regular, routine reviews of administrative practice. Compare "fire alarm oversight."

policy-administration dichotomy: the separation of political decision making from administrative policy implementation.

policymaking: the process of defining the goals that public organizations are charged with seeking. Also referred to as policy formation.

politics-administration dichotomy: the notion, advanced by Woodrow Wilson in a famous 1887 article, that the tools for administering public policy can be separated from the politics of making it. It is often used as the foundation for

neutral competence, the idea that administrators need to have the capacity to administer programs, regardless of their political roots.

position classification: the identification of the specific knowledge a job requires, the job's level of difficulty, and the job's responsibilities.

principal-agent theory: a formal approach to organizations that focuses on the relationship between principals and agents.

principals: the superiors who shape the behavior of agents.

Private Sector Survey on Cost Control: a commission appointed by President Ronald Reagan and chaired by industrialist J. Peter Grace, which focused on efforts to reduce the costs of government, especially by eliminating federal governmental programs and relying more on contracting out. Also called the Grace Commission.

privatization: a strategy for turning over public responsibilities to the private sector, either by selling public assets or transferring responsibility to the private sector, or by relying on private companies to supply a good or service through contracts.

process accountability: a method of accountability that focuses on how an organization pursues its objectives.

program accountability: a method of accountability that focuses on an organization's achievement of its policy objectives.

Program Assessment Rating Tool (PART): a budgeting system, developed during the George W. Bush administration, in which agency managers define their goals and measure their performance in meeting them.

Progressives: reformers who campaigned for stronger government regulation to protect citizens from private power and more public programs to improve the lives of ordinary Americans.

public administration: the process of translating public policies into results.

public-choice approach: a method of decision making that assumes individuals pursue their self-interest and derives propositions about their behavior—and the behavior of organizations—from this assumption. According to this approach, individuals are best motivated by market forces.

randomized controlled trials: a strategy of bringing rigorous assessment to public programs by assigning program participants randomly to control and experimental groups and measuring whether a program has different effects on the different groups.

rational approach: a theory of decision making based on the pursuit of the most-efficient outcomes.

rational decision making: a method of decision making that seeks the most efficient solution for problems.

rational-legal authority: an element of traditional organizational theory that focuses on hierarchy and authority to accomplish an organization's goals.

red tape: a colloquial term for government regulations that tend to impose large costs with few benefits. The term comes from Civil War–era documents, which were tied up with red ribbons.

reductions in force (RIFs): involuntary layoff or termination of government employees.

reengineering: a strategy for improving an organization's results by transforming the organization's basic processes.

regulations: rules set by government to govern the behavior of individuals and organizations.

regulatory commissions: government organizations, typically independent agencies, whose function is to write and enforce rules governing private-sector behavior and whose policies are set by a multimember board.

reinventing government: the Clinton administration's strategy for producing "a government that works better and costs less."

representativeness: the degree to which the employees of a government agency, or of the government overall, reflect the demographic makeup of society at large.

risk assessment: a type of cost-benefit analysis that evaluates whether to regulate risks based on the tradeoffs between expenditures and gains.

risk management: the process of forecasting risks and devising strategies for avoiding or reducing them.

rule of anticipated reactions: a strategy by executives to frame their budgetary requests according to how they believe legislators will react to them.

rule of law: the structure of legal process and precedent that frames agreed-upon strategies for resolving complex social, economic, and political problems.

satisficing: a strategy of decision making that seeks a satisfactory (not necessarily the best or most efficient) alternative.

scientific management movement: an approach to bureaucracy that seeks to improve performance by improving efficiency, especially in transforming inputs into outputs.

sequestration: automatic cuts in federal spending imposed if Congress and the president fail to reach agreement on a budget that meets legislated spending targets.

social regulation: the portion of public-sector rulemaking that affects the health, safety, and well-being of citizens (compare economic regulation).

span of control: the number of subordinates overseen by a supervisor.

special-purpose governments: governments, mostly local, created to pursue particular functions, like airport operations, garbage collection, or education.

spillovers: a term from economics to describe effects of activities on those not directly involved in a market transaction. A factory, for example, might sell its products to buyers, but the pollution it produces is a cost that those living in surrounding areas might have to bear.

staff: the common term used to refer to the employees of an organization, not to be confused with staff activities. Sometimes also called pure-staff to distinguish from auxiliary and control staff.

staff activities: those actions (like personnel and budgeting) that support the mission of an organization (compare line activities).

standing to sue: the legal right of an individual or organization to file a legal action.

structure: a formal arrangement among the people engaged in the organization's mission.

surplus: an excess of revenues over expenditures in any given fiscal year (compare deficit).

system boundaries: the border between a system and the rest of the environment.

system purpose: the function for which a system exists.

systems theory: an approach to organizations that focuses on how they translate inputs into outputs.

tax expenditures: special advantages in the tax code to create incentive for behavior the government wants to encourage. Tax expenditures include deductions (in which individuals can reduce their income by the amount of an expenditure, such as a home mortgage) and credits (in which individuals can reduce the tax due by the amount of an expenditure, such as payments for child care).

Taxpayer Bill of Rights (TABOR): Colorado's effort to reduce the growth of state government. The strategy has since been debated in other states as well.

throughputs: in systems theory, the process of transforming inputs into outputs.

total quality management (TQM): a strategy for improving an organization's results by focusing all of its processes and employees on the goal of increasing the value of the organization's work.

traditional authority: an orientation toward authority that relies on a belief in the sacredness of longstanding customs and that relies on the loyalty of individuals to someone who has become a leader in a long-established way.

transaction costs: the expenses, in time and money, incurred in how an organization conducts its operations.

turnover: the rate at which employees leave an organization.

uncontrollable expenditures: outlays required by law, typically for formula-based payments to individuals (e.g., Social Security). The expenditures are not strictly speaking uncontrollable; they can be changed by law, but such changes are difficult and frequently take a long time.

unionization: the effort by organized unions to increase their membership and bargaining power in government.

user fees: a form of revenue collection in which citizens are assessed fees to pay for government services from which they benefit.

voice: the decision by members of an organization to remain within an organization and protest policies and programs with which they disagree.

Washington Monument ploy: a tactic used by administrators to shield themselves from budget cuts by threatening to eliminate their most popular programs (like tours of the Washington Monument) if legislators reduce appropriations.

whistleblowers: individuals who divulge details about the behavior of other members of their organization who might be in violation of the law.

zero-base budgeting (ZBB): a budget strategy that rejects incrementalism and asks administrators to analyze the implications of different packages of spending, from substantial reductions in current spending (the base) through significant increases.

INDEX